# THE ANCIENT MAYA

The corn god,
from Late Classic
Copan, Honduras.

# THE ANCIENT
# MAYA

SYLVANUS G. MORLEY and
GEORGE W. BRAINERD
Revised by ROBERT J. SHARER

FOURTH EDITION

Stanford University Press, Stanford, California

The first edition of this book, by Sylvanus G. Morley, was published in 1946; the second, with revisions by Morley, in 1947. The third edition, published in 1956, was prepared after Morley's death by George W. Brainerd, except for its final chapter, which was written after Brainerd's death by his editorial assistant, Betty Bell. The present edition, prepared by Robert J. Sharer, preserves as much as possible of the Morley-Brainerd text while incorporating the impressive results of the past quarter-century of research.

STANFORD UNIVERSITY PRESS, STANFORD, CALIFORNIA
© 1946, 1947, 1956, 1983 by the Board of Trustees of the Leland Stanford Junior University
Printed in the United States of America
Fourth edition, 1983

Cloth ISBN 0-8047-1137-2
Paper ISBN 0-8047-1288-3

Last figure below indicates year of this printing:
94  93  92  91  90  89  88  87  86  85

# PREFACE

The foundation of our knowledge about the ancient Maya lies in archaeology, the science that reconstructs past societies from their material remains. In recent decades, a variety of new techniques, better research designs, and more sophisticated theoretical frameworks, not to mention an explosive growth in the sheer number of Maya scholars and studies, have all combined to make the results of archaeological investigation more accurate and complete than was previously possible. This unprecedented growth has fostered considerable advances in our understanding of the ancient Maya.

The archaeological foundation of our knowledge is supplemented handsomely by ethnohistory: a wealth of information about Maya civilization that can never be recovered by archaeology is contained in the early written accounts by and about the Maya. Only a few pre-Columbian Maya books are known to survive, but many documents remain from the era of the Spanish Conquest. The nature of these written sources is best summarized by Sylvanus G. Morley, from his Preface to the first edition of this work:

During the century (1550–1650) following the Spanish conquest, a number of native as well as Spanish writers carry on the story for us. Educated Maya who had been taught by the early Catholic missionaries to write their language in the characters of the Spanish alphabet in order to facilitate their instruction in the Catholic faith set down brief summaries of their own ancient history, probably copied directly from their then still surviving historical manuscripts in the Maya hieroglyphic writing.

In addition to the foregoing native sources, several of the early Franciscan Fathers have left admirable accounts of the Maya as they were in the middle-sixteenth century, by far the most important being the contemporary narrative by Fray Diego de Landa, the second Bishop of Yucatán. His *Relación de las cosas de Yucatán*, written in 1566 and extensively quoted in the following pages, is [and remains today] unquestionably our leading authority on the ancient Maya.

But the ancient Maya remained undiscovered, the spectacular remains of their civilization largely unknown and the documents describing their society generally ignored, until the nineteenth century. To continue with Morley's account:

During the next two centuries (1650–1840) very little new was added to the Maya story, but in 1839–1841 John Lloyd Stephens, the American traveler, diplomat, and amateur archaeologist, accompanied by Frederick Catherwood, an English artist, visited the Maya area twice and embodied his impressions thereupon in two outstanding works: *Incidents of Travel in Central America, Chiapas, and Yucatan* (1841) and *Incidents of Travel in Yucatan* (1843). Both were illustrated by Catherwood's superb drawings; today, more than a hundred years later, they still remain the most delightful books ever written about the Maya area.

Stephens' writings were chiefly responsible for bringing the great cities of the Maya civilization to the attention of the outside world. Before the publication of his two books, the very existence of these cities was unknown outside of Yucatan and northern Central America, but, after their appearance, knowledge of the Maya, who developed our greatest native American civilization, became general on both sides of the Atlantic. With Stephens also begins the period of the modern exploration of this region.

In the years that followed, a series of travelers explored the more accessible ruins of Maya civilization, and scholars began to rediscover many earlier accounts. The study of these documents provided the first information about the organization of ancient Maya society, their customs, myths, and religion, and their calendrical and writing systems. By the early years of the twentieth century, the first archaeological investigations of Maya sites were under way. Quoting once again from Morley's original preface:

Since Stephens' time many scientific institutions as well as individual students have been engaged in piecing together different parts of the Maya picture-puzzle. To mention all would expand this preface beyond reasonable limits, but the three most important should be noted: (1) the English archaeologist, Sir Alfred P. Maudslay, the results of whose fifteen years of exploration in the Maya region (1881–1894) were published in the magnificent section on Archaeology of the *Biologia Centrali-Americana*, the first scientific publication about the Maya civilization; (2) the Peabody Museum of Archaeology and Ethnology of Harvard University, which, between 1888 and 1915, sent many expeditions to the Maya area under able leaders who have made many important contributions to our knowledge of the ancient Maya; (3) the Carnegie Institution of Washington, which . . . [carried] on intensive studies in the Maya field for . . . [over] three decades. No fewer than twenty-five annual expeditions under trained archaeologists have been sent to different parts of the Maya area and a vast amount of new material in many fields—archaeology, ethnology, anthropometry, history, linguistics, agriculture, botany, zoology, geography, medicine, and epidemiology—has been obtained.

Morley, a true pioneer in this era of Maya research, directed the Carnegie Institution of Washington's excavations at Chichen Itza (1924–1940) and became the leading authority on Maya monuments and their calendrical inscriptions. Near the end of his career he wrote the first comprehensive account of Maya civilization, *The Ancient Maya*, published in 1946; a second edition appeared the following year. This work, solidly based on the evidence available at the time, quickly became a landmark in Maya studies. Nonetheless, several archaeological discoveries made in the decade following its first appearance soon rendered the work somewhat out-of-date. These new findings, most notably the investigations at Mayapan, the excavation of the tomb beneath the Temple of the Inscriptions at Palenque, and the discovery of the Bonampak wall paintings, provided the basis for a revision of Morley's work by George W. Brainerd. This was published as the third edition of *The Ancient Maya* in 1956.

As fate would have it, however, that very year marked the beginning of a veritable explosion of archaeological research in the Maya area. In 1956 the Tikal Project was initiated by the University Museum of the University of Pennsylvania. One of the most comprehensive investigations of its kind ever undertaken by New World archaeologists, this project continues today, sponsored since 1970 by the Guatemalan government. During this same period several dozen additional archaeological research programs were undertaken throughout the Maya area. The results of this unprecedented era of investigation have increased our store of information about the ancient Maya many times over. But the most immediate consequence has been the discovery that several basic premises about ancient Maya subsistence, the nature of Maya writing, and Maya social, political, and economic organization were incorrect.

These obsolete notions about Maya civilization formed the basis of the previous editions of *The Ancient Maya*. Thus it became increasingly obvious that there was a need for another, even more thorough, revision of Morley's original work. In addition, there is available to us today a great deal of new information not only about Maya civilization itself, but also about the origins and geographical extent of that civilization. When the previous editions were written, most of the available data pertained to the Classic and Postclassic eras in the Maya lowlands, and there was a heavy emphasis on Yucatan sources. The Preclassic period was little known, and there was little consideration of the Maya of the southern highlands and the Pacific coast.

The present revision thus attempts to retain much of the flavor and organization of Morley's original endeavor, while presenting a synthesis of as much of the available information as is possible and appropriate in a single volume. In order to accomplish this, the present work has been divided into four sections. Part I, on cultural history, offers a description of the Maya area (Chapter 1) and a résumé of the chronological development of Maya civilization (Chapters 2–6), completely rewritten and expanded in light of current evidence. Part II deals with society; the chapters (7–10) in this section have been revised in varying degrees, but retain as much of the original text as possible. Chapter 7 (on subsistence systems) has been completely rewritten; Chapter 8 (on the organization of society) retains the original description of Postclassic Yucatecan society, and adds a new section on Postclassic highland society; Chapter 9 (on everyday life) is essentially unchanged; and Chapter 10 (on trade and external contact) is all new. Part III, on material culture, opens with a substantially expanded description of Maya architecture and archaeological sites (Chapter 11). This is followed by updated treatments of Maya ceramics (Chapter 12) and arts and crafts (Chapter 13). Part IV, on intellectual culture, consists of chapters on ideology (Chapter 14) and arithmetic, calendrics, and astronomy (Chapter 16), which have been revised but retain much of the original text. Chapter 15 (language and writing) is new, summarizing the significant recent advances in understanding ancient Maya script. The book closes with an Epilogue describing the destruction of Maya civilization at the hands of the Spanish conquistadores; this material has been reorganized to include an account of the conquest of Guatemala to balance the original treatment of the conquest of Yucatan.

The present work could not have been completed without the much-appreciated assistance of colleagues, friends, and family. My professional colleagues have generously shared with me both the results of their research and their thoughts about the ancient Maya. Several of my nonprofessional friends, though far removed from Maya studies, have nevertheless been a constant source of encouragement and aid. My wife, Judy, and our children, Daniel, Michael, and Lisa, endured without complaint the long retreats into the seclusion I find necessary for writing, even though this was often done during our summer vacations together. Though it is impossible to acknowledge the contributions of all those who have helped me, I would like to mention those whose assistance was direct and vital to the completion of this work.

Several colleagues kindly agreed to expend valuable time away from their research to read and comment upon the final draft of the text. I am, therefore, extremely grateful to Professors E. Wyllys Andrews V (Tulane University), Wendy A. Ashmore (Rutgers University), David A. Freidel (Southern Methodist University), and Gordon R. Willey (Harvard University) for assuming this task and providing numerous important suggestions that have been of considerable benefit to the book. Two of my associates at the University Museum of the University of Pennsylvania, Dr. Christopher Jones and Dr. Arthur G. Miller, were consulted on a continuing basis, even after they had also read and commented on the text; their assistance has been invaluable. Professor James A. Fox (Stanford University) not only read much of the final manuscript, but rewrote and expanded the coverage of Mayan languages and writing (Chapter 15). Fox also kindly provided material for much of the artwork in this chapter. Several other scholars have been equally generous of their expertise, including Professor William R. Coe (University of Pennsylvania), who kindly allowed me access to the rich sources of drawings and photographs from the Tikal Project; Peter Mathews (Peabody Museum, Harvard University), who read and offered significant suggestions for the same chapter, and who offered unpublished information on the Tonina monuments; Ian Graham (Peabody Museum, Harvard University), who checked and added data on the Maya long-count inscriptions that were used as a basis for Appendix A; and Professor Lyle Campbell (State University of New York at Albany), who provided linguistic information that aided the construction of Fig. 15.2.

Assistance of a diverse and significant kind was also given to me by other colleagues at the University Museum and by several graduate students in the Department of Anthropology at the University of Pennsylvania. Dr. Carl P. Beetz prepared most of the maps, and most of the drawings in Chapter 15 after drawings by Fox. In addition Robert Coffman, Eleanor King, Edward Schortman, Patricia Urban, and Lisa Kealhofer provided appreciated assistance. Too numerous to mention here (see Illustration Credits, pp. 673–77) are the many friends and colleagues who provided me with photographs and drawings resulting from their Maya research. Although space limitations allowed the use of only a portion of these, all were appreciated, and the present work has been considerably enhanced by the inclusion of these new illustrations.

Finally, I am especially grateful to my editors at Stanford University Press: William W. Carver, Senior Editor, who after initiating the project to revise the Third Edition of this book asked me to undertake what became a most challenging and rewarding task; and Jean Doble McIntosh, Associate Editor, who copy-edited the manuscript and attended to logistics with a cheerful outlook and professional expertise. Both have made important contributions, not the least of which was the suggestion to reorganize the book's chapters into their present structure.

*Media, Pennsylvania*                                                    R.J.S.

# CONTENTS

xii    Contents

# TABLES

# xvi    Tables

# A NOTE ON NAMES AND PRONUNCIATION

The term Maya is used throughout this book as both a noun and an adjective in reference to the Maya people, as in "the Maya," "Maya books," "Maya writing," etc., or to the Maya language proper of Yucatan. When referring specifically to the language *family*, however, it is customary to use the term Mayan, as both a noun and an adjective, as in "the Mayan languages," "Proto-Mayan," etc.

The names of some of the ancient Maya centers were recorded in the early colonial chronicles of Yucatan and the southern highlands. It would appear from these that Chichen Itza and Mayapan, for example, are original Maya names retained from the Postclassic era. But apart from exceptions like these, the original Maya names for most sites have been lost, and the names used today are in most cases those applied at the time the sites were discovered: Palenque, for example, was named after a nearby town with a Spanish name (*palenque*, or palisade), and Copan was named for a local chieftain shortly after the Conquest. Many centers have been given Spanish or Maya names that commemorate some outstanding attribute; examples include Piedras Negras ("black stones"), Uaxactun ("eight stone"), Coba ("wind-stirred water"), Tulum ("rampart"), and El Chayal (from "obsidian"). In the highlands, where the Spanish conquerors were accompanied by military allies from central Mexico, most of the Maya site names were translated into Nahuatl (the language of the Mexica, or Aztecs) and are known by these terms to this day (the Quiche Maya capital of Gumarcaaj is known as Utatlan, its Nahuatl name). In some cases, for example Tikal and Quirigua, the origins and meanings of site names remain obscure (though it would appear that Quirigua is from a non-Mayan language that preceded Mayan in that area).

The orthography for the various Mayan and other indigenous Mesoamerican languages was first worked out by Spanish scholars of the colonial period. Thus transcribed, Mayan vowels are pronounced as in Spanish; rough English equivalents for the vowels of Yucatec Maya are:

| | |
|---|---|
| *a* as in f*a*ther | *u* as in r*u*le |
| *e* as in l*e*t | (except before |
| *i* as in mach*i*ne | another vowel, then |
| *o* as in f*o*rty | as an English *w*) |

Consonants are also pronounced as in Spanish, though some need special mention:

| | |
|---|---|
| *c* (hard) as in *c*aught | *x* as *sh* in *sh*e |
| *ch* as in *ch*ur*ch* | *h* as in *h*is |
| *tz* as *ts* in nigh*ts* | |

Also, in Mayan languages there is a significant distinction between *glottalized* and plain consonants (see Chapter 15). The glottalized consonants have no English or Spanish equivalents.

Stress is usually regular in Mayan languages, and is consequently not marked. In Yucatec, for example, it is on the final syllable, whereas it generally occurs on the next-to-last syllable in Spanish and Nahuatl. Though Yucatec does have distinctive pitch accents, or tones, these were usually not marked by colonial lexicographers and are omitted here, as are accents on indigenous words generally, following the usage of Ian Graham, *Corpus of Maya Hieroglyphic Inscriptions* (1975: 11).

The sound *tl* so often seen in words derived from Nahuatl is known as a lateral affricate. It is pronounced with the tongue in position for a *t* but with the release of air at the sides of rather than over the tongue.

# THE ANCIENT MAYA

# INTRODUCTION

> This is the account of how all was in suspense, all calm, in silence; all motionless, still, and the expanse of the sky was empty. . . . There was nothing standing; only the calm water, the placid sea, alone and tranquil. . . . Then came the word. Tepeu and Gucumatz came together in the darkness, in the night, and Tepeu and Gucumatz talked together. They talked then, discussing and deliberating; they agreed, they united their words and their thoughts.   —*Popol Vuh* (Recinos 1950: 81–82)

Deep in the heart of the tropical forest of Guatemala lie the remains of one of the great centers of Maya civilization, one of the foremost archaeological sites in all the world. Hundreds of masonry structures, evidently unknown to the Spanish conquistadores and first seen by outsiders only in the mid-nineteenth century, are still in evidence at Tikal today. There are magnificent temples rising more than 70 meters (230 ft) above the ground, complexes of palaces and administrative buildings, sculptured monuments bearing intricate hieroglyphs and the portraits of powerful rulers and their gods. And there are reservoirs, causeways, and a host of lesser constructions. The elite of Tikal society presided over an elaborate hierarchy of nobles, priests, merchants, artisans, warriors, farmers, and slaves, and reaped the wealth of a network of commerce that extended from South America to Central Mexico. The priestly elite mastered many of the intricacies of mathematics and observational astronomy, and they interceded regularly with their gods in matters of noble destiny, success, and prosperity. Perhaps 100,000 people lived in and around Tikal during its prime, twelve hundred years ago. But Tikal was not alone: the course of Maya history saw the rise and fall of a score or more of centers that approached Tikal in size and power. And there were hundreds of smaller towns and villages scattered across the Maya area.

Just as Troy and Samarkand, Timbuktu and Rome, rose and fell in the Old World, Maya centers such as El Mirador, Tikal, Uxmal, Chichen Itza, Mayapan, and a host of others enjoyed careers of expansion, prosperity, and eventual decline, each in its time. By the time of the Spanish Conquest, in the sixteenth century, Tulum, Tayasal, Utatlan, and Iximche had become the most prominent of Maya powers. But these and the remaining Maya centers were destroyed in a protracted, traumatic conquest that consumed thousands of lives, of soldiers and non-soldiers alike, a scourge marked by appalling brutality, the

The principal buildings of Tikal, rising above the tropical forest of lowland Guatemala.

The centers of Maya civilization, often set deep in the tropical forest, have evoked feelings of mystery for centuries (Temple IV, the tallest structure at Tikal, Guatemala).

But the seeming mysteries of the ancient Maya are being solved by archaeologists and other scholars: (*right*) archaeologists Aubrey Trik and Froelich Rainey (foreground), excavating beneath Temple II, Tikal, Guatemala; (*below*) archaeologist and art historian Arthur Miller and archaeologist George Stuart at Tancah, Quintana Roo, Mexico.

determined mediation of the Church, and catastrophic epidemic disease. Thus did Maya civilization succumb at the hands of Europeans.

Ever since the remains of this brilliant civilization were first brought to light in the eighteenth and nineteenth centuries, the ancient Maya have attracted widespread interest and profound admiration. Part of this fascination undoubtedly derives from the image of a "lost civilization" and the seeming mysteries provoked by the discovery of scores of ruined cities deep in the jungles of Mexico and Central America. The questions posed by these discoveries were obvious. Where had this civilization come from? How could the Maya sustain themselves in such an inhospitable environment? What catastrophes had overwhelmed their abandoned cities? Today, scientific research, in a variety of disciplines, has made considerable progress in answering these and similar questions. The mysteries are being solved.

Still, the allure of the ancient Maya persists. The more we learn of them, the more profound is our respect. For as the research record shows, these were a people of astonishing achievement: in mathematics, astronomy, calendrics, and writing systems; in technology, political organization, and commerce; in sculpture, architecture, and the other arts. For the first time we are beginning to understand the origins of this civilization and the reasons for its growth and prosperity, as well as its setbacks. With this increasing knowledge we can recognize in the rise and decline of Maya civilization the same processes that underlie all human achievement, all human history. And although the ancient Maya may still seem somewhat alien from our point of view, their story is our story, an inherent part of the saga of human cultural development.

The story of the development of Western Civilization is familiar to most of us, for we are heirs to a cultural tradition with its roots in the ancient cultures of the Near East (Egypt, Mesopotamia) and in the Classic World of Greek and Roman civilization. We are aware, too, of the great and enduring civilizations of the Far East. We are less well acquainted, perhaps, with a distinct cultural tradition that gave rise to another series of spectacular civilizations, including that of the Maya. This tradition was unknown to the peoples of the Old World until, less than five hundred years ago, the Western world suddenly encountered a New World, inhabited not only by "savages" (a common term in those days) but by sophisticated peoples living in cities as large as or larger than those of Europe, who practiced the arts of writing, metallurgy, architecture, and sculpture. These discoveries shocked and amazed the Spanish, who were intrigued by the civilizations of Mexico and Peru even as they were destroying them. One of the soldiers in the army of Cortés that marched into the Valley of Mexico in 1519, Bernal Díaz del Castillo, described the moment when the Europeans caught their first view of the Mexica (Aztec) capital of Tenochtitlan from the mountain pass overlooking the sprawling city:

. . . and when we saw so many cities and villages built in the water and other great towns on dry land and that straight and level causeway going towards Mexico, we were amazed and said that it was like the enchantments they tell of in the legend of

Amadis, on account of the great towers . . . and buildings rising from the water, and all built of masonry. And some of our soldiers even asked whether the things we saw were not a dream . . . I do not know how to describe it seeing things as we did that had never been heard of or seen before, not even dreamed about. (1956: 190-91.)

To the Europeans of the sixteenth century, secure in the knowledge that they alone represented civilized life on earth, the discovery of the Mexica of Mexico, the Inca of Peru, and the Maya came as a rude surprise. Perhaps the situation at that time was analogous to what would happen to our present world if, content that we are the only known civilized planet in our Milky Way galaxy, we were suddenly to discover another planet inhabited not only by life, but by a civilization at least as sophisticated as our own. How would we react? Would we seize the advantage, assuming it was we who made the voyages of discovery, as the Spaniards did? The peoples of the New World were innocent to the ways of total, genocidal warfare as practiced by the Europeans, and because of their vulnerability, they were ultimately trampled by the conquistadores.

The Old World of the sixteenth century was not content merely to destroy the Mexica, Inca, and Maya civilizations. Their achievements were belittled, and their "pagan" religious rites, especially the mass human sacrifices of the Mexica, were held up as horrors to justify the Conquest. Lest we too easily decry such practices as human sacrifice among the ancient Maya (Chapter 14), we should remember that Europeans of four hundred years ago were fond of burning people alive for religious reasons, not to mention other activities seen as atrocities today. None of these peculiar Old World practices seems to have existed in the New World prior to European colonization.

But the ultimate disparagement of the peoples of the New World was the denial of their heritage, their own unique cultural tradition. When Europeans began to try to explain the existence of civilization among the "savages," the answer was clear: the impetus had to have originated in the Old World, the known birthplace of all such developments. Thus the Mexica, Inca, and Maya were seen as the survivors of forgotten colonists from the Old World civilizations. Egypt was perhaps the most commonly attributed source, but Greece, Carthage, Phoenicia, Israel, Mesopotamia, Rome, Africa, India, China, Japan, and others have all been invoked for this purpose at one time or another. In the first published description of the important Maya site of Palenque, in Chiapas, Mexico (written at the end of the eighteenth century), we find the following explanation for these mysterious ruins:

The conclusion drawn from thence must be, that the ancient inhabitants of these structures lived in extreme darkness, for, in their fabulous superstitions, we seem to view the ideology of the Phoenicians, the Greeks, the Romans and other primitive nations most strongly portrayed. On this account it may reasonably be conjectured, that some one of these nations pursued their conquests even to this country, where it is probable they only remained long enough to enable the Indian tribes to imitate their ideas and adapt, in a rude and awkward manner, such arts as their invaders thought fit to inculcate. (del Rio 1822: 19.)

This idea, which either explicitly or implicitly asserts that the peoples of the New World were incapable of shaping their own destiny or of developing sophisticated cultures independently from Old World influence, is still popular.

But the facts regarding the origins and development of New World civilization do not support the idea of intervention by peoples from the Old World. Rather, the evidence consistently points to an indigenous cultural development in the New World after the original migrations populated North and South America from Asia via the Bering land bridge, at least twenty thousand years ago.

Not all early scholars held to the view that the Maya and other New World peoples reached their peak of development as a result of influences from the Old World. One of the major figures in the discovery of Maya civilization, John Lloyd Stephens, anticipated the present consensus for indigenous development: "We are not warranted in going back to any ancient nation of the Old World for the builders of these cities. . . . there are strong reasons to believe them the creations of the same races who inhabited the country at the time of the Spanish Conquest, or of some not-very-distant progenitors. . . ." (1841, Vol. II: 455.)

This is not to say that accidental contacts between Old and New World peoples could not have occurred before the age of European exploration. And it is just as likely that lost fishermen or merchants from the New World landed on the shores of Asia or Africa as vice versa (though this possibility is seldom, if ever, mentioned in such discussions). But the archaeological evidence to demonstrate such contact, with one notable exception, has thus far failed to materialize. If firm evidence of early contact *is* discovered in years to come, it will be significant only if it can be demonstrated that the meeting between the Old and the New World affected the cultural development of one or both societies. Obviously, the European contact initiated in 1492 has been significant for the changes wrought in both the Old World and the New thereafter. But there are numerous accounts of earlier voyages to "lands across the sea" and contacts with unknown peoples. For example, the Vikings recorded apparent landings in the New World by Leif Ericson in 1001, and by Thorfinn Karlsefni eight years later. The Viking accounts have been supported by archaeological discoveries at L'Anse aux Meadows in Newfoundland, Canada. But these contacts apparently had no lasting effect on either society, the usual consequence of such limited encounters.

On the basis of the available evidence, then, the courses of cultural development in both the New and Old worlds seem clearly independent of each other and devoid of significant interaction until 1492. This book traces the story of one of the most brilliant of the New World civilizations, the ancient Maya, describing what is known about their society and their accomplishments. And it assumes that we can understand the ancient Maya on their own terms, that Maya civilization was shaped by a combination of internal cultural processes, interactions with adjacent peoples of Mexico and Central America, and to a lesser degree, stimuli from more distant societies as far away as North and

South America. As such, the ancient Maya are to be "explained" not as a product of transplanted Old World civilization, but as the result of the processes that underlie the growth of any culture, including those that develop the kind of complexity we call civilization.

The story will conclude with the Spanish Conquest, for the destruction wrought by the Conquest irretrievably transformed the developmental course of Maya civilization. The wars of the Conquest accounted for much of the immediate destruction, since the Maya resisted the loss of their independence with great tenacity. The prolonged conflict also disrupted agricultural production and commerce, and the resulting famines took their toll. The largest loss of life, however, was due to the diseases introduced by the Europeans, against which the Maya had no defenses. In the face of all these destructive agencies, the Maya institutions that had governed society were swept away and replaced by a colonial civil and religious administration that was part of the Spanish Empire. The former Maya elite class—rulers, priests, military leaders, and merchants—was decimated, and its survivors stripped of their former wealth and power. Religious conversion was a fundamental policy of the new authority, and a variety of measures, including the Inquisition, were used in attempts to crush the vestiges of Maya ritual and belief. In the course of these changes, many of the intellectual achievements of the ancient Maya were lost or severely attenuated. The native books (codices) were burned, and the use of Maya script soon disappeared. As a result, a considerable body of knowledge and beliefs—essential information about the ancient calendar, cosmology, deities, ritual, medicine, and history—was lost forever. Many of the traditional arts—painting, sculpture, metallurgy, lapidary work, and featherwork—disappeared, along with their practitioners.

The Maya economic system, too, was drastically altered. The best lands were seized and plantations established for the new masters. New products (such as coffee and sugarcane) soon replaced the goods that were fundamental to ancient commerce (cacao, obsidian, jadeite, feathers, etc.), and new markets and methods of transport replaced much of the complex network of trade routes that had tied the Maya area together. Not all the changes were violent or forcible. For the most part the Maya readily accepted the new European technology, and iron and steel tools quickly replaced those of flint and obsidian.

Yet, in the face of these profound changes, much of ancient Maya culture survived. Although most of its hallmarks were torn away with the Conquest, the very heart of Maya society—the agricultural family and community—clung to its traditions and preserved many of its lifeways. For the most part the Spanish administrators did not or could not reach the agricultural villages, except in areas where forced re-settlement was instituted; as long as required taxes and labor obligations were met, these communities continued largely to govern their own affairs. The social institutions of marriage and kinship that governed family life continued with little change.

After the Conquest, the Maya family continued to subsist by its own efforts, using the newly arrived steel tools to make agricultural production more efficient. Traditional crafts oriented to household consumption—weaving, basketry, pottery making—continued essentially unchanged. Local agricultural and manufactured products, together with those essentials in scarce supply (salt, tools, etc.), were exchanged in community markets that persisted after the Conquest; native commerce survived, albeit on a more limited scale. In some cases the new masters of the land encouraged the indigenous economy, by ordering and using pottery cooking or storage vessels or other Maya products. Because these items were usually made according to European specifications, their production introduced another avenue for altering ancient traditions.

The most enduring elements of Maya culture have been ideology and language, elements that lie at the heart of all cultures. The traditions of Maya ideology and language permeated and reinforced all facets of family and community life, and today continue to be most resistant to change. Despite the vigorous efforts by the Spanish to convert the Maya to Christianity, the traditional beliefs governing family life and the agricultural cycle often managed to survive even while accommodating the new religion. The Mayan languages, too, continued in the new setting. A secondary knowledge of Spanish is obviously useful in dealing with the wider world—for civil and economic interaction, for example—but the Mayan languages have persisted as the first-learned and sometimes only language in traditional family life.

The direct heirs to this Maya family and community tradition continue to this day to live in the area once occupied by the civilization of their ancestors. Although subdivided by many related dialects and languages, there are more than two million Mayan-speaking people in Mexico, Belize, and Guatemala. Obviously, to the extent that traditional social organization, agricultural practices, technology, and belief systems (including vestiges of the ancient calendar) survive, the study of contemporary Maya communities offers an important source of information for the reconstruction of ancient Maya civilization. The work of anthropologists who have studied these communities, including the pioneering research of Alfonso Villa Rojas, a Maya-born anthropologist, has preserved invaluable data that have improved our understanding of past and present.

The traditional culture of these people, however, altered by Conquest and subsequent colonial policies, is changing today at an unprecedented rate. The influences of the modern world seem capable of affecting profoundly what the Spanish could only partially disturb. Today, in Maya communities from the Yucatan to Guatemala, store-bought clothing has replaced handwoven textiles, plastic containers are often more common than traditional pottery vessels, and the transistor radio spreads the Spanish language and Western ideology everywhere. As a result, the younger generations in formerly isolated communities are turning away from the traditions that formerly assured the survival of Maya culture.

Weaving using the back-strap loom is an ancient craft still practiced in many Maya communities today (woman and daughter, San Pedro Necta, Huehuetenango, Guatemala).

Centralized markets, another activity continuing from ancient times, may still be found in many contemporary Maya communities (market at Chichicastenango, El Quiche, Guatemala).

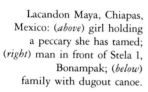

Lacandon Maya, Chiapas,
Mexico: (*above*) girl holding
a peccary she has tamed;
(*right*) man in front of Stela 1,
Bonampak; (*below*)
family with dugout canoe.

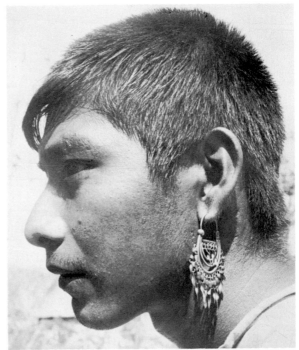

Yucatec Maya, Quintana Roo, Mexico:
(*above*) family; (*left*) wife of the head chief,
Tixcacal; (*below*) Juan Bautista Poot, minor
Tixcacal chief.

Maya people of Yucatan and Guatemala: (*upper left*) young Yucatec boy; (*upper right*) young Yucatec girl; (*middle left*) Quiche man; (*above*) young Quiche man; (*lower left*) Mam municipal officials (San Pedro Necta).

Maya people of Chiapas, Mexico:
(*upper right*) Tzotzil youth (Chamula);
(*middle right*) young Tzotzil girl (Iztapa);
(*lower right*) young Tzotzil man (Chamula);
(*below*) Tzotzil man (Zinacantan).

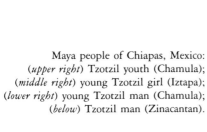

And the traditional culture of the Maya people is not the only heritage of Maya civilization that is disappearing in today's world. The archaeological remains of the ancient Maya also face destruction, for hundreds of Maya sites are being pillaged by looters searching for jade, pottery, and sculpture that can be sold on the thriving antiquities market. Examples of Classic-period Maya "art" fetch the highest prices, with the result that many centers never seen by the Spanish conquistadores, sites that have lain undisturbed for a thousand years, are now being destroyed for a few objects that have commercial value.

A common sight in the Maya area: a looter's trench leading to a plundered tomb at the site of Naachtun, Guatemala, strewn with broken plain pottery of no market value when compared to the prized polychrome vessels inside (photographed in 1976).

Another common form of
destruction from looting:
(*above*) Jimbal Stela 1,
photographed shortly after
its discovery in 1965 by archaeologists from the Tikal
Project; (*below*) the same
stela a few years later, after
looters failed in an attempt
to saw off the sculptured
front surface, destroying
the upper portion of the
monument.

As we shall see, the studies of these sites by archaeologists, epigraphers, and other scholars have produced considerable advances in our understanding of the ancient Maya. The key to this knowledge is archaeological evidence, the careful discovery and recording of the remains of buildings and artifacts which, like pieces of a jigsaw puzzle, reveal a picture only when all are found and properly put into place. The recent advances in deciphering Maya writing and reconstructing dynastic histories at many Maya centers are possible only because the sources of information were known to come from a specific site and were known to be associated with other kinds of evidence. Without this kind of contextual information, these advances in knowledge could not have been made. Thus, when tombs are plundered for their jade and pottery, or sculptures are torn from buildings and sawed off of stelae, their meaning is substantially reduced.

The loss of this kind of archaeological information is irreversible; once a building is torn apart to loot a single pottery vessel, all the evidence accompanying that artifact is also destroyed. And the remains of Maya civilization are a nonrenewable resource. With every site that is plundered, we lose another portion of the archaeological record until, someday very soon, little will remain.

What can be done to stop this destruction? There may be no stopping progress or the cultural changes affecting traditional Maya communities, but most countries have laws against archaeological looting. It is illegal to plunder Maya sites in Mexico, Guatemala, Belize, Honduras, and El Salvador. It is also illegal to import these looted materials into the United States and many other countries. Still, no country can police all of its archaeological sites, or prevent the smuggling of antiquities.

The ultimate answer is economic. Sites are looted for one reason: people will pay spectacular prices for Maya objects. Art collecting is a respectable and rewarding hobby or business, as long as it trades in paintings, sculptures, and other art produced by artists, past and present, for our enjoyment. But the buying and selling of archaeological pieces is not art collecting; a Classic Maya vase does not come from an artist's studio, but from a looted tomb. Perhaps if the demand vanishes—*if people refuse to buy these objects*—so will the pillaging.

It would be ironic if today's world, responsible for the interest and research that has done so much to recover the lost glories of Maya civilization, should also be responsible for the destruction of the ruins of that civilization and the disappearance of the last living links to the ancient Maya. There remains much to study—provided the opportunities are not denied us.

What we do know about these once enigmatic people is prodigious, and as the chapters that follow will demonstrate, their tale is at once fascinating and astonishing.

# PART I
# CULTURAL HISTORY

# 1

# THE SETTING

There is the white sea, and there is a red sea. They say that there is a sea like milk.
... Because they say that there is just water under the earth. And over the water
we are floating. Because they say that where the edge of the world remains . . . there
is just water . . . there they join, the edge of the world and sky.
—Contemporary Chorti Maya view of their world (after Fought 1972: 373)

The Maya area is defined both by the distribution of ancient ruins of Maya
civilization and by the known extent of peoples still speaking Mayan languages.
These criteria bound an area of some 324,000 km² (125,000 sq. mi.), a region
roughly the size of the State of New Mexico, or of the six New England states,
New York, New Jersey, and a quarter of Pennsylvania combined. The area
embraces the southeastern extremity of Mexico, including the whole of the
Yucatan Peninsula, and much of northwestern Central America, including the
nations of Guatemala and Belize and the western parts of Honduras and El
Salvador. Firm geographic boundaries to the Maya area exist only to the south
(the Pacific Ocean) and to the north (the Gulf of Mexico and the Caribbean
Sea). To the southeast and southwest, boundaries are more difficult to fix, since
they correspond not to discrete geographic features, but to zones of cultural
transition between Maya and non-Maya peoples. On the west the Isthmus of
Tehuantepec (almost 200 km, or 120 mi., wide) provides a convenient and
fairly accurate boundary between the Maya and non-Maya areas of southern
Mexico. On the east the zone of transition falls roughly along a line from the
lower Río Lempa in central El Salvador northward to Lago de Yojoa and thence
along the Río Ulúa to the Gulf of Honduras in the Caribbean Sea.

The diffuse nature of these cultural boundaries reminds us that Maya civilization cannot be seen as an isolated development. Beyond sharing common
roots in language and tradition, the ancient Maya were very much a part of a
larger cultural area, one that has come to be known as Mesoamerica.

The Mesoamerican culture area extends from northern Mexico into Central
America as far as Costa Rica. Like the Andean culture area of South America,
Mesoamerica is often referred to as a "nuclear area," for during the last several
millennia prior to European colonization, it was host to a series of crucial

cultural developments. These included the origins of permanently settled villages, the development of agriculture (based on maize, beans, squashes, and other crops), and the emergence of complex societies with urban or semi-urban centers, monumental architecture, calendrical systems, writing, and similar cultural features that are collectively and conveniently referred to as *civilization*. Thus, as part of Mesoamerica, the ancient Maya were influenced by, and in turn exerted an influence upon, their neighboring cultures, such as the Olmec of the Gulf coastal plain, the Zapotec and Mixtec of Oaxaca (west of the isthmus), the cultures centered in Teotihuacan and Tula (to the north, in central Mexico), and the less well known societies to the southeast in Central America.

## Natural and Cultural Subdivisions of the Maya Area

The Maya area has traditionally been divided into two general zones, the highlands in the south and the lowlands in the north (Fig. 1.1). According to this somewhat oversimplified view, the highland zone was seen to be ecologically diverse and rich in a variety of resources, whereas the lowlands were often viewed as ecologically uniform and poor in resources. This distinction was often extended to cultural development in the highland and lowland Maya zones, the view being that the lowland environment was inhospitable or even hostile to human utilization. Thus the ancient lowland Maya were seen as an enigma, an exception to the "rule" that brilliant civilizations could not develop in marginal tropical-lowland environments.

Recent and more thorough studies have laid these preconceptions to rest. It is now known, for example, that the Maya lowlands are not deficient in resources and that, far from being ecologically uniform, the area displays considerable variation. More important, recent ecological and archaeological investigations demonstrate that both the environment of the Maya area and the cultural development it supported are far too diversified to be subsumed under a simple highland-lowland dichotomy.

For its size, the Maya area represents one of the most varied environments on earth. There are contrasts in landform from rugged, almost inaccessible terrain to vast level plains. Differences in altitude produce cool temperate climates in most highland valleys and plateaus, and hot tropical conditions prevail at many of the lower elevations (Figs. 1.2 and 1.3). The traditional climatic subdivisions used in the Maya area reflect these altitude differences: *tierra caliente* (hot country) from sea level to about 800 m (2,625 ft), *tierra templada* (temperate country) from 800 m to about 2,000 m, and *tierra fría* (cold country) above 2,000 m (6,560 ft). But altitude is not the sole determinant of climate. Variations in the amount and timing of rainfall create contrasts across the full range of elevation: dry, almost desert environments are found in certain zones of both highlands and lowlands; and at almost any altitude a superabundance of moisture can produce rain-forest zones. Water is often readily available in free-

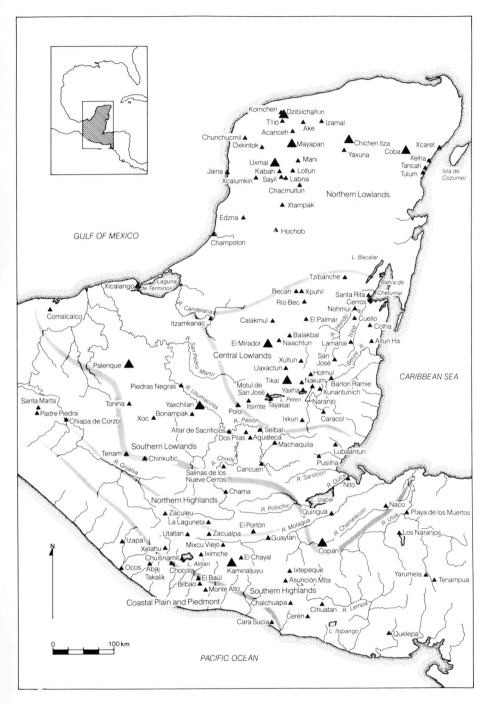

Fig. 1.1. Map of the Maya area, showing principal archaeological sites, major rivers, and generalized natural-cultural subdivisions.

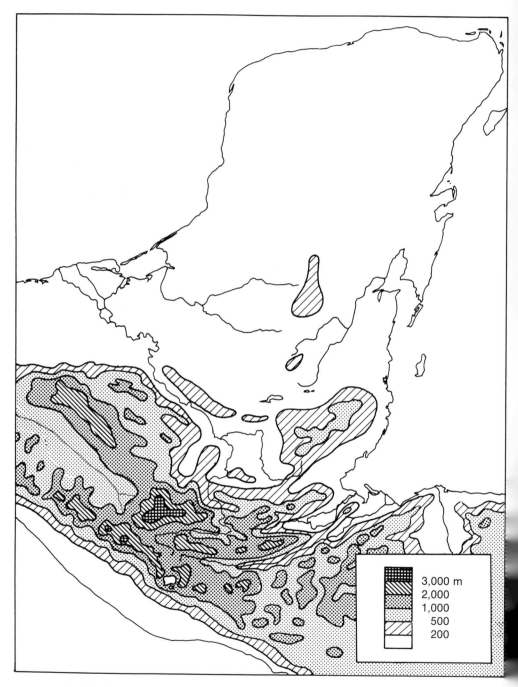

Fig. 1.2. Surface elevations above mean sea level in the Maya area.

3,000 m
2,000
1,000
500
200

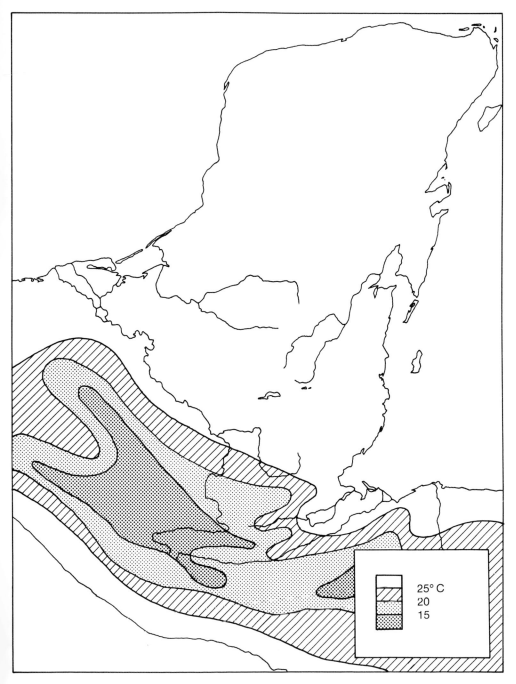

Fig. 1.3. Mean annual temperatures in the Maya area.

flowing rivers, or it may be inaccessible, found only in caverns deep beneath the surface. Highly productive agriculture is possible in areas with deep alluvial or volcanic soils, whereas other regions possess thin, poor soils that support little except thorn and scrub forest.

The southern portion of the Maya area is extremely active geologically. Here three continental plates converge, resulting in frequent and destructive volcanic eruptions and earthquakes that have produced repeated local and regional disasters—some of which have been detected archaeologically.

In order to assess the impact of this varied environment on the ancient Maya, modern investigators often attempt to reconstruct the natural conditions that existed in the past. The starting point for such studies is a description of the present environment, combined with the available archaeological evidence bearing on ancient conditions. By comparing evidence from both past and present, scholars attempt to determine how similar the ancient conditions were to those found today, and to what degree either human interference or natural processes have altered the environment. In a general sense, the findings from such studies indicate that during the past several thousand years the environment of the Maya area has been rather uniform, especially in regard to landform and climatic factors. Some changes have occurred, however; there is some evidence to indicate a general trend toward less rainfall in some areas of the lowlands. More important, perhaps, are indications that short-term variations in seasonal rainfall patterns may have affected living conditions in the past, especially in lowland areas such as the Yucatan Peninsula. In many highland areas the basic form of the landscape has been altered by volcanic deposits and erosion. But the most drastic changes, in the highlands and elsewhere, have taken place in the areas of heaviest recent occupation, where agricultural over-exploitation has resulted in deforestation and soil exhaustion.

In general, however, the Maya area can be characterized according to three basic environmental zones, each of which may be further divided. The boundaries of these divisions are to a large extent arbitrary; each ecological zone actually is bordered by subtle transitions to adjacent zones. Furthermore, because none of the subdivisions is itself uniform, the description of each is generalized. From south to north the environmental zones of the Maya area are: (1) the Pacific coastal plain and piedmont, (2) the highlands, subdivided into the volcanic, or southern highlands, and the metamorphic, or northern, highlands, and (3) the lowlands, subdivided into the transitional, or southern, lowlands, the Peten, or central, lowlands, and the Yucatecan, or northern, lowlands.

## The Pacific Coastal Plain and Piedmont

The broad fertile plain composed of recent (quaternary) sediments that stretches along the Pacific coast—from the Isthmus of Tehuantepec, across southern Guatemala, and into western El Salvador—has long provided rich resources for human existence and an avenue for both migration and commerce. Some of the earliest traces of permanent settlement in Mesoamerica have been found along the margins of the mangrove swamps, coastal lagoons, and meandering river mouths that lie behind the Pacific beaches. Extending inland from the sea lies the gently rising coastal plain proper, known for its rich alluvial and volcanic soils, but long denuded of most of its original forest cover.

The plain is transected by a series of relatively short, swiftly flowing rivers that drain the piedmont and upper slopes of the chain of volcanoes that parallels the coast some 50 to 70 km inland (30–44 mi.). The only major river in this subarea is the Río Lempa in El Salvador, which is also the traditional southeastern boundary of the Maya area.

For far longer than any other peoples of the Maya area, those of the Pacific plain have had to contend with waves of foreign migrants and invaders. The earliest of these appear to have been the Olmec colonizers from the Gulf coastal region to the northwest. Later on, a succession of peoples from Central Mexico settled this plain, and today, after the Spanish Conquest, peoples of European descent are among the inhabitants of the area.

Before the Conquest, the coastal plain was well known for its extensive cacao (chocolate) plantations. Today, the best lands are given over to the cultivation of sugarcane and cotton, and to cattle ranches, and the higher slopes support vast coffee plantations.

The climate of the coastal area is tropical (*tierra caliente*), with mean annual temperatures in the 25°–35°C range (77°–95°F), becoming somewhat cooler with the increasing altitude of the piedmont. There is a relatively dry period from January to April, the hottest days being those at the end of the dry season, and heavy rains fall from May to December. These rains are produced as the warm westerly winds from the Pacific Ocean rise and cool against the slopes of the volcanic highlands. The result is one of the highest rainfall rates in the Maya area: an average of over 3,000 mm of rain (120 in.) per year falls on the Pacific slopes of Chiapas and western Guatemala, and over 2,000 mm of rainfall (80 in.) is typical for most of the rest of the coastal areas (Fig. 1.4).

In the zones of higher precipitation, relic stands of rain forest still exist, usually at altitudes between 150 m and 800 m (500–2,625 ft). The tallest trees may reach 30–40 m in height, and a lower canopy averages 20 m above the ground. Beneath this cover a variety of palms, ferns, shrubs, and small trees, including cacao (the chocolate tree), may be found. As one moves into higher elevations, the rain forest gives way to seasonal growth of the mixed oak and pine typical of the highlands.

Although much of the original animal life of the south coast has been disturbed or destroyed by modern settlement and plantation agriculture, many species remain. The sea and coastal lagoons still abound with fish, shellfish, amphibians, and sea birds. Aquatic reptiles like the sea turtle, water moccasin, and caiman (a relative of the alligator) are still found. Inland, iguanas and various smaller lizards, small mammals, and birds are typical, along with rarer

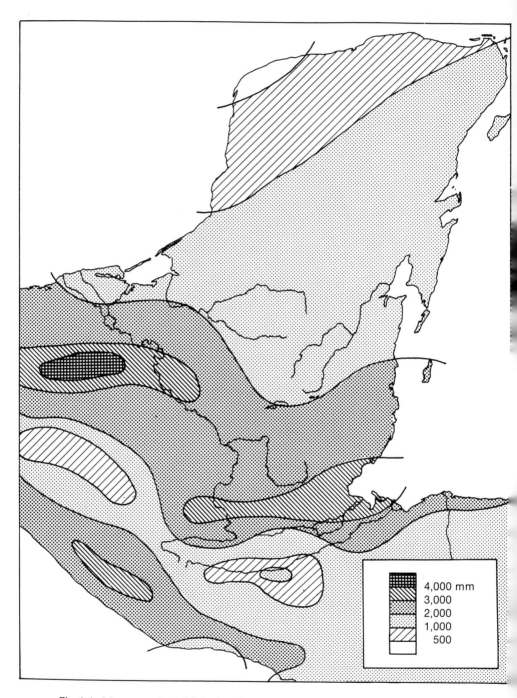

|  | 4,000 mm |
| 3,000 |
| 2,000 |
| 1,000 |
| 500 |

Fig. 1.4. Mean annual rainfall in the Maya area.

Fig. 1.5. Pacific coastal plain: mangrove growth in a coastal lagoon (Guatemala).

species such as the python. And the Pacific coast especially teems with mosquitoes, biting flies, and other insect pests.

The Pacific littoral and lagoons were exploited throughout the pre-Columbian era, for not only is this environment rich in food resources, but the extraction of salt provided a lucrative product for trade. Further inland, a series of sites grew to importance as centers of marketing, ceremonial, and political activity. Early centers such as Izapa, Abaj Takalik, El Baúl, and Cara Sucia (Fig. 1.5) represent the first flowering of Maya civilization, and appear to have prospered from the production of cacao and the control over the important trade routes that transect this region. Their successors were still thriving over a thousand years later, at the time of the Spanish Conquest, although by the beginning of the Christian era the center of florescent civilization had begun shifting to the lowlands to the north. Thereafter, the Pacific plain was clearly peripheral to developments further north.

## The Highlands

The greatest concentration of environmental diversity is found in the highlands, an area generally above 800 m in elevation and characterized by *tierra templada* and *tierra fría* climates. Owing to its diversity, many subdivisions are apparent within this zone. Lowland areas penetrate deep into the highlands along the rivers that flow toward the coasts. But for our purposes two major highland areas will be considered, one to the south, highly populated and dominated by recent volcanic activity, and the other to the north, less disturbed and characterized by older metamorphic formations.

## THE VOLCANIC, OR SOUTHERN, HIGHLANDS

The southern highlands lie in an east-west band between the belt of volcanic cones that parallels the Pacific coast and the great rift-valley system to the north (Fig. 1.1). This rift system marks, at least in part, the junction of the continental plates. As a result, this highland area experiences frequent tectonic activity, in the form of earthquakes and volcanic eruptions. A nearly continuous line of recent volcanoes forms the continental divide from the border of Chiapas, Mexico, through Guatemala, and into Central America (Fig. 1.6). From west to east the major cones are Tacana, Tajumulco, Santa María, Zunil, San Pedro, Atitlan, Toliman, Acatenango, Fuego, Agua, and Pacaya, all in Guatemala, and Santa Ana, Izalco, and San Salvador in El Salvador. The highest is Tajumulco at 4,410 m (14,470 ft). In recent years, Santa María, Fuego, and Pacaya have been especially active; and Izalco, the youngest volcano, has erupted almost continuously from its birth in 1770 until quite recently.

North of the belt of active volcanoes are the rugged older volcanic highlands, capped by thick deposits of lava and ash. In many areas river and stream action has dissected these deposits to form deep, steep-sided gullies, or *barrancas*. Within this area the fertile volcanic soils of the valleys and basins have supported large human populations for thousands of years. The largest of these basins is the Valley of Guatemala, the location of modern Guatemala City. Others include the Valley of Quetzaltenango, in western Guatemala, and the Ahuachapan and Zapotitan basins, both in western El Salvador. Many of the highland basins and volcanic calderas of the region contain lakes, such as Lago Amatitlan in the southern portion of the Valley of Guatemala. The most famous, owing to its extraordinary beauty, is Lago de Atitlan in central Guatemala. Lago Ilopango, near San Salvador, was formed in the caldera left by a violent eruption of about A.D. 200.

Apart from the interior drainage characterizing some of these basins, the principal rivers of the southern highlands flow northward as tributaries of the Río Motagua, which follows the continental rift eastward to the Gulf of Honduras in the Caribbean Sea. In the western portion, a similar drainage pattern forms the Río Grijalva, which flows through the central depression of Chiapas into the Gulf of Mexico.

The volcanic highlands have long provided important resources for their inhabitants. The ancient Maya quarried obsidian (volcanic glass, important as a source for sharp cutting tools) at several locations, the most favored being El Chayal on the upland flanks of the Motagua valley, northeast of the Valley of Guatemala, and Ixtepeque, some 85 km (53 mi.) to the southeast. Another basic necessity for grinding stones (manos and metates) were basaltic rocks such as andesite, available throughout most of the southern highlands. Although steel cutting tools introduced by Europeans have replaced the ancient reliance on obsidian, the traditional mano and metate may still be found as the favored means for grinding maize and other foods.

The climate of the southern highlands is predominantly temperate (*tierra templada*), with mean annual temperatures usually between 15°C and 25°C (59°–77°F). On the sparsely occupied upper slopes of the higher volcanoes, above the 3,000 m level (9,850 ft), much cooler temperatures prevail (*tierra fria*), with frequent frosts and occasional snow accumulations during the winter. Throughout the region a well-defined dry season extends from January to April, followed by a May-to-December wet season. Although the wet season may bring periods of steady rainfall lasting for several days, the usual pattern sees clear skies in the mornings followed by showers or thunderstorms in the afternoons or evenings. Rainfall totals are generally less than in the wetter areas of the Pacific coast, averaging 2,000–3,000 mm (80–120 in.) annually in most areas. Rainfall is much less in areas sheltered from the prevailing easterly trade winds, such as the interior of the Motagua valley and the central Chiapas depression, where annual rainfall is typically less than 1,000 mm.

Today the rich valleys and basins of the southern highlands support the greatest population concentrations in the entire Maya area. The fertile volcanic soils and nearly ideal ("springlike") climate have lured settlers from many other

Fig. 1.6. Southern highlands: Agua volcano, with the colonial capital of Guatemala, Antigua, in the foreground.

areas for at least the past 3,000 years. Yet, the earthquakes and volcanic eruptions would seem to belie the rich promise. Some 1,800 years ago a catastrophic eruption of Ilopango appears to have destroyed all life within 20–30 km, and the widespread ash fall rendered a larger zone (within a radius of 100 km from the volcano) uninhabitable for perhaps 200 years. But even small-scale volcanic eruptions endanger life and livelihood—as witness the recent excavation of a farmhouse and maize field instantaneously buried under several meters of ash released by a nearby volcanic vent at Cerén, El Salvador, sometime around A.D. 600–750 (Fig. 1.7). So-called minor eruptions, bringing ash falls and occasional lava flows, continue to disrupt people's lives today.

Earthquakes have probably taken an even larger toll in lives and property. Historical accounts beginning with the Spanish Conquest document a long series of major quakes during the past five hundred years. The first of these to

Fig. 1.7. Southern highlands: remains of an adobe house (ca. A.D. 600–750) buried by volcanic ash at Cerén, El Salvador. Note the white ash layer beneath the house from the earlier eruption of Ilopango volcano (ca. A.D. 200–250).

be recorded occurred in the southern highlands during the campaign of Pedro de Alvarado in 1526 (see the Epilogue). According to the account written by Bernal Díaz del Castillo, "the next day [we] came upon this valley . . . where now this city of Guatemala is settled. At that time it was altogether hostile and we found many barricades and pits and we fought with the natives to force a passage; and I remember that as we were descending a slope the earth began to tremble so that many soldiers fell to the ground, for the earthquake continued a long time." Among the most significant of these earthquakes are the cluster that destroyed the Colonial capital of Antigua in the eighteenth century, the one in 1918 that all but destroyed Guatemala City, and the recent rupture of the Motagua fault, which took more than 24,000 lives in 1976.

The effect of long-term, high-density human settlement has been to alter or destroy the original flora and fauna in many highland areas. Except for a few remote areas, the populations of many animal species (see the following section) have been reduced or extinguished. Much of the original flora of the highlands appears to have been a mixed evergreen-and-deciduous forest. Although deforestation has advanced into all but the most remote lands and higher elevations, stands may still be found containing various oaks, laurels, sweetgum, dogwood, and many kinds of pine. In higher elevations pines often predominate, sometimes mixed with cypress or juniper.

Beginning with the Spanish colonial era, wasteful agricultural methods and overgrazing by cattle and sheep have led to increased rates of erosion, eventually rendering entire landscapes almost uninhabitable. Efforts have been made recently to halt or even reverse this process. If these efforts are successful, they will ensure that the southern highlands can continue to support sizable populations.

## THE METAMORPHIC, OR NORTHERN, HIGHLANDS

North of the continental rift marked by the Motagua and Grijalva valleys lies a vast belt of highlands (Figs. 1.1 and 1.2). The highest peaks—those in the south, which exceed 3,000 m (9,850 ft)—are composed mostly of metamorphic deposits and range in age from the Paleozoic to the Cenozoic. Further north are the beginnings of Cenozoic sedimentary formations. To the west are the Chiapas highlands and the Altos Cuchumatanes of northwestern Guatemala (Fig. 1.8) and eastern Chiapas, followed by the Sierra de Chuacús in central Guatemala and the Sierra de las Minas that extends eastward almost to the Caribbean. The rich mineral deposits in these highlands have been mined for centuries. Perhaps the most important are the jadeite and serpentine deposits quarried by the ancient Maya, which are found along the southern flanks of the Sierra de las Minas, in the middle Motagua valley.

As one proceeds north, the rugged metamorphic mountains give way to limestone formations, such as those north of the Río Grijalva in Chiapas and in the Alta Verapaz of Guatemala. In this region of spectacular karst topography, typified by "haystack" hills and beautiful underground caverns, waterfalls spring from the sides of mountains, and rivers disappear beneath the porous hills only to reappear miles away.

Although many of the slopes of the northern highlands are poor for agriculture, richer alluvial soils have accumulated in many of the valleys and basins, such as the Rabinal valley north of the Sierra de Chuacús. Farther north, good soils, plentiful rainfall, and cool temperatures make the basins of the Alta Verapaz a prime area for modern coffee cultivation.

Much of the northern highland area is drained by the tributaries of the Río Usumacinta, which in turn flows northwest into the southern lowlands and on into the Gulf of Mexico. Beginning in the west, the Río Jatate flows out of the limestone highlands of Chiapas and joins the Río Lacantun, which originates along the eastern flank of the Altos Cuchumatanes. The main tributary of the Usumacinta, called the Río Chixoy (or Negro or Salinas) in the highlands, drains most of the modern Department of El Quiché, the central portion of the northern highlands. The other major tributary, the Río Pasión, originates farther east, in the Alta Verapaz. The eastern flank of the northern highlands is drained by the Río Polochic, which flows through a lush steep-sided valley into

Fig. 1.8. Northern highlands: view of Altos Cuchumatanes, northwestern Guatemala.

Lago de Izabal in the coastal lowlands of the Caribbean coast. Izabal's outlet to
the sea is via the Golfete and the spectacular gorge of the Río Dulce.

The climate of the northern highlands ranges from annual means below 15°C
(59°F), the *tierra fria* of the Altos Cuchumatanes, the highest mountains of the
region, to the tropical *tierra caliente* typical of the low-lying margins found to
its west, north, and east. Several of the plateaus of the Cuchumatanes support
the highest and coldest modern communities in Guatemala—San Mateo Ixta-
tan and Santa Eulalia lie above timberline at elevations over 2,500 m (8,200
ft). Yet most of the inhabited valleys lie between 750 m and 2,000 m, in
typical *tierra templada* climates. These areas support a varied semitropical
vegetation, whereas the mountain slopes, where rainfall is sufficient, are covered
with pine and oak forests.

For the most part, rainfall follows the same pattern as in the southern
highlands, but the intensity and length of the wet season tend to increase
toward the north. On the northern fringes of the highlands in both Chiapas and
the Alta Verapaz of Guatemala, rainfall totals average over 3,000 mm (120 in.)
per year. The Alta Verapaz is famed for its highland rain forest, the traditional
preserve of the rare and prized quetzal bird. The quetzal, now the national bird
of Guatemala, was of special importance to the ancient Maya, whose ruling
elite used its long, slender, brilliant-green plumes in their headdresses.

Because human disturbance has been less severe than in the areas to the
south, the northern highlands retain more vestiges of the original plant and
animal life. Here one can still find both howler and spider monkeys, kinkajous,
coatimundis, weasels, foxes, peccaries, armadillos, opossums, bats, owls, hawks,
vultures, parrots, and, as mentioned, the rare quetzal. But modern development in the form of highways, logging operations, petroleum exploitation, and
hydroelectric power plants now threatens this once remote and beautiful area.

The development of pre-Columbian settlement in the Maya highlands generally parallels that of the Pacific plain, although many traces of early occupation lie undiscovered beneath deep volcanic and alluvial deposits. Whatever the
effects of those deposits, the northern highlands seem never to have been as
densely occupied as the highlands to the south. The southern highlands share
with the Pacific plain the precocious growth of Maya civilization. During much
of the pre-Columbian era the major population centers were located in the
midst of the largest and richest highland valleys. Kaminaljuyu, situated in the
Valley of Guatemala, dominated the entire southern highlands during the early
development of Maya civilization. Adjacent regions were dominated by important, but less powerful, centers such as Chiapa de Corzo in the central depression of Chiapas to the west, El Portón in the Salama valley to the north, and
Chalchuapa to the southeast on the periphery of the Maya area. Later, during
the peaking of lowland Maya civilization, cultural influences from the north
penetrated the northern highlands, as at Chama in the Alta Verapaz, and
Asunción Mita in the southern highlands. One of the major lowland Maya

• centers of the Classic period, Copan, is located on the eastern margin of the southern highlands.

After the Classic period, highland settlements began to shift away from the valley floors until, shortly before the Conquest, most major centers were located in more secure settings, such as hilltops or plateaus surrounded by ravines. Here the Spanish encountered the capitals of the dominant southern Maya highland kingdoms, such as Zaculeu, Utatlan, Iximche, and Mixcu Viejo.

## The Lowlands

The greater part of the Maya area lies below 800 m in elevation and is characterized by a *tierra caliente* climate. But this lowland zone is far from uniform, for many of the same factors creating the diversity of the highlands are present here. Variations in elevation, rainfall, drainage, soils, and other factors create considerable diversity in the lowland environment, although these are usually less dramatic than in the highlands.

The most conspicuous feature of the lowlands is the tropical forest that still covers the undisturbed portions of the zone. In the drier areas of the Yucatan to the north the forest is stunted or reduced to scrub. Farther south, precipitation increases, and true rain forest is found. These forests are evergreen, or nearly so, with only very brief periods of occasional leaf fall. Rain forests flourish in areas of consistently high rainfall and are characterized by a great diversity of plant species—many unfamiliar to people living in non-tropical zones—that form multi-story canopies. The uppermost canopy, some 40–70 m (130–230 ft) above the ground, is dominated by such giant trees as mahogany and ceiba (a cottonwood). Beneath this, often 25–50 m in height, are found the American fig (amate), sapodilla, bari, Spanish cedar, and many other species. A lower story, usually 15–25 m in height, includes the ramon, or breadnut tree, rubber, allspice, and avocado trees, and a profusion of palms such as the cohune and escoba. Many trees support other plants, including strangler vines, lianas, bromeliads, and orchids. In the deep shade beneath the canopy are ferns, young trees, and many large-leaved plants.

Of course many of these plants were used by the ancient Maya. Ramon and avocado trees furnished food, the vanilla vine and the allspice tree provided condiments, and the palms were used for thatch and many other products. The role that these and other plants played in ancient Maya subsistence will be considered in Chapter 7.

The lowland forest is host to a great variety of animal life, including most of the species already mentioned as inhabitants of the highlands and Pacific coast. In addition there are anteaters, agoutis, pacas (large edible rodents), and other food animals such as tapirs, brocket deer, and cottontail rabbits. There are primates (howler and spider monkeys) and carnivores such as the ocelot, jaguarundi, and the largest New World cat, the jaguar. The ancient Maya held the jaguar in high esteem, especially for its pelt, which was symbolic of elite and ceremonial status. Bird life abounds: doves, parrots, woodpeckers, and toucans; and game birds, including quail, curassows, chachalacas, and the prized ocellated turkey. But the prized quetzal is absent, being confined to the highland rain forests. Reptiles and amphibians are also abundant: many species of toads, tree frogs, turtles, lizards, and snakes, including boas, racers, coral snakes, rattlesnakes, and the deadly pit viper, the fer-de-lance. The emergence of the primitive *Uo* frog each year from its underground habitat continues to signal the onset of the rainy season, just as it did for the ancient Maya. The rivers and lakes of the region provide edible snails (*jute*) and fish such as the mojarra and catfish. Lago de Izabal is famed for its tarpon, as well as róbalo (snook) and snapper. The lowland coasts abound with shellfish—shrimp, spiny lobsters, crabs—and sea turtles, probably the single most important source of food from the sea in ancient times. The manatee is also native to the southern coasts, and recent evidence from coastal Belize, supported by the sixteenth-century narrative of Bishop Diego de Landa, indicates that this animal also was used by the Maya.

Of course the most common forms of terrestrial animal life are invertebrates, including a host of spiders, scorpions, and other insects. Most remain little known, but one commonly sees dragonflies, myriad butterflies (including the famous blue morpho), leafcutting and army ants, termites, and a variety of beetles and bugs. More often felt than seen are mosquitoes, gnats, fleas, ticks, chiggers, biting flies, and wasps and other stinging insects. The ancient Maya raised stingless bees as a source of honey, and their descendants continue to keep hives today. Less beneficial are species that transmit serious diseases: sand flies that carry American leishmaniasis, assassin bugs that carry trypanosomiasis (Chagas' disease), and the malaria mosquito. However, many of these did not plague the ancient Maya; malaria and a host of other diseases were unknown in the New World until they were introduced from the Old World after the Conquest.

The lowlands are usually divided into a series of subzones (Fig. 1.1). At least three major subdivisions can be defined: the transitional (or southern) lowlands, the Peten (or central) lowlands, and the Yucatecan (or northern) lowlands. Each of these comprises further localized subareas, but our discussion will be confined to the three major divisions.

## THE TRANSITIONAL, OR SOUTHERN, LOWLANDS

The transition between highlands and lowlands is often gradual. Thus the rain forest that begins in the karst region of the northern highlands continues without interruption into the lower elevations to the north. A convenient, albeit arbitrary, distinction is the equally gradual transition from *tierra templada* to *tierra caliente* climates, generally marked by the 800–1,000 m (2,625–3,300 ft) elevation contours, which run from northern Chiapas through the northern portions of the departments of Huehuetenango, Quiché, Alta Verapaz, and Izabal in Guatemala.

Fig. 1.9. Southern lowlands: Río Usumacinta near Yaxchilan, Chiapas, Mexico.

This zone constitutes the southern lowlands, an area near to or within the rugged, broken karst terrain composed mostly of Mesozoic and Cenozoic limestone formations. It is typified by high rainfall and good surface drainage. Large rivers flowing out of the adjacent highland regions are available for year-round access to water and canoe transport. Furthermore, much of the southern lowlands possesses deep, rich soils and a high proportion of rain forest. Within this area are found the middle drainage basins of the Río Usumacinta (Fig. 1.9) and its tributaries (Río Jatate, Lacantun, Chixoy, and Pasión), the Río Sarstoon (which forms the southern boundary of Belize), Lago de Izabal, the Río Dulce, and the great alluvial valley of the lower Motagua, as well as the adjacent floodplains and coastal areas of northwestern Honduras (Río Chamelecon and Río Ulúa).

In this region of high rainfall, 2,000–3,000 mm (80–120 in.) fall each year (Fig. 1.4). Temperatures are also very high, averaging in the 25°–35°C range typical of *tierra caliente* climates (Fig. 1.3). In several areas of highest rainfall the dry season may be limited to only a month or two (usually between March and May), but rain may occur even during these periods.

Mangrove and other swamp flora predominate in the low-lying and coastal regions on the edges of this zone, but throughout the rest of the region conditions are often ideal for the growth of true tropical rain-forest species.

## THE PETEN, OR CENTRAL, LOWLANDS

As one proceeds north of the Usumacinta drainage basin, rainfall rates begin to diminish and the landscape becomes less rugged, although still characterized by low, generally east-west ridges of folded and faulted Cenozoic limestone. Within this region is a diverse range of soil and forest types, of lakes and low seasonal swamps (*bajos*). There is less surface drainage, rivers are smaller, and except near lakes, water may not be readily available throughout the year. These features help define the overall environment of the vast central lowland region of northern Guatemala, often referred to as the Peten.

Near the heart of the Peten is an interior drainage basin, some 100 km long from east to west and about 30 km wide (60 mi. long, 18 mi. wide). Along the base of the hills that form the northern side of this basin is a chain of about fourteen lakes, several of which are connected during the rainy season. The largest, Lago Peten Itza, is located about midway within the basin (Fig. 1.10); today, it is some 32 km long and 5 km wide. South of the basin lies a great irregularly shaped savanna (Fig. 1.11). Few trees grow on this grassy plain, and the soil is a compact red clay, apparently not well suited to cultivation. This soil condition, together with the relative sparsity of ancient remains of occupation, suggests that this savanna was not heavily populated in the past, but recent research indicates that at least some Peten savanna lands were occupied in ancient times. The average elevation of the savanna is about 150 m (500 ft), above which the karst ridges rise an average of 300 m.

The few streams rising in the central savanna find their way south and west into the Río Pasión. To the east, along the border with southern Belize, are the jagged Maya Mountains, an outcrop of underlying metamorphic formations (Fig. 1.2). The highest elevation, Cockscomb Peak, rises to a little over 1,100 m. The narrow coastal plain east of the Maya Mountains is watered by a number of short streams flowing into the Caribbean. On the western (Gulf) coast is a large alluvial plain, comprising most of the Mexican states of Tabasco and southern Campeche, that is for the most part a low-lying and often swampy region of lagoons and islands, homeland of the Chontal Maya and their canoe-borne commerce (see Chapter 6).

In the low ranges northwest, north, and northeast of the interior drainage basin, six rivers have their origin. Two of these, the Candelaria and the Mamantel, flowing generally west and north, empty into the great Laguna de Términos on the Gulf of Mexico, on the west coast of the Yucatan Peninsula. Farther south, the San Pedro Martír joins the Río Usumacinta before reaching the sea. The remaining three, the Hondo, the New, and the Belize, flow generally northeast and discharge into the Caribbean on the east coast of the Peninsula; the first two flow into Bahía de Chetumal, the largest bay on the coast of the Yucatan Peninsula.

The ranges of hills surrounding the savanna lands are covered with a dense

Fig. 1.10. Central lowlands: Lago Peten Itza and the island town of Flores, capital of the Peten, Guatemala.

Fig. 1.11. Central lowlands: savanna landscape, Guatemala.

tropical forest that includes all the plant species found in the transitional
lowlands to the south. The southern slopes of the Peten hills are usually sharp,
whereas the northern slopes drop almost imperceptibly from each crest to the
next watercourse. The vegetation of the Peten is usually classified as quasi rain
forest, since the more irregular distribution of rainfall throughout the year
results in extensive dry periods. The variations are subtle, however, and to the
untrained eye, the forest cover in the central lowlands appears little different
from the true rain forests to the south (Fig. 1.12). The tallest trees rise to 50 m
(165 ft) above the forest floor, but for the most part these towering examples of
ceiba, American fig, or mahogany do not form a continuous canopy. The dense
forest canopy, usually lower, is composed of ramon, sapodilla, fig, and numerous other species. A lower story, averaging 10 m in height, often includes
custard apple, allspice, palms, and other species. The shaded forest floor supports a relatively sparse distribution of young trees, ferns, and other broad-
leaved plants. The forest may be interrupted by grassland areas, and here and
there seasonal swamps called *bajos* (*akalche* in Yucatec Mayan) are covered with
low scrub and thorn growth. North of the interior drainage basin, the *bajos*

Fig. 1.12. Central lowlands: tropical forest undergrowth at Tikal, Guatemala.

• become more common, forming a zone of mixed forest and *bajo* growth. Today, the *bajos* of the Peten become swampy or water-filled during the rainy season, and it may be that in the past these depressions held permanent water, forming an area pocked by shallow lakes (see Chapter 7).

Rainfall tends to be somewhat less in the Peten lowlands than in the transitional lowlands to the south, although temperatures are little different (Figs. 1.3 and 1.4). The rainy season extends from May through January, the dry season from February to May (although showers are not infrequent during these months). In most areas annual rainfall averages about 2,000 mm (80 in.). Water never freezes, although cold "northers" in the winter frequently drive temperatures into the uncomfortably cool range. Averages are in the *tierra caliente* range (25°–30°C; 77°–86°F), although dry-season daytime temperatures often rise above 38°C (100°F).

Although many would find this environment to be one of the most difficult in the New World, the ancient Maya found it productive and even hospitable. Extensive areas of good soils were cultivated, using a variety of methods. Rich plant and animal resources supplied food, clothing, and medicine in great abundance. The local limestone made a fine building material; not only was it easily quarried with stone tools (the Maya had no metal tools), but it hardens on exposure to the elements. When burned, it reduces to lime. Throughout the region there are beds of friable granular limestone, which the Maya used, as we use sand and gravel, to make lime mortar. And in several areas the limestone bedrock holds deposits of chert, or flint, which the ancient Maya chipped into a variety of cutting, chopping, and scraping tools.

It is in these central lowlands that the earliest known centers of Classic Maya civilization have been discovered. In this heartland the achievements of the ancient Maya spread throughout the lowlands and reached their apex during the "golden age," from the third to the ninth centuries A.D.

THE YUCATECAN, OR NORTHERN, LOWLANDS

Another subtle transition marks the beginning of the northernmost lowland subarea, roughly corresponding to the northern half of the Yucatan Peninsula (Fig. 1.1). This area is characterized by a general lack of surface drainage, so that access to water becomes an increasingly critical factor in the location of settlements. Except for a wet pocket in the northeastern corner of the Peninsula, rainfall is far less than in the south (Fig. 1.4). Overall, the terrain is quite flat, except for a few ranges of low hills.

The high forest of the Peten becomes the bush of the northern Yucatan Peninsula almost imperceptibly. As one goes north, the giant mahoganies, sapodillas, Spanish cedars, and ceibas give way to lower trees and a much thicker undergrowth (Fig. 1.13). Palmetto grows in abundance along the east coast of the Peninsula. Farther inland there is a long, fingerlike extension of the southern rain forest that contains mahogany, Spanish cedar, sapodilla, and

Fig. 1.13. Northern lowlands: low forest and bush of Yucatan, Mexico.

Fig. 1.14. Northern lowlands: sierra, or low range of hills, Yucatan, Mexico.

other hardwoods. This stand of high forest extends into the somewhat wetter northeastern corner of the Yucatan. The fauna of the northern lowlands is essentially the same as in regions to the south, except that species adapted to drier habitats increasingly predominate farther northward into the Yucatan.

Immediately north of the Peten is the Río Bec–Chenes area, which is geographically and culturally transitional between the central and northern lowlands. As we shall see, the development of the Maya centers in the Río Bec–Chenes area initially paralleled the development of the centers to the south in the Peten, but later followed the course charted by the Maya of Yucatan.

Northern Yucatan is low and flat; the humus is usually not more than a few centimeters in depth, in contrast to the Peten soil, which may be up to a meter deep. There are extensive outcroppings of porous Cenozoic limestone (Tertiary and Recent), and owing to the underground drainage of rainfall, there are almost no surface streams. A low range of hills, generally not exceeding 100 m in height (330 ft), begins at Champoton on the west coast of the Peninsula, runs as far north as the city of Campeche, turns northeast to the town of Maxcanu, and then extends southeastward beyond Tzucacab in central southern Yucatan. This range is known locally as the *serrania*, or *Puuc* hills (Fig. 1.14).

Only a few lakes and rivers are found in northern Yucatan, the rivers little more than creeks. The largest body of water, Laguna de Bacalar in southeastern Quintana Roo, is about 56 km long and only 10 or 11 km wide (roughly 35 by 6 mi.). There are several smaller lakes, such as those around the site of Coba in northeastern Yucatan, and three small rivers, little more than shallow arms of

Fig. 1.15. Northern lowlands: cenote at Valladolid, Yucatan, Mexico.

the sea. On the east coast are two large shallow bays, Ascención and Espíritu
Santo.

The northern lowlands are unusually dry, owing to both low rainfall and
extensive underground drainage. Rainfall averages less than 2,000 mm annually (80 in.) in most areas, most coming during a well-defined wet season (June–
December), and the driest areas of northwestern Yucatan receive less than 500
mm in a given year. Temperatures are typical of the *tierra caliente*. The only
surface water, barring the few lakes and small brackish streams near the coast, is
that afforded by cenotes (from the Yucatec Mayan *dz'onot*). These large natural
wells are found throughout the area, especially in the extreme north. Cenotes
are natural formations, places where the surface limestone has collapsed and
exposed the subterranean water table (Fig. 1.15). Some of these natural wells are
up to 100 m in diameter; their depth varies according to the local water-table
level. Near the north coast the subterranean water is less than 5 m below
ground level, but as one proceeds southward the depth of the cenotes increases
to more than 30 m.

In country as devoid of surface water as northern Yucatan, cenotes are the
principal sources of water today, and they must have been equally important in
determining the location of ancient settlements. Where there was a cenote, there
one can expect to find traces of human occupation.

Recent archaeological discoveries indicate that the Caribbean coastal margins
of the lowlands were exploited long before settled village life emerged. Some of
the earliest Maya villages appeared in this same region, and agricultural settlements seem to have spread into the interior along the rivers of the southern and
central lowlands. The earliest centers of lowland Maya civilization appear in the
interior of the Peten, as at El Mirador and Tikal. The central lowlands were
long dominated by Tikal and a series of adjacent centers. Other important sites
arose in the southern lowlands, such as those in the upper and middle Usumacinta drainage (Seibal, Yaxchilan, Piedras Negras, and Palenque), and far to the
southeast at Copan and Quirigua. At the same time, there were large centers in
the northern lowlands, at Coba and Dzibilchaltun. But after the southern and
central lowland centers declined, the Yucatecan region was dominated in succession by centers such as Uxmal, Chichen Itza, and finally, Mayapan.

Differences in elevation, amount of rainfall, availability of water, temperature, distribution of plant and animal life, and location of natural resources
combine in the Maya area to produce one of the most diverse environments for
its size found anywhere in the world. But in characterizing this diversity by
describing a series of different subareas, we must bear in mind that these
subdivisions merge one into the next almost imperceptibly, and that local
variations within each may sometimes be as great as those that distinguish one
subarea from another.

## 2 THE ORIGINS OF MAYA CIVILIZATION

> This is the history of the world in those times, because it has been written down,
> because the time has not yet ended for making these books, these many
> explanations, so that Maya men may be asked if they know how they were born
> in this country, when the land was founded.
> —*Book of Chilam Balam* of Chumayel (Roys 1967: 98)

Who were the predecessors of the ancient Maya, and what shaped their development? In seeking answers to these questions, it is important to remember that the ancient Maya civilization originated and developed, not in isolation, but in the context of conditions and events in the wider area of Mesoamerica and, ultimately, in the entire New World. Thus, before considering the origins of the Maya, we should set the stage by outlining the chronology that orders these developments.

## The Chronological Framework

New World prehistorians traditionally use a five-stage chronological scheme to span the time from the earliest known peoples to the arrival of European colonists in the sixteenth century (see Table 1). The initial stage, called the *Lithic*, began with the earliest migrations of peoples from Asia across the Bering land bridge during the last ice age, some 20,000 to 40,000 years ago. During this period small bands of people roamed over much of the New World, hunting and gathering food and relying on simple chipped-stone tools. But these early hunting and gathering bands were not unchanging, and archaeologists can discern an increasing reliance on a few particular food resources as the bands in each area became more specialized. This reliance on the seasonal growth cycles of food plants or the availability of food animals was the first step toward two fundamental changes, the establishment of permanent villages and, eventually, the domestication of certain food plant and animal species.

The development of settled communities identifies the next period, the *Archaic* (ca. 6000–2000 B.C.). The earliest known villages appeared along seacoasts, such as those surrounding the Caribbean and along the Pacific, where the rich food resources of the shore and lagoon could support year-round settled life. Thus a rich environment, combined with an efficient food-collecting technology, gave rise to the first villages in the New World. Soon thereafter increasing reliance on certain food plants led to the gradual domestication of maize, squash, beans, and other plant species in highland Mesoamerica, and of manioc, potatoes, and a variety of other crops in South America. These stable sources of food also led to the establishment of permanent village life; and the larger population concentrations that resulted became the foundation for all the civilizations of the New World.

The *Preclassic* era (ca. 2000 B.C. to A.D. 250), which follows the Archaic, is marked by the development of the first New World societies sufficiently complex and sophisticated to be called civilization. These are the Olmec of the Gulf coast in Mesoamerica and the Chavin of the Andean highlands in South America. Both these civilizations appear to have had sophisticated religious and economic institutions, and to have seen in these institutions the basis of authority for hereditary leaders, or *chiefs*. These initial chiefdoms established a basic cultural pattern that most later societies in both Mesoamerica and the Andes were to follow.

During the subsequent *Classic* period (ca. A.D. 250–900) a series of civilizations arose in both Mesoamerica and South America that involved a more complex political organization, the state. States, which often accompany the development of cities, are characterized by having powerful sanctions (standing armies and police forces, for example) to support the political authority. One of the Classic-period civilizations of Mesoamerica was that of the ancient Maya. However, the Maya developed their own unique style of civilization, distinct in many ways from the more urbanized states of Mexico and South America.

The final chronological period is the *Postclassic* (ca. A.D. 900–1500). The Postclassic is marked by the development of the most complex and powerful states in the New World prior to European colonization, including the well-known Toltec and the later Mexica, or Aztec, states in Mesoamerica, and the Inca Empire in the Andes of South America.

## The Origins of Highland and Coastal Cultural Traditions

Where the Maya civilization would arise, two traditions of settled village life, one in the highlands, the other along the coasts, developed during the Archaic and early Preclassic periods. The area where these two traditions emerged was actually somewhat greater than the area ultimately occupied by the Maya.

The most complete record of the development both of village life and of agriculture in the highlands of Mesoamerica comes from outside the Maya area, in the Tehuacan valley of Mexico, southeast of Mexico City. Here, archaeological investigations conducted by Richard MacNeish and his colleagues have documented a sequence of human occupation spanning some 10,000 years. In

# Table 1
## Principal Epochs of Maya Cultural Development

| General cultural periods | Chronology | Areas | | |
|---|---|---|---|---|
| | | Pacific plain and highlands | Southern and central lowlands | Northern lowlands |
| Colonial | A.D. 1500 | Spanish Conquest | Conquest of Tayasal Itza | Spanish Conquest |
| | | Highland conquest states (Quiche, Cakchiquel) | Cortés expedition visits Tayasal and Nito | Political fragmentation / Fall of Mayapan |
| Late Postclassic | | | | Domination by Mayapan |
| | | Quiche warrior elites' entry into highlands from Gulf coast | Itza occupation of Lago Peten Itza region | Chichen Itza abandoned |
| Early Postclassic | | | | Domination by Chichen Itza |
| | A.D. 1000 | Initial occupation of hilltop and fortified sites | Population loss and eventual abandonment of many centers | Reoccupation of Chichen Itza by Itza / Putun Maya Expansion |
| Terminal Classic | | Cotzumalhuapa sculptural style along coast | Putun Maya expansion | |
| Late Classic | | Peak of population and size at many southern sites | Peak of population and size at most lowland centers | Growth in size and population of many centers; ties to central lowlands |
| Early Classic | A.D. 500 | Teotihuacan "colony" at Kaminaljuyu with economic and political ties to lowlands | Teotihuacan withdrawal; "hiatus" at many lowland centers / Expansion of Maya elite culture to peripheries of central lowlands | Initial sculptured stone monuments with hieroglyphic texts and dates; development of dynastic rule / (origins of state systems) |
| Protoclassic | | Ilopango eruption | Initial sculptured stone monuments with hieroglyphic texts and dates; development of dynastic rule | |

Late Preclassic

Middle Preclassic

Early Preclassic

500 B.C.

1000 B.C.

1500 B.C.

2000 B.C.

500

1000

1500

2000

tecture
(origins of complex social, political, and economic systems)

ture, including vaulted tombs, stucco-decorated façades, etc.
(origins of complex social, political, and economic systems)

Expansion of settlement into nonriverine areas

Expansion of settlement along rivers into central lowlands

Early sedentism at Loltun and Mani (?)

Early sedentism at Cuello & Coastal Belize
(origins of village life?)

(Izapan style), often with hieroglyphic texts and dates; probable development of dynastic rule
(origins of state systems)

Olmec influences in Maya area, probable "colonies" along Pacific coastal plain; initial monumental sculpture and architecture
(origins of complex social, political, and economic systems)

Early sedentism along the Pacific coast
(origins of village life?)

this semi-arid highland valley, conditions were right for the gradual domestication of wild maize and other food plants. But the development of highland agriculture was a long, slow process, extending over several thousand years. It took a great deal of time to perfect the agricultural methods that could support a group of people year-round. Thus permanent village life emerged slowly, and it was not until about 1500 B.C. that any firm evidence of permanent settlements in the Tehuacan valley was laid down.

There is less evidence for early human occupation in the Maya highlands. Refuse from Santa Marta cave, in Chiapas, Mexico, reveals that occupation by hunters and gatherers ended by about 3500 B.C. Unfortunately, there is a gap in the cave sequence after this date until around 1300 B.C., when the cave was reoccupied by people who relied exclusively on farming for subsistence. Recent research in the Quiché basin of the southern highlands of Guatemala has located over a hundred preagricultural sites, marked by chipped-stone tools made from basalt. These early hunting and gathering sites have been tentatively dated to a span from about 11,000 B.C. to 1200 B.C. However, the evidence for the transition to the beginnings of village life in this area remains elusive.

This dearth of information appears to be due largely to environmental conditions that have destroyed or obscured archaeological remains. Volcanic activity has deposited deep layers of ash over many areas of the highlands. The heavy rains of the region have redeposited volcanic materials and other soil on valley floors, deeply burying whatever might remain from the earliest settlers. As a result we can only speculate, on the basis of the evidence from other highland areas such as the Tehuacan valley, that the earliest peoples in the Maya highlands also underwent a long, slow development, adapting agricultural methods to a variety of local conditions. Though the environment of the Tehuacan valley is quite different from most of the Maya highlands (the middle Motagua valley and a few other areas in Guatemala have a similar semi-arid climate), the same general process probably took place. Yet because of the variety of soil types, rainfall rates, and terrain, it is likely that it took centuries for human groups to adapt successfully to the diversity of the Maya highlands.

In any case, we do not encounter firm evidence of settled village life in the Maya highlands until well into the Preclassic era. Current theories favor the idea that these first agriculturists were migrants from outside the highlands, probably from adjacent coastal regions, although it remains possible that they represented an indigenous tradition of highland agricultural development, like that documented in the Tehuacan valley.

Archaeological research still under way along the Caribbean coast of Belize, also directed by MacNeish, has reconstructed a long sequence of human exploitation of this shoreline environment. Although these finds come from surface surveys and are not yet verified by excavation, MacNeish reports that Archaic-period hunting and gathering appeared before about 9000 B.C. He also reports that the earliest evidence of settled village life yet discovered in the Maya area comes from this coastal area, during the interval from about 4200 B.C. to 3300 B.C.; thus these villages predate the oldest known permanent villages in the Mesoamerican highlands. Although the data must be interpreted with caution, owing to the fragmentary nature of the record, it appears that these early coastal villagers may have supplemented their diet with agricultural products. But their basic subsistence depended on their gathering the plentiful resources of the sea, lagoons, rivers, and adjacent zones—resources that included fish, shellfish, turtles, sea birds, reptiles, and a variety of other animals (as evidenced by the recovered remains of these species). The concentration and year-round availability of these food sources enabled people to live in permanent villages, rather than having to move from place to place to find adequate food supplies. Indeed, this pattern of coastal subsistence supports small villages along some of these same coasts today.

It is difficult to pinpoint the transition from hunting and gathering to agricultural village life in the Caribbean coastal lowlands. The best available estimate places it in the span from about 3300 B.C. to 2500 B.C., as expanding populations began to move inland. The earliest evidence thus far adduced for these villages also comes from MacNeish's recent Belize research. But it appears that pottery making, a typical characteristic of permanent settlement, did not appear until somewhat later. In northern Belize, permanent settlements in the valleys of the Río Hondo and Río Nuevo (both flowing into the Caribbean) have been marked by pottery making possibly as early as 2000 B.C. The research of Norman Hammond and his associates has revealed a portion of one such village at Cuello. Here the evidence is in the form of a series of associated radiocarbon dates spanning both the third and second millennia B.C., with the earliest at 2448 ± 88 B.C. The finds at Cuello include low house platforms (Figs. 2.1 and 2.2) coated with lime plaster and containing postholes (presumably once supporting pole-and-thatch houses), hearths, human burials, food remains, and a full assemblage of stone tools and pottery. The earliest pottery at Cuello, known as the Swasey Ceramic Complex (ca. 2000–1250 B.C.), is noteworthy because it represents, for its time, a diverse and sophisticated ceramic assemblage. Also of interest is the discovery of at least one mano and one metate fragment, in the earliest levels, and of evidence for maize agriculture, thus far the earliest recovered from the Maya area.

Excavations in northern Yucatan at Mani and the cave of Loltun have recovered pottery seemingly as old as the Swasey ceramics; and the finding of mammoth bones associated with stone tools in occupation levels beneath the earliest pottery in the cave of Loltun raises the possibility of far earlier hunting groups in the Yucatan.

A comparable, but slightly later, village development is known from the Pacific coast at several sites in southern Chiapas (Mexico) and Guatemala. The earliest of these settlements is associated with pottery of the Barra Ceramic Complex (ca. 1700–1500 B.C.), followed by a much more widespread and

Fig. 2.1. Early Preclassic remains from Cuello, Belize: a very low, plastered platform (Feature 262) with postholes from an apparently perishable structure with an interior, circular, clay-lined hearth, about 1800 B.C. (radiocarbon years). The rectangular pit in the upper right corner is a later grave shaft intruded from above.

diverse pottery tradition, the Ocos Ceramic Complex (ca. 1500–1200 B.C.). Subsistence for these early coastal villagers was based on seashore and lagoon gathering, possibly supplemented by agriculture. By Ocos times, population had increased, occupation had spread inland (at least as far as the Grijalva river valley in central Chiapas), and livelihood was clearly dependent on agriculture. On the basis of indirect evidence, such as the discovery of obsidian chips that could have been set in graters used to process roots, it has been suggested that the earliest Pacific coast villagers cultivated manioc, a root crop, but at least some reliance on maize is also probable.

Both the Caribbean and Pacific coastal villagers were culturally precocious, in the sense that they manifested the first indications of part-time craft specialists, social status distinctions, and even long-distance trade networks. For example, jade from the middle Motagua valley of Guatemala was found at Cuello in Belize as early as Swasey times. But neither the Caribbean nor the Pacific coastal village traditions appear to have been related directly to highland developments. Whereas the earliest pottery from the Tehuacan valley appears to have copied the forms of still earlier stone-container prototypes, no immediate ancestors for either the Swasey or Barra ceramic complexes have been discovered.

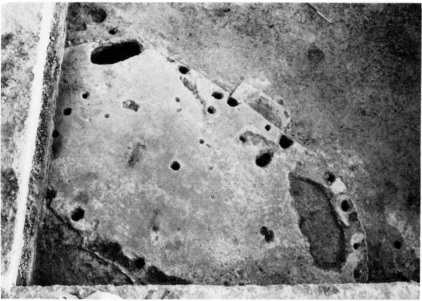

Fig. 2.2. Cuello, Belize: (*above*) a low, plastered platform (Feature 250) overlying Feature 262, with rounded sides and a low frontal step, about 1600 B.C. (radiocarbon years); (*below*) vertical view showing postholes around the perimeter of the platform. Note the same later intrusive grave shaft (Fig. 2.1) in the upper left corner.

The diversity and sophistication of these early coastal pottery traditions argues for yet undiscovered origins, either local or in some distant region. The lack of known prototypes has led some to postulate migrations or other contacts with northern South America, the only New World area with a documented, earlier, pottery-making coastal village tradition. At Puerto Hormiga, Colombia, early village life is dated by radiocarbon methods to at least 3000 B.C. Radiocarbon dating puts similar coastal villages on the Pacific coast of Ecuador, near Valdivia, by the same time, if not earlier. The fact that manioc, a cultigen postulated to be part of the early Pacific coast village tradition in Mesoamerica, originated in South America may be indicative of Archaic-period contacts between these two areas. In addition, evidence of maize, first domesticated in Mesoamerica but found in South America at about the same time, would appear to strengthen the arguments for contact. At present, however, only fragmentary evidence exists for these postulated connections, and only further archaeological research, especially in the intermediate areas of lower Central America, can hope to resolve this problem.

## The Olmec, Mesoamerica's First Civilization

The Pacific coastal village tradition is related to a similar early sedentary development found to the north, across the Isthmus of Tehuantepec, along the Mexican Gulf coast. In this humid, lowland jungle setting, the first true civilization in Mesoamerica, the Olmec, rose and fell long before the Maya achieved comparable status. Although we cannot treat the accomplishments of the Olmec in detail here, it is important to outline their development, for the Olmec established a cultural pattern that in many ways underlay later Maya civilization.

Archaeological investigations at San Lorenzo indicate that Olmec civilization had its roots in the early coastal village tradition of both the Pacific and Gulf coasts. At San Lorenzo, a low hilltop ceremonial center overlooking the Río Coatzacoalcos and its tributaries, the earliest remains of occupation (before ca. 1200 B.C.), includes pottery directly related to the Ocos Ceramic Complex of the Pacific coast. This is followed by a "proto-Olmec" period (ca. 1250–1150 B.C.), during which some Olmec-style motifs, such as incised designs on pottery and hollow baby-faced ceramic figurines, first appear. Then, during the period about 1150–900 B.C., San Lorenzo was transformed into a major center: in a mammoth construction project that required probably hundreds of laborers, the hilltop was leveled and shaped, perhaps to form a giant image of a bird, and surmounted by building platforms and monuments. The most famous of these is a series of carved colossal stone heads. The population appears to have increased rapidly during this time, probably as a result of the perfection of more efficient agricultural methods adapted to the tropical lowland environment, including the cultivation of the rich alluvial soils lining the banks of rivers, and the growing of more productive varieties of maize, originally imported from the highlands.

Evidence of this kind indicates that by around 1200 B.C. the Olmec may have developed a *theocratic* chiefdom, the first known in Mesoamerica. In this system a complex society is managed by an elite class under one ultimate authority, the chief, whose power derives principally from the custodianship of religion and wealth. We infer that the Olmec chief was bestowed a religious power derived from the belief that he provided security for the populace, through rituals to "ensure" proper conditions for agriculture, and that he reinforced the authority of his elite kinsmen. We can perhaps also infer that the chief's economic power had its base in the management of agricultural and other food-producing activities, and in concomitant rights to receive food tribute. Economic power also derived from the control of trade networks; direct archaeological evidence demonstrates that these networks provided the Olmec with a variety of exotic products, including jadeite, serpentine, and magnetite, that were used as symbols of the elite's prestige and authority.

Sites such as San Lorenzo are the remains of Olmec religious and economic centers. Although many similar sites are known, most lie uninvestigated in the almost inaccessible Gulf coast jungle. La Venta, the first Olmec site to be studied archaeologically, lies on an island surrounded by lowland swamp, and appears to have succeeded San Lorenzo as a major power center, after the latter declined about 800 B.C. La Venta was paramount during the period (roughly 1000–600 B.C.) when the power and influence of the Olmec were most extensive and their trade network dominated the exchange of products throughout much of Mesoamerica. Olmec trading centers were established in the central Mexican highlands (the most important being the famous Chalcatzingo site) and along the Pacific coast as far as Chalchuapa in western El Salvador (Figs. 2.3 and 2.4). Obsidian was imported from central Mexico and from the Maya highlands to be manufactured into cutting tools. Most exotic items, many apparently reserved for elite use, included jade from the middle Motagua valley in Guatemala, magnetite possibly from the Valley of Oaxaca in southern Mexico (used to fashion ceremonial mirrors), and fine kaolin clay mined near Chalcatzingo (used to make a distinctive, whiteware Olmec pottery). Perishable commodities were undoubtedly traded also, but no direct evidence has survived. Nonetheless, the Olmec likely imported cacao (the seeds of which are the source of chocolate) from the Pacific coast of the Maya area and quetzal feathers from the Maya highlands, as well as textiles and other products from a variety of sources.

Besides supporting the wealth and authority of the Olmec elite, these trade contacts had an important impact on non-Olmec peoples living in the resource areas. Very likely the Olmec used a variety of means to gain control over the distant resources they desired. Some areas, such as the middle Motagua valley, were apparently uninhabited or only sparsely settled. In such cases, the Olmec traders would have had little difficulty in securing jade or other products. In other cases, the Olmec undoubtedly bartered with local peoples to acquire certain goods.

Research conducted by Kent Flannery and his associates in the Valley of Oaxaca provides an example of a bartering interaction and its effect on the local population. Flannery's research reveals a sequence of occupation by agricultural

Fig. 2.3. Monument 12, Chalchuapa, El Salvador: rubbing of an Olmec-style boulder sculpture (Middle Preclassic, ca. 1000–400 B.C.).

villagers who had developed a degree of social complexity nearly as great as that of the Olmec by the time the latter established a trade relationship with the Oaxacans. Flannery infers that the Olmec treated the Oaxacans as equal trading partners, acquiring local products in exchange not only for material goods but also for both esoteric and practical knowledge. Thus, the Oaxacan elite seem to have sought out, in the Olmec religion, concepts that would better unify their own society, and may have adopted from the Olmec better means of economic and political organization, as well. In this way, Flannery postulates, the Olmec indirectly accelerated the development of Preclassic Oaxacan society.

Many centuries later the power of the Olmec waned, and their control over the trade routes that linked much of Mesoamerica was ultimately lost. But Olmec influence, probably in much the way it did in the Valley of Oaxaca, seems to have stimulated the societies of the southern Maya area, both along the Pacific coast and in the adjacent highlands. As we shall see, it is this area that saw the first flowering of the ancient Maya culture, the New World's most brilliant civilization.

Fig. 2.4. Monument 1, Abaj Takalik, Guatemala: an Olmec-style boulder sculpture (Middle Preclassic, ca. 1000–400 B.C.).

## The Prelude to Maya Civilization

By about 1000 B.C., most of the Maya area was occupied by villagers who subsisted by coastal gathering, swidden (slash-and-burn) agriculture, or a combination of these practices. These villagers, already deeply in touch with their own environment, had no doubt learned much from contact with the powerful, more complex society of the Gulf-coast Olmec. There were undoubtedly many reasons why this circumstance led to the rise of the Maya, and archaeologists have by no means revealed all of them. But recent research has tended to emphasize the search for "causes," and as a result, we can identify many of the most important forces in the development of Maya civilization. The most significant of these factors—ecological adaptation, ideology, trade, and competition—merit closer examination. They did not operate in isolation, of course, but rather in concert, to shape this remarkable civilization.

### ECOLOGICAL ADAPTATION

Ecological adaptation comprises the interrelated factors of environment, subsistence, and population growth. These are obviously important to an understanding of any human society. Environmental conditions and the means used to produce food largely determine the characteristics of a human population, including its health and nutritional status and whether or not it can sustain growth in size, density, or organizational complexity. The Maya area is in many ways an excellent illustration of these relationships, presenting its inhabitants with an extremely diverse environment, one that is rich in resources and blessed with a variety of opportunities for developing means to obtain food. The earliest means of subsistence, hunting and gathering, was greatly facilitated in this environment. Once fully developed, the area supported permanent villages in a few coastal environments and connecting river valleys rich in food resources. Throughout Maya prehistory, in fact, hunting and gathering continued to provide essential protein. Later refinements may have included the development of artificial ponds for the raising of fish, such as those identified along the west coast of the Yucatan Peninsula.

One of the earliest forms of cultivation was undoubtedly *swidden* agriculture, whereby fields were cleared, burned off, and planted with a variety of food crops, including maize, beans, squash, chilis, and such root crops as manioc and sweet potatoes. The fields could also be used to produce nonfood crops such as cotton and tobacco. But whatever the crop, the soil becomes exhausted after several years of cultivation, and new fields must be cleared and planted while the old lie fallow. Swidden agriculture is nonetheless adaptable to a wide range of environments, from highland valleys and mountain slopes to lowland jungle and scrub forest. In fact, it remains the most common agricultural method used by the modern Maya farmer, and is still practiced from the highlands of Guatemala to the lowlands of Yucatan.

Swidden cultivation is an example of *extensive* agriculture: large areas are needed to produce rather low yields per unit area, since a large proportion of land must remain fallow at any given time. More *intensive* agricultural methods usually require some means of replenishing the soils, such as the periodic flooding that revives alluvial river valleys. Probably the oldest intensive method was used by the Maya in the household garden, or dooryard, a plot of land adjacent to each family dwelling that is fertilized by household refuse. Although not as common as swidden agriculture, household gardens are still in use in many Maya communities today. Important garden cultigens include tree crops such as avocado, cacao, guava, papaya, hog plum, palm, and ramon (bread-nut), and some small plots are given over to the many crops grown in the swidden fields. But tree crops were not confined to the household gardens of the ancient Maya, since crops with commercial value, such as cacao and probably oil palm, were grown on plantations located in favorable areas like (in the case of cacao) the Pacific coast, the lower Motagua valley, and the Caribbean coast.

Other ancient intensive methods, techniques rarely found today or no longer used in this area, included raised fields and agricultural terracing; evidence for terracing has been found in parts of the Maya highlands and in hilly portions of the lowlands. Raised fields allowed productive use of swampy or poorly drained land and were similar to the *chinampas* ("floating gardens") of central Mexico. Crops were grown on parallel or intersecting ridges of well-drained, fertile soil built up from the swampy surroundings. The low areas between the raised fields provided drainage and served as a source for rich soil that was periodically scooped up to renew the growing areas. When completely under water, the low areas may have been used for raising fish and other aquatic life. These raised fields could support a variety of crops. It has been suggested that many of the remains of raised fields found in northern Belize were used for growing cacao as well as maize. Relic raised-field systems have been identified in the western lowlands, along the lower Río Usumacinta and Río Candelaria, in the eastern lowlands, and possibly in the *bajos* (seasonal swamps) of the central Peten.

How do these economic variables help us to understand the development of Maya civilization? To begin with, given the diversity of the environment within the Maya area, it follows that there would have been a corresponding variety in the subsistence modes and resources available in each locale and, consequently, a diversity of potentials for growth. Although each of the subsistence methods we have outlined had separate origins—some at an early date, others much later—all undoubtedly followed a similar pattern of development. As a given area was colonized, its environmental potentials led to a sequence of cultural responses: initial experimentation with known resource-acquisition methods, followed by acceptance of these methods (with or without modification) if they proved successful, or by rejection if the methods proved unsuccessful. Ultimately, in areas suitable for population growth, larger and larger settlements produced even greater incentives for the intensification of agriculture.

IDEOLOGY

The ancient Maya made no distinction between the natural and supernatural worlds, and there can be no doubt that their ideology—their concepts of the fundamental character and order of the world—was a significant factor in the development of their civilization. But the difficulties in reconstructing the beliefs of a long-vanished society are formidable, since so little of any ideological system leaves tangible traces for archaeologists to recover. Yet there are clues, and the Maya, through their elaborate calendrical and writing systems and their extensive inventory of sculpture and other art forms, have left a rich symbolic legacy of their ancient ideas and concepts. By combining what we know about contemporary Maya ideology with the knowledge recorded at the time of the Spanish Conquest and the recent advances in deciphering Maya writing, much of this legacy can be interpreted in a general way.

But the farther one ventures into the past, searching for the origins of various concepts, the less evidence there is to work with. Thus, whereas some symbols of ancient Maya ideology are available for study, others are likely to remain forever shrouded in mystery. And, of course, some essential concepts may never have been codified in symbols—perhaps the full inventory of ideas and concepts existed only in the minds of the ancient Maya. Whatever the reason, our attempts to understand those ideas are restricted by our having to rely on only a fragmentary record.

That said, we can nonetheless perceive certain indications of the role of ideology in the development of ancient Maya civilization. In the first place, it is difficult to separate ideology from any other aspect of Maya culture. The supernatural guided all aspects of life, even the daily activities of individual people, and included the ways by which food and other resources were acquired. Thus ideology was embedded in ecological adaptation, trade, and competition, the other factors we are considering.

The structure of Maya society was defined and sanctioned by the cosmological order. Economic transactions, political events, and social relationships, including family and village life, were all seen to be subject to supernatural control. Each individual role and social group had its part in the order, and the elaborate hierarchy of social classes was surmounted by the elite and ruling lords. The ultimate sanction, the threat of supernatural retaliation, helped preserve the structure of society. Most important, the hierarchy appointed specialists, intermediaries between humans and the supernatural who could intervene to gain supernatural favor and discover the meaning of events and what the future would hold (divination). The earliest supernatural specialists were undoubtedly shamans, part-time specialists who cured illness and divined the future. As Maya society grew and elaborated, an elite class with priestly powers emerged: full-time specialists with both supernatural and political authority, conferring on themselves the prerogatives of mediating between the

supernatural and the rest of society. This development marked Maya society as
a theocracy, where rulers were both political leaders and priests. The elite
thereby came to direct *all* activity—the giving of tribute, the building of
temples and palaces, the maintenance of long-distance trade, and so forth, all of
which were ordained by the cosmological order.

## TRADE

Trade among the ancient Maya embraced a complex of economic activity
involving the acquisition and transport of goods and the exchange of goods and
services (often in centralized markets). Although no conclusive physical evidence of ancient markets exists, these trade centers were noted at the time of the
Conquest, and their antiquity is assumed. But direct archaeological evidence for
ancient trade in a variety of commodities does exist. A distinction is often made
between localized trade, that within a single environmental zone such as a
highland valley, and long-distance trade, that between environmental zones.
The ancient Maya were a crucial part of a system of long-distance trade routes
that ran the length and breadth of Mesoamerica and beyond. The Maya
occupied an area intermediate between Mexico and Central America and rich in
highly desirable resources—jadeite, obsidian, salt, quetzal feathers. These assets
established them as essential middlemen.

The development of centralized markets was undoubtedly a crucial factor in
the growth of Maya society. Because goods could be exchanged in a single
centralized location, a village could engage in specialized production (of textiles
or pottery, according to its environmental potential), take its products to the
market center, and exchange them for other necessities from other villages. The
result was an economic unity and interdependency focused on the market
center, and each such market was linked to others by means of long-distance
trade, as well. The long-distance trade networks furnished exotic goods that
were often reserved for limited segments of society, the most important being
the items that furnished wealth and symbols of status for the elite class.

Together, these economic factors were a powerful stimulus for social organization and development. The marketing centers, to which the villages were tied,
were controlled by the emerging elite class, and the resulting economic power
accorded the elites became a crucial foundation for their status and authority.
Those centers in locations favorable to acquiring essential goods or controlling
important trade routes were in an advantageous position, and in most cases
developed the organizations necessary to strengthen the control of the acquisition, transport, and distribution of trade goods. As the managers of these
organizations, the elite increased their wealth, prestige, and power.

The primary long-distance trade routes in the Maya area were those that
connected central Mexico with Central America, the southern route running
along the Pacific coastal plain, the central route running across the Peten, and
the northern route following the Yucatan coast; secondary routes connected the

highlands with adjacent areas to the west, via the Pasión and other river valleys that lead to the Usumacinta or the central Peten. North-south trade routes tied together the Maya area, connecting northern Yucatan and its plentiful salt resources, for instance, with the regions to the south.

## COMPETITION

Even in the initial expansive colonization of the Maya area, competition for land and other resources could have been expected to mount as soon as areas for agriculture and settlement became scarce. Though more intensive methods of cultivation were developed in response to increasing scarcity, another solution emerged, that of competition between centers. The initial competition may well have been economic or religious, as market and ceremonial centers attempted to gain control over larger territories by gaining the allegiance of groups of villagers. But eventually the ultimate competitive option was taken up: military conflict between centers, to expand control over land and resources.

Militaristic expansion necessarily involves certain developmental consequences. In the first place, it creates the need for a new specialty, ultimately a new occupational class, the warrior. In time, the Maya warrior class seems to have become part of the "middle class" between farmer and elite that initially consisted of craftsmen, merchants, and bureaucrats. Second, conflict between centers creates new demands on social organization; and centralized authority is usually the most efficient means of directing a society and its military forces, in either an aggressive or a defensive situation. Thus, for the Maya, competition and conflict also stimulated the development of a more complex society and an increase in centralized authority.

Another consequence, for an area as environmentally diverse as the Maya, was that those centers already holding an advantage in population size and organizational efficiency tended to expand at the expense of the less powerful centers. In such a situation, an expansive power may continue to capture territory from its neighbors until it reaches the limits of its own organization and resources, or until it is checked by an alliance of lesser powers that, once unified, can successfully compete with the aggressive power.

Each of these factors was instrumental in the growth of ancient Maya civilization. The next four chapters trace this development through time, from its earliest manifestations in the Late Preclassic period to the close of the Postclassic, which came to its shattering end with the arrival of the Spaniards in the sixteenth century. In later chapters we shall return to some of these themes as we discuss ancient Maya subsistence, social and political organization, trade, and ideology in greater detail.

# 3 ⟨ •••  ⟩

# THE PRECLASSIC MAYA

The Lords governed the town, settling disputes, ordering and settling the affairs of
their domain, all of which they did by the hands of the leading men, who were
very well obeyed and highly esteemed.
—Landa's *Relación de las cosas de Yucatán* (Tozzer 1941 : 87)

We have seen how the early inhabitants of the Pacific coast established some of
the first settled communities in the Maya area. Archaeological evidence from
this region demonstrates that these people, the precocious and innovative southern Maya, provided an important foundation for what was to become Maya
civilization. Living along the coastal plain and in the adjacent highlands, they
were blessed with a rich supply of natural resources, especially an abundance of
food from the sea and forest and a wealth of minerals such as obsidian, basalt,
jadeite, and serpentine. This region also provides the most direct land routes
between Mexico and Central America.

The Preclassic era is usually divided into three or four periods. The Early
Preclassic (ca. 2000–1000 B.C.) saw the origins of agriculture and settled
communities. The Middle Preclassic period (ca. 1000–400 B.C.) was marked by
the Olmec presence in the southern Maya area. The subsequent Late Preclassic
(ca. 400 B.C. to A.D. 100) saw the emergence of a southern Maya civilization,
ancestral in many respects to the later Classic-period civilization in the lowlands
(Chapter 4). Finally, the end of the Preclassic era, often referred to as the
Protoclassic period (ca. A.D. 100–250), marks an apparent decline of the
southern Maya and the ascent of the lowland Maya to the north.

## Archaeological Investigations

The archaeological study of the Preclassic southern Maya area has enjoyed a
long career, though fewer excavations have been completed there than at sites in
the Maya lowlands. But although numerous Preclassic centers of the Pacific
coast and southern highlands have been known, and unfortunately looted, for

many years, their important role in the emergence of Maya civilization has been recognized only during the past few decades.

Among the first to record their observations of Preclassic sites in the highlands was Alfred P. Maudslay, who published an account of the great center of Kaminaljuyu in the late nineteenth century. However, the realization that Kaminaljuyu represented the largest and most important Preclassic southern Maya center did not take hold until the 1940's, after excavations were conducted by Alfred Kidder and Edwin Shook, under the sponsorship of the Carnegie Institution of Washington. Since then, numerous scholars have undertaken investigations there, culminating in the recently completed Pennsylvania State University project directed by William Sanders and Joseph Michels. Unfortunately, the bulk of the site will never be known, since it has been destroyed by the unremitting urban expansion of modern Guatemala City (Fig. 3.1).

Elsewhere in the highlands, recent programs have been conducted by the French Archaeological Mission in Guatemala and the Central Quiche Project from the State University of New York at Albany, but most of these investiga-

Fig. 3.1. Kaminaljuyu, Guatemala: a relatively undisturbed portion of the site; note the houses of modern Guatemala City, upper right.

tions have looked into the Classic and later periods. The University of Pennsylvania Museum's Verapaz Archaeological Project, in the Alta Verapaz and the Salama valley (Baja Verapaz), emphasized research at Preclassic sites. To the west, in Chiapas, the Brigham Young University–New World Archaeological Foundation, under the direction of Gareth Lowe, has undertaken the most comprehensive program of archaeological investigation in the southern Maya area. Since the mid-1950's, this work has surveyed and excavated numerous sites, the most prominent being Chiapa de Corzo, where occupation spanned the Preclassic period (and later). To the southeast, the University of Pennsylvania Museum sponsored the archaeological investigation of Chalchuapa, in El Salvador, beginning in 1954 and continuing from 1966 to 1970. Several smaller Preclassic sites have been excavated recently in El Salvador, including the Late Preclassic village of Santa Leticia near Chalchuapa, under investigation by Arthur Demarest of Harvard University.

Among the pioneering studies conducted along the Pacific coastal plain was that of Robert Burkitt, who excavated the Preclassic Chocola site in the early twentieth century. More recently, the New World Archaeological Foundation has investigated the important center at Izapa, along with numerous other coastal sites. In Guatemala, Lee Parsons excavated at Bilbao in the 1960's, and Shook has continued his investigations of coastal sites, the most recent being at Monte Alto and El Balsamo. The important Abaj Takalik site is being excavated by John Graham and his colleagues from the University of California at Berkeley.

## The Emergence of Chiefdoms in the Southern Maya Area

It is now generally accepted that the Preclassic era marked the emergence of the first complex societies in Mesoamerica, usually referred to as chiefdoms. Chiefdoms are characterized by permanent social and political status differences, such as social ranking and occupational specialization. As in less complex tribal societies, however, the organization of chiefdoms is also based on kinship. That is, social and political status is usually determined by birth: a person born into a high-ranking lineage acquires the status commensurate with his or her birthright.

The leader, or headman, of the highest-ranking lineage usually assumes the role of chief, the person possessing the highest status and authority within the society. The power of the chief derives from supernatural sanctions and economic control. As leader of the highest-ranking lineage, he inherits the supernatural support of deities and his own illustrious ancestors. Usually, the chief also receives the largest portion of tribute (goods and services) from the economic surpluses produced by others. But his authority is often limited to what can be done by persuasion or by acquiring and maintaining the allegiance of other lineages through the bestowal of favors and wealth, often from collected tribute.

• • •

## The Middle Preclassic

By the Middle Preclassic, the founders of Mesoamerica's first civilization, the Olmec, appear to have entered and even colonized the southern Maya area, so as to control both its natural resources and its trade routes. Archaeological evidence from Olmec sites indicates that obsidian from known sources in the southern Maya highlands was exported to the Gulf coast. It is likely that jadeite, serpentine, hematite, feathers, and other highland products were also traded or simply extracted for use in the Olmec heartland, to the northwest. Furthermore, the Olmec seem to have used the south-coast trade routes as part of an even larger economic network that connected Mexico with southeastern Central America. Olmec artifacts, such as small carved pendants, have been found as far south as Costa Rica.

Although the fragile evidence of cacao cultivation (seeds, pollen, and other plant remains) has not survived, the Olmec were quite likely involved in the production and distribution of this prized crop. Conceivably they were the first to set up cacao plantations on the south coast, a prime growing area for this crop, as later times attest. Olmec interest in the central lowlands and other parts of the Maya area, although less well understood, may have been due to their interest in cacao. The Caribbean coast, for example, was another prime cacao region in later times, and may have been so during the Preclassic.

To control certain natural resources, trade routes, and possibly the cultivation of cacao, the Olmec seem to have established a string of colonies along the Pacific coastal plain from the Isthmus of Tehuantepec to western El Salvador. These colonies were in a position both to secure local agricultural products, such as cacao, and to control the long-distance trade routes from the Maya highlands and from Central America. The evidence for these colonies is provided by a chain of archaeological sites along the south coastal plain that possess dramatic monumental sculptures of Olmec personages and motifs. The portraits on these monuments seem to represent elite rulers, perhaps local chiefs or the founders of colonies. At Padre Piedra, Chiapas, there is an Olmec-style monument with figurines and other artifacts similar to those found at the Olmec homeland sites on the Gulf coast. Just over the modern border at Abaj Takalik, Guatemala, a large boulder sculpture depicts an Olmec personage. Nearby, the excavations directed by Graham have uncovered a series of small monuments carved in characteristic Olmec style. Farthest to the southeast, the Las Victorias boulder at Chalchuapa, El Salvador, contains four carved figures; the two larger ones clearly depict Olmec personages. Nearby excavations revealed a large (22-m-high), conical earthen mound in the El Trapiche group that was built during the Olmec colonial period (ca. 600–700 B.C.) and appears to have been a near replica of the famed "pyramid" at La Venta. The La Venta pyramid, also conical, has been interpreted as representing a mountain or volcano, and the

Chalchuapa construction might have been built for the same purpose (in both ● ● ●
cases there is a small, conical volcano nearby).

These Olmec sculptures, their monumental scale (as at Chalchuapa), and the presence of similar, specialized pottery wares all indicate the presence of an Olmec-dominated, non-egalitarian society on the Pacific coastal plain in Middle Preclassic times. These artifacts suggest that the southern Maya region flourished under a series of chiefdoms dominated by a colonial Olmec elite and maintained by supernatural and economic sources of power.

The Pacific coastal plain was not the only area of Middle Preclassic Olmec presence, although the archaeological evidence is less clear in other parts of the Maya area. In the highlands several Olmec artifacts indicate trade relationships with the Gulf coast, but not necessarily an Olmec presence, and it is likely that centers such as Kaminaljuyu were already powerful enough to resist direct colonization by the Olmec. In the lowlands, an Olmec-style implement described as a "bloodletter" was excavated from a Middle Preclassic deposit at Seibal, demonstrating trade links across the lowlands to the Gulf coast. Farther to the west, at the site of Xoc in the southern lowlands of Chiapas, a spectacularly sculptured rock outcrop depicted an Olmec personage or deity carrying a maize plant. Tragically, the entire Xoc sculpture was destroyed in the early 1970's by looters attempting to remove it for illegal sale.

## The Late Preclassic

Olmec colonization and trade relationships, especially in the southern area where the best archaeological evidence exists, seem to have fostered further independent economic and political development during the Late Preclassic (ca. 400 B.C. to A.D. 100). This subsequent growth in southern Maya society may have followed the pattern reconstructed by Kent Flannery in the Valley of Oaxaca (see Chapter 2). Regardless, it is now apparent that by the beginning of the Late Preclassic, Olmec presence in the Maya area ceased. For the next few centuries the southern Maya centers became the most developed and prosperous of any in the Maya area, and some, such as Chiapa de Corzo, Izapa, El Baúl, Kaminaljuyu, and Chalchuapa, emerged as independent mercantile powers. Each seems to have been the capital of a prosperous regional chiefdom, a center for both ceremonial and economic activities. The economic sphere included the cultivation and distribution of cacao and other crops, as well as commerce in highland minerals and commodities from Central America. Most of these goods seem to have been borne by human carriers along the trails that followed the natural overland routes of the area. One of these, the highland route westward from Kaminaljuyu, followed the central depression of Chiapas, dominated by Chiapa de Corzo, to the Gulf coast. Kaminaljuyu was also a crossroad for north-south routes connecting the northern highlands (a prime source for quetzal feathers) to the Pacific plain. The most important route ran along the Pacific

• • •   coast, from Central America via the string of former Olmec colonies all the way to Tehuantepec, and ultimately to the great centers in the Valley of Oaxaca and Mexico. Thus the extensive trade network first consolidated by the Olmec appears to have continued to prosper under the management of the ruling elites that controlled the separate regional chiefdoms along these routes.

It is thus no accident that the earliest examples of Maya hieroglyphic writing and sculptural style are found at Late Preclassic southern Maya centers. Archaeological investigations indicate a rapid growth in population and the development of stratified, theocratic organizations, as demonstrated by massive ceremonial structures and the artifacts of a variety of ritual activities recognized as typically Maya. It is these southern Maya centers that displayed the first evidences of the flowering of Maya civilization several centuries before the rise of the Classic lowland sites.

Although no single center dominated the entire southern area, Kaminaljuyu, in the largest basin of the southern Maya highlands, appears to have been the

Fig. 3.2. Kaminaljuyu: plan of a Late Preclassic ruler's tomb in Structure E-III-3, showing the remains of the principal burial and of three young, presumably sacrificial companions. Numbered items refer to various grave goods, including jadeite beads, a jadeite mask or headdress, obsidian blades, stingray spines, stuccoed gourds, quartz crystals (most of which were clustered at the feet and along the right side of the principal burial), and 157 pottery vessels (circular objects).

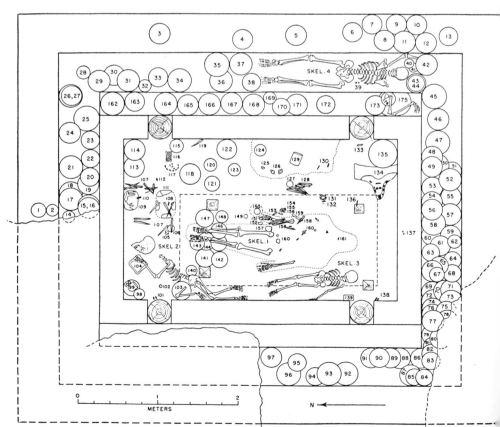

most powerful Late Preclassic site in the southern region, if not the entire Maya area. Its direct control of one of the most important obsidian quarries in the highlands, El Chayal (20 km, or 12 mi., to the northeast), made it the center of a trade network that distributed this prized commodity throughout the Pacific coast, the western highlands, and northward into the lowlands. The power and wealth that accrued to the Late Preclassic chiefs of Kaminaljuyu is vividly demonstrated by the two spectacular tombs excavated by Kidder and Shook. Both were found within the huge earthen mound of Structure E-III-3, which probably served as the platform for the ancestral shrines that were built over the tombs of these powerful chiefs (Fig. 3.2).

Evidence of similar, although often less imposing, constructions has been found at other Late Preclassic highland and coastal centers. The ceramics from these centers (which corresponds to the Miraflores Complex at Kaminaljuyu), the adobe architectural style, and particular characteristics of site planning give evidence of common traditions that may reflect economic or even political alliances with Kaminaljuyu. For instance, burials and caches containing pottery nearly identical to the Miraflores assemblage found in the Structure E-III-3 tombs have been found at many southern Maya sites, including El Baúl (on the Pacific plain), El Portón (in the highlands to the north in the Salama valley; Fig. 3.3), and Chalchuapa (to the southeast on the frontiers of Central America). One diagnostic type of pottery within this assemblage was Usulutan ware, distinctively decorated with swirling "resist" lines, usually in cream against an orange background (Fig. 3.4). Usulutan pottery, its antecedents distributed throughout the Middle Preclassic period at Chalchuapa, apparently developed in the southeastern Maya area. By Late Preclassic times it was probably manufactured at several southern centers, including Kaminaljuyu, Chalchuapa, and Quelepa (eastern El Salvador), and was traded throughout the southern Maya area. Usulutan pottery has been found in Chiapas, in many of the elite tombs of the important Chiapa de Corzo site; in the lowlands to the north, as at El Mirador and Tikal; and in Central America as far as Costa Rica.

The most significant characteristic of southern Maya civilization was the development of hieroglyphic writing and a distinctive sculptural art style. Glyphic symbols were sculptured on stone monuments in the Valley of Oaxaca and on the Gulf coast possibly as early as the Middle Preclassic, indicating that the ultimate origins for the Maya writing system might have lain elsewhere. And in Oaxaca, at Monte Alban, some glyphic notations appearing on stelae (upright stone shafts) may represent the names or titles of individuals, place names, and numbers. The numbers are represented by the common Mesoamerican bar-and-dot numerals (a dot equals one and a bar equals five). Two of the Monte Alban stelae (nos. 12 and 13) may have been carved as early as 450 B.C., although this date is merely an estimate. Both have bar-and-dot numerals and what appear to be calendrical and non-calendrical glyphs. Given the presence of such glyphs outside the Maya area, it is logical to assume that the knowledge of a writing system was brought to the Pacific coastal centers via the same trade

• • •  routes that connected them to the Oaxacan and Gulf coast centers. Once learned, however, the writing system was quickly adapted by the southern Maya to their own uses. Some "foreign" glyphs seem to have been modified and others invented to eventually create the most complex writing system in the pre-Columbian New World (see Chapter 15).

The most significant intellectual achievement of the southern Maya appears to be the invention of a calendrical system with a fixed zero date, known as the long count or Initial Series (see Chapter 16). Both calendrical and non-calendrical symbols were used to record specific events, and sculptured on stone stelae as durable memorials to rulers and other individuals. As such, they appear to have become objects of ancestor worship (a "stelae cult") as well as symbols of political legitimacy. Written records might also have been kept on perishable materials such as bark paper, like that used in later times. The best evidence for

Fig. 3.3. El Portón, Guatemala: Late Preclassic dedicatory cache excavated under the axial staircase (top) of the principal pyramid (Structure J7-2). Note the two incensarios with modeled jaguar heads and long obsidian blades (lying on several vessels) probably used in bloodletting rites.

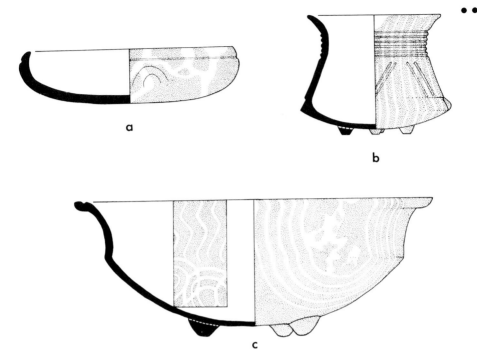

Fig. 3.4. Examples of Usulutan pottery from the southern Maya area: (*a*) Middle Preclassic; (*b, c*) Late Preclassic.

this is that the basic Mayan word for "to write," according to one interpretation, is based on the root for "to paint (with a fine brush)." Portable records in the form of painted tallies and messages could have been used for tribute lists or inventories of trade goods, which would have given an obvious advantage to the southern Maya in their economic competition with other regions.

Apart from the early carved inscriptions from Oaxaca, bar-and-dot numerals found on the Gulf coast seemingly date from the Late Preclassic. Stela C at the site of Tres Zapotes, Veracruz, contains a simple bar-and-dot inscription and sculptured elements in a very late Olmec style (Fig. 3.5). If the Tres Zapotes inscription was based on the same zero date as the one used by the Maya, then the Stela C date corresponds to 31 B.C. (If a different zero date was used on the Gulf coast, the Maya correlation could not be used to convert the Tres Zapotes inscription to a Gregorian date.)

Apart from a few exceptions, such as Stela C at Tres Zapotes and the Tuxtla statuette (Fig. 3.6), the majority of early calendrical inscriptions have been found in the southern Maya area, and it is telling that these southern monuments were sculptured in an early version of a distinctive Maya style. The calendrical notations consist of simple bar-and-dot symbols carved like the

Fig. 3.5. Fragment of Stela C, Tres Zapotes, Veracruz, Mexico. The recently discovered upper portion of this monument bears the initial long-count bar-and-dot number 7.

Fig. 3.6. Tuxtla Statuette, San Andres Tuxtla, Veracruz, Mexico. The crudely incised long-count date on the front appears to be equivalent to A.D. 162.

lowland inscriptions of the earliest Classic period but often without the accompanying day-unit glyphs. The earliest known date, again assuming a consistent Maya zero date, comes from Stela 2 at Chiapa de Corzo; its 7.16.3.2.13 reconstructed date corresponds to December 9, 36 B.C. At El Baúl, on the Pacific coast, Stela 1 has a partially destroyed but readable date (7.19.15.7.12) equivalent to A.D. 36 and a sculptured personage rendered in early Maya style (Fig. 3.7). Stela 2 (Fig. 3.8) at Abaj Takalik, also on the south coast, has a partially preserved date corresponding to this same era, the first century B.C. (probably 7.16.?.?.?). The recent intensive archaeological investigation of this site has yielded several new early Maya monuments, for example, Stela 5, with two long-count dates (8.3?.2.10.5 and 8.4.5.17.11), the latter corresponding to A.D. 126 (Fig. 3.9). Recalling the Olmec monuments uncovered at this site, Abaj Takalik provides clear evidence of Middle Preclassic Olmec colonial occupation followed by Late Preclassic Maya development. A similar sequence has been documented farther to the Southeast at Chalchuapa, and the same pattern can be inferred for several other southern Maya centers.

Many other Late Preclassic sculptured monuments, although without calendrical notations, are known from the southern Maya area. Executed with considerable artistic skill, they demonstrate the ceremonial and political authority vested in their chiefs. The most numerous assemblage of monuments was erected at the major center of Izapa; and because they have been known and studied for many years, the southern Maya style is often referred to as "Izapan" (Figs. 3.10 and 3.11). The great southern highland center of Kaminaljuyu also erected a series of Late Preclassic monuments. Of these, the magnificently sculptured fragment known as Stela 10 is perhaps the most significant, for it contains a rather long (non-calendrical) hieroglyphic text. Another sizable text, although badly battered, was found on the fragmentary Late Preclassic Monument 1 from Chalchuapa (Fig. 3.12).

In sum, it is clear that the Late Preclassic southern Maya were fully literate, possessing a developed hieroglyphic writing system that included zero-date calendrical notation. And since these early dates do not correspond to the ends of calendrical cycles ("period-ending dates"), as do many later lowland monuments (see Chapter 4), the Late Preclassic stelae are undoubtedly part of a Maya tradition to commemorate specific historical events and individual rulers. This inference is supported by the prevalence of defaced or broken stelae (Fig. 3.13), since this kind of destruction was usually a part of rituals held after the death of the person to whom the monument was dedicated, as an expression of Maya ancestor worship (see Chapter 14).

Overall, the archaeological evidence shows that the southern Maya area was the setting for the emergence of civilization during the Late Preclassic. Networks of economic, political, and ideological interaction integrated this varied region, and apparently fostered the growth of an increasingly complex society. The clustering of the same characteristics at each site in the region, seen in

Fig. 3.7. Stela 1, El Baúl, Guatemala: a personage sculptured in the early southern Maya style and a partially destroyed hieroglyphic inscription, including a bar-and-dot long-count date equivalent to A.D. 36.

Fig. 3.8. Stela 2, Abaj Takalik, Guatemala, sculptured in the early southern Maya style, showing a partial long-count date equivalent to the first century B.C.

Fig. 3.9. Stela 5, Abaj Takalik: two personages rendered in the early southern Maya style flanking a hieroglyphic inscription with two long-count dates, the latest equivalent to A.D. 126.

Fig. 3.10. Stela 21, Izapa, Chiapas, Mexico: rubbing showing a decapitation scene and an elite personage being borne in an elaborate sedan chair. The Late Preclassic sculptural style known as Izapan takes its name from this site.

Fig. 3.11. Fragmentary sculpture from Chocola, Guatemala, executed in the early southern Maya style (Late Preclassic).

A    B    C    D    E    F       G    H

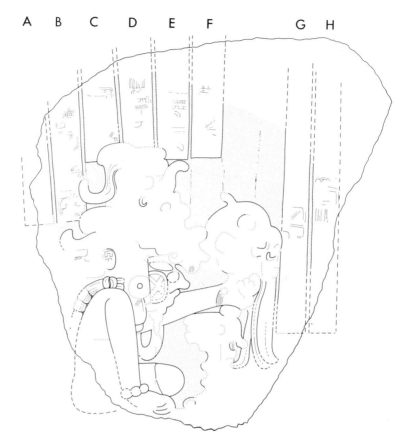

Fig. 3.12. Monument 1, Chalchuapa, El Salvador: drawing of a badly battered sculpture rendered in early southern Maya style, with hieroglyphic text (Late Preclassic, ca. A.D. 0–200).

artifacts (especially ceramics and trade goods), architecture, sculpture, and writing, indicates that continued interaction between centers characterized this period.

The ethnic identity of the Preclassic populations in the southern Maya area is not so clear, however. Although correlating linguistic groups with archaeological remains is in most cases impossible, a few clues are available from the distribution and development of Mesoamerican languages (see Chapter 15). This evidence has been used to propose that the Preclassic peoples of the southern Maya area spoke an early form of Chol, Mam, or Pocomam (all Mayan languages), or a non-Mayan language such as an ancestral Mixe-Zoquean tongue.

Language questions aside, the other elite-associated characteristics used to define Preclassic southern-Maya civilization—architectural elements, sculpture,

Fig. 3.13. El Portón, Guatemala: excavations in Structure J7-4 exposing a monumental basin (foreground) and a partially exfoliated sculpture and hieroglyphic column on Monument 1 (background). Middle to Late Preclassic.

Fig. 3.14. Late Preclassic "pot belly" sculptures provide one of the links between the southern Maya area and the lowlands to the north: (*above*) example from Chocola, Guatemala; (*right*) Monument 40, Abaj Takalik, Guatemala; (*below*) drawings of a miniature example from Tikal, in the central lowlands.

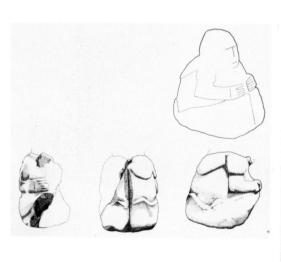

writing, and the calendrical system—are all prototypes of those that later blossomed in the lowlands during the Classic era. Thus the cultural development of the southern Maya can only be seen as directly ancestral to Classic Maya civilization (see Fig. 3.14).

## The Maya Lowlands in the Later Preclassic

The Late Preclassic was a time of prosperity in other portions of the Maya area as well. In the lowlands to the north, the cultural tradition begun by the earliest agricultural settlers, now traced back to the third millennium B.C., continued relatively unchanged through the Middle Preclassic. During this period, equivalent to the Swasey and Xe Ceramic Complexes (ca. 2000–800 B.C.), lowland communities were situated on or near seacoasts, rivers, or lakes that provided stable sources of water and easy routes of communication. An expansion of settlement beyond the confines of riverine environments and into the interior forested regions occurred by the end of the Middle Preclassic (corresponding to the Mamom Ceramic Complex, ca. 800–400 B.C.). Mamom ceramics are found throughout the central and southern lowlands, reflecting the population growth that necessitated the seeking and exploitation of new lands. This expansion was seemingly dependent on the construction of water storage facilities to ensure adequate supplies during the dry season.

The available archaeological evidence points to an egalitarian ("tribal") society in the lowlands from Swasey through Mamom times. Pottery and other artifacts such as chipped-stone tools generally lack specialized forms that would indicate the presence of occupational specialists or social class distinctions. The meager architectural remains reflect a simple division between domestic structures and a few slightly larger public platforms, perhaps used for community festivals or ceremonies. Examples of early lowland "public" architecture include a platform (4 m high) facing a plaza area at Altar de Sacrificios and a limeplastered platform built of boulders at Cuello, both dating to the Middle Preclassic. The Cuello platform was surmounted by a small building with rough, stone-rubble walls faced with plaster; its roof must have been thatched.

The transition from the Middle Preclassic to the Late Preclassic (which corresponds to the Chicanel Ceramic Complex, ca. 400 B.C. to A.D. 100) was marked by the emergence of larger and more complex social units. Sites founded in earlier times appear to have greatly increased in size; and many new centers began, as evidenced by the widespread findings of Chicanel-period pottery throughout the lowlands, perhaps a reflection of better communication between centers or even of political pressures resulting in conformity among the inhabitants. Clear evidence of class distinctions appears in the artifactual remains. Specialized pottery forms became common, and some were clearly used for ceremonial offerings (caches) or burial gifts. Other artifacts show the increasing differentiation associated with the presence of a wealthy ruling class. The

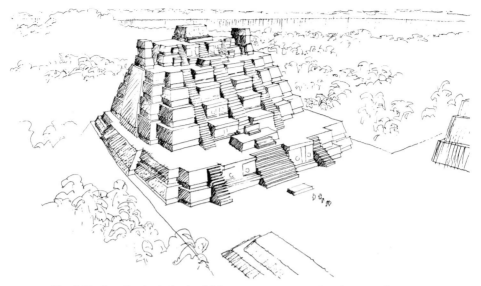

Fig. 3.15. Late Preclassic lowland Maya structure: restoration drawing of Structure N10-43, Lamanai, Belize, with a height of some 33 meters, one of the largest pyramids for its time in the Maya area.

tombs of these high-status individuals contain a varied inventory of imported luxury goods: jadeite, seashells, and pottery (including the prized highland Usulutan ware). Stingray spines, used for ritual bloodletting by the ruling class, are also found. Besides reflecting class and status differences, these goods indicate increased trade contacts with coastal regions, the southern Maya area, and beyond.

The architectural remains demonstrate the same trends. The oldest lowland buildings of monumental size date from the Late Preclassic, and compare in size and energy expenditure with the larger Olmec and southern Maya "pyramids" built in the Middle Preclassic. A platform some 33 m high was built at Lamanai, and one nearly as large (22 m tall) was constructed at Cerros, both in the eastern part of the central lowlands (Figs. 3.15 and 3.16). At Tikal, the Lost World Pyramid (Structure 5C-54) of this period measures some 80 m square at the base and over 20 m high. The oldest ceremonial precinct at Tikal, the North Acropolis, was begun, built out of cut-stone masonry. Within this old complex several Late Preclassic tombs have been excavated; one consisted of a masonry chamber representing the earliest known example of a corbeled vault (see Chapter 11). Also at Tikal, wall paintings were executed in a manner closely related to the southern Maya style, especially that of the Miraflores period at Kaminaljuyu (Fig. 3.17). This link to the south, also evidenced by certain ceramic and other artifactual similarities, may represent the beginning of important connections with Kaminaljuyu, ties that were economic and political in

Fig. 3.16. Late Preclassic Structure 5C-2nd, Cerros, Belize: (*above*) excavation of the richly decorated, terraced pyramid; (*below*) elaborately painted stucco-modeled masks flanking the axial staircase.

Fig. 3.17. Structure 5D-sub-10-1st, a Late Preclassic structure found buried beneath the North Acropolis, Tikal, Guatemala: (*left*) one of the painted figures on the wall of the tomb beneath

nature, and that were to play a significant role in the development of Tikal. But the most impressive constructions are at El Mirador, the largest known Late Preclassic center in the Maya area. As we shall see (Chapter 4), a key to understanding the origins and significance of the southern Maya connection may be found at this huge lowland center north of Tikal that appears to have reached its apogee at the end of the Preclassic and possesses sculpture executed in the southern Maya style. Far to the north, a sculptured relief in the cave of Loltun demonstrates obvious affinities to the southern Maya sculptural style, and probably dates to the end of the Preclassic era (Fig. 3.18).

Despite the rapid growth of the lowland centers in the Late Preclassic, however, there are no known examples of Maya hieroglyphic writing or calendrical notations from this period outside the southern area. From this we conclude that the leading edge of Maya civilization still lay with the southern Maya. Recent archaeological investigations at the lowland center of Cerros, in northern Belize, demonstrate that development there reached a peak in the Late Preclassic. Like other lowland sites, Cerros shows no Preclassic inscriptions, and like other centers such as Uaxactun (Structure E-VII-sub; Figs. 3.19 and 3.20), El Mirador (Structure 34; Fig. 4.3), and Tikal (Structure 5C-54), its Preclassic architecture included large, plastered masonry platforms decorated with huge masks and other relief panels (Fig. 3.16). Glyphic elements are also present, not as part of discrete texts, but rather incorporated into the masks and other building decorations.

the structure; (*center and right*) drawing of the partially preserved murals on the front of the structure.

The director of the Cerros research, David Freidel, has noted that this kind of architectural, artistic, and symbolic unity is typical of the Late Preclassic lowlands, probably reflecting a centralization of religious and civil authority. That is, the representations of both ideological and political power were fused together and presented architecturally, a different custom from that found in the southern Maya area. But the stela cult, originated in the south, reflected a separation of political and religious symbols from architecture. Whether this indicates a less centralized authority among the southern Maya, or merely a different tradition of expressing the symbols of authority, is not yet clear. What is clear is that when the southern custom of erecting commemorative monuments arrived in the lowlands, it brought along a new means for recording the ideological symbols, calendrical dates, and historical texts that would reinforce a preexisting centralized civil and religious authority. But the tradition of using architecture for the same purposes continued in the lowlands throughout the Classic period.

## The Protoclassic and the Decline of the Southern Maya

Seemingly in the midst of their prosperity, the precocious southern Maya fell into a sudden decline at the close of the Preclassic era, a period known as the Protoclassic (ca. A.D. 100–250). The decline was not confined to the south; in the lowlands many Chicanel-period centers underwent a setback at the same

Fig. 3.18. Cave of Loltun, Yucatan, Mexico: rubbing of a sculptured figure executed in a style closely related to that of the southern Maya during the Late Preclassic.

Fig. 3.19. Structure E-VIII, Uaxactun, Guatemala: (*above*) remains of a Classic-period structure before excavation; (*below*) after excavation, which revealed the well-preserved Structure E-VII-sub, with stuccoed façade.

Fig. 3.20. Structure E-VII-sub, Uaxactun: stucco masks.

time, and a few, like Cerros, appear to have been completely abandoned. But the effects of the Protoclassic decline were much more drastic in the southern area. The stela cult ceased to exist, and many sites were completely abandoned. For years, scholars have debated the causes for the demise of the southern Maya. Recent research in El Salvador, beginning at Chalchuapa and continuing in the nearby Zapotitan valley, has provided a promising answer to this vexing question. The downfall of the southern Maya now seems due to two related causes, one natural and the other economic and political. The major natural catastrophe was the eruption of Ilopango volcano (Fig. 3.21), in central El Salvador, which seriously cut agricultural production, depopulated a wide area, and severed the coastal trade connections between Mexico and Central America. Payson Sheets and his colleagues have documented the timing of this disaster (ca. 200–250), one consequence of which was that massive ash falls rendered the area within a 100-km radius of Ilopango uninhabitable for up to 200 years. These investigations indicate that a vast zone within the southeastern Maya areas was depopulated—whether through death or emigration, its inhabitants vanished. Although much of the Pacific coastal agricultural region appears to have escaped heavy damage, ash falls certainly reduced production at least temporarily. It has also been proposed that disastrous flooding from torrential rainfalls spawned by Ilopango's ash cloud affected much of the Maya area, and that far-reaching ash falls could have reduced the aquatic food resources harvested from rivers and coastal areas. Bruce Dahlin has hypothesized that south-

Fig. 3.21. View of the lake-filled caldera of Ilopango, all that remains of the volcano after its catastrophic eruption at the end of the Preclassic era (in the foreground, San Salvador, capital of El Salvador).

• • •  ern Maya refugees from the Ilopango disaster introduced plantation-style cacao production and an era of prosperity into new areas, most notably the eastern Maya lowlands. But the south-coastal trade network certainly could not be maintained without its sustaining population. The subsequent loss of trade connections through the area produced a final economic disaster for those southern Maya not immediately affected by the volcanic eruption.

The second factor in the decline of this region followed closely on the heels of the first: colonization by Teotihuacan, and the consequent loss of economic and political independence. This great center (Fig. 3.22), the first true urban state in Mesoamerica, rose to power in central Mexico during the last few centuries of the Preclassic period. Perhaps taking advantage of the disruption and chaos in the wake of the Ilopango eruption, Teotihuacan appears to have seized control of the Pacific coastal region of the Maya area early in the Classic period. By the Middle Classic, as this region's population and production of resources such as cacao recovered, Teotihuacan seems to have established an alliance with Kaminaljuyu, or a colonial enclave there, in an attempt to monopolize the cacao trade and the distribution of jadeite and obsidian throughout Mesoamerica.

Fig. 3.22. Teotihuacan, Valley of Mexico: view of the "Pyramid of the Sun," constructed during the rise to power of this first large urban state in Mesoamerica (Late Preclassic).

## Reconstructing the Maya Preclassic

The pattern of Preclassic development in the Maya area can be reconstructed in the following manner. The earliest areas to be colonized were lowland coastal zones and connecting river valleys that supported small villages through specialized gathering and, presumably, through limited cultivation of rich alluvial soils. During this Early Preclassic period, total population was very small, and confined to small scattered villages. Though we know little or nothing about the ideology of these early villagers, supernatural affairs were probably the responsibility of a few part-time shamans. Critical items such as salt were traded over long distances, and status items probably were, too, as suggested by the appearance of Motagua valley jade in Swasey-phase deposits at Cuello, Belize.

The southern Maya area was especially important during the Preclassic era because it lay along the principal routes between Mexico and Central America, and in a prime area for cacao cultivation. These aspects of favorable location, combined with the Olmec's desire for access to jadeite, obsidian, and other resources in the adjacent highlands, motivated the Olmec to colonize the Pacific coastal plain during the Early and Middle Preclassic. After the Olmec withdrew from the Pacific coast, toward the end of the Middle Preclassic, the southern Maya assumed control over both the long-distance trade routes through their region and the local critical resources (cacao, jade, obsidian, etc.). The heritage of Olmec presence and economic prosperity resulted in the accelerated development of southern Maya society. This development culminated in the first stable, authoritarian political institutions—hereditary theocracies—that were commemorated by sculptured monuments displaying calendrical dates and hieroglyphic texts. The precocious development of the southern Maya is thus seen as a direct legacy of Olmec colonization, combined with a favored economic position. By contrast, the emergence of a complex society in the Maya lowlands to the north was perhaps a more gradual and enduring process.

By the end of the Early Preclassic era, the adoption into the lowlands of swidden agricultural methods appears to have opened a series of new environments to human occupation, most notably the extensive lowland forests away from previously settled coastal and river margins. A prime motive for this expansion was undoubtedly population growth, an increase fostered by food surpluses.

In many regions of the Maya area, as long as new lands were available and population continued to increase, an excess of people could have moved into virgin areas, cleared new fields, and established new communities, thus continuing the expansion. As a result of this kind of colonization, population could grow without an increase in density, as farming villages became dispersed over the landscape. Eventually, however, this kind of expansion had to slow and eventually stop as new lands became scarce or unavailable. And, of course, not all lands were suitable for swidden agriculture.

• • •     Areas with prime soil and proper rainfall, or locations in control of such critical resources as salt or chert, could support more dense populations than could less well endowed lands. It was in these more favored areas that the more complex societies appear to have first developed. The earliest of these in the lowlands were probably the small chiefdoms that began to appear in the Late Preclassic. The first ceremonial and market centers seem to have grown around the residences of chiefs and an allied elite class that possessed both religious and economic status. These centers functioned as the chief's power base and as the setting for religious and economic activities that bound the elite class to the non-elites, who farmed the land or extracted the resources destined for trade. The power of the chief and the elite class relied on a reciprocal alliance with the people in the surrounding villages. Among the elite, full-time specialists in supernatural affairs emerged, priests who acted as intermediaries between the supernatural and natural worlds, using their esoteric knowledge (including the calendar) to assist or reinforce the farmer in deciding when to plant and harvest his crops. In return for this reinforcement and other kinds of security, the farmers paid tribute in the form of food and labor. The ceremonial precincts, then, provided a measure of well-being, whereas the adjacent markets furnished ready access to a variety of food, goods, and services, as well as centralized places for the exchange of the surpluses and products of each household. Control of the markets was an important source of elite power. And control over long-distance trade was both a source of wealth for the elite and a stimulus for the development of the efficient organizations needed to procure and transport both mundane and high-status goods from faraway lands.

Throughout the Maya area, the earliest religious and economic centers may have been nearly vacant except during days of ritual or market activity. But on those days, they attracted people from the surrounding countryside, much in the way that Maya towns do today. During those times the populace was under the direct authority of the chief and the elite. Yet there was a paradox implicit within this system: whereas the elite centers exerted a centripetal attraction on the populace, population expansion had a centrifugal effect, sending people outward in search of fresh agricultural land. In order to strengthen the ties with the farming class, and perhaps to enhance the wealth (tribute) and power of the chief by increasing the population under his authority, the elite must have taken measures to reduce the centrifugal tendency. One way of doing this, reducing the dependency on swidden agriculture, would have provided an important stimulus for the development of new and more intensive ways of producing food. The drive to increase centralized power also seems to have sparked a search for more efficient means to organize the populace and to have stimulated the growth of larger and more productive trade routes.

Throughout the Preclassic era these tendencies toward centralization can be inferred from the archaeological record by the growth in both size and population density of the Maya centers. This growth probably led the early Maya chiefdoms into direct competition, and perhaps even conflict, in an attempt to gain control over larger territories and populations, as well as trade routes. In the lowlands there may have been conflicts between several central Peten centers, each attempting to monopolize the portages between the Gulf coast and the Caribbean river systems used as trade routes. The site of El Mirador, for instance, may have been prominent for a time in the Late Preclassic, but it appears that Tikal was the ultimate winner in that competition, becoming the primary power during the subsequent Early Classic period. Similar competition and development seem to have existed between Preclassic centers located so as to control coastal commerce, such as Cerros, in Belize, and Komchen, far to the north near the Yucatecan coast.

But, as we have seen, the most important long-distance trade activity in the Preclassic seems to have followed the old Olmec, Pacific coast route. The southern Maya centers along this route and in the adjacent highlands appear to have been inhabited by the wealthiest and most sophisticated chiefdoms of their day. However, a rather sudden shift of emphasis to a trans-Peten route at the close of the Preclassic—probably brought on by the devastating eruption of Ilopango—appears to have contributed to the decline of the Pacific coast centers and, ultimately, to have stimulated cultural development in the southern and central lowlands. Almost certainly, Ilopango severed the old Pacific coastal trade routes to Central America and opened the way for this region to be subjugated by Teotihuacan.

**4**

# THE CLASSIC AND THE RISE OF THE LOWLAND MAYA

In due measure did they recite the good prayers; in due measure they sought the
lucky days, until they saw the good stars enter into their reign; then they kept
watch while the reign of the good stars began. Then everything was good.
—*Book of Chilam Balam* of Chumayel (Roys 1967: 83)

An examination of the Classic period (ca. A.D. 250–900) of the ancient Maya
tends to focus almost exclusively on the central and southern lowland zones. It
is within these areas that the lowland Maya rose to prominence and established
the hallmarks recognized as the flowering of Maya civilization. As with the
Preclassic, archaeologists have established certain chronological divisions as
points of reference in discussing the period, beginning with the Protoclassic (ca.
100–250, actually the transition from the Preclassic). This was followed by the
Early Classic (ca. 250–550), the era of crystallization of lowland Maya civilization. The Middle Classic hiatus (ca. 550–600) represents a pause or possibly an
actual setback in lowland Maya cultural development. But the subsequent Late
Classic (ca. 600–800) saw the revitalization and peaking of Maya civilization.
Finally, the Terminal Classic (ca. 800–900) witnessed the decline of civilization
in the southern and central lowlands.

## Archaeological Investigations

Our present understanding of Classic Maya civilization builds on the results
of more than a hundred years of archaeological research. And the lowlands have
been the focus of that research. The first discoveries and explorations of the
lowlands, in the nineteenth century, were due to the efforts of such trailblazers
as John Lloyd Stephens, Frederick Catherwood, Alfred Maudslay, Teobert
Maler, and Alfred Tozzer. In the early twentieth century, pioneering work was
done by Raymond Merwin at Holmul, and the basic lowland chronological
sequence was established at Uaxactun by the excavations sponsored by the
Carnegie Institution of Washington in the 1930's. The Carnegie Institution also
sponsored Sylvanus Morley's early excavations at Chichen Itza in the Yucatan

and at Copan. Other important investigations of this era included J. Eric Thompson's investigations at San José for the Field Museum and Linton Satterthwaite's research for the University of Pennsylvania Museum at Piedras Negras.

Until the mid-twentieth century, almost all archaeological research in the Maya lowlands was focused on the most prominent remains of past occupation, the clusters of large masonry structures and sculptured monuments that defined Maya sites. The first modern investigation to concentrate on the more humble assemblages of archaeological evidence, including the house mounds and settlement patterns left by ancient Maya farmers, was the Barton Ramie Project in the Belize river valley, sponsored by the Peabody Museum of Harvard University. This approach was incorporated in the largest and most comprehensive archaeological program yet attempted in the Maya area, the Tikal Project sponsored by the University Museum of the University of Pennsylvania (1956–70). Another extensive long-term project was undertaken by Tulane University at Dzibilchaltun (1957–65). During this same era an unprecedented number of lowland sites were investigated, including Altun Ha and Lubaantun in Belize, Altar de Sacrificios and Seibal in Guatemala, and Becan, Chicanna, Palenque, and Edzna in Mexico. More recent programs are under way, or have recently been completed, at the sites of Cerros, Coba, Colha, Copan, Cuello, Lamanai, Pusilha, El Mirador, Quirigua, and Tonina.

The results of this surge of archaeological research during the past 25 years have revolutionized our understanding of the ancient Maya. Even so, the archaeological evidence remains far from complete, so that our present conceptions of Maya civilization are bound to change as new information becomes available.

The archaeological foundation is supplemented by other extremely valuable sources of information, including studies of Maya art, architecture, and epigraphy (inscriptions). Art and architecture have been analyzed to discover the distribution of particular styles across both space and time; a true pioneer in this field was Herbert Spinden. The foremost study of Classic Maya sculpture, undertaken by Tatiana Proskouriakoff in 1950, demonstrated that the style of Maya monuments follows a developmental course consistent with other aspects of lowland culture. The most significant recent discoveries have been in the field of epigraphy. The calendrical inscriptions on Maya monuments and other materials had been deciphered by the end of the nineteenth century, and these texts have provided a most important and detailed chronological control for Maya archaeology. But during the past twenty years, major advances have been made in deciphering the non-calendrical inscriptions, and these have provided a wealth of new information about the political and social history of Maya sites (see Chapters 8 and 15). As a result, the study of the ancient Maya is emerging from the realm of prehistory to that of history.

•••• 
## The Southern Maya Area in the Classic

Compared to the amount of archaeological research that has been done in the lowlands, the investigation of the Classic period in the southern Maya area has been rather meager. Although extensive archaeological surveys have been made of many highland areas, excavations have been less frequent. Those at Kaminaljuyu remain the principal referent for the highland Classic period. Important Classic-period occupation has been revealed by excavations at several other centers, most notably Zaculeu, near Huehuetenango, and Chuitinamit-Atitlan, near Lago de Atitlan; and Zacualpa, Los Cimientos–Sajcabaja, La Lagunita, and Chitinamit, in the Quiche area to the north. On the Pacific coastal plain, Bilbao and Abaj Takalik remain the most thoroughly investigated sites of Classic-period occupation.

The most conspicuous external involvement was the colonization of the areas along the Pacific coast by Teotihuacan, the dominant central-Mexican power during the Early Classic. Teotihuacan was also deeply involved with the major highland power of the Early Classic, Kaminaljuyu. The nature of this involvement is still debated, but it seemingly included a process of increasing economic and political alliance that culminated in the establishment of a Teotihuacan colony at Kaminaljuyu, and perhaps intermarriage between ruling families. Aside from the sporadic occurrence of Teotihuacan artifacts (especially pottery), this external linkage is not well documented in the archaeological record of other highland Maya sites.

Kaminaljuyu seems to have declined during the Late Classic, after the apparent withdrawal of Teotihuacan by about A.D. 600. There are no known Late Classic highland centers of a size to rival the powers of the Maya lowlands during this era. The most common indications point to outside contacts with the lowlands to the north, as evidenced by imported polychrome pottery vessels and other goods. Predictably, highland products, especially obsidian and jadeite, were extensively traded into the lowlands. These and other highland products from the Classic period are usually common at the southern Maya sites, reflecting a well-developed regional trading network.

Overall, however, the southern Maya area seems not to have been densely occupied during the Classic period. In part, this may have been due to the slow recovery from the disruptions that ended the Preclassic florescence there (see Chapter 3); but the area did remain a rich and valuable source for a variety of products that were traded locally and sought by outside powers. Thus the production of cacao on the Pacific coast attracted, for a time at least, the attention of Teotihuacan. During the same period the southern highland center of Kaminaljuyu provided Teotihuacan access to, or control over, the El Chayal obsidian source and other local products. The lowland Maya centers we shall examine also gained access to highland resources by using the principal river systems, especially to the south via the upper Usumacinta–Río Chixoy system and its tributaries and from the Caribbean by way of the Motagua valley. A series of these lowland centers rose to prominence during the Late Classic; significantly, they were the ones situated such that they could control trade along these routes to and from the highlands.

## Primary Centers:
## The Emergence of States in the Maya Lowlands

Implicit in our discussion of the Classic period is the notion that the lowland Maya were organized at a state level of social complexity during this time. A state-system society is stratified into a series of classes, including full-time occupational specialists, topped by a highly centralized, hierarchical government that rules a territory with well-defined boundaries. States characteristically develop political power, not simply an authority derived from economic, social, and religious sanctions. Though typical of chiefdoms, these sanctions may also be found in states, where they are augmented by a stable, well-organized administrative hierarchy of full-time specialists in the management of society. Political authority is, of course, backed by the means to carry out governmental policies and decisions: usually a legal system enforced by a police or military organization.

In most early or preindustrial states the political system is headed by a single office, such as "king." This ruler possesses considerable power by virtue of his position as head of the administrative hierarchy and its institutions of enforcement. Power is also based on economic and religious sanctions, such as the right of tribute collection and the concept of divine right or its equivalent. Political stability is further assured if there is a uniform rule of succession to the rulership, as in father to eldest son (primogeniture). Orderly succession by primogeniture or other means usually results in ruling dynasties like those found in most preindustrial states (ancient Egypt, China, medieval Europe, and so forth). But the continuity of the system may be in jeopardy when there is no uniform rule of succession, or when a ruler leaves no clear heir. Periods of uncertainty and even chaos are often the result (even some modern industrial states may experience such traumas if they lack an established rule of succession).

In the case of the ancient Maya, there is some evidence that rulership was claimed as a kind of divine right, perhaps by a supernatural identity like the god-kings in many preindustrial states of the Old World. Although there was a single office for the highest political authority in each major center, some epigraphic and ethnohistorical data indicate that a measure of power may have been delegated to other officials with specific functions. These offices were probably held by members of the ruling lineage, brothers, sons, and other relatives of the ruler. Other lines of evidence indicate that power was shared by

•••• the leaders of several elite lineages, although one "royal" lineage seems to have furnished a single supreme ruler in most instances.

Among the ancient Maya, the principle of dynastic rule seems to have begun in the southern zone by the end of the Preclassic era. This is evidenced by the use of calendrical monuments that seem to commemorate the achievements of individual rulers (Chapter 3). Thus we may conclude that incipient state systems had arisen among the southern Maya by the beginning of the Classic era. But it is in the lowlands to the north that the recent advances in decipherment of Classic-period hieroglyphic texts provide the most secure evidence for dynastic rule.

Heinrich Berlin first identified "emblem glyphs," or symbols, associated with specific sites (see Chapter 15). Emblem glyphs are composed of a principal element, or main sign, unique to each site (Figs. 4.1 and 4.2). This main sign is accompanied by affixes, including the "ben-ich" prefix, usually translated as "lord" or "lord of the mat," and by the "water group" prefix, which has been translated as "precious" or "in the line of descent." The mat has long been recognized as a symbol of the highest political power among the Maya. The meaning of the main sign remains unclear; it may refer either to a dynastic name or title or to actual place names. Thus a plausible reading of the emblem glyph for the Tikal site might be "in the line of the lords of the mat of Tikal" or "lord of the Tikal dynasty." In either case, the presence and continuity of emblem glyphs in the lowland texts dealing with the political history of a site may be seen as *prima facie* evidence that the site in question possessed a state-level organization. This supposition is supported by additional epigraphic evidence, resulting largely from the pioneering work of Proskouriakoff, that led to the partial decipherment of texts dealing with the succession of individual rulers at several lowland sites. In some cases these glyphs have been identified, so that Mayan words have been proposed as readings for these; one example is Pacal ("shield"), a ruler of Palenque. But in most cases modern researchers have simply assigned to the individual rulers nicknames suggested by the appearance of the glyphs.

Kinship glyphs in the Classic inscriptions, which have also been identified, suggest that the basic rule of succession was primogeniture, although younger

Fig. 4.1. Maya emblem glyph: dog-head main sign, referring to an unidentified site, with the "ben-ich" prefix above and the "water group" prefix to the left (from the façade of Quirigua Structure 1B-1, A.D. 810).

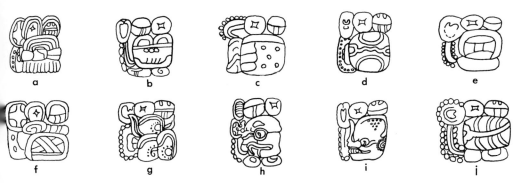

Fig. 4.2. Maya emblem glyphs: (*a*) Tikal; (*b*) Yaxchilan; (*c*) Piedras Negras; (*d*) Palenque; (*e*) Naranjo; (*f*) Tonina; (*g*) Seibal; (*h*) Calakmul; (*i*) Copan; (*j*) Quirigua.

brothers and other relatives might have succeeded in cases where the usual heir could not.

Epigraphic evidence of this kind has led one scholar, Joyce Marcus, to propose the following hierarchy of lowland sites during the Late Classic period (see also Table 7, p. 213):

A *regional center*, first in its region to acquire an emblem glyph, may have had more than one. Its texts refer to other regional capitals, and it is mentioned by its own dependencies.

A *secondary center* had its own emblem, but it is only rarely mentioned by its regional capital, whereas its own texts mention the regional capital, often in conjunction with marriage or other alliances; it might or might not have been mentioned by tertiary centers.

A *tertiary center* had no emblem glyph, but its texts mention the emblem of its regional capital and perhaps of a secondary center.

A *quaternary center* had no emblem glyph, and its texts do not mention its regional capital.

In the discussion that follows, *primary center* refers to any Maya site that appears, on the basis of the date of acquisition and geographical distribution of its emblem glyph(s), to have been the first to achieve a state level of organization within its region. Other sites, classified by Marcus as secondary centers, appear to have achieved the same level of organizational complexity, but seldom seem to have achieved dominance within their region. For convenience, we shall refer to all these sites, together with those that remained dependent on the dominant powers, simply as *centers*.

The information currently available suggests that there was only one primary lowland center for much of the Early Classic: Tikal, which dominated the Peten region of the central lowlands. By the beginning of the Late Classic, a series of additional primary centers seems to have emerged: Palenque in the southwest-

•••• ern region, Yaxchilan in the Usumacinta region, Copan in the southeastern region, probably Calakmul in the northern region of the central lowlands, and Coba and Uxmal in the northern lowlands. Calakmul, Coba, and Uxmal remain largely unknown for lack of archaeological information, but we shall be inquiring into the character and political history of the other primary centers. A selective chronological summary of this historical development may be found in Table 2.

## The Protoclassic

The period of one or two hundred years immediately preceding the beginning of the Classic era is known as the Protoclassic because the archaeological record often shows that to be the time of the first signs of the elaboration of lowland culture, especially in architecture and ceramics and, at some sites, of dramatic increases in population. That is, the Protoclassic appears to be a prelude to the Classic florescence of Maya civilization.

The significance of this Protoclassic development has been the subject of at least two different interpretations. The first of these postulates that the development seen in the Protoclassic was indigenous, representing the emergence of a state society in the lowlands without significant influence from outside areas. This internal pattern of development may be most apparent at Tikal, where the evidence reflects a steady progression of population growth and an elaboration in architecture and other material remains.

The other interpretation sees the Protoclassic as the result of the interaction between indigenous growth and outside influence. The best evidence for this view comes from sites in the eastern lowlands—Holmul, Barton Ramie, and Nohmul. At these sites the archaeological record is marked by rather sudden changes during the Protoclassic: evidence of rapid population increase, new stone tools such as bark beaters, and the appearance of a new ceramic inventory (including diagnostic Usulutan and polychrome decoration, besides vessels with four bulbous supports known as mammiform tetrapods). These changes have been best documented at Barton Ramie, where it was found that twice as many house platforms were occupied during the Protoclassic as in the preceding era. This evidence suggests an influx of new peoples into the eastern lowlands during the Protoclassic. The homeland of these migrants was postulated many years ago to have been the southeastern periphery of the Maya area, what is now western Honduras and El Salvador. Recent archaeological research at Chalchuapa and other sites in El Salvador has discovered that many of the material traits present in the lowland Protoclassic, especially in local pottery traditions, do appear to have originated in this southeastern region. The most probable cause for the apparent migration northward was the same volcanic disaster that devastated southern Maya society around A.D. 200–250 (see Chapter 3).

TABLE 2

*Selected Events in the History of Central-*
*and Southern-Lowland Centers During the Classic Period*

| Date | | |
|------|------|------|
| Maya | Gregorian (A.D.) | Event |
| 8.12.0.0.0 | 278 | Earliest known lowland dynastic monument, Tikal Stela 29 (8.12.14.8.15), displaying initial use of Tikal emblem glyph. |
| 8.13.0.0.0 | 297 | |
| 8.14.0.0.0 | 317 | Leyden Plate (8.14.3.1.12), with probable portrait of "Jaguar Paw," first identified Tikal ruler. |
| 8.15.0.0.0 | 337 | |
| 8.16.0.0.0 | 357 | Uaxactun Stelae 18 and 19, first known to record katun-ending dates (custom introduced by Teotihuacan?). Uaxactun Stela 5 (8.16.1.0.12), displaying Tikal emblem glyph. |
| 8.17.0.0.0 | 376 | Accession of "Curl Nose" at Tikal recorded on Stela 4 (8.17.12.16.7). |
| 8.18.0.0.0 | 396 | Tikal Stela 18, earliest known record of a katun-ending date at this site. |
| 8.19.0.0.0 | 416 | Accession of "Stormy Sky" at Tikal (ca. 8.19.10.0.0). |
| 9.0.0.0.0 | 435 | Tikal Stela 31 (9.0.10.0.0), recording the history of early Tikal rulers. |
| 9.1.0.0.0 | 455 | Quirigua Monument 3 (Stela C, erected in A.D. 775), showing 9.1.0.0.0 long-count date and the name of a probable early (founding?) ruler at this site. Death of "Stormy Sky" at Tikal, recorded in Burial 48 (9.1.1.10.10). |
| 9.2.0.0.0 | 475 | Accession of "Kan Boar" at Tikal (ca. 9.2.10.0.0). Accession of "Jaguar Paw Skull" at Tikal (ca. 9.2.13.0.0). Quirigua Monument 26 (9.2.18.?.?), recording apparent third or fourth ruler at this site. |
| 9.3.0.0.0 | 495 | Tikal emblem glyph on Yaxchilan Lintel 37 (9.3.13.12.19?). |
| 9.4.0.0.0 | 514 | Earliest known Yaxchilan emblem glyph on Stela 27. |
| 9.5.0.0.0 | 534 | Earliest known Piedras Negras emblem glyph on Lintel 12 (ca. 9.5.0.0.0). Accession of "Double Bird" at Tikal recorded on Stela 17 (9.5.3.9.15). Middle Classic hiatus begun at Tikal. |
| 9.6.0.0.0 | 554 | Earliest known Copan emblem glyph on Stela 9 (9.6.10.0.0). |
| 9.7.0.0.0 | 573 | |
| 9.8.0.0.0 | 593 | Earliest known Naranjo emblem glyph on Stela 38. Earliest known Palenque emblem glyph on Hieroglyphic Staircase (9.8.9.13.0). |
| 9.9.0.0.0 | 613 | Accession of Pacal at Palenque (9.9.2.4.8). |

••••

TABLE 2 (*continued*)

| Date | | |
| Maya | Gregorian (A.D.) | Event |
| --- | --- | --- |
| 9.10.0.0.0 | 633 | Approximate date of accession of "Bird Jaguar II" at Yaxchilan. |
| 9.11.0.0.0 | 652 | |
| 9.12.0.0.0 | 672 | Accession of "Ah Cacau" at Tikal recorded on Temple I lintel (9.12.9.17.16); end of hiatus. |
| | | Accession of "Shield Jaguar" at Yaxchilan (ca. 9.12.10.0.0). |
| | | Death of Pacal at Palenque (9.12.11.5.18). |
| | | Accession of "Chan Bahlum" at Palenque (9.12.11.12.10). |
| 9.13.0.0.0 | 692 | Death of "Chan Bahlum" at Palenque (9.13.10.1.5). |
| | | Accession of "Kan Xul" at Palenque (ca. 9.13.10.3.0). |
| 9.14.0.0.0 | 711 | Accession of "Chaacal" at Palenque (9.14.10.4.2). |
| | | Accession of "Chac Zutz" at Palenque (9.14.11.12.14). |
| | | Death of "Ah Cacau" at Tikal (ca. 9.14.11.17.3?). |
| | | Accession of "Cauac Sky" at Quirigua recorded on Monument 10 (Stela J) (9.14.13.4.17). |
| 9.15.0.0.0 | 731 | Copan Stela A, showing emblem glyphs of four primary centers (Tikal, Palenque, Copan, and ?Calakmul). |
| | | Earliest known Quirigua emblem glyph on Monument 13 (Altar M). |
| | | Accession of "Yax Kin" at Tikal recorded on Stela 21 (9.15.3.6.8). |
| | | Earliest known Aguateca emblem glyph on Stela 2 (9.15.5.0.0). |
| | | "18 Rabbit," thirteenth ruler of Copan, captured by "Cauac Sky" of Quirigua (9.15.6.14.6). |
| | | Death of "Shield Jaguar" at Yaxchilan (9.15.10.17.14). |
| | | Accession of "Bird Jaguar III" at Yaxchilan (9.15.11.0.0). |
| 9.16.0.0.0 | 751 | Earliest Seibal emblem glyph on South Hieroglyphic Staircase. |
| | | Accession of "Sun-at-Horizon" at Copan (9.16.12.5.17?). |
| | | Accession of "Kuk" at Palenque (9.16.13.0.7). |
| | | Death of "Yax Kin" at Tikal (ca. 9.16.15.0.0). |
| | | Accession of "Chitam," last identified ruler at Tikal, recorded on Stela 22 (9.16.17.16.4). |
| 9.17.0.0.0 | 771 | Accession of "Yax Sky," last identified ruler at Copan, recorded on Altar F (9.17.4.1.11?). |
| | | Death of "Cauac Sky" at Quirigua recorded on Monument 7 (Zoomorph G) (9.17.14.13.0). |
| | | Accession of "Sky Xul" at Quirigua recorded on Monument 7 (9.17.14.16.18). |

TABLE 2 (*continued*)

| Date | | Event |
|------|------|------|
| Maya | Gregorian (A.D.) | |
| 9.18.0.0.0 | 790 | Accession of "6 Cimi," last identified ruler at Palenque (ca. 9.18.9.0.0). |
| | | Accession of "Jade Sky," last identified ruler at Quirigua (ca. 9.18.10.0.0). |
| 9.19.0.0.0 | 810 | Inscription on Quirigua Structure 1B-1 showing last date in southeastern area. |
| 10.0.0.0.0 | 830 | |
| 10.1.0.0.0 | 849 | Stela 10 at Seibal, recording emblem glyphs of four primary centers (Tikal, Seibal, ?Calakmul, and ?Motul de San José). |
| 10.2.0.0.0 | 869 | Latest known dated monument at Tikal, Stela 11. |
| 10.3.0.0.0 | 889 | Latest known dated monument in the Tikal zone, Jimbal Stela 2. |
| 10.4.0.0.0 | 909 | Latest known dated monument from central and southern lowlands, Tonina Monument 101. |

This interpretation of the Protoclassic thus sees the expansion of lowland population and the elaboration of lowland culture as having been triggered by the arrival of new peoples from the southern Maya area. In this way many of the traits and institutions already present among the southern Maya, such as hieroglyphic writing, long-count calendrical notation, economic systems, and the production of cash crops such as cacao, could have been introduced into the lowlands.

But the development of any society, including the lowland Maya, cannot be explained by the simple imposition of a new order originating from an outside group. It is becoming increasingly clear that important trade contacts and even political ties existed between the southern and lowland Maya *before* the Protoclassic era. It is also apparent that any Protoclassic migrations directly affected only a portion of the lowlands, apparently areas with established trade contacts, such as the eastern lowlands. Tikal and many other centers of lowland Maya culture were not as directly affected by the southern Maya settlers. So that rather than postulate a Protoclassic migration as the cause of the sudden surge in the development of lowland society, it is more reasonable to assume that the contact between the two areas stimulated and accelerated a process already inherent in lowland Maya society. It is the fusion of these two cultural traditions that is reflected in what we call the Protoclassic, not a sudden change in the direction of development.

An important key to the processes of cultural development in the Protoclassic appears to lie in the vast early site of El Mirador, possibly the first primary center in the lowlands. Although the archaeological investigation of this site is only beginning, El Mirador seems to have reached its zenith during this period, for it may have been the focal point for southern Maya economic and political

Fig. 4.3. El Mirador, Guatemala: excavation of Structure 34, revealing a stucco-modeled mask detailed with a jaguar-paw ear flare, flanking the plastered staircase (Late Preclassic; compare Figs. 3.16, 3.19, 3.20).

interest in the lowlands even prior to the Protoclassic (Fig. 4.3). It is located in a position to have secured control of trans-lowland trade and the connections to the south.

The introduction of a ruling dynasty at El Mirador, either by the direct imposition of a southern Maya ruler or by marriage between ruling lineages, is suggested by reports of southern-style sculptured monuments. Whatever the means of introduction, dynastic rule dominated the political fortunes of the lowlands for nearly a thousand years. El Mirador, regardless of its origins and functions and by virtue of its precocious size alone, seems to have been the principal power in the lowlands during the Protoclassic. For reasons still unknown, its ascendancy ended as the Classic period began and a new center emerged to dominate the lowlands.

## The Early Classic

The Early Classic period (ca A.D. 250–550) witnessed the apparent domination of the central lowlands by Tikal, the best-known and longest-enduring primary center in its region. The reconstruction of Tikal's dynastic history uses two kinds of information: the results of the archaeological investigations of the Tikal Project, and the recent advances in hieroglyphic decipherment. The excavation of Tikal's North Acropolis, which unveiled the longest and most complex sequence of construction known in the Maya area, is especially significant to our understanding of this site's Early Classic history (Figs. 4.4 and 4.5). Although the larger, richer body of evidence from Tikal than from other lowland centers may bias our present understanding of this development, it does appear that Tikal's sociopolitical development was more accelerated than that of most other Early Classic sites. Furthermore, it seems likely that in its rise to power Tikal was able to eclipse other centers that had been prominent during earlier periods. A realignment of power in the Early Classic is clearly indicated by the fact that many Preclassic and Protoclassic centers (including the former dominant center of El Mirador) diminished in size and population during the first several centuries A.D. In some cases, as at the recently investigated Late Preclassic center of Cerros, previously important sites were completely abandoned by the time of the Early Classic.

As mentioned in Chapter 3, Tikal first evinced its emerging status as a primary center in the Late Preclassic, when the initial indications of a permanent, ruling elite class appeared. Tikal and other early lowland centers of development, such as nearby Uaxactun, may have been under the domination of El Mirador during this era, but the hallmark of Tikal's attainment of primary-center status appeared in A.D. 292 with the dedication of the earliest known lowland monument, Stela 29, bearing the long-count date 8.12.14.8.15 (Fig. 4.6). By this time, Tikal probably had become master of its own destiny, and the Jaguar Paw lineage was established in power. This lineage was named after its first identified ruler by Clemency Coggins, who with Christopher Jones has worked out much of the dynastic succession at Tikal. Jaguar Paw himself appears to be portrayed on the famous Leyden Plate (Fig. 4.7), with a date of 8.14.3.1.12 (A.D. 320). The earliest example of Tikal's emblem glyph is found on the front of Stela 29. The appearance of this emblem, a symbol that was to endure for some six hundred years, is perhaps the best evidence of Tikal's status as the center of an independent ruling lineage.

Other central-lowland centers asserted their independence and importance by erecting monuments soon thereafter, although none is known to possess an emblem as early as Tikal. Uaxactun commemorated its early political history with a series of six monuments between 328 and 416 (8.14.10.13.15 and 8.19.0.0.0; Fig. 4.8). Balakbal erected a single stela in 406 (8.18.10.0.0). Four

Fig. 4.4. Tikal, Guatemala: base of the North Acropolis trench, looking south, during excavations that revealed an exceptionally long and complex constructional sequence.

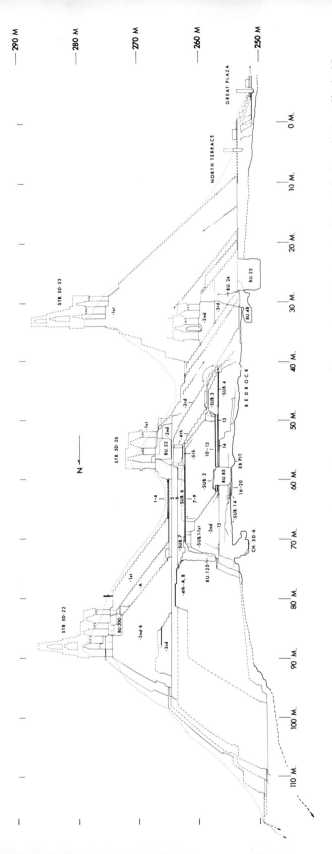

Fig. 4.5. North Acropolis, Tikal: generalized section drawing showing superimposed construction dating from the Late Preclassic to the Late Classic. Note the location of Burial 48 beneath Structure 5D-33-2nd, and Stela 31 interred in the rear room of this buried building (see Figs. 4.11 and 11.9).

Fig. 4.6. Stela 29, Tikal, with the earliest long-count date yet known from the Maya lowlands: (*above left*) drawing of the front, showing the sculptured portrait of an early Tikal ruler carrying a two-headed ceremonial bar; (*above right*) monument front; (*below left*) drawing of the back, showing the long-count date 8.12.14.8.15 (A.D. 292); (*below right*) monument back.

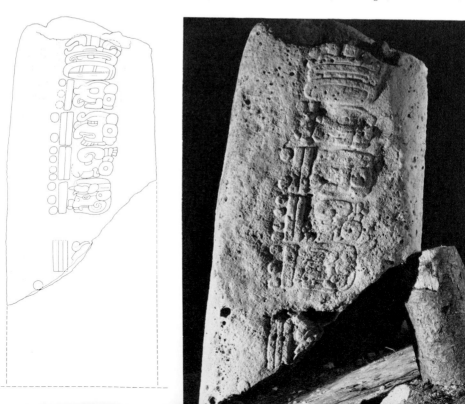

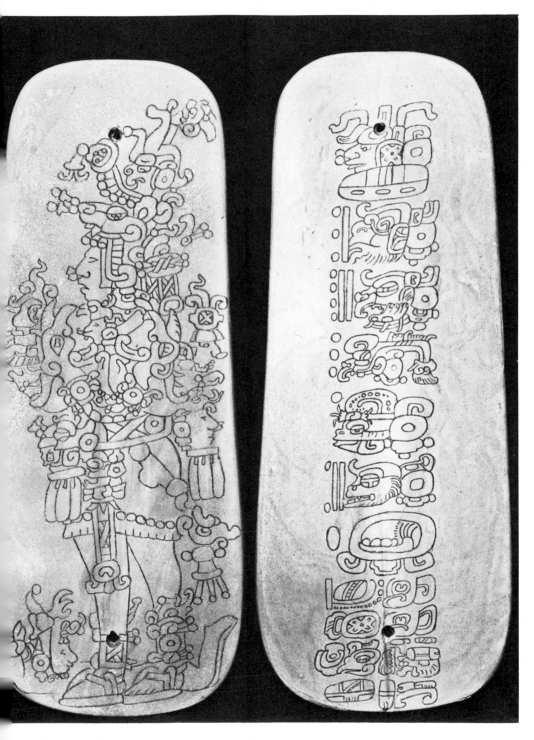

Fig. 4.7. Leyden Plate, a jadeite plaque, probably from Tikal although it was found near the delta of the Río Motagua in the nineteenth century. The front (left) bears a probable portrait of Jaguar Paw, an early Tikal ruler, and the back (right) is inscribed with the long-count date 8.14.3.1.12, or A.D. 320 (compare Fig. 4.6).

additional nearby centers have monuments datable from this same span: Uolan-tun, near Tikal, Stela 1; El Zapote, three monuments (Stelae 1, 4, and 7); Yaxha, Stela 5; and Xultun, Stela 12.

All these lowland centers possessing the earliest known long-count dates are located in the core of the central area. Furthermore, their being generally evenly spaced throughout this region suggests that, at least initially, they were political equals, independent of and competitive with each other. However, it also appears that Tikal soon began to assert its power over the entire central lowlands. In 358 (8.16.1.0.12) Stela 5 at Uaxactun displayed Tikal's emblem, from which we assume that it was under Tikal's jurisdiction by that time.

Fig. 4.8. Stela 9, Uaxactun, Guatemala, the earliest known monument at this site, 8.14.10.13.15 (A.D. 328).

Several other early rivals ceased to erect any further monuments, apparently ••••
losing their sovereignty to Tikal.

Tikal's fortunes were soon joined to those of the southern Maya, specifically
a revitalized Kaminaljuyu and its apparent allies from Teotihuacan. By becoming closely linked to this great urban center in the Valley of Mexico following
the decline at the end of the Preclassic era, Kaminaljuyu had emerged as the
major power in the southern Maya highlands during the Early Classic period. It
appears that in a desire to extend its hegemony over trade from its base in the
southern Maya area into the Maya lowlands, the Teotihuacan-Kaminaljuyu
alliance chose Tikal as its partner.

The apparent economic connection with the southern Maya region is revealed
in the sculptural and archaeological record at Tikal. Stela 4 (Fig. 4.9) marks the
beginning of a Teotihuacan-Kaminaljuyu episode, in both its style and historical record. This monument records the accession to power of a new ruler known
as Curl Nose, named after his presumed name glyph, in 378 (8.17.12.16.7).
The style of Stela 4, and the regalia worn by the sculptured portrait of Curl
Nose, recall the tradition of Teotihuacan. In contrast to the style of earlier Tikal
monuments, in which portrait figures stand in profile, Stela 4 depicts Curl Nose
seated and facing front. The protector figure over Curl Nose's head is a Maya
deity, Chac (God B), god of rain and storms. According to Coggins's analysis,
Chac, who represented the Maya version of Tlaloc, the Mexican god of rain-
storms, became the patron deity of the new ruling dynasty at Tikal, as Tlaloc
was at Teotihuacan. Eventually this patron, or a closely related deity, Bolon
Tzacab (God K), was represented as the "manikin scepter," the symbol of
dynastic rulership, as seen on a Teotihuacan spear thrower, or atlatl (Fig. 4.10).
A later monument dedicated during Curl Nose's reign, Stela 18 of 396
(8.18.0.0.0), was the first at Tikal to commemorate a period-ending date, the
completion of a katun (approximately a twenty-year period), introducing a
custom, possibly of non-Maya origin, that was followed for the rest of the
Classic Period. (The gods and religious customs are discussed in Chapter 14.)

The Tikal tomb identified by Coggins's study as that of Curl Nose, Burial
10, included offerings of items very similar to the furnishings from the Teoti-
huacan-period tombs at Kaminaljuyu. Coggins has proposed that Curl Nose
was in fact from Kaminaljuyu, perhaps a member of the ruling lineage there
who came to rule at Tikal by marrying a woman of the old Jaguar Paw lineage.

A presumed son born of this "royal" union, Stormy Sky, became the
founder of a new line of rulers at Tikal. Stormy Sky rose to power in about 426
(8.19.10.0.0). His first known monument, discovered enshrined and buried in
the temple built over his tomb, is the magnificent Stela 31 (Figs. 4.11 and 4.12)
dedicated in 435 (9.0.10.0.0). This monument proclaims Stormy Sky's right to
rule by portraying his father, Curl Nose, above his headdress as his celestial
protector and ancestor. His reign was marked by a synthesis of lowland Maya
tradition and Teotihuacan-Kaminaljuyu economic and political institutions.

Fig. 4.9. Stela 4, Tikal, recording the accession of Curl Nose in A.D. 378: (*left*) the monument; (*below*) drawings of the front and back. The frontal-portrait technique is in the Teotihuacan style.

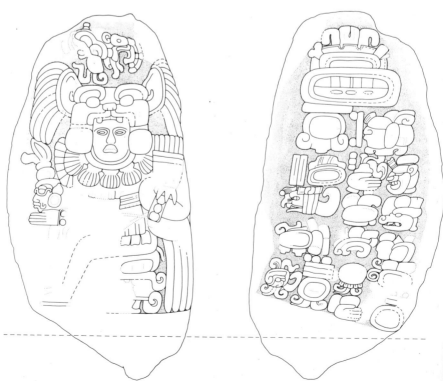

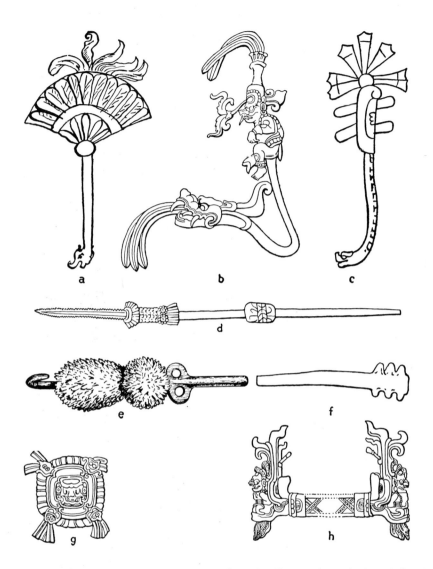

Fig. 4.10. Manikin scepters and other insignia from the Classic and Postclassic periods: (*a*) probable representation of a Late Postclassic manikin scepter from the colonial-period Xiu genealogical tree (see Fig. 8.4); (*b*) Late Classic manikin scepter from Monument 16 (Zoomorph P) at Quirigua; (*c*) Early Postclassic example of the manikin scepter from a fresco in the Temple of the Warriors at Chichen Itza; (*d*) spear; (*e*) atlatl, or spear thrower; (*f*) war club; (*g*) small ceremonial shield (Classic); (*h*) two-headed ceremonial bar, the symbol of supreme authority in the Classic period.

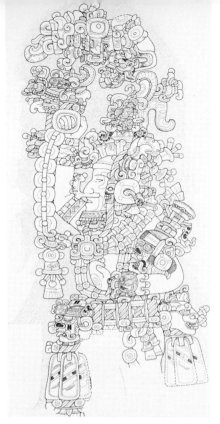

Fig. 4.11. Stela 31, Tikal: (*left*) drawing of the frontal sculptured portrait of Stormy Sky (note the head topped with the Tikal emblem glyph held in the crook of his left arm and Stormy Sky's name glyph adorning his headdress; (*below left*) side view of the monument after the excavation of Structure 5D-33-2nd (note the figure in Teotihuacan-style military garb, his shield adorned with Tlaloc, the Mexican rain god).

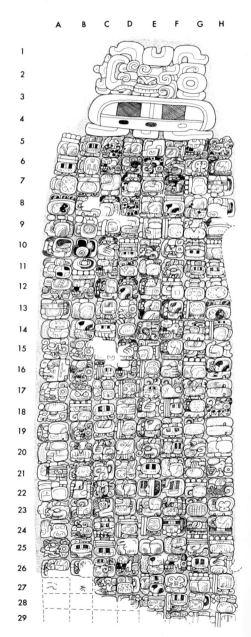

Fig. 4.12. Stela 31, Tikal: drawing of the extensive hieroglyphic text on the back of the monument.

Symbolic of this union, Stormy Sky is portrayed on Stela 31 in standing profile ••••
according to the old Maya fashion, displaying the insignia of traditional Maya
rulers; but more dramatically, he is flanked on either side by figures dressed in
Teotihuacan military regalia, wearing helmets and carrying Mexican atlatls and
shields displaying Tlaloc.

As ruler, Stormy Sky appears to have brought the aggressive mercantile
orientation of Teotihuacan into full development at this dominant Maya center.
During his reign, Tikal reached out beyond the central lowlands to secure
valuable resources and trade routes. Two areas seem to have been of prime
interest, one to the southwest, the other to the southeast. In both regions Tikal
appears to have established its influence by becoming involved in the establishment of ruling dynasties at already-established but minor centers. Interestingly,
this control over distant regions was not maintained, for these centers apparently gained their independence—as indicated by the acquisition of their own
emblem glyphs—shortly after Stormy Sky's death.

In the southwest region, Tikal appears to have been involved in the dynastic
affairs of Yaxchilan by about 475 (9.2.0.0.0), and thereby secured a foothold
on the strategic Usumacinta river route that connects the northern highlands
with the Gulf coast. This is indicated by the presence of Tikal's emblem on
Lintel 37 (dated at ca. 504) in Structure 12 at Yaxchilan, and by the persistence
of a Tikal sculptural style as late as 524 (Stela 14, 9.4.10.0.0). But the earliest
known example of Yaxchilan's own emblem glyph is on Stela 27 (Fig. 4.13),

Fig. 4.13. Stela 27, Yaxchilan,
Chiapas, Mexico, the earliest
known monument with the
Yaxchilan emblem glyph, A.D. 514.

Fig. 4.14. Monument 26, Quirigua, Guatemala: (*above*) front of the upper portion of this broken sculpture, with the portrait of a probable early ruler cradling a two-headed ceremonial bar in his arms, more visible in (*upper right*) a rubbing of the front and sides of the monument (compare Fig. 13.6); (*lower right*) back, showing the long-count date 9.2.18.0.? (A.D. 493).

dated at 514 (9.4.0.0.0), which indicates that independence from Tikal had ●●●●
been secured by this time.

Even farther afield, Tikal seems to have established its influence at Quirigua
and possibly Copan, both of which are in the southeastern periphery of the
Maya area. A newly discovered monument at Copan, Stela 35, has no surviving
glyphs, but its standing figures closely resemble those on several Late Preclassic
sculptures in the southern Maya style. Copan's earliest glyphic inscriptions,
however, indicate that the full calendrical and sculptural tradition of the central
lowlands had expanded to this southeastern center by 500. But the most
specific sculptural tie to Tikal yet known in the southeastern periphery is
provided by another newly discovered stela, Monument 26 at Quirigua (Fig.
4.14). This sculpture preserves an apparent date of 9.2.18.?.? (493), and seems
to be clearly in the stylistic tradition of the Tikal-Uaxactun region. Later
Quirigua monuments appear to have continued this stylistic link to the north.

With a presence in the southeast, Tikal could have secured outposts at the
gateway to Central America and control over the Motagua valley route between
the highlands and the Caribbean. In addition, Copan and Quirigua were
located so as to control access to several valuable resources, such as jadeite from
the middle Motagua valley and obsidian from the Ixtepeque source. In the case
of obsidian, it would seem that Tikal succeeded in breaking the monopoly held
by Teotihuacan through its alliance with Kaminaljuyu, which controlled the
prime source at nearby El Chayal. Of course, it is just as likely that Tikal was
acting on behalf of Teotihuacan and Kaminaljuyu, at least initially, and thus
merely extended Kaminaljuyu's obsidian monopoly. Either way, within a hundred years, or by about 564, Copan acquired its own emblem, and within a
short time developed into a primary center in its own right, apparently controlling Quirigua and the rest of the southeastern region for almost two hundred
years.

As a whole, the Early Classic Maya of the lowlands developed a complex
society characterized by an elite ruling class and a non-elite class of farmers,
craft specialists, and other laborers. Yet, according to an analysis by William
Rathje, there appears to have been considerable social mobility during this
period. Individuals seem to have been able to earn higher social rank by
acquiring wealth and power; and two prime means for gaining wealth were
colonizing new lands or peoples and controlling valuable resources or trade
routes. Thus it is likely that individuals who succeeded in these economic
ventures formed the basis for a new elite class that ruled over a series of newly
founded centers.

These emerging centers appear to have been ultimately dependent on Tikal,
however, for under its Teotihuacan alliance, Tikal seems to have controlled
much of the central lowland trade, possibly acting as the central redistribution
point for lowland goods destined for other regions and for foreign commodities

•••• (such as obsidian) entering the lowlands. Beyond the economic sphere, Tikal certainly became the most important lowland religious center, the primary shrine for pilgrimages. Ultimately it symbolized the supernatural power that stood behind and sanctioned the political and social order, since it was the seat of the oldest dynasty, with all its attendant Teotihuacan associations. As new dynasties established themselves, and new primary centers developed at Yaxchilan, Copan, and elsewhere, Tikal was probably still looked upon as the source of the supernatural power that established and preserved lowland society. Tikal could be viewed, in a sense, as the Rome, "the eternal city," of the lowland Maya.

Why and how did Tikal manage to be so successful in economically and politically dominating the central lowlands during this period? Why was Tikal able to overcome the apparent precocious dominance of El Mirador and emerge as the primary center in the lowlands during the Early Classic era? Although the answers are by no means complete, several known factors must have contributed to Tikal's success.

The first of these is location. Tikal is situated on a series of low hills that form part of the divide between the Caribbean and Gulf of Mexico drainage systems. These hills contain chert, or flint, which for the lowland Maya was a valuable resource for the making of chipped-stone tools—thus from the center's very beginnings, the people of Tikal controlled a critical natural resource. To the east and west of Tikal lie two large seasonal swamps (once, perhaps, shallow lakes), that seem to have been exploited for intensive agriculture. At least portions of these depressions were apparently modified by raised-field systems, providing Tikal with a plentiful local agricultural resource. In addition to this rich subsistence base, each of the shallow lakes is ultimately connected to a major river system, one flowing northeast to the Caribbean, the other flowing west to the Gulf. Much of Tikal's prosperity must have derived from the trade that followed these river systems through its territory. As postulated by Jones, these rivers provided a primary avenue of canoe-borne commerce between the Caribbean and the Gulf of Mexico. And because Tikal was situated on a critical portage between these two drainage systems, it controlled one of the major east-west trade routes passing across the Maya lowlands.

Tikal also occupied a strategic military position, such that in times of conflict it could be effectively defended against attack. The swamps (or lakes) to the east and west effectively eliminated threats from those directions. Approaches from either the north or south were defended by a ditch and rampart that may have been constructed during the apparently turbulent Protoclassic or Early Classic period. The smaller center of Becan, 120 km north of Tikal, constructed a massive defensive ditch and earthwork around its civic core during this period.

Unquestionably, Tikal's connections with Teotihuacan and Kaminaljuyu were a major factor. Probably because of its strategic location, Tikal appears to have been chosen by Teotihuacan, the dominant Mesoamerican mercantile power, to be its principal trading partner for the lowlands. As we have seen, this led not only to Tikal's economic ascendancy, but to its political development as well, as the lowland's first enduring ruling dynasty. The fusion of Teotihuacan and Maya religious and political institutions afforded the prestige and supernatural associations that underlay its dominance of the Early Classic lowlands.

## The Middle Classic Hiatus

Tikal's economic prosperity and political domination during the Early Classic period suffered an apparent setback in the sixth century, at the time of the so-called Middle Classic hiatus, traditionally dated from about A.D. 534 to 593 (9.5.0.0.0 to 9.8.0.0.0), but lasting as late as 692 (9.13.0.0.0) at Tikal. The period is defined by a decline in, or even a complete cessation of, the erection of monuments at most lowland sites. The amount of new construction at many sites also decreased. At Tikal, the furnishings in burials and tombs of this time, even in one obviously belonging to a member of the ruling elite, have been characterized as "impoverished" when compared to the sumptuous offerings of earlier or later times. Gordon Willey has suggested that the hiatus was due to the same factors that would later attend the more severe decline at the end of the Classic period; thus an understanding of the Middle Classic setback might help determine the causes of the failure of lowland civilization some three hundred years later (see Chapter 5).

Willey has proposed that the hiatus seems to have been a repercussion of upheavals in central Mexico. During this period, both Teotihuacan and its sphere of influence began to decline: long-distance trade through the Maya area seems to have fallen off dramatically, the connections with Kaminaljuyu were broken, and control over the southern Maya zone may have been completely relinquished. Certainly the loss of the links to Teotihuacan had serious consequences for the lowland economic system, but must have been especially disastrous for the rulers of Tikal, resulting as it necessarily would in a decline in wealth and prestige. It has recently been suggested by Clemency Coggins that the hiatus brought political struggle to Tikal, as the older Jaguar Paw lineage challenged the power of Stormy Sky's successors and forced, at least for a time, the compromise of a sharing of power.

## The Late Classic

By A.D. 600 the lowland Maya world began to recover from the hiatus. Although the power of Teotihuacan was gone, the benefits of its political and economic system appear not to have been forgotten, and the new order that emerged in the Late Classic lowlands (ca. 600–800) continued to follow the Mexican-derived model of the primary center established at Tikal. But instead of a single primary center as in the Early Classic, Late Classic lowland society

●●●● was organized under the dominion of a series of such centers, each controlling a region within the lowlands. A recovered Tikal regained its position as the primary center of the Peten region, Yaxchilan was the primary center of the Usumacinta region, Palenque dominated the southwestern region, Calakmul probably did likewise in the northern Peten, and Copan became the primary center in the southeast. A host of lesser centers seems to have jockeyed for advantageous positions. Some of these were allied to the more powerful primary centers; others perhaps remained unaligned or gained their independence when the opportunity arose.

As a result, the Late Classic lowlands may have become somewhat less centralized economically and politically, dividing sovereignty among an increased number of centers, all independent of any direct ties with Tikal. Yet the surprising uniformity found in many ways throughout the Late Classic may indicate frequent communication and even alliances between centers. The stylistic and iconographic diversity typical of many Early Classic monuments was replaced by a more uniform tradition. Because the lunar calendar became standardized throughout the lowlands, the era from 672 to 751 (9.12.0.0.0 to 9.16.0.0.0) has been labeled the "Period of Uniformity." Ceramics, at least in the elaborately decorated pottery styles, are also very similar in most regions. Significantly these characteristics are associated with the elite class, and their similarity reflects considerable communication and cooperation among the ruling classes of several centers. Marriage exchanges and even military alliances provide further evidence, as well as the apparent religious importance of certain primary centers.

Using epigraphic evidence it has been proposed that four primary centers enjoyed a special ceremonial status during the Late Classic, suggested by an inscription from Stela A at Copan (Fig. 4.15) dated at 731 (9.15.0.0.0), which records the emblem glyphs of Tikal, Copan, Palenque, and possibly Calakmul (see Fig. 4.16). Each is associated in the text with one of the four cardinal direction glyphs. The same quadripartite principle was in existence at least 150 years later, as can be seen from a similar inscription at Seibal, although two new centers replaced Copan and Palenque on the roster. It can be noted that this quadripartite division recalls the fourfold concept emphasized at Teotihuacan, and thus may be a reflection of continued Mexican influence on the lowland Maya political and religious systems.

Another bond between centers, suggested by several scholars, might have been based on military alliances. The Late Classic center of Yaxchilan stands out as a military power, and there is some epigraphic evidence that this center led an alliance of several primary centers (including Tikal and Palenque) and some secondary centers in the Usumacinta region (Piedras Negras, Aguateca, and possibly others).

Yet it should be reemphasized that despite these kinds of intersite connections, there is no evidence that the Late Classic Maya were unified politically or

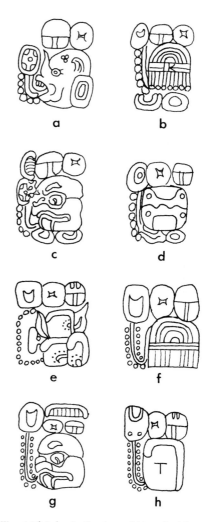

Fig. 4.15 (*left*). Stela A, Copan, Honduras, portraying the ruler 18 Rabbit and dated at A.D. 731, or 9.15.0.0.0 (see Fig. 4.16).

a

b

c

d

e

f

g

h

Fig. 4.16 (*above*). Portions of hieroglyphic texts from Copan and Seibal apparently naming four regional Maya centers. Top four, from Stela A, Copan, showing emblem glyphs of (*a*) Copan, (*b*) Tikal, (*c*) Calakmul (?), and (*d*) Palenque. Bottom four, from Stela 10, Seibal (see also Fig. 4.29), showing emblem glyphs of (*e*) Seibal, (*f*) Tikal, (*g*) Calakmul (?), and (*h*) Motul de San José (?).

•••• even economically. Instead, most Maya scholars see a Late Classic society composed of independent states, each perhaps dominated by a primary center, together with their dependencies.

## TIKAL AND THE PETEN REGION

The Late Classic political history of Tikal has been reconstructed by the efforts of several scholars. The basic outline of the dynastic succession has been presented by both Christopher Jones and Clemency Coggins. These works indicate that the succession of rulers immediately following the great Early Classic leader, Stormy Sky, is not yet fully understood. A ruler named Kan Boar came to power about A.D. 485, and it is probable that he was the son of Stormy Sky. Kan Boar's son, Jaguar Paw Skull, came to power by 488 (9.2.13.0.0) and was portrayed on several Tikal monuments. After that time the dynastic record is obscure, owing to the severe erosion and deliberate destruction of many monuments. Stela 23 depicts a woman, and gives her date of birth and her name, Woman of Tikal. She was the first of many Maya women portrayed on stelae, both in primary and secondary roles. Dynastic breaks and exiles have been proposed for this era, and the tombs in a wealthy residential complex on the far southeastern edge of Tikal have been seen as the burial places of Woman of Tikal and her royal family.

The accession of a new ruler, Double Bird, in 538 (9.5.3.9.15) is documented on Stela 17. A parentage statement in this inscription is badly eroded, but the mother's name appears to be Woman of Tikal and the father's name may be Jaguar Paw Skull. These kin ties would indicate the continuance of the old dynastic line. However, no monuments dated between Stela 17 and 692 have been found at Tikal, defining the hiatus period at this site, so we do not know how long Double Bird reigned or who succeeded him. Toward the end of this interval, Tikal seems to have reasserted its authority to the south, in the Usumacinta region. The inscriptions on the hieroglyphic stairway at Dos Pilas refer to the capture of a local ruler by an important person from Tikal in 643 (9.11.11.9.17). Marcus suggests that the hieroglyphic stairway was commissioned after Tikal's takeover to record the "official" history of Dos Pilas.

Tikal's fortunes were dramatically renewed after the accession of a new ruler, originally designated Ruler A and now named Ah Cacau, which occurred in 682 (9.12.9.17.16). Jones has pointed out that the long inscription on one of the wooden lintels of Temple I, as well as the texts on the carved bones from the tomb of Ah Cacau, name his father as Shield Skull, whose position as ruler of Tikal is shown by the use of the Tikal emblem glyph. Linda Schele has pointed out that painted ceramic dishes from a hiatus-period tomb also seem to provide the name of both Shield Skull's father, the presumed original occupant of the tomb, and his grandfather. Thus it appears that Ah Cacau's family had ruled Tikal for at least two generations during the hiatus. Coggins has proposed that the date of Ah Cacau's inauguration was chosen to occur precisely thirteen katuns (256 years) after Stormy Sky's succession, and thus seems to have been used to commemorate the completion of one round of katuns and the beginning of a new era. Throughout his reign, Ah Cacau's efforts to renew Tikal's prestige and power seem consciously associated with his illustrious ancestor and the first great period of Tikal's history. This phenomenon is known as cultural revitalization, whereby the lagging fortunes of a society are rebuilt by efforts to recall and duplicate past glories.

Ah Cacau's program to revitalize Tikal emphasized a return to the traditional fusion of Mexican and Maya ideology associated with Stormy Sky's reign. An example of this is manifested by the construction of Twin Pyramid groups, intended to commemorate the completion of each katun. According to a study by Jones, three Twin Pyramid groups were built before Ah Cacau's reign. But it was during Ah Cacau's rule and thereafter that the Twin Pyramid groups were used as settings for carved katun-ending monuments. According to Coggins, the public rituals held in these groups to celebrate the end of the katun reflected the heritage of Mexican beliefs associated with the Tikal dynasty, and may be analogous to large-scale public ceremonies formerly held at Teotihuacan.

Ah Cacau's revitalization of Tikal included an expansion of its external realm. In about 683 (9.12.10.5.12) Tikal seems to have secured an important ally in the center of Naranjo through the marriage of a woman from the Tikal dynasty to the ruler of Naranjo. This alliance probably endured until at least 726 (9.14.15.0.0).

The tomb of Ah Cacau, over which was built his spectacular funerary shrine, Temple I (Figs. 4.17 and 4.18), was sumptuously furnished with jadeite, shell, pottery, and beautiful works of art, testimony to Tikal's renewed prosperity (Fig. 4.19). Included in the burial offerings were an exquisite jade mosaic vase (see Fig. 13.51) and a set of beautifully engraved and carved bones, one of which carried inscribed references to the emblems of Copan, Palenque, and two other centers; each emblem is preceded by the Imix, or "capture," glyph, possibly recording military successes against these sites. Others give Ah Cacau's name glyphs and repeat his parentage statements.

The exact date of Ah Cacau's death is unknown, but it appears to have been between 721 and 731. Thus, after a reign of some 50 years, Ah Cacau was succeeded in 734 by his son, Yax Kin (Ruler B). Yax Kin continued, or more likely exceeded, his father's efforts at transforming Tikal into one of the most impressive and powerful centers of the Late Classic Maya world. It was probably he who ordered the construction of the largest temple pyramid at Tikal, Temple IV, marking the western boundary of Tikal's civic and ceremonial core (see Fig. 11.7). The great causeway avenues leading into Tikal were probably built during this period also; one of these leads to the Temple of the Inscriptions (Temple VI), built during either Yax Kin's reign or that of a little-known successor to mark Tikal's eastern perimeter. The roof comb of this temple

Fig. 4.17. Temple I, Tikal: view of the front, facing west toward the Great Plaza, showing the staircase that leads to the funerary temple on the summit, with a seated portrait of Ah Cacau on the roof comb.

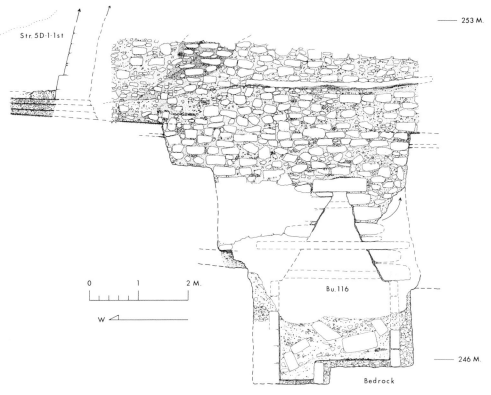

Str. 5D-1-1st

253 M.

0      1      2 M.

W ◁

Bu. 116

246 M.

Bedrock

Fig. 4.18. Temple I, Tikal: archaeological section drawing showing Ah Cacau's vaulted tomb (Burial 116), buried beneath the Temple I pyramid (Structure 5D-1-1st).

Fig. 4.19. Ah Cacau's tomb, as found by archaeologists who entered the chamber through the roof vault; the skeletal remains of Ah Cacau were encrusted with jadeite, shell, and other ornaments and surrounded by pottery vessels.

•••• contains a giant hieroglyphic inscription, apparently recording principal events in the history of Tikal (see Fig. 11.16). The earliest date corresponds either to a mythical founding date for Tikal at 5.0.0.0.0 (1139 B.C.) or, as Jones has suggested, to a long-remembered historical event of the Olmec era, since it is contemporary with Gulf coast sites such as San Lorenzo (see Chapter 2). The next date, 6.14.16.9.16 (457 B.C.), almost certainly records a historical event, one occurring at about the time Tikal was emerging as a Preclassic lowland trading center. The third date, 7.10.0.0.0 (156 B.C.), harks back to the era of the first North Acropolis structures, about the time of the earliest origins of Tikal's ruling dynasty as indicated by the initial tombs in the North Acropolis. Several dates in the Early Classic follow, and the remaining text seems to refer to Yax Kin.

Yax Kin died in about A.D. 768, and may have been succeeded by a little-known ruler. A better-documented successor, and the son of Yax Kin, has been named Chitam (Ruler C), the last known member of Tikal's long and illustrious dynastic line. Chitam seems to have attempted to carry on his forefathers' programs. The last two katun-marking Twin Pyramid groups were constructed during his reign, and both are almost double the size of any of the earlier examples. By this time, however, Tikal's prosperity and power were in decline. Despite the late date of 889 (10.3.0.0.0) on one monument, the history and fate of Tikal and its ruling dynasty after Chitam's reign disappears into obscurity.

### PALENQUE AND THE SOUTHWESTERN REGION

Palenque was one of the first centers to gain prominence in the wake of the Middle Classic hiatus. During the Early Classic it was a minor center, as documented by the archaeological investigations of Robert Rands. The Temple of the Inscriptions at Palenque records the accession dates of seven lords or rulers prior to A.D. 615, two of them women.

The Temple of the Inscriptions was built as the funerary shrine to Palenque's greatest ruler, called Pacal, who was buried in an elaborate tomb beneath the pyramid supporting the temple (Fig. 4.20). The tomb was discovered several decades ago during the archaeological investigations of Alberto Ruz Lhuillier, when he noted that the inner walls of the temple did not end at their junction with the floor, but continued below it. This, together with his deduction that the holes in one large floor slab were finger holds, led him to conjecture that something lay beneath the temple. The slab was lifted, revealing a corbel-vaulted stairway filled with rubble that took some three years to clear. In 1952 the end of the staircase was reached deep beneath the temple floor, and through a doorway Ruz discovered a large vaulted crypt (Figs. 4.21 and 4.22) containing a mammoth limestone sarcophagus topped by a magnificently carved lid (Fig. 4.23). The walls of the tomb were covered with beautiful figures modeled in stucco, and the sides of the sarcophagus lid were carved with portraits and

Fig. 4.20. Perspective drawing of the Temple of the Inscriptions at Palenque, Chiapas, Mexico, showing the vaulted staircase leading to the tomb chamber.

hieroglyphs. Inside lay the skeletal remains of Pacal, covered with jade beads, a disintegrated jade mosaic mask, and other offerings.

The sarcophagus text and other inscriptions at Palenque have been deciphered as recording the death dates of Pacal's predecessors (the same seven individuals whose accession dates are found on the temple above the tomb), along with Pacal's birth date on March 6, 603 (9.8.9.13.0), and his death on August 30, 684 (9.12.11.5.18). Other inscriptions record his accession to power on July 29, 615, when he was merely 12 years old. The epigraphic data indicate, therefore, that Pacal ruled for over 68 years and lived to be well over 80. Ruz has pointed out that Pacal's bones indicate that he lived to be no more than about 40, and the apparent contradiction has yet to be resolved, although it might be noted that age determinations from adult skeletal remains are difficult and often inaccurate.

Fig. 4.21. Interior of the tomb beneath the Temple of the Inscriptions, Palenque: (*above left*) entry; (*above right*) stucco figures on the wall of the tomb; (*below left*) view toward the entry; (*below right*) view from the entry.

Fig. 4.22. Sarcophagus in the tomb: (*above*) the lid removed, revealing the remains of the ruler identified as Pacal with jadeite and other adornments; (*below*) detail of the sculptured relief on the side of the sarcophagus.

Fig. 4.23. Temple of the Inscriptions tomb, Palenque: rubbing of the sculptured sarcophagus lid, depicting Pacal's falling in death into the jaws of the underworld.

•••• 

During Pacal's reign Palenque became a major power, dominating the south-western region of the Maya lowlands and expanding its authority over the surrounding region. The first use of Palenque's emblem glyph occurred at the beginning of Pacal's rule. In 633 an apparent marriage between a woman from the Palenque ruling class and the ruler of the neighboring site of El Tortuguero cemented an alliance between these two centers. Palenque's primacy was formally recognized less than 50 years after Pacal's death, when it was named one of the four primary centers associated with the quarters of the cosmos on Stela A at Copan. The growth of Palenque's power and prestige was probably due at least in part to the political stability engendered by Pacal's long reign. Prosperity was also linked to political longevity in Tikal under Ah Cacau and in several other Maya centers.

Pacal was succeeded some 132 days after his death by his 48-year-old son, Chan Bahlum. During a reign of just over eighteen years, Chan Bahlum expanded the site of Palenque. His most famous monuments are the three beautiful buildings to the east of his father's funerary temple, designated the Temples of the Cross, Foliated Cross, and Sun. Within each are shrines containing sculptured panels interpreted as commemorating each of Palenque's patron deities (the Palenque Triad) and Chan Bahlum's accession to three titles, or offices, as ruler. For instance, the Temple of the Foliated Cross is associated with Bolon Tzacab (God K), the patron of ruling dynasties, whose image appears on the manikin scepter as far back as the Early Classic dynasty at Tikal. The panels in all three shrines show Chan Bahlum's receiving the symbols of office from his father, Pacal.

Chan Bahlum died in 702 (9.13.10.1.5), and his younger brother, Kan Xul, then 57 years old, became the new ruler 53 days later. During Kan Xul's reign Palenque's realm appears to have reached its maximum extent. The royal residence at Palenque, the great palace, was enlarged to include a famed four-story tower in veneration of Kan Xul's father, Pacal. When viewed from the top of the Palace tower on the winter solstice, the sun sets directly behind the Temple of the Inscriptions, appearing to enter the underworld through Pacal's tomb.

The exact date of Kan Xul's death is unknown, but he was succeeded by his son, Chaacal, in 721 (9.14.10.4.2). Chaacal, 43 when he came to the throne, appears to have ruled for only about a year. He was followed by Chac Zutz in 722 (9.14.11.12.14), who reigned for some 9 years. After an interregnum or a gap in the historical record of about 33 years, the son of Chaacal, Kuk, became Palenque's ruler in 764 (9.16.13.0.7), by which time the power of Palenque seems to have waned. In 771 (9.17.0.0.0) a former dependency of Palenque, the center of Pomona, appears to have achieved its independence, displaying its own emblem for the first time.

The historical record at Palenque ends during the reign of Kuk, and the fates of both Palenque and its ruling dynasty are unknown. An inscribed pottery

•••• vessel records the accession of an apparent ruler with the Mexican name of 6 Cimi in 799, which may indicate that Palenque had been taken over by a foreign or Mexican-influenced Maya dynasty by the end of the eighth century.

## YAXCHILAN AND THE USUMACINTA REGION

The centers of the Usumacinta region are arranged linearly along the Río Usumacinta and its tributaries, which once carried the commercial goods that flowed between the highlands and the Gulf coast. This zone first came to prominence with the rise of Yaxchilan, soon after dynastic rule was founded at the site, probably introduced by way of Tikal. Yaxchilan became a primary center by A.D. 514 (9.4.0.0.0), the date of its first known emblem glyph.

The era of greatness for Yaxchilan began after the hiatus with the second ruler with the name Bird Jaguar, who seems to have come to the throne in about 630, perhaps ruling until 681. But Yaxchilan gained its greatest prominence during the later reigns of two aggressive and long-lived rulers of the Jaguar dynasty. Shield Jaguar, who appears to have ruled for at least 50 years

Fig. 4.24. Sculptured lintels from Yaxchilan: (*left*) Lintel 25 from Structure 23, unusual in the fact that its glyphs are reversed (in mirror image), the far-left column recording the capture of Lord Ahau by Shield Jaguar, ruler of Yaxchilan (who may be depicted here emerging from the jaws of a serpent above his consort); (*right*) apparent portrait of Shield Jaguar holding a flaming torch (?) over his consort, who is engaged in a bloodletting ritual.

after coming to power in about 682, extended the realm of Yaxchilan through
conquest and consolidation of nearby centers. The numerous and finely sculptured inscriptions of Yaxchilan (Fig. 4.24) repeatedly record these deeds, for
example, detailing Shield Jaguar's capture of a neighboring ruler named Ahau.
The date of Ahau's capture is recorded as 9.12.8.14.1 (680), just before Shield
Jaguar's accession to power, and this event may in fact have been related to
his attaining the throne. It was Shield Jaguar who seems to have led the
formation of a military alliance, perhaps dominated by Yaxchilan, that included not only centers in the surrounding Usumacinta region, but Tikal, Palenque,
and other primary centers as well. Shield Jaguar's death is recorded as 742
(9.15.10.17.14).

Shield Jaguar was succeeded by Bird Jaguar III, possibly his son, seemingly
soon after his death. Bird Jaguar III continued the military exploits of his
predecessor. The texts at Yaxchilan refer to Bird Jaguar as the captor of the
lords Cauac and Jeweled Skull. Several Usumacinta regional centers that were
previously independent appear to have succumbed to Yaxchilan domination
during the reign of Bird Jaguar III.

One Usumacinta center with a long history of independent rule is Piedras
Negras, located some 40 km (25 mi.) downriver from Yaxchilan. Piedras
Negras acquired its own emblem by 534 (9.5.0.0.0). The beautifully sculptured inscriptions and monuments detailing the political history of its rulers, the
Aac (or Turtle) dynasty, were the first of any lowland site to be deciphered. The
breakthrough was made by Tatiana Proskouriakoff, who noted that the sequence of dated stelae formed at least six groups, beginning with a monument
depicting a male figure seated in an elevated niche, usually with an older female
figure below (Fig. 4.25). This motif was associated with a date glyph and an
event glyph that could be read as "accession to power." Thus the scene on the
monuments depicted the inauguration of the new ruler, along with the partici-
pation in the ceremony by the ruler's mother, probably symbolizing the important role played by the female line in ensuring the dynastic succession. Other
monuments in each group usually commemorated each five-tun (five-year)
period of the ruler's reign. The span of any one of the monument groups did
not exceed a normal human lifetime, so that the sequence of Piedras Negras
rulers worked out by Proskouriakoff represents reigns of 35, 47, 42, 28, 5, and
17 years.

A dispute over the succession of rulers at Piedras Negras appears to have
been settled by intervention in 756 (9.16.6.10.19). At that time an emissary
from Yaxchilan named Bat Jaguar (perhaps a name variant for Bird Jaguar III,
or more likely his representative) held an audience at Piedras Negras even as the
current ruler seems to have lain dying. When the Piedras Negras ruler died a
few days later (9.16.6.11.7), a new ruler probably designated by Bat Jaguar
took office (9.16.6.17.1). These events are commemorated on the famous Wall
Panel 3 from Piedras Negras (Fig. 4.26). Yaxchilan's authority over Piedras

Fig. 4.25. Motifs commemorating ruler accession, on stelae from Piedras Negras, Guatemala, depicting the inauguration of four rulers: (*upper left*) Stela 25, A.D. 608; (*lower left*) Stela 11, 731; (*center*) Stela 6, 687; (*right*) Stela 14, 761 (note the portrait of the maternal figure below the niche).

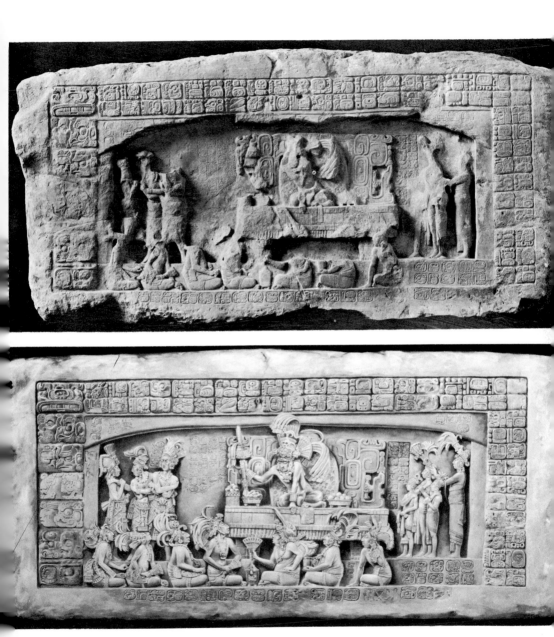

Fig. 4.26. Wall Panel 3, Temple O-13, Piedras Negras: (*above*) wall panel as it was found; (*below*) restoration drawing by M. Louise Baker.

•••• Negras may not have lasted long, however, for according to Proskouriakoff, a new and independent ruler took office five years later.

Although this intervention was peaceful, there are indications that Piedras Negras's independence may have been interrupted by hostilities several decades earlier. A monument at the site of Aguateca (Stela 1) records the capture of a Piedras Negras ruler in 741. Aguateca also appears to have been an aggressive center, probably taking part in the Yaxchilan military alliance and securing its own emblem by 736 (9.15.5.0.0). The somewhat surprising extent of Aguateca's military exploits is detailed on Stela 2, dated at 741 (9.15.10.0.0), which refers to an alliance of Aguateca, Seibal, and Dos Pilas that launched a raid on Tikal, resulting in the capture of a Tikal lord, perhaps a military leader. Seibal did not acquire its emblem until after this raid; at least, the first reference does not occur until 751 (9.16.0.0.0). As we shall see, Seibal appears to have become increasingly important after this date, its power reaching a zenith during the Terminal Classic.

COPAN AND THE SOUTHEASTERN REGION

Copan is the southeasternmost Classic Maya site; together with Quirigua in the adjacent lower Motagua valley, it represented the dominant power on the borderlands with Central America. We have already discussed the probable origins of ruling dynasties, when both centers were Early Classic colonies, from the central lowlands, possibly from Tikal. We know that Copan's emblem was established by A.D. 564 (9.6.10.0.0) and that the ruler portrayed on the newly discovered Monument 26 at Quirigua appears to have been the third or fourth member of that center's dynasty. Although our knowledge of the details of the early political history of these two sites remains meager, it is fairly certain that the rulers of Copan maintained control over most of the southeastern region during the Early Classic period, including, presumably, the center of Quirigua.

Not until the Late Classic, with its more abundant archaeological remains and its fuller textual sources, do some details of the Copan and Quirigua dynasties become apparent. Unlike the more certain base of information provided by the recently completed archaeological and epigraphic research at Quirigua, the political development of Copan remains somewhat uncertain. Combining what is known about both centers permits the only reasonable reconstruction.

The appearance of Quirigua's emblem by 731 (9.15.0.0.0) probably signals its bid for independence from Copan. But the emblem reportedly occurs twenty years earlier at Pusilha, a small site located 100 km to the north in southern Belize. Thus Quirigua may have begun to assert its independence and expand its realm to the north, dominating Pusilha in the process, by the beginning of the eighth century. Quirigua's ambitions, probably motivated by a desire to control the lucrative trade that flowed through its precincts, appear to have led to conflict with Copan.

The Copan ruler of this time is known as 18 Rabbit (Fig. 4.15). His rival at ●●●●
Quirigua, the fourteenth member of the local Sky dynasty according to the
inscriptions, has been named Cauac Sky. Cauac Sky came to power at Quirigua
in 725 (9.14.13.14.17) and apparently continued the expansive policies seemingly begun by his unknown predecessor(s). Matters came to a head in 737
(9.15.6.14.6), a date repeatedly given prominence on Cauac Sky's monuments
(Fig. 4.27), when Cauac Sky captured 18 Rabbit, probably in a raid on Copan.

Fig. 4.27. Monument 5 (Stela E), Quirigua,
Guatemala, portraying the dominant ruler of
this center, Cauac Sky (9.17.0.0.0, or A.D. 771).

•••• As a result, Copan's hegemony over the southeastern region was broken, and a twenty-year gap in Copan's inscriptions may reflect the political and economic confusion that followed.

At Quirigua, a major rebuilding effort for the remainder of Cauac Sky's 60-year reign transformed the entire site, evidence of the newly won wealth and prestige that followed Copan's defeat. In this connection, Berthold Riese has suggested that the Quirigua inscriptions naming Cauac Sky the fourteenth ruler refer not to a local dynastic succession, but to his claim to have been successor to 18 Rabbit, the thirteenth ruler at Copan.

Nonetheless, for approximately a hundred years the rulers of Quirigua appear to have reigned supreme over the lower Motagua valley and its adjacent areas, controlling the critical jade route between the highlands to the west and the Caribbean to the east. Cauac Sky died in 784, and was succeeded 78 days

Fig. 4.28. The Acropolis at Quirigua, showing Structure 1B-1, built during the reign of Jade Sky and containing the latest known date at this site (9.19.0.0.0, or A.D. 810); and Structure 1B-2 (lower right), an earlier building that may have been the first palace of Cauac Sky.

later by his presumed son, Sky Xul, who seems to have ruled for about eleven ● ● ● ●
years. He was followed by a regent or possibly a usurper, who ruled for about
five years.

The last identified Quirigua ruler, Jade Sky, took the throne about 800.
During this reign the power of Quirigua appears to have reached its peak. Jade
Sky launched another massive construction program, rebuilding much of the
Acropolis (palace) compound. It is interesting that throughout more than a
century of construction activity in Quirigua's Acropolis, a small but elaborately
decorated building (Structure 1B-2), tentatively identified as Cauac Sky's original palace, was preserved and probably venerated by his successors. In 810 the
last known date from Quirigua was sculptured on the façade of one of Jade
Sky's new Acropolis buildings (Fig. 4.28). A few years later Jade Sky's presumed palace, the largest building at Quirigua (Structure 1B-5), was completed. Although construction continued thereafter, the historical record disappears.
Quirigua was occupied after Jade Sky's reign, which probably ended sometime
in the mid-ninth century; but this later occupation may have been by peoples
who came as intruders from the Caribbean coast.

At Copan, two rulers with short reigns seem to have succeeded 18 Rabbit.
Stable political direction appears to have been reestablished by the reign of Sun-
at-Horizon, who came to power around 763 (9.16.12.5.17). He appears to
have ruled until his death in about 801. Copan's latest known date is 805, and
the center appears to have been in decline by that time.

## The Terminal Classic

A convenient marker for the apex of Classic Maya civilization corresponds to
A.D. 790 (9.18.0.0.0), when more lowland centers erected dated monuments
than at any other time. After this date the number of sites recording long-count
dates dropped rather dramatically. Three of the Late Classic primary centers,
Palenque, Copan, and Yaxchilan, along with their dependencies, ceased to
record their political fortunes after about 810 (9.19.0.0.0), and the last known
lowland stela with a long-count date was dedicated at Tonina in the southwestern periphery in 909 (10.4.0.0.0).

The majority of the monuments that date from 790 and later are found at
smaller centers. At least ten of these sites appear to have erected stelae for the
first time during the Terminal Classic period. This indicates a shift in population away from the larger Late Classic centers toward smaller, independent
political units. There was also a shift in the geographical distribution of lowland
centers. Terminal Classic sites are concentrated not only in the old core of the
central lowlands, the Tikal region, but also in two other regions, one to the
southwest in Chiapas and the other in the northern lowlands of the Yucatan.
Recently completed archaeological investigations by Don and Prudence Rice
(Proyecto Lacustre) of occupation around four small lakes in the central Peten

•••• have demonstrated that these areas continued to be occupied from the Classic through the Postclassic era. On the basis of the number of structures dated by excavation at sites around Lagos Macanche, Salpeten, Quexil, and Petenxil, there appears to be a significant decrease in occupation (including complete abandonment at several sites) between the Preclassic and Classic periods. Later, after population peaked during the Late Classic, another decrease occurred at the close of the Classic, although there is no indication of complete abandonment at these lake sites. Occupation at these sites then increased during the Postclassic, apparently equaling or exceeding the levels reached during the Late Preclassic period. The shift in the geographical distribution of centers at the close of the Classic period probably corresponded to a breakdown in the established political system as the old state organizations began to disintegrate. It may also reflect the intrusion of a new ruling order that became established at many of these lowland centers.

The Terminal Classic decentralization of population and political organization is best documented at Tikal. On the basis of ceramic distributions analyzed by Patrick Culbert, some 95 percent of the residential house platforms excavated at Tikal were occupied during the Late Classic (9.15.0.0.0 to 10.0.0.0.0). But during the Terminal Classic, after 830, most if not all of these outlying residences were abandoned, and occupation was restricted to the site core area. These late people appear to have been comparatively impoverished. No new buildings were constructed, and the residences that were occupied were not maintained. Total population was greatly reduced; Culbert estimates that it numbered no more than 10 percent of Tikal's Late Classic occupation. At the same time, five small centers around Tikal's periphery rose to comparative prominence. One of these, Jimbal, dedicated the latest known monument of the Tikal zone, in 889 (10.3.0.0.0).

The general decline in the established order was also reflected in the decrease of nonlocal emblem glyphs on Terminal Classic monuments. Furthermore, references to marriage alliances between centers ceased, while stylistic and iconographic diversity increased. The frequency of conflict and capture scenes, along with "foreign" or Mexican motifs and styles, also increased. The smaller centers that continued to commemorate their local histories were apparently no longer allied to or dependent upon the larger centers. In fact, the centers of political power in the lowlands appear to have become increasingly hostile to each other during the Terminal Classic.

Many of these characteristics are best seen at Seibal, in the southern lowlands in the heart of the Río Pasión region. Development of this site seems to have reached its apex during the Terminal Classic period. Between 830 and 930, according to Jeremy Sabloff's studies, Seibal reached its maximum population (ca. 10,000), which probably made it the largest southern lowland center at that time. Its importance is indicated by an inscription dating from 840 (10.1.0.0.0), which, like Copan's Stela A erected 119 years earlier, names four primary lowland centers. The text of Seibal Stela 10 (Fig. 4.29) lists Tikal and possibly Calakmul (or Uxmal?) as the only survivors of the original four (Fig. 4.16). Seibal's emblem replaced that of Copan, and another unidentified center, suggested by Joyce Marcus to be Motul de San José, replaced Palenque. If the problematical identifications are correct, all four Terminal Classic primary centers were located close together in or near the core of the lowlands, reflecting the drastic attenuation of the Maya realm from its extent during the Late Classic period.

Fig. 4.29. Stela 10, Seibal, Guatemala, depicting on its front a ruler with "foreign" characteristics and an inscription naming four regional centers (see Figs. 4.16 and 11.32), 10.3.0.0.0 (A.D. 889).

•••• The Terminal Classic ascendancy of Seibal seems to have been due to its takeover by a "foreign" elite, whose portraits were carved on its latest stelae. Excavations of this site have documented the shifts in ceramic, architectural, and sculptural styles beginning about 830 that reflect this intrusion. Gordon Willey and Sabloff have proposed that the center was taken over by a peripheral Maya group, who originally came from the Gulf coast of the Yucatan Peninsula and seem to have acquired a veneer of Mexican cultural traits. Another scholar, Joseph Ball, identified Seibal with the historic site of Chakanputun, a center recorded in later Yucatecan chronicles as having been founded by the Itza Maya, a group with known Mexican cultural ties. According to both Ball and J. Eric Thompson, the term Itza is the historic Yucatecan name for a Putun Maya group that migrated from the Yucatan south until they eventually settled at the site of Chakanputun. Thus, it is possible that the historically recorded migration of a Mexicanized group, the Itza, can be correlated with an archaeologically documented intrusion at Seibal during the Terminal Classic.

## Reconstructing the Maya Classic

The ancient Maya reached their maximum cultural development of the Classic period in the central and southern lowland zones. This florescence is associated with the emergence of a political and social order typical of the preindustrial state. Although the origins of this development appear to lie with the southern Maya, a shift of fortunes during the Protoclassic era resulted in the ascendancy of the lowland peoples as the dominant powers in the Maya area. The first lowland state organization was probably established at Tikal during the Early Classic period. Tikal's rise to prominence was contemporary with the apparent decline of El Mirador, a huge center with southern Maya connections whose power seems to have reached its peak during the Protoclassic era. The ascendancy of Tikal was certainly aided by economic and political ties with the dominant Mesoamerican power, Teotihuacan, along with its highland ally, Kaminaljuyu. In fact, the establishment of the political dynasty destined to dominate Tikal's history might have originated from a marriage alliance between the old ruling lineage and a Mexicanized lineage, probably from Kaminaljuyu. During the Early Classic this line of rulers seems to have been involved in the establishment of ruling houses at several centers, including Yaxchilan and Quirigua.

Tikal's hegemony was broken during the Middle Classic hiatus, a short period of decline apparently brought about by the withdrawal of Teotihuacan's economic interests in the Maya area. During this period local dynasties in Palenque, Yaxchilan, Copan, and other centers succeeded in establishing or consolidating their own independent state organizations, dominating the smaller centers within their political realms.

During the Late Classic period, the primary centers continued to dominate the smaller independent states. Although perhaps the last center to recover from the hiatus, Tikal regained its former prestige and at least a vestige of its former power under the reign of three Late Classic rulers. Marked by a series of vigorous and long-enduring reigns by rulers at several other centers, Late Classic Maya society enjoyed a period of unprecedented prosperity and power. Yet lowland society at this time was politically fragmented and increasingly culturally diversified as a result of the maneuverings by competing dynastic rulers to secure or increase their power and wealth. At the same time, shifting alliances between ruling families fostered an overall uniformity in elite-level culture, including art styles, regalia, religious symbols, calendrical systems, and historical texts. Compared to the Early Classic, society became more complex, and social mobility was reduced as social status came to be based more on birth than ability. Most significant, Late Classic lowland society was characterized by an expansive growth in population and aggressive competition. The increasing population was accompanied by more centralized authority, and both the size and complexity of society began an upward growth spiral.

By about A.D. 800, the beginning of the Terminal Classic, the former social and political order began to break down. Society in the southern and central lowlands became increasingly decentralized as population levels declined. At Seibal and other late-blossoming centers, new ruling elites became dominant, probably representing Mexicanized cultural backgrounds such as the Putun Maya. The ultimate decline in the fortunes of the southern and central lowland Maya will be examined in the next chapter.

# THE DECLINE OF THE CLASSIC MAYA

> There were no more lucky days for us; we had no sound judgement. At the end of our loss of vision, and of our shame, everything shall be revealed.
> —*Book of Chilam Balam* of Chumayel (Roys 1967: 83)

As we have seen, Maya centers in much of the lowlands suffered a seemingly dramatic decline during the Terminal Classic period. Over a relatively short period, corresponding roughly to the ninth century (A.D. 790 to 889, or 9.18.0.0.0 to 10.3.0.0.0 in the Maya calendar), a slowdown and cessation in intellectual and cultural activities are reflected in the archaeological record over most of the southern and central lowlands. By the end of this era the construction of administrative, residential, and ceremonial structures had ceased at most sites. No further dynastic monuments were erected; hieroglyphic texts and calendrical dates were no longer recorded. The manufacture and distribution of the elaborate traditional luxury and ritual goods made of pottery, jade, wood, bone, and shell ended. From this kind of evidence, it can be inferred that the failure of the Classic lowland Maya involved especially the ruling elite, the class that sponsored and directed the majority of the activities that disappear from the archaeological record.

The spatial pattern of the cessation of these activities indicates that the failure was more complete in the cores of the southern and central lowlands than to the north (Yucatan) and east (Belize). Occupation was continuous in these regions and, in the case of the Yucatan, appears to have increased. But in the great central lowland sites, such as Tikal, the archaeological record reflects a profound decrease in population, although the region remained occupied for several centuries after the end of the old elite-associated activities. Finally, at some point several hundred years before the arrival of the Spaniards, the population centers throughout most of the central lowlands were abandoned to the rain forest, except for small settlements around the lakes of central Peten.

Maya civilization did not terminate with the end of the Classic period. But later developments from the ninth century until the Spanish Conquest in the

sixteenth century, corresponding to the Postclassic period, are devoid of most of
the characteristics that define Classic Maya lowland culture, especially those
traits that distinguish the elite segment of society. Furthermore, Postclassic
Maya society was centered in two distinct regions outside the central and
southern lowlands, the northern half of the Yucatan Peninsula and the southern
highlands of Guatemala.

## Investigations into the Classic Decline

What caused the demise? The question began to be asked as soon as many of
the great centers of the Classic Maya were rediscovered in the lowland rain
forest during the eighteenth and nineteenth centuries. The early answers all
stressed sudden catastrophe, a seemingly obvious conclusion given the dramatic
contrast between the empty and silent jungle-covered ruins and what was
recognized as a once populous and highly developed civilization. To the European mind, a great civilization set in the depths of an inhospitable rain forest
seemed like a contradiction in terms. It seemed only logical, therefore, to
assume that the Maya failed because of the hardships of their environment.
That they succeeded so brilliantly for a time was viewed, sometimes even to this
day, as something of a "mystery." To early scholars, however, the question
about the Maya failure was often not as important as the question of origins.
And *that* question was initially answered, of course, by recourse to migrations
from a host of known civilizations in the Old World.

With the more recent general acceptance of the idea that the Maya represented an indigenous New World development, attention turned to the reasons
for the mysterious abandonment of the lowland cities. Since the turn of the
century, dozens of theories have been advanced, and from these, two general
trends can be discerned. In the first place, there has been a shift away from
theories that propose a single cause toward theories that advance multiple
factors. Second, there has been a shift away from sudden and dramatic catastrophe toward more subtle, longer-acting processes. Both of these trends reached a
culmination at a symposium of Maya scholars in 1970, convened to consider
the collapse question and to reevaluate the problem in light of the rapidly
accumulating new evidence about Maya civilization resulting from the unprecedented amount of new archaeological research.

The results of this conference provide the most comprehensive treatment of
the subject to date. Significantly, one conclusion from the conference was the
realization that a better understanding of the Classic Maya demise could be
achieved only by increasing our information about ancient Maya society. Given
the additional progress made in our knowledge of the ancient Maya since the
collapse conference was held, we should be in a better position today to
understand the demise. That is, as our traditional concepts of the ancient Maya
are modified or replaced by new information, our understanding of the collapse

is also altered, and any evaluation of the Maya collapse issue must be considered with this perspective in mind. For example, results of research completed during the last twenty years have challenged and overthrown traditional concepts about ancient Maya economic, social, and political organization (see Chapters 7, 8, and 11).

Old ideas die hard; in this case Maya archaeology (like the archaeology of many complex societies) had long been dominated by investigations of the largest sites and, within those sites, of the most elaborate or impressive buildings. As a result, our knowledge of Maya society is heavily biased toward the elite class, who occupied the palaces, temples, and tombs. Although it is obvious that a more balanced sampling of archaeological data should produce a better picture of all aspects of ancient Maya society, excavation and funding priorities have tended to preserve this traditional research bias. Until recently there have been few exceptions to the traditional approach. Future work, including more studies based on well-balanced sampling strategies and regional rather than site-oriented research problems, should produce a more complete picture of the ancient Maya. If it does, we can expect that our present assessment of the Maya collapse and, indeed, our view of the whole of ancient Maya society, will need to be further modified.

The various theories concerned with the demise of Maya civilization are conveniently categorized as those that emphasize *internal* factors and those that emphasize *external* factors. Theories emphasizing internal factors view the Classic Maya decline as generally isolated from developments occurring in the wider context of Mesoamerica. Theories emphasizing external factors propose that the demise was due largely to developments originating outside the immediate Maya area.

## Theories Emphasizing Internal Factors

Most of the earliest theories attributed the end of Classic Maya civilization to internal events, but several recent proposals have also emphasized these factors. The themes of the three most useful of these explanations are natural catastrophes, ecological disaster, and sociopolitical disintegration.

Several kinds of natural catastrophes have been advanced as possibly triggering the demise of Maya civilization. Earlier we explored the hypothesis that vulcanism played a role in the decline of Preclassic society in the southern Maya area (Chapter 3). Though most of the Maya lowlands area is not geologically active, earthquakes do occur. The southern fringes of the lowlands are especially vulnerable to tectonic activity. Using the evidence of unrepaired structural damage to a major palace at the site of Xunantunich (Benque Viejo) in the central lowlands, an area of low tectonic activity, it has been proposed that one or more catastrophic earthquakes may have contributed to the downfall and abandonment of lowland sites.

Recent excavations at Quirigua leave no doubt that major earthquakes did indeed plague the inhabitants of the southeastern Maya lowlands. Quirigua was built directly on the Motagua fault, the same one whose rupture in 1976 caused a disastrous earthquake in Guatemala, clearly revealing the fault trace. Evidence of ancient damaged and collapsed construction there, as well as massive second-ary buttressing of masonry buildings, testifies to ancient tectonic activity. But though earthquakes may have affected specific areas including Quirigua and perhaps Xunantunich, there is no evidence and little likelihood that tectonic catastrophes devastated the entire Maya lowlands.

Other natural disasters have been proposed as culprits for the Classic Maya downfall. The Maya lowlands are frequently visited by Caribbean hurricanes. It is likely that a major storm of this kind could easily destroy agricultural production over a wide area. As with earthquakes, however, it is difficult to accept the theory that the relatively localized destructive effects of hurricanes could trigger the failure of the lowland Maya. Furthermore, the destruction of a forest in a hurricane's path could be seen as beneficial, clearing new lands for agricultural exploitation.

Epidemic diseases could have produced catastrophic depopulation of the Maya lowlands. Yellow fever has been among the most often suggested culprits in this regard. The disastrous effect of epidemic disease among New World populations is tragically documented by the consequences of the introduction of malaria, smallpox, and other Old World diseases at the time of the Spanish Conquest. Yellow fever is also usually considered an Old World disease, but its discovery among New World primates (especially howler monkeys) indicates that it may also be indigenous to Central and South America. The historically documented bubonic plague that ravaged late medieval Europe, though obvi-ously not affecting the Maya directly, arguably provides an analogue for the lowland collapse, especially as an illustration of the social consequences of sudden and severe depopulation caused by disease. That the ancient Maya were vulnerable to epidemic disease is indicated by skeletal studies from both Tikal and Altar de Sacrificios. Both sites demonstrate progressive nutritional deficien-cies and increasing disease potentials in lowland populations toward the end of the Classic period.

A variety of ecological disasters has been proposed to explain the Maya demise. The earliest pointed to the harmful consequences of swidden agricul-ture, believed to have once been the basis of lowland subsistence. The assumed destructive effects on soil fertility and the gradual conversion of forested areas into savanna grasslands have been used to explain the failure of Classic Maya civilization. Since the Maya had no tools to cultivate the grasslands, according to this argument, they were eventually forced to abandon the central lowlands. Other supposed effects of swidden cultivation in combination with the heavy tropical rainfall were severe erosion and the deposition of soil into what were formerly shallow lakes, now the swampy depressions (*bajos*) found in many areas of the lowlands. The question whether all these depressions were shallow lakes or not, at least within the span of Maya civilization, has yet to be resolved.

It has been proposed that the Classic Maya declined through a failure to adapt successfully to the lowland environment, although this thesis is flawed by its failure to account for the centuries of successful exploitation of the habitat and by grossly underestimating the subsistence potential of the Maya lowlands (see Chapter 7). Nonetheless, examinations of subsistence capabilities, assuming swidden cultivation, have resulted in the same verdict; that is, over-exploitation of the environment leads to agricultural failure that could account for the Classic Maya collapse. This idea has been modified by proposing that the lowland Maya began to intensify their agricultural base to meet growing population pressures, but that the means used, grassland swiddens, proved to be ecologically disastrous.

The ecological-disaster theories based on swidden cultivation can no longer be supported, given the recent evidence of diversified and intensive agriculture practiced by the ancient Maya. Some investigators, however, never accepted the idea that the ancient Maya relied on swidden agriculture, proposing that intensive agriculture would have been required to support peak populations in the lowlands. But an acceptance of intensive agriculture among the ancient Maya does not necessarily rule out concurrent acceptance of ecological disaster as a cause for the Classic decline. Most Maya scholars now agree that the documented intensification of Maya agriculture was a response to increasing population and ecological pressures. Thus, the collapse may have been due, at least in part, to an overwhelming of the environmental limits of the lowlands. Although no longer based on an overstatement of the destructive effects of a reliance on swidden agriculture or on an underestimation of the lowland potential, this conclusion nonetheless strongly echoes the original ecological-failure proposals.

The third category, which attributes the decline to social and political failures, is based, either implicitly or explicitly, on supposed weaknesses inherent in Classic Maya society. That is, these theories assume that the prestige and authority of the ruling elite were eroded, usually through violent confrontations with the non-elite classes, and that as a result, Classic society fell apart and the lowland centers were abandoned.

The idea of a revolt has been extremely popular. Several investigators have suggested that the increasing size of the ruling class, combined with their abuses of power, led to a popular revolution. The best-known advocate of the revolution theory was J. Eric Thompson. His "peasant revolt" theory received wide acknowledgment and even acceptance among Maya scholars. (It should be noted, however, that although this idea is often found in Thompson's popular writings, it seldom appears in his scholarly publications.) The thesis holds that a combination of factors, including agricultural difficulties, malnutrition or disease, and perhaps even natural disasters, culminated in widespread disillusionment as the Maya peasant class lost confidence in the rulers. The situation was made worse by an increasing dissociation from the concerns of the populace by the elite, as theocratic rulers turned increasingly to esoteric matters instead of to practical solutions to the mounting crisis. The inevitable result was a violent revolt by the peasants, who then destroyed the ruling class.

At Piedras Negras, the discovery of broken "thrones" offered support for the possibility of revolt against the rulers. Later research uncovered smashed or mutilated monuments at Tikal that could also have resulted from acts of violence, but more recent interpretations of the Tikal evidence indicate that monument mutilation was a custom practiced throughout the Classic period, and is thus a weak argument for revolution.

An economic variation on this theme holds that the elite-controlled trade network of the central lowlands (the core area) was eventually cut off from access to critical commodities by the rise of trading centers on the peripheries (the buffer zone). As a result, the core area collapsed, followed thereafter by the buffer zone, which was left with no trading customers. Archaeological evidence indicates, however, that many sites located in the buffer zone collapsed long before those in the core area, quite the opposite of what this theory projects.

Although based on external conditions, another variation of the sociopolitical failure thesis attributes the demise to a changing economic and political environment, specifically, competition from rival Mexican states. This thesis holds that more efficient means to mobilize food resources, manpower, and wealth, developed in the highland states of Mexico, placed the Maya in a disadvantageous position. Specifically, the traditional ruling elite could not or would not institute the changes necessary to ensure the survival of the Classic Maya civilization.

The Maya collapse symposium would later concur: "The Maya of the Late Classic period apparently made no technological or social adaptive innovations which might have mitigated these difficulties." Yet other investigators have indicated that several changes seen in the archaeological record during the Late Classic might well be interpreted as attempts by the ruling elite to adapt to crisis conditions. For instance, the apparent acceleration of monument construction during this era might have been undertaken to appease the supernatural powers believed to control Maya destiny.

The Maya concept of cyclical history is of relevance to the collapse issue, especially its emphasis on fatalistic prophecies associated with a round of thirteen katuns (approximately 256 years; see Chapter 16). Each katun in the cycle was numbered and had a distinctive set of prophecies; the Maya believed that the recurrence of a particular, numbered katun every 256 years brought with it the reenactment of corresponding events and conditions from the past. Recent research has revealed indications of this cyclical concept of history among the elite rulers at Late Classic Tikal, including the deliberate public association of individual rulers with katuns representing earlier periods of prosperity (Chapter

4). This research, in turn, has led to hypotheses that the Late Classic Maya rulers at Tikal were attempting a cultural revitalization aimed at reestablishing past glories, and that an unsuccessful revitalization attempt may have coincided with the decline of that center.

It is also possible that the Maya concept of cyclical history contributed actively to the collapse. Prophecies of fundamental political and religious change associated with specific katuns are known from the ethnohistorical record. For example, the Spanish conquest of the last bastion of Maya independence at the site of Tayasal in 1697 was probably hastened by the approach of a new katun cycle that augured momentous changes (see the Epilogue). The earliest signs of trouble in the Maya lowlands began with the onset of a new katun cycle in A.D. 790; the beginning of the preceding cycle (A.D. 534) corresponded with the Middle Classic hiatus, a time of depressed activity in the lowlands (see Chapter 4). Counting back an additional katun cycle, to A.D. 278, brings us to a time eerily close to the eruption of Ilopango and the demise of the southern Maya's prosperity (Chapter 3). The conclusion drawn from these regularities is that as the Late Classic katun cycle approached its end, the fatalistic Maya failed to resist the forces of change that were sweeping away the old order because of prophecies that foretold fundamental changes in their society.

The final internal theory considers accelerating civil warfare to have been a factor contributing to sociopolitical disintegration and collapse. This thesis ascribes the disruption to attempts to conquer and consolidate the lowland area by one or more of the major Classic centers—a situation analogous to the Peloponnesian wars that debilitated Greece in the fifth century B.C. The battle and judgment scenes on the murals at Bonampak and the captive motifs frequently found in Maya sculpture provide evidence of warfare among the Classic Maya. Mutilated sculpture, the same evidence used to support the idea of a popular revolution, could also be interpreted as a consequence of warfare. Moreover, the inscriptions at Quirigua frequently mention the "capture" of the ruler 18 Rabbit of Copan, the larger and presumably rival center some 50 km to the south, and texts from several other sites, including Yaxchilan, refer to conquest. However, most scholars interpret these kinds of evidence as depicting small-scale raiding or even ritualized conflict between centers, the result of increasing competition for land, labor, trade routes, and other economic resources. It is more difficult to substantiate the idea of conquest on a scale sufficient to bring ruin upon the lowland Maya.

## Theories Emphasizing External Factors

Explanations for the demise of the Classic Maya that lay the cause on external factors have gained increased favor in recent years, perhaps owing to a reaction against the isolationism inherent in the internal theories. But however the several factors ultimately sort themselves out, it no longer seems sensible, in seeking explanations for the demise, to ignore the context of larger issues throughout Mesoamerica.

Foreign invasion of the Maya lowlands has been proposed by several scholars. Militaristic Mexican invaders may have conquered the lowlands and forcibly resettled the survivors in northern Yucatan, nearer the "Toltec" capital of Chichen Itza. The evidence from Altar de Sacrificios, provided primarily by a rather complete shift in the pottery inventory, indicates that the site was invaded and conquered at the close of the Classic period. A similar event, suggested by changes seen in the architectural and sculptural records, as well as the pottery (Chapter 4), has been reconstructed at the site of Seibal. There would seem to be little doubt that Seibal was not only conquered, but occupied as well, by a new ruling group at the end of the Classic period. The homeland for these invaders remains in doubt, but stylistic evidence and the portraits of individual rulers on the post-conquest monuments at Seibal suggest that they were foreigners sharing at least some cultural traditions with the lowland Maya. As will be discussed further in the next chapter, these invaders have been identified as Putun Maya, a Gulf coast people peripheral to Classic Maya civilization who rose to power in the Postclassic period.

Proponents of the foreign-invasion thesis hold that the resulting disruptions in lowland Maya society were sufficient to bring about its demise. On the other side, the lack of evidence for invasion or conflict at most centers other than Seibal and Altar de Sacrificios casts doubt on the cause-and-effect relationship between invasion and collapse. Arguably, the invasion was more an effect than a cause of the collapse, made possible by the already weakened condition of Maya society. At Tikal, for instance, there is little indication of invasion or any other serious incursion from outside until well after the site was in decline.

The economic relationships between the lowland Maya and other peoples of Mesoamerica suggest another theory for the demise. The changes in Mesoamerican long-distance trade networks that mark the Terminal Classic may have isolated the southern and central lowland Maya from the economic and political powers that came to dominate the Postclassic. During this period the Putun Maya rose to power and appear to have monopolized the seacoast trade routes that became increasingly important at the end of the Classic period. The investigation of a Postclassic port-of-trade on Isla de Cozumel, off the east coast of Yucatan, related the demise to the failure of the traditional lowland elite to recognize the importance of the new sea trade around the Peninsula. As a result, the old land routes were largely abandoned, and the lowland Maya became isolated economically. A case for the rise and fall of Tikal, specifically, can be constructed around the site's position of control over trans-lowland canoe routes. When these routes diminished in importance, the site appears to have fallen on hard times and was eventually abandoned.

It has also been suggested that the long-recognized pause in building and monument construction that marks the Middle Classic hiatus (Chapter 4) represented a "little collapse," a rehearsal of events (due to the same causes) that would lead ultimately to the decline some three hundred years later. The cause of both events may have been the severance of symbiotic economic relationships between the lowland Maya and other Mesoamerican civilizations. In the Early Classic the dominant relationship was with Teotihuacan, and its termination after Teotihuacan's destruction seems to have caused the hiatus in the Maya lowlands. After the hiatus, a reorganized Late Classic society established more diverse external economic alliances, but these, too, were ultimately bypassed and superseded by adjacent societies, spawning a lowland collapse. The question, then, is why the Maya recovered from one breakdown in their external economic networks only to fail in a similar situation later. The answer appears to be that by the end of the Classic period the long-distance trade routes, now firmly in the hands of new mercantile powers based on sea commerce, were beyond the control of the traditional powers of the central Maya lowlands.

## Reconstructing the Classic Decline

What do we know about the decline of the Classic Maya? On the strength of the Maya collapse symposium, augmented by data made available since 1970, we may suggest the following:

1. The complexity and growth of Classic lowland Maya society were stimulated by interaction with Teotihuacan, especially at Tikal. Withdrawal of Teotihuacan power from the lowlands precipitated the Middle Classic hiatus, while providing the opportunity for independent development of and competition between the Maya centers of the Late Classic. Tikal, for instance, underwent a revitalization during this era.

2. The lowland elite promoted common training, beliefs, symbols of prestige, and lines of authority, reinforced by increasingly elaborate ceremonialism, to foster cooperation between sites in controlling political alliances, trade, and warfare and to promote the expansion of their power. These factors also served to increase the social distance between the elite and the various non-elite classes, and fatalistic beliefs in prophecies of change coinciding with the katun cycle may have contributed to the elite's loss in popular support, their low morale, and their eventual downfall.

3. Continued population growth intensified the pressures on an increasingly complex and vulnerable subsistence system as the incidence of malnutrition and disease increased and productivity decreased. Certain elite responses to the crises, such as accelerated construction of ceremonial structures, may have exacerbated the situation by placing heavier labor demands on the populace, thus increasing the problems of adequate food production and distribution.

4. The traditional long-distance trade networks (via land and river canoe)

diminished in importance with the increase in seacoast trade around the Yucatan Peninsula. The failure of the established elite to adapt to the changing economic situation led to a loss of wealth, prestige, and power. Several centers, including Altar de Sacrificios and Seibal, seemingly were occupied by the new mercantile elite, eventually to be abandoned when these sites lost their importance as trade centers.

Some combination of these factors brought about a shift in the concentration of economic and political power, from the traditional primary centers to newer, competing centers of power. Much of the population that occupied the lowlands during the Classic period, including those members of the elite class able to adapt to new conditions, gradually moved to the new power centers in areas controlled by the prosperous new states in northern Yucatan and to the new mercantile elite centers along the Gulf and Caribbean coasts (see Chapter 6).

However these factors are ultimately sorted out, it no longer seems profitable to look for single, dramatic causes for the decline of the Classic Maya. Thus, the issue has shifted from one of finding causes for the collapse to one of reexamining the concept of cultural decline. The traditional term "collapse" now clearly seems to be an inappropriate term. The Classic Maya appear not to have suddenly fallen apart; rather, both internal and external processes—multiple, subtle, and simultaneous—yielded a gradual transformation of the social, political, economic, and even ideological foundations of Maya society. Out of these processes emerged a reoriented culture based in areas outside the central lowlands, a culture that would prosper during the Postclassic era and suffer the ravages of the Spanish Conquest.

# 6 ⊡

# THE POSTCLASSIC MAYA

> 6 Ahau was when the discovery of Chichen Itza occurred. 13 Ahau was when the
> mat of the katun was counted in order. 8 Ahau was when Chichen Itza was
> abandoned. There were thirteen folds of katuns when they established their houses
> at Chakanputun.    —*Book of Chilam Balam* of Chumayel (Roys 1967: 135–36)

The Postclassic period, about A.D. 900–1500, has long been characterized as an
era of decline from the cultural florescence of the Classic period. In some cases,
the term "decadent" has been used to describe the Late Postclassic, either to
typify an observable shift in the standards of artistic expression or to characterize other aspects of life in these later times. More properly, perhaps, the
Postclassic is seen as an era when the societies in the Maya area and throughout
all Mesoamerica were dominated by three particular themes of social organization: a reliance on militarism, a prevalence of secularism in political affairs, and
an increasing development of urban life.

To these three themes, all begun in the Classic, we may add a fourth—
integration—for the Postclassic was above all else a time when the boundaries
of traditional regional cultural developments began to break down. Overall,
populations were increasing again, and more numerous and widespread interregional contacts resulted from active communication, commerce, alliances, migrations of groups, and military conquests.

The increased contacts, together with the increased population, enlarged the
sphere of groups that shared common Mesoamerican cultural traditions. The
Postclassic has long been recognized in the Maya area as a period of "Mexicanization," a time when cultural traits from central Mexico and other regions were
increasingly incorporated into Maya art, architecture, ceramics, and the other
products of culture recovered by archaeologists. The Maya chronicles that have
survived speak of this era as a time of invasions and conquests by foreigners,
and the peoples have been identified as coming from the southwest periphery of
the Maya area; they were probably Maya groups heavily influenced by central
Mexican culture, or even led by Mexican elites. These events brought the
ancient Maya into contact with new political ideas, military tactics, and religious
practices, all of which were to cause significant changes in their society.

Thus, the Postclassic period was a complex era for the Maya, a time of profound changes. In many ways, the cultural traditions that began in the Preclassic and developed throughout the Classic were permanently altered. According to the Maya themselves, the Classic period was a time when "they adhered to their reason. . . . At that time the course of humanity was orderly." But the Postclassic era brought "the origin of the two-day throne, the two-day reign. . . . There were no more lucky days for us; we had no sound judgement."

The extant Postclassic Maya chronicles, such as the *Book of Chilam Balam* from which the above quote was taken, reflect the Maya's own view of the past. This view is not so much history in our sense of the word, but rather the reconciliation of actual events with prophecy. As a result, the chronology of events in Maya writings may be distorted, compressed or expanded like a telescope, at times even presented in a contradictory manner. To further the difficulty, the results of archaeological research are not always in accord with the available ethnohistorical accounts. But despite our imperfect knowledge of the Postclassic era, it is nonetheless possible to outline the major sequence of events.

Whereas the focus of major developments during the Classic era was the central and southern lowland areas, the Postclassic period saw the almost uninterrupted development of the northern lowlands of Yucatan (Table 3)

TABLE 3

*Selected Events in the History of Northern-*
*Lowland Centers During the Postclassic Period*

| Date | | Event |
|---|---|---|
| Maya | Gregorian (A.D.) | |
| 10.6.0.0.0 | 948 | Itza Maya abandon Chakanputun (Seibal?) and move north into the Yucatan. |
| 10.8.0.0.0 | 987 | Itza reoccupy Chichen Itza, beginning the era of dominance of that site in the north. Mayapan founded (?). |
| 10.9.0.0.0 | 1007 | Xiu Maya reoccupy Uxmal (?). |
| 11.0.0.0.0 | 1224 | Conquest of Chichen Itza led by Hunac Ceel, ruler of Mayapan; Itza driven from Chichen Itza (ca. 1221); era of Mayapan dominance in the north begins. |
| 11.11.0.0.0 | 1441 | Revolt led by Ah Xupan Xiu; Mayapan and its Cocom leaders (save one) destroyed. |
| 11.13.0.0.0 | 1480 | Civil wars rage between northern centers (ca. 1496). |
| 11.14.0.0.0 | 1500 | Spaniards first seen (1511). |
| 11.15.0.0.0 | 1520 | First two attempts at conquest by the Spanish are defeated (1527-35). Ah Dzun Xiu and party massacred by orders of Nachi Cocom (1536), thus avenging the Xiu-led revolt against Mayapan. |
| 11.16.0.0.0 | 1539 | Spanish Conquest of the Yucatan (1540-46; see the Epilogue). |

reach its climax, along with a return to prominence of the southern area, especially the highlands. We will consider events in the Yucatan first, then briefly review Postclassic developments in the southern Maya area.

## The Earlier Periods in Yucatan in Retrospect

Because both rainfall and soil cover diminish as one proceeds north (Chapter 1), population growth in the northern lowlands must have been constrained by the limited agricultural potential of the region. Yet the archaeological evidence clearly establishes that a series of populous and prosperous centers developed in the Yucatan, beginning in the Preclassic era.

In large measure, these centers owed their existence to valuable local resources, especially salt and probably cotton production. Control over the production and export of these commodities was undoubtedly the foundation of the prosperity seen in the archaeological record of the Peninsula. Several large northern centers, such as those located in areas of very thin soils near the coastal salt sources, were probably dependent on food imports to sustain their populations. Dzibilchaltun and Chunchucmil typify centers that must have received foodstuffs and other goods in exchange for salt exports.

Although there is evidence of very early occupation in Yucatan (Chapter 2), the earliest major center thus far investigated is the site of Komchen (Figs. 6.1

Fig. 6.1. Structure 500, Komchen, Yucatan, Mexico: excavations revealed construction from the Middle through the Late Preclassic eras; the ramp and the short staircase nearest the camera date from the Middle Preclassic.

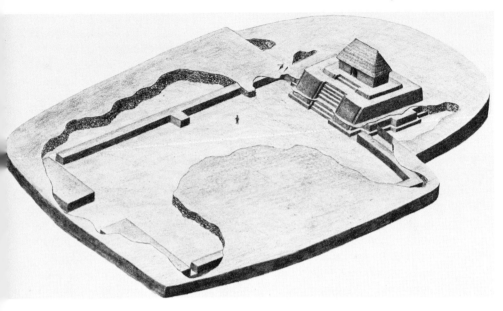

Fig. 6.2. Structure 450, Komchen, built during the Middle and Late Preclassic, connected to Structure 500 (Fig. 6.1) by a 250-meter-long *sacbe* (causeway).

and 6.2), just north of Dzibilchaltun. The growth of Komchen, probably among the first centers to consolidate control over local salt production, spanned some six hundred years, from about 400 B.C. to A.D. 200. On the basis of the inventory of imported artifacts and the remaining architectural characteristics (the site is badly destroyed), Komchen seems to have been a vital link in an early circum-Yucatecan trade route that reached as far south as Chiapas and Belize.

Komchen declined rapidly at the close of the Preclassic era. Interestingly, the same fate befell another prosperous Preclassic center in Belize, Cerros, seemingly a part of the same Late Preclassic circum-Yucatecan trade network (see Fig. 3.16). The downfall of these coastal centers probably resulted from the collapse of the trade network that sustained them. The cause of this collapse, though unknown, was undoubtedly related to the emerging dominance of the inland Classic centers, and the growing importance of the new riverine or overland trade network that characterized the period (Chapter 4).

The Early Classic era remains less well known in the northern lowlands. No single major center seems to have dominated the political and economic events of the period, although several important sites are uninvestigated (such as Ake, Acanceh, and Izamal) that might be able to furnish evidence about this time span. Hieroglyphic texts from the Classic period are also rather scarce in the Yucatan.

The scattering of Early Classic dated monuments that do exist in the area include Lintel 1 at Oxkintok (Fig. 6.3) from 475 (9.2.0.0.0) and Stela 1 at Tulum (found there but undoubtedly moved from elsewhere) from 564 (9.6.10.0.0). But these are isolated occurrences, not portions of the long sequence of dynastic monuments typical of most central and southern lowland Classic sites.

Several northern centers appear to have risen to prominence during the Late Classic era. Dzibilchaltun, located immediately north of Mérida, rapidly expanded during the Late and Terminal Classic periods, until it became one of the largest northern centers for its time. Its growth and prosperity probably resulted from its control over the production and export of local salt resources. This power clearly made Dzibilchaltun heir to the position enjoyed by Komchen during the Late Preclassic era. The presence of sculptured stelae indicates that this center was ruled by an elite dynasty, although no hieroglyphic texts have survived. The prosperity of Chunchucmil, located some 100 km (62 mi.) southwest of Dzibilchaltun, seems to have reached its apogee in this same era.

Two other northern centers have yielded fairly good sequences of sculptured monuments and preserved texts. Coba, a mammoth site situated among a series of shallow lakes in northeastern Yucatan, dedicated a series of monuments beginning in 618 (9.9.5.0.0). Edzna, inland from the Gulf coast of Yucatan, is known for an even longer sequence of monuments, extending from 633 to 810

Fig. 6.3. Lintel 1, Oxkintok, Yucatan, Mexico, showing the earliest known long-count date in the northern lowlands (9.2.0.0.0, or A.D. 475).

Fig. 6.4. Regional architectural styles: (*above*) Structure 1, Xpuhil, Campeche, Mexico, a prime example of the Río Bec architectural style (restoration drawing by Tatiana Proskouriakoff); (*below*) Structure II, Chicanna, Campeche, the excavated and partially restored façade typical of the Chenes architectural style.

(9.10.0.0.0 to 9.19.0.0.0). The sculptural and architectural styles (augmented by the ceramic affiliations at Edzna) indicate that both sites were allied to the major Classic centers to the south. These cultural ties probably reflect a commercial network uniting Coba and Edzna with the southern Classic centers, perhaps as inland collection points for cotton, salt, and other important Yucatecan products.

The Late and Terminal Classic eras in Yucatan were marked by several regional developments, of which the architectural styles are the best known (see Chapter 11). Río Bec, centered at the base of the Yucatan Peninsula and including Becan, Xpuhil, and Río Bec, displays architectural and ceramic traits that combine the styles of the central and northern lowlands. In architecture, for instance, Río Bec is noted for the use of high terraced towers crowned by nonfunctional "temples," thought to imitate the great pyramid temples of the Classic centers in the Peten region, most notably at Tikal. This southern characteristic was combined with elaborate building façades decorated with mosaic masks, typical of Yucatecan architecture (Fig. 6.4a).

Farther to the north, Xtampak and several other sites reflect the same Río Bec architectural style, except for the absence of the "false" pyramid towers. This architecture, emphasizing elaborate mosaic façades and doorways framed by elaborate "monster masks," has been labeled Chenes (Fig. 6.4b). But Chenes is clearly a close relative of the same regional cultural tradition seen at Río Bec.

The best-known regional architectural style was developed in northern and northwestern Yucatan. The Puuc style, named after the low range of hills found in the area, gave rise to some of the most beautiful and most appealing of all Maya buildings (Fig. 6.5). The characteristic, finely fitted veneer masonry

Fig. 6.5. Prominent example of the Puuc architectural style, the Governor's Palace, Uxmal, Yucatan, Mexico.

covers a self-supporting structural hearting held together by lime-based concrete. Typically, the plain lower zones of Puuc buildings contrast with their
upper zones, which are decorated by intricate mosaic designs. The earliest
examples of this style seem to be present at Edzna, Xcalumkin, and Oxkintok,
but its finest examples are found at sites that reached their zenith during the
Yucatecan Terminal Classic period (ca. A.D. 800–1000), such as Uxmal,
Labna, Sayil, and Kabah. The available epigraphic evidence from Uxmal, the
largest of these sites, indicates that a ruling dynasty was in power at this center
during the Terminal Classic period. The striking similarities of Puuc architecture to contemporary or even earlier styles in Mexico, especially in the Valley of
Oaxaca at the site of Mitla, probably reflect the growing contacts between
Maya and Mexican cultures that peaked during the Postclassic era.

## The Transition from Classic to Postclassic in Yucatan

The transition between the Classic and Postclassic periods was marked by the
rise of a new group, the Putun (or Chontal) Maya, whose homeland appears to
have been along the Gulf coast in the Tabasco lowlands. The Putun were not a
single Maya "nation," but comprised several independent groups. They appear
to have been unified only in language (Chontal; see Chapter 15) and in cultural
traditions, which were heavily Mexicanized, especially among the ruling elite.
The political and religious institutions of the Putun reflected many characteristics typical of central Mexico, and at least some Putun groups seem to have
been allied with the major power of Early Postclassic Mexico, the Toltec.

The Putun were both warriors and merchants, and their aggressive movements during the Postclassic seem to have been often motivated by a desire to
seize and control important resources and trade routes. Initially, they seem to
have been concerned with maintaining several of the old riverine and overland
routes in the central and southern lowlands that flourished during the Classic
period. Eventually, however, they controlled the seacoast trade around the
Yucatan Peninsula that connected the east and west coasts and, ultimately, the
commerce between Gulf Coast Mexico and Central America. Most of the series
of ports in this sea-trading network included colonies of resident Putun merchants: Xicalango in the Putun heartland along the Gulf coast, Isla de Cozumel
off northeastern Yucatan, and Nito, on the Gulf of Honduras at the base of the
east coast of the Peninsula.

In the Yucatec Maya chronicles, such as the *Books of Chilam Balam*, an
important group known as the Itza may be identified with the Putun. The Itza
were a specific, famous Maya group whose destiny was central to the fortunes of
Postclassic Yucatan. Given the uncertainties about the ethnic identity of all
these peoples, the term Putun will be used here to refer to the generalized
Mexicanized Maya that clearly seem to have expanded their commercial and
political power during the Postclassic period. A clearer picture emerges at the

time of the Spanish Conquest, when the Putun homeland on the Gulf coast of the Yucatan was known as Acalan, or "land of canoes." The capital of this region, known as Itzamkanac, was described by the Spanish as a substantial and prosperous center. At the time of Cortés's visit in 1524, the ruler of Acalan was both the leading merchant of Itzamkanac and the holder of the ancient title of a supreme ruling lord, *ahau*.

Evidence of Putun movements can be detected as early as the Terminal Classic. During this period Chichen Itza, later the dominant center of the Yucatan, was a relatively minor settlement. But the site is known for some of the earliest examples on the Peninsula of Mexican architectural forms, which may reflect occupation by a Putun group during the Terminal Classic era. The Temple of the Chac Mool, underlying the splendid Toltec-style Temple of the Warriors, was decorated by wall paintings depicting two elite groups. One is clearly Maya, for the leaders are seated on jaguar skins and hold manikin scepters; the others are just as clearly from a Mexicanized tradition. The scene has been interpreted as commemorating an alliance between local Yucatecan rulers and a newly arrived Putun group, perhaps the establishment at Chichen Itza of a Putun colony.

During this period the commercial and even political interests of another Putun group may have penetrated westward into central Mexico, as far as the Valley of Puebla, perhaps to secure a trade network during a period of disorganization between the fall of Teotihuacan and the rise of Tula, capital of the Toltec state. The evidence for this derives mainly from the long-known architectural reliefs in Maya style at Xochicalco and the spectacular newly discovered murals at Cacaxtla in the Valley of Puebla. The Cacaxtla murals depict a great battle between warriors led by war captains who display a combination of Maya and Mexican characteristics. Furthermore, pottery from the Valley of Puebla during this era includes plumbate and fine orange types that are usually associated with Putun sites.

The Putun also appear to have moved into the central and southern Maya lowlands during the Terminal Classic period. The ceramics at Becan, Tikal, and several other sites change during this era in ways that suggest outside influence, perhaps that of Putun. But the principal thrust of the Putun was up the Río Usumacinta, the major trade route between the Gulf coast and the region of the southern lowlands and the adjacent highlands. Here, on the Río Pasión, a strategic tributary of the Usumacinta, sits the site of Seibal, a relatively minor center during the Classic period. Archaeological investigations at Seibal clearly reveal that this center was significantly transformed, beginning about A.D. 830 and continuing through the remainder of the ninth century, to a major population center. The series of new buildings and monuments erected at this time show unmistakable Yucatecan characteristics; and Seibal's new rulers, shown in the sculptured portraits to have adopted many conventions of the traditional Classic elite, are clearly foreigners (see Fig. 4.29).

The Yucatecan chronicles describe the history of this period: "There were thirteen folds of katuns when they established their houses at Chakanputun. . . . For thirteen folds of katuns they had dwelt in their houses at Chakanputun. This was always the katun when the Itza went beneath the trees, beneath the bushes, beneath the vines, to their misfortune." It is quite possible that Chakanputun is Seibal, deep in the southern rain forest ("beneath the trees . . . beneath the vines"), and that the foreigners who took over Seibal were Putun Maya from the Yucatan. The famous wall paintings in the Temple of the Jaguars, above the Great Ball Court at Chichen Itza, may depict scenes from the history of the Putun Maya, one series of which was clearly set in the rain forest of the southern lowlands. This could be a representation of Seibal and the period of Putun domination over portions of the southern lowlands. The other group of murals depicts a highland setting similar to the environment of central Mexico. This setting, together with the theme of the murals themselves—the confrontation between two war leaders and their forces—recalls the Cacaxtla murals.

The archaeological evidence indicates that shortly after 900 Seibal was abandoned, for reasons unknown. Perhaps when the old trans-Peten trade routes broke down, Seibal lost much of its strategic commercial advantage. There are also indications of renewed invasions, probably by competing Putun groups from the Gulf coast, that may have brought about the end of Seibal's Putun dynasty.

By the tenth century the Putun seem to have developed large sea-going canoes, which they used to control the coastal trade routes that were to change the fortunes of Postclassic Yucatan. Former peripheral areas, such as the northeastern coast, began to attract the sizable populations necessary to maintain port facilities and connecting inland routes.

## The Dominance of Chichen Itza

The culmination of the Putun expansion occurred in the tenth century, probably in the interval between 918 and 987. Later Yucatecan chronicles relate that a Putun Maya group of this period, possibly in alliance with Toltec elite warriors from central Mexico, established a new capital at Chichen Itza. The leader of this group was named Nacxit Xuchit and carried the Mexican title Quetzalcoatl ("feathered serpent"), translated into Maya as Kukulcan. Landa describes Chichen Itza in glowing terms:

Chichen Itza is a very fine site, ten leagues from Izamal and eleven from Valladolid. It is said that it was ruled by three lords who were brothers who came into that country from the west, who were very devout, and so they built very beautiful temples and they lived very chastely without wives, and one of them died or went away, upon which the others acted unjustly and indecently and for this they were put to death. . . . It is believed among the Indians that with the Itzas who occupied

Chichen Itza there reigned a great lord, named Kukulcan, and that the principal building, which is called Kukulcan, shows this to be true. They say that he arrived from the west; but they differ among themselves as to whether he arrived before or after the Itzas or with them. They say that he was favorably disposed, and had no wife or children, and that after his return he was regarded in Mexico as one of their gods and called Quetzalcoatl; and they also considered him a god in Yucatan on account of his being a just statesman; and this is seen in the order which he imposed on Yucatan after the death of the lords, in order to calm the dissensions which their deaths had caused in the country.

From the center at Chichen Itza, the Putun dominated the Yucatan for the next two hundred years, but murals and sculptured reliefs show that this domination was not always peaceful. The force of arms and tactics, adopted by the Putun and perhaps even reinforced by contingents of Toltec warriors, subdued any resistance by the Yucatec Maya. Although this domination appears to have ended the Yucatecan florescence, as reflected in the rise of the Puuc architectural sites, there is no evidence of a Putun "empire" in the northern lowlands. Local Maya rulers appear to have continued to rule over their own provinces, provided they paid proper tribute and allegiance to the rulers of Chichen Itza. This is indicated by the chronicles and by the restricted distribution of the Early Postclassic style in architecture and sculpture, which was almost exclusively limited to Chichen Itza itself. The new rulers of Chichen Itza rebuilt this center into a truly splendid capital, its architecture often very similar to the style and forms of buildings from Tula, the Toltec capital, north of Mexico City. Several examples of such innovations can be found:

1. Colonnades, either within or adjacent to buildings (Fig. 6.6), formed either of square or round columns, built of a series of stone drums, and often sculptured in low relief. The form of the colonnades varies widely, and a series, often in rows, may be found at the base of a pyramid that bears a temple on its summit (Temple of the Warriors, Temple of the Wall Panels). Large interior rooms were sometimes roofed on rows of columns (Temple of the Warriors). Colonnades also stand alone, backed by a solid wall and sometimes with end walls (South Temple of the Great Ball Court). Such a colonnade may also be backed by a square or rectangular courtyard surrounding another colonnade, which connects to the colonnade in front by a doorway (e.g., at El Mercado, Fig. 6.7). Colonnades with backing walls often have accessory structures such as benches or a dais attached to the rear wall. Roofing on the colonnades may be either beam-and-mortar roofing (Warriors), thatch roofing (Mercado), or Maya corbeled vaulting (many structures). The vaulted roofs are supported on exceedingly long wooden lintels, the column-lintel arrangement being substituted for the continuous masonry walls of Classic Maya buildings. Beam-and-mortar roofs are typical of Mexican architecture.

2. Round temples, which occurred from early times on the Mexican mainland but first appeared in the Maya area at this period (the Caracol, Fig. 6.8).

Fig. 6.6. Temple of the Warriors, Chichen Itza, Yucatan, Mexico: (*above*) overall view showing the basal colonnades along the front and southern sides; (*below*) summit temple, with feathered-serpent columns at the entrance.

Fig. 6.7. Chichen Itza: interior of El Mercado colonnade.

Fig. 6.8. Chichen Itza: the Caracol, a round temple constructed on a series of platforms.

3. Wide doorways containing two stone columns in the form of feathered serpents; the head is on the surface, the body is vertical, and the tail runs forward and up to support a wooden lintel.

4. General use of feathered serpents as ornaments on balustrades, panels, and other architectural elements.

5. A battered basal zone on the exterior faces of most pyramids and building walls. This zone usually stands at an angle of about 75 degrees, to a height of about a meter, and contrasts with the characteristically vertical Maya walls.

6. Prowling jaguars, full-faced Tlaloc figures, vultures in profile holding a human heart in their talons, and reclining human figures holding long, diagonally placed spears. These motifs are nearly identical at Tula and Chichen Itza in bas-relief carvings.

7. *Tzompantli*, or skull rack (Fig. 6.9). This is a low platform, walled in stone and covered with human skulls sculptured in relief.

8. Atlantean figures, men with hands upraised to support a dais or door lintel, sculptured in full round.

9. Warrior figures in a variety of sculptural treatments, but wearing characteristic clothing, ornaments, and insignia. They are found in processions on altars, or singly on square columns, or as caryatids sculptured in full round at

Fig. 6.9. Chichen Itza: *tzompantli* (skull rack), a platform decorated by shallow reliefs depicting human skulls.

Tula. Insignias include butterfly-shaped gorgets and headdress ornaments; various styles of headgear appear, including those related to the later Mexica (Aztec) military orders of Eagles and Jaguars. Many figures carry spear throwers.

10. Chacmools, full-round figures of men lying on their backs, their knees and heads raised, their hands surrounding a carved, bowl-shaped depression at about the position of the navel.

11. Standard bearers, sculptured standing figures with hands held in front of the body and a perforation between them seemingly designed to hold a pole, which likely bore a banner at its top.

Chichen Itza's buildings of this period also reflect a strong continuation of Yucatecan Maya architecture. They are finely built, using Puuc veneer-masonry techniques, vaults, and mosaic façades. In most cases, the Maya-built masonry at Chichen Itza is far finer than that at Tula. Maya deities, most often the all-important Chac, or rain god, were featured alongside Mexican deities. In essence, Chichen Itza during the Early Postclassic period displayed a fusion of central Mexican and Maya societies in its architecture. The traditional theory holds that this architectural blending at Chichen Itza reflected the conquest of the center by the dominant Early Postclassic power in central Mexico, the Toltec originating from Tula.

In later times, political dynasties throughout Mesoamerica claimed descent from the rulers of a city called Tollan, or Tulan, usually identified with the archaeological site of Tula. The idea of a Toltec invasion and takeover at Chichen Itza has been supported by the Maya chronicles, but those sources also suggest that the foreign invaders spoke a Mayan language, a dialect related to Yucatec. Also, most recent archaeological evidence shows that many Mexican elements in Yucatan had already been introduced by the Terminal Classic period, and perhaps earlier. It has been further argued that, in contrast to the remains in the Yucatan, Tula reveals no prototypes for some of the Mexican architectural features described earlier; and certainly Chichen Itza is the better-constructed center. These pieces of information suggest that Tula was the outpost of Mexicanized Maya expansion, the reverse of the traditional theory, and that mentions of the fabled city of Tollan in later times actually refer to Chichen Itza.

However that might be, when we take into account not only the architecture, but the art styles, pottery, and other artifacts, the archaeological evidence indicates a hybrid of Maya and Mexican cultural elements in the Yucatan during the Early Postclassic, centered on Chichen Itza. It is this hybrid culture that has been most often associated with the Putun Maya and traced back at least as far as the Terminal Classic. During that period there were many incursions of peoples bearing a Mexicanized Maya culture, identifiable in the Yucatan (Chichen Itza), in the southern Maya lowlands (Seibal), in the highlands, on the Pacific coast (Cotzumalhuapa), and even in central Mexico (Xochicalco and Cacaxtla). Assuming that the bearers of this hybrid culture were the Putun Maya groups, we can suggest the following reconstruction of events.

The Putun were successful merchants, warriors, and opportunists. By taking advantage of the power vacuums left in the wake of the decline of the Classic states of Mexico and many lowland Maya centers, they were able to capture the critical resources and trade routes formerly controlled by these Classic-period powers. Certainly control over the lucrative salt trade was a prime objective. Because the Putun groups were not politically unified, they established a series of regional capitals in various areas of Mesoamerica, apparently integrated into a loose commercial confederation. The best archaeological evidence for this economic network is provided by the trade goods, such as fine orange and plumbate pottery found throughout Mesoamerica. Other sites supply additional indications of Putun domination in the Terminal Classic and into the Early Postclassic.

Chichen Itza was the greatest center reflecting Putun associations during the Early Postclassic. Its relationship with Tula and the Toltecs of Central Mexico remains unclear, although it seems increasingly apparent that this Yucatecan center was not a Toltec colonial outpost. More likely, perhaps, the two centers maintained close commercial ties, as well as military and diplomatic alliances.

In large part, the later Maya chronicles are quite uncomplimentary when referring to the period of Chichen Itza's hegemony.

They brought shameful things when they came. They lost their innocence in carnal sin. . . . There was no great teacher, no great speaker, no supreme priest when the change of rulers occurred at their arrival. Lewd were the priests when they came to be settled here by the foreigners. Furthermore they left their descendants here at Mayapan. These then received the misfortunes, after the affliction of these foreigners. These, they say, were the Itza. Three times it was, they say that the foreigners arrived.

Bishop Landa's characterization in the *Relación de las cosas de Yucatán* is at variance with this description. The rulers of Chichen Itza are described as "very devout, and so they built very beautiful temples and they lived very chastely without wives." The *Chilam Balam* of Mani describes the Itzas as "holy men."

The Postclassic chronicles relate that there was a high priest over all of Yucatan, who received no assignment of servants from the political lords but was supported by gifts. He held himself apart from political allegiances and from most sacrifices. He appointed all priests, and his advice on matters of learning was much respected by the lords. The office was hereditary, and possibly derived from the position of ruler or principal lord in the old Classic Maya hierarchy, shorn of direct political power but still influential and respected. The second sons of lords were trained in priestly learning, which included calendrical and related ceremonies, divinations and prophecies, Maya writing, and cures for diseases.

The ruling political groups at the time of the Spanish Conquest prided themselves on their Mexican ancestry, and their leaders periodically conducted a curious sort of interrogation of officials to ensure that no Maya impostors had crept into their ranks, using what was called the language of Zuyua in the *Chilam Balam* of Chumayel. Zuyua, a mythical place associated with Mexica origins, is considered the birthplace of Kukulcan. This "language" must have been taught by father to son among the rulers, and presumably was unknown to those not of Mexican descent. Despite its claim as esoteric Mexican lore, the language of Zuyua is studded with Maya calendrical and religious references, undoubtedly the result of the blending of Maya and Mexican cultures that is often noted to characterize this era.

The spread of the Putun Maya–controlled sea-trade network can be traced during this period. Several pieces of fine orange pottery have been found at Chichen Itza—a dozen or more whole vessels and over a thousand fragments. This pottery, among the best of any made in Mesoamerica, was manufactured on the Gulf coast (see Chapter 12); it must have been shipped by canoe along the coast, a distance of over 1,000 km (620 mi.), plus perhaps another 120 km by land (75 mi.). Its effects on the local artisans are clearly evident. Native pottery of all sorts save the cooking pots shows an imitation of Gulf coast shapes, but the copies are usually inaccurate because of the retention of the old Yucatecan forming techniques. The designs, also copied, capture little of the

Fig. 6.10. Nohmul, Belize: Structure 9, excavation of a round platform dating to the Terminal Classic–Early Postclassic period.

verve and precision of the imported pieces. And the designs were still incised before the application of the slip, a native Yucatecan practice not found in fine orange pottery.

Smaller quantities of Mexican mainland pottery were found at Chichen Itza. A long, fragile clay pipe seems to have been brought from far west of Mexico City. Also found were vessels of plumbate pottery from the south coast of Guatemala. Trade in luxury goods included gold in some quantity from Panama, and turquoise and jadeite from the Mexican and Maya highland areas, respectively.

Architectural remains also provide evidence of the spread of Chichen Itza's influence. On the eastern coast of Yucatan, at Nohmul in northern Belize, recent archaeological work has uncovered two buildings reminiscent of those at Chichen Itza. One is a round structural platform (Fig. 6.10), the other a courtyard building.

Farther south, at the Classic center of Quirigua, Postclassic occupation has been revealed by ceramic refuse that includes pottery imported from the eastern coast of Yucatan. Most significant, a sculptured stone Chacmool, found at Quirigua in the nineteenth century, may indicate a direct link to Early Postclassic Chichen Itza.

## The Late Postclassic and the Dominance of Mayapan

According to the chronicles, in A.D. 1221 the hegemony of Chichen Itza was broken. Mayapan, the new dominant center, was built after the fall of Chichen Itza, and sixteenth-century documents report that it had been abandoned before the Spanish Conquest, about A.D. 1450. Landa described the rule of Mayapan as follows:

After the departure of Kukulcan, the nobles agreed, in order that the government should endure, that the house of the Cocoms should have the chief power because it was the most ancient or the richest family, or because he who was at the head of it was a man of greatest worth. This being done, since within the enclosure there were only temples and houses for the lords and the high priests, they ordered that other houses should be constructed outside, where each one of them could keep servants, and to which the people from their towns could repair, when they came to the city on business. Each one then established in these houses his major domo, who bore for his badge of office a short and thick stick, and they called him caluac. He kept account with the towns and with those who ruled them; and to them was sent notice of what was needed in the house of their lord, such as birds, maize, honey, salt, fish, game, cloth and other things, and the caluac always went to the house of his lord, in order to see what was wanted and provided it immediately, since his house was, as it were, the office of his lord.

The precise circumstances under which Mayapan replaced Chichen Itza are unclear in the chronicles. Political intrigue played a part, as did the kidnaping, by the ruler of Izamal, of the wife of the ruler of Chichen Itza. In the ensuing war Hunac Ceel, ruler of Mayapan, was said to have conquered Chichen Itza, and there is supporting archaeological evidence that Chichen Itza was sacked. Excavations in the Temple of the Warriors indicated that sculptures were intentionally thrown down, and cached offerings seem to have been anciently looted. There is both archaeological and documentary evidence of contacts with Mexico in the political affairs in Yucatan. Hunac Ceel is said to have employed Mexican mercenaries against Chichen Itza, and later Cocom rulers of Mayapan twice brought in Mexican or Putun soldiers from garrisons in Tabasco.

Archaeological excavations have provided a chronological sequence that generally parallels the events recorded in the Yucatecan chronicles. Two sequent architectural eras, the earlier at Chichen Itza, the later at Mayapan, have been worked out. Associated with the Early Postclassic period, buildings at Chichen Itza are a recognizable assemblage of artifacts, including plumbate and other pottery trade wares. Almost entirely postdating these structures, pottery of a later assemblage is found. This same pottery assemblage is also found in the lower levels of Mayapan, mixed with the later pottery characteristic of that site.

Shortly before the abandonment of Chichen Itza (about 1200) a new tempering material was introduced in the pottery-making craft that spread rapidly through the Peninsula. Then, not long after the establishment of Mayapan, a new slip color appeared, which has continued in use in Yucatan until the present day. Using these changes as time markers suggests that Chichen Itza was depopulated gradually, despite the apparent violent end that took place in the site center. The ceramic evidence also entertains the possibility of a time lapse between the abandonment of Chichen Itza and the founding of Mayapan. The ritual importance of Chichen Itza, however, lasted until the Spanish Conquest, and there is abundant evidence, both archaeological and documentary, of pilgrimages to the site.

Mayapan, a smaller center than Chichen Itza, lies about 100 km (60 mi.) almost directly to the west. Landa described Mayapan in the following terms:

Kukulcan established another city after arranging with the native lords of the country that he and they should live there and that all their affairs and business should be brought there; and for this purpose they chose a very good situation, eight leagues further in the interior than Mérida is now, and fifteen or sixteen leagues from the sea. They surrounded it with a very broad stone wall, laid dry, of about an eighth of a league, leaving in it only two narrow gates. The wall was not very high and in the midst of this enclosure they built their temples, and the largest, which is like that of Chichen Itza, they called Kukulcan, and they built another building of a round form with four doors, entirely different from all the others in that land, as well as a great number of others round about joined together. In this enclosure they built houses for the lords only, dividing all the land among them, giving towns to each one, according to the antiquity of his lineage and his personal value. And Kukulcan gave a name to this city—not his own as the Ah Itzas had done in Chichen Itza, which means the well of Ah Itzas, but he called it Mayapan, which means "the standard of the Maya," because they called the language of the country Maya, and the Indians [say] "Ichpa" which means "within the enclosure." This Kukulcan lived with the lords in that city for several years; and leaving them in great peace and friendship, he returned by the same way to Mexico, and on the way he stopped at Champoton, and, in memory of him and of his departure, he erected a fine building in the sea like that of Chichen Itza, a long stone's throw from the shore. And thus Kukulcan left a perpetual remembrance in Yucatan.

The temple described by Landa is identifiable today, its four-stairway platform and flat-topped temple obvious copies of those at the much larger and better-built El Castillo at Chichen Itza.

Intensive archaeological excavations have been conducted by the Carnegie Institution at Mayapan over some five years, producing a variety of information about domestic and religious architecture. Mayapan was a walled settlement covering an area of 4 km² (1.5 sq. mi.), whose gateways show careful planning against military attack. The bow and arrow, as well as quilted cotton armor, may have been brought from Campeche during the occupation of Mayapan, supplementing the spear thrower, which had already been introduced. Within the wall was a religious precinct, as described by Landa, although the low, secondary wall said to have surrounded it has not been located archaeologically. Grouped around the temples of the major center sit rectangular buildings that probably housed the official quarters of the regional rulers; these buildings, styled with colonnades and solid rear walls, face on a series of paved plazas. The Mayapan buildings, unlike those of Chichen Itza, were made of crudely shaped blocks, set in mud or plaster mortar. Not a vaulted roof of this period remains standing at Mayapan, and the sculpture was equally slipshod. Thirty-five hundred buildings have been counted within the wall of Mayapan, and the population must have totaled over fifteen thousand.

Throughout the town are irregularly spaced houses, most of which were at least partially of masonry construction. When available, slightly elevated ground was chosen for their location, presumably for reasons of drainage, which is always a problem in Yucatan during heavy rains. Low, dry-stone property walls surround these houses, enclosing irregularly shaped dooryards that average perhaps a quarter of an acre. Meandering among the haphazardly placed houses are lanes or passages of a sort, their irregular boundaries fixed by whatever property walls chance to be adjacent. This house arrangement varies from that of the larger urban centers in the Valley of Mexico, where houses were built in regular arrangements or blocks. It seems reasonable to speculate that the Maya, even in densely settled conditions, retained the plans of their rural farmsteads as much as possible. At Mayapan, as at earlier large centers, they may have continued to keep bees and raise fruit and garden vegetables as they still do in Yucatecan villages. Although Mayapan was described as dependent on tribute from other parts of the country for subsistence and thus may not be a typical settlement, it fits the description of native towns given by the early Spaniards. In Landa's wording,

Before the Spaniards had conquered that country, the natives lived together in towns in a very civilized fashion. They kept the land well cleared and free from weeds, and planted very good trees. Their dwelling place was as follows: in the middle of the town were their temples with beautiful plazas, and all around the temples stood the houses of the lords and the priests, and then of the most important people. Thus came the houses of the richest and of those who were held in the highest estimation nearest to these, and at the outskirts of the town were the houses of the lower class. And the wells, if there were but few of them, were near the houses of the lords; and they had their improved lands planted with wine trees and they sowed cotton, pepper and maize, and they lived thus close together for fear of their enemies, who took them captive, and it was owing to the wars of the Spaniards that they scattered in the woods.

The rulers of Mayapan were of the Cocom lineage, descendants of Hunac Ceel, destroyer of Chichen Itza. The Cocom held sway over a fairly unified Yucatan for nearly 250 years, by a combination of marriage alliances with the

Fig. 6.11. Tulum, Quintana Roo, Mexico: view, from the north, of the Late Postclassic center showing the Castillo, or principal temple, overlooking the sea, with the landing beach visible below.

other noble lineages of the area, and by the simple means of keeping the heads of each of these local ruling families resident at Mayapan, and thus under their direct control. Just to be sure, the Cocom also employed contingents of mercenaries from central Mexico known as the Ah Canul.

The pottery of Mayapan demonstrates that the influence of Gulf coast shapes continued, and the sizes and forms of vessels are reminiscent of the Late Postclassic Mexica, with a few identical details. Another style of fine orange ware, of poorer quality, was imported in some quantity from the nearby Campeche coast. Two new vessel forms of particular interest were introduced at some time late in the history of Mayapan. Since both seem to have had western origins, they may have come with the Mexicans introduced as mercenary soldiers to help maintain Cocom supremacy at Mayapan. A new cooking pot, the cauldron, was introduced, suggesting that women came with the mercenaries. The figurine incensarios (incense burners), which also appeared at this time, may have stemmed from early roots in the Oaxacan highlands, where such vessels were made from Preclassic times on. These Mayapan incensarios are similar in detail to those of a very wide area, stretching from southern Veracruz through Belize and inland as far as Lago Peten Itza. Over this whole area figurine incensarios are found on the surfaces of more ancient Maya ruins, as well as near temples of their own time period, although the early Spaniards destroyed such "idols" in large numbers during the first years of their stay in the Yucatan.

The best-preserved architectural remains of the period of Mayapan are those at Tulum and other sites on or near the east coast of Yucatan (Figs. 6.11 and 6.12). Others are off the east coast on Isla de Mujeres and Isla de Cozumel, and small shrines of this period have been identified at the Classic center of Coba. Cozumel has been seen as one of the major Putun ports of trade along the sea routes reaching around the Yucatan Peninsula. Tulum undoubtedly served as a major port and trading center during the Late Postclassic. It is situated on a rocky promontory overlooking the sea, opposite a gap in the barrier reef that parallels the east coast of the Yucatan, and is defended from the land side by a stone wall; within the walls is a small beach where vessels could land.

A fine group of murals from Santa Rita (Fig. 6.13), farther down the east coast, shows close similarities to the less well preserved paintings on the Tulum temples. Both show striking similarities to the design of pre-Conquest Mixtec codices from the Mexican highlands and to murals from the same area at Mitla. The presence of these murals attests to the economic prosperity of the east coast sites during this period, for they appear to be the work of expert foreign artists commissioned by the local elite. Figurine incensarios and pottery of the same style as that of Mayapan are also found in these east coast ruins.

The documentary record is frustratingly sketchy concerning the east coast of the Yucatan. The *Books of Chilam Balam*, although they mention the names of eastern towns and give an impression of friendly relations with them, do not

Fig. 6.12. Tancah, Quintana Roo, Mexico: (*above*) Structure 44, a Late Postclassic building (see Fig. 13.33 for the remains of the murals inside); (*below*) Structure B-12, a small Late Postclassic temple pyramid.

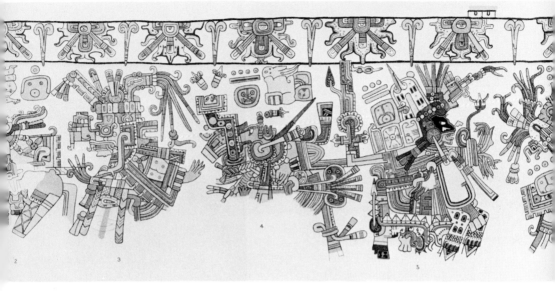

Fig. 6.13. Santa Rita, Belize: restoration drawing of a Late Postclassic mural, about A.D. 1440 or later.

give data about their political affiliations. Tulum, the most spectacular archaeological site of the area, is still a landmark to mariners along the east coast. Occupied until Conquest times, it was probably the Maya center sighted and compared to Seville in an early account of Spanish voyages (see the Epilogue).

## The Fall of Mayapan and the Rise of Petty States

Shortly before 1450 one of the noble lords at Mayapan, Ah Xupan from the Xiu lineage, organized and led a successful revolt against the Cocom. All members of the Cocom lineage were killed, except one who was away on a trading mission. The Xiu, like the Cocom, claimed descent from the Tula-Toltec, and thus could brandish a recognized and legitimate claim to power. The already ruined center of Uxmal was located in the region over which the Xiu were lords, but they appear to have come to the area too late to rule during the Terminal Classic apogee of that center.

As a result of the revolt against the Cocom, Mayapan was sacked and abandoned, an event again verified by archaeology. Excavations revealed evidence of burned buildings, ancient looting, and even the skeletal remains of individuals who may have been killed during the revolt.

Landa, in describing the calamities that befell Yucatan during the century between the fall of Mayapan and the Spanish Conquest, fixed the time of the fall at 1441. Four of the five native chronicles, as well as the two leading early

Spanish authorities—Cogolludo, writing in 1656, and Villagutierre Soto-Mayor, in 1700—corroborate this dating.

Taking the year of his writing, 1566, as his point of departure, Landa says:

> Since the last plague, more than fifty years have now passed, the pestilence of the swelling was sixteen years before the wars, and the hurricane another sixteen years before that, and twenty-two or twenty-three years after the destruction of the city of Mayapan. Thus according to this count it has been 125 years since its overthrow within which the people of this country have passed through the calamities described.

This fixes the date of the plague at 1516 or 1515, the date of the mortality from the wars at 1496, the date of the pestilence at 1480, the date of the hurricane at 1464, and the date of the destruction of Mayapan at 1441. The chronicle from the *Book of Chilam Balam* of Tizimin and the first and second chronicles from the *Chilam Balam* of Chumayel record that there was a pestilence in Katun 4 Ahau (1480–1550), which Landa dated to the very beginning of this katun. The first chronicle from the *Book of Chilam Balam* of Chumayel describes an epidemic of smallpox as having taken place in Katun 2 Ahau (1500–1520). This seems to be Landa's plague "with great pustules that rotted the body," which he reckoned to have occurred in 1515 or 1516. Small though these two items of confirmation may be, they suggest a high degree of reliability for at least this time span in the native chronicles.

After the fall of Mayapan, all the larger cities declined and were soon abandoned. The Chels, a prominent noble family of Mayapan, left after the fall of the city and established their principal settlement at Tecoh. The only surviving son of the slain Cocom ruler, gathering the remnants of his people about him, established his rule at Tibolon, near Sotuta. The victors, the Tutul Xiu, founded a new capital, which they called Mani, meaning in Maya "it is passed."

The last important event in the pre-Conquest history of Yucatan was the ill-fated pilgrimage of the Xiu ruler and his court to offer human sacrifice in the Cenote of Sacrifice at Chichen Itza in 1536. In this year, not a Spaniard remained in Yucatan. After unsuccessful attempts to subjugate the Maya in 1527–28 and 1531–35, the Spaniards had withdrawn completely from the Peninsula (see the Epilogue). By the time the Spanish began their conquest in the sixteenth century, there were some eighteen independent states in the northern lowlands.

Ah Dzun Xiu, ruler of the Tutul Xiu at their new capital of Mani, thought the moment auspicious for undertaking a pilgrimage to appease the Maya gods, who for so many years had afflicted the land with calamities. He applied for a safe-conduct from Nachi Cocom, the ruler of Sotuta, through whose province the pilgrims had to pass. The Xiu ruler no doubt feared reprisals on the part of Nachi Cocom because of the leading part his great-grandfather, Ah Xupan

Xiu, had played in the slaying of Nachi Cocom's great-grandfather, the last ruler of Mayapan.

Nachi Cocom had not forgotten the death of his great-grandfather, for which he held Xiu treachery responsible, and he welcomed the Xiu request as an opportunity for revenge. The safe-conduct was promptly granted, and a pilgrimage headed by Ah Dzun Xiu, his son Ah Ziyah Xiu, and forty other leaders of the Xiu nation set out for Chichen Itza via the province of Sotuta. Nachi Cocom, with a large delegation of his people, met them at Otzmal, five miles southeast of the Cocom capital. The Xiu pilgrims were royally entertained for four days, but at a banquet on the evening of the fourth day the Cocom fell upon their guests and killed them all. This act of treachery split the warring Maya anew, and pitted the two most powerful houses in the northern peninsula against each other.

Even before 1536, the Xiu had offered their submission to the Spaniards, in the second phase of the Conquest (1531–35), but the Cocom had resisted. This probably added fuel to ancient Cocom hatred of the Xiu and provided an additional motive for the Otzmal slaughter.

This massacre, coming so shortly before the final phase of the Spanish Conquest, sealed the fate of the northern Maya by reviving old hatreds and

Fig. 6.14. Tayasal, Guatemala: excavations in 1971 at this Classic-period center on the shores of Lago Peten Itza discovered evidence of Postclassic domestic occupation along the lakeshore.

effectively preventing a united stand against the Spaniards, who returned to Yucatan in 1540 in their successful attempt to subdue the country. Exhausted by civil war, betrayed by some of their own leading native houses, and decimated by disease, the Maya were unable to resist the better-armed Spaniards and finally succumbed to the invaders' superior might.

But the final chapter in the history of the ancient Yucatecan Maya took another 150 years to complete. The Yucatecan chronicles relate that the survivors of the final destruction of Chichen Itza moved southward, back "beneath the trees . . . beneath the vines" into the Peten rain forests still remembered from the Putun sojourn at Chakanputun centuries earlier. There, on a series of islands in one of the lakes of the central Peten lowlands, the Itza built a new capital named Tayasal. Tayasal remained independent, even after the Spanish conquered most other areas of Mesoamerica in the early sixteenth century. Isolated and insulated by the dense rain forest, Tayasal remained beyond the reach of Spanish power until it was finally captured, sacked, and abandoned in 1697 (see the Epilogue). Most scholars have set the location of Tayasal in Lago Peten Itza, on the island of Flores. Certainly Late Postclassic remains exist on Flores, but the archaeological evidence is obscured by the modern capital of the Peten (see Fig. 1.10). Most of the ruins on the adjacent Tayasal peninsula date to the Classic period, although recent excavations revealed Postclassic domestic occupational remains (Fig. 6.14). Another Late Postclassic center exists to the east, on the islands of Lago Yaxha. Known as Topoxte, this large and relatively untouched center might correspond to the historical Tayasal, last capital of the Itzas. If the ruins of Topoxte are not those of Tayasal, they certainly appear to have been occupied during the same interval, and must be related in some way to the Itza occupation of the central Peten.

## The Southern Maya Area in the Postclassic

The rich resources of ethnohistorical information about the Postclassic Maya highlands include the unique chronical of the Quiche Maya, the *Popol Vuh*, and other native documents. But as in the Yucatan, these accounts do not always agree with the available archaeological evidence. The amount of archaeological investigation in the southern Maya area has so far been less than that in the lowlands, and further work may resolve many of the apparent discrepancies. For the time being, only a tentative outline of Postclassic events in the southern area can be offered.

The history of the Postclassic peoples in the southern Maya area seems to parallel events in the northern lowlands. The ethnohistorical accounts mention the conquest of Maya highland areas by outsiders who claimed descent from Tollan, just as in the Yucatan. In fact, the *Popol Vuh* relates that three Quiche Maya princes traveled to their former homeland to gain the authority and symbols of their legitimate right to rule in the highlands. This visit to Tollan

may refer to Chichen Itza, since the *Popol Vuh* records that their journey was to
the east, after which "they crossed the sea," seemingly referring to a route
eastward down the Motagua valley to the Caribbean, and then northward by
boat along the coast of the peninsula. Furthermore, the *Popol Vuh* names the
ruler of Tollan as Nacxit, and the Yucatecan documents record Nacxit-Xuchit
as the ruler of Chichen Itza. The same Yucatecan chronicles also mention gifts
sent to Chichen Itza from Guatemala, probably in deference to the prominent
position of Chichen Itza during the Early Postclassic era. Regardless, it seems
clear that the southern Maya area was affected by the same expansion of
Mexicanized Maya groups that dominated the fortunes of the Yucatan
throughout much of the Postclassic.

In the southern Maya area the earliest evidence of contact with Mexicanized
outsiders occurs no later than the Terminal Classic period. On the Pacific coast
this influence is demonstrated by a monumental sculptural tradition of combined Maya and Mexican elements known as the Cotzumalhuapa style (Fig.
6.15). The chronological position of the Cotzumalhuapa style is a subject of
debate, and some scholars associate it with the Early Classic Teotihuacan
colonization of the Pacific coast (see Chapter 4). It seems to be better linked to
the Terminal Classic and may in fact be related to the expansion of the Gulf
coast Chontal Maya. But both ethnohistorical and linguistic evidence indicates
that by Postclassic times much of the Pacific coast was occupied by migrants
from central Mexico, who spoke a Nahua language (Pipil). Only further
archaeological research can establish the proper dating for the Cotzumalhuapan
development.

As we have seen, the expansion by the Putun up the Usumacinta drainage
appears to have led to their control over several southern lowland centers, such
as Altar de Sacrificios and Seibal. These same movements were probably also
responsible for the first expressions of similar Mexicanized site planning, architecture, and artifacts (including, reportedly, Gulf coast fine orange pottery) that
are seen in the northern highlands. That is, there may have been a further
penetration of Chontal colonists and traders into the highlands by way of the
upper Usumacinta (Río Chixoy and its tributaries) that led directly into the
northern highlands.

Significantly, the available archaeological record indicates a sudden change in
highland society around 800. Some earlier sites were abruptly abandoned;
others were rebuilt and expanded. Both the rebuilt centers and a series of
apparently newly founded Terminal Classic highland centers were often larger
than the older Classic sites, although they continued to be situated in open-
valley settings.

The subsequent Early Postclassic period was marked by a dramatic shift in
settlement pattern. Open-valley sites were largely abandoned, to be replaced by
centers constructed in easily defended locations, usually on hilltops or promon-
tories surrounded by steep-sided ravines. Ditch-and-wall fortifications often

Fig. 6.15. Monument 3,
Bilbao, Guatemala: exam-
ple of the Mexicanized
Cotzumalhuapa sculptural
styles, usually dated to the
Terminal Classic period.

supplemented these naturally defended locations. This shift in site location has
been correlated with a second wave of intrusive outsiders, paralleling the period
of Chichen Itza's ascendancy in the Yucatan. As in the northern lowlands, the
highland documentary sources speak of conquests by warriors who established
new ruling lineages and who married into the local population. The recorded
names of several of the new highland ruling families strongly suggest Mexican
and Yucatecan affinities: Kumatz ("serpent"), Can Sakitzol ("fiery feathered
serpent"), and Xiuj Toltecat ("Toltec Xiu," a name also associated with a
Yucatecan ruling lineage, see p. 173). Thus the Early Postclassic newcomers in
the highlands may be seen as part of the same people who established hegemony over Yucatan from their capital at Chichen Itza, that is, warrior groups of
Mexicanized Putun Maya from the Gulf coast lowlands.

In several cases archaeological excavations support this connection. For instance, the remains from early Postclassic highland sites often include a sculptural motif nearly identical to that associated with the Putun expansion in the
coastal lowlands—an open-mouthed, feathered-serpent head from which human (warrior?) heads protrude. At Chuitinamit-Atitlan, on the south shore of
Lago de Atitlan, a serpent frieze was excavated that compares directly to a
similar motif at Chichen Itza. Architectural parallels are also common. A
possible *tzompantli* has been noted from at least one highland site, at Chalchitan near the headwaters of the Río Chixoy. However, it should be noted that in
some cases, as in the recent excavations at Chitinamit, northeast of Utatlan, no
evidence of Mexicanized sculptural or architectural forms has been found.

Assuming that a new wave of Mexicanized Maya warriors established these
fortified early Postclassic centers, their routes into the highlands seem to have
been via both the upper Usumacinta and Motagua rivers. A series of Early
Postclassic sites has been identified throughout the upper drainage basins of
these rivers and their tributaries. While the Usumacinta gave direct access from
the Putun homeland in the Gulf coast lowlands, the Motagua provided a route
from the Caribbean coast to the east. But it may be recalled that there were ties
with the Putun along the Caribbean coast also. Quirigua, in the lower Motagua
valley, seems to have been occupied during the Early Postclassic by peoples
closely linked to Yucatan's east coast and the Chichen Itza. This tie may reflect
Putun Maya control over the circum-Yucatan coastal trade network, including
the Motagua-valley commerce between the highlands and the Caribbean. In
this way, the Motagua seems to have provided a secondary avenue for Putun
penetration into the Maya highlands.

Whereas the Early Postclassic situation remains somewhat murky, the picture is clearer for the Late Postclassic. The various ethnohistorical sources agree
on the prominence of a series of highland Maya groups and their major
population centers, many of which were encountered and described by the
Spanish in the early sixteenth century. These centers, all located in easily
defended positions like their Early Postclassic precursors, included several pow-

erful regional capitals and many secondary centers, all of which competed for control over the people, products, and trade routes within their regions. Warfare was the common way of settling disputes, and several of these highland groups, notably the Quiche and Cakchiquel Maya, extended their spheres of control at the expense of neighboring societies. Both these groups expanded into the Pacific coastal plain, undoubtedly to gain control over cacao and its other resources.

The major highland centers at the time of the Conquest dominated regions populated by the historically identified linguistic groups found in the area today (see Chapter 15). These included centers in the Pokomam area (such as Mixcu Viejo, Fig. 6.16, and Chinautla Viejo), Atitlan (the major settlement of the Tzutuhil peoples living around the lake of the same name), Zaculeu (in the Mam area; Fig. 6.17), Utatlan (the principal center of the Quiche; Figs. 6.18 and 6.19), and Iximche (capital of the Cakchiquel; Fig. 6.20). Major archaeological investigations have been undertaken at Zaculeu, Mixcu Viejo, Iximche, and Utatlan, as well as at several secondary centers such as Zacualpa.

On the basis of later ethnohistorical accounts, it seems likely that the ancestors of the warrior elite groups that eventually forged the Quiche and Cakchiquel states entered the highlands from the Gulf coastal lowlands shortly after 1200. These warrior groups were probably a new wave of Mexicanized Putun Maya, as evidenced by their own claims of descent from Tollan and by their ideology, which combined Maya and Mexican elements. Although these elite warriors came as conquerors, they seem eventually to have lost their native tongue, adopting the Quiche, Cakchiquel, and other languages of the highland peoples

Fig. 6.16. Mixcu Viejo, Guatemala: Late Postclassic site in the Maya highlands, situated on a series of small plateaus surrounded by ravines in a defensible location typical of this era.

they subjugated. However, throughout their history they carefully maintained their elite status and traditions apart from the indigenous population. The line of Quiche rulers, as reconstructed by Robert Wauchope and Robert Carmack from the *Popol Vuh* and other accounts, is presented in Table 4.

TABLE 4

*Quiche Maya Rulers as Reconstructed from Ethnohistorical Sources*

| Ruler | Approximate dates[a] | Chief accomplishments or events |
|---|---|---|
| Balam Quitze | 1225–1250 | Leads migration into northern highlands. |
| Cocoja | 1250–1275 | |
| Tziquin and E | 1275–1300 | Lead conquest of Pokomam Maya to the east (Rabinal). |
| Ahcan | 1300–1325 | |
| C'ocaib | 1325–1350 | Returns to the east (Tollan?) to gain title of Ahpop. |
| Conache | 1350–1375 | Founds new capital at Ismachi. |
| Cotuja | 1375–1400 | Expands Quiche territory. |
| Gucumatz | 1400–1425 | Utatlan (Gumarcaaj) founded as final Quiche capital. |
| Quicab | 1425–1475 | Quiche conquests reach maximum extent. |
| Vahxaqui Caam | 1475–1500 | Cakchiquel revolt; independent capital at Iximche established. |
| Oxib-Queh | 1500–1524 | Killed by Spanish after conquest of Utatlan (see the Epilogue). |

[a] Estimated by allowing about 25 years per generation (see Wauchope 1949; Carmack 1981).

Fig. 6.17. Zaculeu, Guatemala, a Late Postclassic Mam Maya center; the restored structures are seen here against the Altos Cuchumatanes.

Fig. 6.18. Uratlan, Guatemala, the Late Postclassic capital of the Quiche Maya state: map of the main center. Postulated identification of principal buildings (after Carmack 1981): (*a*) Temple of Tohil, the Quiche sun deity; (*b*) Temple of Awilix, the Quiche moon deity; (*c*) Temple of Jakawitz, the Quiche sky deity; (*d*) Temple of Gucumatz (?), the feathered serpent deity; (*e*) ball court; (*f*) palace, possibly of the Cawek, principal ruling lineage of Uratlan. (Preliminary map based on aerial photographs and surface measurements; D. Wallace and J. Weeks, 1976.)

Fig. 6.19. Utatlan: ruins of the structure identified as the Temple of Awilix, the Quiche moon deity, located on the east side of the main plaza.

Fig. 6.20. Iximche, Guatemala, the Late Postclassic capital of the Cakchiquel Maya state: view toward the east, showing the partially restored Structure 3 facing two small platforms in Plaza A, with the remains of a major palace complex in the background.

Initially, the invading warrior groups occupied mountainous strongholds from which they conducted raids and eventually subjugated the local populace. Their initial capital, known as Jakawitz, has been identified as the archaeological site of Chitinamit. It was during this period that the three Quiche princes returned to their homeland for proper authority to rule over their expanded domain. According to the accounts, one of the returning princes, C'ocaib, appears to have been the first to hold the title of Ahpop ("he of the mat"), the paramount political office of the Quiche state (see Chapter 8).

By about 1350 the Quiche had consolidated their control over the central region between the headwaters of the Río Chixoy and the upper Motagua. There they founded a new capital, Ismachi, on a narrow plateau between two steep-sided ravines, where an unsuccessful revolt was waged against the Quiche during the reign of Ahpop Cotuja. According to the *Popol Vuh* the would-be usurpers "were sacrificed before the gods, and this was the punishment for their sins by order of the king Cotuja. Many also fell into slavery and servitude. . . . The destruction and ruin of the Quiche race and their ruler was what they wished, but they did not succeed."

Early in the fifteenth century, during the reign of Gucumatz ("feathered serpent"), a new capital was founded. This was named Gumarcaaj ("place of the rotten reeds") or, as it is now known, Utatlan. Utatlan was situated on another plateau surrounded by ravines immediately north of Ismachi.

Gucumatz became its first ruler and was glorified in the chronicles, for he extended the power of the Quiche to the north and west of their home region:

The nature of this king was truly marvelous, and all the other lords were filled with terror before him. Tidings of the wonderful nature of the king were spread and all the lords of the towns heard it. And this was the beginning of the grandeur of the Quiche, when King Gucumatz gave these signs of his power. His sons and his grandsons never forgot him.

His successor, Quicab, expanded the Quiche domain through further conquests in the western highlands and southward to the Pacific coast:

He made war on them and certainly conquered and destroyed the fields and towns of the people of Rabinal, the Cakchiquel, and the people of Zaculeu; he came and conquered all the towns, and the soldiers of Quicab carried his arms to distant parts. One or two tribes did not bring tribute, and then he fell upon all the towns and they were forced to bring tribute.

The Quiche state suffered a severe setback in the late fifteenth century, during the reign of Vahxaqui-Caam. About 1470 the Cakchiquel, who had served as subjects and allies of the Quiche during the conquests of Gucumatz and Quicab, revolted against their former masters and established an independent state in the region south and east of Utatlan. The Cakchiquel founded a new capital, Iximche ("ramon tree," the breadnut), also defended by surrounding ravines. From Iximche the Cakchiquel began a new cycle of conquests, subjugating areas formerly controlled by the Quiche. The Quiche made several attempts to reconquer the Cakchiquel, but in vain. In one major battle, recounted in the highland document *Annals of the Cakchiquels*, the attacking army from Utatlan was annihilated, as thousands of Quiche warriors were slaughtered and their leaders captured and sacrificed. The Cakchiquel seem to have been still expanding their domain in the early sixteenth century, when their rise to power was arrested by the Spanish conquerors.

The archaeological reconstruction of the growth of ancient Maya civilization, though still imperfectly known, nonetheless presents a picture of successive regional development, prosperity, and decline.

The prelude to the origins of Maya civilization lies in the wandering hunters and gatherers of the Lithic period. In time, increasing specialization in the subsistence activities and lifeways of these peoples led to the foundations of settled life and agriculture. The earliest known villages emerged along the coastal margins of the Maya area during the Archaic period, and established the basis of the farming family and community that underlay all subsequent growth in Maya society. Building on these developments, the stage was set during the Preclassic era for the emergence of civilization, beginning with the first signs of cultural and social complexity early in this period, a development that culminated in the Olmec, Mesoamerica's first civilization.

The origins of Maya civilization appear to lie in the southern area, the Pacific coastal plain and adjacent highlands. There, probably sparked at least in part by Olmec colonization during the previous era, many of the distinctive hallmarks of Maya civilization emerged during the later Preclassic. One of the primary signs of Maya civilization, dynastic rule commemorated by sculptured stone monuments with hieroglyphic texts, including our initial glimpse of recorded historical dates, first appeared in the southern Maya area.

The thread of history, supplementing the available archaeological evidence, becomes stronger during the Classic period, when the core of cultural development moved northward to the central lowlands, which rapidly became the setting for the florescence of Maya art, architecture, and intellectual achievement. The Early Classic seems to have been dominated by Tikal with its commercial and dynastic ties to the highlands (Kaminaljuyu) and, ultimately, to Teotihuacan. The apparent severing of these connections may have triggered a setback in the Middle Classic, but the Late Classic saw the prosperity and power of a series of lowland centers reach their peak. By the end of this era the first signs of deeper problems emerged, accompanied by the first appearance of Mexicanized Maya peoples in several parts of the lowlands. Ultimately, most of the central and southern lowlands were abandoned, and the center of events moved elsewhere.

The Postclassic era saw the major developments in the ancient Maya world shift to the far north, in the Yucatan, and to the southern highlands far to the south. The Early Postclassic in the Yucatan was dominated by Chichen Itza and the powerful Mexicanized Maya state it represented. By the Late Postclassic a new center, Mayapan, was supreme in the northern lowlands, remaining so until shortly before the Conquest, when centralized authority was fragmented into a series of independent, petty states. A similar course was charted in the southern highlands, where a handful of small kingdoms, dominated by the aggressive Quiche and Cakchiquel states, jockeyed for supremacy until the eve of the Spanish Conquest.

Recently it has been proposed that the occupation of Chichen Itza was contemporaneous with the Terminal Classic Puuc centers. Although there is much to support this hypothesis, resolution of this question must await further research.

# PART II
# SOCIETY

# 7 ⊡

## SUBSISTENCE SYSTEMS

And the greatest number were cultivators and men who apply themselves to
harvesting the maize and other grains, which they keep in fine underground places
and granaries, so as to be able to sell at the proper time.
—Landa's *Relación de las cosas de Yucatán* (Tozzer 1941: 96)

In discussing the major characteristics of ancient Maya society, which we turn to
in the next four chapters, we shall examine in more detail some of the factors
involved in the growth of Maya civilization, as outlined originally in Chapter 2.
These factors—ecology, competition, trade, and ideology, all interrelated—
underlay the cycles of expansion and contraction of ancient Maya society
throughout its history. All of these factors—save ideology, which is the subject
of Chapter 14—will be considered in one form or another in the next four
chapters.

We begin by examining the ancient Maya ecological system, specifically their
means of subsistence, which provided the basic determinant of the growth
potential for their civilization. Competition cuts across all aspects of ancient
Maya society, appearing to have been a factor in the development of subsistence, sociopolitical organization (Chapter 8), everyday life (Chapter 9), and
trade (Chapter 10).

## The Traditional View

Until recently, the ancient Maya were viewed as a civilization whose food
resources relied almost solely on swidden agriculture, a system that makes use
of an extensive land area by alternately burning off each field, cultivating it, and
allowing it to remain fallow for a period at least as long as the time of
cultivation. In most cases at least two years of fallow are required for each year
of cultivation. Thus, a third or less of the available farmland is actually growing
crops in any given year; the bulk lies fallow. For this reason, swidden agriculture cannot support large or dense concentrations of people. It has long been
known that most ancient civilizations, both in the Old World and the New,

relied on subsistence systems that were far more productive and intensive (using less land with little or no fallow periods) than swidden agriculture. Thus the ancient Maya, whose subsistence was believed to have been based solely on that system, were seen as an anomaly: a brilliant civilization whose subsistence relied on "primitive" agricultural practice. But doubts soon arose about the accuracy of viewing the Maya as an anomaly, and scholars began to question the assumption that the ancient Maya were dependent on this one style of agriculture.

The traditional assumption derived from the observation that the present-day Maya practice swidden techniques to produce most of their food. The Spaniards, who first conquered and colonized the peoples of central Mexico, homeland of the Mexica (Aztecs), helped spread the use of the Nahuatl or Aztec word for maize field, milpa, by using it to denote maize fields in other parts of Mesoamerica. The Yucatecan Maya word for maize field is *col*, and other Mayan languages have similar words for it. Shortly after the Conquest, Bishop Diego de Landa described the cultivation of maize by the Yucatec Maya in terms that sound like swidden agriculture:

They plant in many places, so that if one fails the others will suffice. In cultivating the land they do nothing more than clear the brush, and burn it in order to sow it afterward, and from the middle of January to April they work it and then when the rains come they plant it, which they do by carrying a small sack on the shoulders, and with a pointed stick, they make a hole in the ground, dropping in it five or six grains, covering them with the same stick. And when it rains, it is marvelous to see how it grows. (Fig. 7.1.)

But it should be noted that Landa's account does not describe a shifting pattern of cultivation, only that each farmer planted many milpas to be assured of the success of at least some of them. This appears to be a useful adaptation to the dry climate and marginal soil found in northern Yucatan. Even if we assume

Fig. 7.1. Sowing maize with the planting stick, Madrid Codex, p. 36.

Fig. 7.2. A Lacandon Maya man felling a tree, using a modern steel axe (use of the platform is necessary because of the thickness of the tree base).

that Landa did observe a true swidden system in the sixteenth century, such a system may not have been typical of all Maya agriculture. Other techniques could well have been used in different environments and in earlier times.

Today, the swidden agriculture used by the Maya relies on steel tools, especially the machete, sometimes supplemented by the axe. The machete allows the Maya farmer to clear overgrown (fallow) fields with relative ease, and the axe is used to clear new lands of large trees (Fig. 7.2). But the ancient Maya did not have steel tools, only stone axes and blades of obsidian or flint. Without steel cutting tools, clearing new forest or second growth in fallow areas requires considerably more energy and time. Although experiments indicate that stone axes can adequately fell large trees, no ancient Maya tool has been found that would be capable of efficiently dealing with the dense stands of second growth found in milpas after only one or two years of fallow. We assume that once the time and effort had been invested in clearing a new field from the forest, it was maintained for as long as possible by constant weeding. This practice would not require sharp cutting tools, since weeding can be done by hand, and would prevent the growth of competitors to the food plants being cultivated.

Fig. 7.3. Cerén, El Salvador: rows and furrows of a Late Classic maize field preserved under volcanic ash; string tags have been placed in the small holes left by each maize plant (the size of these remains indicates that the ash fall occurred in the spring, when the plants were young).

But this is only an assumption. The traces of an ancient swidden system cannot, of course, be detected today. However, a Classic-era maize field buried by volcanic ash was recently excavated at Cerén, El Salvador (Fig. 7.3). Several lines of archaeological research indicate that ancient Maya population sizes and densities in the central lowlands were far above the levels that swidden agriculture is known to be able to support. A final blow to our assumption has been the discovery and recognition of actual traces of far more complex and productive agricultural methods in the Maya lowlands. Today, most Maya scholars agree that the ancient Maya developed and perfected, over a period of hundreds and even thousands of years, a variety of subsistence methods. The environmental differences found throughout the Maya area allowed the Maya to rely on an array of combinations of these methods, each suited to the particular conditions in any given locale.

We now know the ancient Maya to have been capable of supporting far greater populations than would be possible using swidden agriculture alone. As a result, some of the "mystery" of how the ancient Maya sustained a vast and complex civilization in a supposedly "hostile" environment has been removed. The various subsistence resources used by the ancient Maya follow, as presently understood. But a multitude of unanswered questions remain, enough to keep Maya scholars busy for decades to come.

## Subsistence Systems Available to the Ancient Maya

The ancient Maya relied on a complex array of resources for their subsistence, and the precise combination of ways to acquire food that they used differed from place to place. Although only tentatively understood, the subsistence system can be broadly outlined by dividing it into three major areas according to source and technology: hunting and gathering (wild-food subsistence), animal husbandry, and agriculture. The actual procurement of food undoubtedly incorporated both direct access and exchange. Direct access describes the production and consumption of food by the same individual or family unit, such as a farming family that grows food for its own needs. Exchange brings food acquired from others, possibly specialized producers, using barter or payment. The ancient Maya probably obtained at least some of their food from centralized markets, much like those described by the Spanish in the sixteenth century and used today (see Chapter 10).

With time, as populations grew and increased the pressure on the subsistence system, the ancient Maya probably relied more and more on the marketplace for acquiring both staples and exotic foods. Some evidence suggests that certain lowland areas were cultivated for large-scale food production (on "plantations"); their harvests were then transported to the major population centers.

The same basic technology might have provided important nonfood resources for the ancient Maya from forest, field, and sea. From the forest came

•• one of the most crucial products, firewood, essential as fuel for cooking, firing pottery, and other purposes. Proper maintenance of forest areas also ensured supplies of wood and thatch for buildings, and a multitude of fibers for baskets, rope, and bark cloth. Cotton was cultivated, spun into thread, dyed with a rich array of vegetable and mineral colors, and woven into garments and textiles (Chapter 13). Animal bone, teeth, and pelts were manufactured into a variety of adornments and ritual objects, as were coral and seashells.

## HUNTING AND GATHERING

The ancient Maya, like all pre-Columbian peoples, relied in part on wild-food resources. Lacking a varied inventory of domesticated animals, the Maya supplemented their dietary needs for protein by fishing and hunting (see Table 5). Deer, tapir, agoutis, rabbits, monkeys, and other animals were hunted or trapped for food. One ancient source illustrates the use of a snare to trap deer. Interestingly, some foraging species, such as deer, may have experienced an increase in population concurrent with that of the ancient human residents. Archaeological evidence in the form of skeletal remains found at Tikal indicates

TABLE 5

*Common Wild-Animal Resources Available to the Ancient Lowland Maya*[a]

| Birds | Chachalaca (*Ortalis vetula*) | Edentates | Armadillo (*Dasypus novem-cinctus*) |
|---|---|---|---|
| | Crested guan (*Penelope purpurascens*) | | Tamandua (*Tamandua tetradactyla*) |
| | Curassow (*Crax rubra*) | | |
| | Ocellated turkey (*Agriocharis ocellata*) | Lagomorphs | Forest rabbit (*Sylvilagus brasiliensis*) |
| | Scarlet macaw (*Ara macao*) | Marsupials | Opossum (*Didelphis marsupialis*) |
| Artiodactyls | Brocket deer (*Mazama americana*) | | |
| | White-tailed deer (*Odocoileus virginianus*) | Perissodactyls | Collared peccary (*Tayassu tajacu*) |
| Carnivores | Cacomistle (*Bassariscus sumichrasti*) | | White-lipped peccary (*Tayassu pecari*) |
| | Coati (*Nasua narica*) | | Tapir (*Tapirus bairdii*) |
| | Cougar (*Felis concolor*) | Pinniped | Manatee (*Trichechus manatus*) |
| | Gray fox (*Urocyon cinereo-argenteus*) | Primates | Howler monkey (*Alouatta villosa*) |
| | Jaguar (*Felis onca*) | | Spider monkey (*Ateles geofroyi*) |
| | Jaguarundi (*Felis jaguarondi*) | | |
| | Kinkajou (*Potos flavus*) | Rodents | Agouti (*Dasyprocta* ssp.) |
| | Margay (*Felis wiedii*) | | Paca (*Agouti paca*) |
| | Ocelot (*Felis pardalis*) | | Porcupine (*Coendou mexicanus*) |
| | Raccoon (*Procyon lotor*) | | Squirrel (*Sciurus yucatanensis*) |

[a] After Wiseman (1978).

that the Maya consumed an increasing proportion of deer meat through time. Perhaps the greater availability of deer was due to the expansion of agricultural areas in the lowlands, which provided increased cleared fields to feed a growing deer population.

Apart from snares and traps, weapons like the blowgun were apparently used to hunt birds and monkeys, kinkajous, and other arboreal animals. Small, hard clay pellets found in archaeological remains may have been used as the projectiles.

Aquatic resources made an important contribution to the ancient Maya diet. Archaeologists have found fired-clay net weights and bone fishhooks, as well as artistic representations of dugout canoes, that reflect the Maya technology used to collect food resources from the sea, lakes, and rivers. Both fish and shellfish provided a steady diet for people living along the coasts, and it is likely that dried fish were traded far inland, just as is done today throughout the Maya area. The freshwater lakes and rivers of the highlands and of the southern and central lowlands provided a variety of fish and shellfish. Evidence from the lake region of the central lowlands indicates that the consumption of freshwater mollusks decreased over a period of nearly a thousand years (Middle Preclassic to the Late Classic) before suddenly increasing again at the end of the Classic period. The decrease may have reflected the expansion of agriculture, in that the clearing of forested areas led to increased sedimentation in the lakes, reducing the mollusk populations. A variety of fish species was also available for human consumption, and their importance is indicated by their frequent representation in Maya art.

Wild plants abound in the Maya area, and the present-day collection of many of these for food, medicines, and other uses undoubtedly represents an ancient practice. Common wild food plants include species of papaya, *Annona*, sapodilla, cherimoya, and coyol, as well as condiments like allspice, vanilla, and oregano. It is likely that many of these trees and plants, though not fully domesticated, were tended and cultivated in household gardens (see below).

## ANIMAL HUSBANDRY

Domesticated animals were not a prime source of food for the ancient Maya, who raised a few species, including the dog, which like today was used as a guardian of the household and a companion in hunting. The Maya may have tended or managed certain wild animals, possibly for food, and it is also likely that certain species of dog were fattened and eaten, as was the custom in ancient central Mexico. Other domesticated species seem to have included the dove, the turkey, and the Muscovy duck. The duck was originally from South America, however, and may not have been known to the Maya until after the Spanish Conquest.

The Maya today often raise a variety of wild animals as pets, including

●● parrots and other birds, monkeys, coatis, kinkajous, and the like. Landa notes that the sixteenth-century Maya of the Yucatan did likewise: "Some people raise doves as tame as ours and they multiply rapidly . . . there is an animal which they call *chic* [coati, and] the women raise them and they leave nothing which they do not root over and turn upside down. . . ." Animals such as these were probably raised for food before the Conquest. Several scholars have suggested that the ancient Maya raised herds of deer for food in large penned areas. Landa reported that women "raise other domestic animals, and let the deer suck their breasts, by which means they raise them and make them so tame that they never will go into the woods, although they take them and carry them through the woods and raise them there." Recently discovered artificial channels along the Río Candelaria in the central lowlands (see below) raise the possibility that ponds were constructed in which to raise fish. Supporting archaeological or ethnohistorical evidence would suggest that the ancient Maya may have had a far greater potential for controlling sources of dietary protein than can currently be demonstrated.

### AGRICULTURE: FALLOW SYSTEMS

There can be little doubt that agriculture provided the major source of ancient Maya subsistence (Table 6), using a complex combination of cultivation methods that resulted from a long period of gradual development and environmental adaptation.

For convenience we describe these methods under two categories: fallow systems, in which fields are cultivated for a time and then allowed to lie fallow, or "rest," for a period before cultivation is renewed; and intensive systems, in which fields are cultivated continuously, the fallow periods either not present or lasting less than a year for each year of cultivation.

Fallow periods for short-term swidden agriculture are generally from one to three years for each year of cultivation; for long-term swidden agriculture, generally three to six years for each year of cultivation. For the ancient Maya, both methods probably involved the arduous task of clearing fields with stone tools and allowing the cut vegetation to dry, after which it was burned and the field planted. Large trees and species that provided wild foods were probably left or allowed to grow with the stands of maize, beans, squashes, manioc, and other planted species. Each field was planted and harvested for several successive seasons, depending on local conditions of rainfall, soil quality, and so forth. Once the field became unproductive, owing to competition from weeds and to soil depletion, it was abandoned to lie fallow while new fields were cleared.

Long-term swidden methods are probably among the oldest forms of agriculture in the Maya area. Many scholars believe that the original colonization of forested areas was made by agriculturists practicing long-term swidden cultivation. Because of its reliance on low maintenance and long periods of fallow, this

TABLE 6
*Common Plant Cultigens Available to the Ancient Lowland Maya[a]*

| Cultigen | Month planted | Month harvested | Yield[b] |
|---|---|---|---|
| Amaranth (*Amaranthus*) | | | |
| Avocado (*Persea americana*) | | | |
| Ayote (squash) (*Cucurbita pepo*) | Feb.–May | Oct. | 9,557* |
| Bean, common (*Phaseolus vulgaris*) | June–Aug. | Nov. | 24,013 |
| Breadnut (*Brosimum alicastrum*) | | Dry season | 1,100–2,700[c] |
| Cacao (*Theobroma cacao*) | | | |
| Cassava (*Manihot esculenta*) | | Jan.–Mar. | 2,600 |
| Chili (*Capsicum annuum*) | Mar. | June | |
| Guava (*Psidium guajava*) | | | |
| Maize (*Zea mays*) | Apr.–May | Nov.–Jan. | 1,600 (first-year milpa) 1,134 (second-year) 468 (third-year) |
| Mombin (*Spondias mombin*) | | | |
| Nance (*Byrsonima crassifolia*) | | | |
| Papaya (*Carica papaya*) | | | |
| Pineapple (*Ananas comosus*) | June | Any | 7,718* |
| Sapodilla (*Achras zapota*) | | | |
| Soursop (*Annona* sp.) | | | |
| Sweet potato (*Ipomoea batatas*) | May | Dec. | 22,469 |
| Vanilla (*Vanilla fragrans*) | | | |
| Yautia (*Xanthosoma violaceum*) | | | 40,909 |
| Yucca (*Yucca elephantipes*) | | | |

[a] After Wiseman (1978), with additions.
[b] Given in kg/hectare, except those marked by an asterisk (*), which are given in fruits/hectare.
[c] Lower figure given in Wiseman, the higher figure in Puleston (1978).

method gives relatively low yields while requiring large areas of land, and is therefore best suited for small, scattered populations. In time, as populations increased and more efficient methods developed, long-term swidden cultivation diminished in importance until it was confined to marginal environments.

Short-term swidden agriculture necessitates increased maintenance of the fields, by periodic weeding and intercropping (growing a variety of complementary species together). These techniques reduce competition for the food plants, diminish the rate of soil depletion (or even replenish nutrients if the proper crops are used for intercropping), and thereby reduce the fallow period. In areas of moderate soil quality and good rainfall, short-term fallow systems can be highly productive. Although the ancient Maya apparently lacked the means to efficiently clear dense stands of second growth from fallow fields, making swidden methods increasingly difficult to maintain, they might well have been helped by their climate. In areas with long dry seasons such as northern

Yucatan, the underbrush usually becomes sufficiently combustible to allow clearing by burning, without the need of extensive cutting by stone tools.

No direct evidence exists for the use of either kind of swidden agriculture by the ancient Maya. Indirect evidence comes from the analyses of pollen samples in sediment cores from the beds of several lakes in the central lowlands, which demonstrate that the early Preclassic settlers of that region grew maize; swidden techniques are indicated by remnants of ash fallout, possibly from field burning. It may well be that some of the relic field systems found mostly in the northern lowlands, consisting of stone boundary walls and water-flow deflectors, were cultivated by short-term swidden methods.

The modification of sloped landscape by terracing has been identified in several areas of the lowlands. The largest areas of terracing seem to be in the Río Bec region, where estimates based on ground surveys indicate that some 150,000 hectares of agricultural land were modified by constructed terraces. Another zone has been found along the eastern slopes of the Maya Mountains in Belize, where at least 40,000 hectares of terraced land have been identified. Archaeological excavations in both areas reveal that these terraces were constructed during the Classic period. However, the heavy investment of labor reflected by these agricultural features implies that they may have been used for more intensive agricultural methods. The Maya seem to have used hillside terracing to help retain water in the soil and thus increase productivity.

## AGRICULTURE: INTENSIVE SYSTEMS

The intensive agricultural methods used by the ancient Maya include continuous field cultivation, household gardens, arboriculture, and hydraulic modifications.

In continuous field cultivation crops are grown without fallow periods of sufficient duration to allow the fields to become overgrown, a method that requires constant labor to weed out the competitors of the food crops. Continuous cultivation could have been practiced by the ancient Maya in areas with well-drained, fertile soils and plentiful rainfall. Prime areas for this method are alluvial valleys, like those found in various parts of the southern and coastal lowlands. There, on the natural river levees and the older terraces found above localized or extensive floodplains of such rivers as the Usumacinta, Motagua, Belize, and their tributaries, continuous field cultivation could have been very productive. Periodic flooding in these areas replenished soil fertility by depositing new alluvial soils. The lowest portions of active floodplains (backswamps) are often too wet for much of the year to allow cultivation without hydraulic modifications (see below). Depletion of older alluvial soils no longer replenished by flood deposits could have been controlled by proper intercropping.

As with swidden agriculture, little direct evidence can be found to demonstrate ancient continuous cultivation. Today, local areas of rich soils—volcanic basins of the southern highlands and along the Pacific coastal plain, the deeper soil pockets of the northern highlands and southern lowlands, and flood-plains—support continuous or near-continuous cultivation. Intensive weeding or frequent intercropping are not used, even after centuries of agricultural exploitation; presumably conditions in the past should have been more produc-tive. It seems likely that some of the relic agricultural features, such as the bounded fields and terraces, could have been used for continuous cultivation. Present knowledge about the peak sizes and densities of Maya populations in the central lowlands during the Classic period suggests that some continuous cultivation may have been a necessary part of the ancient system. Given the potential of the alluvial plains found in the southern lowlands, continuous field cultivation could have transformed these and similar fertile areas into "bread-baskets" supplying large amounts of staples for trade with the population centers of the Classic period.

As the name implies, household gardens are cultivated in open spaces adja-cent to and between family residences. In the tropics household gardens may contain a great variety of food plants: annual root crops, maize, beans, and other field species; and perennial shrubs, vines, and trees. The potential of this kind of intensive cultivation is made possible by the array of native plants grown in contemporary Maya household gardens. Household gardens continu-ously supply high yields of foods and condiments per unit of land. The neces-sary care is minimal (mostly weeding), and the rate of soil depletion is low, owing to intercropping. Most important, the soil is conveniently supplied with nutrients from the plant residues, augmented by human and animal wastes originating in the household.

Descriptions of Maya household gardens are known from the sixteenth-century Spanish accounts and from contemporary practice. This form of cultiva-tion may well have existed in earlier times as well. Indirect but persuasive evidence for the use of gardens by the ancient Maya is provided by botanical and settlement pattern studies. At many archaeological sites in the lowlands, investigators have long noted disproportionately heavy stands of food-produc-ing trees such as the ramon, or breadnut. Furthermore, at Tikal and Coba, settlement studies show a near-uniform spacing of residential clusters through-out the site. The spaces between these residential compounds, not large enough for efficient field agriculture, are comparable with those found in contemporary tropical settlements where household gardens are cultivated. The high propor-tion of ramon and other food trees at Maya sites may represent relics of species grown around the residences of Tikal and other Classic-period centers.

Arboriculture is the cultivation of tree crops, like the ramon mentioned above, but in extensive stands rather than household gardens. The variety of productive tree species available to the ancient Maya included the ramon, cacao, sapodilla, and avocado. Studies of the potential harvests from ramon produc-tion indicate that orchards of these trees produce ten times the amount of food per unit of land that maize does. Ramon is a starchy food that can be processed and used like maize to make tortillas or tamales, although contemporary people familiar with this food consider it much less desirable than maize. Importantly, many tree crops require much less labor; weeding is not necessary and the fruit or nuts of some species (such as ramon) may be collected from the ground as they fall. Ramon or cacao might have been grown in monocrop plantations, just as coffee or bananas (imported Old World species) are cultivated in the Maya area today. But the most efficient ancient method would likely have been a form of intercropping, producing what is sometimes called an artificial rainforest by cutting out the unwanted species in the forest and planting a mixture of desirable species in the free spaces. The mingling of different kinds of food trees discourages pests or diseases that favor a single species from spreading throughout a stand of trees and destroying a large part of the population. Intercropping has the same advantages in field cultivation as in household gardens, of course, and monocrop plantation agriculture is possible in the tropics today only through the use of chemical pesticides.

Fig. 7.4. Edzna, Campeche, Mexico: aerial photograph showing the remains of ancient canals used for drainage and irrigation (dark lines). The main ruins of Edzna are located in the lighter area (upper center), at the focus of several radiating canals.

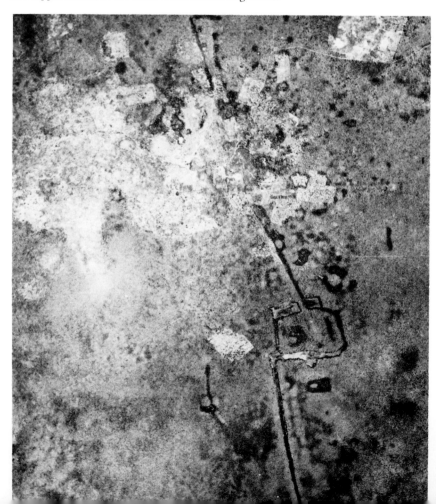

Although occasional food remains and ethnohistorical accounts indicate that tree crops were once important to the Maya, direct archaeological evidence is again difficult to obtain. Cacao was unquestionably one of the prime tree crops grown in suitable lowland environments, but its pollen is extremely perishable, so that traces of ancient cultivation may be impossible to detect. Ceramic images of cacao pods have been found at Copan, Quirigua, Lubaantun, and other Maya sites, indicating that the surrounding valleys were important areas of cacao production. But any evidence of great artificial rain-forest plantations maintained by the Classic Maya has long ago been absorbed into the natural forests of the lowlands.

Hydraulic modification of the landscape serves either to furnish water for crops (irrigation) or to drain excess water from saturated soils to allow better growth. There is evidence that the ancient Maya constructed irrigation networks, but on a much smaller scale than the notable examples elsewhere in the New World along the Pacific coast of Peru and in the southwestern United States.

Evidence of an ancient irrigation system in the Maya lowlands comes from Edzna, in the drier transitional zone between the central and northern lowlands. Investigations directed by Ray Matheny revealed an impressive canal and reservoir system capable of serving a minimum of 450 hectares of cultivated land (Fig. 7.4). The archaeological evidence from these excavations indicates that the Edzna hydraulic system was constructed during the Late Preclassic era (ca. 300–50 B.C.).

In addition, a growing body of evidence shows that the Maya once used raised fields in low-lying areas to provide fertile, yet well-drained, growing conditions for a variety of crops. Raised fields are constructed by digging narrow drainage channels in water-saturated soils and heaping the earth in continuous mounds, forming ridges on which crops may be grown. Continuous cultivation is possible, since periodic hand dredging of muck from the drainage channels brings fresh soil and organic debris to the growing areas (Fig. 7.5). These channels may have been used as sources for the harvest of fish, mollusks, and other aquatic life, or may even have been stocked.

Raised fields can be used to grow a variety of crops, and we possess some direct evidence from Maya times. Recent excavations at Pulltrouser Swamp, Belize, have revealed clear remnants of raised fields dating from the Classic period (Fig. 7.6). From the plant remains recovered by this work, it appears that the Maya used these raised fields to grow maize, amaranth, cotton, and possibly cacao.

Fortunately, the distinctive ridged pattern of ancient raised fields can in many cases be detected by aerial photography (Fig. 7.7). The first to be recognized in the Maya area, those on the floodplain of the Río Candelaria in southern Campeche, Mexico, covered an area estimated at some 2 km² (Fig. 7.8). A larger zone of raised fields (estimated to cover an area of about 75 km²

Fig. 7.5 (*above*). Pull-trouser Swamp, Belize: ground view showing relic raised fields; the shallow standing water fills the silted-in drainage canals during the rainy season.

Fig. 7.6. Dry-season excavations at Pulltrouser Swamp; the far test pit is on the shore of the *bajo,* or swamp, with the line of excavations going down into a relic canal and up onto a raised field (foreground). The excavator is cutting into the artificial fill used to elevate the field plot above the ancient water level.

Fig. 7.7. Aerial view of Pulltrouser Swamp, showing relic raised fields (dark) and canals (light) along the southern edge of the *bajo*.

Fig. 7.8. Aerial view of the Río Candelaria, Campeche, Mexico, showing relic raised fields (regular clumps of vegetation) and canals in the back swamps along the river.

or 30 sq. mi.) has been found on the opposite side of the Yucatan Peninsula, in the valleys of the Hondo and New rivers in northern Belize. North of this region, more recent studies of aerial photographs have tentatively identified a series of raised field systems in the *bajos* of southern Quintana Roo, Mexico, covering an area of over 200 km² (77 sq. mi.). And a recently completed aerial survey using a NASA radar mapping system has revealed an even larger network of drainage canals in the Maya lowlands.

## Reconstructing the Patterns of Subsistence

It is very likely that all of the subsistence alternatives reviewed here, together with others not yet recognized, were used by the ancient Maya. Research on this subject is still too incomplete to reconstruct in any detail how these various methods were developed and recombined within the variety of environments in the Maya area. We can, however, suggest some logical steps that may have taken place.

The development of ancient Maya subsistence involved two complementary processes: expansion and intensification. Expansion describes an increase in the land (or water) areas being exploited for food. As Maya populations grew, the food supply could be increased by colonizing new regions, thus tapping a larger area for food. Intensification increases crop yields without increasing the land (or water) areas exploited for subsistence. Since there were real limits to the expansion of the subsistence system, continued population increases eventually could be accommodated only by increasing the amount of food produced from the same land or water areas.

Environmental differences guarantee that there was no single original Maya subsistence method. We know that prior to the Preclassic period, agricultural techniques were added to the far older inventory of hunting-and-gathering methods. As populations grew, new areas were opened for agricultural exploitation. The initial expansion and colonization of most new areas probably led to a subsistence strategy that supplemented hunting and gathering with long-term swidden cultivation. Raised fields may have been used on a limited scale in some river valleys, perhaps those of the southern and central Maya lowlands. The need for an intensification of agriculture seems to have led to progressively shorter fallow periods within a swidden system, to the development of household gardens, and ultimately to continuous field cultivation, arboriculture, and the expansion of raised fields into new environments, such as *bajos*. At the same time, an intensification of hunting and gathering led to new capabilities in animal husbandry, such as the raising or penning of wild animals or, in combination with raised fields, the raising of aquatic species. This scenario appears logical, but only through further archaeological research into ancient Maya subsistence methods can we hope to improve our present imperfect understanding.

# 8 ⟨ ⦂⦂ ⟩

## THE ORGANIZATION OF SOCIETY

> Before the Spanish had conquered that country, the natives lived together in towns in a very civilized fashion . . . [and] in the middle of the town were their temples with beautiful plazas, and all around the temples stood the houses of the lords and priests, and then the most important people. Thus came the houses of the richest and of those who were held in the highest estimation nearest to these, and at the outskirts of the town were the houses of the lower class.
> —Landa's *Relación de las cosas de Yucatán* (Tozzer 1941 : 62)

Our understanding of ancient Maya social and political organization is based largely on two complementary forms of research: archaeology and ethnohistory (often supplemented by ethnography). The archaeological approach usually centers on ancient settlement research, in that it considers the spatial distribution of the remains of ancient occupation, from the smallest hearth or trash pit to the largest building complex or site. The distribution and patterning of these remains are taken to be a reflection not only of ancient social and political relationships, but also of the residents' interaction with their environment (ecology). In the Maya area, this kind of settlement research has been complemented by epigraphic studies that have enabled scholars to reconstruct dynastic histories for several Classic-period sites (see Chapter 4).

Ethnohistorical research is based on a variety of surviving documents from the Spanish Conquest and early colonial periods that describe the organization of Maya society during its final era. The descriptions of present-day Maya communities (ethnography) have also been used to assist in the reconstruction of ancient Maya organization.

Although these two approaches, archaeological and ethnohistorical/ethnographical, build on different sources of information, as we shall see in reviewing what is currently known about the organization of ancient Maya society, the results obtained from one source may be used to amplify or test the conclusions derived from the other.

## Evidence from Settlement Studies

The patterning of remains that the archaeological approach uses to reconstruct the organization of ancient Maya society was obviously conditioned by environmental conditions: availability of water, good agricultural soils, and access to other necessary resources. In fact, settlement studies are also used to reconstruct ecological relationships. In addition to those relationships, settlement patterns can be used to reconstruct ancient social and political organizations. For instance, the distribution of archaeological remains from a single household (cooking vessels, tools, hearths, burials, and the remains of the house structure itself) may reflect the activities that once took place there, and thus may provide information about the size and organization of a single family.

On a larger scale, the patterning of all such household remains within a single site may reflect the social and political ties that once defined a functioning community. A pattern that reveals a series of clusters of individual houses may indicate that the ancient society was organized according to family groupings such as lineages. Differences observed within a class of residential structures, such as those based on variations in size, elaborateness, or type of construction, may reflect past distinctions like social and economic classes. Beyond this, the pattern of residential structures in relation to buildings with non-residential functions—temples, storage facilities, courts, administrative structures, and so forth—allows the reconstruction of ancient political organization.

In order to undertake these kinds of reconstructions, the archaeologist must be able to identify the kinds of ancient activities that took place; that is, he must be able to determine the function of ancient buildings from their remains. In addition, the archaeologist must be able to ascertain which of the activity areas were contemporary, ensuring that the ancient structures for which functions have been assigned were used at the same time. Although identifying function may at times be difficult, it is usually less of a problem than determining the concurrent use of archaeological remains. The issue of contemporaneity is crucial, since in order to reconstruct the organization of ancient society, the

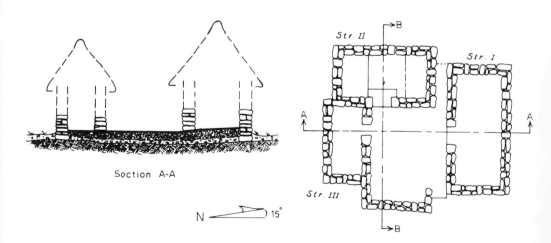

Section A-A

N ⟶ ) 15°

Str. II

Str. I

Str. III

A   A

B

B

archaeologist must have some assurance that the activity areas being studied were part of the same functioning system. For instance, a cluster of family residences might represent a lineage system if they were all occupied at the same time. However, if the residences were occupied at different times, the same cluster might represent a sequential series of houses occupied by a single family.

Most methods used by archaeologists to furnish the necessary chronological control—radiocarbon dating, pottery style analysis, and other techniques—are rarely accurate enough to define time spans of less than a hundred years. An exception occurs, as far as Classic Maya sites are concerned, when a structure can be associated with a Maya calendrical date, but most inscriptions of this kind are limited to the higher-status portions of sites. Thus, for the majority of cases, ancient Maya occupation is assumed to have occurred at the same time within periods averaging about a hundred years in length, equivalent to approximately four human generations at that time.

## Settlement Units in the Maya Lowlands

The Maya area in which settlement has been most thoroughly studied is the generalized lowland zone, including sites in the central and northern lowlands. For this reason, conclusions about archaeological settlement units here are based on lowland data, although they can be considered generally applicable to other regions, with allowances for regional cultural and environmental differences. For the same reason, most of these units are from the Classic period.

The minimal settlement feature is the *residential unit*, usually defined by a low earthen or rubble platform that supported oblong or rectangular structures of one or more rooms with stone walls roofed by pole and thatch (Fig. 8.1), or built entirely of perishable materials. The minimum size of these structures

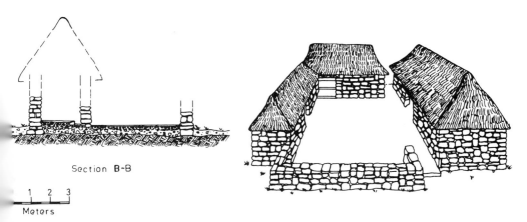

Section B-B

1  2  3
Meters

Fig. 8.1 (*facing page and above*). Ancient Maya residential group east of Xpuhil, Campeche, Mexico, with reconstructed view at the right.

appears to be about 20 m² of roofed space. Some of these structures, built without platforms, are much more difficult to detect archaeologically (their only trace usually being corner postholes). In some cases residential units had walls built of adobe blocks; or only the lower portion of the walls was built of more durable materials, adobe or even masonry blocks, with the upper walls and roof constructed of perishable materials. In the highest-status residential units, the structures were often larger, built completely of masonry blocks, including the vaulted roofs, and were placed on larger, higher, masonry-faced platforms.

Items found in association with residential units include burials under the floors, burned areas or hearths, workshop areas where chipped-stone tools and

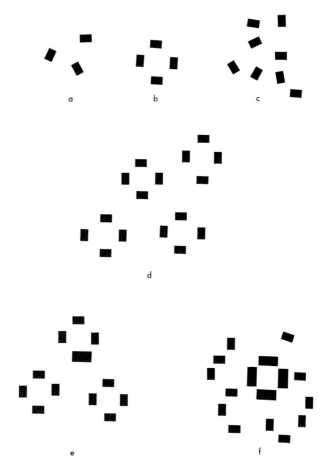

Fig. 8.2. Schematic plans of typical Maya settlement units: (*a*) informal residential group; (*b*) residential patio group; (*c*) informal residential cluster; (*d*) homogeneous patio cluster; (*e*) structure-focused patio cluster; (*f*) group-focused patio cluster.

various other products were made, storage pits (*chultuns*), and debris such as
pottery sherds, broken grinding stones (manos and metates), worn-out flint or
obsidian tools, and even food remains. Evidence of this kind indicates that these
structures were in fact residential in function, probably housing nuclear families
(husband, wife, and children). However, an unknown percentage of structures
that might be labeled residential units could have served specialized functions
as storage sheds, detached kitchens, or household shrines. Occasionally, a flood,
volcanic eruption, or other sudden catastrophe overwhelmed a household, preserving both the building and the tools and other furnishings as they were at the
moment of the disaster. An example of this kind of event has recently been
discovered at the Classic site of Cerén, El Salvador, where the walls of an adobe
house, along with the household articles and adjacent maize field, were suddenly buried and sealed under a thick blanket of volcanic ash (Figs. 1.7 and 7.3).

Two or more residential units found in proximity define a *residential group*
(Fig. 8.2*a*). Commonly averaging two to six units, groupings of this kind are
assumed to have been occupied by an extended family, that is, two or more
nuclear families related by close kinship ties. Extended family groupings may be
generational, when grandparents, parents, and married children maintain separate but proximate residences, or collateral, when siblings or cousins do the
same; combinations of the two types may of course be found.

Craft specializations, such as stone working or pottery making, may have
been associated with some residential groupings, meaning that certain occupations may have followed family lines in ancient Maya society. Non-residential
specialized structures have also been found within residential groups. In some
cases the presence of a leader or headman of the extended family may be
indicated by a single larger or more elaborate residential structure within a
residential group. In some groups, the units are arranged around a central open
space, or patio (Fig. 8.2*b*). A particular residential-group pattern repeatedly
found at Tikal, called "plaza plan 2," consists of a rectangular central patio
bordered on three sides by residential units and enclosed by a smaller but often
higher-platformed structure on the east side. This special building has been seen
as the household shrine for the extended family, where ancestral rituals were
performed above the burial place of the family's "founder."

Larger aggregates of structures have been detected from settlement pattern
studies. A *cluster* consists of two or more residential groups separated by open
space from other such clusters (Fig. 8.2*c, d*). Usually these clusters embrace five
to twelve groups; one group, or one structure, is often larger or more elaborate
than the others (Figs. 8.2*e, f*). If these residential clusters were occupied by
larger kin groups, such as lineages, we assume that the lineage head and his
extended family lived in the largest residential group within a given cluster,
which may have included a lineage shrine in the largest ceremonial structure in
the cluster. The other residential groups within a cluster might have been
occupied by the remaining extended families of the lineage. Some scholars have

•••  suggested a slightly different interpretation of clusters, postulating that the surrounding smaller residential groups housed the retainers, servants, and other individuals dependent on the larger, more elaborate residential group. Both views may in fact be correct.

Beyond the residential level, with the inferred reconstruction of its social organization, Maya sites are dominated by central concentrations of special-purpose structures, including platforms, causeways, temples, ball courts, palaces, occasional fortifications, and plain or sculptured stone monuments. These items usually define most familiar Maya archaeological sites, and the neutral term *center* is now preferred to former labels, such as "ceremonial center," whose functional implications are restrictive. These centers, appropriately named because they are usually spatially central to the residential groupings that surround them, must have served a variety of functions; there are areas for public gatherings, ceremonies, ball games, and markets, and facilities for political and administrative activities like receiving visitors, collecting tribute, and hearing grievances. It is usually possible to discern these various functional areas, especially the distinction between public and restricted areas. Many centers, such as Lubaantun and Quirigua, consisted of two definable areas: one open, spacious, and public; the other closed in, restricted, and private. Larger centers like Tikal include many such contrasting areas. Certainly the largest and most elaborate residences were in or near these centers, which were usually constructed so as to restrict access to and maintain privacy for the courtly and domestic activities of the ruling families and their rituals.

In a very real sense, however, the Maya centers merely represented larger and more complex versions of residential clusters. In fact some scholars have viewed the basic core of even the largest Maya sites as the residences (palaces) for the most wealthy and powerful ruling lineages, the large temple pyramids representing their ancestral shrines. Regardless of the varying emphases given to different functional aspects of Maya sites, the centers and their surrounding residential clusters define the remains of an ancient social and political system, or *community*.

The ancient Maya community provided the setting for the organizational networks that gave society its basic structure. These organizational networks were certainly based on kinship: the nuclear family, extended family, and lineage bonds that were the foundations of Maya society. But the centers were also the setting for levels of organization that transcended kinship ties, including economic and religious systems that attracted people from all levels of society to the centers to participate in ceremonies and to exchange goods and services. In time, the centers took on increased political functions as they became the headquarters for a centralized administrative organization, probably with a series of hereditary offices culminating in a single position of authority at its head.

Maya centers varied considerably in size, arrangement, and architectural style. The smallest may have covered less than a square kilometer, whereas others, such as Tikal (the largest known Maya site), extended over an area of some 123 km², or 50 sq. mi. (see Chapter 11). Size, together with the elaborateness of buildings, the number of monuments and hieroglyphic inscriptions, and other characteristics, undoubtedly reflected the relative political and economic power held by each center. Scholars have long recognized variations in arrangement and architectural style between sites, using the differences between them to divide the Maya area into regions; however, the ancient social and political significance of these divisions is debatable.

The obvious differences in size and complexity support the conclusion that some Maya centers exerted a political dominance over others (see Chapter 4). The primary centers certainly exerted varying degrees of control over smaller centers by means of economic, social, and political alliances. The evidence also suggests that dominant centers such as Tikal sponsored the founding of colonial centers in outlying regions. Military raids or even open warfare certainly seems to have been used to dominate the satellite centers. The distance between the larger sites averages 20–30 km (12–18 mi.), whereas a whole range of smaller centers are found at lesser intervals. Yet attempts to rank sites according to their size and complexity, using both subjective and objective criteria, have proved quite unfruitful and bear no assurance that they accurately assess political power. When combined with criteria of size and location, however, epigraphic

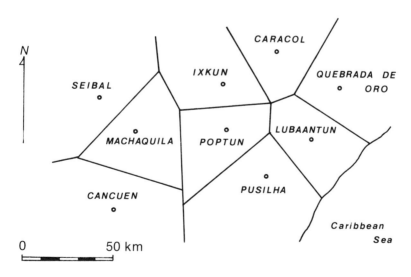

Fig. 8.3. Thiesson polygons drawn around a series of centers in the southern lowlands to arbitrarily define approximate boundaries between centers.

evidence seems to provide some important clues for the reconstruction of ancient intersite political relationships; for example, this kind of evidence indicates that a conflict between the small, relatively simple center of Quirigua and the much larger center of Copan resulted in Copan's defeat.

The reconstruction of ancient Maya political realms and relationships has been approached from several directions. One technique for inferring the extent of each center's realm is the use of maps to construct Thiesson polygons, in which boundaries around sites are drawn through the midpoints between each pair of centers (Fig 8.3). Another is based on the distribution of emblem glyphs in the inscriptions of many Maya centers (Table 7). Emblem glyphs appear to represent the seats of sovereign political authority, and were distinctive for each center (see Chapter 15). Primary centers displayed only their own emblems (see Chapter 4). Secondary centers often mentioned the emblem of the nearest large center in addition to their own, but not those of smaller centers. The smaller centers used only the emblems of larger sites, if they mentioned any emblem at all. This pattern implies a political hierarchy in which lesser centers displayed the emblems from more powerful sites. Recently, a method of ranking lowland Maya sites on architectural criteria (number of courtyard groups) has been proposed. This has led to an ordering of sites within several lowland regions (Table 8) that is suggestive of political and economic hierarchies.

The distribution of Maya road (sacbe) systems has also been used to infer the extent of political realms in the past. This is especially true in Yucatan, where the remains of sacbeob are relatively easy to spot and trace. At Coba, for example, an extensive network of roadways connects the site core with a series of outlying sites, clearly reflecting its ancient centralized authority.

Overall, the location and prosperity of Maya sites, as for all human settlements, were undoubtedly determined by access to essential resources such as water and food. Other factors, such as strategic positions along trade routes, or defensible locations in times of conflict, were probably important as well. A number of Maya sites seem to have been located to take advantage of special circumstances, and at least some of these apparently enjoyed considerable prosperity as a result. In the southern lowlands, many important centers are situated along major rivers (Yaxchilan, Piedras Negras, and Quirigua, to name only a few) that served as important routes of communication and trade, besides providing productive alluvial soils for agriculture. In the central lowlands several sites (such as El Mirador, Tikal, and Uaxactun) are at or near the divide between drainage basins, indicating that they controlled the portages for canoe transport across the Peten. In addition, most centers in this region are associated with bajos, the shallow lakes or swamps that probably provided water and yielded rich harvests when modified by raised fields (Chapter 7). Seacoast trade seems to have determined the location of other Maya sites from the Preclassic era onward. Along the rivers and Caribbean littoral of the east coast of the

TABLE 7

*Example of a Lowland-Site Hierarchy Based on Emblem-Glyph (EG) Distribution*[a]

| | | | | |
|---|---|---|---|---|
| Primary centers (may display own and other primary centers' EG's) | Tikal | Yaxchilan | Copan | Palenque |
| Secondary centers (possess EG; display EG of primary center) | Aguateca Machaquila Naranjo | Piedras Negras | Quirigua | Pomona |
| Tertiary centers (no EG; display EG of primary or secondary center) | Ixlu Jimbal Uaxactun | Bonampak El Cayo | Pusilha | El Retiro Jonuta Miraflores Tortuguero |
| Quaternary centers (no EG; no EG display) | El Encanto Xultun | La Florida La Mar Morales | Los Higos Río Amarillo Santa Rita | Chinikiha Chuctiepa Tila |

[a] After Marcus (1976).

TABLE 8

*Example of a Lowland-Site Hierarchy Based on Number of Architectural Plaza Units (Tikal Region)*[a]

| Site | Number of plaza units | Site | Number of plaza units | Site | Number of plaza units |
|---|---|---|---|---|---|
| Tikal | 85 | Ucanal | 11 | Hatzcab Ceel | 5 |
| Naranjo | 42+ | Tayasal | 10 | Holmul | 5 |
| Uaxactun | 23 | Chochkitam | 8 | Ixlu | 5 |
| Kinal | 20 | Ixkun | 8 | Cahal Pichik | 4 |
| Yaxha | 20 | Xultun | 7 | Itsimte | 4 |
| Caracol | 17 | Xunantunich | 5 | Río Azul | 4 |
| La Honradez | 16 | Chunhuitz | 5 | Motul de San José | 3 |
| Nakum | 16 | San Clemente | 5 | Uolantun | 1 |

[a] After Adams and Jones (1981).

Yucatan Peninsula these include Cerros (Preclassic), Lamanai (Preclassic through Postclassic), and Tulum (Late Postclassic).

Single resources with widespread demand seem to have determined the location and prosperity of several centers. Examples are Dzibilchaltun in northern Yucatan (access to coastal salt), Colha in Belize (good-quality flint), Salinas de los Nueve Cerros in the southern lowlands (salt), Guaytan in the middle Motagua valley (jadeite), and Kaminaljuyu in the southern highlands (obsidian).

•••
___

## Evidence from Ethnohistorical Studies

The ethnohistorical and ethnographical approach to ancient Maya organization draws on the rich resource of documents describing Maya society at the time of the Spanish Conquest and the additional information from more recent studies of ongoing traditional Maya communities. In both cases there are weaknesses inherent in the sources. First and most obvious, the accounts of the sixteenth century must be projected back in time for at least seven or eight hundred years if they are to be used to reconstruct Classic-period Maya society. Obviously this must be done with caution, for there is good reason to assume that the organization of the Maya changed from the eighth to the sixteenth centuries. Projections into the past can be made more accurate by comparing the ethnohistorical accounts with the archaeological data, attempting to isolate correspondences between descriptions and the archaeological remains. A second weakness derives from the biases of the accounts themselves. Some accounts were written by Maya scholars; others by Spanish soldiers, priests, and administrators. Each had his own axe to grind, so that distortions surely resulted. Many documents have been recopied and translated several times, resulting in numerous errors, omissions, and later additions. Cross-checking within the ethnohistorical record itself, and comparison with the archaeological evidence, can often minimize these difficulties.

In considering the ethnohistorical approach, there are two well-documented and thoroughly researched Maya regions. The first is the Postclassic Maya area of northern Yucatan, known best from the excellent accounts written by Bishop Diego de Landa in the sixteenth century and from a series of native chronicles known as the *Books of Chilam Balam*. The second is the Postclassic Quiche Maya area of the central Guatemalan highlands, well known from the survival of the most remarkable native Maya book, the *Popol Vuh*, and other highland Maya chronicles. It should be noted, however, that by Postclassic times, the Maya of both areas were heavily influenced by Mexican culture, so that in some cases it is difficult to separate those aspects of society that were Maya in origin from those that were imported from Mexico.

### THE MAYA OF POSTCLASSIC YUCATAN

According to Bishop Landa, Yucatecan society was divided into several classes, including *almehenob* (nobility), *ahkinob* (priests), *ah chembal uinicob* (commoners), and *ppentacob* (slaves).

At the time of the Conquest, at least nine of the eighteen Yucatecan political units was led by a *halach uinic* ("true man"), although there were important variations in the political organization from one of these petty states to another. This position was hereditary. Landa, describing conditions in Late Postclassic times, states that the lords were succeeded by their oldest sons:

If the lord died, although his oldest son succeeded him, the other children were always very much respected and assisted and regarded as lords themselves; . . . if, when the lord died, there were no sons [old enough] to reign, and he [the deceased lord] had brothers, the oldest of the brothers, or the best qualified, reigned, and they taught the heir their customs and feasts against the time he should become a man; and these brothers [paternal uncles of the heir], although the heir was [ready] to reign, commanded all their lives; and if he [the deceased lord] had no brothers, the priests and principal people elected a man proper for the position.

The *halach uinic* was also called *ahau*, a word the sixteenth-century Maya manuscript-dictionaries define as "king, emperor, monarch, prince, or great lord." This was the title used by the Maya of the colonial period in referring to the King of Spain. *Ahau*, or its equivalent, was probably the supreme title held by the rulers of the great Classic centers of the Maya lowlands. The powers enjoyed by the *halach uinic* were broad. He probably formulated foreign and domestic policies with the aid of a council composed of the leading chiefs, priests, and special councillors (*ah cuch cabob*). He appointed the town and village chiefs (*batabob*), who stood in a sort of feudal relation to him, and the most important of whom were no doubt his close blood relatives.

In addition to being the highest administrative and executive officer of the state, the *halach uinic* was most likely the highest ecclesiastical authority as well. It has been suggested that Classic-period government may have been theocratic, the highest civil and religious powers being combined in the person of one individual who perhaps even then was called the *halach uinic*.

Below the *halach uinic* stood the *batabob*, or lesser chiefs. They were the local magistrates and executives, who administered the affairs of the towns and villages. In the Postclassic and probably in the Classic era as well, they were appointed from among the members of the hereditary nobility, the *almehenob*. They exercised executive and judicial authority in their communities, and although in times of war all served under one supreme military chief, each *batab* personally commanded his own soldiers. He presided over the local council and saw to it that the houses were kept in repair and that the people cut and burned their fields at the proper times. In his capacity as judge he sentenced criminals and decided civil suits. If these were of unusual importance he consulted the *halach uinic* before passing judgment. No tribute was paid directly to the *batab*, being rendered only to the *halach uinic*, but he was supported by the people. One of the *batab*'s principal duties was to see that his town or village paid its tribute promptly to the *halach uinic*.

The *batab* title has been translated from glyph T1030, one element of which is an axe (*baat*). This glyph appears in many Classic lowland texts associated with the names of rulers (see Fig. 15.12). The *batab* title appears to have been held by the supreme ruler (*ahau*), who was the political and military leader of a major center, and by lesser leaders of tributary towns under the jurisdiction of

● ● ●
▬▬

an *ahau*. At the time of the Conquest the highest authorities in several Yucatec states held the *batab* title.

There were two kinds of war captains: one hereditary, presumably the *batab*; the other, of greater importance, was elected for a period of three years and given the title of *nacom*.

This one, called the *nacom*, could not, during these three years, have relations with any woman, even his own wife, nor eat red meat. They held him in great veneration and gave him fish and iguanas, which are like lizards, to eat. In this time [his tenure of office] he did not get drunk, and he kept separate in his house the utensils and other objects which he used, and no women served him and he had but little communication with the people. At the end of these three years [all was] as before. These two captains [the *nacom* and *batab*] discussed the affairs of war and put them in order. . . .

They bore him [the *nacom*] in great pomp, perfuming him as if he were an idol, to the temple where they seated him and burned incense to him as to an idol.

It would seem that the elected *nacom* formulated the strategy of war, whereas the *batabob*, the hereditary chiefs, led their respective contingents into battle.

Next below the *batab* were the town councillors, the *ah cuch cabob*, two or three in number. Each had a vote in the town government, and without their assent nothing could be done. Each stood at the head of a subdivision of the town, and they were likened by Spanish writers of the sixteenth century to the *regidores* in Spanish town governments.

The *ah kulelob*, or deputies, accompanied the *batab* wherever he went and were the assistants who carred out his orders; there were usually two or three of them.

The duties of the *ah holpopob*, meaning in Yucatec "those at the head of the mat," are not so clear. These officials are said to have assisted the lords in the government of their towns and served as intermediaries through whom the townspeople approached the lords. At least two towns in Late Postclassic Yucatan were ruled by a *holpop*. As we shall see, the holder of this title was the supreme ruler of the sixteenth-century Quiche Maya. In the Yucatan the *holpopob* were the advisers of the lords on matters of foreign policy, and are said to have been, after the Conquest, masters of the *popolna*, the house where the men met to discuss public affairs and to learn the dances for the town festivals. The *ah holpopob* were also the chief singers and chanters in charge of the dances and musical instruments in each town during the colonial era.

The *tupiles*, or town constables, stood at the bottom of the law-enforcement structure.

In describing conditions in the Late Postclassic, Landa says that both chiefs' and priests' offices were hereditary and were derived from the nobility: "They taught the sons of the other priests and the second sons of the lords who [were] brought them from their infancy, if they saw that they had an inclination for this profession; . . . and his [the high priest's] sons or his nearest relatives succeeded him in office." A. Herrera, the official historian of the Indies for the Crown of Spain, writes, "For the matters concerning the worship of their gods they had one who was the high-priest, whose sons succeeded him in the priesthood." There is little doubt that both the highest civil and religious offices were hereditary, being filled from the members of one family in each state.

Landa says that the high priest in Late Postclassic times was called Ahaucan Mai. This, however, seems to be a combination of the title *ahaucan* and the family name Mai, which is common in the Yucatan. The high priest may have been called simply the *ahaucan*, since this word in Maya means "the Lord Serpent." In combining the surname Mai with it, Landa was doubtless referring to a specific family in which the office seems to have been hereditary. Landa says further that

He was very much respected by the lords and had no *repartimiento* of Indians [no Indians specially set aside for his personal service], but besides the offerings, the lords made him presents and all the priests of the town brought contributions to him. . . . In him was the key of their learning and it was to these matters that they [the high priests] mostly dedicated themselves; and they gave advice to the lords and replied to their questions. They seldom dealt with matters pertaining to the sacrifices except at the time of the principal feasts, or very important matters of business. They provided priests for the towns when they were needed, examining them in the sciences and ceremonies and committing to them the duties of their office, and set good example to people and provided them with books and sent them forth. And they employed themselves in the duties of the temples and in teaching their sciences as well as writing books about them. . . .

The sciences which they taught were the computation of the years, months and days, the festivals and ceremonies, the administration of the sacraments, the fateful days and seasons, their methods of divination and their prophecies, events and the cures for diseases and their antiquities [history] and how to read and write with their letters and characters [hieroglyphics] with which they wrote, and [to make] drawings which illustrate the meaning of the writings.

Another class of priests were the *chilanes*, or diviners, whose duty it was to give the replies of the gods to the people. The *chilanes* were held in such high respect that the people carried them on their shoulders when they appeared in public.

Another priest was the *nacom* (not to be confused with the war chief of the same title), who was elected for life. According to Landa, he was held in little esteem because he was the functionary who slit open the breasts of the sacrificial victims and plucked out their hearts:

At this time came the executioner, the *nacom*, with a knife of stone, and with much skill and cruelty struck him [the sacrificial victim] with the knife between the ribs of his left side under the nipple, and at once plunged his hand in there and seized the heart like a raging tiger, tearing it out alive, and having placed it on a plate, he gave it to the priest, who went quickly and anointed the face of the idols with that fresh blood.

The *nacom* was assisted in the ceremony of human sacrifice by four aides called *chacs*, respectable old men chosen anew on each occasion. Wrote Landa, "The *chacs* seized the poor man whom they were going to sacrifice and with great haste, placed him on his back upon that stone and all four held him by the legs and arms so that they divided him in the middle." The *chacs* also assisted at the puberty ceremony, kindled the new fire at the beginning of the Maya New Year, and fasted and anointed idols with blood in the month of Mol, which was dedicated to making new idols.

*Ahkin* was the general name for "priest" in Maya. The word means literally "he of the sun." Some of the *ahkins* had specialized duties, for example, as prophets of the thirteen differently numbered katuns. At a sanctuary on Isla de Cozumel and at the sacred Cenote at Chichen Itza, an *ahkin* served as the oracle. It was also an *ahkin* who received the hearts of the sacrificial victims from the hands of the *nacom* and offered them to the idols of the Maya gods.

The modern Maya of northern Yucatan, when they practice the few ancient ceremonies that have survived among them, employ the service of an *ahmen*, or him "who understands." The *ahmen* is a prophet and, at the same time, the inflicter as well as the healer of diseases.

The great mass of the people in Postclassic times were humble maize farmers, whose toil supported not only themselves but also their supreme ruler, their local lords, and the priesthood. In addition, they were the builders of the great complex ceremonial centers and the raised stone highways (*sacbeob*) that connected the principal cities.

Other obligations of the lower class were to pay tribute to the *halach uinic*, to give presents to their local lords, and to make offerings to the gods through the priests. The tribute and offerings consisted of all kinds of vegetable produce, a kind of woven cotton cloth called *pati*, domesticated fowls, salt, dried fish, and all kinds of game and birds. It also included cacao, *pom* (copal) for incense, honey and wax, strings of jade and coral beads, and shells. Their lands were held and tilled in common, probably on the basis of lineage ownership. Landa says:

The common people at their own expense made the houses of the lords. . . . Beyond the house, all the people did their sowing for the lord, cared for his fields and harvested what was necessary for him and his household; and when there was hunting or fishing, or when it was time to get their salt, they always gave the lord his share, since these things they always did as a community. . . . They also joined together for hunting in companies of fifty, more or less, and they roast the flesh of the deer on grills, so that it shall not be wasted [spoil] and having reached the town, they make presents to their lord and distribute [them] as among friends. And they do the same in their fishing.

The common people lived on the outskirts of the towns and villages, and, as suggested earlier, the distance of a man's house from the central plaza may have depended on his position in the social scale.

We do not know what term was used to describe the common people in ancient times, though sixteenth-century Maya dictionaries give *ah chembal uinicob*, *memba uinicob*, and *yalba uinicob* as meaning "the common people, the plebeians"; these terms in Yucatec Mayan mean "the inferior or lower men." At the time of the Spanish Conquest the common people were called *mazehualob*, a Nahua word that means the lower classes, as compared with the nobility. It is still used in northern Yucatan, but it now carries a distinct connotation of social inferiority.

At the bottom of the social scale were the slaves, *ppentacob*. Slavery seems to have been practiced in both the Classic and Postclassic eras. Landa's assertion to the contrary, that it was introduced in Late Postclassic times by one of the Cocom rulers of Mayapan, is difficult to believe in view of the frequent representations of so-called "captive figures" on Classic Maya monuments. These captive figures are very likely representations of enslaved prisoners of war, though they may represent the people of a whole town rather than any specific individual.

In Postclassic times, when we have documentary evidence for slavery, the condition would seem to have arisen in one of five different ways: (1) by having been born a slave; (2) by having been made a slave in punishment for stealing; (3) by having been made a prisoner of war; (4) by having become an orphan; or (5) by having been acquired by purchase or trade. Provision was made by law and custom for the redemption of children born into slavery. If a person was caught stealing, he was bound over to the person he had robbed and remained a slave for life or until he was able to repay the value of the stolen articles. Prisoners of war were always enslaved. Those of high degree were sacrificed immediately, but those of lower rank became the property of the soldier who had captured them. Slaves of this kind are represented in a mural painting from the Temple of the Warriors at Chichen Itza, where they are portrayed as naked, their bodies painted with black and white stripes.

Orphans were acquired for sacrifice either by purchase or by kidnaping. If purchased, the price of a small boy varied from five to ten stone beads. Orphans who had been brought up by rich lords were frequently sacrificed, especially if they were the children of slave women. Finally, slaves could be acquired. Landa, in enumerating the vices of the Maya, mentions "idolatries and repudiation of their wives and orgies of public drunkenness and buying and selling slaves. . . . they were accustomed to buy slaves or other beads because they were fine and good."

At the time of the Spanish Conquest, the five leading families of the Peninsula were: (1) the Xiu, or Tutul Xiu, with their capital at Mani; (2) the Cocom, with their capital at Sotuta; (3) the Canek, with their capital at Tayasal

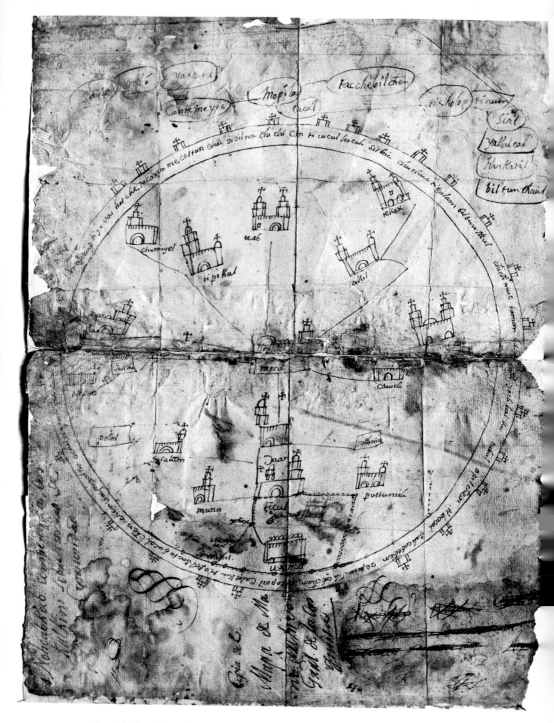

Fig. 8.4. Spanish-colonial-period map of the province of Mani, Yucatan, Mexico.

Fig. 8.5. Colonial-period genealogical tree of the Xiu lineage of Mani.

●●●
in central Peten; (4) the Chel, with their capital at Tecoh; and (5) the Pech, with their capital at Motul.

The foremost of these was the Xiu, perhaps because this family had taken the leading part in the successful revolt against Mayapan in 1441. The Peabody Museum of Archaeology and Ethnology at Harvard University holds a portfolio of 145 documents, the proofs of nobility of the Xiu family, which were accumulated during the Spanish colonial period. The three earliest—a map, a land treaty, and a genealogical tree—date from 1557, only fifteen years after the Spanish Conquest.

The map (Fig. 8.4) shows the province of the Xiu with its capital, Mani, at the center. The symbol for each town and village is a Catholic church with a tower surmounted by a cross; in the cases of the smaller villages there are only crosses. The symbol for Uxmal, which was entirely abandoned by the middle fifteenth century, is the representation of a Maya temple.

The treaty of the Maya lords, which accompanies the map and bears the same date, is the earliest known document to be written in Spanish script in the Mayan language. It describes the boundaries between the Xiu state and the adjoining provinces.

The genealogical tree (Fig. 8.5) shows Hun Uitzil Chac Tutul Xiu seated at its base, holding a fan. Because its handle terminates in the head of a serpent, the fan is thought to be a Late Postclassic form of the manikin scepter. At Hun Uitzil Chac's right side kneels his wife, Yx—— of Ticul; she points to their joint achievement—the spreading Xiu family tree. It is to be noted, however, that the tree rises from *his* loins and not from hers, a graphic insistence on patrilineal descent. The object of the tree was to claim before the Spanish Crown the descent of the Conquest-period Xiu from their purported former capital at Uxmal. For this reason the "founder" of Uxmal, Hun Uitzil Chac, appears as the progenitor of the family. The papers in the portfolio carry the Xiu story down to the time of Mexican Independence in 1821, and from living members of the family it has been possible to continue their history to the present day. The present members of the family live at Ticul, in Yucatan.

### THE POSTCLASSIC QUICHE MAYA

The Maya of the central Guatemalan highlands on the eve of the Spanish Conquest possessed an organization similar in many respects to that of Postclassic Yucatan. The best-documented Postclassic highland society is that of the Quiche Maya, who like the Yucatecans were heavily influenced by central Mexican cultures.

At the time of the Conquest, the Quiche were organized into several social classes. The *ahauab* (plural of *ahau*, or "great lord") were the nobility descended from the original, founding Quiche conquerers, who in turn claimed their origins from the mythical city of Tollan (Chapter 6). The *ahauab*—the political rulers and their officials, priests, and military leaders—lived in masonry palaces located in fortified centers, were considered sacred, and controlled most of the wealth by collection of tribute.

A less well defined middle class was composed of merchants (*ahbeyom*), professional warriors (*achij*), estate managers (*uytzam chinamital*), bureaucrats, artisans, and other specialists. The lower class consisted of commoners (*al c'ahol*), the farmers and laborers making up the bulk of the population. The commoners lived outside the fortified centers in thatched wattle-and-daub houses, were not associated with the sacred origins of the *ahauab*, and provided the food and tribute for the nobility. The *al c'ahol* worked their own land, held in common by their lineage, and lived there or on land rented from the *ahauab*. In addition, a group of landless peasants, *nimak achi*, worked in the fields owned by the nobility and were inherited along with the land. At the bottom of the social scale were the *munib*, or slaves owned by the nobility. The *munib* consisted of commoners captured in war, sentenced criminals, and impoverished individuals sold into slavery by their families. Slaves were usually sacrificed when their masters died, so that they could continue in their service.

All Quiche society, regardless of class, was based on patrilineal descent groups, that is, lineages in which children belonged to the same group as their father. Marriage was exogamous, so that an individual married outside his or her patrilineage. The *ahauab* of Utatlan, the most important Quiche center, were organized into 24 lineages at the time of the Spanish Conquest, each a branch of the four original patrilineal descent groups: the Cawek (9 lineages), Nihaib (9 lineages), Ahau Quiche (4 lineages), and Sakic (2 lineages). The *ahauab* lineages held rights over one or more *chinamits*, the territorial and residential units consisting of the principal administrative structure, or "big house" (*nimha*), parcels of land, and their *nimak achi* and resident *al c'ahol*, in common. The *chinamits* constituted the basis of the organization that bound Quiche society together.

Each *ahauab* lineage was associated with specific political, military, or religious offices. One lineage, with the Mexican name Yagui Winak, furnished many of the priestly offices. Priests (*chalamicat*) were highly esteemed, although they held little secular power. Their chief duties, apart from conducting the specialized and often bloody sacrificial rituals, lay in their role as caretakers of the sacred codices that recorded the ritual calendar and divination tables.

The head of each noble lineage occupied the principal office of that lineage, holding the ultimate authority over its members. At the same time, the *ahauab* lineage heads, together with other specialists including several high priests, formed a council that advised the ruler and helped formulate policy for all Quiche society. Thus a noble lineage head functioned in two capacities: as leader of his kinsmen, and as part of the highest-ranking body of state officials.

But the *ahauab* lineages were not all of equal status, for they were ranked according to differing degrees of authority and prestige. At Utatlan, it appears that three descent groups held a higher status, the Cawek, Nihaib, and Ahau

• • •
Quiche. Each seems to have been associated with one of the Quiche deities. The Cawek patron was Tohil, the male sun deity. The Nihaib patron was Awilix, the female moon deity. The Ahau Quiche patron was Jakawitz, the male sky deity. The heads of each held the most powerful offices. The *ahpop* ("lord of the mat") was head of the Cawek and, at the time of the Conquest, supreme ruler of Utatlan and all Quiche society. Besides possessing the power to make political appointments and leading the religious rituals held for the well-being of the population, he was the head of the army and the most important speaker in the ruling council. The *ahpop* was a hereditary office, usually succeeded to by whichever son of the ruler held the office of *nima rahpop achij* ("great military captain"). Another Cawek official, the *ahpop c'amha* ("he of the mat of the receiving house"), was an assistant to the ruler. As his title suggests, the *ahpop c'amha* received visiting officials in the name of the ruler, and may have acted as interim ruler upon the death of the *ahpop* until the new ruler took office. According to the *Popol Vuh*, there were a total of nine Cawek offices, one for the headman of each Cawek lineage.

The other high officials were the *k'alel* ("courtier"), head of the Nahaib, who acted as a judge and counselor, and the *atzij winak* ("speaker"), head of the Ahau Quiche. There were nine Nahaib offices, four Ahau Quiche offices, and two Sakic offices, again, one for the head of each constituent lineage.

In addition to Utatlan, there were two adjacent Quiche centers (Chisalin and Ismachi), each with its own ruling noble lineages and populations organized according to social classes. Owing to marriage alliances with these lineages and the military supremacy exercised by the *ahpop* in Utatlan, Quiche society functioned as a fairly unified kingdom at the time of the Spanish Conquest. Yet Quiche society had a built-in structural weakness, in that it was possible for another lineage and its leader to gain the military strength to challenge the power of the *ahpop*. This indeed happened on several occasions, and culminated in the revolt of the Cakchiquel and their subsequent establishment of an independent state centered at Iximche (see Chapter 6).

At the time of the Conquest, the Maya highlands were occupied by a series of other Maya groups who appear to have been organized in a manner similar to that of the Quiche. Some of these peoples, such as those in the neighboring Cakchiquel and Tzutuhil, were often at war with the Quiche. Although the Quiche were able to expand their authority to the north and to both the east and west of Utatlan, extending their power over the Mam of Zaculeu and others, the Cakchiquel successfully resisted Quiche attempts at conquest. Despite these hostilities, Utatlan maintained mutual relationships with its neighbors through peaceful commerce, religious pilgrimages, gift exchanges, and marriage alliances among the nobility. Thus, though far from politically unified, the Postclassic Maya highlands were tied together by economic, religious, and kinship bonds.

**∴**

## Reconstructing the Organization of Society

A variety of schemes has been presented to describe ancient Maya social and political organization. A review of several of these will convey a synopsis of our present understanding of ancient Maya society.

### MODELS OF SOCIAL ORGANIZATION

It is possible to discern three general models when seeking to reconstruct ancient Maya society. Each of these schemes represents a position about one of the most enduring questions in Maya studies, namely, the organization and function of Maya centers.

At the simplest level Maya society can be modeled as basically egalitarian. According to this view the Maya centers were temple complexes without significant numbers of permanent residents. Although the idea of vacant ceremonial centers has a long history, its most thorough documentation comes by way of ethnographical studies of the organization of contemporary Maya communities in the Chiapas highlands. The community of Zinacantan, for instance, is organized around an egalitarian *cargo* system, whereby the positions of political and religious authority are held for one-year terms by male officeholders who rotate from one position to another. By taking office once every few years, each individual advances in the community hierarchy with age, so that the positions of highest authority are held by the elders of society. In such a system all levels of power are shared and there is no permanent ruling class. To apply this system to the ancient Maya, one has to assume that the male occupants of outlying residential clusters held the political and religious offices in the centers for predetermined periods, then returned to their homes and fields to await the next call to serve the community. However, the archaeological data are too laden with evidence of differences in wealth and status, as well as indications of sizable and permanent occupation within the centers, to lend much support to the egalitarian model, except perhaps for the lower eschelons of authority.

The archaeological evidence is in better accord with non-egalitarian descriptions. One of the most popular schemes in this category is the "two-class model" of ancient Maya society, which is basically in accord with the foregoing descriptions of Postclassic Yucatan. By this view, the outlying residential clusters were settled by peasant agriculturists, while the centers were occupied by a small but permanent class of priestly rulers along with their servants and retainers. The peasantry supported the ruling class by providing labor for the construction and maintenance of the temples, palaces, and other facilities in the centers and by supplying food, goods, and services. In return, the ruling class provided for the peasantry leadership, direction, and security derived from their

●●●
‒‒‒

knowledge of calendrics and supernatural prophecy. This knowledge allowed the rulers to determine the proper times to plant and harvest crops, thus ensuring agricultural success for the common good of society. In this view, the Maya centers, though not vacant, could not be likened to anything approaching cities; rather they were often termed "ceremonial centers," whose function was primarily that of providing a religious focus for the surrounding and dispersed peasantry. Overall, this position models Maya society as a theocracy, ruled by a peaceful and intellectual class of priest-rulers.

More recently, the vast accumulation of archaeological evidence indicating that ancient Maya society was far more complex than called for in the two-class model has resulted in the emergence of a third description of Maya society. This view, which might be termed the "multiclass model," portrays the Maya centers as having once been populated by concentrations of non-agricultural specialists representing many occupational groups and social classes and by large numbers of outlying agriculturists. In this sense, the Maya centers are considered to have functioned as cities, albeit not marked by the degree of population concentration typical of the urbanism in central Mexico or common in Western civilization. Nonetheless, by this model the Maya centers, occupied by far more than the ruling classes, thus performed far more functions than called for in the previous schemes. Maya society can then be seen as having been composed of at least three major classes: a ruling elite, the commoners, and an emerging middle class. It is probable that further class distinctions existed within each of these basic levels. The commoners inhabited the most humble dwellings, generally located on the peripheries of the centers (except, perhaps, for the service personnel needed by the ruling class), and the group probably included servants, bearers, and maintenance workers, in addition to full-time agriculturists. A middle class composed of such full-time occupational groups as bureaucrats, merchants, warriors, craftsmen, architects, and artists probably lived closer to the civic and religious core. This core was inhabited by the ruling class: the ruler, his family, and other members of the nobility that presumably held the major positions in the political, religious, and economic institutions.

Using the multiclass model as the best current description of ancient Maya, although the details are still only beginning to be fleshed out by continued research, we can sketch a picture of Classic Maya society on the basis of the available archaeological and ethnohistorical data. Not surprisingly, areas of disagreement continue to plague Maya scholars, so that any treatment of this subject must be considered provisional.

As in most human societies, the nuclear family most likely formed the elementary organization for the ancient Maya. This assumption is supported by the archaeological evidence we have reviewed, including the prevalence of residential structures of a size suitable to house a single married couple and their children. The same conclusion may be drawn from the ethnohistorical record; indeed, contemporary Maya societies invariably are built around the nuclear family. In this kind of family organization today, the father or eldest male member is the authority figure for the family, and the same can be assumed for the past. This does not mean that women are or were without status in Maya society; in fact, the domestic authority of the mother or eldest female member of the family is an important factor in the Maya social system today. Both the male and female lines of descent were apparently considered important in ancient Maya society.

Larger kin groups were based on the nuclear family. We have reviewed the archaeological and ethnohistorical evidence that argues both for the presence of extended-family residential groups and for the existence of lineages in ancient Maya society. The bulk of the evidence indicates that these kin groups were linked by the patrilineal principle of descent through the male line. Other evidence suggests that there was also a complementary matrilineal principle, although the role of the female lineage in Maya society is not yet clearly understood. We have noted that patrilineal descent groups, important in Post-classic times in both Yucatan and highland Guatemala, remain discernible in many contemporary Maya communities. Corporate groups defined by patrilineal descent (patrilineages) were strongly developed by the Quiche Maya, for instance, and are still found in several highland areas, most notably in Chiapas. If patrilineal descent is combined with patrilocal residence (married sons continuing to reside near their father), then the lineage becomes a residential group. That is, the patrilineage maintains its residential integrity. This may have happened in ancient times, so that the residential clusters seen at many Maya sites could represent discrete patrilineages.

## FACTORS OF ECONOMIC AND POLITICAL ORGANIZATION

Patrilineages may also exist without providing the basis for residential groupings; other functions may include agricultural landholding and the maintenance of ancestral cults. Thus, the ancient Maya residential clusters might have been occupied by groups defined according to other criteria, such as feudal obligations or occupational specialties. It is likely that, given the acknowledged complexity of Classic Maya society, no single organizing principle formed the basis of all residential groups. We think that patrilineal residential groups were commonplace at one time, perhaps in the Preclassic period. But since Maya society was not egalitarian, and became increasingly stratified into a series of social classes, the traditional residential kin groups might have been weakened.

As the class distinctions between the nobility and commoners strengthened, the ruling classes would likely have encouraged means to make the peasantry increasingly obligated to, and dependent upon, the elite classes. This is because the nobility required the services of the peasantry as a source for labor, tribute, and even military forces. The relationship could have been sealed through a feudal organization with religious sanctions, as in an estate system. Under this system each noble lineage might have held the agricultural lands, protected the vassals that worked the land, and granted enough land for each vassal family to support itself, apportioning the rest of the produce to itself. In addition to growing crops, the vassals would have been obliged to serve their lord with labor and military service. In times of obvious insecurity—and there is evidence of raiding, military fortifications, and the like in the Classic period—the protection of a powerful noble lineage would have been of great advantage to the agricultural peasant. Thus, at least some of the Classic Maya residential clusters might be interpreted as feudal estates. With this kind of system the largest and most elaborate residential group might have housed the landholding noble lineage, the largest residence being that of the lord and the others being those of his kinsmen (sons, younger brothers, and so forth). The lesser groups within the cluster might have housed the extended families of the vassals.

The feudal-estate model would complement some of the interpretations already made from excavated residential clusters. At Tikal, for instance, William Haviland has interpreted the 7F-1 group (see Fig. 11.6) as including the "dower house" of a noble family "out of power" at that center, along with the family's retainers. The dower house could be the main house of a feudal estate, the smaller adjacent residences those of the vassals. The feudal-estate construct might also be applied to the large agricultural plantations established in outlying areas by the Classic Maya. The ridged-field plantations newly discovered in northern Belize and Quintana Roo (see Chapter 7) may have been run as feudal estates by the noble lineages at established Maya centers. Newly colonized areas such as the lower Motagua and Copan valleys may have been established by imposing this organization upon the indigenous inhabitants, much as the colonizing Quiche Maya seem to have done in the highlands during the Postclassic. Not only would such a system have facilitated control over these rich agricultural regions, it would have provided an "outlet" for the younger members of the growing noble lineages from Tikal and the other Maya centers. In this way the younger brothers and sons of the noble houses could have founded their own estates in "frontier" areas.

Another factor that could have weakened residential kin groups was the emergence of occupational specialization. As specialized occupational groups became more common, they undoubtedly would have formed guilds for the promotion and protection of their own interests. It is quite possible, given some archaeological evidence of this nature, that occupational guilds formed residential groups. And, of course, some lineages may have specialized in certain crafts. In addition, occupational groups such as warriors, merchants, and artisans apparently formed the nucleus of a middle class by Classic times. This class had fewer obligations to the nobility and, as in other feudal societies, may have ultimately weakened the power of the traditional ruling class.

A feudal system tends to produce a decentralized political system, for each noble lineage controls its own land and resident vassals, from which it exacts tribute, labor, and armies. Yet the archaeological evidence, including dynastic monuments and huge centralized palace complexes epitomized at Classic Tikal, demonstrates that primary Maya centers were dominated by strong centralized political authorities. Maya society must have been ruled by lords who held unique and supreme powers, men who were in a sense "kings." Thus, a feudal-like organization among the Classic Maya must have been counteracted or controlled to a significant degree by a centralized source of power. The rulers must have had a means of controlling the nobility. Possibly the nobles were vassals of the rulers, in a hierarchy of obligations like that in medieval Europe.

Countering this speculation, the ethnohistorical evidence from such groups as the Postclassic Quiche indicates that the ruler held power mostly by virtue of being the headman of the most prestigious lineage. This prestige was based on supernatural associations and on an ancestral heritage proclaimed by recorded accomplishments and by military leadership and success. The Quiche case also shows the political instability of such a system, for one ruling lineage could lose its supremacy and be replaced by another.

Perhaps each Classic Maya center was dominated by several noble lineages, each jockeying for the prestige that would yield to its leaders the supreme power. Certainly the Classic Maya monuments include proclamations of individual rulers' accomplishments and their rights to rule by virtue of their prestigious ancestry, but it is perhaps misleading to overemphasize the instability of the ancient Maya political system. The Postclassic situation cannot guide all our understanding of earlier society. The Classic Maya did not seem to stress military accomplishment as much as did the later Quiche. Furthermore, the Classic inscriptions indicate that most Maya centers were ruled by successive members of a single lineage, for example, the dynasties of Tikal and Yaxchilan.

The establishment of reasonably permanent ruling lineages was probably a developmental step of considerable significance to the Classic Maya. The political stability fostered by this development would have put these centers at an advantage over those ruled by competing local lineages. Alliances forged between ruling dynasties, often sealed by marriage exchanges, were undoubtedly important contributors to political stability. The earliest known stelae associated with dynastic inscriptions suggest that Tikal was the first lowland Classic center to develop this more stable, centralized political organization (Chapter 4). Clemency Coggins further proposes that this innovation was introduced from outside, probably ultimately from highland Mexico, where the earliest Mesoamerican centralized political institutions were formed, at about the time of the rule of Curl Nose and his successor, Stormy Sky, from around A.D. 378-455. As we have seen (Chapter 3), however, the origins of dynastic rule may have been far earlier, at Kaminaljuyu, Abaj Takalik, and other southern Maya sites. These southern centers preserved sculptured stelae, dating to the end of the Preclassic era, that seem to be prototypes for the later Classic-period dynastic monuments of the lowlands, long before any contacts with Teotihuacan.

•••
¯¯¯

In the lowlands, the period around 455–682 seems to have been politically unstable, marked possibly by the lack of a uniform succession rule and perhaps by episodes of dual rulership. It is during this period that dynastic rule seems to have been established at many other Maya centers. Some of these, like Quirigua and Copan, may have been founded as colonies of larger centers in the central lowlands. Palenque, under the leadership of Pacal, saw its power and prosperity rise dramatically during this era. And at Tikal, not until another outstanding leader, Ah Cacau (a probable descendant of Stormy Sky) came to power in 682 did strong, centralized political authority and economic prosperity return. The Tikal example is the best available case to illustrate the struggle between centralized dynastic rule and the dispersed power of a feudal system. But similar tensions, owing to a variety of causes, may have typified the political systems of all Classic Maya centers.

The obvious differences in size and complexity between Maya centers indicate that certain centers exerted considerably more power than others. The ebb and flow of confederacies, composed of temporarily allied centers, seems to have characterized Classic Maya political history. And the archaeological record contains evidence of competition and conflict. Yet, it must be reemphasized that there is little or no basis for supposing that a permanent political organization existed above the level of the largest centers. Although some centers under the leadership of outstanding rulers underwent periods of expansion and prosperity, none succeeded in unifying the vast Maya area under a single political power. Following Thomas Barthel's thesis of a quadripartite organization based on the cardinal directions, Joyce Marcus has suggested that the distribution of emblem glyphs reflects regional political realms. From this, she has proposed that there were four primary Maya centers that enjoyed ideological, if not political, superiority throughout the Classic period and beyond. Just which centers were the primary ones in a particular period was affected by shifting fortunes, but during most of the Classic period they were Tikal, Calakmul (?), Palenque, and Copan. These centers enjoyed ideological and ceremonial prestige, as well as economic advantage, but probably not political dominance.

# 9

# EVERYDAY LIFE

The Yucatecans are very liberal and hospitable, since no one enters their houses
without their offering him food and drink.
—Landa's *Relación de las cosas de Yucatán* (Tozzer 1941: 98)

The best sources of information about everyday life among the ancient Maya
are the descriptions of sixteenth-century Maya society written immediately after
the Spanish Conquest. These accounts are often usefully supplemented by
archaeological discoveries, as well as ethnographical descriptions of customs
surviving from the past and still practiced today.

## Birth and Early Childhood

The life cycle and behavior of each individual in ancient times were set by
custom and governed by religious beliefs, much as they are today among
traditional Maya families. The ritual obligations of each individual were determined by the 260-day sacred almanac (Chapter 16). The date of birth according to this almanac controlled a person's temperament and destiny, because it
determined which gods were well disposed and which hostile. Among many
highland Maya peoples, such as the Cakchiquel, all given names were fixed
automatically, since they were the same as the day of birth. This practice, if ever
present among the Yucatec Maya, had disappeared in the northern area by the
time of the Spanish Conquest.

The Maya of today love their children deeply and usually treat them with a
great deal of indulgence. The same was undoubtedly true in ancient times.
Children were greatly desired and the women even "asked them of the idols
with gifts and prayers." In order to induce pregnancy, a woman placed under
her bed an image of Ix Chel, goddess of childbirth.

Depressed foreheads were considered a mark of beauty among the ancient
Maya, and this deformation was achieved by binding the heads of babies
between a pair of flat boards, one at the back of the head, the other against the

•••• forehead. These boards were left in place for several days, after which the head
▬▬ remained flattened for life. Maya representations of the human head in profile
show that this practice must have been almost universal, at least among the
upper class.

Another mark of distinction was crossed eyes, which mothers tried to bring
about by hanging little balls of resin to the hairs falling between their children's
eyes. Persistent focusing on these pellets tended to cross their eyes. The ears,
lips, and septum of the nose were pierced to hold ornaments.

A ceremony performed among the modern Maya of Yucatan that may have
survived from ancient times is the *hetzmek*, when the baby is carried astride the
hip for the first time. This is done at three months old for a girl, and at four
months for a boy. The difference in time is said to be because the Maya hearth,
symbolic of woman's activities in the home, has three stones; and the maize
field, symbolic of man's activities in the field, has four corners.

Usually two godparents participate in this ceremony, a husband and wife. If
there is only one, it is a man for a boy and a woman for a girl. Nine objects,
symbolic of what the child will use in later life, are placed on a table. The father
hands the baby to the godfather, who sets the child astride his left hip and
makes nine circuits of the table, each time selecting one of the nine objects and
putting it into the child's hand, reciting instruction in the object's use. He then
turns the child over to the godmother, who repeats the procedure. The child is
then given back to the godfather, and then back to the father, while the
godfather says, "We have made the *hetzmek* for your child." The parents kneel
before the godparents in a sign of gratitude, and an assistant distributes food,
rum, boiled fowls, and tortillas to those present.

In ancient times the young child was carried to a priest, who performed a
divining ceremony and determined the childhood name. The ancient Maya had
three or four different names: (1) *paal kaba*, the given name; (2) the father's
family name; (3) *naal kaba*, the father's and mother's family names combined;
and (4) *coco kaba*, the nickname.

Until the age of three or four, children were brought up by their mothers.
When a boy was about four or five, a small white bead was fastened to the hair
on the top of his head. When a girl reached the same age, a string was tied
around her waist, from which hung a red shell as a symbol of virginity. To
remove either of these before the puberty ceremony was thought to be highly
dishonorable.

## Puberty

According to Bishop Landa, the day for the puberty ceremony was carefully
selected; pains were taken to ascertain that it would not be an unlucky day. A
principal man of the town was chosen as sponsor for the children participating;

his duty was to assist the priest during the ceremony and to furnish the feast. Four honorable old men were selected as *chacs*, to assist the priest and sponsor in conducting the ceremony. On the appointed day, all assembled at the sponsor's house in the court, which had been newly swept and strewn with fresh leaves. An old man was assigned to act as godfather for the boys, and an old woman as godmother for the girls. Then the priest purified the dwelling and conducted a ceremony to expel the evil spirit.

When the spirit had been expelled, the court was swept out again, fresh leaves were strewn about, and mats were spread on the floor. The priest exchanged his vestments for a handsome jacket and a miter-like headdress of colored feathers, taking in his hand a finely worked short stick with rattlesnake tails hanging from it for sprinkling sacred water. The *chacs* approached the children and placed on their heads pieces of white cloth, which their mothers had brought for this purpose. The older children were asked if they had committed any sin or obscene act. If they had, they were separated from the others (Landa does not say whether they were refused permission to participate further in the rite). This concluded, the priest ordered everyone to be seated and to preserve absolute silence, and after pronouncing a prayer for the children, he sat down. The sponsor of the ceremony, with a bone given him by the priest, tapped each child nine times on the forehead, moistening the forehead, the face, and the spaces between the fingers and toes with water.

After this anointing, the priest removed the white cloths from the children's heads. The children then gave the *chacs* feathers and cacao beans that they had brought as gifts. The priest next cut the white beads from the boys' heads. The attendants carried pipes, which they smoked from time to time, giving each child a puff of smoke. Gifts of food, brought by the mothers, were distributed to the children, and a wine offering was made to the gods; this wine had to be drunk at one draught by a specially appointed official.

The girls were then dismissed, each mother removing from her daughter the red shell she had worn as a symbol of purity. With this, the young woman was considered to have reached a marriageable age. The young men were dismissed next. When the youths had withdrawn from the court, their parents distributed among the spectators and officials pieces of cotton cloth that they had brought as gifts. The ceremony closed with feasting and heavy drinking; called "the descent of the gods," it is much more likely to have been a puberty ceremony than the baptismal rite Landa called it.

As they grew older, young unmarried men of the community began to live in a house set apart for them. They gathered there for their diversions and usually slept there until marriage. They painted themselves black until they were married, but were not supposed to tattoo themselves before that time. The youths were constantly with their fathers and at an early age accompanied them to work in the family maize field. Wrote Landa, "In all other things they always accompanied their fathers, and thus they became as great idolators as they, and served them very well in their labors."

After the puberty ceremony, the young women, in preparation for marriage, were taught to be modest: whenever they met a man they turned their backs to him, stepping aside to allow him to pass; when giving a man a drink of water, they lowered their eyes. Mothers taught their daughters how to make tortillas, an occupation that consumed a great part of every woman's time. The women were the housekeepers, cooks, weavers, and spinners. They raised fowl and went to market to buy and sell the articles they produced. When need arose, they carried burdens alongside their menfolk and assisted them in sowing and cultivating.

## Marriage

Bishop Landa says that formerly the Maya married when they were 20 years old, but that in his time they married when they were 12 or 14. In the eighteenth and early nineteenth centuries young men of the Yucatan married at about 17 or 18, and young women at about 14 or 15. Today in the villages of the northern peninsula the average age of the men at marriage is 21, and that of the women nearly 17.

The fathers took great care to find suitable wives for their sons, preferably young women of the same social class and of the same village. Certain relationship taboos existed. It was considered incestuous to marry a girl who had the same surname, or for a widower to marry his stepmother, the sister of his deceased wife, the widow of his brother, or his maternal aunt, though first-cousin marriages were not forbidden.

It was thought to be mean-spirited for a man to seek a mate for himself or for his children personally, instead of employing the services of a professional matchmaker (*ah atanzahob*). This custom has survived in rural districts in northern Yucatan. The matchmaker having been selected, the ceremony was discussed and the amount of the dowry agreed upon. This usually consisted of dresses and other articles of little value, for which the young man's father paid. His mother at the same time made clothing ready for her son and prospective daughter-in-law. Today, in northern Yucatan, the groom or his family defrays all expenses of the wedding, even including the bride's trousseau. This is true of all classes of society from the most aristocratic *hacendado* (plantation owner) to the humblest laborer.

When the day of the ceremony arrived, the relatives and guests assembled at the house of the bride's father. As soon as the priest entered the house, the fathers of the couple presented the young people to him. The priest made a speech setting forth the details of the marriage agreement, after which he perfumed the house and blessed the bridal pair, and the company sat down to the feast that concluded the ceremony. From this time forward the young couple were allowed to live together, and the son-in-law lived and worked in the house of his wife's parents for six or seven years. His mother-in-law saw to it that her daughter gave the young husband food and drink as a token of the parental recognition of the marriage, but if the young man failed to work for the appointed time, he could be put out of the house.

Marriages were often arranged between families while the boy and girl were still very young; the arrangement was then carried out when they came of age. Widows and widowers remarried without ceremony; the man simply went to the house of the woman of his choice, and if she accepted him, she gave him something to eat. Custom decreed that widowers and widows should remain single for at least a year after the death of their previous mates.

Although the Maya were monogamous, divorce was easy, consisting of little more than a simple repudiation. It was a common occurrence, as an early Spanish witness indicates: "They did not have marital relations with more than one woman [at a time], but they left her for trifling reasons, and married another, and there were men who married ten and twelve times; and the women had the same liberty to leave their husbands and take another, but the first time they got married it was by a priest." And Landa says, "And on this account they repudiate more easily, since they marry without love and ignorant of married life and of the duties of married people."

## Clothing and Appearance

The principal garment of the men was the loincloth, called *ex* in Mayan. It was a band of cotton cloth, five fingers wide and long enough to be wound around the waist several times and passed between the legs. These loincloths were woven on hand looms, and the ends were often elaborately embroidered with feathers: "They wore the *mastil* [probably a corruption of *maxtli*, the Mexica word for the same garment] between their legs, which was a large strip of woven *manta*, which, tying it on the abdomen and giving it a turn below, covered their private parts, the two long points having on them much plumage hanging before and behind." The *ex* is represented everywhere in Maya graphic arts, from the gorgeously decorated loincloths worn by the rulers, priests, and nobles to the simple, unadorned versions of the lower classes (Fig. 9.1).

In addition to the *ex*, the men sometimes wore a large square cotton cloth called the *pati*, knotted around the shoulders. More or less elaborately decorated according to the station of the wearer, this garment also served the poor as a covering for their beds at night.

Sandals made of untanned deer hide and tied with hemp cords completed the costume of the common people. On sculptured monuments of the Classic period, the sandals shown are exceedingly elaborate. One important difference may be noted between representations of ancient Maya sandals and the sandals now in use (Fig. 9.2): in ancient times they were bound to the feet by two

Fig. 9.1. Examples of Maya loincloths, or *ex*, from Classic-period monuments.

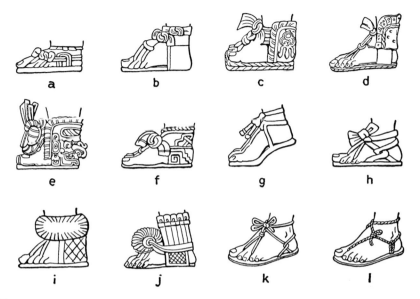

Fig. 9.2. Maya sandals, or *xanab*: (*a–f*) from Classic-period monuments; (*g–j*) from Postclassic-period monuments; (*k*) ancient method of fastening sandals with two cords; (*l*) modern method of fastening sandals with one cord.

thongs, one passing between the first and second toes, the other between the third and fourth toes (Fig. 9.2*k*); today, from the highlands of Guatemala to northern Yucatan, only the first of these thongs is still used (Fig. 9.2*l*).

Except for a bare spot burned on the top of the head, the men wore their hair long. The hair was braided and wound around the head like a coronet, except for a queue that fell behind. Warriors painted themselves black and red, prisoners were painted in black and white stripes, and the priests were painted blue. In preparation for one of the most important ceremonies of the year, the celebrants painted with a blue pigment everything from the utensils of the priests down to the spindles with which the women wove. The priests and sacrificial victim depicted in a fresco from the Temple of the Warriors at Chichen Itza are painted blue from head to foot (Fig. 14.1*f*). Many of the balls of *pom* incense found in the Cenote of Sacrifice at Chichen Itza were also painted a bright turquoise blue. Blue was the color associated with sacrifice among the late Postclassic Maya just as it was among the Mexicans, from whom they may have derived this association.

Paint was also used in tattooing: "Those who do the work, first painted the part which they wish with color, and afterwards they delicately cut in the paintings, and so with blood and coloring-matter the marks remained on the body. This work is done a little at a time on account of the extreme pain, and afterwards also they were quite sick with it, since the designs festered and matter formed. In spite of all this they made fun of those who were not tattooed."

Several accounts of the principal garment worn by Maya women have come down to us. Landa's account says, "The women of the coast and of the Provinces of Bacalar and of Campeche are more modest in their dress, for, besides the covering which they wore from the waist down [a kind of skirt], they covered their breasts, tying a folded *manta* [*pati*] underneath their armpits. All the others did not wear more than one garment like a long and wide sack, opened on both sides, and drawn in as far as the hips, where they fastened it together, with the same width as before." The official Spanish historian Herrera writes, "They wore a dress like a sack, long and wide, open on both sides and sewn as far as the hips." A third early source states, "The Mayan women wore their kind of petticoats, which is like a sack open at both sides, and these, tied at the waist, covered their private parts." A cotton kerchief was worn over the head, "open like a short cowl, which also served to cover their breasts."

Although none of these descriptions is complete, together they give a fair idea of the costume of contemporary Maya women (Fig. 9.3). Today this garment is known as the *huipil*, a Mexica (Nahuatl) word. In the highlands of Guatemala the *huipil* is a blouse, worn with a wraparound skirt. In the Yucatan the *huipil* is a white, loose-fitting cotton dress, of the same width from top to bottom and sewn at the sides, with holes for the arms and a square opening for the head. The armholes, neck opening, and bottom of the garment are beautifully embroidered in cross-stitch. This garment, with its unusual embroidery, almost certainly survives from ancient times (Fig. 9.3, lower illustrations).

Underneath is worn a very full, long petticoat (Maya, *pic*), which hangs below the *huipil*. This is sometimes embroidered around the bottom, always in white. A Maya woman never leaves her house without her rebozo (Maya, *booch*), a scarf she wears draped around her neck or thrown over her head; this may be a survival of the cotton kerchief mentioned above. Today, slippers of European style are worn by the women, but formerly they no doubt used sandals for festive occasions, going barefoot the rest of the time.

Women and girls wore their hair long and took great care of it. The hair was arranged in various ways, the style for married women differing from that for the young girls. The women, like their husbands, anointed themselves with a sweet-smelling red ointment, the odor of which lasted for many days. They tattooed themselves from the waists up, except for their breasts, with designs more delicate than those tattooed on the men.

Much could be written about the dress of the rulers, nobility, and priesthood, drawing from the material in the sculptures, frescoes, and vase paintings. The robes of the *halach uinic*, the festive and war apparel of the nobility, and the insignia and vestments of the priesthood were of great splendor. Yet these

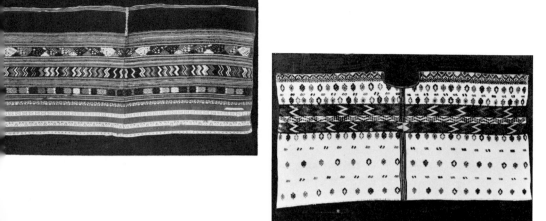

Fig. 9.3. Modern Maya huipils: (*upper left*) from Comalpa, Guatemala; (*upper right*) from San Pedro Sacatepequez, Guatemala; (*lower left*) from Tixcacal, Quintana Roo, Mexico; (*lower right*) from Mérida, Yucatan, Mexico.

•••• articles of dress, though elaborately decorated, were basically the same as the garments of the common man—loincloth, cape, and sandals, with the addition of a headdress.

The loincloths of the upper classes portrayed in the sculptures are of great intricacy. The ends are richly worked with feathers, and the part around the waist is heavily encrusted with ornaments. The simple square cotton *pati* of the common man becomes a magnificent cape of embroidered cotton stuff, jaguar skin, or even brilliantly colored feathers. The beautiful, iridescent tail feathers of the quetzal seem to have been reserved for the nobility. Sandals, too, became increasingly elaborate as the wearer rose on the social scale; those of rulers, as represented on Classic-period monuments, are extremely ornate.

It was in the headdresses, however, that the greatest magnificence was displayed. The framework was probably of wicker or wood, carved to represent the head of a jaguar, serpent, or bird, or even one of the Maya gods. These frames were covered with jaguar skin, feather mosaic, and carved jades, and were surmounted by lofty panaches of plumes, sometimes in the form of a stiffly feathered crest. Always the most striking part of the costume, the panache indicated the rank and social class of the wearer.

Costume accessories consisted of collars, necklaces, wristlets, anklets, and knee bands. They were made of feathers, jade beads, shells, jaguar teeth and claws, crocodile teeth, or in later times gold and copper. Other kinds of jewelry were nose ornaments, earrings, and lip plugs of jade, stone, obsidian, and less valuable materials. Ornaments of the lower classes were confined largely to simple nose plugs, lip plugs, and earrings of bone, wood, shell, or stone.

## The Round of Daily Life

The daily preparation of corn for household use is a major activity of Maya women, and doubtless was so in the past. This household duty may be divided into five steps:

1. The dried, shelled corn is put into an olla (Maya, *cum*), or cooking pot, with sufficient water and lime to soften the kernels. The mixture is brought nearly to the boiling point and kept at this temperature until the hull is softened, being stirred occasionally. The olla is then set aside and allowed to stand until the following morning. This softened corn is called *kuum* in Yucatec Maya.

2. Sometime after breakfast the next morning, the *kuum* is washed until it is perfectly clean and free of hulls.

3. The *kuum* is then ground. In ancient times this was done by hand with the mano and metate, but today hand-operated metal mills have generally replaced them. The ground corn (Maya, *zacan*) is covered with a cloth and allowed to stand until later in the morning.

4. About an hour before the main meal of the day, which takes place in the

early afternoon, a small round table about 40 cm high (15 in.) is washed. This
table always stands near the *koben*, the typical Maya three-stone hearth. Next, a
round griddle (*xamach*) is also wiped clean, placed on the hearth, and allowed
to heat. A section of plantain leaf (*u lee haas*), roughly 15 cm square (6 in.), is
heated on the *xamach* until it becomes soft and pliant; it is then placed on the
table with a pinch of ashes underneath to make it turn easily on the low table.
After these preliminary preparations the Maya woman is ready to make her
tortillas (*uah*).

5. She pinches off a lump of *zacan* about the size of a hen's egg and places it
on the piece of plantain leaf. The left hand forms the edge of the tortilla, and
the right flattens the lump of *zacan* while giving it a rotary motion on the table.
A round, thin, flat cake rapidly takes form under her fingers. The almost
continuous pats produce a characteristic sound, heard throughout all Maya
villages at midday. When shaped, the tortilla is laid on the heated *xamach* to
bake. It is next placed on the hot fagots of wood below the *xamach* until it
puffs out, when the woman picks it up and flattens it again with a blow on the
table. Finally, the tortilla is placed in a gourd (*lec*) to keep it hot; the average
Maya man eats nearly twenty at one meal, and demands that they be piping
hot.

A sixteenth-century account of the eating habits of the ancient Maya has the
following to say:

As to the meals which they ate in the time of their antiquity, they eat the same today.
This is corn boiled in water and crushed. When made into dough, they dissolve it in
water for a drink [posol], and this is what they ordinarily drink and eat. An hour
before sunset it was their custom to make certain tortillas of the said dough. On these
they supped, dipping them into certain dishes of crushed peppers, diluted with a
little water and salt. Alternately with this they ate certain boiled beans of the land,
which are black. They call them buul, and the Spanish, frijoles. This was the only
time they ate during the day, for at other times they drank the dissolved dough
mentioned above.

The principal difference between ancient and modern Maya eating habits appears to be the hour for the main meal of the day. Formerly, to judge from this
account, it was in the late afternoon, "an hour before sunset." There is also
evidence that before the Conquest, tamales, or *zacan* wrapped in corn leaves
and boiled in water, were more typical fare in the Maya area than tortillas,
which appear to have a Mexican origin. Still common in the Maya highlands,
tamales are especially favored for ceremonial meals.

Maya men and women even today do not eat together. The men of the
family eat first, and afterward the women and girls have their meal. The
tortillas eaten at breakfast are those left over from the day before, but toasted
crisp for the morning's meal. The fresh tortillas are not ready until the main
meal of the day.

The men leave for the maize fields between four and five o'clock in the morning, after which the women turn to their principal task of the forenoon—preparing the *zacan* and making tortillas. Spare time is devoted to other household duties.

For refreshment before his return to the house, the man working in the maize fields takes with him a lump of posol (or pozole) wrapped in a piece of plantain leaf. About ten, the man stops work for a few minutes to mix a lump of posol in a half-gourd cup filled with water; the resulting drink looks like milk. If he works until two or three in the afternoon, he may drink posol two or three times.

The men return from the fields in the early afternoon, and eat their main meal—fresh tortillas, beans, eggs, a little meat if it is available, and perhaps a few vegetables and chocolate if the family can afford it. After this meal the man takes his daily bath. Bathed and dressed, the men sit around talking until the evening meal, which is light—tortillas, beans, and chocolate or atole, a hot drink made by mixing *zacan* with water, sometimes sweetened with honey.

The family retires by eight or nine o'clock unless some special business is afoot. Everybody sleeps in one room, in modern times in hammocks but formerly on low platforms of poles. Landa wrote, in this connection:

And then they build a wall in the middle dividing the house lengthwise, and in this wall they leave several doors into the half which they call the back of the house, where they have their beds, and the other half they whitened very nicely with lime [this outer room would seem to have been a sort of porch open at the front and sides] . . . and they have beds made of small rods [saplings] and on the top a mat on which they sleep, covering themselves with their mantas [*patis*] of cotton. In summer they usually sleep in the whitened part of the house [the porch], on one of those mats, especially the men.

A seventeenth-century writer described a bed, in a house in the lowlands of the Río Usumacinta, that was made of a crude wooden framework sufficiently large to hold four persons; and an eighteenth-century writer reported of the Yucatan Maya, "His bed is the floor, or a framework of boards, supported by four sticks."

Today the Maya in lowland regions, and most of the mestizos, sleep in hammocks. The hammock was probably imported by the Spaniards from the Caribbean region. It seems almost certain that had they been in general use at the time of the Conquest, Landa would have mentioned them, but he states explicitly that they "had beds made of small rods." In the highlands, the traditional mat is often still used for a bed.

The food needs of the average Maya family today can be supplied in less than two months of eight-hour workdays. In ancient times it likely took much longer to fell the bush, plant a first-year maize field, and keep it free of weeds. In any event it is evident that the ancient Maya had a great deal of time when they were not engaged in raising food for the family's needs.

That this non-subsistence time of the common people was highly organized by the ruling classes is abundantly proved by the programs of public works that were carried out. These vast constructions of stone and mortar depended on a highly organized and ably directed society. Much labor was needed to quarry the stone for these projects and to transport it to the building sites, to fell wood for the thousands of limekilns, and to gather gravel for the seemingly endless tubs of mortar. Time and skill were required to carve the worked-stone elements, to sculpt the monuments, and to construct the pyramids, temples, and palaces. And all this was in addition to serving the needs of the ruler, the nobility, and the priesthood. In view of all that they did, the common people could have had but little time to call their own.

## Life and Death

When a man was ill he summoned a shaman. This curer of ills used a combination of prayers, ceremonies, and administration of herbs to cure his patients. The Maya area has many medicinal herbs and plants, and an extensive pharmacopoeia was at the disposal of these shamans. Several seventeenth-century Maya manuscripts, listing many ills and their corresponding cures, have come down to us, and some of their remedies have merit. Many of them, too, smack of medieval European superstition mixed with Maya magic, as in this remedy for toothache: "You take the bill of a woodpecker and bleed the gums a little with it; if a man, thirteen times; if a woman, nine times. [The gum] shall be slightly pierced by the bill of the woodpecker. Thus also a piece of a tree struck by lightning is to be grated with a fish-skin and wrapped in cotton-wool. Then you apply it to the tooth. He will recover by this means."

This bleeding of the gums might alleviate some kinds of toothache, but the thirteen times for a man and the nine times for a woman are surely ritualistic survivals from the ancient Maya, the former corresponding to the number of Gods of the Upper World and the latter to the number of Gods of the Lower World.

By contrast, some of the native plants undoubtedly possess medicinal properties, for example, the *kanlol* (*Tecoma stans*), which grows in northern Yucatan. A dose of an extract made from this plant, two to ten drops taken hourly, acts as a strong diuretic and probably a mild heart stimulant as well.

We learn from Landa that, "There were also surgeons, or better said, sorcerers, who cured with herbs and many superstitious rites. . . . The sorcerers and physicians performed their cures by bleedings of the parts, which gave pain to the sick man . . . [the Maya] believed that death, sickness and afflictions came to them for their wrong doing and their sin; they had a custom of confessing themselves, when they were already sick."

According to the same authority, the Maya had great fear of death, and when it took friends or kin, their grief was profound and enduring:

•••• This people had a great and excessive fear of death and they showed this in that all the services, which they made to their gods, were for no other end, nor for any other purpose than that they [the gods] should give them health, life and sustenance. But when, in time, they came to die, it was indeed a thing to see the sorrow and the cries which they made for their dead, and the great grief it caused them. During the day they wept for them in silence; and at night with loud and very sad cries, so that it was pitiful to hear them. And they passed many days in deep sorrow. They made abstinences and fasts for the dead, especially the husband or wife; and they said that the devil had taken him away since they thought that all evils came to them from him [the devil], and especially death.

The body was wrapped in a shroud, and the mouth filled with ground maize and one or more jadeite beads, "which they use for money, so that they should not be without something to eat in the other life." The common people were buried under the floors or behind their houses; and the houses were usually then abandoned. Into the grave were thrown idols of clay, wood, or stone, and objects indicating the profession or trade of the deceased.

The burial customs of the ruling classes were more elaborate. Landa says that the bodies of the nobles and persons of high esteem were burned, their ashes placed in great urns, and temples built above them. The practice has been confirmed by excavations in the pyramid supporting the High Priest's Tomb at Chichen Itza, in the substructures of Temples A-I and A-XVIII at Uaxactun (Fig. 9.4), and in the pyramids of the Temple of the Inscriptions at Palenque (see also Figs. 4.20 and 4.21) and Temple I at Tikal. Cremation must have been instituted late, however, for these excavations of Classic-period structures have revealed that the remains of rulers were not burned.

Graves of important persons (again, uncremated) have also been found in small, stone-lined burial vaults, with corbel-arched roofs, that were built under plaza floor levels at Chichen Itza, Palenque, Uaxactun, and Copan. Most of these pyramid and plaza subfloor burials were accompanied by elaborate mortuary furniture, exquisitely painted pottery vessels, carved jadeite beads and pendants, and ornately chipped objects of flint and obsidian.

In northern Yucatan, another burial custom among the nobility, according to Landa, was that of enclosing the ashes of the dead in hollow statues of pottery or wood. A wooden statue was made to look like the dead man. Ashes from a part of the cremated body were placed in a hollow at the back of the statue's head; the rest of the ashes were buried. These statues and crematory urns were venerated among the family idols.

Among the Cocom, the ruling house of Mayapan, a special burial custom obtained. The bodies of dead lords were boiled until the fleshy parts could be completely removed from the bones. The back half of the head was sawed off, leaving the front half intact. Then, where the fleshy parts of the face had been, a new face was built up with resin. These restored faces were kept, together with the wooden effigies, in the oratories of their houses with the family idols. They

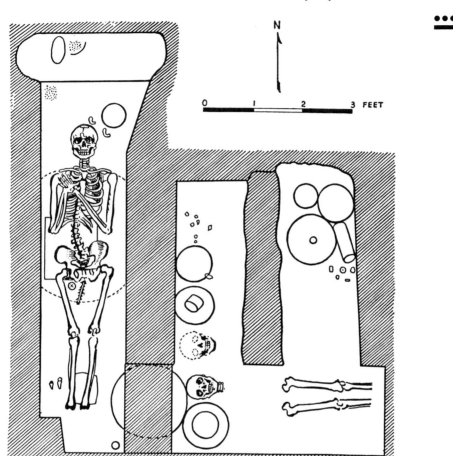

Fig. 9.4. Plan of an elite burial in Structure A-1, Uaxactun, Guatemala (Late Classic).

were held in great veneration, and on feast days offerings of food were made to them so that the lords might lack for nothing in their afterlife.

Archaeology would seem to support Landa's account. In dredging the Cenote of Sacrifice at Chichen Itza a skull was recovered that had the crown cut away. The eye sockets were filled with wooden plugs, and there were the remains of painted plaster on the front. Excavation in the Department of El Quiché, Guatemala, uncovered the front part of a human skull covered with a thick coat of lime plaster modeled to represent a human face.

# 10

# TRADE AND EXTERNAL CONTACT

> The occupation to which they had the greatest inclination was trade, carrying salt
> and cloth and slaves to the lands of Ulua and Tabasco, exchanging all they had for
> cacao and stone beads which were their money.
> —Landa's *Relación de las cosas de Yucatán* (Tozzer 1941 : 94-95)

Archaeologists are concerned with understanding the origins and development of past human societies, and their research has defined several factors that played an important role in the development of Maya civilization (Chapter 2). The agricultural subsistence systems allowed population growth, and the sociopolitical organization saw to the management of society. The third factor was trade and external contact. In considering this subject and its role in the development of Maya civilization, we must widen our focus beyond the Maya area and include all of Mesoamerica, for trade provided the principal means by which the ancient Maya maintained contact with neighboring societies in Mesoamerica. As such, trade networks were a conduit not only for goods, but also for people and ideas, and therefore affected all aspects of Maya society— and even the ebb and flow in the fortunes of the major centers.

## Prehistoric Trade in Mesoamerica

In contrast to the Andean area of South America, which was eventually integrated by highly centralized political powers, Mesoamerica was never united under a single political system. One of the forces making for integration in prehistoric Mesoamerica was commerce: archaeological evidence and ethnohistorical data (such as surviving native tribute lists and Spanish accounts) describe a complex system of exchange networks and mechanisms ranging from simple barter to large-scale redistribution through centralized markets.

Mesoamerica possesses a wealth of environmental contrasts and diversity. This diversity gave the prehistoric inhabitants the opportunity to develop a multitude of local economic specializations, which in turn fostered the development of exchange networks to distribute resources, goods, and services.

*Regional trade* is exchange within a major environmental area; the Central Mexican Symbiotic Zone in the Valley of Mexico is a widely accepted example. *Long-distance trade* is exchange between major environmental areas. Seen in this way, all of prehistoric Mesoamerica can be viewed as a single symbiotic area, integrated by long-distance trade.

It is convenient to distinguish two broad classes of trade, exchange either of utilitarian goods (food and tools) or of exotic items (ritual, wealth, and status goods). Regional trade networks throughout Mesoamerica certainly provided the means for the exchange of both utilitarian and exotic commodities. Long-distance trade networks, on the other hand, appear to have been devoted primarily to the exchange of exotic items. There were exceptions, of course, of certain critical resources with limited and specific sources, such as obsidian. But obsidian served both utilitarian (tool) and exotic (ritual) purposes.

Recently, William Rathje has postulated that the exchange of utilitarian goods (salt, obsidian, and grinding stones) played a central role in the origins of Mesoamerican civilization. This thesis holds that in certain resource-deficient regions, such as the Gulf coast and central Maya lowlands, prehistoric populations developed complex organizations to manage the acquisition and redistribution of utilitarian goods; this development ultimately led to social stratification and a permanent ruling elite (two characteristics of chiefdoms and, ultimately, of state organizations). In contrast, other scholars see trade in exotic goods as the crucial factor in the emergence of social stratification and ruling elites. Control of such items as jadeite, magnetite, and feathers by the elite segment of society marked and reinforced their elevated status, especially within the theocratic system typical of most early civilizations. Although neither model has been rigorously tested by archaeological research, Rathje's scheme may be modified in light of the inventory of local utilitarian items recovered in the Maya lowlands from the Preclassic era, especially from the dominant center Tikal, and the long-overdue recognition of the diversity and economic potential of the Maya lowland environment. Salt, for instance, was readily available in the southern lowlands at Salinas de los Nueve Cerros. Regardless of specific theories, it may be concluded that long-distance trade, comprising both utilitarian and exotic exchange, was vital to the development and integration of all prehistoric Mesoamerican civilizations, including the Maya.

Opinions differ about the importance of trade in the development of the ancient Maya. The model of Classic Maya society as a feudal organization (Chapter 8) implies a relatively weak system of long-distance trade because, with feudalism, economic interaction usually follows the lines of authority established by the obligations of vassalage. Archaeological and ethnohistorical evidence, however, certainly testifies to the importance and persistence of both regional and long-distance trade among the Maya, so that if feudalism contributed to the organization of ancient Maya society, it must have coexisted with a strongly developed system of trade.

Two factors made the ancient Maya prominent in Mesoamerican long-distance trade networks. First, the Maya occupied a strategic position astride the routes that connected Mexico in the northwest to Central America in the southeast. Because trade to supply the populous Mexican states with goods originating in Central America and beyond had to pass through the Maya area, the ancient Maya were able to control this commerce as "middlemen." The second factor stems from the fact that the Maya area was blessed with a plentiful variety of resources that could be used not only by the local inhabitants

TABLE 9

*Principal Trade Goods from the Maya Area*

| Type of goods | Principal place of origin | Type of goods | Principal place of origin |
|---|---|---|---|
| PRIMARILY UTILITARIAN | | | |
| Agricultural products | Various | Obsidian | Southern highlands (specifically, El Chayal, Ixtepeque, and Jilotepeque) |
| Balsam | Pacific coast | | |
| Bark cloth | Pacific coast, lowlands | Ocote or pitch pine | Highlands |
| Basketry | Various | Pottery | Various |
| Condiments | Various | Salt | Northern (coastal) lowlands (lesser sources in southern low- lands, highlands, and Pacific coast) |
| Cotton | Lowlands, Pacific coast, Yucatan | | |
| Dyes and pigments | Various | | |
| Fish and sea products | Coastal areas, lakes | | |
| Flint (chert) | Lowlands (for exam- ple, Colha) | Sugar (honey and wax) | Caribbean coast, Isla de Cozumel |
| Game | Various | Textiles | Various, especially northern lowlands |
| Henequen (maguey) | Northern lowlands | Tobacco | Lowlands |
| Lime | Lowlands | Tortoise shell | Coastal areas, espe- cially Gulf coast |
| Manos and metates | Southern highlands | Volcanic ash | Highlands |
| PRIMARILY EXOTIC | | | |
| Amber | Chiapas | Jadeite | Northern highlands (middle Motagua valley) |
| Cacao | Lowlands, especially Caribbean, Gulf, and Pacific coasts | | |
| | | Jaguar pelts, teeth, etc. | Southern and central lowlands |
| Cinnabar | Southern highlands | | |
| Copal (*pom*) | Lowlands | Pyrite | Highlands |
| Feathers | Highlands, lowlands, and Bay Islands | Serpentine, al- bite, diorite | Highlands |
| | | Shark teeth | Coastal areas |
| Feathers, quetzal | Northern highlands (Verapaz) | Shell, coral, etc. | Coastal areas |
| Hematite | Southern highlands | Stingray spines | Coastal areas |

(see Chapter 1), but by those in foreign lands, such as the highland valleys of Mexico. The most important exports were jadeite, serpentine, obsidian, salt, cacao, and quetzal feathers (see Table 9).

## Goods and Mechanisms in Long-Distance Trade

The most important variables of long-distance trade in prehistoric Meso-america included the most frequently exchanged and most valuable items, the primary sources for these items, the means of transport, the primary routes, the methods of exchange, and the control centers. Identification of these factors is based on extant archaeological records and ethnohistorical literature.

The basic goods exchanged from the Maya area in long-distance trade are listed in Table 9. Other products traded through the Maya area from outside areas are in Table 10. The principal means of transport on land or water in prehistoric Mesoamerica relied on manpower; burdens were carried on the backs of porters (sometimes organized into human caravans) or packed into dugout canoes that may have been augmented by sails during later periods.

Ancient Maya trade was in the hands of several classes of merchants. The majority were members of a non-elite middle class, and these individuals seem to have handled the bulk of the local trade within the Maya area. This group included professional peddlers and itinerant traders who bought and sold a variety of goods in markets or in interactions with individual producers and consumers. Many other members of society engaged in trading activities on a part-time basis. These were the people who manufactured and sold their own goods: farmers and craftsmen, such as potters, weavers, and knappers. But it was a smaller group of wealthy merchants, members of the elite class, that possessed the means to organize and maintain long-distance trade operations. These elite merchants managed the foreign exchanges and controlled most of the movement of goods that passed through the Maya area.

The most important economic institution of the ancient Maya was the centralized market. Markets still provide the principal means for the exchange of food and other goods in both Guatemala and Yucatan; held on scheduled days each week (often on Sundays in rural communities) or daily in the large

TABLE 10
*Goods Traded to or through the Maya Area*

| Goods from Mexico | | Goods from Central America | |
|---|---|---|---|
| Kaolin (?) | Pottery | Chalcedony (?) | Pottery |
| Magnetite (?) | Textiles | Cotton | Rubber |
| Metal (especially copper) | Turquoise | Feathers | Slaves |
| Pelts (especially rabbit) | | Metal (gold, silver, copper, and alloys) | |

urban centers, markets provide a central meeting ground for direct dealings between producer and consumer. The same must have held true in prehistoric times, although obtaining direct archaeological evidence is difficult. Markets in the past, as today, were seldom associated with permanent structures; most were undoubtedly held in open plazas, with only pole-and-thatch stands for shelter. At Tikal, an enclosed rectangular arrangement of multi-doorway structures in the East Plaza (Fig. 11.6) has been identified as the probable central market for this largest of Classic Maya centers. Yet, the evidence is too sparse to rule out other functions.

At the time of the Spanish Conquest, centralized markets were prospering in Mesoamerica, Yucatan, the Maya highlands, and elsewhere. The largest and most spectacular market described by the Spanish was that in Tlatelolco, adjacent to Tenochtitlan, capital of the Mexica (Aztecs) in the Valley of Mexico (and present-day Mexico City). The market square was surrounded by an arcade. The stalls were arranged along a grid of "streets" around a central elevated platform used for public announcements and the execution of thieves. On one corner stood the court of the market officials, where disputes were settled. Goods from all over Mesoamerica were available at Tlatelolco, including a variety of food and drink, jewelry made from precious metals (gold or silver) and stones (jadeite or turquoise), medicines, clothing, rubber, paper, building materials, baskets, mats, pottery, and obsidian blades and other tools. In addition, one could find stalls for the purchase of slaves and prostitutes.

The descriptions of Postclassic markets in the Maya area are similar, although none were as elaborate. Postclassic centers such as Iximche in the highlands also had a permanent plaza area set aside for the market, and government officials to enforce rules, settle disputes, and collect taxes. Larger markets even maintained facilities to house foreign merchants. The markets were well organized, with designated areas for various commodities like those at Tlatelolco.

The ancient Maya may have held fairs to facilitate economic interaction with foreign powers. Held periodically, perhaps once or twice a year in mutually accessible areas, the fairs could have allowed commercial relationships with hostile or rival powers under the protection of local or neutral authorities. The best analogy for this institution is that provided by the fairs of medieval Europe. During the Postclassic period, for instance, long-distance trade for the Mexica was handled by a government-sanctioned guild of merchants, the *pochteca*. The Maya had no comparable organization, since long-distance trade was in the hands of individual entrepreneurs. Furthermore, since the *pochteca* were known to act as military spies for the Mexica, they were usually not welcome in Maya centers. It has been suggested that biannual fairs, held in intermediate areas such as Soconusco (the Pacific coast of Chiapas), allowed the Maya elite merchants and the *pochteca* to carry out their commercial exchanges.

The fair, combining ritual and even recreational activities with commerce, may have existed during earlier times in the Maya area. It is probable that the fair provided a primary means for interaction between Classic-period Maya centers. Fairs may have been scheduled according to the ritual calendar, and undoubtedly coincided with pilgrimages to locally important religious shrines, just as in medieval Europe. In Postclassic times the shrines on Isla de Cozumel, off the Yucatan coast, provided a principal attraction to that important port of trade.

At various times during the prehistoric era in Mesoamerica, long-distance trade was dominated by a particular power. In some cases this domination was manifested by the presence of foreign trade colonies within the Maya area, and other times by the establishment of trading alliances with foreign powers. The Olmec, centered in the Gulf coast lowlands and representing the first chiefdom in Mesoamerica, appear to have created the first integrated Mesoamerican long-distance trade network. Later, competition from former source regions, including highland Mexico and south-coastal Guatemala, appears to have contributed to the decline of the Olmec, ultimately resulting in the rise of the first state organization in Mesoamerica, Teotihuacan. The Teotihuacan state reestablished the integration of Mesoamerica in the Early Classic through long-distance trade, and controlled this network until its demise at the beginning of the Late Classic. Competition from new centers in Mexico that emerged along the long-distance trade routes, Cholula, El Tajin, Xochicalco, and others, probably contributed to Teotihuacan's downfall. After a hiatus, a succession of power centers in central Mexico, the Early Postclassic Tula-Toltec and the Late Postclassic Triple Alliance of the Mexica, controlled much of the long-distance trade in Mesoamerica until the Spanish Conquest.

The primary long-distance routes ran east-west, to the major consuming power centers in Mexico from the major source regions in the Maya area and beyond. Specifically the earliest routes, associated with the Olmec, appear to have been primarily land-based, radiating from the Gulf coast south and west to the Mexican highlands and eastward along the Pacific coastal plain to tap resources in the Maya highlands and Central America. The Early and Middle Classic routes, controlled by Teotihuacan, extended more directly eastward through the Maya lowlands, using both land and river-canoe transport, also to tap resources in the Maya highlands (via the Usumacinta drainage) and beyond (via the Caribbean) into Central America. The old Olmec land route across the southern coastal plain appears to have been reduced to secondary importance during this period. By the Postclassic, the central Mexican centers maintained a diverse network of long-distance commerce, including sea trade controlled by the Putun Maya, who used larger and more efficient seagoing canoes that expanded the water routes around the Yucatan Peninsula. Although many land routes continued to be important, the major one was the old south-coast access to the Maya highlands and Central America.

In addition to these generally east-west routes, an important north-south trading axis connected the southern Maya area and its resources with the lowland areas to the north. The close relationship between Kaminaljuyu and Tikal that can be seen in the archaeological record from the Late Preclassic and Early Classic eras (see Chapter 4) probably reflected economic interaction between the southern highlands and the central lowlands.

## Late Preclassic Trade

Olmec civilization disappeared during the Late Preclassic era, or at least declined relative to the highland powers emerging throughout Mesoamerica (see Chapter 2). Loss of control over the long-distance trade network may have been a major factor in this process, especially if control were relinquished to the rising highland powers. Loss of control over trade and the resulting loss of access to exotic trade goods would have been disastrous to the wealth and prestige of the Olmec ruling elite. Significantly, as the Olmec declined, following much the pattern of the later Classic Maya decline (see Chapter 5), social development accelerated in many of the very regions that previously were the focus of Olmec trade interest. These included the Valley of Mexico, the Valley of Oaxaca, the Central Depression of Chiapas, the Pacific coastal plain, and the Valley of Guatemala. That is, the power and prestige of a theocratic society, such as the Olmec, can be maintained only as long as access to exotic trade items is secure. Olmec society, structurally fragile as most theocratic chiefdoms are, was especially vulnerable because of its reliance on distant sources for most of its exotic goods. As populations in the original Olmec source regions gradually increased in size and complexity (ironically fostered, at least in part, by their contact with the Olmec), these newly emerging societies may have been able to challenge the economic domination by the Olmec, ultimately severing the trade connections with the Gulf coast.

Two former Olmec resource areas are especially significant: the Valley of Mexico, which saw the beginnings of the first urban state (Teotihuacan) in Mesoamerica; and the Pacific coast region of the southern Maya area, which saw the earliest manifestations of Maya civilization. The origins of Maya civilization were marked by the recording of calendrical and dynastic hierogylphic texts, in the distinctive "Maya style," on upright sculptured monuments within ceremonial centers (see Chapter 3; Figs. 3.10–17). This development, the hallmark of Classic Maya culture, is documented from a series of Pacific coastal sites during the Late Preclassic, including Padre Piedra, Izapa, El Baúl, Chalchuapa, and several adjacent regions (Chiapa de Corzo in the Central Chiapas Depression and Kaminaljuyu in the Valley of Guatemala). The most recent and dramatic evidence of this development has been revealed at Abaj Takalik.

The growing prosperity of the southern Maya was cut short at the end of the Preclassic era (around A.D. 100–200). Several theories have been advanced to explain their sudden demise: popular revolt, catastrophic volcanic event, exhaustion of the soil (see Chapter 5). If the eruption of Ilopango was of sufficient magnitude to shatter the structure of southern Maya society, as seems likely, agricultural activities throughout the fall area would have been severely retarded for a considerable period, perhaps for several generations, and the impact on the existing exchange networks in the southeastern Maya area would have been equally devastating. The explosion might well have severed the ancient Pacific-coast trade route to Central America by extinguishing the exchange links in central El Salvador. Because of the extent and duration of depopulation in much of this region, the route could have been disrupted for several centuries. Though ash-free areas of the Pacific coast may have remained an important resource zone for cacao, the loss of the trade link to Central America would certainly have had a significant and lasting effect on the future of the entire Maya area, and all of Mesoamerica.

To the north during this era, recent research by David Freidel and others has revealed evidence of a Late Preclassic coastal trade network that followed the margins of the Yucatan Peninsula. Based on excavations at Cerros, near the Caribbean coast in northern Belize (Fig. 3.16), and recent investigations of northern Yucatecan coastal sites and the rise of the salt trade (Fig. 10.1), it is

Fig. 10.1. Dzemul, Yucatan, Mexico: aerial view of the Xtampu salt evaporation pans on the Caribbean coast, of the type used in pre-Conquest times. Archaeological evidence indicates that this resource was important from the Late Preclassic on.

apparent that circumpeninsula canoe trade provided an important means for both communication and economic exchange by the Late Preclassic period. Although modest in scale compared to later times (see below), this formative coastal trade network seems to have brought prosperity to Komchen and other Yucatecan sites (see Chapter 11), which in exchange for salt received jadeite and other exotic goods from the south. The rapid growth of Cerros in the Late Preclassic, together with the evidence of ties to regions located both north and south of this center, testifies to the importance of the coastal Caribbean route by this time. Sites located along this route obviously prospered, and some may have been able to adapt to the changes that marked the Classic era. But Cerros appears to have been unable to survive these changes, most notably an apparent realignment of trade routes, for the site was abandoned at the close of the Preclassic period.

The dominant Maya lowland center in the Late Preclassic was undoubtedly El Mirador. Although the economic role of this precocious power is only beginning to be documented, it appears that El Mirador served as a major redistribution node and probably controlled trans-Peten commerce in its heyday.

From all indications, then, long-distance trade was well established in the Maya area during the Preclassic. Two primary axes can be inferred: an east-west axis in the south, connecting Mexico with the resources of the Maya highlands and Central America by way of the Pacific coastal plain; and a north-south axis, connecting Yucatan and its salt supplies to the markets and resources to the south by way of both the Gulf and Caribbean coasts.

## Classic Trade: Teotihuacan and the Lowland Maya

The Classic period saw two developments that profoundly affected long-distance trade in Mesoamerica and the developmental course of Maya civilization. The first of these was a shift in the bulk of east-west commerce from the ancient Preclassic trade routes along the Pacific coastal plain and the coast of Yucatan to central-Maya routes through the highlands and, more important, along rivers across the lowlands. The second development was the emergence of a new Mesoamerican power center at Teotihuacan, which was able to reunify the long-distance trade network during the Early Classic period.

During its prime, Teotihuacan was one of the greatest cities of the ancient world (ca. 100 B.C. to A.D. 700; see Fig. 3.22). By A.D. 400 this new power appears to have gained control over much of the long-distance trade between the Maya area and central Mexico. Among Teotihuacan colonies and alliances in the Maya area, the most notable was Kaminaljuyu, where a major portion of the site was rebuilt in a style duplicating the civic architecture of Teotihuacan. Several colonies also seem to have existed on the Pacific coastal plain south and west of Kaminaljuyu. In this region at least one ceramic manufacturing center mass-produced elaborate Teotihuacan ritual vessels and incensarios. Teotihuacan products were imported throughout much of the Maya area, and even pottery and other locally produced items often emulated central Mexican styles.

The colonization of the southern Maya area assured Teotihuacan of control over several critical commodities, providing the central Mexican state with a near-monopoly in these resources throughout Mesoamerica. From Kaminaljuyu, Teotihuacan could obtain obsidian from the nearby quarry at El Chayal, and may have managed the local trade networks throughout the southern Maya highlands. On the south coast, Teotihuacan could control the valuable cacao plantations, as well as the principal route for highland products destined for central Mexico.

In Chapter 4 we saw how the first centers to rise to prominence in the central lowlands were situated on the portages between river systems flowing east to the Caribbean and west to the Gulf of Mexico. Thus, centers such as El Mirador and Tikal were in a position to control the modest east-west commerce that crossed the base of the Yucatan Peninsula throughout the Preclassic. With the disruption of the Pacific-coast connection to Central America, these lowland routes took on new importance. Before long, lowland colonies were established at Copan and Quirigua, which thereafter could tap the Central American trade that bypassed the devastated southeastern zone. New routes from Central America probably moved northward overland through western Honduras or along the Caribbean coast. From this region products could be transported by canoe up the coast of Belize and then west across the lowlands by river. At this same time, the east coast of the lowlands appears to have become a major cacao production area. Southern Maya refugees from the Ilopango disaster may have helped establish this traditional southeastern cash crop in the eastern lowlands, a possibility supported by the indications of increased contacts from the southeast at this time at Barton Ramie, in the Belize river valley. The market for much of this lowland cacao lay in Mexico, and the same riverine routes across the lowlands must have been used to transport it westward.

El Mirador seems to have been the first lowland center to have reaped the benefits of this increasing commerce. The period of its greatest prosperity corresponds to the Late Preclassic and Protoclassic, after which it seems to have declined rapidly. Thereafter, another site astride the lowland portages, Tikal, became the dominant power in the lowlands. It is tempting to conclude that Mirador and Tikal were commercial rivals, and that the decline of the former was related to the rise of the latter. One could suggest that Tikal's location farther south gave it an advantage over Mirador, or that Mirador was vanquished in a time of conflict. But at this point we know too little about Mirador to support a discussion about rivalry in either economic or political terms.

Nonetheless, it does appear that Tikal gained an important advantage by securing an alliance with Teotihuacan. The early Tikal inscriptions record that Curl Nose came to power in the fourth century A.D., apparently by marrying a woman from the Tikal ruling lineage. Curl Nose may have been a member of the ruling elite from the Teotihuacan-dominated highland center of Kaminal-juyu, or even from Teotihuacan itself. Regardless, this marriage seems to have established an alliance between Tikal and Teotihuacan. We can surmise that as a result Teotihuacan gained direct access to such lowland products as cacao, thus furthering its monopolistic hold over Mesoamerican trade. Reciprocally, not only did Tikal gain considerable prestige from its alliance with the domi-nant power in Mesoamerica, but the leverage afforded by Teotihuacan's back-ing allowed Tikal to control trade throughout the lowlands.

Thus, during the Early Classic a series of new lowland centers was established in locations suitable for controlling the principal lowland trade routes. Many, if not all, were probably founded by Tikal or allied to Tikal by marriages between ruling families. We have already mentioned Copan and Quirigua in the south-eastern area, which secured the Central American trade connections; Quirigua also controlled the important Motagua jade route to the Caribbean. Other centers, such as Yaxchilan, would have secured the valuable Usumacinta route between the highlands and the Gulf coast. Far to the northeast, Coba may have been established to control resources and monitor trade in northern Yucatan.

The Middle Classic hiatus in the economic and political prosperity of the lowland Maya seems to have been caused by the decline of Teotihuacan, followed by a breakdown in the Mesoamerican long-distance trade network. Tikal, as Teotihuacan's principal ally, seems to have suffered the most from this decline (see Chapter 4). But other lowland Maya centers, including Tikal's former colonies and allies, appear to have gained new prosperity and power in the wake of these developments. In the southwestern lowlands, Palenque took over the position from which to control commerce between Mexico and the interior lowlands. By this time the Pacific coastal route to Central America was undoubtedly reestablished as the southeastern area was resettled. Copan ap-pears to have maintained control over much of this commerce, perhaps increas-ing its efforts to control trade through the area to the south. Copan's rival, Quirigua, probably still controlled the Motagua jade route. The Usumacinta routes continued under the authority of Yaxchilan and its allies.

Thus, during the Late Classic period, although the power centers in the lowlands were reoriented and probably competitive, the overall pattern of long-distance trade that had developed during the Early Classic appears not to have changed significantly.

## Trade in the Postclassic

A crucial change did begin to occur, however, by the Terminal Classic period (ca A.D. 800–1000). By this time a group of seacoast traders, the Putun (or Chontal) Maya, from the Gulf-coast region of Tabasco, were increasing their hold over commerce along the coasts (see Chapter 6). The Putun Maya were established at Xicalango, a major port on Laguna de Términos. There, as documented by Spanish colonial sources, the land-based merchants from central Mexico traded a variety of products with the Putun sea merchants, who brought their goods from as far as lower Central America.

The source of the Putun Maya's prosperity and power lay both in their strategic location on the Gulf coast and in an apparent technological break-through, the development of large oceangoing canoes capable of transporting huge loads of goods at less cost than by former methods.

Water-borne commerce was undoubtedly an ancient tradition among the Maya, extending back at least as far as the Late Preclassic. Besides plying the riverine routes across the southern and central lowlands, the smaller canoes of this time seem to have begun to exploit the islands off the east coast of Belize and the other coastal margins of the Yucatan Peninsula. But it appears that by the Postclassic era much larger vessels were developed. A single large seagoing canoe could carry more goods with less manpower than land-based porters or even river craft, which required large crews for portages. The oceangoing canoes apparently had sails to propel them when the winds were right, although paddlers were needed to keep the vessels moving when sails could not be set.

Using these sea-trading vessels, the Putun Maya soon extended their trade routes all the way around the Yucatan Peninsula, establishing their own ports at several strategic points. During the Postclassic period, Isla de Cozumel, off the northeastern coast, was perhaps the most important port of trade for the new sea-borne commerce. Other Putun colonies were established at Champoton on the west coast of Yucatan and at Nito on the mouth of the Río Dulce, near the base of the east coast of the Peninsula.

Although almost any product could be transported by sea, this mode of travel especially favored the heavier and bulkier products, such as salt, grinding stones, cacao, and so forth. A famous encounter with a Maya trading canoe off the north coast of Honduras near Islas de la Bahía (Bay Islands), recorded by Columbus on his fourth voyage, is our best eyewitness account. The canoe, described as being as long as a galley and eight feet wide, had a cabin amid-ships, and a crew of some two dozen men, plus its captain and assorted women and children. It carried a cargo of cacao, metal products (copper bells and axes), pottery (including crucibles to melt metal), cotton clothing, and *macanas* (Mexican-style wooden swords set with obsidian blades).

The dominance of sea trade in the Postclassic produced, as one would expect, a shift in human settlement toward the seacoasts of the Yucatan Peninsula. This reorientation in long-distance trade routes might have precipitated the decline of lowland Classic Maya society. The Classic "collapse" seems to correspond to the decline of the older lowland centers, especially those like Tikal that were located far inland and dependent on the older trans-Peten trade routes (Chapter 5). Yet the opposite can also be argued. That is, that the chaos resulting from the breakdown of Classic lowland society disrupted the older riverine and land-based trade routes, thus necessitating the growth of seacoast commerce.

Despite the critical role of sea trade during this period, porter-borne overland trade in the Yucatan and throughout the Maya area continued to be important during the Postclassic period, and even into the early colonial era—in the sixteenth and seventeenth centuries, unconquered Maya groups such as the Tayasal Itza (Chapter 6) maintained a vestigial overland trade network through the central and southern lowlands.

# PART III
# MATERIAL CULTURE

# ARCHITECTURE AND ARCHAEOLOGICAL SITES

It was then that they built temples in such numbers as are seen today on all sides, and in passing through the forests, there are seen in the midst of the woods the sites of houses and buildings of marvelous construction.
—Landa's *Relación de las cosas de Yucatán* (Tozzer 1941 : 40)

Our knowledge of ancient Maya social and political organization rests, in good measure, upon inferences derived from the physical remains of past activity, namely, the archaeological sites scattered across the Maya area. In this chapter we shall consider the principal features of ancient Maya architecture and describe briefly some of the better known archaeological sites. Chapter 12 then explores the ceramic remains, and Chapter 13 surveys the other arts and crafts.

## Architecture

The variation in form of Classic Maya buildings has long suggested that they served various functions. The functions so posited have given rise to labels commonly applied to many structures, the most familiar being "temples," buildings elevated on high pyramidal platforms with restricted interior spaces and large free-standing façades called roof combs. There are also "palaces," elongated multiple-room buildings usually situated on lower platforms, typically possessing benches, doorway niches ("curtain holders"), small windows, and other features that suggest a residential function. These (and similar) labels, though often justified by the available archaeological evidence, must be used with caution, for they are frequently oversimplified. Buildings in both categories undoubtedly hosted a variety of activities, and not all "temples," for instance, seem to have been used for the same purposes. In addition, of course, there are other types of specialized Maya buildings, some of which are not easily subsumed under these or other functional categories. But for convenience these labels will be used here, together with other commonly used constructional designations, such as ball courts, causeways (*sacbeob*), sweat baths, shrines, and the like (see Table 11).

TABLE 11

*Functional Classification of Maya Architectural and Constructional Features, with Examples*

| | | Area | |
|---|---|---|---|
| Features | Pacific plain and highlands | Southern and central lowlands | Northern lowlands |
| **BUILDINGS AND BUILDING ASSEMBLAGES** | | | |
| Pyramid temples | Awilix Temple, Utatlan (Fig. 6.19) | Temple II, Tikal (Figs. 11.10 and 11.11) | El Castillo, Chichen Itza (Fig. 11.67) |
| Pyramid temples with tomb | Structure E-III-3, Kaminaljuyu (Fig. 3.2) | Temple I, Tikal (Figs. 4.17–19); Temple of the Inscriptions, Palenque (Figs. 4.20 and 4.21) | High Priest's Tomb, Chichen Itza (Fig. 11.65) |
| Necropoli | Structure D6-1, Los Mangales | North Acropolis, Tikal (Fig. 4.5) | |
| Palaces | Cawek Palace, Utatlan (Fig. 6.18) | Central Acropolis, Tikal (Fig. 11.6) Palace, Palenque (Fig. 11.38) | Governor's Palace and Nunnery, Uxmal (Figs. 6.5 and 11.59) |
| Ball courts | Ball Court, Utatlan (Fig. 6.18) | Structures 8 & 9, Copan (Fig. 11.43) | Ball Court, Chichen Itza (Fig. 11.69) |
| Sweat baths | Structure B-12, Los Cimientos-Chustum | | |
| Skull platforms | | | *Tzompantli*, Chichen Itza (Fig. 11.65) |
| Astronomical assemblages | Plaza A platforms, Iximche | Group E, Uaxactun (Fig. 11.21) | |
| Twin Pyramid groups | | Group 4E-4, Tikal (Figs. 11.18 and 11.19) | |
| **PUBLIC AREAS** | | | |
| Monument plazas | Monument Plaza, Izapa | Great Plazas at Copan and Quirigua (Figs. 11.43 and 11.48) | Terrace of the Monuments, Uxmal (Fig. 11.58) |
| Elevated plaza-platforms | | Terrace of Temple IV, Tikal; Danta Platform, El Mirador | Terrace of the Governor's Palace, Uxmal |
| Reviewing stands | | Ball Court Plaza, Quirigua (Fig. 11.48) | |
| Market areas | Plaza C(?), Iximche | East Plaza, Tikal (?) | |

Although some Maya buildings were built on level terrain, most were constructed on elevated surfaces. These ranged from low earthen platforms that supported the simplest houses to the terraced masonry-faced "pyramids" crowned by the loftiest structures at sites such as Tikal. The remains of most domestic buildings throughout the Maya area indicate that they were constructed in the same manner as contemporary Maya houses. Typically, a pole framework supports a thatched roof; walls are usually wattle and daub, a lattice of sticks plastered with a thick coating of adobe (mud mixed with straw or other binder). In the hottest regions, house walls are often unplastered, allowing the passage of cooling breezes. More substantial houses may have foundations of stone, or rough stone walls smoothed with plaster.

Ancient building platforms in the southern Maya area were usually earthen-cored and faced with adobe plaster (typically mixed with volcanic ash, abundant in the southern area). Owing to the scarcity of easily worked and suitable building stone, even the largest and most elaborate southern Maya buildings were usually constructed of perishable materials, such as pole and thatch or adobe blocks. Stonework, when encountered, was usually used for pavements, steps, and occasional decorative elements. In a few cases, as at Asunción Mita in the southeastern highlands, the natural cleavage planes of the local stone provided convenient-sized masonry for structures.

The most durable and best-known examples of Maya architecture are represented by the elaborate masonry structures found at most of the major centers in the southern, central, and northern lowlands. These regions are endowed with plentiful and easily obtained building materials, soft limestone beds that can be cut into blocks or reduced by burning to produce lime for plaster. Some regional variations occur; for instance, in the southeastern lowlands, sandstone, rhyolite, and marble were used as building stone at Quirigua, whereas trachyte masonry was used at Copan. Masonry decorations were often integrated with architecture, so that adornments such as inset corner moldings, apron moldings, mosaic corner masks, and friezes are commonly found.

From Preclassic times on, lime-based plaster was frequently used to pave level expanses ("plazas") between structures in the heavily built areas of most sites. Plaster almost invariably covered both exterior and interior masonry to provide a smooth finished surface on Maya buildings. Surfaces of platforms and building floors also received a thick coat of plaster. At many sites, three-dimensional modeled plaster decoration ("stucco reliefs") was used to adorn walls, building façades, and roof combs. The best-known examples of such decoration are the beautiful plastered relief panels at Palenque (Fig. 13.19). These modeled scenes were once further embellished by painting. Plastered surfaces were either left an unpainted white to cream, or painted in one or more colors. Occasionally the evidence indicates that an entire building was covered by colored plaster, as in the case of the red-painted Structure 5D-22 at Tikal. Interior painted scenes or murals are rarely preserved, but fragmentary examples have survived from the Preclassic era at Tikal (Fig. 3.17), from the Classic era at several sites, including Uaxactun, and from the Postclassic period at Chichen Itza, Tulum, and several other northern sites. But the most spectacular examples are the Late Classic murals at Bonampak (Figs. 13.25–27).

Although masonry styles vary throughout the Maya area, a core of traits is common to most or all lowland Classic Maya buildings. The supporting platforms were usually built up with rubble and earth and faced with cut-stone masonry. Summit access is often gained by a medial staircase. Most platforms surmounted by only one building have either a single frontal staircase or four medial staircases. At many sites, substructural platforms support more than one building, and in some cases modifications and additions eventually unified the separate platforms into a single mass. A large and complex multi-building platform of this kind is usually termed an acropolis; a good example is the North Acropolis at Tikal (Fig. 4.5). Superimposed construction is a hallmark of Maya architecture; when one building had outlived its usefulness, it was often partially or totally covered by a new and larger structure.

The masonry buildings situated on these platforms usually have relatively little interior space in proportion to their bulk (Fig. 11.1). This feature follows from the predominant building technique of rubble-filled walls, cut-stone facings, and corbeled vaults (Fig. 11.2). Rather than solid-masonry block walls, most Maya wall surfaces consist of a single layer of masonry that serves as a facing for a rubble hearting. The result is a relatively thick wall, necessary to support the corbeled vaulting and roof. The corbeled, or "false," arch typically has the form of an inverted "V." It is constructed of a vertical series of overlapping blocks, each of which projects farther inward until the intervening space between the two walls can be bridged by a single capstone. The earliest vaults are of rough masonry, thickly plastered to provide a smoothed soffit, or slope to the ceiling. Later vaults used beveled vault stones to provide a finished soffit. In a true arch, each block is supported by the vault stones on either side, so that it forms a strong, integrated unit. Corbeling is a form of cantilever, in which the only support is from the overlap with the block below, although each vault stone is counterbalanced by the weight of the hearting that holds it in place. It is much weaker than a true arch, thus necessitating the thick walls typical of Maya buildings. The width of Maya corbel-vaulted rooms rarely exceeds 3 m (10 ft).

Because of the limitations of corbeled vaulting, most Maya buildings are single-story. However, by the use of massive walls and narrow vaults, two- and even three-story masonry buildings were constructed, as in the Central Acropolis at Tikal. In addition, the roofs of many Maya structures supported decorative elements, façades or roof combs. Roof combs are masonry backdrops for front-facing decorative elements, usually constructed of mosaic or stucco work, that add to the height of the building. Sometimes of solid masonry, they are often supported and lightened by narrow, one- or two-story corbeled vaults.

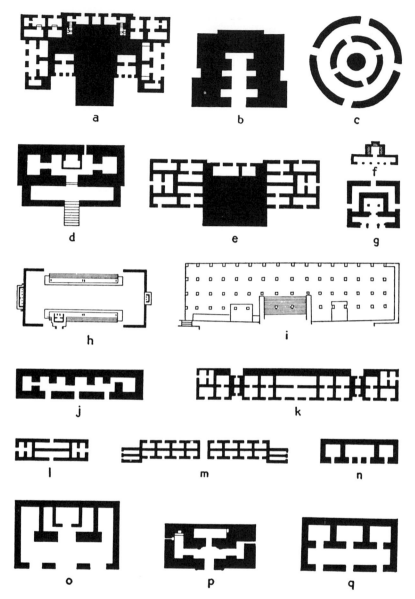

Fig. 11.1. Plans of various Maya structures: (*a*) Palace, Xtampak; (*b*) Temple IV, Tikal; (*c*) Caracol, Chichen Itza; (*d*) Structure E-II, Uaxactun; (*e*) Akabtzib, Chichen Itza; (*f*) Sweat Bath No. 2, Chichen Itza; (*g*) El Castillo, Chichen Itza; (*h*) Ball Court, Chichen Itza; (*i*) Northwest Colonnade, Chichen Itza; (*j*) Structure 33, Yaxchilan; (*k*) Governor's Palace, Uxmal; (*l*) House of the Turtles, Uxmal; (*m*) House of the Pigeons, Uxmal; (*n*) Structure 21, Yaxchilan; (*o*) Temple of the Sun, Palenque; (*p*) Structure 22, Copan; (*q*) Red House, Chichen Itza.

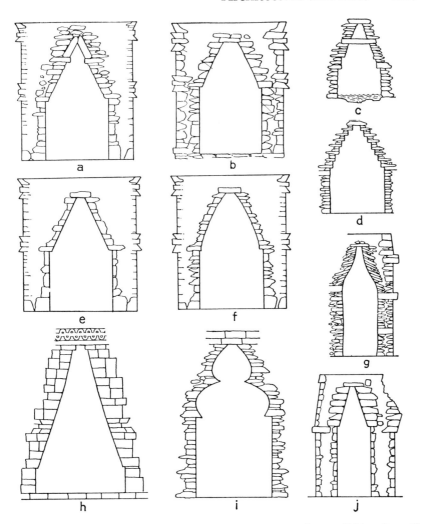

Fig. 11.2. Cross sections of Maya corbeled vaults: (*a*) Monjas Annex, Chichen Itza; (*b*) characteristic Classic-period arch with irregular vault stones and plastered sides; (*c*) viaduct, Palenque; (*d*) Structure E-X, Uaxactun; (*e*) characteristic Terminal Classic, or Puuc, arch with dressed sides, or (*f*) with "shore-shaped" vault stones and curved soffit; (*g*) Structure A-V, Uaxactun; (*h*) arcade through the Governor's Palace, Uxmal; (*i*) trifoil arch, Palace, Palenque; (*j*) second story, Monjas, Chichen Itza.

Most roof combs rise above the midline of the building, but some are supported by the front wall, giving the building a false front, called a "flying façade."

The best exemplars of roof-comb architecture are the great temples at Tikal (Fig. 4.17). Serving as funerary monuments to that center's Late Classic rulers, each is capped by a huge roof comb bearing the mosaic-sculptured portrait of the commemorated individual. As such, Tikal's great temples culminate the lowland tradition of integrating platform, building, and roof comb into a single monumental structure.

Despite these overall architectural similarities, considerable variation in style and even technique appear in Maya masonry buildings. For instance, at Palenque, in the southwestern lowlands, temple structures typically have two parallel vaulted rooms that are noticeably larger and more open than most of their contemporaries (Fig. 11.1*o*). Rather than being vertical, the upper façades of Palenque's buildings slope inward (the mansard roof), generally following the angle of the interior vaulting (Fig. 4.20). This reduced the weight born by the exterior walls, and allowed them to be less massive. As a result, the front wall could be opened by multiple doorways and the vaults made wider. A single transverse interior wall supports the bulk of the roof, which includes a reduced roof comb made lighter by being an open lattice rather than solid masonry. The vaults in the palace at Palenque display considerable variety in shape, including a doubly rounded soffit (Fig. 11.2*i*).

Perhaps the most consistent and pleasing variation in Maya architecture, the Puuc style, developed in the northern lowlands and culminated during the Terminal Classic era (Figs. 11.3 and 11.4). Although obviously related to styles outside of the Maya area (most explicitly, those of Mitla and similar sites in the Valley of Oaxaca), Puuc architecture retains many features of earlier Maya buildings. The hearting of Puuc buildings is a solidified lime-based concrete, which gives considerable strength to the structure. The masonry consists of finely shaped, limestone veneer blocks applied to this concrete hearting. This veneer masonry provides no structural support, as can be seen in ruined Puuc buildings that have lost their veneer. In such cases the concrete hearting usually continues to support the structure. The vaults of Puuc buildings retain the form of the corbeled arch (with either straight-sided or rounded soffits), but they are not technically corbeled, since the vault stones, usually shoe-shaped to secure a better purchase in the hearting, are a veneer over the concrete that actually supports the vault (Fig. 11.2*f*).

On the exterior, the lower façade of Puuc buildings is usually devoid of decoration (Figs. 11.3, lower illustration, and 6.5). Single or multiple doorways are found; multiple doorways were easily formed by using round or square columns to divide the opening. A variation generally found south of the Puuc region is traditionally treated as a separate architectural style called Chenes, and typically differs in having elaborately decorated lower façades, especially doorways incorporated into elaborate mosaic sculptures of monster masks (Fig. 6.4, lower illustration; see also Fig. 11.5). Another variation, the Río Bec style, adds false towers to the building façade (Fig. 6.4, upper illustration).

Upper façades often have a negative batter, that is, they slope slightly outward to compensate for distortions in visual perception. The upper façade of Puuc buildings is decorated by elaborate precut sculptured mosaics. Common

Fig. 11.3. Puuc-style buildings and architectural details: (*upper left*) corner mask, House of the Magician (Adivino), Uxmal; (*upper right*) mask at the top of the west staircase, same building; (*below*) La Iglesia, Nunnery Group, Chichen Itza.

Fig. 11.4. Puuc-style buildings and architectural details: (*left*) corner masks, temple of the Great Pyramid, Uxmal; (*upper right*) mask step, same building; (*immediately above*) north façade, same building.

motifs include x-shaped lattices, multiple columns (plain or banded "spools"), stepped frets, and the like (Figs. 11.3 and 11.4). Although curvilinear and naturalistic designs persist—serpents, masks, and other motifs typical of most Classic Maya building decorations—it is this geometric mosaic style that most strongly recalls the architecture of Mitla and other Oaxacan sites. The use of plaster decoration appears to be rare or nonexistent on Puuc buildings. Frontal roof combs are typical, but the overall scale is reduced, and these roof ornaments may often be completely absent.

## Archaeological Sites

The lowland Maya centers that are described in the rest of this chapter are only a sample of the several hundred known, some one hundred of which possess inscriptions with calendrical dates. This sample was selected not by size or splendor, but in an attempt to give a representative picture of Maya sites from the Classic and Postclassic periods. Most of these are easily accessible today; others remain difficult to reach. We know a great deal about some, owing to archaeological research, and very little about others. But the sample does include those sites that have been comprehensively investigated by archae-

Fig. 11.5. Palace of the Masks, Kabah, Yucatan, Mexico.

ologists and other specialists, and that have thus come to furnish the basis for much of what is known about the ancient Maya.

We will begin our descriptions with the centers in the core of the central lowlands: Tikal, Uaxactun, El Mirador, Nakum, Naranjo, Yaxha, Calakmul, and Becan. The description of Tikal will be the most detailed, for in addition to its being the largest Classic Maya site, more is known about it than any other center. We will move on to the eastern periphery of the central lowlands and briefly consider Altun Ha, Caracol, and Xunantunich, all in Belize. From there, we will examine several sites in the southern lowlands (Lubaantun, Seibal, Altar de Sacrificios, Yaxchilan, Piedras Negras, and Bonampak); in the southwest (Palenque and Tonina); and in the southeast (Copan and Quirigua). We will close with descriptions of the major sites of the northern lowlands: Coba, Dzibilchaltun, Uxmal, Kabah, Sayil, Labna, Chichen Itza, and Tulum.

## Tikal

The largest known Maya center, Tikal (Fig. 11.6), has been subjected to the most comprehensive archaeological investigation of any Maya site to date. Tikal remained unknown to the outside world for centuries, far from any settlement and isolated by thick jungle growth, despite the fact that Cortés and his soldiers must have come very close to the ruins in 1525 during their march from Mexico to Honduras (see the Epilogue). The official discovery was made by a Guatemalan government expedition led by Modesto Mendez and Ambrosio Tut, which reached Tikal in 1848 and recorded some of its ruins. Later in the nineteenth century several of the magnificently carved wooden lintels from Temples I and IV were removed to the Museum für Völkerkunde in Basel by an expedition under Gustav Bernoulli. Alfred Maudslay's visits in 1881 and 1882 were the first to photographically record the sculpture and architecture at Tikal. This work was continued by Teobert Maler in 1885 and 1904, as part of his efforts to record Maya sites for the Peabody Museum of Harvard University. Maler's work at Tikal was finished by Alfred Tozzer and R. E. Merwin of the Peabody Museum, who successfully completed the first map of the site (published in 1911). The monuments and inscriptions of Tikal were systematically recorded by Sylvanus Morley as part of his pioneering study of Maya hieroglyphic texts, after visits in 1914, 1921, 1922, and 1928. During the first year of the Carnegie Institution of Washington's excavations at nearby Uaxactun (see below), Edwin Shook visited Tikal and discovered a building complex, Group H, and two new causeways (named after Maler and Maudslay). At this time Shook began to formulate plans for an archaeological investigation of Tikal that were realized nearly twenty years later.

During these times Tikal could be reached only by an arduous journey on foot or muleback using the trails blazed by chicleros, collectors of raw chewing gum. But in 1951 the Guatemalan Air Force cleared a dirt airstrip adjacent to

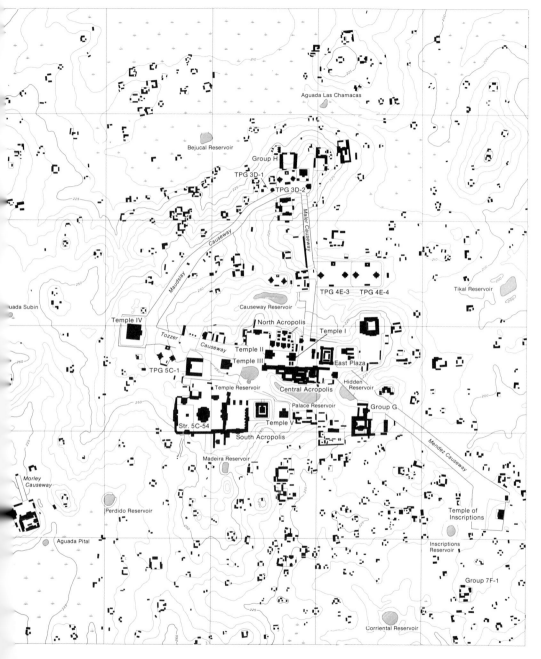

Fig. 11.6. Map of the central portion of Tikal, Guatemala (TPG = Twin Pyramid Group). Grid 500 meters square; elevation in meters.

the ruins. This made possible the large-scale movement of people and supplies into Tikal, and as a result, an archaeological research program became feasible. In 1956, after several years of planning, the University Museum of the University of Pennsylvania initiated the Tikal Project, which it was to continue for the next fifteen years. Shook served as the first field director for this research, and William Coe directed the project during its last seven years. Judged by almost any standard, the Tikal Project was conducted on an unprecedented scale for Maya archaeology. By its final year, in 1970, its professional staff over the years had totaled 113 archaeologists. The final results of the project's research are to be published in 28 volumes of reports (eleven preliminary reports are already in print, including a new site map). To date well over a hundred scholarly articles and other publications based on data gathered at Tikal have appeared.

With the close of the University of Pennsylvania's project in 1970, excavations of the buildings and their consolidation (reinforcement) continued under the auspices of the Instituto de Antropología e Historia of Guatemala. Under the direction of two expert Guatemalan archaeologists, Carlos Rudy Larios and Miguel Orrego, this work has concentrated on Group G, a large palace com-

Fig. 11.7. Aerial view of Tikal, looking northwest to the major buildings towering above the tropical forest: Temple IV (upper left), Temple V (lower left), Temple III (center left), and to the right, Temples I and II facing the Great Plaza, with the North Acropolis beyond and the palaces of the Central Acropolis in the foreground.

plex southeast of the Great Plaza. A new and expanded program of investigations at Tikal was initiated in 1980, directed by Jean Pierre LaPorte, and work is expected to continue at the site for many years to come.

The core area of Tikal is strategically situated on a series of low ridges (average elevation 250 m, or 820 ft) that rise about 50 m above two swampy depressions (*bajos*) lying to the east and west. Most of the great buildings presently visible (Fig. 11.7), clustered on the high ground of the site core, date from the Late Classic period, the time of Tikal's most pronounced power and construction activity. Although excavations revealed that many earlier buildings lie encased within Late Classic structures, the North Acropolis (Fig. 4.5) remained largely free from renovation, and its buildings are mostly from the Early Classic era. Another example of early construction is the Lost World Pyramid (Structure 5C-54), a massive Late Preclassic platform unaffected by later building activity.

The outlying groups of structures lie scattered over an area of residential occupation covering some 60 km² (23 sq. mi.), mostly on the higher and better-drained terrain. A system of earthworks, consisting of a shallow moat and interior rubble wall, connects the two swampy depressions (that once may have been shallow lakes), to protect Tikal from both the north and south. The area within these defensible boundaries totals some 123 km².

The most intensive excavations of the Tikal Project took place in the North Acropolis, located immediately north of the Great Plaza (Fig. 11.7). The North Acropolis is essentially a huge platform, measuring 100 by 80 m (330 by 260 ft), comprising numerous rebuildings and expansions, ultimately supporting a symmetrical arrangement of eight funerary temples (Fig. 11.8) constructed over a 300-year period (ca. A.D. 250–550). Older buildings lie buried beneath this platform, revealed by extensive trenching and tunneling (Figs. 4.4 and 4.5). The earliest appears to have been built during the Late Preclassic (ca. 200 B.C.). Four additional temples, each elevated by high pyramidal platforms, were later constructed one by one along the southern edge of the acropolis. Their staircases once led southward toward the Great Plaza below. Once constructed, these structures effectively screened off the North Acropolis from easy access during the final centuries of Tikal's occupation. Three smaller shrines flank the southeastern corner of the platform.

The North Acropolis excavations revealed not only a complex sequence of construction, but a succession of richly furnished tombs, indicating that this precinct of Tikal served as a necropolis, the burial place for Tikal's rulers from the Late Preclassic through the Early Classic. Our knowledge of the dynastic history of Tikal runs through the Classic era, minimally from the death of the first identified ruler around A.D. 376 to the inauguration of the last known ruler in 768 (see Chapter 4). This dynastic reconstruction is based on deciphered inscriptions from Tikal's monuments and lintels, together with evidence excavated from a number of rulers' tombs. Several of these in the North Acropolis have been identified as those of specific Early Classic rulers.

Fig. 11.8. Structure 5D-22, Tikal, one of the apparent funerary temples of the North Acropolis; the corner terraces of the Early Classic pyramid are decorated with "apron" moldings and masks flanking the axial staircase to the right.

Fragmentary wall paintings found in two Late Preclassic tombs from the North Acropolis (Burials 166 and 167) closely resemble the style and iconography of the southern Maya area (see Chapter 3). This is certainly evidence of contact between the two regions, perhaps resulting from obsidian and jadeite trade, or even indicating that the original Tikal ruling family came from a southern Maya center such as Kaminaljuyu. The earliest known dynastic monument in the Maya lowlands, Tikal Stela 29 (A.D. 292), reflects a sculptural heritage from the south in its portrayal of a standing profile figure accompanied by a historical long-count date (Fig. 4.6).

A tomb under Structure 5D-26 (Burial 22) can be dated to the Early Classic, probably the late fourth century A.D. Unfortunately, it appears to have been opened and looted during the Late Classic, but from what remained it has been tentatively proposed that it originally contained the burial of Tikal's first known ruler, Jaguar Paw. No monuments have been identified from this ruler's reign, but the later Stela 31 appears to give his death date in A.D. 377.

Two monuments are known from the next reign, that of Curl Nose, and both (Stelae 4 and 18) are near the front of Structure 5D-34, on the west front of the North Acropolis. This structure covers a deeply buried tomb (Burial 10), most likely that of Curl Nose, who died about 425 after being in power for some 47 years. The tomb contained the skeletal remains of the ruler and a variety of offerings that demonstrate close connections with the Early Classic elite tombs of Kaminaljuyu. During this era Kaminaljuyu was closely allied to Teotihuacan in central Mexico, and these links are also apparent in Curl Nose's tomb. Burial 10 contained a variety of pottery vessels with southern Maya associations, including several with stucco-painted decoration executed in a Teotihuacan style, a grotesque ceramic effigy of the "old god" (a deity of great importance in the southern area), and animal offerings (turtle carapaces, a crocodile skeleton, and bird remains) reminiscent of the contents of contemporary tombs at Kaminaljuyu. Finally, a small carved jadeite head from Burial 10 has been interpreted as a representation of the ruler's name glyph. From this evidence it has been concluded that Curl Nose reestablished the southern Maya connections seen in the Late Preclassic, possibly after Kaminaljuyu had recovered from the Ilopango disaster several centuries earlier (see Chapter 3). In fact, Curl Nose himself may have been a prince from there or from another Teotihuacan ally. According to this theory, proposed by Clemency Coggins, his rule at Tikal was validated or strengthened by his marriage to a woman from Tikal's established ruling lineage. Regardless, his connections to the south and with the powerful city of Teotihuacan are further attested to by the style of his inaugural monument, Stela 4 (Fig. 4.9).

These ties continued during the reign of the next ruler, recorded on Stela 31 as Curl Nose's son, Stormy Sky. Stormy Sky was the most important of Tikal's Early Classic rulers, since during his reign Tikal's power and dominance over much of the central lowlands was established (see Chapter 4). His tomb is probably Burial 48 (Fig. 11.9), found deep beneath the tall central pyramid (33 m high) fronting the north-south axis of the North Acropolis. This tomb also contained materials linked to both Teotihuacan and Kaminaljuyu, including a vessel painted with the butterfly motifs closely tied to central Mexican art. On the plastered walls of the tomb is a painted long-count date of 9.1.1.10.10 (A.D. 456), which occurs after the events of his reign mentioned on Stela 31 and is probably the date of Stormy Sky's death. The structure above the tomb, known as 5D-33, was built during the early years of the Late Classic period, but was so badly preserved that it was dissembled by excavation to reveal the earlier

Fig. 11.9. Chamber of Burial 48, Tikal, beneath Structure 5D-33-2nd in the North Acropolis (see Fig. 4.5); the decorated walls of this tomb included the presumed death date of Stormy Sky, 9.1.1.10.10 (A.D. 456).

structures buried beneath. The first of these, Structure 5D-33-3rd, was built over Stormy Sky's tomb, probably as a mortuary shrine for his ancestral cult. Not long after, this building was replaced by another (Str. 5D-33-2nd), possibly to commemorate an important anniversary of Stormy Sky's death. Finally, the great ruler of Late Classic Tikal, Ah Cacau (also known as Ruler A), seems to have marked his illustrious ancestor's death on its thirteenth-katun anniversary in 713 (9.14.1.10.10) by dedicating the largest North Acropolis building, 5D-33-1st. But before this latest building was constructed, Stormy Sky's magnificent monument, Stela 31 (Fig. 4.11), which may have stood in front of his mortuary temple, was carried up the staircase and reset within the rear room of 5D-33-2nd, almost directly over his anciently concealed tomb. There, after rituals that left the broken base of the monument burned, and smashed incensarios strewn about the room, the stela was carefully encased in rubble fill and the partially dismantled building buried beneath the new shrine. Here Stela

31 was found during the excavations of the Tikal Project just as the Maya had left it. It portrays Stormy Sky in traditional Maya regalia, complete with his name glyph attached to his headdress. In the crook of his left arm he carries a head with Sun Jaguar attributes and the Tikal emblem glyph attached. When Stormy Sky's tomb was opened by archaeologists, the ruler's remains were found flanked by the bones of two retainers, probably sacrificed upon his death. On Stela 31 Stormy Sky is similarly flanked by two guardians dressed in Teotihuacan-style military garb, carrying shields, spear throwers, and feathered darts. The lengthy hieroglyphic inscription on the back of the monument records nothing less than the early dynastic history of Tikal, including the apparent death date of Jaguar Paw (8.17.1.4.12), the inauguration of Curl Nose (8.17.2.16.17), and the commemoration of the first katun of Stormy Sky's own reign (9.0.10.0.0, or A.D. 445).

Fig. 11.10. Temple II, Tikal: consolidated after excavation.

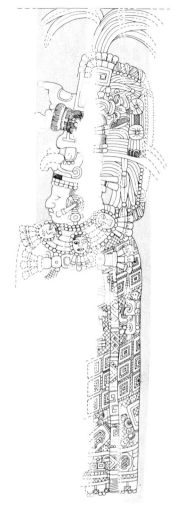

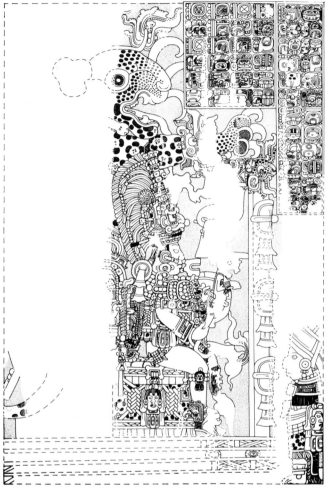

Fig. 11.11. Temple II, Tikal: drawing of a carved wooden lintel showing the portrait of a woman, possibly the wife of Ah Cacau.

Fig. 11.12. Carved wooden lintel from Temple I, Tikal (see Fig. 4.17), with the portrait of Ah Cacau seated in front of a giant jaguar "protector."

Immediately south of the North Acropolis is the Great Plaza, flanked by two magnificent structures, Temple I on the east and Temple II on the west. Both were built in the Late Classic period, although Temple II appears as an enlarged version of Tikal's typical Early Classic architectural style (Fig. 11.10). The wooden lintel of Temple II seems to portray a woman and may have commemorated the wife of the ruler Ah Cacau (Fig. 11.11). Temple I, rising some 47 m (155 ft) above the plaza, is innovative in its location outside the traditional necropolis and in its architecture (Figs. 4.17 and 4.18). Its proportions depart from the Early Classic style, the nine stepped terraces stressing its height. It may have been modeled after the slightly earlier Structure 5D-33-1st, probably built by Ah Cacau to honor Stormy Sky, and thus may have been symbolic of the thirteen-katun link between the two reigns. But Temple I was actually built after Ah Cacau's death, probably by his instructions to his son and successor, Yax Kin Caan Chac. Ah Cacau's tomb was discovered underneath, north of the centerline of the pyramid. On its summit is a three-room temple, surmounted by a huge roof comb portraying the ruler seated on his throne, which undoubtedly served as his mortuary shrine. A carved wooden lintel inside this shrine (Fig. 11.12) depicts Ah Cacau seated before an immense jaguar-protector deity, and records the inauguration of his rule on 9.12.9.17.16 (May 4, 682).

His tomb (Burial 116) consists of a large vaulted sepulcher constructed within a nearly 7-m-deep excavation, over which Temple I was then built. Measuring some 5 by 2.5 m and over 4 m high (16 by 8 by 13 ft), the chamber floor was mostly taken up by a masonry bench. On the bench were found the skeletal remains of Ah Cacau, lying on what once had been a woven mat (*po*, a symbol of rulership) bordered by ornaments of oyster shell and jadeite (Fig. 4.19). Gathered about the remains was an array of offerings, including polychrome pottery vessels, shells, pearls, and jade. Ah Cacau himself was adorned by a massive jadeite necklace made of large round beads, like that depicted around his neck in his sculptured portraits on Stelae 16 and 30. Among the more than sixteen pounds of jadeite in the tomb were a jade-mosaic cylindrical vase with a cover bearing his hieroglyphic name and possibly a miniature of Ah Cacau's head (Fig. 13.51). A bundle of carved bones lay nearby. When cleaned, 37 were found to include finely incised hieroglyphic inscriptions, including Ah Cacau's name glyphs and passages seemingly referring to events of his life and journey to the underworld after his death. The underworld journey is depicted as having been in a canoe borne by animal deities.

South of the Great Plaza lie several massive architectural complexes and the adjacent Central Acropolis, consisting of a maze of multi-room and multistory residential structures arranged around a series of internal courtyards (Fig. 11.13). This area surely housed Tikal's ruling dynasty and their retainers during much of the Classic period. Farther to the south, across one of the reservoirs constructed to ensure water supplies during each dry season, lies Temple V, the apparent mortuary shrine to an unknown ruler. This structure is some 57 m high (187 ft), the second tallest of Tikal's temples (after Temple IV). West of Temple V is the still-unexcavated South Acropolis, and the Plaza of the Seven Temples, named after a row of nearly identical shrines on its east side. This plaza is also notable for the unique triple ball court on its northern edge. Still farther west

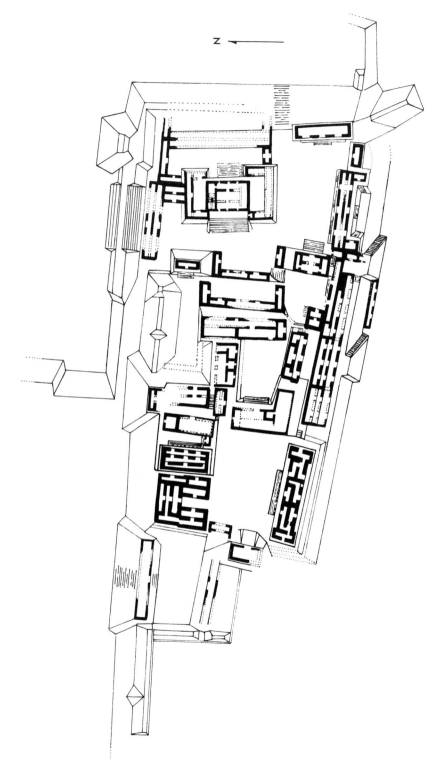

Fig. 11.13. Plan of the Central Acropolis at Tikal, the probable residential complex for the Lake Classic rulers of this center.

lies a large enclosed plaza centered around the huge Late Preclassic Lost World Pyramid, seemingly associated with Tikal's early history and maintained, because of its importance, throughout the center's occupation.

Immediately north of the Central Acropolis, and just behind Temple I, lies the East Plaza. Its most conspicuous feature is a large rectangular assemblage of multiroom buildings (Structures 5E-32 to 5E-36) that seems to have served as Tikal's major market. Just to the west of this is Tikal's largest ball court. The East Plaza provides an intersection for two *sacbeob*, the Maler Causeway leading northward to Group H, and the Mendez Causeway leading southeast to Temple VI (Temple of the Inscriptions). The Mendez *sacbe* also provides an avenue to Group G, a major palace complex nearly as large as the Central Acropolis. Recent excavations in Group G have revealed a buried building under Structure 5E-55; its rooms were unusually well preserved because of the obvious care with which rubble fill was packed into them before construction covered them. The interior walls of several of these rooms were decorated by a variety of incised and painted graffiti, including several finely executed, short hieroglyphic texts and a gruesome human sacrificial scene. A red sun symbol was found painted on the vault of the central room, reminiscent of the same sort of sign painted on the vault of Ah Cacau's tomb under Temple I. The walls of an adjoining room were covered with handprints of red paint and mud slurry; the mud-slurry prints depict two *ahau* glyphs, one formed by three handprints, all done at the time the rooms were being filled and abandoned.

The reign of Ah Cacau was marked by the construction of the first two dated Twin Pyramid groups, a symmetrical architectural assemblage originating in Early Classic Tikal (only one example is known from another site; see Yaxha, below). The assemblage consists of two flat-topped pyramids with four staircases flanking the east and west sides of a plaza. On the south side is a single building with nine doorways, and on the north, a walled enclosure containing a stela and altar. Twin pyramid groups were constructed for the rituals commemorating the passage of each katun (see Chapter 14), a period of twenty 360-day years.

The first katun ending of Ah Cacau's rule was marked by Twin Pyramid Group 3D-1, situated in Group H, 1 km north of the Great Plaza. Group 3D-1 was razed by later construction, but its monuments have survived. Stela 30 retains its portrait of Ah Cacau, and its companion Altar 14 has a giant 8-Ahau glyph, naming the current katun, and a long-count date of 9.13.0.0.0, corresponding to March 18, A.D. 692, nearly ten years after his accession to power. The next katun ending of 9.14.0.0.0 (December 5, 711) is commemorated by Twin Pyramid Group 5D-1, located to the west of the Great Plaza, adjacent to the Tozzer Causeway and near the base of Temple IV. In the remains of the enclosure are Stela 16, bearing its portrait of Ah Cacau (Fig. 11.14), and Altar 5, whose text and sculptured scene might refer to the death of his wife or an important woman from the ruling dynasty.

Fig. 11.14. Stela 16 from Twin Pyramid Group 5D-1, Tikal, portraying Ah Cacau (9.14.0.0.0, or A.D. 711).

The Tozzer Causeway leads west from the rear of Temple II to the massive Temple IV, the largest structure at Tikal, towering some 70 m high (230 ft; Fig. 11.7). Temple IV appears to mark the reign of Ah Cacau's son and successor, Yax Kin Caan Chac. The two carved wooden lintels over the wide doorway leading into the narrow-roomed shrine on its summit record the date 9.15.10.0.0 (741). They depict elaborate portraits of the ruler (Fig. 11.15), and of the name glyphs of him and his father, who was noted as living into his fourth katun (between 60 and 80 years old). The exact date of Ah Cacau's death is not known, but it was apparently between 721 and 734. One of the carved bones in his tomb bears the date 9.14.11.17.3 (723), which may refer to his death.

We do know that Yax Kin (Ruler B) was inaugurated 9.15.3.6.8 (December 10, 734), a date commemorated on Stela 21, located at the base of Temple VI far to the southeast. This structure, also built during or immediately after Yax Kin's reign, is notable for the extensive hieroglyphic text on the sides and back of its roof comb (Fig. 11.16), dated 9.16.15.0.0 and recording much of the dynastic history of Tikal (see Chapter 4). Yax Kin marked the end of the first katun of his reign with Twin Pyramid Group 3D-2, at the northern terminus of the Maler Causeway in Group H (Fig. 11.17). Its enclosure contains Stela 20 and Altar 8, dedicated to the katun ending 9.16.0.0.0 (751).

The tomb of Yax Kin has not been positively identified. Several scholars have suggested that it is probably located either in Temple IV or Temple VI, both likely candidates as mortuary shrines. During the Tikal Project excavations, however, a richly furnished tomb (Burial 196) was found beneath a small pyramid, Structure 5D-73, immediately south of Temple II in the Great Plaza. This building is unusual in having no masonry structure on its summit. But the contents of the tomb were fully as sumptuous as those of Ah Cacau's Burial 116. In fact, as William Coe has pointed out, the contents and organization of Burial 196 duplicated those of Burial 116 in many ways. The most striking parallel was the presence of a cylindrical jadeite mosaic vessel (see Fig. 13.51). Although there are no hieroglyphic texts to positively identify its occupant, its contents included a carved bone with the date 9.16.3.0.0, not long before the time of Yax Kin's death, or around 766. Thus, Yax Kin's tomb has probably already been found, and his mortuary shrine seems to have been built apart from his final resting place.

The last identified ruler of Tikal, known as Chitam (Ruler C), marked two katun endings with Twin Pyramid Groups during his reign. The first of these, and the largest at Tikal, is Twin Pyramid Group 4E-4, located east of the Maler Causeway, halfway between the East Plaza and Group H. Dedicated in 9.17.0.0.0 (771), it contains Stela 22 and Altar 10 (Figs. 11.18 and 11.19). The stela, bearing a portrait of Chitam, records the date of his accession to power in 9.16.17.16.4 (768). One katun later (9.18.0.0.0, or 790), Twin Pyramid Group 4E-3 was built next to 4E-4; it includes Stela 19 and Altar 6.

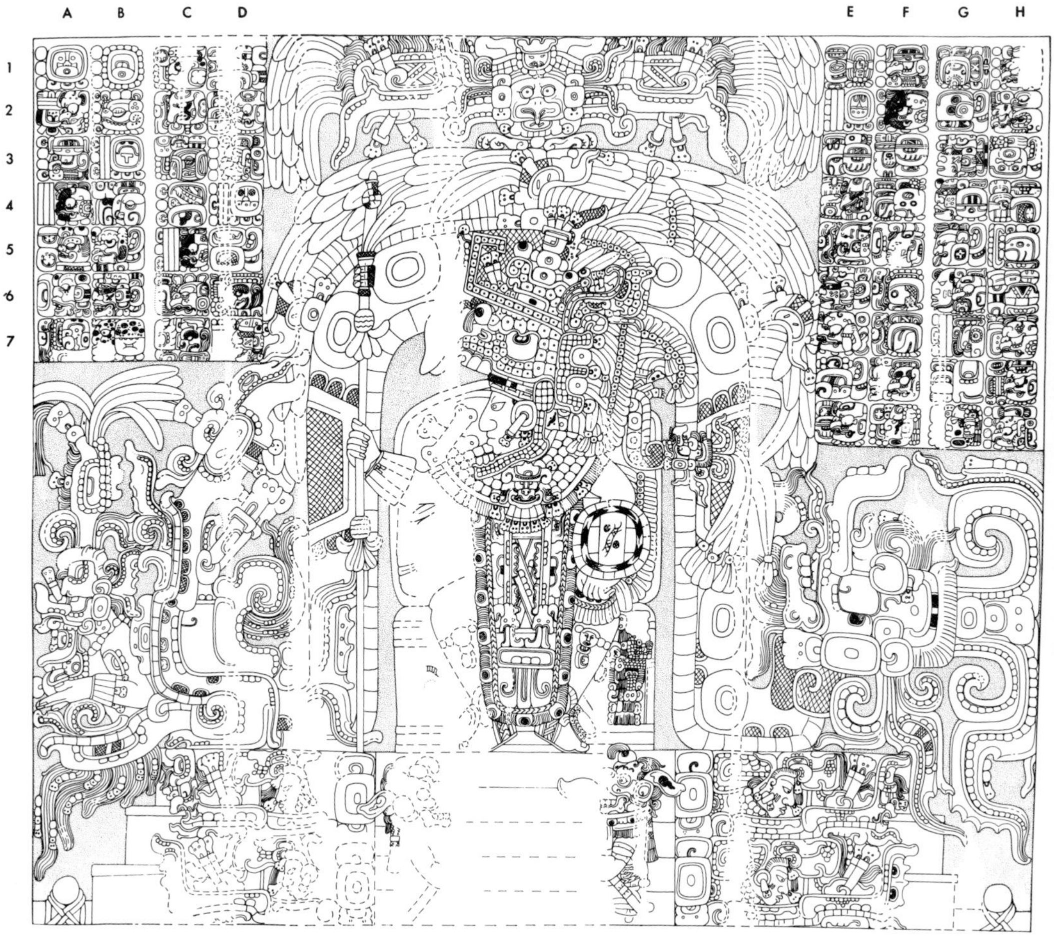

Fig. 11.15. Drawings of carved wooden lintels from Temple IV, Tikal: (*above*) Yax Kin, ruler of Tikal; (*facing page*) Yax Kin holding a manikin scepter, seated in front of a giant "protector" figure.

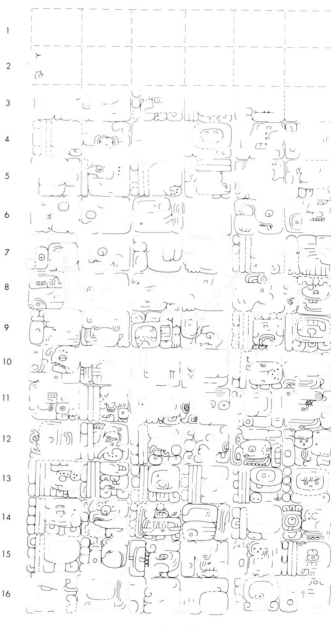

Panel W

Fig. 11.16. Drawing of the partially preserved inscription on the roof comb of Temple VI (Temple of the Inscriptions), detailing events in the history of Tikal.

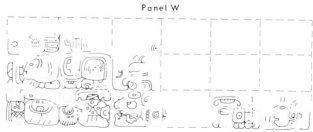

Panel X

A

1
2
3
4
5
6
7
8
9

Fig. 11.17. Stela 20 from Twin Pyramid Group 3D-2, Tikal, portraying Yax Kin holding a war-club staff. Note the jaguar throne.

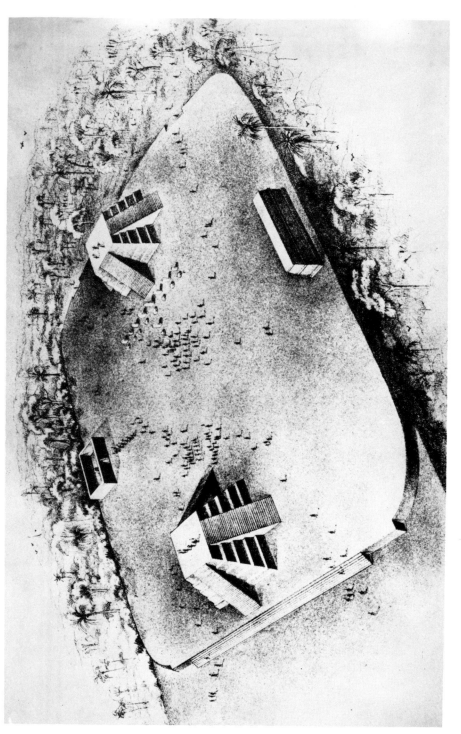

Fig. 11.18. Tikal Twin Pyramid Group 4E-4: restoration view, the monument enclosure holding Stela 22 and Altar 10 in upper left (drawing by Norman Johnson).

Fig. 11.19. Tikal Twin Pyramid Group 4E-4: within the enclosure, a view of Altar 10 backed by Stela 22, which portrays Chitam (9.17.0.0.0, or A.D. 771; see Fig. 15.16 for decipherment of the Stela 22 text).

The latest of Tikal's Late Classic pyramid temples, Temple III, may have served as Chitam's mortuary shrine, or it might be associated with a subsequent, and still unidentified, ruler. Temple III is located west of the Great Plaza, and its summit shrine contains a carved wooden lintel depicting a corpulent ruler, dressed in a jaguar skin (Fig. 11.20). There are a pair of monuments at its base, Stela 24 and Altar 7, which have been dated to 810

Fig. 11.20. Drawing of a carved wooden lintel from Temple III, Tikal, presumably showing the portrait of a ruler (Chitam?) dressed in a jaguar pelt.

(9.19.0.0.0). Only one monument at Tikal has a later date, Stela 11 in the Great Plaza, with a 10.2.0.0.0 (869) inscription. This may refer to yet another ruler, but by this time construction activity had long since ceased, and the center was rapidly losing population. Its days of glory and power past, Tikal seems to have been totally abandoned by the end of the tenth century.

## Uaxactun

Uaxactun is located some 40 km (25 mi.) north of Tikal. Meaning "eight stone," the name was coined by archaeologists in recognition of Stela 9, which dates from the eighth baktun at the site (Fig. 4.8). Although substantially smaller than Tikal, Uaxactun's span of occupation seems to have been about the same, with origins in the Middle Preclassic and abandonment by the Early Postclassic.

The first comprehensive archaeological investigations in the central lowlands were conducted at Uaxactun over twelve years (1926–37) by the Carnegie Institution of Washington. Participants in this project included Franz Blom, Oliver Ricketson, A. Ledyard Smith, Robert Smith, Edwin Shook, and Robert Wauchope. The pioneering research of these scholars provided a series of firsts in lowland Maya archaeology. For example, the basic cultural chronology for the central lowlands was founded on the available calendrical inscriptions, the pottery sequence, and architectural development. This chronology has been used as a starting point for almost every other chronological sequence in the region. As a case in point, the chronology of pottery forms and types at Tikal, owing to their similarities to those from Uaxactun, is founded on the work done by the original Carnegie research.

Uaxactun, mapped during the Carnegie investigations, consists of a series of architectural groups situated on five low hills or ridges, surrounded by the remains of house platforms. The house mound survey at Uaxactun, directed by Ricketson, discovered an apparent density of occupation far higher than a swidden subsistence system would allow, resulting in one of the first suggestions that Maya agriculture must have been more productive than contemporary theories had held (see Chapter 7).

Excavations in Group E revealed the first known Maya architectural assemblage aligned so as to function as an astronomical observatory. In the years since, a series of similar building alignments has been found at other Classic centers. These observatories seem to have been used primarily for determining the positions of equinoxes and solstices. A pyramid was built on the west side of a court, facing due east (Fig. 11.21). On the opposite side, three temples were erected on a terrace, their façades running north and south, arranged so as to establish lines of sight when observed from the stairway of the pyramid on the west side. From this observation point, the sun, on its way north, rose directly

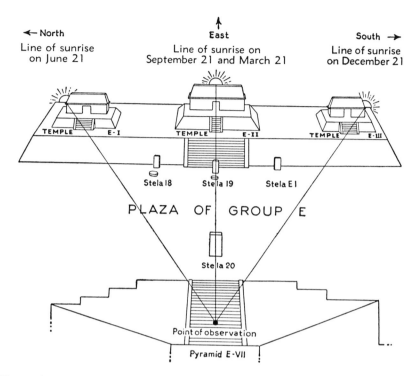

Fig. 11.21. Perspective diagram of Group E, Uaxactun, Guatemala, showing alignments apparently used to determine the dates of solstices and equinoxes.

behind the middle temple (E-II in the figure) on March 21, the vernal equinox; behind the north front corner of the north temple (E-I) on June 21, the summer solstice; behind the middle temple again on its way back south on September 23, the autumnal equinox; and behind the south front corner of the south temple (E-III) on December 21, the winter solstice. This assemblage of buildings was a practical instrument for determining the longest and shortest days of the year, and the two intermediate positions when day and night are of equal length.

Excavation of the badly ruined Structure E-VII revealed a well-preserved earlier platform underneath, dubbed E-VII-sub. The substructure dates from the Late Preclassic era, and at the time of its discovery it was the earliest building known from the Maya lowlands. The terraced surfaces of E-VII-sub were completely covered with lime-based plaster, as were its four stairways and sixteen side masks (Figs. 3.19 and 3.20). The platform surface never held a masonry building. Four postholes were found in the plaster flooring, and these no doubt supported the corner posts for a thatched-roof structure. Since E-VII-sub's discovery, several buildings of the same age have been excavated, includ-

Fig. 11.22. Drawing of the mural in Uaxactun Structure B-XIII, dating to the end of the Early Classic era: (*above*) left half; (*below*) right half.

ing the larger Lost World Pyramid at Tikal, and Structure 5C-2nd at Cerros in Belize, a center that reached its apogee in the Late Preclassic.

Work was also conducted in Uaxactun's Group A, a complex of temples, palaces, and monuments. A *sacbe* leads north from Group A, past an ancient water reservoir, to Group B. There, in the excavation of Structure B-XIII, a mural was found dating to the end of the Early Classic period (Fig. 11.22). The painting has since perished, but fortunately it was accurately copied by Antonio Tejeda. It depicts a flat-roofed building within which are seated three women. Just outside is a black-painted male, with his arm across his chest in the sign of greeting. He faces another man, dressed in Mexican attire, holding an atlatl (spear thrower). These figures, together with the more than twenty others depicted, are accompanied by hieroglyphic texts. The scene appears to represent a meeting or ceremony between local elite and a foreign representative, perhaps from Kaminaljuyu or even Teotihuacan.

At present Uaxactun remains much as it was; no consolidation or restoration was undertaken by the Carnegie project. Recently, however, Shook returned to the site to direct the consolidation of E-VII-sub, so that this important example of early Maya architecture has been preserved.

## El Mirador

El Mirador is a vast site in the Peten of Guatemala, some 65 km (40 mi.) north of Tikal and about 7 km (4 mi.) south of the present Mexican border. The center is situated on high ground among an area of *bajos* that may have formed shallow lakes in the past (Fig. 11.23). A series of *sacbeob* radiates from Mirador across several of the *bajos* and appears to connect outlying groups or nearby sites.

The ruins of Mirador were first reported in 1926. In 1930 its forest-covered temples were photographed from the air by Percy Madeira, Jr., as part of his aerial reconnaissance of Maya sites. In 1962 Ian Graham spent ten days at the site, conducting a ground survey and preparing a preliminary map. The current program of archaeological investigation began in 1978 (Fig. 11.24), facilitated by the recent construction of an airstrip near the ruins. This research, directed by Bruce Dahlin and Ray Matheny has already added a great deal to our meager understanding of this very significant Maya center.

The known extent of the main group of architecture covers an area of at least 2 km² (0.8 sq. mi.). Many of the buildings within this area were constructed on a grand scale (Fig. 11.25). The portion depicted on the map is dominated by the second-largest architectural complex at the site, known as El Tigre. This complex is composed of a massive pyramidal platform surmounted by three smaller pyramids, together rising to a total height of some 55 m (180 feet) above the surrounding terrain. This triadic architectural pattern is found repeatedly at El Mirador, and is usually seen as reflecting an ancient Maya tradition, in contrast

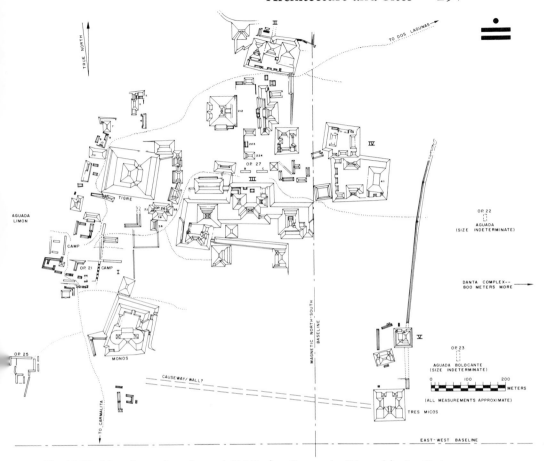

Fig. 11.23. Map of a portion of central El Mirador, Guatemala. (Mapped by Ian Graham, 1967, with additions by Glenna Nielsen.)

to the quadratic pattern interpreted as a Classic-period Mexican introduction and seen, for example, in the Twin Pyramid groups at Tikal.

To the south of El Tigre is another, slightly smaller triadic complex known as Monos (some 40 m high, or 130 ft). The area west of El Tigre is dominated by a large building complex labeled the Acropolis, which includes yet another triadic platform. In the court north of this platform are the fragmentary remains of several Late Preclassic–style sculptured monuments, apparently devoid of hieroglyphic texts. A host of smaller structures, including Late Preclassic domestic platforms, surrounds these prominent constructions.

The eastern boundary of this entire group is marked by a north-south masonry wall, joining a little-known complex known as Tres Micos to the southeast. In 1982, excavations in this boundary wall indicated that it dates to the Late Preclassic and revealed a sculptured monument fragment (re-used as part of the wall). This fragment appears to be the broken top portion of a Late Preclassic stela.

An east-west causeway links a portal in this wall to the largest single architectural complex at El Mirador, known as Danta. A plain stela and altar have been found at the base of this complex, just north of the termination of the causeway. The Danta Complex rises above a basal terrace in three stages. The lowest platform, measuring some 300 m on each side and about 7 m high (985 by 23 ft), supports a series of buildings, including a large (11-m-high) triadic platform on its southwestern corner. The second, smaller platform rises another 7 m, and in turn supports a third platform, some 21 m high. Crowning this

Fig. 11.24. El Mirador: excavation of an Early Classic elite residence recently plundered by looters, who left the irregular pit seen in the center of the trench.

Fig. 11.25. South side of Structure 34, El Mirador, rising some 20 meters, the smaller structure located immediately southeast of the major pyramid (El Tigre) in Fig. 11.23. Recent excavations indicate that Structure 34 was constructed in Late Preclassic times.

third stage is another triadic arrangement of pyramids, the largest (easternmost) rises yet another 21 m to its summit. The total height of this, the highest point at El Mirador, is some 70 m (230 feet) above ground level at its eastern base, making this the tallest (and most massive) Maya construction known. If superimposed on Tikal's Great Plaza, the Danta Complex would cover the entire plaza, both Temples I and II, and the North Acropolis. The east-west distance from Danta to El Tigre (ca. 2 km) is about the same as the east-west distance from Temples IV to VI at Tikal.

The Danta structures are faced with cut-stone masonry, and excavations here and elsewhere at El Mirador (Fig. 4.3) reveal that they were elaborately decorated with stucco masks in the Late Preclassic lowland style. These investigations also indicate that Late Classic peoples who re-occupied the site used some of this masonry to build domestic structures that cover portions of the first and second platforms at Danta. Excavations beneath these later superficial constructions consistently revealed Late Preclassic materials.

The results of the archaeological investigations at El Mirador conducted thus far demonstrate that occupation there originated during the Middle Preclassic, with a peak of population and constructional activity in the Late Preclassic, and ended during the Protoclassic era. The several fragmentary sculptured monuments show stylistic affinities to the Late Preclassic tradition of the southern Maya area. This link is reinforced by the finding of ceramic modes, including Usulutan and Usulutan-related types, closely allied to the Late Preclassic traditions from the same southern Maya region. Classic-period pottery is also present, but this later occupation seems to have built only domestic structures and to have rapidly declined by the end of this era.

In summary, present evidence indicates that El Mirador was the single largest and most powerful Maya center during the Late Preclassic period, a role seemingly ancestral to the later dominance enjoyed by Tikal in the Classic era and clearly on a par with that of Teotihuacan and other large contemporary highland urban centers. Further investigation of El Mirador is obviously essential to better understand the origins of Maya civilization—and the entire question of the genesis of urban states in Mesoamerica.

## Nakum, Naranjo, and Yaxha

These three central lowland sites are located southeast of Tikal. Although none has been subjected to comprehensive archaeological investigation, all represent important centers of Classic occupation.

Nakum was reported to the outside world as a result of the explorations of Maurice de Perigny in 1905–6. A preliminary study and partial site map were published in 1913 by Alfred Tozzer. Additional mapping was done at Nakum by Nicholas Hellmuth in 1973, but no overall settlement map has been done. These maps reveal that the site core (central area) of Nakum is composed of two large architectural complexes, connected by a *sacbe* (the Perigny Causeway). The southern complex contains a Group-E astronomical alignment (see Uaxactun, above). Temple A, on the east side of this group, is noteworthy in having two unusual corbel-vaulted doorways flanking a central doorway with a wooden lintel. To the south is a large acropolis supporting a series of apparently residential structures and courts, comparable to the Central Acropolis at Tikal. Near its center is a higher platform surmounted by four buildings facing an inner court, possibly the residence of Nakum's ruling family.

Nakum appears to be largely a Late Classic center, but earlier remains may of course be revealed when archaeological excavations are conducted. Unfortunately, however, the site has apparently been heavily looted. Nakum's three dated stelae, of some fifteen known from the site, correspond to A.D. 771, 810, and 849. Located only 25 km (15 mi.) east of Tikal, near the headwaters of the Río Holmul, it probably once served as an important trade link between Tikal and the Caribbean coast.

The site of Naranjo, about 25 km east of Nakum, was reported by Teobert Maler after his explorations in 1905. On the basis of the information available, Naranjo contains impressive architectural remains. Its rather numerous monuments (47, of which 36 are sculptured) span the Late Classic period (9.8.0.0.0

to 9.19.10.0.0). One of the earliest in the sequence, Stela 25 from 9.9.2.0.4, is shown in Fig. 11.26. The local dynastic sequence, worked out from Naranjo's hieroglyphic texts, indicates close ties to Tikal.

First reported by Maler after his visit in 1904, Yaxha lies on the north shore of the lake by the same name, about 30 km (19 mi.) southeast of Tikal. It was mapped during the 1930's by the Carnegie Institution of Washington, and in the early 1970's further mapping and test excavations were conducted in the site core under the direction of Hellmuth. The architectural core consists of a series of plazas and acropolis groups, with access to several outlying groups and the lakeshore provided by three *sacbeob*. There is an architectural alignment similar to Group E at Uaxactun, and the only Twin Pyramid Group identified

Fig. 11.26. Stela 25, Naranjo, showing a frontal portrait of the first identified local ruler, holding a double-headed ceremonial bar (9.9.2.0.4, or A.D. 615).

outside of Tikal. The sculptured monuments indicate elite occupation from the Early to Late Classic (8.16.0.0.0 to 9.18.3.0.0).

## Calakmul

Calakmul is situated about 120 km (74 mi.) north of Tikal. Judging from what is known about the site's sculpture and its extensive architecture, it must have been a large and important center. Though Calakmul remains relatively unknown, it contains more stelae than any other center in the Maya area. In some instances, several monuments were dedicated at the same time; for example, in 9.15.0.0.0 (A.D. 731) seven stelae were erected to commemorate the katun ending. Calakmul's monuments span 9.4.0.0.0 to 9.18.0.0.0, or 514 to 790. It has been identified as one of the four regional centers whose emblem glyphs appear on Stela A at Copan (see Chapter 4).

One interesting feature is a sculptured limestone outcrop, measuring some 6.5 by 5 m, depicting seven captive figures with their hands bound behind their backs. The largest figure in the group stands nearly 3 m (10 ft) tall.

## Becan

Becan is situated in the heart of the Yucatan Peninsula, some 150 km (93 mi.) north of Tikal. The site was discovered in 1934 by two archaeologists, Karl Ruppert and John Denison, who named it after its most conspicuous feature, an encircling moat and rampart (Becan: "ditch filled with water"). Three seasons of archaeological investigations in the Río Bec region were carried out from 1969 to 1971, and much of this work focused on Becan. The project was sponsored by Tulane University and the National Geographic Society, under the overall direction of E. Wyllys Andrews IV. The research also examined the settlement and subsistence activities around Becan, and the nearby, unfortified, elite center of Chicanna.

The core of Becan is defined by the moat and rampart, which enclose an oval-shaped area of about 46 acres (Fig. 11.27). Excavations revealed that the moat was originally some 5 m deep and about 16 m wide (16 ft deep, 52 ft wide), its interior rampart rising another 5 m. Access to the site was by seven narrow and solid causeways across the moat, formed by leaving strips of the limestone bedrock intact. The rampart was built of the underlying soft limestone rubble (*sascab*). There is no evidence of a parapet and interior walkway, as found at the smaller fortifications of Mayapan and Tulum. Construction of the moat and rampart is dated to the first part of the Early Classic, or possibly even slightly earlier.

Ceramic evidence indicates that Becan and its surrounding region were first settled near the end of the Middle Preclassic (by ca. 550 B.C.). Rapid population growth seems to have occurred throughout the Late Preclassic, when an

Fig. 11.27. Becan, Campeche, Mexico: aerial view showing the surrounding massive ditch and earthen rampart.

elite center first emerged. Structure IV-sub, some 15 m high, was built during this era. This expansion appears to have been due to a combination of the good agricultural potential in the region and Becan's strategic position in controlling local trade routes. The defensive facilities were eventually constructed to maintain Becan's political and economic control over the region.

Population seems to have contracted during the Early Classic, beginning shortly after the moat-and-rampart system was constructed. Trade contacts with Teotihuacan are indicated by the presence of central-Mexican obsidian and by a famous cache of a slab-leg cylindrical vessel (with Maya style decoration) containing a hollow Teotihuacan figurine, excavated from Structure XIV (see Fig. 12.11, lower illustration). Becan's population seems to have continued to decline through the end of the Early Classic.

In the Late Classic Becan was revitalized, as the population dramatically increased and vigorous building activity resumed. The majority of the civic structures at the site, and the nearby centers of Chicanna and Xpuhil, reflect the Río Bec architectural style that developed during this period (Fig. 6.4, upper illustration). The architectural activity of the Late Classic ceased by the beginning of the Terminal Classic (ca. 830). Changes in the ceramic inventory, however, indicate that peoples from northern Yucatan settled at Becan during the Terminal Classic. By Early Postclassic times Becan and its surrounding region saw the beginning of a steady population decline, and the elite centers of the Río Bec region were soon abandoned.

## Altun Ha

The next three centers are located in the eastern periphery of the central lowlands, in what is now Belize. All three have received some archaeological investigation, the most comprehensive being the recent research at Altun Ha.

The site of Altun Ha is located in northern Belize, near the Caribbean coast, adjacent to the town of Rockstone Pond, from which it was named Altun Ha, or "place of stone water." Archaeological investigations directed by David Pendergast, and sponsored by the Royal Ontario Museum, took place at Altun Ha from 1964 to 1970. This research revealed that this center had been occupied since the Early Preclassic (ca. 1000 B.C.), but that the currently visible construction results largely from expansion dating from the Classic era. Population probably peaked at about 3,000 during that time.

The core of the site is clustered around two plazas, one to the north (Group A; Fig. 11.28) and the other to the south (Group B). The excavation of

Fig. 11.28. Altun Ha, Belize: view of Group A after excavation and consolidation of the structures.

Fig. 11.29 (*above*). Altun Ha: Structure B-4, which contained a jadeite carving of Kinich Ahau, the sun deity.

Fig. 11.30. The head of Kinich Ahau from Structure B-4; this figure, the largest known Maya jadeite carving, weighs 4.42 kilograms (9.7 pounds).

Fig. 11.31. Altun Ha: the grave goods in the Structure A-1 tomb.

Structure B-4 (Fig. 11.29), on the east side of Plaza B, revealed a richly furnished tomb, probably that of one of Altun Ha's rulers. Among its contents
was the largest Maya jadeite sculpture yet found (Fig. 11.30), a representation
of Kinich Ahau, the sun deity (God G), weighing 4.42 kg (9.7 lb). Another
tomb (Fig. 11.31) was discovered in Structure A-1, containing some 300 jadeite
objects and the decomposed residue of a codex, or Maya book. All this is

evidence of considerable wealth and power held by the rulers of Altun Ha, an unexpected finding in what was previously thought to be a minor and unimportant center on the eastern edge of the lowlands. But the evidence excavated from Altun Ha indicates that this center participated in, and reaped the benefits from, a trade network connecting the Caribbean coast with the core of the central lowlands, probably dominated by Tikal.

## Caracol

Caracol is situated adjacent to the foothills of the Maya Mountains, in south-central Belize. Its location provided close access to the resources of the area, especially crystalline rock for grinding stones. This undoubtedly contributed to the development and prosperity of Caracol as a trading center. Discovered in 1938, the site was initially investigated by an expedition from the University Museum, University of Pennsylvania, directed by Linton Satterthwaite during two field seasons in 1951 and 1953. The principal objective of this work was to record and preserve the recently discovered sculptured monuments and to map the site. Clearing and excavations undertaken to locate additional monuments uncovered four new stelae and a series of elite tombs associated with the monuments. In 1958 another season was conducted by A. H. Anderson, Archaeological Commissioner of Belize, resulting in the discovery of more burials and an additional stela.

Forty monuments are now known from Caracol, spanning most of the Classic period, from A.D. 485 (9.2.10.0.0) to 849 (10.1.0.0.0) or possibly 889 (10.3.0.0.0). A long hiatus occurs in this record from 692 to 771 (9.13.0.0.0 to 9.17.0.0.0), but an important dynastic sequence has been worked out from the inscriptions on these monuments.

## Xunantunich

Xunantunich is a small site (also known as Benque Viejo) near the headwaters of the Río Belize, just east of the Guatemala-Belize border. After a visit by Teobert Maler in 1905, brief archaeological work was conducted at the site by several investigators, including J. Eric Thompson (1938) and Linton Satterthwaite (1951), before an expedition from the Museum of Archaeology and Ethnology, Cambridge University, excavated and consolidated portions of the site core in 1959–60. This work revealed evidence of structural damage caused by an earthquake near the end of the Classic-period occupation of Xunantunich, which led to the development of the theory that earthquakes may have caused the Classic Maya "collapse" (see Chapter 5). Xunantunich is dominated by Structure A-6, a large building complex that rises to a height of some 40 m (130 ft), and contains an elaborate stucco-and-stone mosaic façade. The site has only one known dated monument, from the Terminal Classic period (10.1.0.0.0, or A.D. 849).

## Lubaantun

Lubaantun is a small Late Classic center located in the dense rain forest of southern Belize, well within the southern lowlands. The site is situated close to the Río Grande, a small river that provided access to the Caribbean only 30 km (19 mi.) to the southeast. The ruins, discovered in 1903 by Thomas Gann, were sporadically investigated by Gann and others, including R. E. Merwin, whose explorations for the Peabody Museum of Harvard University brought him to Lubaantun in 1915. In 1926 and 1927 T. A. Joyce led a British Museum expedition to excavate the site. In 1928 the British Museum work was abandoned to give priority to surveying the newly discovered site of Pusilha, about 32 km to the southwest. Pusilha generated more interest at the time since unlike Lubaantun it contained sculptured stelae with hieroglyphic inscriptions.

The investigation of Lubaantun was resumed in 1970 by a project jointly sponsored by Cambridge and Harvard universities, directed by Norman Hammond. This research produced a new map of the site core, and verification of the conclusions based on the earlier work that Lubaantun had been occupied relatively briefly, only from about A.D. 700 to 870. Thus, Lubaantun seems to have been the result of a Late Classic colonization of the Río Grande region. The recent research suggests that this was done to administer the production of the principal export item of the region, cacao.

The site does not display the two hallmarks of Classic lowland Maya centers: vaulted buildings and sculptured monuments. Lubaantun is essentially a single acropolis unit, constructed on a low ridge between two streams. There is a ball court to the south, and two high, terraced platforms near its center. To the north is another ball court, directly west of a large plaza. The plainness and monumentality of many of Lubaantun's masonry terraces, especially in the use of large stone blocks, recalls the latest architectural style of Quirigua to the south (see below).

## Seibal

Seibal is another small center, situated on a bluff overlooking the Río Pasión, in the southern lowland rain forest, about 60 km (37 mi.) east of Altar de Sacrificios. The site was reported and photographed by Teobert Maler in the early twentieth century. From 1963 to 1969 Seibal was the subject of a comprehensive archaeological investigation conducted by the Peabody Museum of Harvard University, with excavations directed by A. Ledyard Smith and the project under the overall direction of Gordon Willey.

Most of the core of Seibal (Group A) is arranged around two plazas. The northern plaza contains a ball court on its west side. The southern plaza has a central platform with four stairways (Structure A-3), a stela at the base of each side (Fig. 11.32).

Fig. 11.32. Structure A-3, Seibal, Guatemala: (*above*) before excavation; (*below*) after excavation and restoration, with Stela 10 at the base of the staircase (see Fig. 4.29).

The archaeological research at Seibal revealed that the site reached its zenith during the Terminal Classic, at a time when it appears to have been taken over by a powerful outside group, identified as Mexicanized Putun Maya (see Chapter 6). The architectural and ceramic remains reflect this foreign heritage. Some of Seibal's late masonry buildings have strong ties to the Puuc veneer style of the northern lowlands, also linked to the Putun expansion. A round masonry platform, reached by a *sacbe* east and south of Group A, also testifies to the site's Mexicanized Maya connections. But the well-executed carved monuments provide the most vivid evidence for Seibal's non-Classic-Maya heritage in the Terminal Classic. Most of the known stelae at the site, dating from A.D. 800–900, portray individuals (rulers) whose manner and costuming are often a mixture of Classic Maya and foreign elements. The magnificent Stela 10 (849) depicts a ruler dressed in very Late Classic Maya regalia, holding a double-headed ceremonial bar, but his mustached face appears distinctly non-Maya (Fig. 4.29). Even more alien-appearing are Stelae 2, 14, and 19, all dating to approximately 870. Stela 14 portrays an impersonator of the Mexican wind deity, Ehecatl. Several of the portraits of Seibal's apparent Putun rulers from the Terminal Classic strongly resemble in style the painted figures on the recently discovered murals at Cacaxtla, in central Mexico (see Chapter 6).

## The Usumacinta Centers: Altar de Sacrificios, Yaxchilan, and Piedras Negras

Altar de Sacrificios was the subject of an archaeological research program from the Peabody Museum, Harvard University, again led by A. Ledyard Smith and Gordon Willey, from 1958 through 1963. The site is strategically located at the junction of the Pasión and Usumacinta rivers in the southern lowlands, along the trade routes between the highlands to the south and the lowland regions to the north, and (via the Usumacinta) to the northwest (Gulf coast). The Peabody Museum excavations revealed a long sequence of occupation at Altar de Sacrificios, beginning earlier than at Tikal or most other central lowland centers. The evidence for this was provided by pottery dated to the Early Preclassic era (the Xe Ceramic Complex). The site reached its peak development in the Late Classic era, although its architectural remains are not large or extensive. The famous Altar Vase, discovered during the excavation of Structure A-III (Fig. 11.33), appears to commemorate a particular historical event at the center (see Chapter 12). The dated monuments from Altar de Sacrificios span much of the Classic era, from 9.10.0.0.0 (455) to 10.1.0.0.0 (849). Ceramic evidence indicates that the site was occupied during the Terminal Classic period by outsiders, probably Putun Maya groups, perhaps at the same time as their takeover of Seibal (see Chapter 6).

Yaxchilan, a large and seemingly dominant center of the Usumacinta region,

Fig. 11.33. Altar de Sacrificios, Guatemala: (*above*) Structure A-III during excavation; (*below*) elite tomb discovered under the staircase of Structure A-III, its occupant commemorated by the Altar Vase, found in a grave nearby (see Fig. 12.14).

Fig. 11.34. Structure 19, Yaxchilan,
Chiapas, Mexico.

Fig. 11.35. Stela 11, Yaxchilan, probably
portraying the ruler Bird Jaguar and captives (9.16.1.0.0, or A.D. 752).

is located about 80 km (50 mi.) downriver from Altar de Sacrificios, naturally defended by a nearly closed loop on the Mexican side of the river. A preliminary survey and recording were done by both Alfred Maudslay and Teobert Maler. The site is notable for its impressive architectural remains, including excellent sculpture (Figs. 11.34 and 11.35), which date from 9.0.0.0.0. (435) to near the end of the Late Classic period (9.18.12.12.6). During the Late Classic, four important buildings were constructed, Structures 21, 23, 42, and 44. These were embellished with twelve sculptured stone lintels, three in each building. These lintels and the other monuments at Yaxchilan record the reigns and conquests of the Jaguar dynasty (see Chapter 4).

Recently, Yaxchilan has been investigated by archaeologists from the Instituto Nacional de Antropología e Historia of Mexico. This work has succeeded in consolidating and preserving at least the central portion of the site.

Piedras Negras (Fig. 11.36) lies some 50 km (30 mi.) northwest of and downriver from Yaxchilan, or about 180 km (110 mi.) due west of Tikal, along the eastern bank of the Usumacinta. It was investigated by an archaeological project from the University Museum of the University of Pennsylvania from 1931 to 1939, led by J. Alden Mason and Linton Satterthwaite. This research revealed new information about Maya architecture, including the fact that

Fig. 11.36. Piedras Negras, Guatemala: restoration drawing by Tatiana Proskouriakoff.

many of the often badly deteriorated structures at Piedras Negras were built without masonry vaults and were probably roofed by beam and thatch.

Piedras Negras is justly famed for its excellent sculpture (Fig. 11.37), which culminated, in the opinion of most, in Wall Panel 3 from Temple O-13 (see Fig. 4.26 and Chapter 4).

The practice of erecting period markers at the ends of the successive hotuns, or 1,800-day periods, was more consistently followed at Piedras Negras than at any other Maya center. From 9.8.15.0.0 to 9.19.0.0.0 (608 to 810), each of the 22 consecutive hotun endings was celebrated by the erection of a sculptured monument, every one of which has survived. It was this series of stelae (see Fig. 4.25) that provided the key to the first reconstruction of a dynastic history for a Maya center (see Chapters 4 and 15).

## Bonampak

This small center is located in the valley of the Río Lacanha, about 30 km (19 mi.) south of Yaxchilan. The site and its famous murals were reported to the outside world in 1946 by Giles Healey. A subsequent reconnaissance was conducted by the Carnegie Institution of Washington to record the murals and other features of the site. The murals were photographed, and excellent color copies were painted by Antonio Tejeda. On the basis of the known dated inscriptions, elite activity was confined largely to the Late Classic era (9.8.9.0.0 to 9.18.0.0.0), probably under the control of nearby Yaxchilan. The Bonampak murals are described and illustrated in Chapter 13.

## Palenque

The site of Palenque is dramatically situated at the foot of the northernmost hills of the Chiapas highlands (Fig. 11.38), overlooking the vast forest-covered Gulf coast plain. It occupies a position on the southwestern periphery of the Maya area, with Tortuguero, an apparently subsidiary center, and Comalcalco the only sizable Maya centers located farther west.

Palenque has been well known to the outside world since the eighteenth century, when a succession of explorers, including Antonio del Rio, reported the site. In the nineteenth century, Palenque became the most studied of all Maya sites, owing to the efforts and publications of men such as William Dupaix, Frederick Waldeck, John Lloyd Stephens, Arthur Morley, Désiré Charnay, and others. Alfred Maudslay's superb photographic record remains a valuable resource for scholars studying Palenque and the other sites he visited. Many of these nineteenth-century scholars recorded the famous stucco relief panels in

Fig. 11.37 (*facing page*).  Piedras Negras stelae: (*left*) Stela 12, 9.18.5.0.0 (A.D. 795); (*right*) Stela 40, 9.15.15.0.0 (746).

drawings and photographs. Because these fragile panels have suffered further disintegration in the intervening years, these early records have proved to be invaluable.

Investigations at Palenque continued in the early twentieth century, with further studies by Edward Seler, Sylvanus Morley, Franz Blom, and Oliver LaFarge. The Mexican government began a program of conservation and restoration of the site before World War II that has continued to the present day. Although Palenque has yet to be the subject of comprehensive archaeological research, limited excavations have been undertaken in conjunction with the restoration program. The most notable of these were directed by Alberto Ruz Lhuillier, primarily in the Temple of the Inscriptions. Recent archaeological investigations of the surrounding area, directed by Robert Rands of Southern Illinois University, have centered on an innovative study of pottery manufacturing zones. This work has provided valuable chronological information and data on the development of settlement in the Palenque region. Epigraphic studies by a series of scholars, including Floyd Lounsbury, David Kelley, Linda Schele, and Peter Mathews, have focused on the texts from Palenque, reconstructing in detail the center's dynastic history during the Late Classic period.

Today, as in the past, the visitor cannot help but be captivated by the beauty of Palenque's temples and palaces, placed like finely wrought jewels in a vivid

Fig. 11.38. Palenque, Chiapas, Mexico, located at the foot of the northern highlands: the multi-doorway Temple of the Inscriptions on the right (see Fig. 4.20), the Palace with its tower, and, beyond, the Temples of the Cross, Foliated Cross, and Sun.

tropical-green setting. Entering from the west, two of the site's most impressive structures invite exploration: the Temple of the Inscriptions, with its strangely uneven number of five doorways, and the multi-room Palace with its unique four-story tower (Fig. 11.38). Immediately, Palenque's distinctive architectural style is apparent. Despite the use of block masonry and corbel-vaulted rooms similar to those of most Classic-period lowland sites, the multiple doorways, sloping upper façades, and low, open-work roof combs—all decorated with stucco relief panels—give Palenque a delicate and serene atmosphere. When compared to the vertical thrust of the lofty and dominating structures at Tikal, Palenque's structures emphasize the horizontal dimension.

One remarkable feature of Palenque is the absence of free-standing sculptured monuments. Rather than appearing on stelae or altars, the portraits of Palenque's rulers were either carved on stone panels or modeled in plaster and placed on the walls of buildings. Most of these are now fragmentary (Fig. 13.19), but the stucco work was once brightly painted, and many interior walls show traces of these modeled and painted decorations. Fortunately, some portraits and most of the hieroglyphic texts carved on stone panels remain largely intact inside several of the site's most prominent buildings.

The Temple of the Inscriptions, rising some 25 m (80 ft) on a rectangular, terraced platform (Fig. 4.20), was built soon after the death of Palenque's greatest ruler, Pacal, who died in A.D. 683. It was constructed during the reign of Pacal's son and successor, Chan Bahlum, as a mortuary shrine for his father. (Chapter 4 describes the discovery of Pacal's tomb beneath the building platform by Ruz.) Today, one can follow the corbel-vaulted staircase that leads from inside the temple down nearly 30 m beneath the pyramid to the burial crypt. The tomb chamber is about 10 by 4 m in size, with a vaulted ceiling over 7 m high. The walls are decorated by nine stucco figures (Fig. 4.21, upper right illustration), representing the nine lords of the underworld, the Bolontiku (see Chapter 14). Most of the floor space is occupied by a huge sarcophagus, in which Pacal's jade-adorned remains were found, covered by a magnificently carved lid (Fig. 4.23). The scene on the lid depicts the dead ruler falling into the underworld, represented by the fleshless jaws of the earthly aspect of Itzamna, the reptilian Maya deity. Above Pacal are depicted the tree of life, symbolizing the earthly realm, and the celestial two-headed serpent, the sky aspect of Itzamna. Sculptured figures and hieroglyphs on the sides of the sarcophagus record Pacal's ruling ancestors and his death date in 683 (9.12.11.5.18).

The inauguration of Chan Bahlum is recorded on the Temple of the Inscriptions above. But the major shrines dating from his reign are the three small structures known as the Temples of the Sun, Cross, and Foliated Cross (Fig. 11.38). These are located on a large elevated plaza along the eastern side of the site. The Temple of the Sun sits on a low, terraced platform on the east side of the plaza. Opposite this is the Temple of the Foliated Cross, its platform incorporating part of the hill behind; its front room is now collapsed. On the north side of the plaza is the Temple of the Cross, supported by the highest platform of the group. Each building is architecturally similar, with three doorways leading to a front room, and a central rear chamber flanked by two small side rooms. The central rear room contains a roofed shrine chamber, a room within a room. The back wall of each shrine is decorated with an extraordinary carved panel, the central motif of which gives each temple its popular name (Fig. 11.39).

The composition of each sculptured panel is similar, depicting the deceased Pacal facing a larger portrait of the new ruler, Chan Bahlum, both figures flanked by extensive hieroglyphic texts. Pacal is depicted on the left and Chan Bahlum on the right in two of the panels, with their positions reversed in the Temple of the Foliated Cross. The Temple of the Cross seems to have served as an ancestral shrine for Palenque's ruling lineage. Its text records the mythological origins of the three patrons of Palenque's dynasty, the Palenque Triad, and the birth and inauguration of Chan Bahlum and his ancestors. The Temple of the Foliated Cross, in keeping with its location on the east, the life-giving direction of the rising sun, commemorates the earthly realm, and in particular, Chan Bahlum's reign and Bolon Tzacab (God K), the principal deity of Maya

Fig. 11.39. Sculptured tablet from the inner shrine, Temple of the Cross at Palenque, depicting the deceased ruler Pacal (left) and his successor, Chan Bahlum (right).

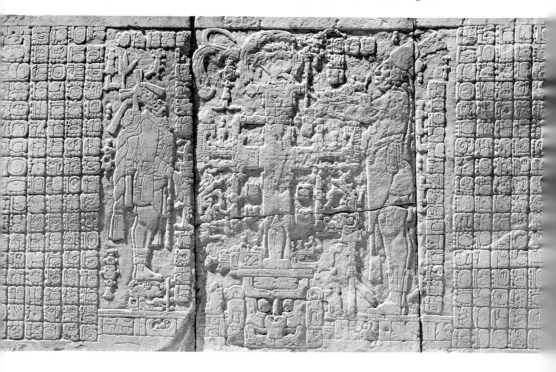

ruling lineages. The western building, the Temple of the Sun, associated with the setting sun and death, commemorates warfare, the underworld, and the underworld's jaguar patron.

Palenque's largest and central building complex is the aptly named Palace. These buildings, situated on a large 10-m-high platform (100 by 80 m in extent, or 330 by 260 ft), undoubtedly served as the residences for most, if not all, of Palenque's historically identified rulers. The main entrance was by way of a wide staircase on the northern side of the platform. The exteriors of most buildings are decorated by carved stone and stucco reliefs. Even the vaults are elaborated, each major building marked by a different style of vaulting. The buildings comprise a series of galleries and rooms arranged around several interior courts or patios. In the southwest court are a steam bath and three latrines, as well as the famous four-story tower. The largest interior court is located in the northeastern portion of the Palace. The interiors of the rooms, too, were decorated with modeled stucco masks.

The earliest visible buildings in the Palace most likely originated with the reign of Pacal, although earlier structures lie buried beneath the platform. Pacal's accession to power is commemorated on the Oval Palace Tablet, where he is attended by his mother, Lady Zac Kuk. Subsequent rulers rebuilt and expanded the Palace complex. The northern part (Houses A, D, and AD) is associated with the reign of Chan Bahlum's brother and successor, Kan Xul. Here a stone panel carved with an extensive hieroglyphic text and an accession scene was found during the excavations conducted by Ruz. The text reviews the preceding reigns and appears to depict Kan Xul's inauguration, attended by his mother.

The Palace tower may date from this reign or immediately thereafter, during the rule of Kan Xul's successors. Two carved tablets found flanking the tower stairs appear to depict the next two rulers. The first of these, Chaacal, may be represented on the Orator Tablet. The next ruler, Chac Zutz, seems to be depicted on the Scribe Tablet.

The reign of Chaacal is also recorded on Structure 18, located south of the Temple of the Foliated Cross, and on Temple 21, situated south of the Temple of the Sun. Temple 18A, adjacent to Temple 18, was built over a deeply buried crypt, possibly the tomb of a ruler such as Chaacal, but its identity remains unknown. The accession of Chac Zutz appears to be depicted on the Tablet of the Slaves, found in Group IV, a smaller palace complex located west of the main site. Excavations in this group directed by Rands revealed it to contain a cemetery area.

To the north of the Palace and its platform staircase is a plaza with a small ball court on its east side. The north side of the plaza is bounded by a series of small temples. One, the Temple of the Count, was named after Count Frederick Waldeck, who reportedly lived there for several years while studying the ruins of Palenque in the early nineteenth century.

Fig. 11.40. Stela 12, Tonina, carved in the round like the other monuments from this center, with a probable date of 9.12.0.0.0 (A.D. 672).

## Tonina

The location of Tonina, at an elevation of 800–900 m about 50 km south of Palenque (2,625–2,950 ft, 30 mi.), in the Ocosingo valley, gives it a transitional lowland-highland environmental setting. The site has been the focus of recent research by the French Archaeological Mission in Mexico.

The site is known best for its monuments, which are considered stylistically the least typical of all Classic Maya sculpture. The sixteen known monuments are all small when compared to the average 2.5–3-m height of those from other Maya centers; most of the Tonina stelae are less than about 2 m tall. They also differ, importantly, in being carved fully in the round, like statuary (Fig. 11.40). The dated monuments reportedly span most of the Classic period, from 9.3.0.0.0 to 10.4.0.0.0 (A.D. 495 to 909), although the earliest surely dated inscription (Monument 106) is 9.8.0.0.0 (593). The recently discovered Monument 101 has the latest long-count date of any Maya Stela (10.4.0.0.0).

## Copan

Copan is the major Classic Maya center of the southeastern lowlands, the frontier region with Central America, although its setting in a fertile valley surrounded by mountains is certainly transitional to a highland environment (Fig. 11.41). Justly famed for its splendid sculptural and architectural style, it represents another variation within the Maya realm.

Copan has been known since shortly after the Spanish Conquest, and was described by Don Diego Garcia de Palacios in 1576. In the nineteenth century, Copan was brought to the attention of the outside world through the descriptions and illustrations of John Lloyd Stephens and Frederick Catherwood. Later, Alfred Maudslay's photographic record of Copan's sculptures rekindled interest in the site. From 1891 to 1894 the Peabody Museum, Harvard University, conducted investigations at Copan under the direction of George Gordon This work was followed by excavations and restoration work conducted by the Carnegie Institution of Washington for several years beginning in 1935.

One of the most interesting archaeological features at Copan is the cross section of the Acropolis exposed by the Río Copan (Fig. 11.42). Since the city was abandoned in the early ninth century, the river has changed its course and cut away a great portion of the eastern base of the Acropolis, exposing a vertical face some 37 m high (121 ft) at the highest point and 300 m long (985 ft) at

Fig. 11.41. Aerial view of Copan, Honduras, situated on the banks of the Río Copan.

the base. This is one of the largest archaeological cross sections in the world, and a number of earlier plaza-floor levels can be clearly distinguished in it.

Reconstruction was an important part of the Carnegie work at Copan. Most significant, a diversion rechanneled the river, so that the site is no longer threatened with destruction. In addition, more than a dozen fallen and broken monuments were repaired and re-erected. Temples 11, 21a, 22, and 26 and the ball court (Structures 9 and 10) were excavated and repaired, and several tunnels were driven through the Acropolis to find earlier constructions.

In 1975 and 1976, the Peabody Museum returned to Copan under the direction of Gordon Willey to investigate the distribution of Classic-period settlement in the valley region surrounding the main group of ruins. Shortly thereafter, the Instituto Hondureño de Antropología e Historia began a new program of research and consolidation, Proyecto Copan, and this work is continuing.

The site core of Copan, covering an area about 600 by 300 m (2,000 by 1,000 ft), is composed of a massive elevated complex on the south, the Acropolis, and a series of connecting plazas and smaller structures to the north

Fig. 11.42. Section of the Acropolis at Copan exposed by the Río Copan before it was diverted.

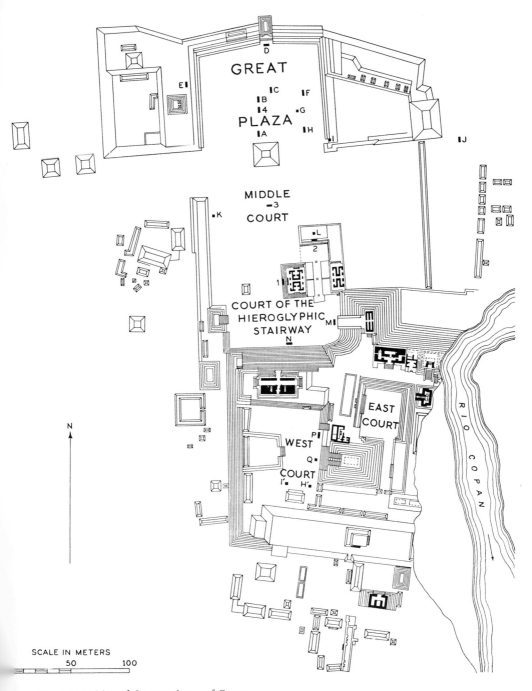

Fig. 11.43. Map of the central area of Copan.

Fig. 11.44. Copan: (*above*) Jaguar Stairway in the East Court; (*lower left*) sculptured figure of a jaguar standard bearer adorning the stairway; (*lower right*) the Hieroglyphic Stairway, Structure 26, on the platform summit.

(Fig. 11.43) that includes the Court of the Hieroglyphic Stairway (flanked by the famous ball court) and the Monument Plaza (formed by the Main and Middle courts) separated by Structure 4, a platform with four stairways recently excavated and restored. South of the Acropolis is a series of smaller plazas and buildings, the Cemetery Group, mostly elite residential structures. A *sacbe* leads northeast to another series of elite residences, including Structure A in the CV-43 group, site of the discovery by the recent Peabody Museum excavations of a sculptured bench panel with a full-figure glyphic inscription.

The Acropolis comprises two enclosed plazas, the West and East courts (Fig. 11.44), and a series of elevated structures, only one of which (Structure 22) clearly appears to have served as a residence. Projecting to the north is Structure 26, dated to A.D. 756, which is reached from the west by the Hieroglyphic Stairway from the court below. This Court of the Hieroglyphic Stairway is 95 by 38 m (312 by 125 ft); at one end, just behind Stela M and its altar, rises the Hieroglyphic Stairway, 62 steps, 10 m wide. A large anthropomorphic figure sits at the midpoint of every twelfth step. The faces of the steps are sculptured with 1,500–2,000 individual glyphs, the longest inscription in Maya hieroglyphic writing, but which is, unfortunately, largely jumbled by its collapse. Structure 11, apparently dedicated in 756 also but covering several earlier structures, is reached by a broad monumental staircase on the south side of the same court. Structure 22, dated to 771, faces south toward the East Court of the Acropolis. This building, its inner doorway framed by a magnificent sculptured relief and corner masks, bears a resemblance to the Chenes architecture of the Yucatan.

The highest point on the Acropolis is the summit of Structure 16, facing the West Court. The recent excavation of Structure 18, located on the southeastern corner of the Acropolis, with its eastern edge swept away by the old course of the Río Copan, revealed another building elaborately decorated with sculptured reliefs (Fig. 11.45). On Structure 18's rear (southern) side, a flight of stairs was discovered that leads down to a sepulcher roofed by a four-sided vault (a corbeled "dome"). In its floor the excavators found a sunken burial chamber. But when cleared, this tomb, perhaps that of one of Copan's last identified rulers, Sun-at-Horizon, was found to be virtually empty, probably looted not long after it was constructed and dedicated.

The dated monuments of Copan span the entire Classic Period (Fig. 11.46). A newly discovered stela, found broken and reused in the rubble of Structure 4 in the Monument Plaza, is without a hieroglyphic inscription. But the style of the sculptured portrait of the lower part of a human figure is very early, reminiscent of the monuments from the southern Maya area, so that its age is certainly equivalent to the oldest known lowland stela. A subsequent dynastic sequence has been worked out, although its beginnings and the reigns of the first eleven rulers are still unclear. Several monuments appear to record the accession of a ruler in A.D. 564. This is a period of apparent contact between Copan and Kaminaljuyu, and perhaps Teotihuacan, as indicated by ceramics

Fig. 11.45. Structure 18, Copan: (*right*) sculptured doorjamb; (*below*) doorway of the structure, with the remains of a decorative façade.

Fig. 11.46. Copan stelae: (*left*) Stela H, 9.17.12.0.0 (A.D. 782); (*below*) Stela P, 9.9.10.0.0 (623).

and some elements of sculptural style. Many later Copan stelae maintain elements derived from Teotihuacan, long after its power waned in the Maya area. For instance, the twelfth Copan ruler, depicted on Stela 6, dated at 682 (9.12.10.0.0), wears a headdress decorated with a Tlaloc mask and the Teotihuacan year sign. There are several indications of the founding of a new dynasty during the latter part of the Early Classic, and later rulers may have retained some of the symbols of power imported during that time.

In 702 a new ruler named 18 Rabbit was inaugurated at Copan (see Fig. 4.15). Evidence from the neighboring center of Quirigua (discussed below) indicates that this ruler's reign ended with his capture by Cauac Sky, ruler of Quirigua in 737. 18 Rabbit disappears from Copan's historical record, eventually succeeded by Sun-at-Horizon, the last securely identified ruler at that site. It was during Sun-at-Horizon's reign that Structure 22, possibly this ruler's palace, was constructed. An additional ruler may be recorded in the inscriptions, but the available archaeological evidence indicates that Copan's end, shortly after 800, was rather abrupt.

## Quirigua

Quirigua is a small center situated in the southeastern lowlands, along the lower Río Motagua, within the most extensive alluvial valley in the Maya area. This location was strategic, lying between the sources of jadeite and obsidian farther up the Motagua and the trade connections to the north with the central lowlands and the Caribbean coast or to the east with Central America.

In the nineteenth century, after a visit to the ruins by Frederick Catherwood, John Lloyd Stephens reported Quirigua's existence to the outside world. Alfred Maudslay spent several seasons there, photographing the famous monumental sculptures and sponsoring the first excavations at the site. In the early twentieth century, the Archaeological Institute of America conducted excavations, directed by Edgar Lee Hewett and Sylvanus Morley, followed by further work by the Carnegie Institution of Washington. From 1974 to 1979 the University Museum, University of Pennsylvania, conducted a comprehensive program to investigate the site core, its surrounding settlement, and coeval sites within the lower Motagua valley. In addition, this project worked with the Guatemalan government through the Instituto de Antropología e Historia to conserve the site's monuments and consolidate its major buildings.

These recent investigations combined archaeological and historical research by integrating excavation with studies of Quirigua's hieroglyphic inscriptions. This effort revealed that Quirigua was founded during the Early Classic era, probably by elite colonists from the central lowlands, possibly Tikal. The period is marked by at least two fifth-century monuments, among the earliest outside the central lowlands to combine portraiture and dated hieroglyphic texts (Fig. 4.14). Settlement and construction seems to have begun during this era at

Group A, high on a hilltop overlooking the valley, and on the flood plain itself, along the banks of the Motagua. All remains of this early settlement on the floodplain are now covered by deep deposits of alluvium.

The main group at Quirigua (Figs. 11.47 and 11.48), comprising the structures and monuments visible today, are largely the product of a flurry of building activity in the Late and Terminal Classic periods. The site developed two principal areas, built along the bank of the Motagua (today, after changing its ancient course, the riverbed is about 1 km south of the main group). In the south is the Acropolis, a quadrangle of residential buildings on the north, west, and south sides of a central court. The east side of the court, reflecting an ancient residential pattern found at Tikal, was reserved for a series of smaller shrines. These shrines probably served as the focus for rituals venerating the ancestors of Quirigua's ruling lineage. The oldest of these, dating from the Middle Classic period, covered a deeply buried crypt, in which the remains of a single male adult were found, possibly the ancestral founder of the residential complex. Under the west side of the Acropolis, excavations and tunnels uncovered a completely buried ball court, dating from the first part of the Late Classic. Structure 1B-2 was a small residence, located in the southwestern corner of the Acropolis, nearly buried by later construction. This building is elaborately decorated with sculptured masonry reliefs, and probably served as the initial residence of Quirigua's greatest ruler, Cauac Sky, in the mid-eighth century. The two largest structures, 1B-1 on the south side (Fig. 4.28) and 1B-5 on the north, were constructed during the reign of Quirigua's last historic ruler, Jade Sky, whose portrait appears on Monument 11 (Stela K). An earlier wall, decorated with sculptured mosaic heads of Kinich Ahau, the Maya sun deity (God G), was discovered in 1975 along the west side of the Acropolis (Fig. 11.49), from which it must have once overlooked the Río Motagua.

North of the Acropolis is a plaza enclosed on three sides by stepped "reviewing stands," in the center of which is a small later ball court. The ball-court plaza also contains the magnificent zoomorphic sculptures and altars dedicated during the reign of Cauac Sky's successor (see Fig. 13.10). The ball-court plaza is bounded on the north by a badly ruined, terraced pyramid, and on the west by a deep basin, now silted in but once perhaps providing facilities for Quirigua's river port.

North of the Acropolis and ball-court plaza lies the Great Plaza, the most extensive setting for monuments in the Maya area, where eleven of the largest Maya sculptures known are located (Fig. 11.50). All but two of these pertain to the long reign of Cauac Sky (see Fig. 4.27), who was inaugurated in A.D. 724, and one of these monuments (Zoomorph G) marks the date of his death in 784. Cauac Sky's portrait adorns most of the monuments in the plaza (Stelae A, C, D, E, F, H, and J). Most of the terraces and staircases at Quirigua are monumental in size but devoid of embellishment. Architectural sculpture seems to have been reserved for vaulted buildings, using either masonry (as in Structure 1B-2 and the mosaic-decorated wall) or stucco-façade reliefs (found as ruined fragments in structural debris).

Most of this construction occurred after 737, the year the Quirigua inscriptions record that Cauac Sky captured 18 Rabbit, ruler of Copan (see Chapter 4). Prior to this, Quirigua may have been under some sort of control by Copan. The expansion of Quirigua, lasting for about a century during the reigns of Cauac Sky and his successors, appears to have been directly stimulated by the new-found wealth and power derived from gaining control of the Río Motagua commerce.

During the Terminal Classic period Quirigua's traditional ruling dynasty seems to have been usurped, and both the center and its commercial interests passed to the control of outsiders. Construction in the Acropolis continued, but no more Classic-style monuments were erected, and Quirigua seems to have been abandoned during the Postclassic era.

Fig. 11.47. Quirigua, Guatemala: aerial view of the Motagua valley, showing the main group of Quirigua ruins in the forested area in the center of the photograph, Sierra de las Minas in the background.

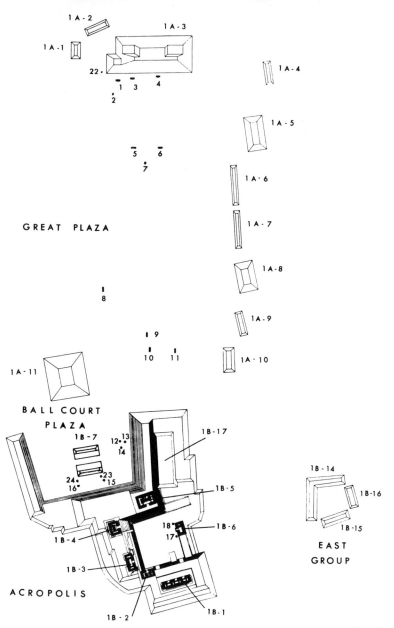

GREAT PLAZA

1A-2

1A-1

22

1 3 4

2

1A-3

1A-4

1A-5

1A-6

1A-7

5 6

7

1A-8

8

1A-9

9

10 11

1A-10

1A-11

BALL COURT
PLAZA

1B-7

12 13

14

1B-17

24 23

16 15

1B-5

18

17

1B-6

1B-4

1B-3

ACROPOLIS

1B-2

1B-1

1B-14

1B-16

1B-15

EAST
GROUP

Fig. 11.48. Quirigua: map
of the main group. (After
Morley.)

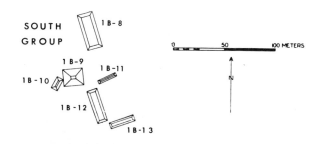

SOUTH
GROUP

1B-8

1B-9

1B-11

1B-10

1B-12

1B-13

0        50        100 METERS

N

Fig. 11.49. Quirigua: Late Classic sculptured-mosaic mask of Kinich Ahau, the sun deity, part of a decorated wall discovered during excavations in the Acropolis in 1975.

Fig. 11.50. View of the Great Plaza at Quirigua, looking south toward the Acropolis, with Monument 4 (Stela D) at the far right, and Monument 7 (Zoomorph G) between Monuments 5 (Stela E, right) and 6 (Stela F, left) in the middle distance.

# Coba

Coba is situated in northeastern Yucatan amid five small lakes, a rare physiographic feature in the almost waterless plain of the Yucatan (Fig. 11.51). First surveyed by the Carnegie Institution of Washington, more recently the center and its outlying dependencies were investigated under a program sponsored by the Instituto Nacional de Antropología e Historia of Mexico.

The site is most worthy of comment for its long period of occupation. It was founded by A.D. 623 (9.9.10.0.0) and occupied, at least intermittently, until late Postclassic times, around the fourteenth or fifteenth centuries. Coba possessed more Classic-era stelae—32 (23 sculptured)—than any other northern Yucatan center. One of the best preserved of these monuments is Stela 20, with a date of 9.12.12.0.5 (684). It was found near the base of Structure 1, the Nohoch Mul pyramid, northeast of the main group. Structure 1 is a Late Classic construction, some 24 m in height (80 ft), capped by the addition of a Late Postclassic building similar in style to those of Tulum (see below).

The main group at Coba, located between lakes Coba and Macanxoc, is dominated by the Castillo, another 24-m-high pyramid. A series of *sacbeob* radiates in five directions from this group to other areas of the site, connecting the central section with its outlying groups. Coba is famed for these raised artificial roads, of which sixteen are known.

The word *sacbe* (*sacbeob*, plural) means "artificial road" in Mayan (*sac*, "something artificial, made by hand"; *be*, "road"). These limestone roads vary in height from 0.5 to 2.5 m above the ground level (Fig. 11.52) and run in straight lines between the groups. The sides are built of roughly dressed stone,

Fig. 11.51. Aerial view of Coba, Quintana Roo, Mexico, set amid the small lakes in the northeastern lowlands.

Fig. 11.52. *Sacbe* connecting Coba and Yaxuna: (*above*) side of the causeway at its highest point; (*below*) stone roller (?) found on top of the causeway.

and the tops are covered with a natural lime cement called *sascab*, which hardens under wetting and pressure. The roads are about 4.5 m wide (15 ft) and vary in length from less than a kilometer to a little over 100 km (60 mi.). The longest causeway runs generally westward from Coba to Yaxuna and is straight except for a few slight deviations, which may indicate that when it was constructed—probably in the Late Classic period—Coba was the most important center in northeastern Yucatan; the first six of the seven changes in highway direction occur within 32 km of Coba, apparently in order to pass through smaller dependent settlements. Two causeways that intersect each other just south of the isthmus between the two largest lakes at Coba appear in the aerial photograph as two straight lines across the forest.

An interesting discovery in connection with the Coba–Yaxuna highway was an ancient Maya road roller. This cylinder of limestone, now broken into two pieces (Fig. 11.52, lower illustration), measured 4 m long and 0.7 m in diameter and weighed 5 tons. It is large enough for fifteen men to have pushed it at one time, and when rolled along the highway it must have packed the surface into a hard layer.

## Dzibilchaltun

Dzibilchaltun is an extensive and important site situated far in the northwestern corner of the Yucatan, only 20 km (12 mi.) from the coast. Its location so near the salt-producing shores of the Caribbean certainly indicates that one of its ancient roles involved the salt trade (see Chapter 6). It is only some 5 m above sea level, and within one of the driest portions of the northern lowlands. Its water supplies were furnished by the Xlacah Cenote, located in the southwestern corner of the main plaza of the site.

A major program of archaeological investigation at Dzibilchaltun began in 1956 and continued for the next ten years. This research was directed by E. Wyllys Andrews IV, who along with George Brainerd had reported the site in 1941, after its discovery by Alfredo Barrera Vasquez. The Dzibilchaltun project was sponsored by the Middle American Research Institute of Tulane University.

These investigations revealed that the entire region surrounding the site was densely settled in ancient times. In fact, the near-continuous extent of settlement remains made it difficult to determine the boundaries of the site. The mapped area of Dzibilchaltun covers more than 19 km$^2$ (7 sq. mi.) and includes over 8,000 identified structures, most of which are apparently house platforms that probably once supported pole-and-thatch dwellings. About 2,000 platforms preserve the remains of low stone walls, enclosing either one or two rooms, that undoubtedly were once covered by thatched roofs. The central 0.5 km$^2$ of the site contains close to a hundred masonry structures, including vaulted buildings on low platforms and terraced pyramids clustered around several plaza areas. Many of these core-area buildings seem to have housed the ruling elite of Dzibilchaltun.

A series of *sacbeob* connects nearby and outlying groups with the central area. The surrounding 3-km² zone contains smaller clusters of structures, some with masonry vaults, often distributed continuously or linked by *sacbeob*. Beyond this zone lies an area of some 13 km² that includes scattered groups of ruins, some including vaulted buildings. Outside this area, and stretching over some 100 km², are the remains of the bulk of the house platforms and plentiful open areas that probably served as the ancient agricultural sustaining area for Dzibilchaltun's population.

The completed archaeological research reveals that occupation at Dzibilchaltun spanned about two thousand years. The earliest remains, identified by Middle Preclassic pottery, date from as early as 500–600 B.C. Settlement at that time included a small agricultural hamlet, named the Mirador Group (Fig. 11.53), and includes the earliest known example of a Maya sweat bath. Population grew during the Late Preclassic, when several ceremonial complexes developed within the area.

The largest Preclassic center, Komchen, was recently excavated for the Middle American Research Institute, Tulane University, under the direction of E. Wyllys Andrews V. This research revealed that Komchen was a sizable site during the Middle and Late Preclassic periods, with approximately 900 to 1,000 structures covering a 2-km² area at its maximum by about A.D. 150. The site has been heavily looted, so that details of architectural form are difficult to determine. As at the Mirador Group, however, Komchen was marked by large-scale public architecture from the Middle Preclassic, with expansion continuing through the Late Preclassic (see Fig. 6.1). The earliest known *sacbe* in the Yucatan has been identified at Komchen, dating from the Late Preclassic era. Komchen's largest building platforms are comparable in size to those at Late Classic Dzibilchaltun, with three known to have been at least 8 m high. But in contrast to those at Dzibilchaltun, structures here do not form clusters, sitting rather evenly over the site in a dense, concentric pattern, with the largest buildings at or near the core.

Occupation at both Komchen and the Mirador Group appears to have ceased by the end of the Preclassic period, and the populations drastically declined, so that during the Early Classic era the Dzibilchaltun area was nearly abandoned.

The site recovered during the Late and Terminal Classic, however, and Dzibilchaltun grew to its maximum size, reaching a population of 25,000 or more by 800 (Fig. 11.54). During this time of expansion nearly all the masonry-vaulted buildings were constructed, and some 90 percent of all residential structures appear to have been occupied. Also during this time, most if not all of the more than 25 monuments known from the site were erected. One period-ending date survives (probably 10.1.0.0.0, or 849) on Stela 9. The front of Stela 19 depicts a ruler holding a manikin scepter, the symbol of high office at most Classic Maya sites.

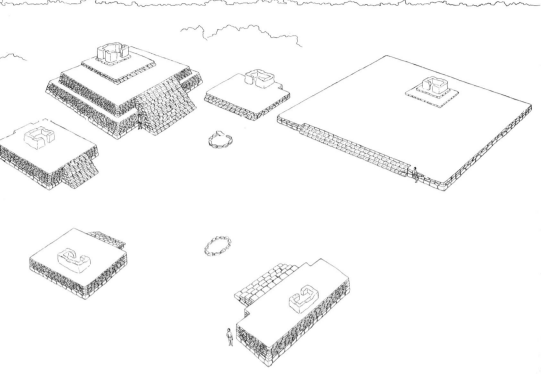

Fig. 11.53. Dzibilchaltun, Yucatan, Mexico: restoration drawing of the Mirador Group platforms dating from the Middle to Late Preclassic; the summit buildings were added in the Late
Postclassic, and the two oval house platforms in the plaza are post-Conquest.

Fig. 11.54. Dzibilchaltun, looking southeast and showing the cenote Xlacah and the causeways connecting the south plaza (right), central plaza (left), and other architectural groupings
(restoration drawing by George Stuart).

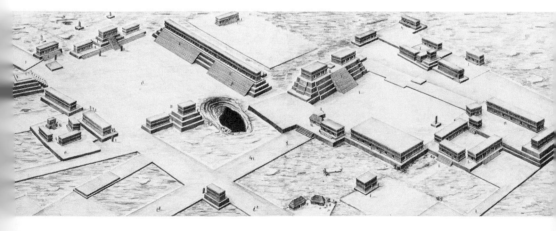

During the Late Classic the masonry buildings were constructed in typical lowland style, using stone blocks and true corbeled vaulting. During the Terminal Classic era, the Puuc architectural style appeared at Dzibilchaltun, represented by veneer masonry and carved-mosaic façade decoration instead of the earlier stucco. Total population during the Terminal Classic may have decreased slightly, but the concentration at the site core seems to have increased.

In the Early Postclassic, or after about 1000, population declined rapidly and building activity ceased for a time. A modest revival occurred around 1200, when several new buildings were constructed of reused masonry. A small population continued to dwell at Dzibilchaltun during the Late Postclassic, reusing earlier buildings as residences and shrines.

One of the most notable buildings at Dzibilchaltun is the Temple of the

Fig. 11.55. Seven Dolls Group at Dzibilchaltun: (*above*) as it appeared about A.D. 700–750 (restoration drawing by George Stuart and Lisa Biganzoli); (*below*) excavated and consolidated Temple of the Seven Dolls (note the remains of the later overlying structure at the right corner).

Seven Dolls, architecturally unique in several important respects (Fig. 11.55). Built about 700, it represents one of the earliest vaulted buildings at the site. It is a square temple on the summit of a platform with four stairways. Four wide doorways lead into a continuous vaulted corridor that surrounds a central room, which is roofed by a high four-sided vault that forms a low tower above the roof. Rectangular windows flank the eastern and western doorways. The upper exterior façades were decorated with elaborate stucco masks, apparently unpainted. Before the end of the Classic era the temple and its platform were completely encased in a much larger four-stairway pyramid. Centuries later, during the Late Postclassic, when the pyramid was in ruins, its west side was trenched and the long-buried Temple of the Seven Dolls was reopened and used as a shrine. An altar was erected inside, and painted with four successive hieroglyphic medallions over the years of its use. In front of the altar an offering was placed in the floor, containing seven crudely fashioned clay figurines, after which the temple was given its present name.

## Uxmal

Uxmal is situated in western Yucatan, about 80 km (50 mi.) south of Dzibilchaltun. Judging by its location and size (Fig. 11.56), it was an important political and economic center, especially impressive for its superb assemblage of buildings, most of which were constructed in the Puuc architectural style. Unfortunately, however, no systematic archaeological excavations have been conducted, so that we know relatively little about the site. A series of undated stelae has been located there (Fig. 11.57). The predominance of Puuc architec-

Fig. 11.56. Aerial view of Uxmal, Yucatan, Mexico.

Fig. 11.57. Drawing
of Stela 7, Uxmal.

ture at the site indicates that Uxmal reached its apogee during the period around A.D. 800–1000, but the length of occupation before and after this era is undocumented. The lack of later architectural styles points to a probable decline in the beginning of the Postclassic.

The core of Uxmal is dominated by extensive and complex multi-room structures, undoubtedly the residences of the ruling elite (Fig. 11.58). The largest of these palace-type complexes is the badly ruined South Group, in which three palace quadrangles were built on a series of ascending terraces, the highest and southernmost constructed around a pyramid. Just to the east is the Great Pyramid, and beyond that the Governor's Palace (Fig. 6.5) which is the largest single structure of its kind at Uxmal and often considered the finest example of Puuc architecture extant. It surmounts a triple terrace 15 m high and covering five acres of ground; the palace itself is nearly 100 m long, 12 m wide, and 8 m high (330 by 40 by 26 ft), and contains 24 chambers. The elaborate mosaics decorating its four facades are composed of some 20,000 elements. A recent probe near the northeastern corner revealed the existence of an earlier, Chenes-style palace beneath the building. Southeast of the Governor's Palace lies another pyramid, the House of the Old Woman.

On the northwestern corner of the terrace is a smaller palace, known as the House of the Turtles because of its upper façade decoration, a small gem of Puuc architecture. From this point there is a spectacular view to the north, past the ball court toward the most famous residential complex at Uxmal, the so-called Nunnery Quadrangle (Fig. 11.59). Immediately to the east is a high platform with rounded corners that supports two temples and is known as the Adivino (House of the Diviner, or Magician).

The Nunnery Quadrangle consists of four buildings with sculptured façades, arranged around the sides of a court measuring 76 by 61 m (250 by 200 ft). This court is entered through a central corbeled arcade in the building on its south side. The structure on the north side surmounts a terrace 5.5 m high and is reached by a stairway 27.5 m wide; architecturally it is the most important unit of the quadrangle, though the two flanking units, the East and West ranges (Fig. 11.60), are scarcely less impressive. The mosaic façade of the western building, for instance, includes feathered-serpent motifs, models of thatched-roof houses, and a central throned pavilion that may have once held the sculptured portrait of a ruling personage.

The Adivino seems to have been built in at least four stages, incorporating earlier buildings within its mass. The penultimate construction is represented by a Chenes-style temple that crowns the first terrace of the platform. This terrace is reached by a steep western staircase (Fig. 11.61) that gives access to the temple, elaborately decorated to represent a giant monster mask, its mouth forming the west-facing doorway. The uppermost temple, in Puuc style, faces a higher, eastern staircase.

West of the Nunnery is another quadrangle, known as the Cemetery Group,

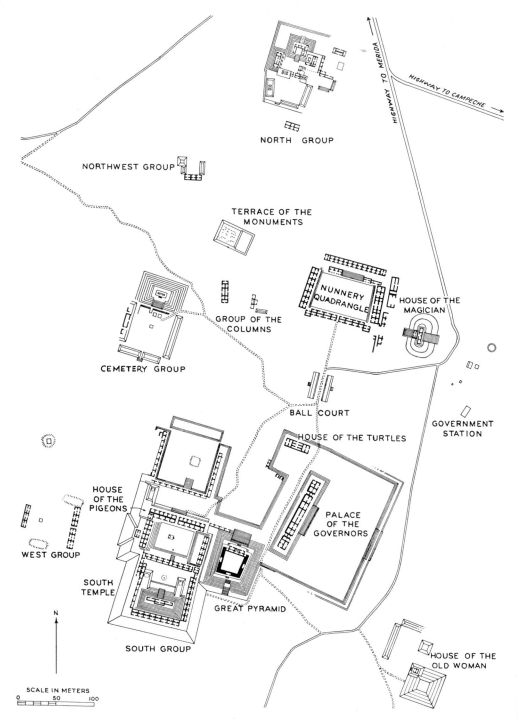

Fig. 11.58. Map of the central area, Uxmal.

Fig. 11.59. Nunnery Quadrangle, Uxmal: (*above*) looking north, the Ball Court in the foreground; (*below*) the south wing, the Governor's Palace in the background.

Fig. 11.60. Nunnery Quadrangle, Uxmal: (*above*) east wing; (*below*) west wing.

Fig. 11.61. Uxmal: staircase and Chenes-style temple of the Adivino, or House of the Magician.

facing a pyramid on its north side. Farther to the north is a large platform supporting a series of broken stelae, and beyond that is another ruined complex, the North Group.

Unusual among Maya sites, Uxmal possesses a quantity of phallic sculpture. Phallic motifs exist on the rear façade of the Nunnery Quadrangle's north building, and on the front façade of the west building. There is also a collection of phallic sculpture east of the platform supporting the Palace of the Governors, and this motif adorns the façade of the aptly named Temple of the Phallus, located farther to the south.

Recently Uxmal's emblem glyph has been tentatively identified in several inscriptions from the site. One of the most productive historical texts is on a small cylindrical altar found just south of the Governor's Palace. This monument appears to record the name of an Uxmal ruler, Lord Chac, and his parents (Chac Uinal Kan and Lady Bone). Lord Chac may also be named on Stela 7 (Fig. 11.57); its portrait of a richly clad ruler standing on a double-headed jaguar throne is like that found sculptured in stone on the platform east of the Governor's Palace. These monuments are without identifiable dates, but a painted capstone from the Nunnery Quadrangle records a calendar-round date (4 Eb 5 Ceh) that probably corresponds to 10.3.18.9.12, or A.D. 907, and appears to name both Lord Chac and his father, Chac Uinal Kan. The location of these inscriptions suggests that both the Governor's Palace and the Nunnery Quadrangle were associated with Lord Chac's reign at Uxmal.

## Kabah, Sayil, and Labna

These three somewhat smaller sites are also justly famous for their examples of Puuc architecture. About 18 km (11 mi.) of stone causeway connect Kabah with Uxmal to the north. Another tie to Uxmal is suggested by a hieroglyphic text that records two emblem glyphs, one possibly that of Kabah, the other the same as that tentatively identified as belonging to Uxmal. The latter is associated with the name glyph of Lord Chac, apparent ruler of Uxmal.

The most interesting structure at Kabah is the Palace of the Masks (Fig. 11.5), which contains ten chambers arranged in two rows of five each, for an overall length of 46 m (151 ft). The chambers of each pair are built one directly behind the other, with a single doorway to the outside.

The exteriors of most Puuc-style buildings are devoid of sculptural decoration below the medial molding, the intricate mosaics being concentrated in the upper half of the façades. The Palace of the Masks, however, stands on a low platform, the face of which is decorated with a single row of mask panels; above this is a carved molding, surmounted by the lower half of the façade, which is in turn composed of three rows of mask panels running across the front of the building. Above an elaborate medial molding there are again three rows of mask panels, the topmost being surmounted by a terminal molding.

Another unique feature of Kabah is the stone arch (Fig. 11.62). Standing

Fig. 11.62. Kabah, Yucatan, Mexico: arch at the perimeter of the site.

Fig. 11.63 (*left and right*). Structure 2C-6, Kabah: sculptured doorjambs.

apart from any other building, at the beginning of the causeway leading to Uxmal, it spans nearly 5 m (now restored). Its use is unknown, although it probably marked a formal boundary and the entrance to the civic core of Kabah.

Sayil is located only a few kilometers south of Kabah. Like its neighbor, it has not been subjected to thorough archaeological investigation. Sayil's most famous feature is the three-terrace palace, surmounted by a broad central staircase that appears to be a later addition. A small Puuc-style palace at Sayil has a sculptured hieroglyphic inscription over one of its doorways.

Labna is situated about 18 km (60 mi.) to the southeast of Sayil. Its two-terrace palace, similar in style to the Sayil example, is connected by a short *sache* to another architectural group that includes a pyramid capped by a partially fallen temple with a high flying façade or frontal roof comb. Adjacent to the pyramid is a small palace group entered by way of a famous archway, one of the most beautiful examples of Puuc architecture. Labna was briefly investigated by Edward Thompson in the late nineteenth century, and its principal buildings have been partially restored, as at Kabah and Sayil.

## Chichen Itza

Chichen Itza, located in north-central Yucatan, is one of the largest centers in the northern lowlands, its known extent covering an area of at least 5 km$^2$ (2 sq. mi.) of relatively dense architectural remains (Fig. 11.64). The pre-Columbian name for the site, recorded by Bishop Landa (see Chapter 6), means "mouth" or "opening of the wells of the Itza." It also appears to have been named Uucyabnal, "seven great rulers," and may have been the mythical Tollan referred to in later epics (see Chapter 6).

The first large-scale archaeological investigations by the Carnegie Institution of Washington, directed by Sylvanus Morley, were at Chichen Itza, beginning in 1924 and continuing for two decades. This work concentrated on the excavation and restoration of the site's major buildings, but in the process several nearly intact structures were discovered beneath subsequent constructions. Much valuable work was done in architectural recording, but the site still lacks some critical information of the kind obtained from modern archaeological research, including data about population size, settlement patterns, and building functions. A basic chronological scheme for the site remains a problem in some respects, since several major buildings cannot be dated with any precision.

Most of the visible structures at Chichen Itza are assigned to one of two architectural periods: the "florescent" (Terminal Classic), associated with a Puuc style, or the "modified florescent" (Early Postclassic), associated with the addition of certain Mexican architectural traits (listed in Chapter 6) to a continuing Maya masonry tradition. The florescent-period buildings are located in the southern portion of the site, and though some of these were rebuilt or added to during the Early Postclassic, most of the modified florescent structures are in the northern part of the site (Fig. 11.65).

The oldest known buildings at Chichen Itza were constructed in an early Puuc style. Mosaic-decorated upper façades and block masonry walls, rather than the fine veneer work of later times, can be seen in the terrace supporting the Caracol, the House of the Deer, and the Red House. The Puuc style also appears in a series of non-elevated palace structures, including the original buildings in the Nunnery Group (Monjas, Annex, and Iglesia) and in the Akabtzib. Radiocarbon dates from the wooden beams in the Red House and Iglesia are about A.D. 600–780, but these may refer to the growth period of the wood, rather than to later building construction. The later additions to the Akabtzib have been dated from a sculptured inscription over one of its inner doorways (Akabtzib: "dark writing") as either 10.2.0.0.0 or 10.3.0.0.0 (869 or 889). The Carnegie excavations found that the upper platform of the Caracol was associated with a stela dated to about 840.

The Caracol (see Fig. 6.8), located in the heart of the Terminal Classic architectural area, is a distinctive round structure crowning two superimposed rectangular platforms. It is something of an architectural mismatch, characterized by J. Eric Thompson as "a two-decker wedding cake on the square carton in which it came." The round superstructure appears to be somewhat later than its supporting platforms, probably dating from the beginning of the modified-florescent period, and seems to have been refurbished later during the Post-

Fig. 11.64. Aerial view of Chichen Itza, Yucatan, Mexico.

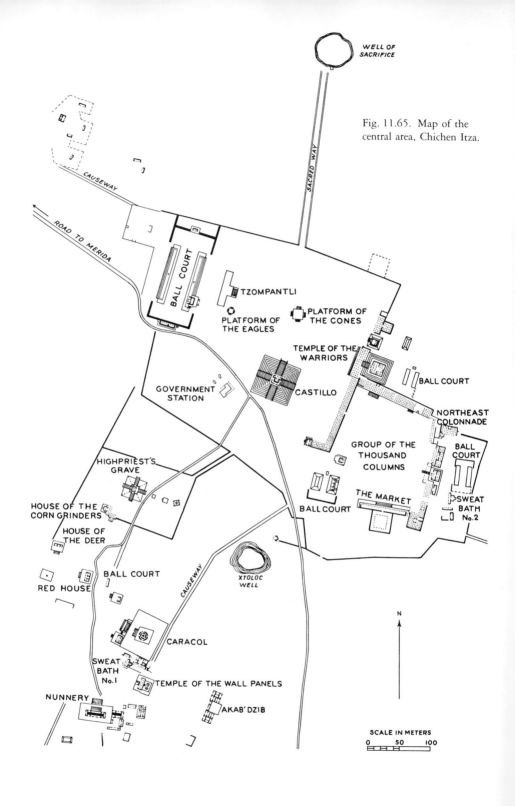

WELL OF
SACRIFICE

Fig. 11.65. Map of the
central area, Chichen Itza.

CAUSEWAY

SACRED WAY

ROAD TO MERIDA

BALL COURT

TZOMPANTLI

PLATFORM OF
THE EAGLES

PLATFORM OF
THE CONES

TEMPLE OF THE
WARRIORS

CASTILLO

BALL COURT

GOVERNMENT
STATION

NORTHEAST
COLONNADE

BALL
COURT

GROUP OF THE
THOUSAND
COLUMNS

HIGHPRIEST'S
GRAVE

HOUSE OF THE
CORN GRINDERS

THE MARKET

SWEAT
BATH
No.2

HOUSE OF
THE DEER

BALL COURT

BALL COURT

RED HOUSE

CAUSEWAY

XTOLOC
WELL

N

CARACOL

SWEAT
BATH
No.1

TEMPLE OF THE WALL PANELS

NUNNERY

AKAB'DZIB

SCALE IN METERS
0    50    100

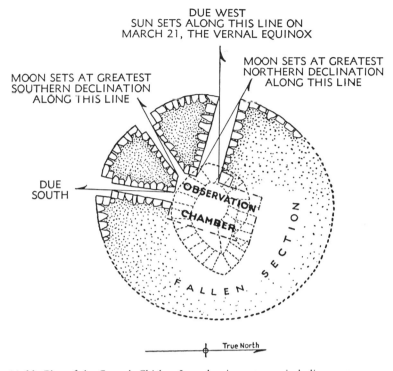

DUE WEST
SUN SETS ALONG THIS LINE ON
MARCH 21, THE VERNAL EQUINOX

MOON SETS AT GREATEST
NORTHERN DECLINATION
ALONG THIS LINE

MOON SETS AT GREATEST
SOUTHERN DECLINATION
ALONG THIS LINE

DUE
SOUTH

OBSERVATION
CHAMBER

SECTION

FALLEN

True North

Fig. 11.66. Plan of the Caracol, Chichen Itza, showing astronomical alignments.

classic era. Round structures were associated with Ehecatl, the wind-deity aspect of Quetzalcoatl (Kukulcan) in central Mexico, so it is reasonable to assume that the Caracol had this kind of function at Chichen Itza. Some 12.5 m high (41 ft), its central core of masonry conceals a spiral staircase, which winds up to a small chamber near the top of the building. The Spanish name for such a stairway is *caracol*, because of its fancied resemblance to the convolutions of a snail shell. The square openings through the thick walls of the chambers (Fig. 11.66) seem to fix certain astronomically important lines of sight. For example, one line of sight through the west wall bisects the setting sun on March 21, the vernal equinox; other lines coincide with the moonset on this same date.

The northern or Early Postclassic part of Chichen Itza is dominated by El Castillo, a large four-stairway pyramid supporting a flat-topped temple (Fig. 11.67). Like several Late Classic Maya pyramids, El Castillo has nine terraces (compare Temple I at Tikal). But the four stairways are usually seen as reflecting a Mexican architectural style, although this was already common in Late Classic centers such as Tikal (for example, in the Twin Pyramid groups). The temple of El Castillo has four doorways, but the wider northern doorway is divided by two feathered-serpent columns. Similar columns are known from six other buildings at the site. Inside the buried temple of an older structure encased within El Castillo, Carnegie archaeologists found a Chacmool and a red-painted jaguar "throne," which has fangs of chert, jadeite eyes, and inlaid jadeite disks to represent its spots (Fig. 11.68).

To the west is the Great Ball Court, incorporating an earlier building, the Lower Temple of the Jaguars with its murals under its southeastern corner (Fig. 11.69). The Upper Temple of the Jaguars, corresponding to the last construction stage of the ball court, sits above the same corner; its murals may depict episodes in the history of the Putun Maya (see Chapter 6). The Great Ball Court is the largest in Mesoamerica, measuring 166 by 68 m overall (545 by 223 ft), with a playing alley 146 by 36 m. The vertical playing surfaces are different from the long sloping zones typical of earlier courts at Copan and

Fig. 11.68. Red Jaguar Throne from the buried temple beneath El Castillo, Chichen Itza.

Fig. 11.67 (*below*). El Castillo, Chichen Itza, the principal pyramid temple of the Early Postclassic period at the site.

Fig. 11.69. Great Ball Court, Chichen Itza: (*above*) playing alley, looking south, the Temple of the Jaguars at upper left; (*below*) Temple of the Jaguars, with feathered-serpent columns.

other Classic lowland sites, indicating that the Postclassic game differed from the earlier contest.

Seven ball courts are known at Chichen Itza: six that were still in use when the city was last occupied, and an earlier one buried under a later terrace behind the Monjas. A stone ring was usually set into the middle of each long facing wall, and the object of the Postclassic game was to drive the ball through one of the rings, the openings of which were parallel to the ground. The balls were solid rubber, and the description of them given by the early Spanish historians marks the first European notice of rubber. The ball could not be thrown by the hand but had to be struck by the elbow, wrist, or hip, and leather pads were fastened to these parts of the body. The winning stroke was made so rarely that, by an ancient rule of the game, the player making it had forfeited to him all the clothing and jewelry of the spectators. When the ball was thus driven through the ring, all the spectators took to their heels to avoid paying the forfeit, and the friends of the lucky player ran after them to exact it.

Relief sculptures along the basal terrace of the Great Ball Court's walls may depict a more gruesome outcome. On the left stands an apparent victorious ball player or warrior with a knife in one hand and the head of his vanquished foe in the other. The decapitated foe kneels to the right of a disk, or shield, bearing a death's head, with streams of blood transformed into serpents spurting from his neck.

To the north of El Castillo is a vast plaza containing two small platforms

Fig. 11.70. Platform of the Cones, Chichen Itza, located north of El Castillo.

Fig. 11.71. Chichen Itza: (*above*) turquoise mosaic disk found in the Temple of the Chac Mool, encased within the Temple of the Warriors; (*below*) limestone box in which the disk was found.

(Fig. 11.70) and a *tzompantli* (Nahuatl for a rack used to display trophy heads from sacrifice and warfare; see Fig. 6.9). On the east side of this plaza sits the Temple of the Warriors (Fig. 6.6). Although larger and more finely built, its architecture parallels Pyramid B at Tula, the site identified as the Toltec capital north of Mexico City. The staircase leading to the large summit structure, its perishable beam-and-mortar roof having disappeared long ago, was reached by passing through a spacious colonnaded building. These colonnaded halls, also once roofed with beam and mortar, extend to the south and east of the Temple of the Warriors; they may have been used as council halls. Colonnades completely surround the Court of the Thousand Columns, a great open plaza of 4.5 acres, which may have been the marketplace of the ancient city.

An earlier building was found during the excavations under the Temple of the Warriors. Known as the Temple of the Chac Mool, it contained murals representing Maya and Mexicanized Maya (Putun Maya?) elites (see Chapter 6). Beneath the floor of this temple a cache was discovered containing a mosaic disk made of turquoise, a substance not found in the Maya area, but usually imported from central Mexico (Fig. 11.71).

In the northern part of Chichen Itza are two large natural wells, or cenotes, which no doubt contributed greatly to the importance of this site in ancient times. The Xtoloc Cenote was formerly the water supply for the center's population. A *sacbe* leads north from El Castillo to the edge of the Cenote of

Fig. 11.72. Sacred Cenote (well) of Sacrifice at Chichen Itza.

Sacrifice (Fig. 11.72). During Chichen Itza's ascendancy, and even after its downfall in the Late Postclassic, pilgrimages were made to this sacred cenote from all parts of the Maya area and beyond in order to cast offerings into its depths. Dredging of the cenote did produce jadeite, gold, pottery, human bone, and other items; but contrary to popular belief, there is no evidence that virgins were sacrificed in this way (see Chapter 14).

## Tulum

The ruins of Tulum are situated on the sea cliffs overlooking the Caribbean on the east coast of the Yucatan (Fig. 6.11), just south of the channel between Isla de Cozumel and the mainland. The site appears to have been occupied at the time of the Spanish Conquest, and was probably sighted by Juan de Grijalva during his reconnaissance of this coast in 1518. Tulum was visited by John Lloyd Stephens and Frederick Catherwood, who discovered the fragments of a reused Early Classic stela at the site (Fig. 11.73). In the early twentieth century the buildings were mapped and investigated by Samuel Lothrop. Later studies of the region's settlement were conducted by William Sanders. Recently, Arthur Miller directed a program of archeological and art-historical research focused on the mural paintings at Tulum and adjacent east-coast sites.

These investigations reveal that Tulum was occupied in the Late Postclassic, beginning about A.D. 1200. Its principal structures show several parallels with the earlier modified-florescent period at Chichen Itza and the later buildings of Mayapan, except that Tulum's architecture was executed on a much reduced scale. Quite likely, one motivation for its founding was to establish a trading center on Yucatan's east coast, probably by a Putun Maya group in alliance with the rulers of Mayapan.

The site is bounded on its landward sides by a stone wall that was once equipped with a walkway and parapet and averages some 6 m thick and 3–5 m high. In all, the wall circumscribes a roughly rectangular area about 385 m from north to south and 165 m from east to west (1,263 by 541 ft). Approach from the east is protected by sea cliffs averaging some 12 m in height. The wall is broken by five narrow gateways, one on the west side and two each on the north and south. Small structures ("watch towers") mark the landward corners.

Within the wall lies a series of masonry platforms and buildings, including colonnaded palaces and elevated temples. Traces of at least one "street" can be detected by a north-south alignment of structures just inside the western gate. In general, Tulum's masonry is very crude and often covered with thick coatings of plaster.

The largest palace-type buildings, Structures 21 and 25, lie along this alignment. Both have colonnades and once had beam-and-mortar roofs. Just to the south of Structure 21 is the Temple of the Frescoes (Structure 16), which

Fig. 11.73 (*above*). Tulum,
Quintana Roo, Mexico: the
Castillo, or principal temple, as depicted by Frederick Catherwood in the
mid-nineteenth century
(see Fig. 6.11).

Fig. 11.74. Tulum: por-
tion of the murals on the
interior walls of Structure
16, about 1450 or later.

consists of a small lower gallery, opened by a colonnade to the west, and an even smaller second-story temple. On the inner wall of the lower gallery are frescoes dating, according to Miller's analyses, to some time later than A.D. 1450 (Fig. 11.74). The style of these murals is similar to that of the Paris Codex, one of the few surviving Maya books (see Chapter 15). The façade of Structure 16 is decorated with stucco reliefs, including niched figures of the "diving god," identified as representations of Xux Ek, the Maya "wasp star," or Venus deity.

To the east is a central precinct, defined by a low masonry wall. Its principal building, the Castillo (Structure 1), is a 7.5-m-high platform that supports a small vaulted two-room temple, which is reached on its western side by a staircase with a wide balustrade. The temple building has a single western doorway supported by two circular columns. Later modification transformed these into feathered-serpent columns, similar to those common at Chichen Itza. The Castillo platform was built over an earlier colonnaded palace with a beam-and-mortar roof. The wings of this palace extend north and south from beneath the platform (Fig. 11.73).

Immediately north of the Castillo is a tiny elevated structure, also reached by a staircase on its western side, known as the Temple of the Diving God, or Structure 5 (Fig. 11.75). Its walls have a pronounced negative batter, and traces of a splendid mural painting on its interior (eastern) wall can still be discerned (Fig. 11.76). Above its single western doorway is its namesake, a stucco figure of the diving god.

Structure 45 is dramatically situated to the north of the central precinct, on a promontory above the sea (Fig. 11.77). Resting on a circular platform, it contains an altar still being used by the local Maya populace when Lothrop conducted his research at Tulum in 1924. A small shrine in front of Structure 45 appears to have been used as a beacon for seagoing canoes. A break in the offshore barrier reef occurs opposite the site, and canoes seeking to make port at Tulum could have used such beacons to guide their safe passage through the reef. Between the Castillo and Structure 45 a gap in the sea cliff forms a cove and landing beach suitable for Maya trading canoes.

Finally, it should be noted that a small cenote near the northern wall provided a source of water within Tulum's walls. A small building (Structure 35) is perched on the limestone ledge overhanging this water source.

Although a cluster of architectural features—such as platform supports for buildings and the arrangements around courts or plazas—characterizes most Maya sites, the overall impression is one of considerable architectural diversity. Each site briefly examined here has its unique attributes, manifesting its own individual variations on one of the several Maya architectural styles: the central Peten, the southeastern and southwestern lowlands, or to the north, the Río Bec, Chenes, and Puuc traditions.

Architectural variations are, of course, only one reflection of the diversity seen in the remains of Maya civilization. Similar patterns of variety are manifested in

Fig. 11.75. Tulum: view north from the front of the Castillo staircase, with Structure 5 and a portion of the encircling wall in the distance (note the corner tower at left).

Fig. 11.76. Tulum: portion of the murals on the interior wall of Structure 5.

Fig. 11.77. Tulum: view from the rear of Structure 5, with Structure 45 on the promontory beyond the landing beach.

the styles of sculpture, pottery, and other artifacts (see Chapters 12 and 13). But in a larger sense these are but variations upon a theme, for all are part of a recognizable Maya tradition, from the first glimmerings of Maya civilization seen in the Preclassic period, through the florescence of the Classic, and into the latest manifestations in the Postclassic.

# 12

## CERAMICS

The trades of the Indians were making pottery and carpentering. They earned a great deal by making idols out of clay and wood, with many fasts and observances. —Landa's *Relación de las cosas de Yucatán* (Tozzer 1941 : 94)

Ceramic remains have long been one of the most valuable evidences of past human society. Because of their durability, artifacts made of fired clay—pottery vessels, figurines, beads, and other items—usually survive long after most human products have disappeared. The Maya area is no exception, and even in the humid lowland conditions that destroy most cultural remains, ceramic materials often survive. The most ubiquitous ceramic artifact is the potsherd. Even though ceramic materials resist decay, everyday experience testifies that pottery vessels are very fragile. Thus it is not surprising that a welter of potsherds litter most sites of ancient habitation.

## Ceramics and Archaeology

Pottery remains have many uses for the archaeologist. The differences in vessel size and shape are clues to their functions. Ultimately, the determination of function leads to the reconstruction of ancient human activity (see Chapter 8). Thus the remains of a structure strewn with potsherds from a recognizable set of vessel shapes (storage jars, cooking pots, griddles, and so forth) indicate that it was once a residence. Another building littered with sherds from distinctly nondomestic pottery forms (incensarios, bowls for offerings, etc.) reveals that ritual activity once took place there.

But the most traditional, and perhaps the most valuable, use of the potsherd has been as a marker of time. Because of the nature of pottery itself—a plastic medium sensitive to the subtle manipulations of the potter, but controlled by the prevailing traditions of vessel form and decoration that gradually change and shift through time—a knowledgeable archaeologist can give a rather accurate date for most well-preserved ancient pottery fragments. Thus, the finding of potsherds during archaeological excavations provides an immediate and convenient chronological check for the investigator. For instance, the archaeologist can usually quickly verify that an excavation has reached soil levels that date from the Late Preclassic, for example, by simply examining the potsherds from that level.

The changes in pottery shapes and decorations through time are usually determined from the excavation of stratified archaeological deposits. As broken vessels are discarded, they may be swept or thrown, along with other trash, into refuse heaps called middens. In some cases midden deposits may accumulate for hundreds or even thousands of years, the earliest material at the bottom of the deposit, the latest at the top. Each stratum or visible layer in the midden describes an interval of past time, an episode of trash deposition. These provide an inventory of the kinds of pottery and other surviving artifacts used at a particular time, and a key to overall changes in form and decoration through time.

Only a few long-term middens have been excavated in the Maya area. The Maya were fond of recycling their own refuse. In refurbishing and expanding their centers, they found that both middens and demolished structures made excellent construction fill for new buildings. As a result, relatively few long-term accumulations seem to have survived undisturbed; most that have been excavated were used for relatively short periods of time. Yet, by piecing together evidence from a series of such short-term middens, along with information from pottery found in construction fill and other places, Maya archaeologists have succeeded in defining pottery sequences at many sites.

The blocks of time that these sequences represent, ranging from several decades to several hundred years in duration, are defined by *ceramic complexes*, distinctive and relatively stable kinds of pottery made and used in a particular area during a given period. Pottery of a single complex stands in contrast to the pottery made and used in earlier or later times. Of course most shifts in the pottery inventory of any society do not occur simultaneously but at different rates through time, so that ceramic complexes must be defined arbitrarily. This is analogous to any convenient ordering of eras in history, such as the sequence of periods known as the Dark Ages, medieval period, and Renaissance in European history.

The many local ceramic chronologies that have been worked out in the Maya area are relatively accurate and valid in reflecting the shifts in ancient pottery inventories through time (Table 12). Many have been cross-checked by radiocarbon (C-14) analysis and other means of dating the past. Although these ceramic sequences are the most common and complete time indicators available, they are not cultural chronologies. It is not valid to equate ceramic complexes with history, saying in effect that changes in traditions of pottery form and decoration reflect changes in political, social, religious, or other institutions of a past society. No doubt certain events, such as a shift in

TABLE 12

Ceramic Sequences from Selected Maya Sites

| General cultural periods | | Pacific coast — Salinas la Blanca and Bilbao | Southern highlands — Chalchuapa | Southern highlands — Kaminaljuyu | Southern lowlands — Altar de Sacrificios | Uaxactun | Central lowlands — Barton Ramie and Cuello | Becan | Dzibilchaltun | Northern lowlands — Mayapan | Date (Gregorian) A.D. |
|---|---|---|---|---|---|---|---|---|---|---|---|
| Postclassic | Late | | | | | | | | | Chikinchel | |
| | | Peor es Nada | Ahal | Chinautla | | | Lobo | Chechem | Tases | 1400 |
| | | | | | | | | | – – Hocaba – – | |
| | Early | | Matzin | Ayumpuc | Jimba | | New Town | Xcocom | Zipche | Sotuta | 1200 |
| | | | | Pamplona | | | | | Copo 2 | | 1000 |
| | | – – Santa Lucia – – | Payu | Amatle | Boca | Tepeu 3 | Spanish Lookout | Chintok | Copo 1 | Cehpech | |
| Classic | Late | | | | Pasión | Tepeu 2 | Tiger Run | Bejuco | | Motul | 800 |
| | | | | | Chixoy | Tepeu 1 | | Sabucan | | | |
| | | Laguneta | Xocco | Esperanza | Ayn | | Hermitage | Chacsik | Piim | Cochuah | 600 |
| | Early | | | | Salinas | Tzakol | | | | | |
| | | Mejor es Algo | Vec | Aurora | | | Floral Park | | | | 400 |
| | | | | Arenal | | | | | Xculul | | 200 |

Chronological chart (B.C. 0–2000), Preclassic periods.

| B.C. | | | | | | | | |
|---|---|---|---|---|---|---|---|---|
| 0 | | | | Mount Hope | Chicanel | Plancha | Miraflores (Verbena) | Caynac · Crucero |
| 200 | Tihosuco | Komchen | Paklum | Barton Creek | | | Providencia · Chul · 2 | |
| 400 | | Nabanche | Acachen | Jenney Creek | Mamom | San Felix | Las Charcas · Kal · Conchas | |
| 600 | | | | | | Xe · Colos · 1 | | |
| 800 | | | | | | Tok · Jocotal | | |
| 1000 | | | | | | Cuadros | | |
| 1200 | | | | Swasey | | | | |
| 1400 | | | | | | Ocos | | |
| 1600 | | | | | | Barra | | |
| 1800 | | | | ? | | | | |
| 2000 | | | | | | | | |

Late · Middle · Early

Preclassic

economic fortunes within a pottery-making village, produce some changes in the pottery made by that society. But profound social changes that affect nearly all aspects of society, such as political conquest, may have a rather minor effect on the pottery of the conquered society. Until further study has more fully explored the dynamics of pottery stability and change, we should not assume that the sequences of ancient Maya pottery necessarily reflect shifts in other aspects of culture. Overall, these sequences constitute an important tool for the archaeologist as a convenient and practical aid to dating artifacts and buildings.

Recent research to identify the sources of clay used in ancient Maya ceramics (based on neutron-activation and other analytic techniques) has begun to define major production centers and clarify pottery distribution and trade patterns. As a whole, Maya ceramic studies have contributed priceless information about the origins and development of the early Maya, their trade networks, the development of social and occupational distinctions, ancient diet and culinary practices, religious beliefs and rituals, kinship relationships, funeral practices, and other aspects of the lives of both elite and commoner.

## A Chronological Review of Maya Pottery

The ancient Maya developed a remarkable ceramic tradition, one of the most varied and diverse of any known to the archaeological record anywhere in the world. An exhausting variety of pottery types, forms, and decorative techniques were produced during the some 3,500 years that span the time from the earliest origins of the Maya to the Spanish Conquest. Among the outstanding features of pre-Columbian Maya pottery are ceramics exhibiting deeply polished red and brown slips, lustrous blacks, unusual resist-decorated wares, sensitive and grotesque modeling, delicate thin-walled creams and oranges, mass-produced molded vessels, and beautiful polychromes, including the exquisite portrait vases of the Late Classic period.

### EARLY PRECLASSIC

As in the Old World, pottery first appeared in Mesoamerica with the emergence of settled village life. The technology of making containers of clay probably owes its ultimate origin to the human capacity for experimenting with and manipulating the environment. Learning to fire clay to produce the characteristic hardness and durability of pottery may well have been accidental. Whatever its origins, it is probable that the earliest pottery in Mesoamerica was modeled into forms that imitated preexisting containers; globular neckless jars (the *olla* of today) were modeled after containers made from gourds, and wide, flat-bottomed bowls may have been formed after pans made of wood or stone (similar to the *sarten* of today).

The technical excellence and variety of decorations of this early Mesoamerican pottery might indicate ultimate origins or influences from elsewhere. Indeed, the earliest pottery yet discovered in the New World is from northern South America (Colombia and Ecuador). Perhaps the first New World peoples to practice village life, by farming manioc and fishing the coast lagoons, developed to the south, and these new techniques spread north by means of migration and diffusion along the coasts of Central America (see Chapter 2).

The oldest known pottery from the Maya area has been found along the east coast of Yucatan in northern Belize (Swasey Ceramic Complex), and along the Pacific coast (Barra and Ocos ceramic complexes) where the modern nations of Mexico and Guatemala meet. The remains of a series of early villages dating from the second and third millennia B.C. have been excavated in these areas. The earliest pottery thus far discovered in the highlands appeared soon thereafter, apparently representing the first penetration of the highlands proper by agricultural peoples using a shifting pattern of maize cultivation. These first highland settlers may have moved up the Motagua valley from a still-undiscovered center of coastal villages along the southern Caribbean coast. Similar highland agricultural adaptations resulted in population movements from the Pacific coast into the highlands via the major valleys (such as the Río Paz). This movement was demonstrated by archaeological research at several sites, including Chalchuapa, just across the Guatemalan border in El Salvador, where occupation was established by 1200–900 B.C. Similar early occupation is documented on the western flank of the Maya highlands, in the central depression of Chiapas. The earliest occupation at the major highland site of Kaminaljuyu followed shortly.

This early pottery is generally well fired, hard, and durable. Some wares are slipped and well polished (black, red, and ivory wares dominate). Other, more utilitarian wares (storage and cooking vessels) are unslipped. Decoration includes punctations (in both rows and zones), appliques and modeling (heads and faces on jar shoulders), incising, fluting, differential firing effects (white-rim black ware), resist lines, and painting (red-rim neckless jars). (See Fig. 12.1.)

The ceramic inventory from this early period is well developed; findings include many of the vessel forms used for basic subsistence functions throughout the pre-Columbian era. The large neckless jar forms are well suited for the storage of water and possibly food products. The general scarcity of smaller jars and suitable handles indicates that pottery vessels were not often used for the transport of water or other substances at this early date. A relative lack of external burning on some pottery has led investigators to conclude that cooking was probably done by placing hot stones inside large vessels to heat liquids and solid foods (such as tamales).

Hand-modeled figurines, usually anthropomorphic (Fig. 12.2) but occasionally zoomorphic, first appear during this period. The earliest examples were

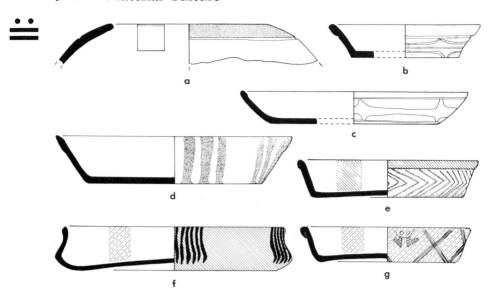

Fig. 12.1. Early Preclassic pottery. From the southern Maya highlands: (*a*) red-rimmed *tecomate*; (*b*) red-painted incised brown bowl; (*c*) incised brown bowl; (*d*) resist-decorated gray bowl. From the eastern lowlands (Cuello, Belize): (*e*) red-rimmed bowl with chevron grooving; (*f*) red bowl with black paint; (*g*) incised buff bowl.

Fig. 12.2. Early Preclassic clay figurine heads from the southern Maya highlands.

usually modeled in a rather free, naturalistic style that is both individualistic and unstereotyped. The function of these fascinating clay effigies has never been satisfactorily explained. Some researchers suggest a religious function, as idols for a village-level, agricultural fertility cult. Others propose more mundane explanations, such as toys or dolls for children. Whatever their ancient function, these figurines have a sporadic distribution in both time and space, appearing rather commonly in several regions of Mesoamerica (including the southern Maya highlands) during the Preclassic, then nearly disappearing in the Early Classic era only to reappear and flourish during the Late Classic period.

MIDDLE PRECLASSIC

The Middle Preclassic, characterized by occupation of much of the Maya area, saw the beginnings of widespread settlement across the central lowlands (Chapter 3).

Many of the pottery traditions of the Early Preclassic were not only maintained but elaborated during this period. New elements (especially prevalent in the highlands) include the first attempts at polychrome painting (black, white, red, and yellow paints applied after firing), the first bichrome slipping (for instance, red-on-cream and red-on-orange), and the beginnings of the Usulutan tradition of resist decoration. Red, black, orange, and streaky brown slipped wares are typical; the streaky-brown pieces were often highly polished. Forms include necked jars (with handles on the neck or high on the shoulder), composite wall bowls, bowls with labial and medial flanges, bowls with vertical tubular spouts, and elaborately modeled, cylindrical incense burners (three-pronged incensarios). (See Fig. 12.3.) These incense burners constitute the earliest clear indication of specialized ritual pottery.

Fig. 12.3. Middle Preclassic pottery. From the southern highlands: (*a*) red-rimmed spouted vessel; (*b*) polychrome stucco-painted bowl; (*c*) Usulutan decorated bowl; (*d*) incised ivory-gray bowl; (*e*) punctated, incised jar. From the central lowlands: (*f*) grooved orange bowl.

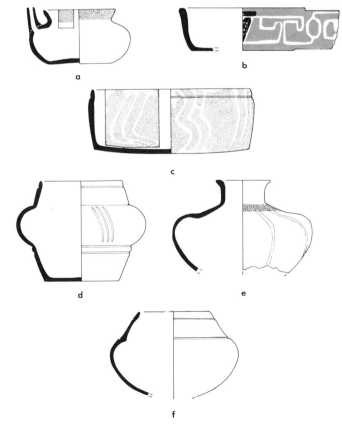

Other distinctive Middle Preclassic pottery includes shoe-shaped cooking pots, spouted vessels, bowls with grater bottoms, and peculiar cup-shaped vessels with long, tripod legs, which lasted in use through all periods in some areas of Mesoamerica. Both cylindrical and flat clay stamps, whistles in animal form, and hand-modeled figurines are also found. Clay figurines increased in popularity during this era, but lost their individualistic character, becoming stereotyped and uniform in style (Fig. 12.4).

### LATE PRECLASSIC AND PROTOCLASSIC

The ceramic inventory became even more elaborate and diverse in the Late Preclassic (Figs. 12.5 and 12.6). Black-brown, lustrous-red, orange, and cream slipped wares predominate. The distinctive Usulutan decorated pottery, typified by swirling patterns of parallel resist lines, was produced in the southeastern periphery of the Maya area and traded widely during this time. This decoration was apparently produced by application of narrow bands of wax or pitch to the vessel surface. When fired, this substance melted away, leaving a lighter-colored surface in its wake. Other features of the vessels included supports (tripods and tetrapods with solid or hollow conical supports), shallow modeled decorations (for example, "toad effigies"), stucco, bichromes, and trichromes. Typical forms included necked jars (with handles on the jar shoulder), tall cylinders with flaring walls, bowls with grooved everted rims, and

Fig. 12.4. Middle and Late Preclassic clay figurine heads from the southern highlands: (*top row*) Middle Preclassic; (*bottom row*) Late Preclassic.

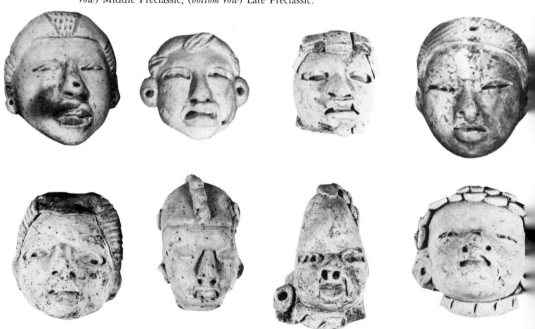

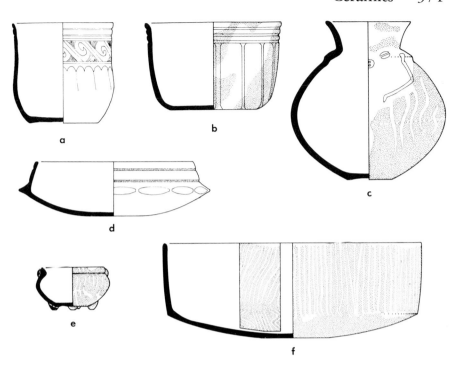

Fig. 12.5. Late Preclassic pottery from the southern highlands: (*a*) finely incised black-brown bowl; (*b*) fluted Usulutan bowl; (*c*) Usulutan jar; (*d*) fine red bowl with faceted shoulder and graphite-painted grooves; (*e*) miniature Usulutan bowl; (*f*) Usulutan bowl.

bowls with covers. The incensario tradition was elaborated by modeling and postfiring polychrome painting. The pottery tradition of the southern and central lowlands, dominated by a distinctive type called Sierra Red, became unusually uniform from site to site during this period.

Certain highland pottery common in Late Preclassic times, such as the toad bowls and modeled mushrooms in both clay and stone, seems to indicate the ritual use of psychotropic substances by religious specialists, probably during divinatory ceremonies. Since similar practices are documented in the ethnographical literature of Mesoamerica (as well as other areas of the New World), this example provides another example of the continuity of religious practices in the Maya area (see Chapter 14).

The pottery figurines of the Late Preclassic continued the trends of the previous era, generally appearing even less expressive and more uniform (Figs. 12.4 and 12.7).

At the close of the Preclassic, a series of new pottery elements appears to have spread over much of the eastern Maya area. This Protoclassic assemblage (Chapter 3), probably originating in the southeastern periphery (eastern Guate-

Fig. 12.6. Late Preclassic pottery from the central lowlands: (*above*) Usulutan bowl; (*below*) spouted vessel with painted imitation Usulutan design.

Fig. 12.7. Late Preclassic clay figurine heads from the central lowlands.

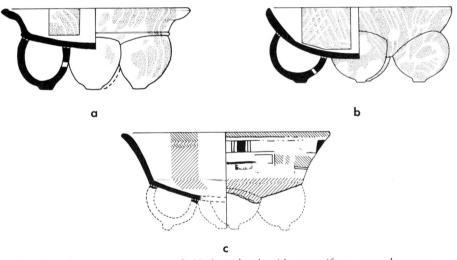

a                                                                          b

c

Fig. 12.8. Protoclassic pottery: (*a, b*) Usulutan bowls with mammiform tetrapod supports, from the southern highlands; (*c*) a polychrome bowl with mammiform tetrapod supports, from the central lowlands.

mala and western El Salvador), includes the "mammiform tetrapod" bowl (bowls with four bulbous supports; Fig. 12.8), Usulutan and red-on-orange bichrome decoration, and in the eastern and southeastern lowlands, the first orange polychromes (red and black on orange).

EARLY AND MIDDLE CLASSIC

The Classic period is noted for the development and spread of polychrome pottery, in both highland and lowland areas. The Early Classic polychromes of the lowlands are typically red and black on orange or cream, with painted motifs executed in geometric patterns. Both red-painted and red-and-black-painted Usulutan pottery is distinctive of this period in the highlands and southeastern lowlands. Monochrome slipped wares are dominated by polished black, cream, and orange types. Stucco painting (postfiring) is common, although one distinctive highland utilitarian type is decorated with scraped slip (the slip is swirled with the fingers while still wet to produce an effect like finger painting). Common and distinctive forms include ring-based bowls and basally flanged bowls. Toward the end of this period (the Middle Classic) several new forms enjoyed a widespread distribution. These included tripod-supported cylindrical vessels and small pitchers emulating forms typical of those from Teotihuacan (see Figs. 12.9–11).

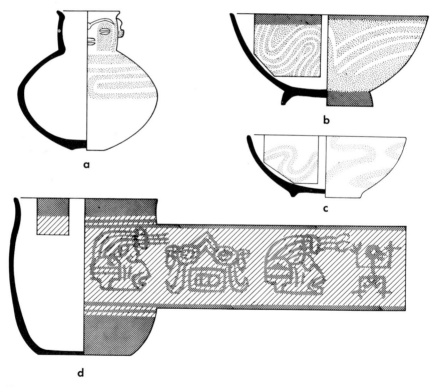

Fig. 12.9. Early Classic pottery from the southern highlands: (*a*) red-on-cream jar with effigy-modeled neck; (*b*) red-rimmed Usulutan bowl with ring base; (*c*) scraped-slip cream-colored bowl with ring base; (*d*) red-on-orange painted bowl with Tlaloc-like motifs.

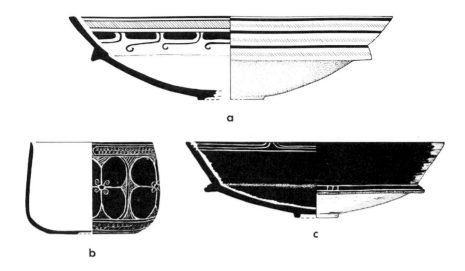

Fig. 12.10. Early Classic pottery from the central lowlands: (*a*) basal-flange polychrome bowl; (*b*) incised black bowl; (*c*) incised, black, basal-flange bowl; (*below*) basal-flange polychrome bowl with ring base and effigy-handled lid (Tikal).

Fig. 12.11. Early Classic pottery from the central lowlands: (*upper left*) stuccoed, polychrome, cylindrical tripod bowl with Tlaloc motif and effigy-handled lid (Tikal); (*upper right*) incised, orange, cylindrical tripod bowl and lid (Tikal); (*below*) carved and incised, black, cylindrical tripod bowl and Teotihuacan-style hollow figurine (Becan).

The near absence of pottery from the Early Classic period in many areas of the Maya highlands may result from the disruptions in this region mentioned in Chapter 3. But the pottery from many sites, including many in the lowlands, is characterized by a relative lack of development and elaboration.

In the northern Yucatan plain the ceramics of the Classic stage were sharply divided into two traditions: the earlier (regional-stage) pottery is closely similar to the Early Classic pottery of the central lowlands; the later (florescent-stage) is a separate tradition developed in Late and Terminal Classic times. Regional pottery consisted of monochromes that are strikingly similar to those of the Peten, but polychrome decoration was less frequently used. The Yucatan has produced, however, one of the best-documented ceramic sequences leading from Preclassic into Classic times, not to mention sizable Middle and Late Preclassic structures. These accomplishments are the work of well-organized communities of considerable size. It is also notable that nearly every archaeological site sampled on the northern plain produced Late Preclassic ceramics. The centers of northern Yucatan were thus established well before "Maya civilization" developed, and continued to be occupied until after the collapse of the Peten centers.

The long tradition of clay figurines nearly vanished throughout most of the Maya area at the beginning of the Classic period. The decline of this familiar Preclassic tradition has been equated with the suppression of the local village-agricultural cults by an increasingly powerful (and jealous) state-controlled elite religion. The figurines known from this period are almost invariably associated with elite ritual contexts, such as the Teotihuacan-related cache from the lowland site of Becan (Fig. 12.11, lower illustration). These Mexican-influenced figurines were often molded, in contrast to the Preclassic tradition of hand modeling.

## LATE AND TERMINAL CLASSIC

The Late Classic period is noted for its fine polychrome pottery. Although some of this pottery was poorly or incompletely fired, the painted scenes are justly noted for their artistic merits (Figs. 12.12 and 12.13). Motifs include both naturalistic and geometric designs, glyphic texts, and individual portraits. The polychrome vases and dishes (on tripod supports) were created by sophisticated resist techniques and painted black, orange, red, white, and a variety of other colors. Most notable examples come from the lowlands (see Figs. 13.35–38 and the discussion of the Altar Vase below), but significant centers of the art were located in the northern Maya highlands (see the Chama, Nebaj, and Ratinlinxul vases, Figs. 13.39–41) and along the southeastern periphery (Copador polychrome produced at Copan; Fig. 12.12c).

The culmination of the ceramic portrait artistry is epitomized by the Late Classic, lowland, polychrome cylindrical vases (Fig. 12.13, lower illustration). Ceramic art was also well expressed in the delicately modeled and painted Late

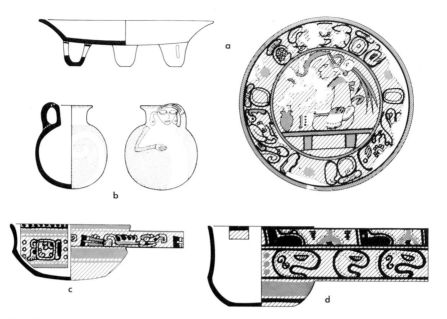

Fig. 12.12. Late Classic pottery from the southern highlands: (*a*) polychrome tripod vessel imported from the lowlands; (*b*) white or orange jar with modeled monkey figure; (*c*) Copador polychrome bowl; (*d*) purple polychrome bowl.

Fig. 12.13. Late Classic pottery from the central lowlands: (*above*) polychrome bowl with glyph band (Tikal); (*right*) polychrome portrait vase (Tikal).

Classic incensarios. Resist and negative-painted decoration, two other typical Late Classic characteristics, appeared on tall cylindrical vases, ring-stand vessels, and tripod-supported dishes. Generally speaking, there were two size ranges of slipped-ware jars: one large enough to carry a full backload of water, the other of two- to three-liter capacity. Hemispheroid basins are common, and low platters are found in some areas; both have thickened rims. Bowls are of two types, both smaller than the preceding shapes. Most bowls hold one to three liters, their bottoms are nearly flat, their sides flare, and they sit on specialized supports, either a ring or three legs. Hemispheroid bowls, which hold half a liter to a liter, have either a flattened bottom or a ring base. The unslipped, externally striated cooking pots continued the traditions begun in earlier times. Although incensarios for religious ceremonies were also unslipped, they were decorated with appliqué and painted with white clay or plaster. Among the thin, finely made, and elaborately decorated vessels that were widely traded, the most common shape is cylindrical; some flare slightly, some are barrel-shaped.

Because the Late Classic period is the most thoroughly studied era of Maya civilization, more data has been collected about the pottery of the Late Classic than any other. Some of these studies have provided new and important insights not only into our knowledge of Maya ceramics, but into the nature of Maya social and political organization as well (see Chapter 8).

One of the most beautiful examples of Classic lowland polychrome pottery, the Altar Vase (Fig. 12.14), was excavated by archaeologists at Altar de Sacrificios. The meaning of its painted scene was interpreted by R. E. W. Adams, and provides a vivid portrayal of the ritual activity and customs of the Maya ruling elite. The Altar Vase depicts a funeral rite that occurred in A.D. 754. The subject of the funeral, a middle-aged woman of obvious importance, was probably from the ruling dynasty at Altar de Sacrificios. The scene on the vase depicts an elaborate ritual of dancing, singing, and sacrifice involving six individuals; at least three were members of the ruling dynasties of other centers: Tikal, Yaxchilan, and an unknown center in the Chama region of the northern Maya highlands. The offerings brought by these visitors (including several pottery vessels) were apparently placed in the woman's tomb. The vase also depicts the auto-sacrifice of a young female, possibly a member of the dead woman's family. The Altar Vase, together with the knife that was presumably the cause of her death, was buried with the young sacrificial victim in a simple grave near the tomb.

Several famous polychrome vessels (the Chama, Nebaj, and Ratinlinxul vases), all from the adjacent northern Maya highlands, appear to depict the merchant elites that rose to power in the Late Classic, for their scenes often portray mercantile themes and symbols. On the Ratinlinxul Vase (Fig. 13.41), a merchant prince arrives, borne in a palanquin and accompanied by some of his bearers. This scene may illustrate the kind of power structure that developed on the southern periphery of the Maya lowlands, an area of independent enclaves established and maintained by aggressively competitive merchant "princes."

Fig. 12.14. Photographic roll-out of the scene on the Altar de Sacrificios Vase (Late Classic), found buried with the remains of a young woman who appears to be depicted at the lower left, her throat cut and her hand still holding a leaf-shaped flint knife.

Their power was seemingly based on control of the lucrative trade routes between the resource zones of the highlands and the markets in the lowlands.

Other important studies of Late Classic pottery delineated the localized pottery manufacture and distribution at the largest Maya site, Tikal, and at Palenque and its surrounding dependencies. The stereotyped scenes on Terminal Classic, mold-made fine orange pottery (Fig. 12.15) have been interpreted as representing the conflict and eventual takeover of several Usumacinta sites (Altar de Sacrificios and Seibal) by Mexicanized Maya groups from the Gulf coast region (Chapter 6).

During the Late Classic period, figurines reappeared in the central Maya lowlands; their center of development seems to have been along the Gulf of Campeche in the states of Tabasco and Campeche. The finest figurines, which are usually found in graves, come from Isla de Jaina (Fig. 12.16), although good examples also come from the region of Palenque and Jonuta. The figurines, about 10–25 cm high (4–10 in.) and made of a fine-textured orange clay, often bear a white wash with traces of paint in blue and other colors. These solid pieces were hand-modeled or mold-made (Fig. 12.17). Mold-made specimens often contain pellets to make a rattle, or a whistle and stops to form an

Fig. 12.15. Fine orange pottery from Yucatan (Terminal Classic to Early Postclassic): (*a*) Uxmal; (*b, c*) Chichen Itza.

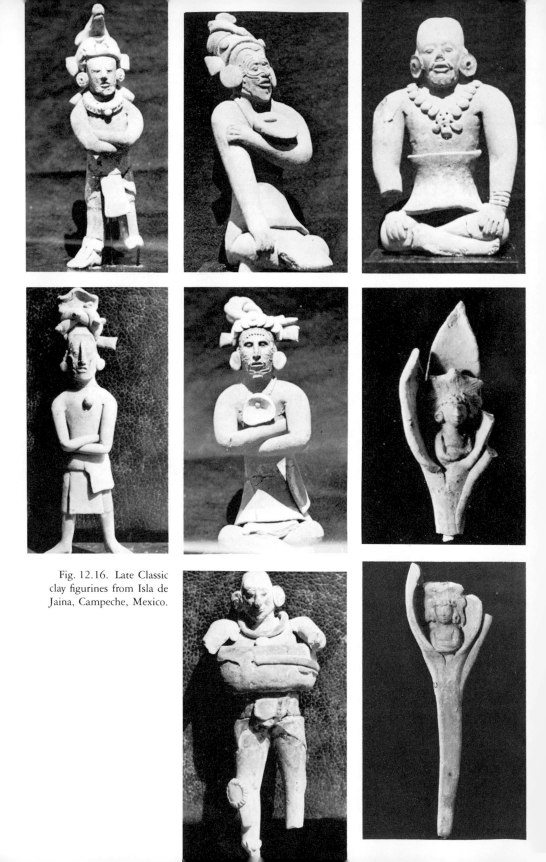

Fig. 12.16. Late Classic clay figurines from Isla de Jaina, Campeche, Mexico.

ocarina. Detailing on these figurines is amazingly fine; tattooed designs show clearly on faces no larger than a thumbnail. Without question these are the most intricate and detailed work in clay in pre-Columbian America. Figurines, flageolets, and other small pottery objects, generally similar in style to the Jaina mold-made figurines, are found over a larger area, including the Peten, Puuc, and Gulf coast regions.

In the Yucatan, the pottery of the Late and Terminal Classic is largely devoid of polychrome decoration. The distinguishing and diagnostic remains are the slatewares, characterized by a waxy gray to brownish slip, occasionally ornamented with a pale, crudely applied grayish paint. Despite their drab coloring, the characteristically fine, smooth finish, the careful forming, and the technical excellence (Fig. 12.18) seem to derive from a carefully organized, competent

Fig. 12.17. Figurine shaped by an ancient mold found near the Río Chixoy, Chiapas, Mexico.

Fig. 12.18. Slateware, Terminal Classic period: (*above*) excavated fragment, Uxmal; (*upper right*) bowl from Dzan; (*lower right*) jar of unknown provenance; (*below*) carved bowl found near Tikal.

group of craftsmen, whereas the Peten polychromes are creations of talented individual artists. Further evidence of the "industrialization" of Maya pottery is found in the use of the *k'abal* among modern Yucatecans. The *k'abal* is a wooden disk that rests on a smooth board and is spun between the soles of the potter's feet, in a procedure very close to the wheel throwing used by Old World potters from as early as 3000 B.C. Although the true potter's wheel was never used in pre-Columbian America, vessels made on a *k'abal* have the even, elaborate contours characteristic of wheel-made pottery, and this feature characterizes much of the pre-Conquest Maya ceramics from the northern lowlands.

### EARLY POSTCLASSIC

At the close of the Classic new types of pottery began to appear throughout the Maya area. Technologically superior, hard, thin walled, and fine pasted, these remains include the fine orange pottery found in the lowlands and the Yucatan, which was apparently produced on the western periphery of the Maya area, and the Yucatecan slateware already discussed (Figs. 12.15 and 12.18). The most distinctive Early Postclassic pottery is the only truly vitrified (glazed) pottery in pre-Columbian America, plumbate ware (Fig. 12.19), produced along the Pacific piedmont in southwestern Guatemala. Pottery of this tradition must have been fired in enclosed kilns (probably pits) capable of reaching the high temperatures required for vitrification. Plumbate pottery was frequently elaborately decorated by molding or by a combination of modeling and carving. Plumbate ceramics, which underwent several hundred years of development and were widely traded even beyond the Maya area, are hallmarks of the Early Postclassic period. An apparent production center for an early form of plumbate pottery (San Juan plumbate), recently discovered in this area, should provide invaluable new data about the manufacturing technology of pre-Columbian pottery.

Despite the technological excellence of these particular ceramics and the lingering of a simple polychrome tradition in the lowlands (Fig. 12.20), in other respects the pottery of the Early Postclassic period demonstrates an overall decline in quality from that of earlier times.

### LATE POSTCLASSIC

The pottery of the Late Postclassic has been found at a variety of sites, including the capitals of the independent, highland Maya "kingdoms" destroyed during the Spanish Conquest. In addition, several investigators have traced the Late Postclassic wares of Yucatan and the Maya lowlands (the latter largely restricted to the areas around Lago Peten Itza, Lago Yaxha, and other lakes).

The Late Postclassic fostered the continued, widespread tradition of monochrome utilitarian pottery (Figs. 12.21 and 12.22). Paste variations probably reflect regional or local production centers. In the highlands, wares continued to

Fig. 12.19. Plumbate pottery from the northern lowlands (Early Postclassic).

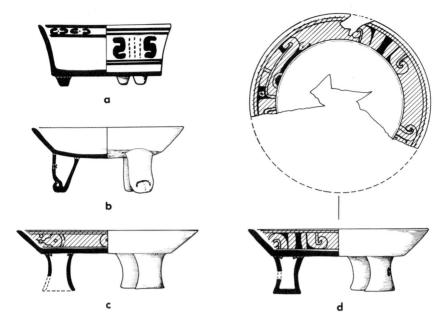

Fig. 12.20. Pottery from the central lowlands. Terminal Classic: (*a*) polychrome bowl with solid tripod supports. Early Postclassic: (*b*) red bowl with hollow-scroll tripod supports; (*c, d*) polychrome bowls with hollow "trumpet" supports.

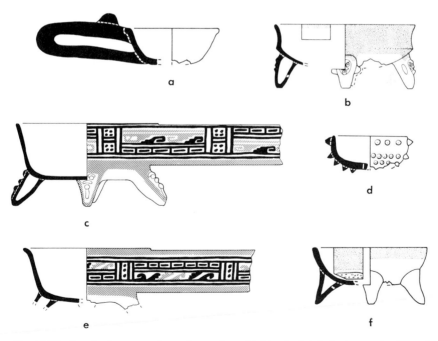

Fig. 12.21. Postclassic pottery from the southern highlands: (*a*) ladle incensario; (*b*) red-painted bowl with mold-made figures for supports; (*c*) Chinautla polychrome bowl with mold-made, figured supports; (*d*) miniature bowl with appliqué spikes; (*e*) Chinautla polychrome bowl; (*f*) red-on-buff bowl with grater interior.

Fig. 12.22. Late Postclassic pottery from the northern lowlands: (*above*) coarse red-ware tripod bowls; (*below*) effigy incensario found near Chichen Itza.

be tempered with volcanic ash. Surfaces often appear to be unslipped and smoothed, but exteriors are usually polished to a low gloss. Other examples have a thin, polished slip or wash. Colors range from red, tan, or cinnamon to brown, depending on local clays and firing conditions. Common shapes include necked jars (*tinajas*), with two strap handles placed low on the jar body, and a variety of unsupported bowls similar to contemporary shapes. Bowls with plain or elaborately modeled tripod supports are also found.

Bichrome wares accompany the prevalent monochrome pottery described above, but with the addition of white-painted motifs. The primarily geometric designs include bands, circles, dots, scrolls, frets, zigzags, triangles, diamonds, chevrons, and sunbursts, either singly or in combination, although some may represent stylized animals. Common shapes are water jars, with designs painted on the vessel shoulders and handles, and tripod-supported bowls with flaring walls, often painted white on both interior and exterior surfaces.

During the Late Postclassic simple, polychrome-decorated pottery flourished. In the highlands a range of similar polychrome pottery was produced and exchanged over much of the area. This ware, generally defined by red and black motifs painted on a white or cream background, is usually referred to as Chinautla polychrome (Figs. 12.21c, e). In fact, this polychrome tradition can be divided into at least three categories based on the style of painting. One of these, a "dull paint style," is generally associated with sites in the northern and western portions of the highlands (from Chiapas in Mexico to the Verapaz in Guatemala). It occurs at the Conquest-period sites of Zaculeu, Utatlan, Chuitinamit, and Iximche. Another style, the "bright paint style," appears to be distributed in the southern highlands and may be found at Mixcu Viejo, Chinautla, Chimaltenango, and Chalchuapa. Finally, a black-outlined style appears to be a companion to the bright-paint tradition, although there are similarities to Mexican motifs found on the Marihua red-on-buff type found in the southeastern highlands of El Salvador. The vessel forms of this polychrome tradition are generally the same for each style; tripod-supported bowls and water jars displaying exterior-painted zones on the shoulder, handle, and neck are common.

Widely spread throughout the Maya highlands are vessels made of a highly "micaceous" paste. This distinctive specular component in the clay has been identified as a form of talc, mined in Baja Verapaz and used today in several pottery production centers. Forms of this Late Postclassic ware include jars, a variety of bowl shapes, and most typically, *comales*, or tortilla griddles. Vessels may be unslipped or, often in the case of *comales*, slipped on the interior with talc to provide a nonstick cooking surface.

In the Yucatan there were changes in the method of preparing the pottery clay and later a change to the red slip color that is still used in the northern area (Fig. 12.22, upper illustration). Later still, the introduction of a new form of cooking pot might suggest the arrival of foreign women, and the introduction of figurine incensarios indicates a striking change in religious custom. Several categories of apparently ritual vessels were used during the Late Postclassic, including mold-decorated ladle censers, flanged censers, and hourglass-shaped or pedestal-based vessels. These elaborate incensarios (Fig. 12.22, lower illustration) were often destroyed as heathen idols by the Spanish conquerers.

## Patterns of Household and Industrial Ceramic Production

During the pre-Conquest era, the Maya appear to have developed four related kinds of pottery production. By Postclassic times all four systems were probably in use. The earliest and most persistent pattern, inferred from the archaeological data for all time periods, can be described as nonspecialized household production. Under this system, households produced pottery for their own needs, perhaps producing an excess for consumption by local non-pottery-making households by selling vessels through a market or merchant distribution system. This kind of pottery production was a secondary household activity to the primary function of subsistence farming. The second type, which appears to have developed by Late Preclassic times in the Maya area, can be described as semi-specialized household production, whereby households began to specialize in particular pottery forms or types. This production, too, was a part-time activity, secondary to subsistence farming. By the Classic period, at least in the Maya lowlands, specialized household production appears to have developed alongside continuing nonspecialized or semi-specialized production. In this case, pottery production became the primary economic activity of the household unit, usually through one or more family members as artisans, and these households probably no longer undertook subsistence farming. The final development in the Maya area saw the emergence of specialized industrial production, during the Terminal Classic–Early Postclassic era. With this system, production of certain pottery types took place in a specialized facility, often using pottery molds and other mass-production methods.

The use of molds to impart standardized motifs on vessels indicates the existence of specialized pottery production during the Postclassic. This specialized production was probably centered in both households and specialized facilities. Plumbate pottery and, perhaps, effigy incensarios and certain polychrome-decorated vessels were mass-produced in specialized facilities for widespread distribution. Certainly the finding of these kinds of vessels throughout much of the Maya area supports this conclusion. However, only a few technological studies designed to define actual production centers and patterns of trade have been conducted.

Although specialized manufacture of certain classes of vessels is strongly indicated, truly industrialized production remains unverified by archaeological excavation, with the exception of plumbate vessels. The disappearance of plumbate pottery by the Late Postclassic remains unexplained, but was doubtless related to a major shift in political and economic alliances associated with the emergence of the independent, highland Maya "kingdoms" during this period.

In terms of technology, the advances in pottery mass-production and firing procedures, which reached their highest development with Tohil plumbate, appear to have declined during the Late Postclassic. All pottery was unvitrified by this time, so that low-temperature, open-firing methods may be inferred. One significant new development in the Late Postclassic is the production of highland pottery using a high proportion of talc, as both a slip and as an ingredient in the pastes of vessels. This mineral has the ability to impart a nonstick surface to cooking vessels, so its use in pottery represents an important technological breakthrough.

13

# ARTS AND CRAFTS

They had little axes of metal . . . which they fitted to a wooden handle, and it
served them as a weapon and in turn for carving wood.
—Landa's *Relación de las cosas de Yucatán* (Tozzer 1941: 121)

It is appropriate, when surveying ancient Maya arts and crafts, to concentrate on
those works that tend to be preserved in the archaeological record. The subject
of Maya art has deservedly received a great deal of attention from scholars, and
can be only briefly considered here.

## Stone Sculpture

Ancient Maya sculpture may be divided into two basic categories, free-
standing monuments and architectural elements. The monuments include upright stone shafts (stelae), flat, often rounded stones ("altars"), and more rarely,
boulder sculptures (such as the "zoomorphs" found at Quirigua). Architectural
sculpture may be found on lintels, wall panels, door jambs, steps, façades, and
roof elements.

It has often been noted that ancient Maya sculpture tends to "abhor a
vacuum"; in other words, there is very little free space, and most areas are filled
with sculptural detail. The motifs of Maya sculpture usually consist of a
combination of portrayals of natural human and animal forms with supernatural symbolism. The natural forms appear recognizable and "normal" to our
eyes; the supernatural elements often seem grotesque and alien. But given what
we know about Maya ideology (see Chapter 14), we can assume that the
distinction we see between the natural and the grotesque was not given the
same significance by the ancient Maya.

Limestone, being the most plentiful, was the principal stone used in ancient
Maya sculptures. A few sites like Quirigua, Pusilha, and Tonina employed
sandstone, the native rock in their localities, and Copan used trachyte, a volcanic tuff. However, these are exceptions.

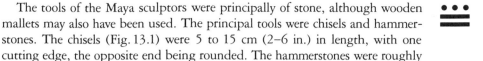

The tools of the Maya sculptors were principally of stone, although wooden mallets may also have been used. The principal tools were chisels and hammerstones. The chisels (Fig. 13.1) were 5 to 15 cm (2–6 in.) in length, with one cutting edge, the opposite end being rounded. The hammerstones were roughly spherical in shape and varied from 5 to 7 cm (2–3 in.) in diameter. It is likely that the flaked flint chisels, so plentiful in some Maya sites, were used for stone cuttings. Massive amounts of debris from ancient flint working found in recent archaeological excavations at Colha, Belize, indicate that this was a major center for the manufacture of chipped-flint tools.

The native limestone is relatively soft as it occurs in the ground, but hardens after exposure. It was quarried with comparative facility, and was easily carved while still fresh from the quarries. The sandstone of Quirigua, Tonina, and Pusilha was also soft in its native state, but the trachyte used in Copan is of about the same hardness before being quarried as afterward. Trachyte is so fine-grained and even-textured that it is admirably adapted to carving; however, it has one serious drawback: it contains nodules of flint so hard that stone chisels could not have worked them. When such nodules were encountered they were either removed, leaving a depression in the face of the monument, or left protruding. Examples of both practices may occur on the same monument. Sometimes, when the inclusion was too difficult to remove entirely, the projecting part was battered off. In the case of the human head in the long-count introducing glyph on Stela 2 (Fig. 13.2), clever manipulations incorporated a stubborn nodule into the design itself. The heads represented in Maya inscriptions almost always face the observer's left, but this profile faces to the right. By thus reversing the direction, this flinty inclusion fell in the right position to serve as an earplug.

Maya sculpture was doubtless finished by abrasion and then painted, usually a dark red. This red pigment was probably made from an oxide of iron obtained from anthills, which abound in the forest. Blue was the next most

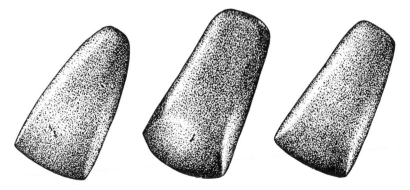

Fig. 13.1. Maya ground-stone celts, or chisels.

Fig. 13.2. Long-count introducing glyph
on Stela 2, Copan, Honduras.

common color. The pigments were ground and probably mixed with copal, for the paint still adheres to the stone in many places with the tenacity of a good varnish. Although the colors have for the most part worn off, traces of the original paint can still be found where the relief is high and undercut.

In quarrying the shafts of stone from which the stelae were made, advantage was taken of natural cleavage planes in the rock. This is best seen in the case of some of the Quirigua stelae, the cross sections of which are trapezoidal in shape, with no single corner a true right angle. The method of quarrying at Calakmul (Fig. 13.3) was to free the blocks from the surrounding limestone by digging down along their sides and ends, preparatory to prying them loose from the bedrock. Several of the Quirigua stelae still show "quarry stumps" on their plain undressed butts (Fig. 13.4).

The French artist Jean Charlot has made four original drawings illustrating the principal steps in making a Maya stela: (1) quarrying the shaft, (2) transporting the stone, (3) erecting the monument, and (4) sculpturing it (Fig. 13.5). The forests of Peten abound in hardwood trees, sections of which would have served admirably for rollers, and fiber-yielding plants for making ropes and cables are equally common. A masonry socket to fit the butt of the shaft was made. Then, probably by means of a ramp and an A-frame of beams, the shaft was pulled upright and the fourth side of the socket filled in. It is important to note that the shafts were brought from the quarries in an unfinished state and carved after being set up.

As we have already seen (Chapter 3), the earliest Maya sculptures are found in the southern area. The monuments of Izapa, Abaj Takalik, Kaminaljuyu, and other sites demonstrate that the custom of carving portraits and hieroglyphic inscriptions, including calendrical dates, on stone stelae and their companion altars was established by the Late Preclassic. At El Mirador and other lowland sites were found fragmentary sculptures that may date from the end of the Preclassic era. Thus far, however, the first dated examples of the sculptured-monument tradition in the lowlands appear in the central Peten from the Early Classic period. Stela 29 at Tikal possesses the earliest long-count calendrical date in the lowlands, A.D. 292. This monument, and a series of slightly later

Fig. 13.3. Two partially quarried stelae shafts, Calakmul, Campeche, Mexico.

Fig. 13.4. Quarry stumps on the butt of Monument 10 (Stela J), Quirigua, Guatemala.

Fig. 13.5. Steps in the making of a Maya monument, after the original drawings by Jean Charlot: quarrying, transporting, raising, and sculpturing the monument.

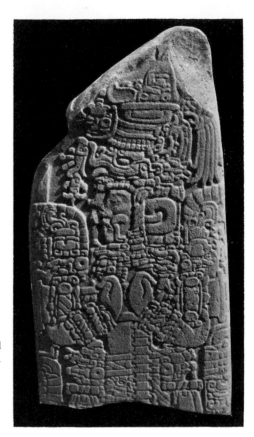

Fig. 13.6. Stela 2, Tikal
(ca. 9.3.10.0.0, or A.D. 504).

Baktun 8 stelae from the core of the central lowlands, belongs to a sculptural tradition with direct affinities to the earlier southern Maya monuments. The human figures on these monuments are often shown in the same position—head, legs, and feet in profile; torso and arms in full front; and feet in tandem (Fig. 13.6). A little later the position became more natural. The toes of the back foot advanced slightly, overlapping the heel of the front foot, but the rest of the body remained unchanged. This position also appeared before the close of Baktun 8 (435). The profile presentation of the human figure persisted throughout Maya history with little change, and remained a common position in Maya art.

The earliest lowland dated monument with a sculptured, fully frontal view of the human figure is Stela 4 at Tikal. It records a calendar-round date corresponding to 378. A long-count date of 396 is sculptured on Stela 18, which portrays a seated full-front figure. Both of these Tikal monuments depict the ruler Curl Nose (see Chapters 4 and 11). A similar frontal style can be seen on Stela 26 at Uaxactun, dedicated in 9.0.10.0.0 (445). This monument was discovered beneath the floor of Shrine II in one of the earliest levels of Structure A-V. The figure on its front is badly eroded (Fig. 13.7, left), but it is still possible to distinguish the lower half of the face, the arms, and the feet.

The full-front view of the human figure is common at Tonina (Fig. 11.40), Copan, Quirigua (Fig. 4.27), Piedras Negras, Palenque, Yaxchilan, Naachtun, and Seibal. It reached its greatest perfection at Copan and Quirigua; at the latter site frontal portraiture was established by 475. The front view of the human figure seated cross-legged is best expressed at Piedras Negras.

The four Piedras Negras monuments, shown in Fig. 4.25, depict the inaugurations of successive rulers (see Chapters 4 and 15), who are seated cross-legged

Fig. 13.7. Early Classic monuments at Uaxactun: (*left*) Stela 26 (9.0.10.0.0, or A.D. 445); (*right*) Stela 5 (8.16.1.0.12?, or ca. 358).

in a niche. The earliest of these four monuments, Stela 25, was dedicated in 9.8.15.0.0 (608); the portrait is within a niche too shallow to permit treatment of the figure in high relief. On Stela 6, dedicated in 9.12.15.0.0 (687), this same composition is seen again. Considerable advance in sculpture had been made, and the niche is deeper, permitting the figure to be treated more successfully. The face is well done but out of proportion to the rest of the body. By the time this composition was executed on Stela 11, dedicated in 9.15.0.0.0 (731), notable improvement had been made. The niche had become so deep that the proportions of the seated figure are more lifelike, and the details are beautifully executed. The design was again sculptured on Stela 14, dedicated in 9.16.10.0.0 (761), which is perhaps the finest stela at this site. The niche is sufficiently deep to present the figure in the half round; its anatomical proportions are correct, and the details are exquisitely carved. This monument also presents a masterly combination of high- and low-relief carving.

The front presentation of the standing human figure was brilliantly achieved at Copan and Quirigua. The figures at the latter site are probably more to modern taste because they are more restrained; the Copan stelae certainly include the finest examples of nearly full-round sculpture produced by the ancient Maya, but they are also among the most ornate (Fig. 11.46).

The last vestiges of the early style disappeared by the beginning of the Late Classic, from about 630 to 730, though in provincial centers some sculptors did not follow the prevailing naturalistic trends of this period. The figures on Stela 21 at Naachtun (Fig. 13.8), dedicated in 687, are misshapen for such a late date. The contrast between this monument and Stela A at Copan (Fig. 4.15), dedicated in 9.15.0.0.0 (731), is arresting. Such stylistic differences between monuments erected so close together in time may be explained by the provincial status of smaller centers as compared to the larger centers.

The century and a half from 731 to 889 of the Late Classic witnessed the most brilliant development of New World sculpture in pre-Columbian times. This period was in many ways the golden age of the Maya civilization, and its cultural flowering is perhaps best exemplified in sculpture. By this time centuries of sculptural achievement lay behind, and technical difficulties had long since been mastered; creativity was free to express itself within the framework of its traditions and experience.

Among the wealth of sculptures from the Late Classic period, it is difficult to select those that are most typical. One of the most beautiful monuments at Piedras Negras, Stela 14, has already been illustrated (Fig. 4.25, right). Another almost equally striking monument, Stela 12 (Fig. 11.37, left), dedicated in 9.18.5.0.0 (795), shows a profile presentation of the human figure exclusively.

At Palenque, in the crypt below the Temple of the Inscriptions, the carving of the slab covering the sarcophagus is exceptional for its delicacy and sureness of line (Fig. 4.23).

Fig. 13.8. Stela 21,
Naachtun, Guatemala
(9.12.16.17.12?, or
ca. A.D. 689).

One of the most beautiful sculptures produced is Wall Panel 3 from Structure O-13 at Piedras Negras (Fig. 4.26). This masterpiece, a perfect combination of high and low relief, was executed in 9.16.10.0.0 (761). In a number of
places on the panel, arms and legs are sculptured in the full round. The
composition represents a personage seated on a throne, the back of which is a
mask panel; he is flanked on each side by three standing figures. On the ground
before the throne seven figures are seated cross-legged, facing an altar. The
figure on the extreme right is the only one in the composition that has its face
still preserved. M. Louise Baker has made a restoration of this wall panel (Fig.
4.26), although her drawing uses the three-quarter view of figures, a stylistic
device seldom seen in Maya art. The original is in the Museo Nacional in
Guatemala City.

The University of Pennsylvania Museum discovered a throne in Palace J-6 at

Piedras Negras (Fig. 13.9) that was almost identical to the one represented in the wall panel, although the two front supports of the throne on the wall panel are undecorated, whereas those of the actual throne are covered on three sides with hieroglyphic inscriptions. It was dedicated in 9.17.15.0.0 (785), 25 years later than the wall panel, and was so located in the principal hall of the palace that it could be seen from any point in the court below. It now resides in the Museo Nacional in Guatemala City.

At Yaxchilan, sculpture reached its highest point in the lintels of Structure 23: Lintels 24, 25, and 26, the first two of which are now in the British Museum (Fig. 4.24). Lintel 24 is the most outstanding example of sculptural art at Yaxchilan in its harmony of composition, balance of design, and brilliance of execution. Structure 23 was dedicated in 9.14.15.0.0 (726). The finest monuments at Yaxchilan—Stelae 1, 3, 4, and 7—fall short of the lintels, though most of them date about 35 years later, when Yaxchilan was already past the peak of its artistic achievements.

Fig. 13.9. Throne from Palace J-6, Piedras Negras, Guatemala; its condition upon discovery, smashed in pieces, has provoked theories of a violent end to the ruling elite at this and other Classic centers (see Chapter 5).

There is more Late-period sculpture at Copan than at any other Classic site. Many fine monuments were sculptured there: Stelae A (Fig. 4.15), B, C, D, F, H (Fig. 11.46, left), M, N, and 4, and Altars Q, R, S, and T. There were also some other spectacular constructions: Temples 11, 22, and 26, the Jaguar Stairway (Fig. 11.44, upper illustration), and the Reviewing Stand. All were erected and carved between 731 and 782. The longest hieroglyphic inscription in the Maya area—the Hieroglyphic Stairway of Structure 26 (Fig. 11.44, lower right)—was dedicated in 9.16.5.0.0 (756). The exquisite head and torso of the corn god (God E) illustrated in the frontispiece was also carved during this half-century.

Quirigua, although a small site, has 27 sculptured monuments. Stela E, from 771 (Fig. 4.27), and 8 other stelae and zoomorphs were dedicated during the reign of Cauac Sky (Chapter 11). Zoomorph P (Fig. 13.10), perhaps the most massive stone monument in the Maya area, is completely covered with an intricate sculptured design; it was dedicated in 9.18.5.0.0 (795). Perhaps the finest glyphs ever carved on stone are to be found at Quirigua, especially (Fig. 13.11) those on Stela F, dedicated in 9.16.10.0.0 (761), and the rare full-figure glyphs on Stela D, dedicated in 9.16.15.0.0 (766).

By the end of Baktun 9 (830), however, the crest had been passed and there followed an artistic recession from which the ancient Maya never recovered.

Examples of Terminal Classic sculpture reflect this decline. Stela 10 at Xultun (Fig. 13.12), dedicated in 10.3.0.0.0 (889), is one of several monuments erected on this katun ending. The loss in inspiration and technical skill is evident, and the composition is cluttered and flamboyant. The figures are poorly proportioned and a mass of detail obscures the design.

In the Yucatan during Late and Terminal Classic times, distinctive local sculptural styles developed. There are sixteen sculptured stelae at Uxmal, but even the best of them, Stela 7 (Fig. 11.57), is overly ornate as compared with the sculptures of the central and southern lowlands. Another piece is a well-executed human head, with tattooing on its right cheek, emerging from the jaws of a conventionalized serpent (Fig. 13.13). The head can hardly be called independent sculpture, however, for it is attached to the façade of a range of chambers at the western base of the pyramid supporting the House of the Magician and forms an element of the architectural decoration. This head is now in the Museo Nacional de Antropología in Mexico City.

During the Postclassic, carved monuments became rare, and sculpture was confined almost exclusively to the embellishment of architecture. At Chichen Itza no Postclassic stelae have been found, but there are the following categories of statues: (1) Chacmool figures, reclining human figures (Fig. 13.14) whose heads are turned to the right or left, (2) jaguar thrones, (3) standard bearers, and (4) Atlantean figures. At least a dozen Chacmools have been discovered at this site, and two of them still retain inset pieces of polished bone to represent the whites of the eyes and the fingernails and toenails. Each holds a stone plate

Fig. 13.10. Monument 16 (Zoomorph P), Quirigua, Guatemala (9.18.5.0.0, or A.D. 795).

Fig. 13.11. Quirigua stelae noted for their excellent stone carving: (*left*) Monument 6 (Stela F), 9.16.10.0.0 (A.D. 761); (*right*) Monument 4 (Stela D), displaying full-figure glyphs, 9.16.15.0.0 (766).

Fig. 13.12. Drawing of
Stela 10, Xultun
(10.3.0.0.0, or A.D. 889).

Fig. 13.13 (*above*). Front and side views of sculptured architectural element, House of the Magician, Uxmal (Terminal Classic?).

Fig. 13.14. Chacmool, Chichen Itza (Early Postclassic).

Fig. 13.16 (*below*). Atlantean figure, Chichen Itza (Early Postclassic).

Fig. 13.15. Standard bearers, Chichen Itza (Early Postclassic).

clasped by the two hands and resting on the abdomen, and this position suggests that their function might have been to receive offerings.

The jaguar thrones are life-sized figures of jaguars with flat backs to serve as seats. Sculptured representations of them are found at Tikal, Piedras Negras, Palenque, and Xultun, but the actual thrones have been found only at Uxmal and Chichen Itza (Fig. 11.68). They also occur in the frescoes in the Temple of the Warriors at Chichen Itza.

The purpose of the standard bearer was to support a staff, from the top of which hung a feather banner. These standard bearers are in the form of small human figures about a meter high (Fig. 13.15), with the forearms extended horizontally in front, the hands forming a hole through which the staff passed. Another standard bearer found at Chichen Itza shows a figure kneeling on his left knee and grasping the staff in his right hand.

The fourth group, the Atlantean figures, are anthropomorphic statues with arms raised above their heads. They were used to support daises or door lintels in buildings (Fig. 13.16).

## Wood Sculpture

Wood carving seems to have reached its most perfect expression at Tikal in the door lintels of the five pyramid temples at that site. Only the hardest species of wood have survived the damp climate of the Maya lowlands, and then the only wooden objects recovered are from places that are protected from the weather.

The lintels are each composed of from four to ten beams of sapodilla with an overall length of 2 to 5.3 m (6.6–17.4 ft). The design on the lintel in Fig. 13.17 shows an elaborately decorated serpent, its body arching in the middle to form a central niche. The head is to the left, and issuing from its open mouth is the upper body of a god; the serpent's tail is at the right, terminating in two scrolls. A hieroglyphic inscription fills the upper left and right corners of the composition, and across the top between the glyph panels stretches a great bird with spreading wings, the *kukul* (quetzal), sacred bird of the Maya. In the niche formed by the upward curl of the serpent's body is the figure of Yax Kin, ruler of Tikal, seated on a throne. This lintel originally spanned one of the doorways of Temple IV (see also Fig. 11.15), which was dedicated in 9.16.0.0.0 (751). Another Classic-era lintel was found in Temple VII at Tzibanche, west of the southern end of Laguna de Bacalar. It bears an inscription of eight hieroglyphs but no figures, and probably dates from the early Late Classic, perhaps about 9.9.5.0.0 (618).

Occasionally the wooden poles spanning the vaults have also been carved. One of these was found at Tikal in a fourth-story rear chamber of the Palace of the Five Stories.

Carved wooden lintels have been found at Chichen Itza and Uxmal. The best-preserved lintel at Chichen Itza spans the inner doorway of the Temple of the Jaguars on top of the west wall of the ball court (Fig. 13.18). Each of the two beams forming this lintel has the same design carved on it: the sun disk, with a human figure inside it, and outside it another human figure enveloped in the coils of a feathered rattlesnake. Both figures face a centrally placed altar. The lintels in El Castillo at Chichen Itza were carved originally, but most of the low relief has been hacked off with machetes.

John Lloyd Stephens, the American diplomat and amateur archaeologist who visited Uxmal in 1840 and 1841, found in the Governor's Palace a sapodilla beam that he took to the United States when he left the Yucatan. It was subsequently destroyed by a fire in New York—an irreparable loss. Stephens says it was the only beam at Uxmal that was carved, and the inscription might have dated this structure, one of the most beautiful in pre-Columbian America.

Other small objects of carved wood were taken from the Cenote of Sacrifice at Chichen Itza, among them the handle of a wooden sacrificial knife, carved in the likeness of two intertwined rattlesnakes (Fig. 14.11). A chipped-flint blade was hafted to this, and its handle covered with a thin sheet of gold.

Fig. 13.17 (*above and facing page*). Two carved wooden lintels from Temple IV, Tikal (Late Classic).

Fig. 13.18. Drawing of carved wooden lintels, Temple of the Jaguars, Chichen Itza (Early Postclassic).

## Stucco Modeling

Stucco seems to have been used to face platforms in the lowlands from Early Preclassic times (see Figs. 2.1 and 2.2). By the Late Preclassic period it was widely used in exterior decoration (Figs. 3.16, 3.20, and 4.3) and continued to be used on Classic buildings and, to a lesser extent, in Postclassic façades. Stuccowork reached its highest development at Palenque, and the tablets and panels there are the finest examples of this plastic art in the Maya area. Two panels from the west façade of House D of the Palace are illustrated in Fig. 13.19.

In the sealed crypt that Alberto Ruz Lhuillier discovered beneath the Temple of the Inscriptions, the walls are decorated with handsomely modeled reliefs of nine figures, which possibly represent the Bolontiku, the Nine Gods of the Lower World. Under the sarcophagus itself were two excellently modeled stucco heads, which illustrate the Classic Maya ideal of beauty (Fig. 13.20).

Fig. 13.19. Late Classic stucco reliefs from House D of the Palace, Palenque.

Fig. 13.20. Two stucco heads from the tomb of Pacal, Temple of the Inscriptions, Palenque.

Even provincial centers within the Palenque sphere of influence showed this mastery of the stucco technique. Some years ago a tomb was found at Comalcalco, about 160 km (100 mi.) northwest of Palenque. On three walls were representations of standing human figures in stucco, three to a side; two, as restored, and the same two, as found, are shown in Fig. 13.21. Although less finely executed than the stucco figures at Palenque, these Comalcalco figures are not without considerable merit. The best example of stuccowork in northern Yucatan is at Acanceh, where the upper half of a façade shows the remains of a handsome stucco panel of animals, birds, and serpents (Fig. 13.22). When it was uncovered, this Early Classic frieze still retained many traces of its original coloring, with a bright turquoise-blue predominating. For Postclassic times Tulum furnishes examples of stucco decoration, in the form of recessed panels above the doors of buildings.

Fig. 13.21 (*facing page*). Late Classic stucco reliefs from the tomb at Comalcalco, Tabasco, Mexico: (*above*) restored figures; (*below*) figures as originally found.

Fig. 13.22. Early Classic stucco reliefs from Acanceh, Yucatan, Mexico: (*above*) figure of a squirrel; (*below*) figures of a bat, eagle (?), jaguar (?), and serpent.

# Painting

Among the ancient Maya, the fine art of painting reached a high degree of excellence. Frescoes were used in wall decoration, and painting was also used in the decoration of ceramics and in illustrating the codices.

The Maya palette was extensive. There were several reds, ranging from an opaque purplish red to a brilliant orange. A coppery tan color was used extensively for preliminary outlining, and varying mixtures of red with opaque white gave a number of pinks. The yellows ranged from a pale greenish yellow to a dark yellow. A dark brown resulted from mixing yellow and black. There seems to have been but a single blue; this was painted over an opaque ground to obtain a Prussian blue or laid directly on white plaster for a bright cerulean blue. There are many greens, from olive to almost black. No basic green has been found and the different shades probably result from varying mixtures of blue and yellow. A brilliant, lustrous black was used for final outlining, and an opaque white for mixing.

The substance with which the colors were mixed in many examples seems to have been viscous. Chemical analyses of the pigments in the Chichen Itza frescoes show no trace of this carrying substance. It was probably organic and has disappeared with time. It may have been the resin of the *pom* tree from which copal varnish is now made.

The colors were of both vegetable and mineral origin. A number of trees in the Yucatan Peninsula yield excellent dyes. Analysis of Chichen Itza pigments shows that they were largely of mineral origin, but this may be due to the fact that vegetable colors are more perishable. The reds were made from hematite, and the yellows from ocherous earths and clays. Charcoal and other carbonized organic matter was the essential ingredient of the black pigment. The strong blue was inorganic, derived from a particular type of clay.

The brushes with which these pigments were applied have not been found, but the quality of the painting indicates their excellence. Some brushes were so delicately made that fine tapering lines could be drawn with them; coarser brushes filled in backgrounds and broader spaces. The materials used were probably fine feathers or hair. A brush in the hand of an artist is depicted on a fragmentary incised bone from Tikal (Fig. 13.23).

Fragments of wall paintings dating from the Late Preclassic or Protoclassic have been discovered at Tikal (Fig. 3.17). These frescoes show stylistic similarities to the art of the southern Maya during this period. The fresco in Structure B-XIII at Uaxactun, excavated by the Carnegie Institution in 1937, dates from the Early Classic. This building had undergone several changes in ancient times; some of its chambers show beam-and-mortar roof construction. The fresco is colored black, red, orange, yellow, and gray and measures 3 m (10 ft) high. Twenty-six human figures are shown, arranged in two horizontal panels and interspersed with several panels of hieroglyphs. Beneath the lower figure panel

Fig. 13.23. Finely incised bone from the tomb of Ah Cacau, Temple I, Tikal, Guatemala, showing a hand holding a scribe's or artist's brush.

is a horizontal line of 72 day signs (not shown in Fig. 11.22), beginning with the day 12 Imix and ending with 5 Eb.

Hieroglyphic inscriptions are painted on interior walls of the palace at Palenque, and the walls of the shrine in Structure 33 at Yaxchilan show traces of scrolls and figures in red and blue.

By far the most spectacular, as well as the most informative, Maya murals yet discovered are those of Bonampak, Chiapas. These paintings, assigned the Late Classic date of 790 and discovered in 1946 by Giles Healey, cover the three vaulted chambers of a single small building (Fig. 13.24). When found, they were in excellent condition, preserved by the formation of a heavy coat of stalactitic limestone deposited by the constant seepage of water over more than a thousand years.

The scenes, room by room, show a series of activities, probably a record of actual historical events (Figs. 13.25–27). Room 1 shows the preparations, including the gathering of an orchestra, and a series of conferences between a ruler and his noble assistants. Room 2 continues with a raid on a neighboring center, the taking of captives, and their "judgment" before their captors on the stairs of a temple or palace substructure. Room 3 shows the culmination of these events in a ritual dance on the steps of a pyramid, the participants adorned in magnificent costumes, and a bloodletting ceremony by the ruler and his family. The murals contain a number of hieroglyphic texts, which date and explain the scenes and give the names or titles of the participants.

The murals stand in sharp contrast to the sculpture of the stelae, where the principal figure remained stylized in attitude and accouterments for over five hundred years. The scenes are narrative in a forthright yet sensitive style. Naturalism was held so important to the artist that the faces of certain of the participants in the murals can be recognized from room to room as they recur in parts of the story. The moods of the scenes vary: postures and facial expressions are relaxed during the preparations, ferocious in the raid, cold and forbidding during the judgment and sacrifice. Foreshortening and superposition give an effect of depth. The naturalism is stronger and the drafting more skillful than in any Old World art of the same period.

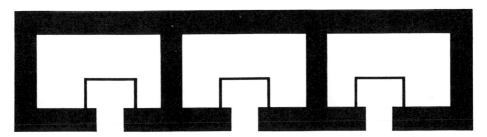

Fig. 13.24. Structure of the Murals, Bonampak, Chiapas, Mexico: (*above*) exterior doorways (left to right) of Rooms 1, 2, and 3 (note the remains of stucco reliefs on the upper façade and the figure in the niche above the central doorway); (*below*) plan of Rooms 1, 2, and 3, showing the size of the dais within each room.

Fig. 13.25. Interior of
Room 2, Bonampak: (*above*) perspective
view toward the entrance, with a "judgment" scene
on the front wall; (*below*) detail of the reconstructed
mural, the ruler at the center holding a spear.

Fig. 13.26. Detail of the unreconstructed Room 2 murals, Bonampak: attendants and captives to the left of the ruler in Fig. 13.25.

Fig. 13.27. Detail of the unreconstructed Room 2 murals, Bonampak: attendants to the right of the ruler.

The first overpowering effect of the Bonampak murals is the magnificence of costuming. Headdresses of delicate featherwork nearly double the height of each principal figure, and the variety of materials used is dazzling—featherwork, cut stone, furs, intricate woven fabrics. The next impression is that of complete lack of self-consciousness in the performers. Each figure is portrayed in an attitude of conversation, and given a relaxed and individual posture. Such detailed information on the life of the Maya ruling class is nowhere else to be found. That the wife and children of the ruler participated in the ceremonies is particularly interesting.

The central capstones in corbel-vaulted chambers were sometimes painted with designs of human figures and single rows of glyphs above and below the humans. These painted capstones are not common; such remains are confined exclusively to northern sites and probably date to the Late and Terminal Classic periods (Figs. 13.28 and 13.29). Wall paintings are also more commonly preserved at northern centers than in the central area and have been found at Chichen Itza, Tancah, Tulum, Santa Rita Corozal, Chacmultun, and Xtampak.

The frescoes from the Temple of the Warriors, the Temple of the Jaguars, and the Monjas at Chichen Itza all date from the Terminal Classic and Early Postclassic periods and show Mexican influence. Two scenes of human sacrifice are illustrated (Fig. 14.1e, f), and a wall painting of a coastal village from the Temple of the Warriors is shown in Fig. 13.30. The sea occupies the lower third of this scene, and there are three canoes, each with an oarsman in the prow and two men fishing. A variety of marine life swarms in the water. On the shore at the right is a flat-roofed temple, a feathered serpent rising from the inner chamber, and two worshipers kneeling in the outer chamber. There are several thatched houses of typical Maya design interspersed with trees. A number of people go about their daily tasks, and the whole picture is peaceful and domestic.

Another mural from the Temple of the Jaguars portrays a vigorous assault on a village (Fig. 13.31). Only two of the attackers show in the lower left corner; a serpent curls behind one of them, apparently his patron deity. The defending warriors swarm out of their village, and behind them, among the thatched houses, are the women. The composition is full of action and there are no superfluous lines.

A mural from the Temple of the Warriors shows another battle. A temple stands in a lake in the upper left corner, and several fish, a snail, a crab, and a jaguar appear in the water. Half a dozen nude captives, their bodies painted with stripes and their arms tied behind their backs, are being led off by warriors or priests. Other warriors seem to be defending a temple in the lower right corner (Fig. 13.32).

Recently, several fragmentary murals have been discovered at Tancah (Fig. 6.12) on the east coast of the Yucatan. These paintings (Fig. 13.33) date from

Fig. 13.28. Drawing of the painted capstone from the Temple of the Owls, Chichen Itza, Yucatan, Mexico.

Fig. 13.29. Drawing of the painted capstone from a tomb, Chichen Itza.

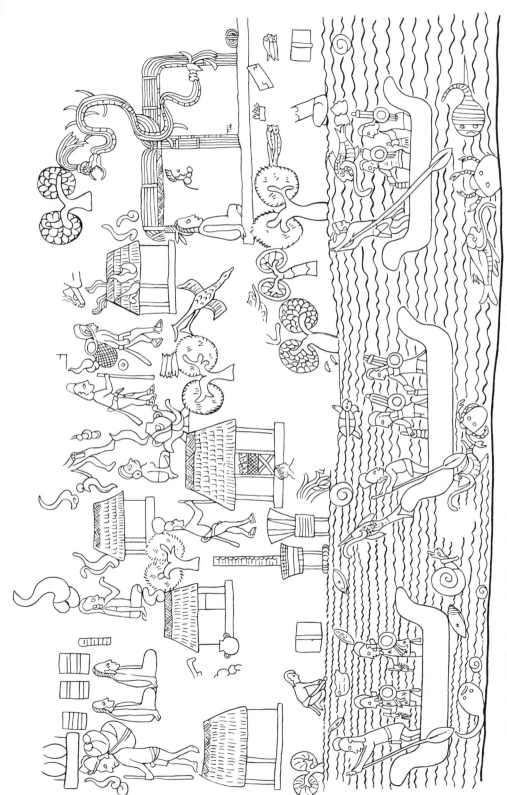

Fig. 13.30. Wall painting of a fishing village from the Temple of the Warriors, Chichen Itza.

Fig. 13.31. Detail from a
wall painting of a battle,
Temple of the Jaguars,
Chichen Itza.

Fig. 13.32. Battle scene from a wall painting in the Temple of the Warriors, Chichen Itza.

Fig. 13.33. Details from a Late Postclassic mural, Structure 44, Tancah, Quintana Roo, Mexico: (*above*) figure of a maize deity; (*below*) figure of a North Star deity.

Fig. 13.34. Drawing of a Postclassic polychrome vase from northern Yucatan.

the Late Postclassic and are stylistically related to the Madrid Codex (Fig. 15.5). The wall paintings at Tulum (Figs. 11.74 and 11.76) and Santa Rita (Fig. 6.13) depict ceremonial and mythological scenes. Also dating from Late Postclassic times, they show such striking resemblances to Mixtec art as to assure connections between eastern Yucatan and Mexico during this period (see Chapter 6).

A few painted vases have been found in the Yucatan, although they may not have been made there; one of the best is shown in Fig. 13.34. At the right is a tree whose trunk shows the outline of a human face; a figure is seated on each of the two branches, while a serpent coils around the trunk. At the right a standing figure blows on a conch shell. Beneath the branches two deer are seated, the one at the right completely swathed in bandages. The left half of the composition shows two figures facing a deer, which seems to be shedding its horns. The figure in front of the deer grasps an antler, and the deer has a blanket on its back decorated with crossbones. The two figures at the left both wear short jaguar-skin skirts or kilts. Above the deer hovers a white bird of prey with hawklike beak. The scene may represent a ceremony held at the time the deer shed their horns, which in the Yucatan is in March.

Some of the best paintings of the Classic period are on the polychrome vases and bowls of the Late Classic found in the central and southern lowlands, and in the adjacent northern highlands in the Chama region along the Río Chixoy. One of the finest vessels, the Altar Vase, was found in a Late Classic burial at Altar de Sacrificios (see Chapter 12). Other finely painted vessels have been excavated from burials and tombs at Tikal, Holmul, Seibal, Tayasal, Altun Ha, and other sites. One of the finest assemblages of polychrome-painted pottery was found in a stone-lined tomb in Structure A-I at Uaxactun, the burial of a ruling personage, judging from the magnificence of his burial offerings. The skeleton lay at full length, with the head pointing to the north and both hands clasped against the right shoulder (Fig. 9.4). At the head stood a painted vase, the extended design of which is shown in Fig. 13.35. The background is a brilliant orange-red; the figures are outlined in black and painted with black and several shades of yellow. Around the top is a line of glyphs, and glyph panels are interspersed between the figures. The principal panel of sixteen glyphs makes up the center of the design, which all the figures face. These glyphs denote a mathematically incorrect Maya date, 7.5.0.0.0 8 Ahau 13 Kankin. It is possible that the date intended was 8.5.0.0.0 12 Ahau 13 Kankin, which would involve two relatively simple changes in the original inscription. Nevertheless, the date must refer to a past event, since stylistically the vase dates about five hundred years later.

The design shows a ruler or elite official seated on a throne, facing the central glyph panel. Behind him stands an attendant, painted black and holding an eccentric-shaped flint (see Fig. 13.56, upper left); another figure holds a feather canopy over the priest's head. To the left of the glyph panel are three figures. The two standing figures, wearing elaborate cloaks, are also painted black; one

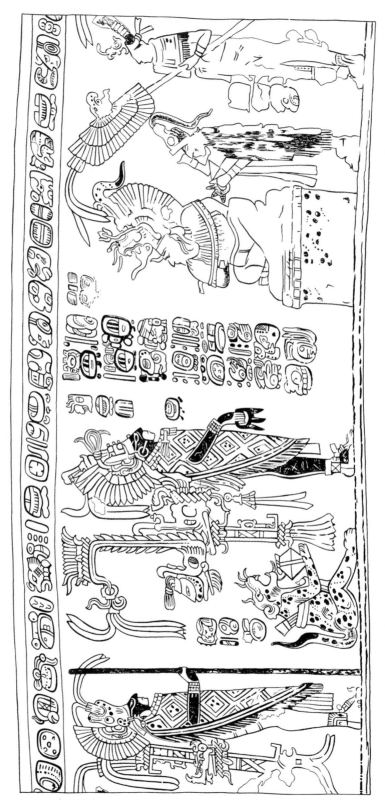

Fig. 13.35. Drawing of the painted scene on a Late Classic polychrome vase from the Structure A-I tomb, Uaxactun, Guatemala (see Fig. 9.4).

carries an eccentric-shaped flint and the other holds a spear. Between them is a seated jaguar offering two bowls, one inverted over the other.

This tomb also contained other polychrome vessels of equal beauty. There were eleven pieces of pottery, nine of them painted. A flat plate with three supports (Fig. 13.36) has an unpainted background, and the design is outlined in black and painted in black and red. A dancer, poised on his toes, is executing a step; his right arm rests lightly on his hip and his left is turned outward in a graceful gesture. The sure sweep of line and the admirable fitting of the design to the circular space indicate mastery of the art. This plate has a small hole broken in the bottom, apparently a ceremonial "releasing of the spirit" of the vessel so that it might accompany the owner on his journey to the other world. Two other painted plates from this same tomb are shown in Figs. 13.37 and 13.38.

A famous painted vase from Chama in the upper Chixoy valley in the northern highlands of Guatemala is shown with its design extended in

Fig. 13.36. Drawing of a polychrome plate from the Structure A-I tomb, Uaxactun: portrait figure with a glyph band.

Fig. 13.37. Drawing of a polychrome plate from the Structure A-I tomb, Uaxactun: stylized head.

Fig. 13.38. Drawing of a polychrome plate from the Structure A-I tomb, Uaxactun: head with a feather headdress.

Fig. 13.39. Chama Vase, Chixoy valley, Guatemala (Late Classic).

Fig. 13.40. Nebaj Vase, Chixoy valley, Guatemala (Late Classic).

Fig. 13.39. The colors are black, red, and brown on a background of pink. Seven figures, interspersed with as many glyph panels, are portrayed. The two principals, painted black, face each other; the one on the right wears a jaguar-skin cloak. The black body paint may symbolize associations with Ek Chuah (God M), patron of Maya merchants. Three of the remaining figures carry fans. Personal characteristics are faithfully rendered, which makes it likely that the figures are portraits.

A similar vase from Nebaj (Fig. 13.40) displays five human figures, five glyph panels, and four larger glyphs at the back of the design. Two figures sit on a dais, with a ruling personage occupying the central position.

A third vase from Ratinlinxul in the same region shows a noble, identified as a merchant, borne in what appears to be a basketry palanquin suspended from carrying poles on the shoulders of retainers (Fig. 13.41). A dog stretches himself realistically below the palanquin. Five retainers follow: the first carries a jaguar-cushioned throne; the next three carry what appear to be canoe paddles; and the last grasps a fold of cloth in his left hand.

Among the codices, the brushwork of the Dresden Codex (Fig. 14.3) is of the highest quality; the lines are bold and fluid. The Paris Codex (Fig. 15.6) is not quite as well done but the difference is not great. In the Madrid Codex (Fig. 15.5), however, both figures and glyphs are poorly drawn. All these codices are suspected to be Postclassic copies of Classic-period originals (see Chapter 15).

Fig. 13.41. Ratinlinxul Vase, Chixoy valley, Guatemala (Late Classic).

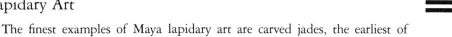

## Lapidary Art

The finest examples of Maya lapidary art are carved jades, the earliest of which were made during Preclassic times. The earliest dated piece is the Leyden Plate, engraved in A.D. 320 (Fig. 4.7), on which the carving is little more than incised.

Another early piece from Copan, dating perhaps two hundred years later, is carved in the round. This piece (Fig. 13.42, upper left), a 7–8-cm pendant (3 in.), shows a seated human figure in left profile. The hole for the suspension cord enters at the mouth of the figure and emerges at the back of the neck; the drilling was done from both sides.

A fine example of Early Classic carved jadeite was excavated at Kaminaljuyu, the important highland center on the outskirts of Guatemala City (Fig. 13.42, lower left). It presents a standing human figure rather than a seated one, and the design is more elaborate. This piece is 15 cm high (6 in.); the body appears in front view and the head and headdress in left profile. The head has a typical Maya profile, and the headdress is formed by the head and foreleg of a crocodile.

A jadeite head (Fig. 13.42, upper pair), although found at Chichen Itza, was probably carved at Piedras Negras. The historical (non-period-ending) date it presents, 9.12.2.0.16 (674), is recorded three times; this date appears nowhere else in the Maya area except at Piedras Negras. The pendant, measuring 9.5 cm high (almost 4 in.), is hollowed out behind. The headdress is formed of a jaguar head, and the inscription is incised on a flat edge surrounding the hollow at the back.

A jadeite head of unknown provenance (Fig. 13.42, lower pair) belongs to the Late Classic, when jade carving was at its best. The features are Classic Maya and technically excellent.

The plaque shown in Fig. 13.43 also dates from very late in the Classic period. It is wedge-shaped, perforated longitudinally near the top, and about 10 cm high (4 in.). A handsomely dressed ruler is seated on a throne, body in front view and head in left profile. The headdress consists of a serpent with opened jaws, from which emerges a small figure with a grotesque face. Another figure kneels before the throne, and an elaborate "speech scroll" issues from the ruler's mouth. This lovely blue-green piece is of Maya origin, although it was probably traded to the great urban center of Teotihuacan, 40 km (25 mi.) northeast of Mexico City, where it was found.

A statuette of a human figure (Fig. 13.44) carved in the full round from fuchsite, a softer jadelike stone, was found under the stairway leading to Temple A-XVIII at Uaxactun. The eyes are rectangular and painted a brilliant red. A number of small holes were drilled in the figure, possibly for attaching ornaments. A similar figure (Fig. 13.45), carved from the same material al-

Fig. 13.42. Carved jadeite from the Classic period: (*upper left*) Early Classic pendant, Copan, Honduras; (*two above*) Late Classic pendant, Chichen Itza, with incised date equivalent to A.D. 674 and probably originally from Piedras Negras; (*lower left*) Early Classic pendant, Kaminaljuyu, Guatemala; (*two below*) Late Classic pendant, provenance unknown.

Fig. 13.43. Late Classic jadeite plaque depicting a probable Maya ruler, found at Teotihuacan, Valley of Mexico.

Fig. 13.44 (*below*). Statuette carved of fuchsite, a softer, jadelike stone, from Temple A-XVIII, Uaxactun, Guatemala.

though fitted with a jadeite nose, was excavated from a cache at El Portón in the Salama valley of the Maya highlands.

The largest jadeite sculpture known from the Maya area was discovered in the tomb of a ruler from Altun Ha, Belize. It portrays the Maya sun god (God G), Kinich Ahau (Fig. 11.30). The tomb of Pacal at Palenque yielded a carved jade of excellent workmanship (Fig. 13.46). This figurine, which was found in the sarcophagus itself, also represents Kinich Ahau.

A large, waterworn boulder of unworked solid jade weighing slightly over 90 kg (200 pounds) was discovered under the stairway of a pyramid at Kaminaljuyu. Many small pieces have apparently been sawed from it, perhaps for making into ornaments.

Three pieces of engraved jadeite from Chichen Itza are shown in Figs. 13.47 and 13.48; although somewhat inferior to the jades previously illustrated, they are excellently carved. The two largest were found in a stone box at the base of the stairway that leads to the early temple buried inside the El Castillo pyramid.

Natural deposits of jadeite have been found in the middle Motagua valley of Guatemala. Pieces of jade were probably found in streams as waterworn peb-

Fig. 13.45. Statuette of a jadelike stone, from a cache in Structure J7-4, El Portón, Guatemala.

Fig. 13.47 (*above*). Carved jadeite head and necklace from the cache lying on the Red Jaguar Throne, Chichen Itza. Postclassic period.

Fig. 13.46 (*left*). Jadeite figurine from the Pacal tomb, Temple of the Inscriptions, Palenque, Mexico.

bles or boulders, ranging in weight from a few grams to several hundred kilograms. The shape and size of the original piece often influenced the design into which it was carved. A study of Middle American jades by mineralogists of the Carnegie Institution of Washington has shown that Maya jades are jadeite, different in chemical composition from Chinese jade, or nephrite. They thus differ somewhat in appearance from Chinese jades: Maya jade is slightly harder, less translucent, and more mottled. It varies from dark green to light blue-green, although all shades from near black to white are known.

Jadeite is extremely hard—6.5 to 6.8 in the mineralogical scale (the diamond is graded 10)—and when we consider that the ancient Maya had no metal tools, their mastery of jade carving is a remarkable technical achievement. Pieces of jadeite were sawed by drawing cords back and forth through grooves and by using hard stone particles and water as a cutting agent. Holes were bored from both ends with drills of bone or hardwood, again using finely crushed stone and water as the cutting agent, with the perforations meeting in the middle. Hollow bird bones were used for drilling circles. In the finer pieces a modeled effect was probably achieved by careful incising, followed by deepening and smoothing the grooves.

Fig. 13.48. Carved jadeites from Chichen Itza, Postclassic period: (*left*) head from the cache under the Castillo Stairway; (*right*) figure from the same cache.

## Mosaics

Few mosaics from either the Classic or Postclassic periods have survived. Mirrors made of fitted pieces of pyrites attached to backs of wood or stone have been found at Piedras Negras, Quirigua, Kaminaljuyu, and several highland sites. There are suggestions of jadeite mosaics in Classic-stage reliefs, and a fine mask has been reconstructed from the jadeite pieces found in the tomb of Pacal at Palenque. A spectacular life-sized mosaic mask of jadeite, shell, and pyrite was excavated from a tomb at Tikal (Fig. 13.49), and a miniature jade mosaic mask in the same style was found in an earlier-period cache at El Portón in the

Salama valley (Fig. 13.50). The apogee of Maya jadeite mosaic work is represented by two similar, cylindrical vessels found in two Late Classic rulers' tombs at Tikal (Fig. 13.51). Originally constructed on wooden backings, they have been reconstructed from the fragmentary states they were discovered in.

Examples of turquoise mosaic from the Postclassic are four disks found buried in ceremonial caches at Chichen Itza. These were not made in the Yucatan, which lacks deposits of turquoise, but were brought from central Mexico, where the technique was common in the fourteenth to sixteenth centuries. The first disk was found by the Carnegie Institution of Washington in a covered limestone jar (Fig. 11.71) beneath the floor of the Temple of the Chac Mool, which was later incorporated into the pyramid of the Temple of the Warriors. The wood backing of this disk was almost rotted away. The restored disk is in the Museo Nacional de Antropología, Mexico City. Three similar disks were later found in the buried temple under El Castillo at Chichen Itza—two in the same box with the carved jadeite illustrated in Figs. 13.47 and 13.48, and the third on the seat of the Red Jaguar Throne. One of the two disks found with the jadeite is in the Museo de Arqueología e Historia at Mérida; the third still rests on the seat of the Red Jaguar Throne (Fig. 11.68).

Fig. 13.49 (*below*). Early Classic life-sized mosaic jadeite mask from Burial 160 (9.4.13.0.0?, or ca. A.D. 527), Tikal, Guatemala.

Fig. 13.50.  Miniature jadeite mosaic mask from a cache in Structure J7-4, El Portón, Guatemala (terminal Preclassic).

Fig. 13.51. Late Classic jadeite mosaic vessels, Tikal, Guatemala: left, a vessel from the tomb of Ah Cacau (Burial 116), with his presumed portrait on the lid; right, a vessel from the probable tomb of his successor, Yax Kin (Burial 196), with his presumed portrait on the lid.

## Metalwork

Metal objects from Classic-period Maya centers are rare. A pair of legs belonging to a small, hollow figurine made of a gold-copper alloy (Fig. 13.52c) was found at Copan. Analysis of this alloy, and of the casting technique employed, suggests that it was made in lower Central America (Costa Rica or

Panama). The legs were recovered from the dirt fill of the foundation vault under Stela H, dedicated in A.D. 782 (Fig. 11.46, right). The other parts of the figurine were not located, and the pieces recovered may have found their way into the vault some time later than the dedicatory date. Copper bells and ornaments have been found at Quirigua dating from the Terminal Classic or Early Postclassic period.

Metal objects from the Postclassic are more common. The greatest number recovered have been dredged from the Cenote of Sacrifice at Chichen Itza, though copper bells have been found elsewhere. Gold and copper objects from the Cenote include disks decorated with repoussé work, a cup and saucer, necklaces, bracelets, masks, pendants, rings, earplugs, bells, and beads (Figs. 13.52–54). The most common objects are small copper bells of the sleigh-bell type; these bells were a common ornament of the death god, Yum Cimil (God A), and are usually associated with him. The style and workmanship of many of the smaller objects indicate that they also were made in lower Central America.

Most of these metal objects probably reached Chichen Itza as articles of trade. Chemical analyses have established that they came from as far south as Colombia, Panama, Honduras, and Guatemala, and from as far west and north

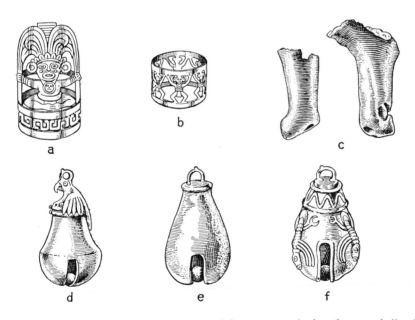

Fig. 13.52. Examples of metalwork: (*a, b*) gold finger rings and (*d, e, f*) copper bells, all dredged from the Cenote of Sacrifice, Chichen Itza, Yucatan, Mexico; (*c*) a pair of gold legs found in the cruciform vault below Stela H, Copan, Honduras.

Fig. 13.53. Gold and copper objects from the Cenote of Sacrifice, Chichen Itza: (*a, d, e*) disks decorated in repoussé technique; (*b*) gold bracelet; (*c*) gold cup and saucer.

as Chiapas, Oaxaca, and the Valley of Mexico. The copper pieces that contain tin and arsenic came from Oaxaca and the Valley of Mexico; those containing only tin are from Honduras. The purest copper came from Guatemala and Chiapas. These origins testify to the extent of the Postclassic trade networks of the Maya.

All objects that show casting are of foreign origin. The only technique with which Maya goldsmiths were familiar was the hammering for repoussé work. The gold used in the few objects actually made at Chichen Itza was probably

Fig. 13.54. Postclassic goldwork from the Cenote of Sacrifice, Chichen Itza.

Fig. 13.55. Central designs from three repoussé-technique gold disks from the Cenote of Sacrifice, Chichen Itza, depicting conflict between Mexicanized Maya warriors.

obtained by reworking cast-gold objects of foreign origin. These local pieces are usually thin disks portraying scenes of battle. The scenes represent conflicts between Maya warriors and Mexicanized (Putun?) warriors. The central designs from three such disks are reproduced in Fig. 13.55. The figures are similar to those in the reliefs and frescoes of the Early Postclassic at Chichen Itza, and the disks probably date from that period.

## Chipped Stone

The production of chipped-stone tools from either obsidian or flint (chert) was developed to a fine art among the ancient Maya (Fig. 13.56). Substela caches of eccentric-shaped flints and blades are often found buried under Maya monuments. Perhaps the finest examples of this craft are the elaborate but delicately chipped staff heads excavated at El Palmar in Quintana Roo and at Quirigua. A small piece broken from the bottom of the El Palmar flint was not found, but in its original condition it was a completely closed design. Three human heads in profile are shown on the Quirigua piece.

## Textiles

Only a few examples of ancient Maya textiles have survived. Fragments of white cotton cloth, thought to date from before the Conquest, are reported from Tenam in eastern Chiapas; the supposed Late Postclassic dating of this cloth is based on the associated pottery. Numerous small pieces of carbonized cloth were recovered from the Cenote of Sacrifice at Chichen Itza. They show many complicated weaves, and date from Late Postclassic times.

Classic-period sculptures indicate that the cotton fabrics of the period were of rich and complicated weave and that elaborate embroidery was employed. A few representations of these textiles, taken from the monuments, are shown in Figs. 13.57a–d. Textiles from the Postclassic are illustrated in Figs. 13.57e–h. The Bonampak murals portray a variety of Late Classic–period fabrics (Figs. 13.25–27).

Hand-woven cotton materials (*patis*) of fixed length and width were used as articles of trade in ancient times, and after the Conquest became the principal form of tribute exacted by the Spanish.

The Classic and Postclassic sculptures bear witness to the former abundance and variety of Maya weaving. The modern Maya of the highlands of Guatemala have a rich textile art, which no doubt derives from their pre-Conquest ancestors. This is a craft that disappeared in northern Yucatan only recently, but the Lacandon Maya of eastern Chiapas, whose technology closely resembles that of the ancient Maya, still spin cotton thread and weave a coarse cloth, using the same techniques as did their ancestors. Spinning and handloom weaving are done by the women. They gather the cotton and spin it into thread, using as a

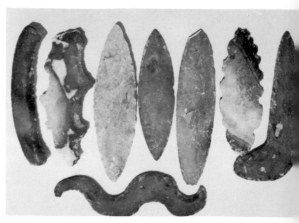

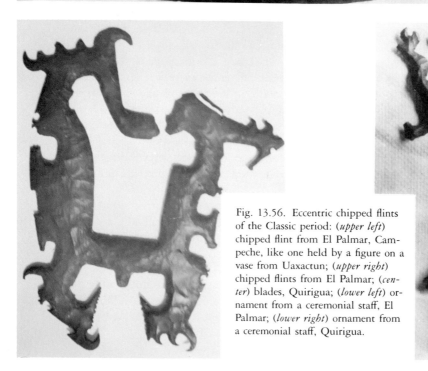

Fig. 13.56. Eccentric chipped flints of the Classic period: (*upper left*) chipped flint from El Palmar, Campeche, like one held by a figure on a vase from Uaxactun; (*upper right*) chipped flints from El Palmar; (*center*) blades, Quirigua; (*lower left*) ornament from a ceremonial staff, El Palmar; (*lower right*) ornament from a ceremonial staff, Quirigua.

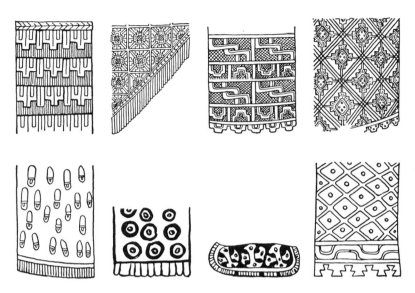

Fig. 13.57. Classic textiles (*top row*) drawn from the monuments; Postclassic textiles (*bottom row*) drawn from wall paintings and pottery.

spindle a slender pointed stick about 25 cm long (10 in.), weighted near the lower end with a disk of pottery. These disks, or spindle whorls, are all that has survived of ancient Maya spinning and weaving implements. They gave balance and weight to the spindle as it was twirled in the right hand, while the lower end of the spindle rested in a gourd on the ground; the unspun cotton was held in the left hand or thrown over the left shoulder (Fig. 13.58).

The Maya loom was of the same general type as those of modern American Indian groups. One wooden rod is fastened to each end of the warp to keep the cloth stretched to the desired width. A thick hemp cord (*yamal*), attached to each end of the lower rod, passes behind the weaver, permitting her to tighten the warp by leaning backward. The upper rod is attached to a tree or post. The strip of cloth may be made as long as 2.4 m (8 ft), and as it lengthens it is wound around the upper rod. The weaver sits as far back from the post as possible in order to hold the loom horizontally at the required tension (Fig. 13.58, right). The looms are about a meter wide, and when wider cloth is desired two strips are sewn together. An ancient representation of this technique appears in the Madrid Codex (Fig. 13.59), where Ix Chebel Yax, patroness of the art, is shown weaving.

Many Maya communities in highland Guatemala are still characterized by the different kinds of cloth they weave and by their traditional designs. Although wool has been introduced since the Conquest, most native clothing is still made of hand-loomed cotton cloth. Today silk is generally used for embroidery, but colored cotton threads and feathers were used in earlier times. No two designs are ever identical, but the weavers of each village generally conform to a distinctive traditional pattern (Fig. 9.3, upper illustrations).

The color symbolism used in highland Guatemalan textile designs still bears some relation to that used by the ancient Maya. Black represents weapons because it is the color of obsidian; yellow symbolizes food because it is the color of corn; red represents blood; and blue means sacrifice. The royal color is green because that is the color of the quetzal bird's plumage, which was reserved for the rulers.

In coloring textiles the thread is dyed, rather than the finished fabric. Although organic and mineral colors are now being replaced by aniline dyes, a few are still in use. Perhaps the most highly prized native dye was a deep purple obtained from a mollusk found along the Pacific coast (*Purpura patula*), a large sea snail related to the Mediterranean mollusk that gave the famous "royal purple of Tyre."

In the Yucatan the type of embroidery used by the modern Maya is cross-

Fig. 13.58.  Spinning and weaving among the Lacandon Maya, Chiapas, Mexico.

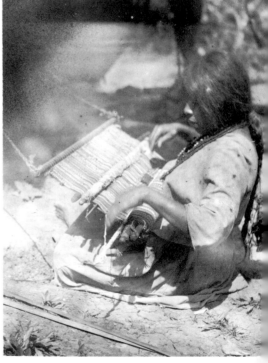

Fig. 13.59. The deity identified as Ix Chebel Yax weaving, Madrid Codex, p. 79.

stitch (*xoc bil chui*, or "threads that are counted"). The earlier designs may have been geometric like those still used in central Quintana Roo, but geometric designs have now been generally displaced by floral motifs (Fig. 9.3, lower illustrations).

Today, native weaves and colors are everywhere giving way to machine-made fabrics and aniline dyes. Even in the highlands of Guatemala, the native textile art is rapidly disappearing.

## Basketry and Matting

No early Maya baskets have been discovered, but they are depicted in Classic-stage graphic art. An elaborate basket appears in Lintel 24 at Yaxchilan (Fig. 13.60*a*). The upper half is worked in a twilled pattern, the middle section shows a design of stepped frets and small squares, and the bottom seems to be ornamented with featherwork. Representations of two Late Classic baskets from the Nebaj Vase are shown in Figs. 13.60*b*, *c*. A Postclassic basket from a wall painting in the Temple of the Jaguars at Chichen Itza (Fig. 13.60*d*) is more elaborate.

Modern Maya baskets are relatively crude. Those woven from thin, tough vines are large and coarse, suitable for carrying corn. Split-cane baskets, smaller and more neatly woven, are used in the home.

Fig. 13.60. Classic and Postclassic baskets from monuments, wall paintings, and pottery: (*a*) on Lintel 24, Yaxchilan; (*b*, *c*) on the Nebaj Vase; (*d*) on the fresco in the Temple of the Jaguars, Chichen Itza.

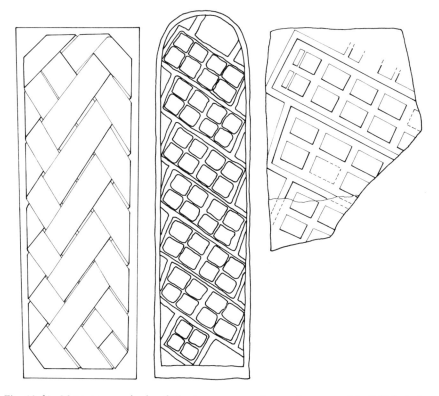

Fig. 13.61. Mat pattern on backs of Classic monuments (not at the same scale): (*left*) Stela J, Copan, the glyph sequence following the interwoven pattern of a mat; (*center*) Monument 7 (Stela H), Quirigua; (*right*) Stela 3, Cancuen, on which the glyph sequence follows a nonwoven diagonal sequence.

No pieces of ancient matting have survived, but imprints have been found on pottery and plaster. A small heap of disintegrated material, apparently the remains of a palm-fiber mat, was found below the plaza floor at Uaxactun. The imprint of another piece was found in the temple beneath El Castillo at Chichen Itza; the Red Jaguar Throne had rested upon this matting. The weave of this Postclassic piece was identical to that of mats still made in Mérida.

Mats played an important role in ancient Maya life. A piece of matting with the sun symbol beside it (Fig. 16.5*a*) is the hieroglyph for the first month of the ancient Maya year, Pop, which means "matting." Sitting on a mat was a mark of authority, and throughout the *Book of Chilam Balam* of Chumayel the words "mat" and "throne" appear interchangeably. The title *ahpop*, "he of the mat," was used by rulers. The sequence of the hieroglyphic inscription on the back of Stela J at Copan follows the weave of a mat pattern in the order of its reading, whereas the superficially similar designs on two other monuments do not (Fig. 13.61).

Baskets and matting must have been common among the ancient Maya, and the materials from which they were made occur in abundance throughout the area.

## Featherwork

A few examples of Mexica (Aztec) featherwork from central Mexico have been preserved, but none of the ancient Maya work has survived. The graphic art of the Classic and Postclassic periods shows how rich and highly developed it must have been, as in the Bonampak murals (Figs. 13.25–27), and early Spanish writers frequently allude to it.

The forests of the Peten teem with birds of gorgeous plumage, and the northern highlands of Guatemala are the habitat of the beautiful quetzal. Feathers were used in making panaches, crests, capes, and shields and in decorating canopies, fans, personal ornaments, and pendants for spears and scepters. Featherwork was also used in embroideries and fringes for cotton fabrics.

One of the loveliest examples is the panache of the headdress worn by a ruler on Wall Panel 3 at Piedras Negras (Fig. 4.26). Such long plumes must have been the tail feathers of the quetzal. On Stela 12 at Piedras Negras (Fig. 11.37, left), a similar headdress is worn by the ruler, who also wears a short feather cape. The graceful and slightly stylized treatment of the featherwork lends distinction to these fine reliefs.

Northern-area representations of featherwork are not as fine. Some featherwork is shown on the wooden lintels from the Temple of the Jaguars at Chichen Itza (Fig. 13.18), and another example from Xculoc, Campeche, is illustrated in Fig. 13.62.

Father Bernardino de Sahagún, our greatest authority on the Mexica, tells us that they had two kinds of featherwork:

They [the Mexica] make the devices which they wear on their backs in dancing, all the costumes of the dance, and the trappings with which they dance [of feathers] and they executed the craft and profession of feather-workers in two different ways: the first kind of work consists of fastening the feathers to the background with paste in order thus to finish the work; the second way consists in doing the work and finishing it with the help of thread and cord.

In describing this latter technique Father Sahagún writes further: "There is another kind of work, the handicraft of thread and cord. In this way they make their fans out of the plumes of the quetzal, their feather bracelets, the devices they wear on their backs and other things, their tunics blazoned with their arms etc.; and in addition pendants, panaches, balls, tassels of feathers, with all of which they adorn themselves and decorate their fans."

He also says that this art was relatively recent among the Mexica, especially the use of the brightly colored feathers of tropical birds. These feathers came from the southern provinces, which were not subjugated until the reigns of the last two Mexica emperors before the Spanish Conquest.

Early Spanish writers relate the importance of this craft among the Quiche Maya of the Guatemala highlands, who had aviaries where birds were bred for their plumage. Fuentes y Guzmán, the seventeenth-century historian of Guatemala, says that the Quiche rulers at Utatlan had "places set apart for the breeding of ducks, for the sake of their plumage which they employed in weaving." Another early authority, describing the same place, states: "The throne of the king was notable because it had a canopy of very rich plumes and above this protection or covering, other coverings of different colors, in such a way as to give an effect of great majesty. The prince, or he who was to succeed, had three canopies and the other brothers or sons, two."

Besides weaving the feathers into their cotton fabrics, the Maya attached them to wood and wicker frames for headdresses. Father Moran in his manu-

Fig. 13.62. Examples of feather headdresses carved on doorjambs of Structure 2, Xculoc, Campeche, Mexico.

script dictionary of Pokomam Mayan defines the *mayut* as a "framework of wood adorned with plumage, which they wear on their backs in their dances." The Museum of the Cinquantennaire in Brussels displays an ankle-length cape of macaw feathers built on a framework of wickerwork; this cape supposedly belonged to Moctezuma II, the Mexica ruler at the time of the Spanish Conquest. A quetzal-plume headdress, certainly belonging to the same ruler, is in the former Imperial Museum in Vienna.

Feathers, cotton fabrics, seashells, and semiprecious stones were used not only personally but for trade and for payment of legal penalties; in Postclassic times turquoise, copper, and gold were similarly used: "they exchanged mantas [*patis*] of cotton for gold and for certain axes of copper, and gold for emeralds, turquoises and plumes. . . . At the end [the man who had committed the injury] was sentenced to pay a certain quantity of rich plumes, or mantas, or cacao, which went to the treasury."

The most highly prized feathers were the tail plumes of the quetzal, which were reserved for royal use. According to Bartolomé de Las Casas, to either capture or kill one was a capital offense: "in the province of Vera Pas [Guatemala], they punish with death him who killed the bird with the rich plumes, because it is not found in other places and these feathers were things of great value because they used them as money."

# PART IV

# INTELLECTUAL CULTURE

# 14

# IDEOLOGY

You are God our Father. You are our master in the Sky. Sun, Sun, you shed your light on us. Never can we pay for your blessings which you give to us. Everything is the sun; there is no way we can pay you.
—Contemporary Chorti Maya prayer (Fought 1972: 489)

They had a very great number of idols and temples, which were magnificent in their own fashion. And besides the community temples, the lords, priests and the leading men had also oratories and idols in their houses, where they made their prayers and offerings in private.
—Landa's *Relación de las cosas de Yucatán* (Tozzer 1941: 108)

Each society holds, more or less, to a particular ideology, a body of concepts that provide order and explain the unknown. The Maya of today continue to maintain the vestiges of an ancient ideology quite different from our Western concepts of life and the universe. We conceive of our world as being composed of discrete components, the natural and supernatural realms. The natural world corresponds to that which is observable, divided into an animate (living) realm of creatures on this earth and an inanimate (nonliving) realm of objects on the earth and beyond, organized into the solar system, our galaxy, and the entire universe. We reserve the unobservable realm to something called the supernatural, be it concepts like luck and superstition or the codified philosophy, beliefs, and faith we call religion.

Although the ideological concepts of the ancient Maya were severely disrupted by the trauma of the Spanish Conquest, and then by subsequent events, it is possible to reconstruct some aspects of this belief system from what we know of present-day Maya culture combined with ethnohistorical accounts from around the time of the Conquest and an analysis of archaeological evidence. The resulting picture, although imperfect, is reasonably complete and coherent.

The world of the ancient Maya was governed by a cosmological order that transcended our distinction between the natural and supernatural realms. All things, animate or inanimate, were imbued with an unseen power. This invisible power was amorphous in the case of the "spirits" inhabiting rocks, trees, or other objects (animism). In other cases this power was embodied in a "deity" in animallike (zoomorphic) or humanlike (anthropomorphic) form. This fusion of the observable and unobservable is best expressed by the Maya concept of *cuxolalob*, the knowledge of that which is both rational and supernatural.

Above all, the world was seen as an ordered place in its normal state. This order stemmed from the predictable movements of the "sky wanderers," the sun, moon, planets, and stars that marked the passage of time. Each of these celestial bodies was animate, a deity by our definition.

The basic unit of this order was the day, the *kin*, in which the sun passed out of the underworld at dawn and across the sky only to be swallowed once again by the underworld at dusk. A succession of twenty *kins*, each of which was represented by its own anthropomorphic deity, collectively formed a *uinal*, also represented by an anthropomorphic deity. (See below for a discussion of Maya time deities.) The central importance of time in the world order is indicated by the fact that *uinic* means "man" in Yucatec Maya, perhaps because it was men who "knew the rhythm of the days in themselves," as recorded in the *Book of Chilam Balam* of Chumayel. Thus in the ancient Maya scheme of things, time itself was animate, and the *cuxolalob* of time provided the fundamental order for the universe (the Maya calendar is described in Chapter 16).

## Origins of Maya Ideology

The origins of these and other ideological concepts undoubtedly lie in the distant past, even as far back as the hunters and gatherers, who needed to be intimately acquainted with their total environment to assure themselves of adequate shelter and food and to survive its dangers. Under such conditions the concept of animism helps explain a world that inspires both security and fear. The discovery of order in one's surroundings, perhaps especially in the predictable movements of the sun and moon, increases understanding and reduces insecurity. An ideology based on these fundamental and observable phenomena requires no specialists. Each family head was probably responsible for ensuring that the animistic forces in the environment were satisfied, so as to guard against accident, illness, or other disasters.

But as any society grows and becomes more complex, occupational specialists begin to emerge. One kind of specialist, the shaman, is responsible for the relationships between humans and the surrounding animistic forces. In the Maya area shamanism was probably well developed before the Preclassic era, emerging with village life and agriculture, if not before. The shaman's medicinal substances, knowledge of illness, and appeals to unseen forces were used to cure the sick. The shaman's ability to communicate with these forces by divination provided a measure of power over other members of society. The earliest Maya shamans probably also developed the beginnings of the calendrical system, and were therefore charged with maintaining the world order by keeping track of the various cycles reckoned by the movements of the "sky wanderers." The most practical benefit of this knowledge was the ability to predict the coming of the seasons, and thereby to choose the proper time to plant and harvest crops.

Later in the Preclassic period, as society became larger and more complex, full-time specialists and leaders became established. In the case of the Maya, the management of unseen forces became a fundamental concern of the ruling elite, both to reinforce and support their own elevated status and to ensure prosperity. Those aspects of shamanism involved with societal matters—the management of the calendar to maintain the world order, public divination, and other rituals to ensure success and prosperity—soon became the responsibility of a priesthood that in time became an intrinsic part of the ruling class.

The Maya priesthood became an institution both self-contained, at the heart of the Maya elite class, and self-perpetuated, through the recruitment and training of acolytes. By the beginning of the Classic period, Maya priests had developed a body of esoteric knowledge, probably codified and recorded by a written system in books (codices; see Chapter 15). This body of knowledge, centered around astronomical observation and recording, was used primarily to develop and maintain an ever increasingly complex calendrical system whose principal purpose seems to have been astrological, that is, as a divining technique to predict events and determine the destiny of the world.

The priesthood performed a variety of often spectacular public ceremonies to inspire awe and obedience in the populace. Such ceremonies usually involved music, dancing, the burning of incense, and offerings, which often included the blood of priests and, on certain occasions, human sacrifices. The ruler of each Maya center seems to have served as principal priest, responsible for certain rituals and divinations held to ensure the success and well-being of the state. Because the functions of political and religious leadership seem to have been fused, the Maya order is usually termed a theocracy.

## Transformations by Outsiders

Later Maya writings, in addition to the Spanish accounts, often refer to Postclassic-era religious changes that were introduced by outsiders, either Mexican peoples or Mayan-speaking groups influenced by Mexican customs. The principal changes seem to be greater emphasis on the worship of the images of deities ("idolatry") and increased human sacrifice.

The old men of these provinces [Yucatan] say that anciently, near to eight hundred years ago, idolatry was not practiced, and afterwards when the Mexicans entered it and took possession of it, a captain, who was called Quetzalquat [Quetzalcoatl] in the Mexican language, which is to say in ours, plumage of the serpent . . . introduced idolatry into this land and the use of idols for gods, which he had made of wood, of clay and of stone. And he made them [the Maya] worship these idols and they offered many things of the hunt, of merchandise and above all the blood of their nostrils and ears, and the hearts of those whom they sacrificed in his services. . . . They say that the first inhabitants of Chichenyza [Chichen Itza] were not idolators, until a Mexican captain Ku Kalcan [Kukulcan] entered into these parts, who taught idolatry, and the necessity, so they say, to teach and practice it.

Herrera, the official historian of the Indies for the Crown of Spain, leaves no doubt about this point, stating bluntly that "the number of people sacrificed was great. And this custom was introduced into Yucatan by the Mexicans."

But it should be borne in mind that both of these practices were known to the Maya long before they were "introduced" by foreigners. Pottery incensarios adorned with masks or images of deities are frequently found in archaeological remains dating from both the Preclassic and Classic periods. Representations of human sacrifice are found on Classic monuments, polychrome pottery, and the graffiti inscribed on building walls (Fig. 14.1). Raiding and the taking of "trophy heads" appear to have had ritualistic associations during the Preclassic and Classic periods; one such trophy is depicted on the Bonampak murals. A spectacular example of early mass human sacrifice has been excavated from beneath a Late Preclassic platform at Chalchuapa, in the southern Maya area. In this case, a total of 33 individuals, mostly young males (probably captives), were buried together, many with unmistakable signs of sacrifice and mutilation (decapitation, and severing of limbs). A Late Preclassic monument from Izapa (Stela 21) depicts a decapitated individual.

Maya ideology underwent its greatest transformation at the hands of the Spaniards, when Christianity was imposed, sometimes forcibly, upon the native population. The greatest change was the disappearance of the esoteric cult perpetuated by the Maya priesthood, for this was the most visible aspect of "paganism," and therefore most vulnerable to elimination by the Spaniards' program of conversion. Public shrines and their "idols" were destroyed, books were burned, and the priests themselves were either forcibly converted or executed. And along with the formal and public aspects of Maya religion went much of Maya learning, including the writing system. Fortunately, some native accounts survived, preserving a partial record of ancient Maya ideology.

The less public elements of the Maya belief system often escaped detection and have been perpetuated within Maya family and village life down to the present. In areas where the Spanish pressure for conversion was most intense— in colonized regions of northern Yucatan and in the southern highlands, for example—Maya beliefs and rituals were often kept secret and apart from Christianity. Although baptized and thus officially "converted," many Maya people learned to accept the new religion in its public setting, the church, while continuing the old family rituals in the house and the agricultural rituals in the fields. Of course when elements of Christianity happened to correspond to aspects of native ideology, the Maya could "accommodate" their conquerors by seeming to accept Christian concepts, all the while maintaining their old beliefs under a new guise. For instance, the cross existed as a Maya symbol for the "tree of life," the sacred ceiba supporting the heavens, so that the Christian cross was readily accepted, although often worshiped for its ancient Maya connotation.

Fig. 14.1. Scenes of human sacrifice. From the Classic period: (*a*) Stela 11, Piedras Negras; (*b*) Stela 14, Piedras Negras. From the Postclassic period: (*c*) Dresden Codex; (*d*) Madrid Codex; (*e*) Temple of the Jaguars, Chichen Itza; (*f*) Temple of the Warriors, Chichen Itza.

In northern Yucatan, when evidence for the secret continuance of Maya beliefs was discovered, the Inquisition was brought in to extinguish all vestiges of "paganism." The Maya response was often to flee from the Spaniards. As a result, a series of refugee settlements were formed deep in the bush of southeastern Yucatan, where the traditional way of life could be pursued without interference from the Spanish authorities. A fierce tradition of Maya nativism and independence flourished in these areas of Quintana Roo. At the heart of this nativistic Maya tradition was a cult centered around the worship of a "talking cross," a wooden image that served as an oracle. Efforts in the nineteenth century by the newly independent government of Mexico to assert its control over the region resulted in a protracted conflict, the War of the Castes. Many villages in Quintana Roo remained isolated and independent of outside control until well into the twentieth century.

The Lacandon Maya of the southern lowlands have remained relatively untouched by Western contact until the present century. Much of the ancient Maya ideology survives in the Lacandon belief system, albeit in greatly attenuated form. At least until recently, for instance, the Lacandon still manufactured and used pottery incensarios, similar in form to some types used during the Classic era. Rituals are still held in sacred caves and even in the Classic-period ruins found in the area (Fig. 14.2).

Fig. 14.2. Ritual burning of *pom* (copal) incense by the Lacandon Maya at the ruins of Yaxchilan. The man holds a prayer board on which are small nodules of *pom* to be burned as an offering in the ancient temples.

In other regions, however, including the Alta Verapaz in the highlands of Guatemala, Christianity was peacefully introduced, owing to the efforts of Father Bartolomé de Las Casas. As a result, Maya and Christian ideologies have tended to blend into a single system that is neither indigenous nor Western. In many highland Maya communities, isolated until recently from outside interference, the ideological system has been controlled by native shamans. These officials assumed control of public ceremonies, such as baptisms and masses held in churches and divining and curing rituals undertaken on behalf of individuals. In several of these highland communities the Maya shamans have maintained elements of the ancient calendrical system, such as the 260-day almanac, still used to determine the birthday names of infants and the proper days for ceremonies.

In Yucatecan cosmology, the archangel Gabriel and other Christian saints become the Pauahtuns of ancient Maya mythology, the guardians of the four cardinal points; the archangel Michael leads the Chacs, the former rain gods. In Belize it is St. Vincent who is the patron of rain, and St. Joseph the guiding spirit of the cornfields.

The cosmological order in the Maya highlands links Kinich Ahau (see below) with the Christian God, called "Our Father Sun" or sometimes "Our Father Rain." A female counterpart, equated with the Virgin Mary, is "Our Mother Moon" or "Our Mother Maize." Christ is identified with Hunapu, a familiar figure from the *Popol Vuh*, and the cross, worshiped as a deity, is sometimes associated with the deity of the Maya day Ahau. Other anthropomorphized powers, directly descended from ancient Maya counterparts, dwell in the physical world, including mountains, volcanoes, caves, and lakes, and in animals and other forms of life.

## Cosmology

The Maya believed that there had been several worlds before the present one, and that each had been destroyed by a deluge. Bishop Diego de Landa records this tradition but fails to state the number of worlds thus destroyed:

Among the multitude of gods which this people adored, they worshiped four, each of whom was called Bacab. They said they were four brothers whom God [Hunab Ku], when he created the world, placed at the four points of it, to hold up the sky, so that it should not fall. They also said of these Bacabs, that they escaped when the world was destroyed by the deluge. They gave to each one of them other names and [thus] designated by them the part of the world where God placed him [each one] to bear up the heavens.

This tradition, the end of the world by a deluge, is depicted on the last page of the Dresden Codex (Fig. 14.3), according to one interpretation. Across the sky stretches a serpentlike creature; symbols of the constellations are on its side,

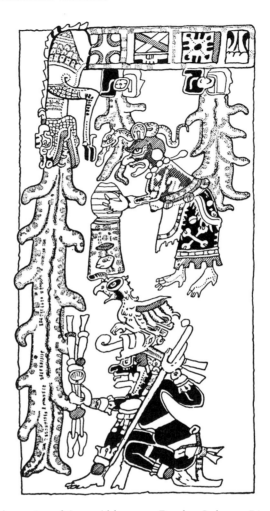

Fig. 14.3. The destruction of the world by water. Dresden Codex, p. 74.

and signs for solar and lunar eclipses hang from its belly. From its open jaws, and from the two eclipse signs, a flood of water pours earthward. Below the heavenly serpent, the Old Woman Goddess with long talonlike fingernails and toenails, the patroness of death and destruction, holds an inverted bowl from which also gushes a destroying flood. At the bottom the Muan bird of evil omen rests on the head of the black war and death deity (see under "Other Deities"). In his right hand he holds two javelins and in his left a long staff, all pointing downward.

The modern Maya of northern Yucatan believe that there have been three worlds previous to this one. The first world was inhabited by dwarfs, the *saiyam uinicob* or "adjuster men," who are thought to have built the great ruined cities. This work was done in darkness, for the sun had not yet been created. As soon as the sun rose for the first time, the dwarfs were turned to stone. This first world was ended by a universal deluge, the *haiyococab*, or "water over the earth." The second world, inhabited by people called the *dzolob*, or "offenders," was ended by the second flood. The third world was populated by the Maya themselves, the common people or *mazehualob*; this world was ended by the third flood, called the *hunyecil* or *bulkabal*, which means the "immersing." This last deluge was followed by the present or fourth world, peopled by a mixture of all the previous inhabitants of the Peninsula, and this too will eventually be destroyed by a fourth flood.

The Maya religion had strong elements of dualism, the eternal struggle between the powers of good and evil over the destiny of man. The benevolent powers, bringing thunder, lightning, and rain, fructify the corn and ensure plenty. The malevolent ones, characterized by death and destruction, cause drought, hurricanes, and war, which ruin the corn and bring famine and misery. This contest is depicted in the codices, where Chac, the rain deity, is shown caring for a young tree; behind him follows the death god, who breaks the tree in two (Fig. 14.4).

The Maya conceived of the world as having thirteen heavens, arranged in layers, the lowest being the earth itself. Over each presided one of the Thirteen Gods of the Upper World, or Oxlahuntiku (in Yucatec Maya, *oxlahun* is "thirteen," *ti* is "of," and *ku* is "god"). There were nine underworlds, also arranged in layers, over each of which presided its own deity, one of the Bolontiku, or Nine Gods of the Lower World (in Maya, *bolon* is "nine").

The Maya apparently believed in an afterlife. According to Landa, the future was divided into a place of suffering and a place of rest, although there is some suspicion of European influence in his statement.

People who committed suicide by hanging or were sacrificed, warriors killed in battle, women who died in childbirth, priests, and rulers went directly to the Maya paradise: "They also said and held it as absolutely certain that those who hanged themselves went to this heaven of theirs; and thus there were many who on slight occasions of sorrows, troubles or sicknesses, hanged themselves in order to escape these things and to go and rest in their heaven, where they said

Fig. 14.4. A rain deity nourishes a tree; a death deity uproots it. Madrid Codex, p. 60.

that the Goddess of the Gallows, whom they called Ixtab, came to fetch them."

What we know from the circumstances discovered in the excavations of rulers' tombs at Palenque, Tikal, and other Classic-period centers suggests that these most powerful of individuals were believed to have been transformed into supernatural beings upon death. In a sense, they became deities, and their passage to this status seems to have been commemorated in the funeral rituals, the trappings of which have been found in these tombs. This deification seems to have been an expression of ancestor worship, a theme that probably permeated ancient Maya religion. Several sculptures associated with the death of rulers, such as the sarcophagus lid from Pacal's tomb (Fig. 4.23) at Palenque, or perhaps Monument 24 at Quirigua, depict rulers at the moment of death and deification falling into the underworld, usually depicted by jaguar symbolism. Jaguars seem to have been both lords of the underworld and protectors of rulers during their reigns.

In the Postclassic, the Maya paradise was described as a place of delights, where there was no pain or suffering and an abundance of food and drink. There grew the *yaxche*, sacred tree of the Maya (the ceiba), in the shade of which they could rest forever from labor. Those whose lives had been evil descended into the ninth and lowest underworld, Mitnal, the Maya hell. There devils tormented them with hunger, cold, weariness, and grief.

## Maya Deities

To the ancient Maya, the cosmos represented both unity and diversity simultaneously. The power inherent in all things, whether natural or supernatural in our terms, could be manifest in supernatural beings we label "deities." Inasmuch as all Maya deities were aspects of the same power, the Maya supernatural realm can be viewed as monotheistic. Inasmuch as each aspect could be represented in a distinct manner, the definition of individual deities supports the view of the Maya supernatural realm as polytheistic.

These aspects of the Maya supernatural may be characterized according to a variety of criteria, including function (a war deity as opposed to a sun deity), sex (male and female aspects), direction (commonly east and west, but also north, south, and center), age, color, and so forth. This inherent diffuse quality of sacredness has inevitably led to confusion in attempts to identify individual deities. A series of studies, made to classify and describe these deities, used the Maya codices, where the portraits and associated glyphs representing particular anthropomorphic deities are most clearly represented. But although there is a general consensus about the identity of a dozen or so of these deities, there is confusion about the remainder and even disagreement over the total number of "separate deities."

Since these codices date from the Postclassic period, and some attributes of the deity portraits they contain can be linked to non-Maya (Mexican) supernatural beings, it can be argued that the deities in the codices derive in some measure from the belief systems of ancient Mexico. This position seems to be supported by the relative rarity of comparable representations of anthropomorphic deities prior to the Postclassic era. Thus the seemingly ordered polytheistic character of Maya ideology apparent from the studies of the Postclassic codices may reflect, at least in part, the incorporation of non-Maya beliefs, rather than indigenous Maya ideological concepts.

Several studies of Maya ideology have explored the painted scenes on some Classic pottery vessels. Most of the scenes are difficult to interpret, but they appear to represent aspects of ancient Maya myth and ritual. They occasionally show anthropomorphic deities, such as God N (see under "Other Deities"), in settings that are suggestive of myth. More often, they depict humans engaged in apparent ritual, sometimes wearing costumes, masks, and headdresses to impersonate deities. As such, these studies add to our understanding of Maya ideology. It must be noted, however, that their usefulness is limited by the fact that most of the vessels upon which these studies are based were looted from Maya sites, thus losing any information about how, where, and with what they were found. Unfortunately, therefore, the interpretations of the painted scenes on these vessels, however intriguing, remain limited and unverified (see the Introduction for a discussion of the destruction wrought by the looting of Maya archaeological sites).

With these qualifications in mind, we can briefly consider the principal anthropomorphic deities represented in the codices, in approximately decreasing frequency. The letter designations proposed by Paul Schellhas at the beginning of the twentieth century, and still in general use with some modifications, are noted here for convenience.

## ITZAMNA, A REPTILIAN DEITY (GOD D)

Itzamna, the all-pervasive reptilian deity of the ancient Maya, embodies the monotheistic-polytheistic duality of the Maya supernatural. Itzamna means "reptile (or iguana) house," referring, it would seem, to the fact that both earth and sky were reptilian in Maya cosmology. The earth and sky corresponded to the terrestrial and celestial aspects of Itzamna. In perhaps the most fundamental aspect, Itzamna was Hunab Ku, the creator of the universe. "They worshipped a single god who was named Hunab and Zamana, which is to say one only god." Hunab Ku means precisely that in Yucatec Maya (*hun*, "one"; *ab*, "state of being"; *ku*, "god"). This creator aspect of Itzamna was so remote from everyday affairs that Hunab Ku seems to have figured little in the life of the ancient Maya. No representations of Hunab Ku have been identified in the codices or elsewhere. In the *Popol Vuh*, the sacred book of the Quiche Maya of the highlands, the creator fashioned humankind out of maize.

In the codices, Itzamna is represented as an old man with toothless jaws and sunken cheeks (Fig. 14.5*a*). He has two name glyphs: one may be a convention-alized representation of his head; the other contains as its main element the day-sign Ahau. Since *ahau* meant "king, monarch, prince, or great lord," Itzamna's name glyph verifies his supernatural primacy. He was patron of the day Ahau, the last and most important of the twenty Maya days.

Itzamna was considered lord of the heavens, and lord of day and night. Credited with inventing books and writing, he is said to have been the first to name the places in the Yucatan and to divide the lands there.

As early as the Late Preclassic (as on Stela 19 at Kaminaljuyu), Itzamna was depicted as a two-headed serpent. These representations continued on the sculpture of the Classic and Postclassic eras. In this manifestation as the celestial serpent, his body represents the sky; his front (right-hand) head faces east, symbolizing the rising sun, the morning star (Venus), and life itself; his rear (left-hand) head represents the west, the setting sun, and death, usually depict-ed by a fleshless lower jaw (see Fig. 11.15, p. 286). The so-called ceremonial bar, held by rulers in the sculptured portraits on many Classic Maya stelae such as those at Copan, is clearly a representation of the two-headed, celestial-serpent aspect of Itzamna.

Itzamna appears to be associated with the ruling lineages of Maya centers, probably as their chief patron. This is especially apparent from the identification of rulers with Kinich Ahau (also called Ah Kinchil and God G), the sun aspect of Itzamna in his role as lord of the day (see below). The Temple of the Cross at Palenque, the building supposedly dedicated to the birth of the gods and the origins of that center's three patrons (known as the Palenque Triad; see Chapter 11 and Fig. 11.39), appears to have been associated with Itzamna. The inscrip-tions in this building record a mythical date (1.18.5.3.2 9 Ik 15 Ceh) that may refer to his birth. The two companion temples are linked to the other members of the Palenque Triad and also seem to record similar, though later, mythical dates for these deities.

Another reptilian deity, the feathered serpent Kukulcan, may be but another aspect of Itzamna. Kukulcan was especially prominent in the Postclassic era, in keeping with his strong associations with Mexican ideology. In Mexico the feathered serpent, known by his Nahuatl name, Quetzalcoatl, was the super-natural patron of rulers. A recent study has shown that part of the birth date recorded in Palenque's Temple of the Cross, 9 Ik, corresponds to an alternative name for Quetzalcoatl, 9 Wind. It has also been suggested that there are twin aspects of Kukulcan/Quetzalcoatl, one associated with good omens, the other with evil ones. The duality manifest in the good/evil aspects of Quetzalcoatl parallels the life/death aspects of Itzamna symbolized in his two-headed, celestial-serpent representation.

During the important ceremonies in connection with the Maya New Year, Itzamna was especially invoked to avert calamities. In the month of Uo, at a ceremony in honor of his manifestation as the sun god, the priests consulted the sacred books to learn the auguries for the coming year. In the month of Zip he

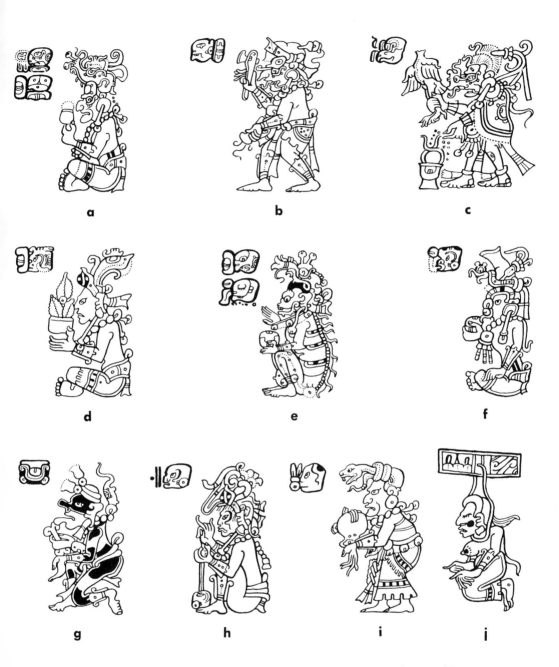

Fig. 14.5. Maya deities as represented in the codices: (*a*) Itzamna, the primary deity (God D); (*b*) Chac, a rain deity (God B); (*c*) Bolon Tzacab, a ruling-lineage deity (God K); (*d*) Yum Kaax, a maize deity (God E); (*e*) Yum Cimil, a death deity (God A); (*f*) Ah Chicum Ek, a North Star deity (God C); (*g*) Ek Chuah, a merchant deity (God M); (*h*) Buluc Chabtan, a war and human-sacrifice deity (God F); (*i*) Ix Chel, a rainbow deity (Goddess I); (*j*) Ixtab, a suicide deity. Kinich Ahau (God G) is not figured.

was invoked as the god of medicine, together with Ix Chel. In the month of Mac he was worshiped by the old men in a ceremony with the Chacs. In these ceremonies Itzamna was benevolent, never connected with destruction or disaster; in the codices he never appears with the symbols of death.

### KINICH AHAU (AH KINCHIL), A SUN DEITY (GOD G)

Although this deity, known as Kinich Ahau or Ah Kinchil, "the sun-faced one," has been considered a distinct figure, he seems clearly to have been the day aspect of Itzamna. As such, symbolizing the period of the sun's life in its daily journey across the sky, and hence all life, this aspect of Itzamna was closely associated with Maya rulers. The rulers of several Maya centers appear to have assumed an identity with Kinich Ahau, either because they wanted to associate themselves with their powerful supernatural patron or because they fostered the belief that they were a manifestation of the sun god.

God G was the patron of Muluc days and the number four.

### CHAC, A RAIN DEITY (GOD B)

The figure identified as Chac, the Maya rain deity, is represented in the codices with a reptilian face, a long, often down-curling snout, and two curved fangs projecting downward from the mouth (Fig. 14.5b). Although the portraits of God B in the codices have also been identified as Kukulcan and Itzamna, it seems more likely that God B represents Chac, his reptilian appearance indicating a close relationship to Itzamna or perhaps a manifestation of him.

God B's name glyph in the Madrid Codex has a T-shaped eye, probably reflecting an association with Tlaloc, the Mexican rain god. This sign is also the glyph for the day Ik, of which God B was probably patron.

God B was of obvious importance in the codices. His portrait occurs some 218 times in the three extant codices. In contrast, God D, the anthropomorphic Itzamna, appears only half as often (103 occurrences), and not at all in the Paris Codex.

Chac had four principal aspects, each linked to a cardinal direction and each associated with its own color: Chac Xib Chac, the Red Chac of the East; Sac Xib Chac, the White Chac of the North; Ek Xib Chac, the Black Chac of the West; and Kan Xib Chac, the Yellow Chac of the South.

In the months of Chen or Yax a great festival was held in honor of the Chacs, which was called *ocna*, meaning "enter the house." The four gods known as the Bacabs, who were closely associated with the Chacs, were consulted to determine a propitious day for the ceremony, which was devoted to renovation of the Temple of the Chacs. During this annual ceremony, the idols and incense burners were renewed, and if necessary, the temple itself was rebuilt. A tablet commemorating the event was set into the temple wall.

The rain god, benevolent like Itzamna, was associated with creation and life. For the ordinary Maya farmer whose paramount interest was his maize field, Chac was the all-important deity, and his friendly intervention was sought more frequently than that of all the other gods combined. The mask panels with long curling noses found throughout the Maya area, but especially in Puuc architecture, are probably representations of the head of this god (Fig. 11.3 and Fig. 11.4, upper right).

God B was the patron of Ik days and the number thirteen.

## BOLON TZACAB, A RULING-LINEAGE DEITY (GOD K)

Bolon Tzacab is also portrayed in the codices with a reptilian face. His long snout is more elaborate than that of God B, and usually upturned (Fig. 14.5c). He is usually depicted with an axe or smoking cigar in his forehead in Classic-period representations. As might be expected, God K is associated with both Itzamna (God D) and Chac (God B), and thus can also be viewed as a manifestation of Itzamna. Bolon Tzacab, "he of nine (many) generations," is mentioned in the *Books of Chilam Balam*, and his name glyph (recognizable from the codices) appears with the numeral nine as a prefix in the texts from several Classic-period Maya sites.

God K is the image portrayed on the manikin scepter, often held as a symbol of office by rulers on the sculptured stelae of the Classic era (Fig. 4.10b). In fact, the act of acquiring the manikin scepter is usually seen as the equivalent to inauguration for ancient Maya rulers. The first known representations of God K on the manikin scepter appear at Tikal, where the figure appears to be related to Tlaloc, the Mexican rain deity. It has been suggested that this symbol of rulership developed from Tlaloc or from the emblem associated with the Mexican-related dynasty that assumed power at Tikal during the Early Classic (see Chapters 4 and 11). The manikin scepter itself seems to have been derived from the atlatl (spear thrower) carried by the Teotihuacan (or Kaminaljuyu) personages in the sculptures from the lowlands of this period. The role of God K as patron-protector of ruling families is supported by the association with Itzamna and by the procreative role reflected in the name Bolon Tzacab, with its implications for the continuity of the dynasty.

At Palenque, God K is closely linked to the Temple of the Foliated Cross, where his probable (mythical) birth date (1.18.5.4.0 1 Ahau 13 Mac) is recorded. This temple commemorates the origins and reign of Palenque's ruling lineage.

God K was the patron of Kan days and a year patron.

## YUM KAAX, A MAIZE DEITY (GOD E)

The third deity in frequency of representation in the codices is God E, associated with agriculture (especially maize), who occurs 98 times in the three manuscripts. He is always represented as a youth (frontispiece), sometimes with an ear of corn as his headdress (Fig. 14.5*d*). Occasionally the corn is shown sprouting from the glyph for the day Kan, which is itself the symbol for corn in the codices. Kan was also the day of which this god was the patron. Of all the deities represented in the codices, God E shows the greatest amount of head deformation. His name glyph is his own head, which merges at the top into a highly conventionalized ear of corn, surmounted by leaves.

God E, as patron of husbandry, is shown engaged in a variety of agricultural pursuits. Rulers impersonating God E are occasionally depicted in Classic-period sculpture scattering grains of maize (or drops of blood). Like the maize he typified, he had many enemies, and his destiny was controlled by the gods of rain, wind, drought, famine, and death. In one place he is shown under the protection of the rain god and in another in combat with a death god.

Although the specific name for a maize deity is unknown, in later Postclassic times his identity seems to have merged with that of a more general agricultural deity known as Yum Kaax. Like one aspect of Itzamna and Chac he was benevolent, representing life, prosperity, and abundance.

### YUM CIMIL, A DEATH DEITY (GOD A)

The fourth god in frequency of representation is God A, identified as Yum Cimil (as he is known in the Yucatan), who occurs 88 times in the three codices. He has a skull for a head, bare ribs, and spiny vertebral projections; if his body is clothed with flesh, it is bloated and marked with black circles, suggesting decomposition (Fig. 14.5*e*). The principal accessories of the death deity, his "sleigh-bell" ornaments, sometimes appear fastened in his hair or to bands around his forearms and legs, but more often they are attached to a stiff, rufflike collar. These bells, of all sizes and made of copper or sometimes gold, were found in quantity during the dredging of the Cenote of Sacrifice at Chichen Itza, where they may have been thrown with sacrificial victims (Figs. 13.52*d–f*).

Only Itzamna and God A, his antithesis, have two name glyphs. The first glyph of God A represents the head of a corpse, its eyes closed in death; the second is the head of the god himself, with truncated nose, fleshless jaws, and a flint sacrificial knife as a prefix. A frequent sign associated with God A is not unlike our own percentage sign %. God A was patron deity of the day Cimi, which means "death" in Maya, and of the number ten.

God A appears to have had several manifestations, one of which presided over the lowest of the nine Maya underworlds, Mitnal. God A is frequently associated with the god of war and human sacrifice (God F), and his companions include the Muan bird and the owl, both considered creatures of evil omen and death. Today the Yucatecan Maya believe that Yum Cimil continues to prowl around the houses of the sick, looking for prospective prey.

## AH CHICUM EK, A NORTH STAR DEITY (GOD C)

God C is the fifth most common in the codices, occurring 61 times in the three manuscripts. He has been identified as Ah Chicum Ek, "the guiding star." He is always portrayed with a snub-nosed face and peculiar black markings on his head (Fig. 14.5*f*). He has only one name glyph, which has been likened to the head of a monkey. This head, with a different prefix than that of his own name glyph, is also the hieroglyph for the direction north, thus tending to confirm his association with the North Star. The nature of the occurrences of his name glyph in the manuscripts also indicates that he must have personified some important heavenly body.

In one place the North Star is spoken of as the guide of merchants, which is appropriate because the North Star is the only star in the latitudes of the Peten and Yucatan that does not change its position radically through the year. Merchants are also said to have offered *pom* incense to him at altars along roadsides. He was benevolent and is found in association with the rain god; he was probably patron of the day Chuen.

## EK CHUAH, A MERCHANT DEITY (GOD M)

God M is the sixth most commonly represented deity in the codices, occurring 40 times. He has a large, drooping underlip; he is usually shown painted black (Fig. 14.5*g*), and his name glyph is an eye rimmed with black. God M is usually identified as Ek Chuah, "black scorpion," the black deity of merchants. He appears with a bundle of merchandise on his back like an itinerant merchant, and in one place he is shown with the head of God C, the North Star deity and the guide of merchants. Ek Chuah was also the patron of cacao, one of the most important products traded by Maya merchants. Those who owned cacao plantations held a ceremony in his honor in the month of Muan.

## BULUC CHABTAN, A WAR AND HUMAN-SACRIFICE DEITY (GOD F)

Portraits of God F occur 33 times in the codices, and always in connection with death. His constant characteristic is a black line partly encircling his eye and extending down his cheek (Fig. 14.5*h*). His own head, with the number eleven in front of it, is his name glyph. God F has been identified as Buluc Chabtan, "eleven faster," although other manifestations (or separate deities) with similar functions appear to have existed. God F seems to have been the patron of the Maya day Manik, the sign for which is the grasping hand. He is sometimes shown in company with God A at scenes of human sacrifice. A war god in his own right, he is often shown burning houses with a torch in one hand, while he demolishes them with a spear in the other. The concept of a war god, a god of death by violence and human sacrifice, seems to be embodied in God F.

## IX CHEL, A RAINBOW DEITY (GODDESS I)

Goddess I is often associated with serpents and destruction, perhaps because of her association with the black war deity (God L). But her identification as Ix Chel, "she of the rainbow," implies the more benevolent side, healing, childbirth, and divination (Fig. 14.5*i*). The focal point for the veneration of Ix Chel was Isla de Cozumel, off the east coast of Yucatan.

### OTHER DEITIES PORTRAYED IN THE CODICES

A variety of additional deities are portrayed in the codices, and although some have been classified and described, few enjoy a clear consensus on their identity.

God L, the black war and death deity, is often linked or confused with God M, the black deity of merchants, and at least two additional black-painted deities. God L, identified as the third member of the Palenque Triad, is associated with the Temple of the Sun at Palenque, apparently dedicated to warfare and the underworld. God L's probable (mythical) birth date is recorded in this building as 1.18.5.3.6 13 Cimi 19 Ceh (note that Cimi means "death").

God N often has underworld associations also, and has been identified as Mam, a highland-Maya earth deity, and as Pauahtun, a lowland Maya deity with unknown functions. Often depicted as an old man, God N has been identified on several painted Classic vessels, sometimes accompanied by a retinue of young and beautiful women.

Goddess O, probably named Ix Chebel Yax, seems to have been the patroness of weaving. Other, less well defined female deities also appear in the codices. One of these, often confused with Ix Chel, seems to have been associated with the moon. Ixtab, the suicide deity, is depicted in the Dresden Codex (Fig. 14.5*j*), hanging from the sky by a halter looped around her neck; her eyes are closed in death, and a black circle, representing decomposition, appears on her cheek.

### THE THIRTEEN DEITIES OF THE UPPER WORLD AND
### THE NINE DEITIES OF THE LOWER WORLD

As we have seen, the ancient Maya conceived of their deities as both single and composite entities. Although the Oxlahuntiku, or Thirteen Gods of the Upper World, were regarded collectively as a single deity, they were also considered to be thirteen separate gods; the Bolontiku, or Nine Gods of the Lower World, were regarded in the same fashion.

In certain myths preserved in the *Book of Chilam Balam* of Chumayel, this unity and the composite character of the Oxlahuntiku and Bolontiku are clearly set forth, whereas in the inscriptions of the Classic period the multiple conception of the Bolontiku is repeatedly emphasized. Each of the nine Bolontiku was,

|       |        |       |
|-------|--------|-------|
| First | Second | Third |
| Fourth | Fifth | Sixth |
| Seventh | Eighth | Ninth |

Fig. 14.6. Glyphs identified as representing the nine deities of the lower world.

in turn, the patron of a day of the Maya calendar, and it was believed that these nine gods followed each other in endless succession throughout time. Thus, if God X were patron of the first day, he would again be patron of the tenth day, the nineteenth day, and so forth; if God Y were patron of the second day, he would again be patron of the eleventh, the twentieth, etc. We do not know what the nine Bolontiku looked like, since no representations of them have yet been identified in the codices, but their name glyphs have been identified (Fig. 14.6).

Against an inner wall of Temple 40 at Yaxchilan there seems to have been a row of nine seated anthropomorphic figures, each about two-thirds of a meter high, which may have represented these nine gods, but unfortunately all of them have been destroyed except for their ankles and feet. Along the eastern base of the tower of the Palace at Palenque were found the badly destroyed remains of nine similar figures, but all details by which either series might have been identified have disappeared.

We do not even know the name glyphs for the thirteen Oxlahuntiku, although together with the Bolontiku they must have constituted one of the most important groups of Maya deities. It has been suggested that thirteen of the head-variant numerals of the Maya arithmetical system (all but zero) represent the heads of these gods.

### THE THIRTEEN DEITIES OF THE KATUNS

Each of the thirteen different katuns, or twenty-year periods, had its special patron. Although the names and name glyphs of these gods are unknown, they seem to be shown in the fragmentary Paris Codex, one side of which presents a succession of katuns with their corresponding patron deities. Some of these may be recognized, such as the rain god and the wind god in the representation of Katun 7 Ahau (Fig. 14.7).

### DEITIES OF THE NINETEEN MONTHS

Another group of deities whose names we do not know are the patrons of the nineteen months of the Maya year. Here, however, we do know most of their corresponding name glyphs (Fig. 14.8). Some of these are the signs of heavenly bodies, and others the heads of animals or birds; still others are total mysteries.

### DEITIES OF THE TWENTY DAYS

In addition to the Bolontiku patrons for the Maya days, each day was presided over by a particular deity (Chapter 16). God D was the patron of the days called Ahau, the last and most important day in the twenty-day uinal; God B, of the Ik days; God E, of the Kan days; God A, of the Cimi days; God

Fig. 14.7. Ceremony celebrating the end of the twenty-year period of Katun 7 Ahau (perhaps A.D. 1323–42). Paris Codex, p. 6.

Fig. 14.8. Glyphs identified as representing the deities of the nineteen Maya months.

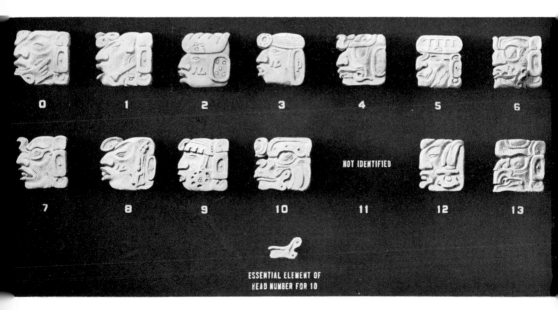

Fig. 14.9. The deity representations serving as head-variant numerals.

C, of the Chuen days; God F, of the Manik days; and Kinich Ahau, of the Muluc days. The remaining thirteen days doubtless had their own patron deities, which have not yet been identified.

### DEITIES OF THE NUMERALS 0-13

Another important series of gods included the patrons of the fourteen head-variant numerals. The numerals are the heads of these fourteen deities, each associated with one of the numbers. God A was patron of the number ten, which is depicted as the fleshless skull of the god himself (Fig. 14.9). God G was the patron of the number four, and God B, patron of the number thirteen. The heads of the numbers one to thirteen inclusive, as already suggested, may be those of the thirteen Oxlahuntiku.

## Rituals and Ceremonies

To the ancient Maya, the main purpose of ritual was the procuring of life, health, and sustenance. A number of early authorities express this idea: "They worship idols . . . in order to petition [the gods] for health and good seasons"; or, in this prayer, "All powerful god, these sacrifices we make to thee and we offer these hearts so that thou mayest give us life and temporal goods." Sacrifices were made "in order to buy food from the gods so that they [the people] might have much to eat."

The gods were invoked and placated by a number of different offices. The rulers of Maya centers performed sacrifices of their own blood, presumably to symbolize the blood of the ruling lineage. Classic sculptures sometimes depict rulers with an implement identified as a bloodletter, used to draw blood from the penis, a ritual of seemingly obvious symbolic meaning for human fertility. Although Landa reports that only men practiced bloodletting, several Classic scenes show elite women drawing blood, often from the tongue (Fig. 4.24, right). The Madrid Codex shows both a man and a woman in the act of drawing blood from their ears (Fig. 14.10). The blood thus obtained, and that from human and animal sacrificial victims, was liberally sprinkled over the idols.

They make sacrifices of their own blood, sometimes cutting the edges [of their ears] in pieces, and thus they left them as a sign [of their devotion]. Other times they pierced their cheeks, other times the lower lips; again they scarify parts of the body; or again they perforate their tongues in a slanting direction from side to side, passing pieces of straw through the holes, with horrible suffering; and yet again they slit the superfluous part of the virile member [the foreskin], leaving it like their ears, which deceived the general historian of the Indies [Oviedo] into saying that they practiced circumcision. . . . The women do not practice these blood-lettings although they were very devout; furthermore, of all things that they have, whether it be birds of the sky, animals of the earth, or fish of the sea, they always anointed the face of the demon {their idols} with the blood of these.

Rulers and other members of the elite seem to have performed these and other rituals in which they impersonated, or perhaps actually assumed the identity of, supernatural powers. A case in point is preserved in the scene depicted on a sculptured panel from Palenque, which is directly parallel to a portion of the Madrid Codex. In the Palenque scene, a human figure, probably a ruler, wears a maize headdress and holds an axe. In the Madrid Codex a figure is portrayed representing the maize deity (God E); he too holds an axe. Similar hieroglyphic inscriptions accompany both scenes and include the same date glyphs, verb, and axe.

According to Landa, almost all important ceremonies began with fasts and other abstinences. They were scrupulously observed, and to break one's fast was considered a great sin. These preparatory purifications, which also included sexual continence, were mandatory for the priests and those who assisted directly in the ceremonies, and voluntary for others. In their fasting, they observed restrictions on flesh foods and the seasonings salt and chili pepper.

Sacrifices were an important part of Maya worship; they ranged from simple offerings of food to the presentation of all kinds of ornaments and valuables to the practice of human sacrifice. The offerings varied according to the urgency of the occasion. If the sacrifice was to cure a sickness or to avert some minor trouble, offerings of food or ornaments might be made. In times of great common need human victims were sacrificed, especially in order to bring rain to such dry areas as the Yucatan.

The burning of incense formed an indispensable part of every ceremony. It was made principally of copal (*pom*), a resin extracted from the copal tree (*Protium copal*) and less frequently of rubber, chicle, and another resin called *puk ak* in Maya; such trees were grown on special plantations. The incense, highly prized for personal use and as an article of trade, was made into small cakes decorated with cross-hatching and painted a bright turquoise blue. Scores of such cakes were recovered in the dredging of the Cenote of Sacrifice at Chichen Itza. The priest's assistants prepared balls of fresh incense, laying them

Fig. 14.10. Bloodletting rituals.
Madrid Codex, p. 95.

out on small boards made for the purpose, as the Lacandon Maya of Chiapas still do today. The incense was then burned in specially shaped pottery vessels, which had the head or figure of some deity modeled on the outside.

*Pom* burns with a fragrant odor. If the hearts of large animals were not available for offerings, Landa says, imitation hearts were sometimes molded out of *pom* incense: "And if they were not able to have large animals like tigers [jaguars], lions [pumas], or crocodiles, they fashioned hearts out of their incense." Landa's statement has been corroborated by the discovery of a human-shaped heart, made of some vegetable substance, in the center of one of the incense cakes recovered from the Cenote of Sacrifice. Faint memories of the ancient beliefs and the holy places linger among modern Maya in remote regions. Until recently the Lacandon still burned *pom* incense in typical Maya incense burners in the principal temple at the ruins of Yaxchilan (Fig. 14.2), and the Maya of eastern Yucatan offered incense in the ruins of Tulum on the east coast of the Peninsula.

Another religious observance was dancing. There were many kinds, varying with the different ceremonies, but social dancing was entirely unknown. Each sex had its own dances, and only rarely did men and women dance together. In one of their war dances some eight hundred dancers took part: "There is another dance [*holcan okot*] in which eight hundred Indians, more or less, dance with small banners, taking long war-steps to the beat [of a drum], among them there is not one who is out of step." In another dance, great skill was shown in catching reeds with a little stick:

One is a game of reeds, and thus they call it *colomche*, which means that. In order to play it, they form a large circle of dancers, whom the music accompanies, and two of them enter the circle in time to the music, one with a handful of reeds with which he dances holding himself upright; the other dancer crouches, both of them always inside the circle. And he with the reeds throws them with all his strength at the other, who with great skill, catches them, by means of a small stick. Having finished throwing, they return in time to their places in the circle, and others go out to do the same thing.

Another sixteenth-century writer wrote, "There were many other dances of which there would be more than one thousand kinds, and they considered this as an extremely important thing and so great a number of people assemble to see it that more than fifteen thousand Indians would gather, and they came from more than thirty leagues [120 km] to see it, because, as I say, they considered it an extremely important affair."

There were many ceremonies for individual and group needs, but a similarity of pattern runs through all of them. All were preceded by fasting and abstinence, symbolic of spiritual purification, and priestly divination always determined the auspicious day for the rite. And the ceremonies themselves shared common features: an expulsion of the evil spirit from the worshipers; incensing of the idols; prayers; and the sacrifice, if possible, of some living thing, animal or human. In the Postclassic era, after the sacrifice the victim's blood was smeared on the idol of the god in whose honor the ceremony was being held. The priests themselves were also smeared with blood, their hair becoming clotted, gory mops. Most of the ceremonies closed with feasting and general drunkenness—according to Spanish sources an inevitable conclusion to every Maya ceremony.

### DIVINATION AND ALTERED CONSCIOUSNESS

The drunkenness reported by the Spanish was undoubtedly related to an aspect of Maya ritual not well described in the ethnohistorical documents: divination, or ritual acts designed to communicate directly with supernatural powers. Divination is used to foretell future events and to determine causes for events otherwise not understood, the reasons for illness, misfortune, and so forth. A variety of divinatory rituals is still practiced by highland-Maya shamans today, including the interpretation of repetitions in the 260-day calendar and, in Mam Maya communities, the casting of *mech*, the sacred red beans (in which an odd count may mean a positive answer, and an even count a negative one). The ancient 365-day Maya calendar certainly served to foretell future events (see Chapter 16). And the Classic-period sculptures that show rulers "sowing maize" may depict divination analogous to the *mech* ritual of present-day Maya shamans.

But the ancient Maya also seem to have used substances that altered the individual's normal state of consciousness, almost certainly as a part of divinatory ritual. Thus the ingestion of narcotics, hallucinogens, and other psychotropic substances was seen as a way to transform existence and to meet or communicate with unseen powers. These experiences could then be interpreted to answer specific questions and determine future events. Psychotropic substances may have been used for other ritual purposes, but divination seems to have been the most important.

The Maya, like most Mesoamerican peoples, made fermented alcoholic beverages, using maize and agave (pulque); especially favored for ritual purposes was the drink balche, made from fermented honey and the bark of the balche tree (*Lonchocarpus longistylis*). Leaves from the wild tobacco plant (*Nicotiana rustica*), much more potent than today's domestic varieties, and other species were rolled into cigars and smoked, inducing a trancelike state. There is a variety of depictions of cigar-smoking in Classic-period contexts from the Maya area.

The Maya highlands are the natural habitat for several mushroom species containing hallucinogens. Stone figures of mushrooms are found in the southern Maya area as early as the Late Preclassic era, as in the Kaminaljuyu tombs (Fig. 3.2). Dictionaries of highland languages compiled immediately after the Spanish Conquest mention several mushroom varieties whose names clearly indicate their use. One type was called *xibalbaj okox*, "underworld mushroom," in reference to the belief in being transported to a supernatural realm. It was also named *k'aizalah okox*, "lost-judgment mushroom."

Other hallucinogenic substances were certainly available to the ancient Maya for divinatory rituals, although their use is not securely documented. These include peyote, the morning glory, the poison gland of the tropical toad (*Bufo marinus*), and perhaps the water lily.

Landa recorded that alcoholic beverages were drunk at every ritual occasion. In the seventeenth century, Thomas Gage reported that the highland Pokomam added tobacco or toads to their fermented beverages to strengthen the result. In earlier times, some of these substances were probably consumed as part of specialized divinatory rituals. During the Classic period at least, these substances were not always administered orally. Several painted pottery vessels graphically depict the use of an enema apparatus in apparently ritual settings; the direct introduction of alcoholic or hallucinogenic substances into the colon results in immediate absorption by the body, thereby hastening the effect.

## HUMAN SACRIFICE

Human sacrifice was performed in several ways; the most common manner in the Postclassic period was according to the Mexican custom of removing the heart (Figs. 14.1*c–f*). Women and children were sacrificed as frequently as men. The intended victim—stripped, painted blue (the sacrificial color), and wearing a special peaked headdress—was led to the place of sacrifice, usually either the temple courtyard or the summit of the pyramid supporting the temple. After the evil spirits were expelled, the altar, usually a convex stone that curved the victim's breast upward, was smeared with the sacred blue paint. The four *chacs*, also painted blue, next grasped the victim by the arms and legs and stretched him on his back over the altar. The *nacom* advanced with the sacrificial flint knife and plunged it into the victim's ribs just below the left breast. Thrusting his hand into the opening, he pulled out the still-beating heart and handed it to the *chilan*, or officiating priest, who smeared blood on the idol to whom the sacrifice was being made. If the victim had been sacrificed on the summit of a pyramid, the *chacs* threw the corpse to the court below, where priests of lower rank skinned the body, except for the hands and feet. The *chilan*, having removed his sacrificial vestments, arrayed himself in the skin of the victim and solemnly danced with the spectators. If the sacrificial victim had been a valiant and brave soldier, his body was sometimes divided and eaten by the nobles and other spectators. The hands and feet were reserved for the *chilan*, and, if the victim was a prisoner of war, his captor wore certain of his bones as a mark of prowess.

Archaeological corroboration of this ceremony was found several times in the wall paintings at Chichen Itza (Fig. 14.1*e, f*). One such scene portrays a human

Fig. 14.11. Sacrificial knife from the Cenote of Sacrifice, Chichen Itza

sacrifice to Kukulcan, the feathered serpent, patron deity of the center. A lower coil of the serpent-god's body forms the sacrificial altar, while the upper coils and the head rise in front of the doorway of his temple. Only two *chacs* are shown, perhaps because of the difficulty of drawing one figure directly behind another. The *chilan* stands between the altar and the god, his upraised hand holding the sacrificial knife. Several of these knives have been recovered from the Cenote of Sacrifice. One has a blade of finely chipped flint and a handle of wood, carved in the likeness of two intertwined serpents, their bodies overlaid with gold (Fig. 14.11).

In other representations of human sacrifice the victim's breast is shown already opened. Rising out of it is a portrayal of the dead man's soul, conceived in one case as a tree ascending toward the heavens, a bird perched on its branches (Fig. 14.1c).

A bow and arrow were also used in human sacrifice:

If he [the victim] was to be sacrificed by arrows they stripped him naked and anointed his body with a blue color, and put a pointed cap on his head. When they had reached the victim, all of them, armed with bows and arrows, made a solemn dance with him around the stake, and while dancing they put him up on it and bound him to it, all of them keeping on dancing and looking at him. The foul priest in vestments went up and wounded the victim with an arrow in the parts of shame, whether it were a man or woman, and drew blood and came down and anointed the face of the idol with it. And making a certain sign to the dancers, as they passed rapidly before him [the prisoner] still dancing, they began one after another to shoot at his heart, which had been marked beforehand with a white sign. And in this manner they made his whole chest one point like a hedgehog of arrows.

This type of sacrifice is depicted in an incised drawing from the walls of Temple II at Tikal (Fig. 14.12), most likely scratched there long after the center had been abandoned. Probably imported from central Mexico in late Postclassic times, the same ceremony is also shown in the Mexican codices.

But human sacrifice was clearly practiced during the Classic period, as evidenced by sculptured scenes and other depictions. An example of auto-sacrifice by cutting the throat is depicted on a ceramic vessel recovered by archaeological excavations at Altar de Sacrificios. The significance of the sacrificial scene in the funeral ritual can be interpreted using the information recorded during careful excavation (see Chapter 12 for a résumé of this interpretation).

Fig. 14.12. Graffiti from Temple II, Tikal, showing sacrifice by arrow or spear.

A glimpse of a most gruesome form of human sacrifice was recently discovered in the excavations of Group G at Tikal. There, in a building buried by later construction, well-preserved graffiti dating from the Late Classic era were revealed. These graffiti include finely executed black-painted glyphs and motifs incised in the plaster walls. One scene vividly depicts a man who, his hands tied to a post behind his head, has been disemboweled.

An unusual ceremony of human sacrifice was practiced in the Cenote of Sacrifice of Chichen Itza during the Postclassic, and perhaps in earlier periods as well. In times of famine, epidemic, or prolonged drought, victims were hurled into this great pocket in the limestone. More or less oval in shape, the Cenote of Sacrifice (see Fig. 11.72) averages about 50 m wide (165 ft) and is some 20 m (65 ft) from ground level to the surface of the water. The depth of the water averages another 20 m, and the sides of the well are either vertical or undercut. Pilgrimages were made from great distances to attend these sacrifices, and valuables were hurled into the well with the living victims in order to appease the angry rain gods. The cenote is connected with El Castillo, the principal temple dedicated to Kukulcan, by a stone causeway 300 m long and 6 m wide, varying in height from 1 to 4.5 m above ground level. Wrote Landa,

Into this well they have had, and then [middle-sixteenth century] had, the custom of throwing men alive, as a sacrifice to the gods in times of drought, and they believed they did not die though they never saw them again. They also threw into it many other things, like precious stones and things that they prized. And so if this country had had gold, it would be this well that would have the greater part of it, so great was the devotion which the Indians showed for it.

This prediction has been confirmed by archaeology. In 1905–8 the Peabody Museum of Archaeology and Ethnology of Harvard University carried on dredging operations in the Cenote of Sacrifice, bringing to the surface a treasure of sacrificial offerings. These articles include masks, cups, saucers, gold and copper repoussé plates, and gold jewelry. Many copper sacrificial bells of different sizes were found, and small ceremonial axes. There were numbers of

polished jade beads, as well as carved jade ornaments, sacrificial knives, and
several throwing sticks. Fragments of cotton textiles were found, and ornaments
of carved bone and shell. There were also about 50 human crania and numerous human long bones. Some of the bones were carved, perhaps for use as
trophies of war. Most numerous of all were the cakes of *pom* incense, usually
found in the bottoms of crude pottery vessels and painted a bright turquoise
blue. Study of the gold and copper objects found in the Cenote of Sacrifice
indicates that they were brought to Chichen Itza from points as far distant as
Colombia and Panama to the south and from as far north as Oaxaca and the
Valley of Mexico.

In addition to appealing to the gods by these offerings and human sacrifice,
worshipers extracted a prognosticative element from these ceremonies. The
victims, especially children, their hands and feet unbound, were thrown into the
Cenote by their masters at daybreak. If any survived the plunge, a rope was
lowered at midday to haul them out, and the children were asked by the lords
what manner of year the gods had in store for them. If a child did not survive
the ordeal, "all that lord's people [that is, the retainers of the child's master] as
well as the lord himself threw large stones into the water and with great hue and
cry took flight from there."

### THE THIRTEEN KATUN ENDINGS

An old and important ceremony, probably with Mexican origins and introduced at Tikal during the Early Classic era (see Chapter 4), was the erection of
the katun stone, or monument, at the end of each katun, or 7,200-day period.
Each of the thirteen differently named katuns had its own patron deity and its
special rites. Although this ceremony started as a katun-ending rite during the
Early Classic period at some central lowland sites such as Uaxactun in 357
(8.16.0.0.0), it soon came to be celebrated twice each katun, at the halfway
point and at the end. The celebration at the intermediate lahuntun, or 3,600-
day-period ending, was of less ceremonial significance. In a few centers of the
Classic era, notably Quirigua and Piedras Negras, the quarter-katun endings
(the hotun, or 1,800-day-period endings) were also commemorated. In late
Postclassic times, however, when a number of contemporary sources made
reference to this ceremony, it was again celebrated only on the katun endings.

One of the most constant features of the ceremony, and one which persisted
for nearly twelve centuries (357–1519), was the erection of a monument,
usually inscribed with hieroglyphics giving the date and additional historical
information. The most elaborate version of the katun ceremony was celebrated
at Tikal during the Classic period. A series of katuns were marked at that site
not only by the construction of sculptured monuments, but by an entire
architectural complex, the Twin Pyramid Group, constructed especially for the
occasion (see Chapter 11).

The Late Postclassic version of the ceremony was spelled out by Landa. Katun 7 Ahau, for example, possibly represented on page 6 of the Paris Codex (Fig. 14.7), ran from 1323 to 1342. During the first half of this 7,200-day period (1323–32), the idol of Katun 7 Ahau ruled alone in the temple, after having been a guest there for the ten years preceding his actual rule. During the second half (1332–42) the idol of the following katun, 5 Ahau (who was to rule from 1342 to 1362), was placed in the same temple as a guest and was shown respect as the successor. In 1342, when the rule of 7 Ahau was finished, his idol was removed and the idol of 5 Ahau was left to rule alone for ten years (1342–52). Thus the idol of each katun was worshiped for 30 years: the first decade as the guest of his predecessor, the second decade when he ruled alone, and the third decade when he shared the rule with his successor.

### NEW YEAR CEREMONIES

Another important group of ceremonies centered around the Maya New Year. At the time of the Spanish Conquest the Maya year-bearers, the days upon which a New Year could begin, were Kan, Muluc, Ix, and Cauac (in earlier times, other sets of days had been year-bearers). Each was associated with one of the cardinal points: Kan years with the east, Muluc with the north, Ix with the west, and Cauac with the south. The New Year ceremonies began in the closing five days of the preceding year; the five days of the last month, Uayeb, were unlucky days, when everyone stayed at home lest misfortune befall. The celebrations corresponding to the four kinds of Maya New Years, although differing in details, follow the same general pattern. (For a résumé of the ceremonies and dances of the Maya year, see Table 13.)

*Kan years.* The New Year ceremonies for Kan years began during the five closing days of the preceding, or Cauac, year. A pottery idol of the god Kan U Uayeb was set up temporarily on a pile of stones at the south entrance to the town, because south was the cardinal point of the dying Cauac year. A lord was chosen at whose house all the feasts connected with the ceremony were to be held, and there the idol of Bolon Tzacab (God K), who was to be patron of the new Kan year, was erected. Next the whole community went to the south entrance where the idol of Kan U Uayeb had been set up, and there the priest offered it an incense mixture of ground corn and *pom*; cutting off the head of a turkey, he offered the fowl to the idol. The idol, amid rejoicing and dancing, was then carried to the house of the lord who was donor of the feast. Here the idol of Kan U Uayeb was placed in front of that of Bolon Tzacab, and many gifts of food and drink were offered to them. Afterward these offerings were distributed among those present, and the officiating priest was given a haunch of venison. The devout drew blood from their ears and smeared the idols with it, offering heart-shaped loaves of cornmeal and squash seeds to the idol of the New Year.

The two idols were kept at the lord's house for the five days of Uayeb. It was believed that failure to incense them regularly during this period would be followed by the special sicknesses that afflicted mankind during Kan years. As soon as the five Uayeb days had passed, the idol of Bolon Tzacab, patron of the Kan year, was taken to the temple; that of Kan U Uayeb was set up at the east gate, east being the cardinal point associated with Kan years. Here the idol of Kan U Uayeb stood until the end of the Kan year. Kan years were considered good ones "because the Bacab Hobnil who ruled with the sign Kan, they said, had never sinned as had his brothers [especially the two who presided over the Ix and Cauac years], and it was on this account that no calamity came to them in it [a Kan year]."

Later in the year, if misfortunes began to happen, the priests ordered another idol to be made and erected to Itzamna (God D). This was placed in the temple; three balls of rubber were burned before it, and a dog, or if possible a human, was sacrificed to it. This sacrifice was effected by hurling the victim from the summit of the pyramid onto a pile of stones in the court below. The heart was removed and offered to the new idol, together with gifts of food. This second ceremony closed with a dance given by the old women of the community, dressed in special garments. Landa says that this ceremony was the only one celebrated in a temple at which women could be present.

*Muluc years.* In Muluc years, which followed Kan years, the idol Chac U Uayeb was taken to the east entrance where the idol of Kan U Uayeb had been left the year before. The same ceremonies were repeated, but in Muluc years the idol set up in the house of the lord chosen to give the feast was Kinich Ahau, the sun deity (God G). The same dances were performed, offerings of food and incense were made, and when the five unlucky days were over, the idol of Chac U Uayeb was carried to the north entrance and set up on one of the two piles of stone. Muluc years were thought to be good years because the Bacab who presided over them was believed to be "the best and greatest of the Bacab gods." If Muluc year turned out badly, however, the priests turned to the god Yax Cocay Mut, "the green firefly pheasant," whose image was made and worshiped. The special evils that were prone to happen in Muluc years were a scarcity of water and an abundance of sprouts in the corn. The old women had to perform a special dance on high stilts (Fig. 14.13) and to offer pottery dogs bearing food on their backs.

Fig. 14.13. Person on stilts, associated with Muluc-year rituals, Madrid Codex, p. 36.

## TABLE 13

### Yucatecan Maya Ceremonies of the Postclassic Period, According to Bishop Landa

| Month | Patron of month | Name of ceremony | Patron god or gods | Object of ceremony | Group or groups participating in ceremony | Kind of dance |
|---|---|---|---|---|---|---|
| Pop | Jaguar | | All gods | New Year rites and renewing all utensils | General | |
| Uo | God of Number 7 | *Pocam* | Itzamna | Ascertaining prognostications for the year | Priests, physicians, sorcerers, hunters, fishermen | *Okot uil* |
| | | | Ix Chel, Itzamna, Cit Bolon Tun, Ahau Chamahes | Appealing to these gods of medicine for their help | Physicians, sorcerers | *Chan tuniab* |
| Zip | A serpent god | | Acanum, Suhui Dzipitabai | Appealing to these gods of the hunt for successful hunting | Hunters | |
| | | | Ah Kak Nexoy, Ah Pua, Ah Cit Dzamal Cum | Appealing to these gods of fishing for successful fishing | Fishermen | *Chohom* |
| Zotz | Bat | No special ceremonies reported; devoted to preparation for that of the following month | | | | |
| Tzec | God of the Day Caban (?) | | Four Bacabs, but especially Hobnil, Bacab of Kan years | Appealing to the god of bees for an abundance of honey | Owners of beehives | |
| Xul | Unknown | *Chic kaban* | Kukulcan | Blessing of the idols | General | |
| Yaxkin | Sun | No special ceremonies reported; devoted to preparation for that of the following month | | | | Sacred |

| | | | | | | |
|---|---|---|---|---|---|---|
| Mol | An old god (?) | *Olob zab kamyax* | All gods | Anointing all utensils with sacred blue ointment | General | |
| | | | Four Acantuns | Flowers for the bees | Owners of beehives | |
| | | Idol-making ceremonies continued | | Making new idols of the gods | Individual having new idols made for him | |
| Chen | Moon | | | | | |
| Yax | Venus | *Ocna* | Chacs | Renovating the Temple of Chac | General | |
| Zac | God of the uinal (twenty-day time period) | | Acanum, Suhui Dzipitabai | Appeasing the gods of the hunt for having shed blood in the chase | Hunters | |
| Ceh | New fire | No special ceremony reported | | | | |
| Mac | A young god (?) | *Tupp kak* | Chacs, Itzamna | Securing rains for the corn and a good year | Old men | |
| Kankin | Unknown | No special ceremony reported | | | | |
| Muan | A young god (?) | | Ek Chuah, Hobnil | Ensuring a successful year for the cacao plants | Owners of cacao plantations | |
| Pax | A god with a Roman nose | *Pacum chac* | Cit Chac Coh | Obtaining victory in war | Warriors | *Holcan okot* |
| Kayab / Cumku | A young god (?) unknown | *Sabacil than* | | Pleasure and diversion | General | Unknown |
| Uayeb | Unknown | | Chac (red) U Uayeb, Sac (white) U Uayeb, Ek (black) U Uayeb, Kan (yellow) U Uayeb | Preparing for the New Year ceremonies, one for each of the four kinds of years: Kan, Muluc, Ix, and Cauac | General | |

*Ix years.* In Ix years the idol Sac U Uayeb was erected at the north entrance of the town and a statue of Itzamna, the patron of the Ix year (God D), was set up in the house of the lord selected to give the feast. The same series of rites was performed; at the end of a Muluc year the idol of Itzamna was carried to the temple and that of Sac U Uayeb to one of the piles of stone at the west gate. Ix years were considered unfavorable: people were especially prone to fainting fits and eye troubles; and there were supposedly more hot suns, drought, famine, thefts, discord, changes of rulers, wars, and plagues of locusts. If any of these calamities occurred, the priests ordered an idol made to Kinich Ahau (the sun aspect of Itzamna), and again the old women executed a special dance.

*Cauac years.* In Cauac years an idol called Ek U Uayeb was made and carried to the west entrance of the town, and another of Uac Mitun Ahau was placed in the house of the lord who was giving the New Year's feast; the same ceremonies followed. Uac Mitun Ahau was lord of the sixth hell of the underworld. When the ceremonies had been performed, the idol of Uac Mitun Ahau was carried from the house of the lord to the temple, and the idol of Ek U Uayeb was carried to the south entrance of the town, where it was installed for the coming year.

Cauac years were considered the most dangerous of all; they were years when heavy mortality was to be expected, as well as hot suns, flocks of birds, and swarms of ants to devour the young seeds. But again the priests came forward with their remedy. This time the people had to make idols of four gods—Chic Chac Chob, Ek Balam Chac, Ah Canuol Cab, and Ah Buluc Balam—which were installed in the temple; one ceremony required burning a huge fire of fagots and dancing among the embers on bare feet.

Throughout the year other ceremonies were celebrated to propitiate various gods, in order to obtain rain or good harvests and to ensure success in hunting, trading, war, and other activities. Most of these have long since been forgotten, and only a few of the most important are discussed here.

## CELEBRATIONS OF THE VARIOUS MONTHS

*The month of Pop.* On the Maya New Year's Day, the first day of the month of Pop, which fell on July 16 of the year 1556 in the Julian calendar (July 26 of the Gregorian calendar), a solemn renovation ceremony was held in which all the articles in daily use were renewed. Houses were swept clean and old utensils were thrown out upon the town refuse pile. The four *chacs* who were to serve the priest for the ensuing year were chosen, and the priest himself prepared the balls of incense for the New Year ceremony.

*The month of Uo.* During this second month, the priests, physicians, sorcerers, hunters, and fishermen celebrated festivals in honor of their respective patron gods. A priest consulted the sacred books to learn the auguries for the coming year, and after feasting and drinking, the festivities closed with a dance in honor of the month. The special ceremonies of these five vocations were continued into the following month, Zip.

*The months of Zotz and Tzec.* During the fourth month, Zotz, the owners of beehives began to prepare for their feast, which was held in the following month, Tzec. Their divine intercessors were the four Bacabs, and Hobnil, the Bacab who was patron of the Kan years, was their special friend. Incense was burned and pictures of honey were painted on the incense boards. The object of the feast was to increase the yield of honey, and the owners of hives contributed an abundance of it, from which a wine was brewed with the bark of the balche tree; heavy drinking of this beverage concluded the ceremony.

*The month of Xul.* On the sixteenth day of the sixth month, one of the most important festivals of the Maya year was celebrated, in honor of Kukulcan. This ceremony was formerly observed all over Yucatan, but after the fall of Mayapan in 1441 it was held only at the Xiu capital of Mani. Other provinces sent gifts, among them the magnificent banners of featherwork used in the rite.

People from surrounding towns and villages assembled at Mani on the day of the feast, having prepared for it by preliminary fasting and abstinences. At evening a great procession of lords, priests, common people, and clowns (a special feature of the celebration) set out from the house of the lord who was giving the feast and proceeded to the Temple of Kukulcan. The exorcisms and prayers were made, the feather banners were broken out from the summit of the temple pyramid, and the participants spread out their personal idols of wood and clay in the court in front of the temple. A new fire was kindled, incense was burned, and offerings were made of food, cooked without salt or chili pepper, and of a beverage composed of ground beans and squash seeds.

The lords and all those who had fasted stayed at the temple for the remaining five days and nights of the month, making offerings to their idols, praying, and performing sacred dances. During these five days the clowns passed among the houses of the well-to-do, playing their comedies and collecting gifts, which were divided among the lords, priests, and dancers. The banners and idols were then gathered up and taken to the house of the donor lord; from there each participant departed for his own home. It was believed that Kukulcan himself descended from heaven on the last day of the feast to receive the offerings of the worshipers. This feast was called *chic kaban*, which may mean "clown-named."

*The months of Yaxkin and Mol.* During the seventh month, Yaxkin, preparations were made for another general ceremony in honor of all the gods, which was celebrated in the eighth month, Mol, on a day fixed by the priests. It was called, according to Landa, *olob zab kamyax*, which is probably a corruption of the Maya phrase *yolob u dzab kamyax*, meaning "they wish to administer the receiving of the blue color." After the people had assembled in the temple and the exorcism and incensing had been carried out, the principal object of the ceremony, which was to anoint everything with the sacred blue ointment, was begun. All sorts of utensils and even the doorjambs of the houses were smeared with blue ointment. The boys and girls of the town were assembled, and the backs of their hands were struck nine times to make them skillful in the occupations of their parents. An old woman, called the *ixmol*, or "conductress," did this for the girls, and a priest did it for the boys. The beekeepers also celebrated a second festival in the month of Mol in order that the gods should provide flowers for the bees.

Another important ceremony was held in Mol, or in some other month if the priests found that the omens of Mol were not propitious. Called "making gods," it was the occasion for making the wooden idols. The sculptors who carved these idols were fearful of their own art, since it was thought very dangerous to make representations of the gods. They consented to do it with great reluctance, fearing that some member of their families would fall ill or die. As soon as the sculptor who was to make the idols had been selected, the priest, the four *chacs*, and the sculptor began to fast. The man for whom the idols were to be made built a thatched hut in the forest, cut the wood from which the idols were to be carved, and installed a covered pottery urn so that the idols could be decently kept under cover.

The wood used was always the same—cedar, the most easily carved of all native woods. The Maya word for cedar is *kuche*, which means "god tree," perhaps because such idols were made from it. Incense was taken to the hut to offer to four gods, called Acantuns, each of whom presided over one of the cardinal points. Instruments for scarification were provided, and tools for carving.

The priest, the *chacs*, and the sculptor were shut up in the hut and went to work, first cutting their ears and smearing the images of the Acantuns with blood, incensing, and praying. This was kept up until the idols were finished, while the man for whom they were being made carried food to the hut. Complete sexual abstinence was required of all, and no outsider was allowed to approach the place.

*The month of Chen.* By the next month, Chen, the idols were finished. The man for whom they had been made paid the priest, *chacs*, and sculptor with gifts of food and beads, and removed the idols to an arbor in his own yard. Here the priest and sculptor cleaned themselves, and the priest blessed the idols with prayers. The evil spirits having been exorcised and incense burned, the idols were wrapped in cloth, placed in a basket, and turned over to the owner, who received them with great devotion and reverence. The ceremony, as usual, closed with feasting and drinking.

*The month of Yax.* A renovation ceremony, already described in connection with the rain god, Chac (God B), was celebrated in the month of Yax. Clay idols and incense burners were renewed, probably with ceremonies similar to those described in connection with the making of wooden idols.

*The month of Zac.* During this eleventh month, the hunters again celebrated a festival like the one in the month of Zip, to make amends to the gods for any blood they might have shed in the chase. Any bloodshed, except in sacrifice, was believed to be an abomination for which atonement had to be made.

*The months of Ceh and Mac.* There is no special ceremony described for the twelfth month, Ceh, but in the next month, Mac, the old men celebrated a feast in honor of the four Chacs and Itzamna (God D). This was called *tupp kak*, or "the killing of the fire." A great hunt was organized, in which many animals and birds were caught. On the day of the ceremony these were brought to the courtyard of the temple, where a great pile of fagots was set up. After the usual exorcisms and incensing, the animals and birds were sacrificed and their hearts thrown into the fire. When the hearts were consumed, the *chacs* extinguished the fire and the ceremony proper began. For this feast only the lord who gave it was obliged to fast. All assembled in the court of the temple, where a stone altar had been built with a stairway on one side. When the altar had been ceremonially purified, mud was smeared on the bottom step and the sacred blue ointment on the other steps. Incense was burned, and the Chacs and Itzamna were invoked with prayers and offerings; eating and drinking closed the ceremony. The *tupp kak* was celebrated in order to obtain a year of good rains; the month Mac fell in the latter part of March and early April, not long before the beginning of the rainy season, and it was thought that the ceremony would ensure plentiful rain for the corn.

*The months of Kankin and Muan.* No special ceremony is reported for the fourteenth month, Kankin, but in the following month, Muan, a festival in honor of Ek Chuah (the merchant and cacao deity, God M) and Hobnil (Bacab of the Kan years) was celebrated by owners of cacao plantations. A dog with cacao-colored spots was sacrificed on one of the plantations, incense was burned, blue iguanas, blue feathers, and game were offered to the idols of these gods, and the long pods of the cacao beans were given to each official who participated in the rite. When the offerings and prayers were over, the ceremony closed with the usual feasting and drinking, but this time without drunkenness. Landa says, "there were three drinks of wine for each one and no more."

*The month of Pax.* In the month of Pax there was a ceremony called *pacum Chac*, "the recompensing of Chac," in honor of the god Cit Chac Coh, "Father Red Puma." Judging from the nature of the ceremony, this god was a patron of warriors. This was a general ceremony; the lords and priests of the smaller towns and villages went to the larger centers, where the celebration was held in the Temple of Cit Chac Coh. Sometime before the fifth day preceding the festival, everyone went to the house of the war captain, the elected *nacom*, and with great pomp bore him in a palanquin to the temple, where he was seated and incensed. The next five days were spent in offering prayers, gifts, and incense at the temple and in feasting, drinking, and dancing the *holcan okot*, or dance of the warriors. Then the ceremony proper began, and since it was a rite to secure victory in war, it was celebrated with great solemnity.

The ceremony opened with the same sacrifices by fire as practiced in the month of Mac, which were followed by prayers, offerings, and incensing. The lords carried the *nacom* on their shoulders in his palanquin around the temple, incensing him as they went. A dog was sacrificed and its heart offered to the idol of Cit Chac Coh. When the *chacs* opened a large jar of wine, the festival was over. The other celebrants escorted the *nacom* back to his home, where everybody but the *nacom* himself got ceremoniously drunk. The next day the *nacom* distributed quantities of incense among the participants in the feast, and urged them to observe all the festivals of the coming year with diligence and fidelity in order that the year should be prosperous.

*The closing months of Kayab, Cumku, and Uayeb.* The strenuous program of religious ceremonies in the first sixteen Maya months dictated a need for some relaxation before the exacting rites of the New Year began. The lighter festivities, held during the last three months—Kayab, Cumku, and Uayeb—were called the *sabacil than* and were celebrated in this manner:

They sought in the town among those who were the richest for someone who would be willing to give this festival, and advised him of the day, in order that these three months that remained before the New Year should have more diversion. And what they did was to assemble in the house of him who gave the festival, and there they performed the ceremonies of driving out the evil spirit, and burned copal [pom] and made offerings with rejoicings and dances, and they made wine-skins of themselves, and this was the inevitable conclusion. And so great was the excess which there was in the festivals during these three months that it was a great pity to see them, for some went about covered with scratches, others bruised, others with their eyes enflamed from much drunkenness, and all the while with such a passion for wine that they were lost because of it.

In judging Landa's constant complaints about the drunkenness of Maya ceremonies, it must be remembered that every observance of the ancient religion was anathema to him. The bishop's observations about the drunken orgies with which he says these ceremonies always concluded should probably be taken with a grain of salt.

**15**

# LANGUAGE AND WRITING

America, say historians, was peopled by savages; but savages never reared these
structures, savages never carved these stones . . . standing as they do in the depths of
a tropical forest, silent and solemn, strange in design, excellent in sculpture, rich in
ornament . . . their whole history so entirely unknown, with hieroglyphics explaining
all, but perfectly unintelligible. . . . No Champollion has yet brought to them the
energies of his inquiring mind. Who shall read them?
—John Lloyd Stephens (1841, Vol. I: 104, 158, 160)

There are today about 2.5 million speakers of 28 Mayan languages. Except for
the Huastecs of Veracruz and San Luís Potosí, they occupy a compact zone in
the Mexican states of Chiapas, Tabasco, Campeche, Yucatan, and Quintana
Roo, in most of Guatemala, and in parts of Belize, Honduras, and El Salvador
(Fig. 15.1). Many are at least minimally bilingual in Spanish, and all Mayan
languages have been influenced by (and have influenced) Spanish. Nevertheless, a Mayan language is still the language of the home for most of the Indians
of this area. Despite the Conquest, and centuries of social change, the Mayan
languages have survived well: although a few have become either extinct or
nearly so, others (e.g., Kekchi) are actually expanding in number of speakers
and territory.

Studies of the modern Mayan languages and their colonial antecedents
provide a rich source of historical inferences about the ancient Maya. Most
directly, they provide crucial tools for the decipherment of Maya writing. They
provide much more, of course, but these are the aspects emphasized in this
chapter.

## History of the Mayan Languages

The Mayan language family takes its name from the Maya language of
Yucatan, which is now commonly referred to by scholars as Yucatec. The
Mayan languages are so similar that the propriety of grouping them as a
language family is readily apparent, and was recognized in colonial times.

As their geography suggests, the Mayan languages (except Huastec) have
been in contact with each other for many centuries, and often grade into each

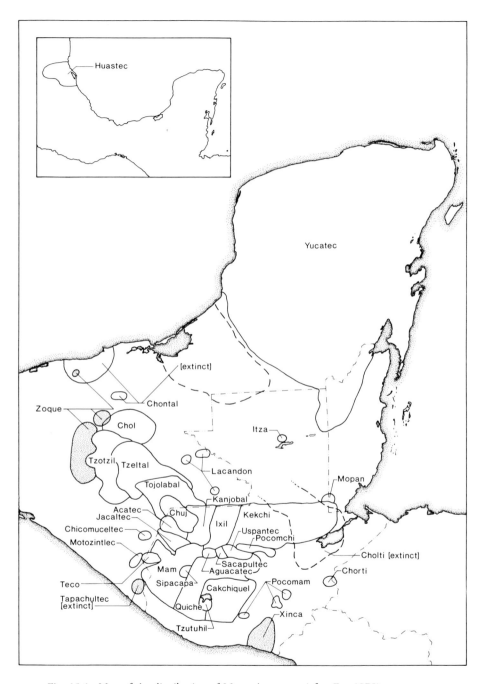

Fig. 15.1. Map of the distribution of Mayan languages (after Fox 1978).

other just as the environmental zones of the area do (Chapter 1). Changes have spread from one language to another in different degrees of penetration according to social factors that pertained at various times. It is therefore impossible to assign all Mayan languages to unequivocal places on a family tree; this is so partly because not enough is known of their linguistic history, but also because a family tree does not adequately represent their complex relationships. It is possible, however, to provide a weighted subgrouping (Fig. 15.2) that permits some historical inferences.

Linguists generally recognize three major subgroups of Mayan: Huastecan, Yucatecan, and the rest of Mayan (which we may call "Southern Mayan"). It is commonly supposed that Proto-Mayan first diverged into Huastecan and the ancestor of the other Mayan languages, and that the latter then diverged into Yucatecan and Southern Mayan. At first inspection, it seems obvious that Huastecan is the most remote subgroup; it certainly is separate spatially, and this is consistent with the relatively small amount of vocabulary that Huastecan shares with other Mayan languages. Indeed, Huastecan was the last major subgroup to be recognized as a part of the Mayan family. Recently, however, several linguists have pointed out that Huastecan shares many phonological innovations with the Tzeltalan-Cholan subgroup, and this occasions some hesitation in accepting the antiquity of Huastecan. Such a radical revision of its position would imply that its sharply divergent vocabulary is due to an intense, recent influence from non-Mayan languages.

But assuming a Proto-Mayan speech community that became differentiated through migration or some other social disruption, and assuming also that the resulting communities (say, the antecedents of Huastecan and the rest of Mayan) themselves eventually diverged, and so on, whether according to a neat family tree or not, how can such differentiations be dated, and where did these early communities live? Where no direct historical evidence is available, the first question is usually answered impressionistically, by an intuitive comparison of the amount of change to be accounted for with the amount of change that has occurred in language families for which there *is* such evidence, e.g., Romance or Germanic.

However, attempts are now being made to quantify both the amount and rate of linguistic change. In one technique, known as *glottochronology*, it is posited that an original basic vocabulary that is relatively immune to borrowing (i.e., body-part terms, kin terms, numerals, pronouns, etc.) will tend to be replaced in the original meanings by new words at a constant and universal rate (derived from the rate of change in Romance; roughly 80 percent of this basic vocabulary remains after one millennium). The degree of separation of languages can therefore be given an absolute time depth by collecting the relevant words from each language, noting the percentage of shared cognates, and applying the retention rate in a simple formula.

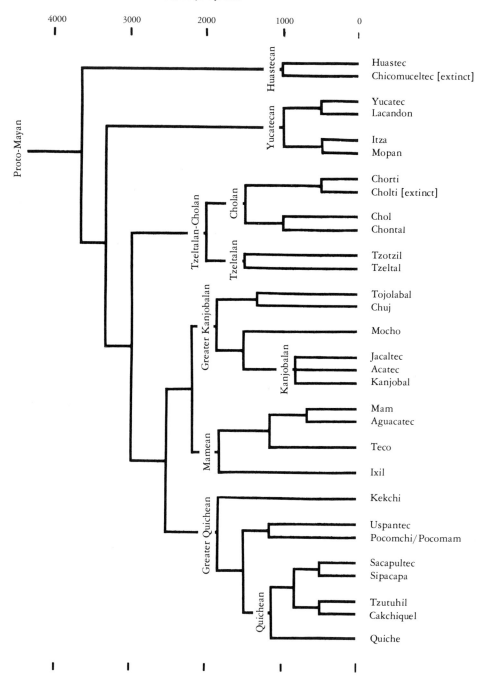

Fig. 15.2. Subgrouping of the Mayan languages.

Though the assumptions are vulnerable to many criticisms, and the results therefore are at best only approximations, such calculations have been carried out for Mayan several times, and tend to be in agreement on an important point: all the major Mayan subgroups (i.e., Huastecan, Yucatecan, Tzeltalan-Cholan, Greater Kanjobalan, Mamean, and Greater Quichean) appear to have become distinct between about 2000 B.C. and A.D. 100, that is, during the Preclassic era (see Chapter 2). Lesser distinctions (e.g., among the Cholan languages) arose later.

The location of the Proto-Mayan homeland has also been the subject of some inquiry, and the conclusions here are just as speculative. According to the principles pioneered by Edward Sapir, the greater the degree of differentiation present, the longer the period of time we should assume for the development of that differentiation, other factors remaining equal. The geographical center of gravity is determined by postulating a homeland requiring the least possible number and distance of migrations to get the major divisions to their current locations. As we noted above, however, problems persist in the determination of Mayan subgrouping. Generally, Mayanists remain convinced that the homeland was in the Guatemala-Chiapas highlands. This conclusion is based on the relative lack of differentiation in Yucatecan, given its remote genetic position and large area, and on the comparatively greater differentiation in the highlands. But in this case other factors are pertinent; the greater differentiation in the highlands may also be due to terrain barriers (compare Fig. 15.1 with the physical map, Fig. 1.1), and conversely, the linguistic homogeneity of Yucatan may be partly due to the more passable terrain there.

The homeland issue has in some cases (e.g., Indo-European) been addressed through comparison of the reconstructed vocabulary of the protolanguage with the natural environment at the time insofar as that can also be reconstructed. If one can demonstrate that ancestral words referred to natural items whose ancient ranges were quite limited, an area may then be indicated within which the speech community must have resided or with which it had other very close contact. Using such techniques it is easy to show that the ancient Maya inhabited an area in Mesoamerica, but that determination is of course trivial. A more precise location is sought, but for several reasons it is quite difficult to obtain for the ancient Maya. In addition to the usual problems of determining the ancient meanings of words and natural environments, we are faced with the distinctive geography of southern Mesoamerica. Its flora and fauna are associated not so much with particular areas as with particular elevations, and the Maya speech communities, well adapted as they were to this situation, tended to inhabit several ecological zones within a relatively small horizontal area or to engage in intense trade back and forth, so that all are likely to have been familiar with words for natural objects that were themselves narrowly delimited.

The few cases that have been made also point to the highlands as the Proto-

Mayan homeland, but these arguments are not without weaknesses. At the end of the nineteenth century Karl Sapper used the Proto-Mayan word *tyax, for which he reconstructed the meaning "pine," to rule out the Yucatec lowlands as a part of the Proto-Mayan homeland. According to Sapper, the pine (several species of which have a high resin content, and are used throughout the highlands for tinder and torches) does not, and very likely did not, occur in Yucatan. Yucatec still has a descendant (or *reflex*) of the ancestral word, namely *tah* "torch"; Sapper explained this as a natural consequence of the Yucatec migration, which left the Yucatecs with no referent for *tah* other than what was originally only one of many in its semantic range. The weakness, even if one accepts Sapper's opinion concerning the ancient range of the pine, is that the highland meanings could have been extensions from "torch" in a migration going the other way. More evidence is needed before this approach can be said to implicate one area conclusively. Similar studies have shown some promise for establishing more precise dating of linguistic innovations by correlating loan-words with the archaeologically verified introduction of the objects.

Mary Haas recently characterized a reconstructed protolanguage as a "glorious artifact"; for the purposes of cultural as well as geographical inference, this holds especially for the reconstructed vocabulary. The meanings of the reconstructed words tell us much about early society and culture, and much of this information is not amenable to archaeological investigation. Not unexpectedly, the Proto-Mayan speech community had a rich vocabulary for maize agriculture, with separate words for generic maize, the green ear, the mature ear, the cob, maize flour, maize dough, the tortilla, a toasted maize drink, the grindstone, and for the first, second, and third (increasingly fine) grindings of maize. The earliest word for slaked lime (used in softening maize and giving consistency to the dough, as well as for processing other foods) was closely related to the word for ashes, suggesting that ashes may have preceded slaked lime in this function. Alternatively, since limestone is not found in most highland areas, this may be additional evidence of a highland origin for Mayan. Expectably, there was also a weaving complex (to weave, the spindle, cotton, etc.).

Most of the cognates that provide the evidence for reconstructing the maize complex in Proto-Mayan vocabulary are shared by most Mayan languages, and have obviously not been readily replaced through borrowing or other processes. Other strong cognate sets also seem to indicate culturally important items: salt, chile, bean, squash, sweet potato, sweet manioc, avocado, tobacco, honey, etc. Finally, terms reflecting material culture and social structure are well represented: sling, blowgun, hammock, bridge/ladder, sharpening stone, fireplace stones (trivet), plate, varnish worm (crushed insect used for lacquer), bench, mat, sandal, comb, to write, book, mother's brother, sister's son, etc.

Since 1861, when E. G. Squier first suggested that Zoque is related to Yucatec, it has become clear that the adjacent Mixe-Zoquean family (Mixe, Sayula Popoluca, Sierra Popoluca, Zoque, and Tapachultec; for the last two, see

Fig. 15.1) forms a higher-order linguistic family with Mayan. Though some scholars still believe that the striking similarities are due entirely to borrowing, many of the cognates and correspondences now proposed are not likely to have been due to contact. In particular, there is deep grammatical evidence for the relationship, including several Mayan kinship and body-part terms that contain fossilized pronominal prefixes identical to the reconstructed pronouns of Mixe-Zoquean. This is not to say there was no borrowing between these groups, for there certainly was. Much like the impact of Norman French on English, the borrowing was between related languages; consequently, arguments for either common descent or borrowing must take into account both possibilities. But the genetic classification of Mayan with Mixe-Zoquean is of only marginal relevance to our understanding of the ancient Maya, for the divergence between these ancient families must have been great even by the Early Preclassic. The borrowing between the two groups almost certainly took place in the Preclassic, and reflects an extraordinary cultural influence of the Mixe-Zoqueans on the Maya, since most of the borrowing was in that direction. Terrence Kaufman has noted the close correspondence between the current distribution of Mixe-Zoquean languages and the distribution of Olmec archaeological sites, and proposed that the Olmec were speakers of a Mixe-Zoquean language. The identification of the archaeological Olmec with early Mixe-Zoquean speech communities certainly explains the influence of Mixe-Zoquean on Mayan, for archaeology has indicated that the Olmec exerted such influence (see Chapter 2).

Most Mayan languages also have at least a small number of loanwords from Nahuatl (the language of the Mexica, or Aztecs) and closely related languages; these loanwords presumably reflect the rising prominence of the central Mexican states from the Late Preclassic on.

The early Maya were not just receivers of cultural influence, however. Lyle Campbell has shown that Xinca, a nearly extinct non-Mayan language of southeastern Guatemala, has a fairly large number of loanwords from Mayan, reflecting a cultural influence of the Maya on the Xinca comparable to that of the Mixe-Zoqueans on the Maya.

The same techniques used in the dating and geographical location of early Mayan have been applied, with considerably more reliability, to the issue of the linguistic identity of the Classic Maya. Until recently, the former heartland of Classic lowland Maya civilization—the central Peten and upper Usumacinta drainage—had been largely depopulated, because the massive extermination and forced resettlement of the Acalan Chontal, the western and eastern Chol, and various Yucatecan-speaking groups in late colonial times effectively removed what small population had remained after the Classic period. Now the Itza, Lacandon, and Mopan, who are thought to have entered the Peten long after the Classic, and who partly escaped the colonial depopulation, have been joined by scattered settlements of Kekchi and Spanish speakers, and the area is enjoying a vigorous in-migration. But what were the languages of their predecessors in this region?

Hyacinthe de Charencey, Karl Sapper, and William Gates independently established the close relationship of modern Chorti, Chol, and Chontal in a Cholan subgroup of Mayan that may well have begun to diversify in Classic times. Sapper and, independently, J. Eric Thompson concluded that the modern distribution of the Cholan languages, and the large number of Cholan loanwords in Kekchi (which absorbed some colonial Cholan resettlements and is today expanding into the Peten), indicates the former existence of a belt of Cholan speakers from the Laguna de Términos through the Usumacinta and Pasión drainages to the Golfo Dulce on Guatemala's Caribbean coast and the area around Copan still occupied by the Chorti. This belt of Cholan was confirmed with Gates's discovery of a colonial manuscript dictionary from the now-lost village of Delores, generally supposed to have been somewhere near the Lacantun and Ixcan rivers in southwestern Peten (i.e., in the middle of the belt). This dictionary was of the now-extinct Cholti language, which was virtually a dialectal variant of Chorti, as the names suggest.

It seemed justified, therefore, to infer that Cholan, perhaps already dialectally differentiated, was the language of the Classic Maya heartland. John Justeson and James Fox have recently proposed from inscriptional evidence that Cholan was indeed the language used at several sites (Palenque, Dos Pilas, Aguateca, Copan) along the southern edge of the proposed belt, but they also show that Yucatecan was being used much farther south than anticipated, namely, in Piedras Negras, Bonampak, Yaxchilan, Seibal, and Naranjo. Tzeltalan, too, is at least geographically implicated as a language that may have been used at highland Chiapas sites, but it has not yet been possible to distinguish it hieroglyphically. Inscriptional evidence is the only hope for such precise definition of ancient language borders, since place names are mostly new in the depopulated area and give no evidence of the language of the earlier inhabitants.

Notwithstanding our subgrouping of Mayan (Fig. 15.2), in which Yucatecan is shown as only distantly related to Cholan and Tzeltalan, these language families have been geographically adjacent to one another for a long time, during which their speakers shared the cultural advancements of Classic Maya civilization. They had a significant influence on each other, especially in loanwords and writing, and for this reason they may be treated as a cultural subgroup, which may be termed Greater Lowland Mayan.

## The Structure of Mayan Languages

Although the study of Mayan linguistic structures is relevant to many disciplines, including theoretical linguistics, we are here concerned mostly with those aspects that have been directly applicable to the decipherment of Maya writing. The focus, therefore, will be on the structures of the Greater Lowland Mayan languages, and upon those features of linguistic structure that are most relevant

TABLE 14
*Yucatec Sounds and Transcription*

| CONSONANTS | Labial | Dental | Palatal | Velar | Glottal |
|---|---|---|---|---|---|
| Plain stops | p | t | | c | ʔ (doubled vowel) |
| Plain affricates | | tz | ch | | |
| Glottalized stops | p' (pp) b | t' (th) | | k | |
| Glottalized affricates | | tz' (dz) | ch' | | |
| Spirants | | s | x | | h |
| Nasals | m | n | | | |
| Lateral | | l | | | |
| Semiconsonants | w (u) | | y | | |

| VOWELS | Front | Central | Back | | |
|---|---|---|---|---|---|
| High | i | | u | Length | V: (not marked in traditional transcription) |
| Mid | e | | o | High pitch | V́ |
| Low | | a | | Low pitch | V̀ |

NOTE: Unlike some phonetic alphabets, this Spanish-based traditional orthography sometimes uses more than one letter for a single distinctive sound. Sounds used only in Spanish loanwords are omitted from this table. Yucatec has two glottalized stops in the labial position; these differ in the type of glottalization (explosion versus implosion). The symbol "V" represents any of the five vowels of Yucatec. Colonial Yucatec had the velar spirant *j* as well as *h*, but they were not differentiated in transcription; modern Yucatec has only *h*. Where colonial orthography differed from the transcription used here (as in the old use of both *s* and *z* for our *s*), the most common versions are placed here in parentheses following the modern symbol. See also "A Note on Names and Pronunciation" in the front matter.

to decipherment. In so restricting ourselves we miss much, but unavoidably; the field is large, and even the most cursory general summary would require a volume in its own right.

The sound systems of the Mayan languages, like other aspects of their structure, show close similarities. We are perhaps best served by the example of Yucatec, since so many Yucatec words have become traditional in Maya scholarship. The Modern Yucatec sound system (Table 14) includes five vowels, each of which may be either short or long. Yucatec is also one of the few Mayan "tone" languages: its long vowels carry distinctive pitch, which may be either rising-falling or low-level, marked with acute and grave accents, respectively.

Yucatec has eighteen consonants, some of which involve a feature that is not unusual in the languages of the world as a whole, but is unfamiliar to English speakers: the "glottalized" consonants. These are made like their non-glottalized ("plain") counterparts, except that simultaneously, or nearly so, the vocal folds of the larynx are closed tightly. The release of this closure has a phonetic effect that is often heard as "explosive" and "guttural," both of which terms accurately describe part of what is going on. All Mayan languages have plain and glottalized series of consonants, though some have more than others. Mayan languages also have a "glottal stop," which is simply the closing and blowing apart of the vocal folds without accompanying oral articulation. English has this same sound, but it is used only expressively (it is the "constricted" sound in expressions like "uh-uh" and "oh-oh"), whereas in Mayan it distinguishes words as a normal consonant. The Cholan languages have essentially the same sounds as Yucatec, though they do not have distinctive pitch. Chorti also has the consonant *r*, which is lacking in Yucatec (except in Spanish loanwords and, in some dialects, as a predictable alternant, or allophone, of *l*).

One of the main tasks of the early colonial friars, who became fluent in Yucatec and other Mayan languages, was to devise an orthography so that these languages could be written down in dictionaries, sermons, catechisms, legal documents, etc., without recourse to the seemingly cumbersome (and dying) indigenous writing. The systems they developed were based on Spanish spelling augmented by a few new letters and various small marks, or "diacritics," attached to the old letters. These systems ignored some distinctions in the native languages (notably, in Yucatec, distinctive pitch), but were effectively (if sometimes inconsistently) used and survive today in scholarly works as traditional spellings of Mayan words. These have been modified for use with modern type fonts, but are essentially direct descendants of the colonial versions. A traditional orthography is used in this book, except in representing sounds not distinguished by traditional spelling (see Table 14 and "A Note on Names and Pronunciation" in the front matter).

The root morphemes (that is, the roots of words) of Mayan are of interest from the points of view of both theoretical linguistics and decipherment. They are generally regular in their sound structure, consisting predominantly of three sounds, namely a consonant ($c_1$) followed by a vowel (v), followed by a consonant ($c_2$); that is, they have the shape $c_1vc_2$. There are statistical tendencies governing the consonants that co-occur within the same morpheme. From the point of view of Maya writing, we will see below that the cvc structure of Mayan root morphemes presented some challenges to the inventors of the Maya syllabary.

Mayan languages are polysynthetic; i.e., there is a high ratio of morphemes per word, and one complex word may often express what we know in English as a complete sentence.

Typical Mayan word order, reflected in both written pre-Columbian texts and spoken language, is verb-object-subject in transitive sentences, verb-subject in intransitive sentences. Mayan verbs are accompanied by pronominal markers of subject and object, even if there are separate nouns serving these functions. In Mayan languages the pronominal markers are of two basic types, the *ergative*, used for possession and the subject of transitive verbs, and the *absolutive*, used for the object of transitive verbs and the subject of intransitive verbs. Their use contrasts with that of English pronouns, which are differentiated according to whether they represent subject, object, or possessor, without regard to the nature of the verb. In a pseudo-English version of Mayan, it is as if one were to say "*my* father" (possessor) and "*my* shot the turkey" (transitive subject), but his struck *me*" (transitive object) and "*me* slept" (intransitive subject). Compare

TABLE 15
*Yucatec and Chol Expressions with English Translation Equivalents*

| | English | Yucatec | Chol |
|---|---|---|---|
| **INTRANSITIVE** | | | |
| 3rd person subject | he slept | *wèːn-Ø-i* "sleep"-3rd person absolutive-demonstrative | *wäy-ä-Ø* "sleep"-past-3rd person absolutive |
| **TRANSITIVE** | | | |
| 3rd person subject | he wrote the book | *t-u-tz'iːb-ah-Ø huʔn* past-3rd person ergative-"write"-perfect-3rd person absolutive "book" | *t-i-tz'ihb-ä-Ø hun* past-3rd person ergative-"write"-past-3rd person absolutive "book" |
| **POSSESSIVE** | | | |
| 3rd person possessor | her father | *u-yùːm* 3rd person ergative-"father" | *i-tat* 3rd person ergative-"father" |

NOTE: Chol has six vowels: *i, e, a, o, u,* and *ä*; the last is a high central vowel derived historically from short *a*.

the expressions in Yucatec and Chol with their translations in English (Table 15), noting the pronoun usage ("Ø" indicates that the absence of a marker is significant, and implies the third person).

Mayan languages thus distinguish between actors in transitive events and actors in intransitive events, and treat transitive verbs and possessive constructions similarly. This type of structure, called "ergative," is quite common in the languages of the world, though its specific mode of expression (through pronouns, case, etc.) may vary. Many Mayan languages are ergative only in some grammatical constructions, "accusative" (i.e., English-like) in others; Yucatec, for example, is not ergative in the present, present progressive, and future tenses, or in subordinate clauses. This "split" ergativity is common. From the point of view of decipherment, the importance of Mayan ergativity, with the split in its implementation, lies in the probability that it will be observable in the ancient texts, and indeed, the ergative third-person pronominal prefix *u* has been identified.

Given the Maya preoccupation with calculations, it is important to understand Mayan numeral systems, which were among the most interesting and rarest in the world. We describe here the systems as they were recorded in colonial times; they have since become more like Spanish. The colonial numeral systems were *vigesimal* (base twenty) rather than *decimal* (base ten); that is, the Maya counted by twenties, four hundreds, eight thousands, etc. (see Chapter 16), rather than by tens, hundreds, and thousands, and their numeral expressions reflect this. In English, we find new words (ten, hundred, thousand, etc.) at the appropriate decimal multiples, with combinations of these and the numerals below ten filling in the intervening counts except eleven and twelve, which are fossils from former expressions meaning "one left over" and "two left over." In Mayan languages, we find the new words at the vigesimal multiples (twenty, four hundred, eight thousand, etc.). The Mayan numerals one through nineteen, however, were quite like our own, with unique numerals up to and including ten, and the "teens" produced as combinations of one through nine with ten. Use of a lesser base for lower numerals in a high-base system like a vigesimal one is common in world systems, and obviously functional, since it reduces the number of unique lower numerals needed. The Greater Lowland Mayan languages had unique numerals through twelve, astonishingly like English; the etymology of their "eleven" is obscure, but their "twelve" differed from the structure of thirteen through nineteen only in employing an archaic morpheme order.

What was rare about the Mayan systems was not their vigesimal base or subordinate decimal base, but their use of an *anticipatory* method of counting above twenty. This is best explained by example. Instead of saying the Mayan equivalent of "twenty-one" (21), "twenty-sixteen" (36), or "two-twenty-nine-teen" (59), as we might expect by analogy with our own system, the Maya used numeral phrases equivalent to "one going on two-twenty" (21), "sixteen going on two-twenty" (36), and "nineteen going on three-twenty" (59).

The Mayan system was capable of an efficient expression of very large numbers, and one might hope to find it in the hieroglyphic texts, except that the Maya adopted a written notation that was even more efficient, and used a modified vigesimal base in calendrical records. With only two exceptions (both in the Dresden Codex), Mayan numerals have not been found "spelled out" in the pre-Columbian texts.

Another feature of the grammar of both colonial and modern Mayan numerical expressions is that one of a large class of words, termed *numeral classifiers*, is inserted between the numeral (or other quantifier, such as "many," "some," etc.) and the thing numbered. This word encodes information about the shape, position, or size of the numbered object(s); a pseudo-English equivalent would be something like "four arranged-in-a-straight-line stones," where our hyphenated phrase stands for a single Mayan numeral classifier. Such classifiers are obligatory in the expression, though there are several general classifiers that can be used when the speaker does not wish to be so precise. A few numeral classifiers have been identified in Maya writing, and these seem to be of the generic, or less discriminating, type.

The obligation to encode for shape and position in Mayan does not stop with numeral classifiers. Mayan languages also have special conjugations for *positional* verbs, that is, a class of verbs that refer to various ways of taking position, for example, Chorti *a?-cha-wan* "he-lies-(positional)." The positional suffix *-wan* in our example has been identified in the hieroglyphic texts. In addition, Mayan languages employ demonstrative pronouns and adjectives that make fine distinctions in the distance and direction of movement of their referents. Such grammatical concern for the semantics of space is not uncommon in the languages of the world, though it perhaps strikes us as unusual. We may infer that this sort of information was and is important in the culture of the speakers, whether Classic or not; but no studies have confirmed this independently of language.

Finally, Mayan languages in colonial times had well-developed systems for personal names and titles, including two morphemes (the masculine and feminine *proclitics*, also found in modern Mayan languages) that began male and female names, hereditary and occupational titles, and titles of place of origin. They were also found, usually in a diminutive sense, as the first morphemes of many animal and plant terms. Both have been identified in the inscriptions. Mayan languages did not distinguish gender in the pronouns, as does English, but they did so in such titular expressions and in kinship terms.

Dictionaries of Mayan languages, sometimes highly specialized, appear frequently, and attest to the richness of the modern vocabularies. Some of the earliest colonial dictionaries were also the most comprehensive, and these are invaluable in decipherment, since they reflect language closer to the actual time the hieroglyphic texts were written, and preserve terms that have been lost in the spoken languages since the colonial era. Mayan vocabularies have been subjected to intensive investigation, especially with an eye to making cultural and cognitive inferences about the speakers. For example, there are comprehensive treatises on the botanical and zoological nomenclatures of several Mayan languages, as well as specialized works on numeral classifiers, color terminology, and kinship terminology. Studies of colonial dictionaries have achieved considerable success in reconstructing culture through vocabulary, and much of this work has been of great value in the decipherment and interpretation of Classic Maya texts.

The Mayan languages today are parts of sophisticated local repertoires of verbal and nonverbal communicative strategies, and some studies now emerging promise to elucidate these matters in a way that will also benefit research into ancient Maya civilization. In many areas the Maya still use poetic and ritual language reminiscent of the discourse structure of the pre-Columbian codices. John Fought has recently demonstrated how the structure of modern Chorti folklore follows many of the ancient poetic conventions found in the *Popol Vuh* (see below). We are learning more about Maya discourse, especially in the Tzeltalan area, site of the productive Chicago and Harvard Chiapas projects. There are monographs on Tzotzil folklore, tales, dreams, gossip, and humor, and growing collections of tales, dreams, and ritual discourse in many Maya areas. John Du Bois has studied gestural systems among the modern Maya of highland Guatemala, and these have already suggested hypotheses for the origins of sign values in some of the many hand-form signs of Maya writing.

It must be emphasized that most of these studies, from phonological to ethnographical, were not made with the sole or even major purpose of learning

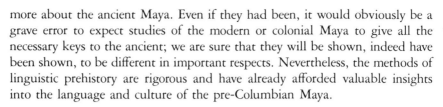

more about the ancient Maya. Even if they had been, it would obviously be a grave error to expect studies of the modern or colonial Maya to give all the necessary keys to the ancient; we are sure that they will be shown, indeed have been shown, to be different in important respects. Nevertheless, the methods of linguistic prehistory are rigorous and have already afforded valuable insights into the language and culture of the pre-Columbian Maya.

## Maya Documents of the Colonial Period

One of the first concerns of the Spanish friars after the Conquest was to teach the Maya to write their own languages, using the letters of the Spanish alphabet and a few innovations. The natives were supposed to use this new writing only for Christian purposes, but they managed to record in it a considerable number of native prophecies, myths, rituals, current events, synopses of their own history, and petitions to the Crown.

During the century following the Conquest, many of these native manuscripts were written in Yucatan. The most important were the *Books of Chilam Balam*. The *Chilan* (the final *n* changed to *m* before a following labial consonant like *b*) were native seers, a class of priests or shamans. *Balam*, meaning literally "jaguar," was an honored personal name as well as a title in pre-Columbian and colonial Yucatan. Ralph Roys believed that Chilam Balam was an individual seer whose fame was so great (because he prophesied the coming of the white man) that many local communities named their accounts after him. These books, kept by local religious leaders, were distinguished from each other by the addition of the name of the town where each was written. Only a few of them have survived. The most important are the *Books of Chilam Balam* of Mani, Tizimin, Chumayel, Kaua, Ixil, and Tusik, and the Codex Pérez, which is a nineteenth-century compilation of rescripts from others that are now lost.

For history, the most significant sections of the *Books of Chilam Balam* are the *u kahlay katunob*, the "count of the katuns" (the katun was a unit of 20 tuns, or 20 × 360 days) or native chronicles, which briefly set forth the leading events of the Yucatec past in the context of a belief in the cyclic nature of history. Five such historical accounts are preserved: one in the Mani, one in the Tizimin, and three in the Chumayel *Books of Chilam Balam*. The astrological and numerological almanacs found in the *Books of Chilam Balam* strongly resemble those in the pre-Columbian books (see below), and we have little doubt that these colonial manuscripts are at least partly translations of pre-Columbian sources, the originals of which are now lost. However, it is also clear that there is much purely colonial influence in the *Books of Chilam Balam*, including Spanish loanwords and concepts. Moreover, each account was influenced by the political motives of the rulers of the respective towns. In short, the interpretation of the *Books of Chilam Balam* is subject to the usual historiographical concerns of cultural and personal bias, and the same is true of the other colonial (and pre-Columbian) documents.

There was also a rich colonial literary tradition among the Quichean peoples of the highlands of Guatemala. The *Popol Vuh* ("book of the mat") of the Quiche state is not only the single most outstanding Maya literary work, it is one of the truly great products of all Native American literature and oral tradition. A brilliant poem of over nine thousand lines, the *Popol Vuh* preserves a coherent cosmogony, mythology, and traditional history of the Quiche, one of the most powerful peoples of the Guatemalan highlands (see Chapter 6). The elegance of the language and the literary style of the *Popol Vuh* emphasize the loss we and the Quiche have suffered in the annihilation of Quiche learning during the colonial period. The poetic structure of the *Popol Vuh* is essentially semantic and grammatical rather than phonetic. Little use is made of rhyming, alliteration, or meter; rather, elaborate couplets, triplets, etc., are built up of semantically and grammatically parallel lines. The mythology of the *Popol Vuh* has been used as a key to the interpretation of Classic Maya funerary ceramic vessels, which bear elaborate depictions of a complex world of the dead that in many cases have direct parallels in the *Popol Vuh*. The themes of the *Popol Vuh* and the ceramic vessels were also depicted in Izapan, Mixtecan, and Central Mexican iconography.

The *Popol Vuh* was evidently written in sixteenth-century Utatlan, the Quiche capital, by a Spanish-trained native Quiche, very probably using a combination of oral and written (pre-Columbian) sources. It shows some evidence of colonial Spanish influence. The manuscript was evidently copied several times; the original was lost by the mid-1800's. We owe the discovery of our copy of this manuscript, which is now in the Newberry Library in Chicago, to a keen and enthusiastic nineteenth-century student of Mesoamerican prehistory, the Flemish Abbé Charles Brasseur de Bourbourg, one-time parish priest of Rabinal, Guatemala. If Brasseur had given us only the *Popol Vuh* his fame would have been secure, but we are also indebted to him and the local collectors who helped him for the discovery of (to name only the most significant) the *Annals of the Cakchiquels* (a short but otherwise *Popol Vuh*–like history of the Cakchiquel state); the *Rabinal Achi* (a Quiche dance-drama that Brasseur learned was still known by the people of his parish; he paid out of his own pocket for a last performance, during which he wrote detailed notes, later published); the Tro portion of the Madrid Codex; the only surviving copy of Bishop Diego de Landa's *Relación de las cosas de Yucatán*; and the *Diccionario de Motul*, an enormous colonial Yucatec dictionary. These works, together with other fragmentary colonial documents from both the highlands and the Yucatan Peninsula, provide a priceless source of information about Postclassic Maya language, history, social and political institutions, religion, and other facets of a long-vanished way of life.

## Ancient Maya Writing

Scholars have traditionally considered the use of writing to be one of the hallmarks of civilization, and the ancient Maya writing system is often and justly hailed as one of the most significant achievements of the pre-Columbian New World. By allowing its users to keep relatively permanent records, writing greatly increases the efficiency of the transmission and accumulation of knowledge from generation to generation. The ancient Maya, for example, were able to record seasonal and astronomical information over long periods of time, and these records contributed to the development of accurate calendars and to impressive breakthroughs in their understanding of astronomical events and mathematics.

Civilization does not presuppose such an advanced record-keeping system, however. The Maya developed writing to an extraordinary peak, but theirs was not the only Native American writing system. The Postclassic Mixtec and Mexica (Aztec) states recorded a large body of historical and commercial information using essentially pictographic writing systems far less tied to their spoken languages than the Maya system was to theirs, and these scripts, like that of the Maya, were but the latest in a long tradition of writing going back to the Mesoamerican Preclassic. In fact, the Mixtec and Mexica systems had the advantage (over a more language-bound one like that of the Maya) that they could be read by speakers of different languages, once a few basic orthographic conventions were understood. This is precisely the advantage of modern Chinese writing over phonetic systems. The latter, of course, have their own advantages (including ease of learning and efficiency), but it is important to realize that the interethnic flexibility of the Mixtec and Mexica systems made them efficient for handling the trade and tribute records of these expanding states. Similarly, the Inca *quipu* system, which many scholars consider to have been at best a marginal form of writing, was well adapted for the bookkeeping functions of a state that was more centralized than any other in pre-Columbian America.

In fact, the most eminent scholars of the mid-twentieth century believed until recently that the surviving Maya texts were devoted entirely to astronomy, astrology, and calendrics, in spite of colonial accounts that spoke of pre-Columbian Maya histories, genealogies, medical texts, treatises on plants and animals, and maps. As recently as 1950, J. Eric Thompson asserted that the Maya did not record history on their stone monuments, and could describe the Maya as "excelling in the impractical, yet failing in the practical." Sylvanus Morley was generally so unconcerned with noncalendrical glyphs that he did not draw them in his records of inscriptions. These scholars had their precursors in men like J. T. Goodman, who also believed that the stone monuments would not yield records of "a single historical event," but the general nineteenth- and early twentieth-century view was that the texts contained undeciphered historical records. In Herbert Spinden's words, which have proved remarkably accurate,

> we may expect to find in the Mayan inscriptions some hieroglyphs that give the names of individuals, cities, and political divisions and others that represent feasts, sacrifices, tribute, and common objects of trade as well as signs referring to birth, death, establishment, conquest, destruction, and other fundamentals of individual and social existence.

Later scholars, understandably swept up in the rapid progress being made in deciphering the astronomical and calendrical parts of the inscriptions, became more and more inclined to the view that what remained to be deciphered would prove to be of the same nature. Similarly, traditional scholarship rejected early colonial assertions that there was a phonetic component in Maya writing.

All that is changed now. With recent advances in the decipherment of Maya hieroglyphs, it can be stated with certainty that the suppositions of the earlier scholars, based partly on colonial accounts, were correct. Many ancient Maya texts, especially those from the Classic period, deal with historical events in addition to calendrical and other esoteric matters. Thus, like the records of ancient Egypt, Sumer, and other early states, they deal with the histories of specific centers and the reigns of their rulers, their political fortunes, genealogy, marriages, alliances, and conflicts. The recognition of this historical information has significantly altered our understanding of Maya civilization.

It is also certain that Maya writing had a phonetic component, and that the relative importance of phoneticism increased with time. Thus, Maya writing was not static, and great progress has been made in elucidating its principles and their origins. Our increased understanding of the nature of Maya writing, notably the phonetic component, offers crucial evidence for future decipherment, and a new approach to understanding the history of several Mayan languages—the first for which we have significant pre-Columbian documentation. In both the sociocultural and linguistic senses, then, advances in decipherment have begun to move the study of the ancient Maya from the realm of prehistory to that of history.

## Pre-Columbian Maya Texts

Knowledge of Maya writing did not long survive the Spanish Conquest, owing to the diligence of church and government officials who rooted out any manifestations of this visible symbol of "paganism." Landa, in a passage that ironically accompanies his invaluable eye witness description of Maya writing, described his own role in its suppression: "We found a large number of books in these characters and, as they contained nothing in which there were not to be seen superstition and lies of the devil, we burned them all, which they regretted to an amazing degree, and which caused them much affliction." Most of the

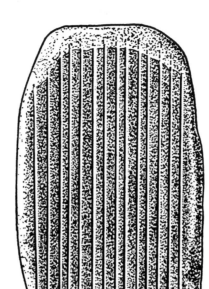

Fig. 15.3. A stone bark beater from Seibal, Guate-mala; natural size.

books that escaped deliberate destruction eventually succumbed to neglect and the ravages of the climate.

By extraordinary good fortune, however, early colonists sent a few books to officials and friends in Europe. Three of these pre-Columbian Maya books, dated to the Postclassic, have survived to the present day. They are now known as the Dresden, Madrid, and Paris codices (a codex is an important manuscript volume), named for the cities where they now reside. The Maya codices, of which there were once whole libraries, were made of paper manufactured from the inner bark of several species of the amate (Yucatec *kopo²*), or native fig tree (*Ficus cotonifolia, F. padifolia*), pounded into a pulp and held together with natural gums as a bonding substance. This paper was also used for costumes, and as a receptacle for blood in bloodletting rites. Ancient stone bark beaters— hand-sized, oblong, and with closely spaced parallel grooves (see Fig. 15.3) —have been found in great numbers in Maya archaeological sites. Bark beaters of wood may also have been used, as they are still among the Jicaque Indians of Honduras.

Each sheet of book paper was made in a long strip and folded like a screen. The individual leaves of the Madrid Codex average about 23 cm high by 9 cm wide (9 by 4 inches), those of the Paris Codex about 22 cm by 12.5 cm. The Dresden Codex is a little smaller and more regular, with leaves about 20.4 cm by 9 cm. A coating of fine white lime was applied to both sides of the paper sheet, and on the smooth finish thus obtained were painted a number of columns of glyphs and, often in bright colors, various pictures of gods, animals, and other objects evidently involved in ceremonies or other activities. The pages were divided into horizontal sections by red lines, and the order of reading was usually from left to right, top to bottom, remaining in the same horizontal section through one to as many as eight folds, then descending to the next section. The books were thus organized into chapter-like sections, and since they were painted on both sides, read all the way along one side of the strip, then turned and read along the reverse. They were bound between decorated boards, and when completely opened were quite long. The Madrid Codex is the longest, at 6.7 m (22 ft) with 56 leaves (112 pages); the Dresden Codex is 3.5 m (11 ft) long and has 39 leaves (78 pages, 4 of them blank); and the Paris Codex, which is only a fragment, is 1.45 m (4.8 ft) long and has 11 leaves (22 pages). There have been several facsimile editions of each codex.

The Dresden Codex was bought for the Dresdener Bibliothek in 1739 by its director, Johann Christian Götze, who found it in a private library in Vienna. Its earlier history is unknown. Since it was obtained in Vienna, and since Austria and Spain had a common sovereign at the time of the Conquest, the book may well have been sent back to the emperor Charles V by some priest or soldier (we know that Cortés himself sent examples of Mesoamerican books to Charles V in 1519). Charles V's residence was in Vienna; much of the Moctezuma treasure (originally gifts to Cortés) and the five letters from Cortés to Charles V were eventually discovered there. By the early 1800's, the Dresden Codex had fallen into three parts, leading to early confusion in pagination. Now in the Sächsische Landesbibliothek in Dresden, East Germany, it suffered some water damage as a result of bombing during World War II, but has been restored. A sample page has been shown in Fig. 14.3.

The Paris Codex was rediscovered by León de Rosny in the Bibliothèque Nationale at Paris in 1859, in a basket of old papers in a chimney corner, its existence apparently forgotten after earlier discoveries in the 1830's and in 1855. It was wrapped in a piece of torn paper with the word "Pérez" written on it, which led to its earlier name, Codex Peresianus (now changed to prevent confusion with the Codex Pérez described above, which is also owned by the Bibliothèque Nationale). The Paris Codex, which is only a small fragment of the original book, is in much worse condition than the other two codices. The lime coating has eroded away at the page margins, taking with it all the pictures and glyphs except those in the middle of the pages. A sample page is shown in Fig. 15.4.

The Madrid Codex, divided into two unequal parts, was found in Spain in the 1860's. Although both parts were found at different places, León de Rosny discovered early in the 1880's that they were parts of the same original manuscript. The larger section, found in 1866 by Brasseur de Bourbourg in the

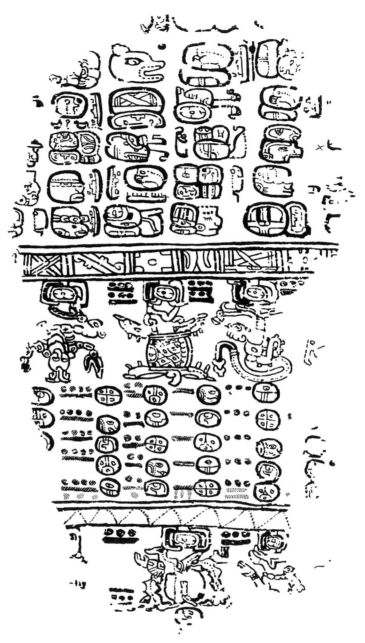

Fig. 15.4. Paris Codex, p. 24, one of two pages depicting the Maya zodiac. Of the seven zodiacal animals originally found on this page (there were thirteen in all), three are clear—the scorpion, turtle, and rattlesnake in the middle section—and a fourth, probably a bat, is preserved in the lower section. Note the right-facing human/deity and animal heads in the glyphic text, one of the unusual examples of right-to-left reading order.

possession of Professor Juan de Tro y Ortolano, of Madrid, was given to Brasseur for publication and for some time went under the name of Manuscrit Troano, or Codex Tro. The smaller part belonged to José Ignacio Miro, who had acquired it from Juan Palacios (who had offered to sell it to the Bibliothèque Nationale in 1867) and sold it in 1875 to the Museo Arqueológico in Madrid, which now owns both parts. The second part was supposed to have come from the province of Extremadura and was first called the Codex Cortesianus under the assumption that it had been brought there by Cortés. Since the conqueror of Yucatan, Francisco de Montejo, and many of his soldiers were from Extremadura, one of these men may have brought the whole codex from Yucatan. The combined sections, for some time known as the Codex Tro-Cortesianus, are now known as the Madrid Codex. A page is shown in Fig. 15.5.

The Dresden Codex can be characterized as a treatise on divination and astronomy. The Madrid Codex, likewise, is devoted to horoscopes and almanacs to assist the Maya priests in their divinations and ceremonies, but it contains fewer astronomical tables. What we have of the Paris Codex is also ritualistic, one side being completely devoted to a katun sequence and its patron deities and ceremonies; it also contains a depiction of the still poorly interpreted Maya zodiac (Fig. 15.4). All three codices, therefore, are of a similar nature, and contain little if any history.

Internal evidence from the codices points to origins in Yucatan. According to J. Eric Thompson, most of the glyphic and iconographic associations in the Dresden Codex are with central and eastern Yucatan, especially Chichen Itza, which he considered the most likely point of origin. He believed the book to be a product of the early thirteenth century, though it, like the other two, was probably at least partly copied from earlier books. Günter Zimmermann found evidence for the work of eight different scribes in the Dresden Codex.

Both the Paris and Madrid codices show stylistic associations with the murals of Tulum and those recently found at Tancah, both on the east coast of Yucatan, indicating possible origins in those areas. However, the year-bearers (the days on which Maya years could begin; see Chapter 16) of the Madrid Codex are shifted one day forward (from Akbal, Lamat, Ben, Etz'nab to Kan, Muluc, Ix, Cauac) from those prevalent in Classic times and in the other two codices. This shift is traceable to western Yucatan, which persuaded Thompson that the codex probably originated there; the Postclassic east-coast year-bearers are not known, however. Thompson assigned both the Madrid and the Paris codices to the period 1250–1450, that is, later than the Dresden Codex.

None of these codices was found through archaeological excavations; the climate in most of the Maya area is so moist, and the mildew so destructive, as to virtually preclude the survival of a buried book. Nevertheless, fragments have been found in several Classic-period tombs, including those at Uaxactun,

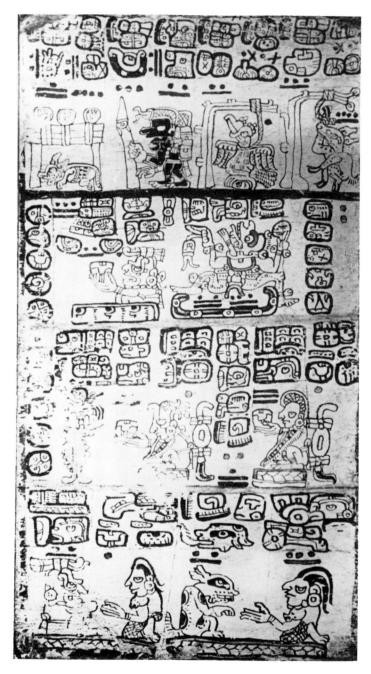

Fig. 15.5. Various almanacs, Madrid Codex, p. 91. The bird hanging from a noose in the top section is an ocellated turkey; its glyph group appears over the tree branch that holds the noose (see text).

Altun Ha, and Guaytan in the Maya area and at El Mirador, Chiapas, in an area of uncertain ancient linguistic affiliation. Except for the El Mirador Codex, all of these buried books were found in a nearly disintegrated state, and were not recoverable. The El Mirador Codex, much smaller in format than the intact Mayan codices, today lies unopened in the Museo Nacional de Antropología in Mexico City. Exposed to pressure and water percolation, the paper of the book had long since rotted away, and the lime page coatings had coalesced into a solid block. Experiments on minor fragments revealed intact painting inside, but were not successful enough to allow risking the main block.

An intact fragment of another possible pre-Columbian Maya book (the Grolier Codex, named after the Grolier Club in New York City, where it was first placed on public display) recently appeared in a private collection. Although tests indicate that the paper is pre-Columbian, the authenticity of the Grolier Codex is doubted by some scholars who feel that the style of the pictures is incorrect, and who point out that caches of blank pre-Columbian paper have been found in dry Mexican caves and are presumably available to forgers. Moreover, the Grolier Codex deals entirely with Venus almanacs in a simplistic fashion, adding almost no new information to the sophisticated treatment of Venus in the Dresden Codex; this in itself is suspicious, since the content would therefore have been easy to fake. The issue is still undecided. Scholars remain hopeful that more Mayan books will yet be found in recoverable condition, but we obviously cannot expect to find libraries like the clay-brick archives of the ancient Near East.

In contrast to the state of affairs in the Maya area, over four hundred native Mixtec-Mexica manuscripts have come down to us, of which about thirteen are of pre-Columbian origin. Some of these are made of deerskin, others of cotton or paper. If materials other than paper were ever the primary ones used in a Maya book, no examples have survived, nor does Landa mention them. Remains of an animal-hide binding connecting separate sections of the paper strip have been found in the Dresden Codex, but it is not known whether this was original or a subsequent repair job. Colonial texts claim that maps were made with a cotton backing.

Fortunately, a large number of Maya texts on more permanent media have survived both time, neglect, and the Spaniards' destructive efforts, though they are faring less well at the hands of modern smugglers of pre-Columbian art. All the earliest known texts from the Late Preclassic were carved on stone, as part of free-standing monuments, i.e., stelae and altars. Most of the texts surviving from the Classic were also carved on such monuments, or on parts of masonry buildings (lintels, wall panels, etc.). At Tikal and a few other sites, wooden lintels bearing carved texts have survived. Other Classic texts were incised on portable artifacts made of bone, stone, or pottery, or were fashioned on the stucco façades of buildings. In other cases they were painted on walls and on elaborately decorated ceramic vessels. Many of these have not been published, however, and those that have been are scattered through an almost hopeless tangle of out-of-print literature. Recently Ian Graham and his associates at Harvard University's Peabody Museum began the formidable task of assembling photographs and drawings of all the inscriptions in a single set of publications, the *Corpus of Maya Hieroglyphic Inscriptions*, which will run to 50 volumes and take many years to complete. Roll-out photographs and drawings of the beautiful renderings on polychrome ceramic vessels have also begun to appear, but there is still no prospect for a published set of the magnitude of the *Corpus*.

## Deciphering Maya Writing

The decipherment of Maya writing has been one of the most enduring studies undertaken by Maya scholars. We begin our account with a brief introduction to the basic typological dimensions used in classifying and explaining writing systems and to the basic elements and structure of Maya writing.

Traditionally, writing systems have been classified into several different major types: *pictographic, ideographic, logographic, syllabic,* and *alphabetic.* These have often been seen as increasingly sophisticated stages of the evolutionary development of all writing systems. Essentially, these types include two different dimensions of classification: the type of unit that an element of the writing system represents, and the mode of representation—whether through signs that resemble or otherwise make clear what their meanings are, or through signs whose shapes have no current relationship to their meanings. Alphabetic units represent the individual distinctive sounds, or phonemes, of language, and syllabic units represent syllables; both of these types are *phonetic.* Logographic units (*logograms*) represent whole morphemes or words. Pictographic scripts are supposed to represent words, ideas, or groups of words or ideas by means of elements that picture their associated meanings, whereas ideographic scripts do so by means of signs whose relationships to their meanings are less or not at all obvious. Most scripts are actually combinations of these (e.g., *logosyllabic* scripts like Sumerian), and the historical development of scripts is much more complicated, though it is true that individual phonetic signs are typically descended from logograms, and the mode of representation typically passes from the pictographic to the arbitrary sign.

Maya writing is built on a system of individual elements, or *glyphs,* that are themselves generally grouped into *glyph groups* having a generally squared or oval appearance (see Fig. 15.6). Commonly, Mayanists refer to both glyphs and glyph groups as glyphs; proposals have been made to make usage more precise, but none has won acceptance. The individual glyphs, like Maya art generally, appear quite elaborate to Western eyes. Some are obviously "pictures" of some natural object, but many others seem strictly arbitrary in appearance, though of

Fig. 15.6. Structure of the accession compound (*a–d*) and the initial-date indicator "was born" (*e–g*): (*a*) prefix T59 *ti/ta* "at"; (*b*) superfix T168 *ahpo* (see text); (*c*) main sign T684b, depicting a vulture with a knotted band, formerly known as "toothache"; (*d*) subfix T188; (*e*) main sign T740, also known as "upended frog"; (*f*) subfix T126 *ih*; (*g*) postfix T181 *ah*, a verbal suffix, also known as the "lunar postfix."

course they may not have been so to the Maya. According to their size and normal position within glyph groups, Maya glyphs have been classified as *main signs* (the largest and central glyphs within a group) and *affixes*, which are joined to the main sign and are themselves subclassified into *prefixes, superfixes, subfixes,* and *postfixes,* according to whether they are positioned to the left of, over, below, or to the right of the main sign. Both prefixes and superfixes are usually referred to as prefixes, and subfixes and postfixes as postfixes. Glyphs can also be fused within the main sign, in which case they are known as *infixes.* Main signs can themselves be compounded. The reading order of glyphs within a glyph group is typically in the order prefix, superfix, main sign, subfix, and postfix, though factors such as the nature of the affixal attachments, scribal variation, etc., could affect the normal order.

There are about 800 known Maya glyphs; these have been catalogued and are referred to by their catalogue numbers (usually in J. Eric Thompson's system, in which their numbers are preceded by "T") or by nicknames based on

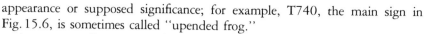

appearance or supposed significance; for example, T740, the main sign in Fig. 15.6, is sometimes called "upended frog."

A text normally consists of several such glyph groups organized into rows and/or columns. Glyph groups within a single text are read from left to right in the row and top to bottom in the column. In even numbers of columns, the groups are read in columns of two:

| | | | |
|---|---|---|---|
| 1 | 2 | 7 | 8 |
| 3 | 4 | 9 | 10 |
| 5 | 6 | 11 | 12 | etc.

For odd numbers of columns, the order is usually either

| | | | | | | | |
|---|---|---|---|---|---|---|---|
| 1 | 4 | 5 | | | 1 | 2 | 7 |
| 2 | 6 | 7 | | or | 3 | 4 | 8 |
| 3 | 8 | 9 | etc. | | 5 | 6 | 9 | etc.

Frequently one column is longer than others, especially when the inscription wraps around a carved figure; these are finished before going on to the next set of columns:

| | | | | | |
|---|---|---|---|---|---|
| 1 | 2 | 10 | 11 | 16 | 17 |
| 3 | 4 | 12 | 13 | 18 | 19 |
| 5 | 6 | 14 | 15 | 20 | 21 |
| 7 | | | | | 22 |
| 8 | | | | | 23 |
| 9 | | | | | 24 |

For easy reference to a particular glyph group in a text, the text is given a set of coordinates, with letters for columns and numbers for rows, so that any group has a unique coordinate identity (e.g., A1, B1, A2, etc.):

```
      A    B    C    D
   ┌──────────────────
1  │
   │
2  │
   │
3  │
```

The most common variation from the normal reading order is right-to-left (e.g., on pp. 23–24 of the Paris Codex; see Fig. 15.4); in such cases, those glyphs with recognizable faces (as on animal or human depictions) or orientations are found to be faced in the opposite direction, i.e., to the right, though the influence of normal order on the scribes can often be seen in orientation errors.

Until the 1950's, most experts on the subject were convinced that Maya writing was logographic, differing from other Mesoamerican scripts only in the size of the vocabulary, in its heavy representation of grammatical affixes and particles as well as the usual nouns and verbs, and in its supposedly greater use of the "rebus" principle (using a logogram to stand for a similar-sounding word), the only phoneticism then believed to have been characteristic of the system. The roughly 800 glyphs in the script exceeded the maximum number needed for an alphabet (about 30 in this case) or a syllabary (about 125), and its failure to reach the proportions of well-known logographic scripts like Chinese, with thousands of characters, was attributed to its limited range of use, i.e., in calendrical and astronomical matters. The number of different Maya glyphs is in fact very similar to that of known mixed scripts.

The groundwork for Maya decipherment was laid by the Franciscan friar and Bishop of Yucatan, Diego de Landa, who included significant information about Maya writing in his *Relación de las cosas de Yucatán* (written about 1566), a detailed history and description of the Maya of Yucatan. Landa based much of his account on interviews with learned Maya informants. There is also evidence that part of Landa's account was literally translated from at least one source written in Yucatec, presumably in Spanish characters. From Landa we have our most important account of the Maya calendar, together with the Maya signs for the twenty days, the eighteen 20-day uinals, and a "Maya alphabet." After Landa's death in 1573, his original manuscript was kept in the Franciscan convent at Mérida, and is now lost. The present edition stems from an abridged copy made in the early seventeenth century. This copy was discovered in 1863 by Brasseur de Bourbourg in the library of the Academía de Historia in Madrid, and first published in 1864. From Landa's death until the discovery of this abridged copy the study of Maya hieroglyphic writing was practically dormant, though a growing interest in the ancient Maya provided documentation of the inscriptions that would prove crucial to later scholars. Among these early explorers we are especially indebted to John Lloyd Stephens and his companion, Frederick Catherwood, a technical artist (see Fig. 11.73), who recorded Maya inscriptions in the rugged frontiers of Guatemala and Mexico in the 1830's and 1840's.

Brasseur also discovered the Tro portion of the Madrid Codex in 1866, and familiar as he was with the Landa manuscript, recognized that the characters were so similar to those of Landa that the codex had to be a Maya book, the first that was so identified. In 1869–70 Brasseur published the Tro along with his interpretation based on the Landa manuscript. Although he was able to recognize Landa's day signs, the sign for "sun" or "day," and the bar-dot numeric notation, Brasseur's conclusions regarding the supposed phonetic signs were almost completely in error; the major exception was his reading of Landa's *u* as the Yucatec ergative third-person pronoun. Though these contributions were important, Brasseur's claims to be able to translate line after line of the codex were decidedly premature; we now know that he was reading the codex backwards! Other early scholars, such as León de Rosny and Cyrus Thomas, would keep trying to apply the Landa "alphabet" to achieve phonetic solutions to the puzzle of Maya writing, but these attempts all foundered on the problems of (1) difficulty in recognizing the poorly drawn glyphs in the Landa copy;

(2) ignorance of what constituted the critical features of a glyph, and hence its range of variation in the renderings of the Maya scribes; and (3) failure to consider counter-evidence. By the turn of the century, understanding of the astronomical and calendrical portions of Maya texts had progressed so far, and the phonetic readings were so uncertain, that the whole phonetic approach to Maya writing was repudiated, even by some of its own previous adherents.

Although Brasseur and Rosny (who in 1876 deciphered the four directional glyphs north, south, east, and west) had some early success in the calendrical and astronomical interpretations, the scholar to whom most credit is due for the success of this approach was Ernst Förstemann, head librarian of the Dresdener Bibliothek and an accomplished Germanic philologist. Förstemann began in 1880 (in his late fifties) a study of the Dresden Codex and other Maya texts that would occupy him for the rest of his life. Within a few years, he had published an insightful commentary on the codex and many articles, in which he identified Landa's month signs, correctly interpreted the signs for "zero" and "twenty," explained the abbreviated almanacs in the codices, and interpreted Maya vigesimal and positional notation, the Venus tables of the Dresden Codex, the long count, the base of the long count at 4 Ahau 8 Cumku, the basic reading order of texts (independently discovered by others, including Cyrus Thomas), the signs for time periods and their head variants, and the workings of the inscriptional distance numbers (see Chapter 16 for calendrical details).

Förstemann's work partly overlapped that of J. Thomas Goodman (once owner and editor of the Virginia City, Nevada, newspaper *The Territorial Enterprise*) and a lifelong friend of Mark Twain (Goodman gave Twain his first job as a journalist). Goodman scorned the decipherment efforts of the scholars of his day, and published (in 1897) an important volume in which many of Förstemann's discoveries are stated as if they had been made independently by Goodman. We are still unsure of the extent of Goodman's knowledge of Förstemann's accomplishments, but it is at least clear that Goodman made several important discoveries on his own, including the head variants for the Maya numbers (see Chapter 16), and, in 1905, the correlation for the Maya and Western calendars that today is the most widely accepted (the Goodman-Martínez-Thompson, or GMT, correlation; Martínez and Thompson made minor modifications).

By this time Eduard Seler had deciphered the color glyphs, Paul Schellhas had catalogued the deities pictured in the codices and linked them with their glyphic names, and Daniel Brinton had produced the first summary of what was known about Maya writing in *A Primer of Maya Hieroglyphs* (1885). Knowledge of the inscriptions had begun to accumulate, largely due to the efforts of two indefatigable Maya explorers, Alfred P. Maudslay and Teobert Maler. In the 1880's, Maudslay recorded hundreds of inscriptions with both photographs and plaster casts, and published the photographs along with good drawings (by Annie Hunter) at great difficulty. In the early 1900's, Maler, who had fought in the emperor Maximilian's army, published several volumes of excellent photographs of many less accessible sites.

By the early years of the twentieth century, epigraphers were emphasizing calendrical and astronomical decipherment, and had gone beyond their earlier preoccupation with the codices to the now increasingly accessible inscriptions of the Classic period. Many refinements were made in the understanding of the calendar, and with them came better site chronologies. The explorations throughout the Maya lowlands undertaken by Sylvanus Morley resulted in the discovery and recording of a greatly expanded corpus of Classic texts. Morley also produced a more complete summary of Maya writing, *An Introduction to the Study of Maya Hieroglyphs* (1915). John Teeple deciphered much of the "supplementary series" (now "lunar series") that followed the long count in many Classic-period inscriptions, showing its relationship to a lost lunar calendar. Hermann Beyer established that the "variable element" in the introductory glyph for long-count dates represents the deity for the current 20-day period in the 365-day year.

By the mid-twentieth century, great progress had been made in establishing the critical features of the Maya glyphs and in cataloguing and making concordances of them. This work was led by Thompson, whose monumental *Maya Hieroglyphic Writing: An Introduction* (1950) became the most widely used summary of Maya writing. Günter Zimmermann produced the first good catalogue of the glyphs in the codices, but this was soon all but superseded by Thompson's *A Catalog of Maya Hieroglyphs* (1962), which encompassed both the codices and the inscriptions and proposed the referencing system still used by Maya scholars. Thompson also identified glyphs for several grammatical morphemes, including numeral classifiers. Largely because of his and Morley's influence, scholarly opinion on Maya writing had crystallized by the 1950's into the view that the system was logographic and contained no historical information. By systematizing the identities, ranges of variation, and locations of Maya glyphs, Thompson succeeded in opening the study of Maya writing to new scholars as no one before him had.

But the modern era of decipherment was opened by two major developments in the late 1950's: the discoveries by Heinrich Berlin and Tatiana Proskouriakoff of historical content in the Classic inscriptions, and the first convincing demonstration of phoneticism by Yurii V. Knorozov.

Berlin (1958) had noticed that a certain type of glyph group (see Fig. 15.7), characterized by a consistent set of prefixes but with a highly variable main sign, was not randomly distributed at Maya sites. Several major sites exhibited such glyph groups, and in each case the main signs were found to be practically unique to that site. This distribution led him to the conclusion that these groups

Fig. 15.7. Typical emblem glyph affixes (*a–c*) and various emblem glyphs: (*a*) prefix T36 with *kan* cross; (*b*) superfix T168 *ahpo*; (*c*) subfix T130 *wa* (see text for reading of T168 + T130); (*d*) main sign T756, depicting a bat, the emblem glyph of Copan; (*e*) main sign T559, possibly depicting an avocado tree with fruit, the emblem glyph of Quirigua; (*f*) main sign T562, known as "cleft sky," one of two emblem glyphs of Yaxchilan; (*g*) main sign T569, depicting a topknot of hair, or some sort of bundle, the emblem glyph of Tikal; (*h*) main sign T585, known as "Quincunx," the emblem glyph of Piedras Negras; (*i*) main sign T570, thought to depict a bone, one of two emblem glyphs of Palenque; (*j*) main sign T1040, apparently depicting a skull, the other emblem glyph of Palenque; (*k*) tripled main sign T528, the day sign Cauac, the emblem glyph of Seibal; (*l*) main sign T553, known as "crossed bands, sky variant," the emblem glyph of Naranjo; (*m*) main sign T716, depicting some sort of bundle, the emblem glyph found at several sites near Lake Petexbatun (Aguateca and Dos Pilas, for example).

actually constitute expressions identifying their sites, and he called them *emblem glyphs*. Subsequent work by Berlin and other scholars has confirmed the pattern at site after site.

Berlin was not sure whether the emblem glyph was a place name or perhaps the name of a ruling dynasty or lineage; he inclined to the latter view. The emblem glyphs of some sites do appear at other sites, but these have been explained as evidence of various sorts of relationships between one site and another (see Chapter 8). More than one main sign for the emblem glyph occurs at a few sites (Tikal, Yaxchilan, and Palenque); multiple emblems may indicate that the rulership at a particular site was in some way linked to two lineages. Yet the presence in the inscriptions of other glyphs that are almost surely family names argues against the emblems as current names. The best hypothesis seems to be that they represent a founding lineage.

The identification of the emblem glyph constituted the first demonstration that the Classic inscriptions contain anything as mundane as a local, completely non-calendrical name, and it seemed to make the Maya inscriptions resemble their Old World counterparts more than had been expected. This impression was soon confirmed in a more significant breakthrough. Proskouriakoff, an expert on Maya art, had been studying the inscriptions of Piedras Negras, and found that they exhibit a singular pattern with a compelling historical interpretation. At the site are several stelae with glyphic texts surrounding carved scenes of a person seated within a niche formed of the body of the "celestial dragon" (see Fig. 4.25). Proskouriakoff noticed that each monument of this type was the first to be erected in a given location, and that monuments grouped with it, with other motifs, had been set up every five tuns (360-day years) until another group was started at another temple. Within each group of monuments is recorded not only the erection date but also two earlier dates. One, which she termed the "inaugural date," precedes the date of the first stela in the group by only a short time, and is nearly always followed immediately by a glyph group whose most prominent main sign is T684 (dubbed "toothache" by Thompson, because its main characteristic is a cloth wrapped around the jaw of a vulture and tied off on top of the head; see Fig. 15.8). The other, which she termed the "initial date," might be anywhere from 12 to 31 years prior to the inaugural date, and is usually followed by a glyph group with the main sign T740, the "upended frog" (see Figs. 15.6 and 15.8). Both of these dates are referred to in later texts ("anniversaries"). In Proskouriakoff's words:

Doubtless there are various events in history that are paired in this way, but surely the most common is the birth of some person who in his mature years acquires great prestige or political power. But if the "upended frog" date is a birth date, the fact that it was celebrated for only a limited period suggests that that period was the person's lifetime, and effectively refutes my original notion that the "toothache glyph" expresses the human sacrifice shown on "niche" stelae. More likely, these stelae portray the accession of a new ruler, the "seating on high of the Lord," as the Maya books put it.

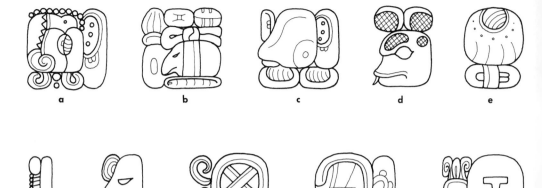

Fig. 15.8. Various glyph groups and glyphs with historical interpretations: (*a*) "was born," or initial-date indicator; (*b*) accession, or inaugural-date indicator; (*c*) capture; (*d*) captor; (*e*) captive; (*f*) prefix on names of males; (*g*) prefix on names of females; (*h*) wife; (*i*) count of the rulers; (*j*) death.

Proskouriakoff discovered that the time covered by any single group of inscriptions in no case exceeded 60 years, a normal human lifetime (a conclusion also reached by Charles Bowditch in 1901 and Morley in 1915, both of whom had correctly guessed the nature of Piedras Negras Stela 1 but never followed up on it). In a series of logical conclusions based on her brilliant original insight, Proskouriakoff went on to propose that each group of inscriptions documents the life of the then ruling lord of Piedras Negras; that the initial date is his birth date or the date of an associated ritual; that the inaugural date and niche motifs are records of his accession to power; that anniversaries of these dates were celebrated later; that the male figure dominating the front of a monument is a depiction of the ruler; that the female figure on the back of a monument is a depiction of the ruler's wife or, in one case with two female figures, his wife and daughter; that their names and titles follow the glyph groups for birth and inauguration; and that female names are prefixed by a glyph that resembles a woman's face, with a characteristic lock of hair (see Fig. 15.8).

It is difficult now to imagine the shock engendered by Proskouriakoff's work. The dominating male figures on the monuments had been thought to be gods, and the females were thought to have been males in priestly garb. The various secondary dates in the texts were thought to be corrections for the difference between the 365-day year and the true solar year. Now the texts were seen to be historical, and there was even the prospect that the associated buildings had been built by or for these rulers (in some cases, as tombs).

Proskouriakoff's evidence included similar texts from other sites. After the publication of her initial discoveries in 1959, she went on to a detailed study of the inscriptions of Yaxchilan, in which she was able to demonstrate her decipherment of glyphs for death, capture, and captor (see Fig. 15.8), and to show the relevance of her interpretations to inter-site relationships. Thompson accepted her conclusions enthusiastically, and today they are accepted as the basis for current progress in historical decipherment.

It will be noticed that Proskouriakoff's decipherments did not involve actual *readings* of Mayan words; instead, she was able to *interpret* glyphs without positing the actual phonetic identity or particular word involved. This distinction between semantic or grammatical interpretations and phonetic readings is important, and it is clear that the latter would not readily be forthcoming if the Maya script were strictly logographic. It is also evident that the discovery of any sort of phonetic system in the script would aid greatly in semantic interpretation, and vice versa. As recently as 1972, however, no less a scholar than Thompson could confidently state as his first "rule" of decipherment,

Maya writing is not syllabic or alphabetic in part or in whole. Some early students, bemused by Landa's so-called alphabet, supposed that they had found an alphabetic-syllabic system in the Maya glyphs, but such ideas were soon abandoned as untenable, only to be revived in recent years amid strident claims to have read the Maya glyphs.

Except for the brief and aberrant advocacy of Benjamin Whorf in the 1930's and 1940's, the last real try for a phonetic breakthrough had ended with Cyrus Thomas's admitted failure near the turn of the century. Thomas had actually hit upon what we now know to have been a few nearly correct solutions, but they were couched in an alphabetic hypothesis that, along with his faulty standards of glyph recognition and proof (see above), turned him in the wrong direction. Whorf, an American linguist with a considerable reputation in other circles, wrote a series of papers in which he claimed to be able to read whole passages from the codices phonetically, but his work met devastating and mostly deserved criticism. Nevertheless, he had made one advance over Thomas's earlier work by pointing out that the Maya phonetic system was likely to have involved a syllabary rather than an alphabet.

The "recent strident claims" referred to by Thompson were those of Knorozov (1952, etc.), the Soviet linguist who, using a "Marxist-Leninist" approach, began the other revolution of the 1950's. This revolution would be slower to develop, partly because Knorozov's arguments were not nearly as careful as Proskouriakoff's. Knorozov tried to demonstrate how a system of signs for cv syllables could have been used for writing a language with predominantly cvc roots. The basic problem is: How is the final consonant to be represented, given that there are no signs for single consonants? Knorozov proposed that the final consonant was written with a second cv sign that agreed with the vowel of the first, in a principle he called *synharmony*; thus a Mayan word *cutz*, "turkey," would be spelled *cu-tz(u)*.

Knorozov, using the Landa "alphabet" as his key, proceeded in the grand tradition of Whorf, Thomas, and Brasseur to bury his key insights in a veritable mountain of incorrect identifications, assumptions, and decipherments, making it easy for Thompson to demolish his arguments as he had done with Whorf's before. But Knorozov had succeeded, we now know, in deciphering several glyphs correctly, and, perhaps even more important, succeeded in convincing a few scholars that he was on the right track. Among these was David Kelley, who defended Knorozov's principles and some of his decipherments in a series of papers that culminated in his 1976 summary of the state of the art, *Deciphering the Maya Script*. Kelley took Knorozov's insights and constructed a more conservative argument for the existence of a Maya syllabary, only a small part of which was claimed to have been ascertained. Kelley also added a few new syllabic signs to the list.

We can appreciate the logic of the phonetic argument if we construct a chain of hypotheses somewhat similar to those encountered in the solution of an ordinary cryptogram. To be sure, the Maya texts are not really enciphered in a secret system; but the method of decipherment in either case is similar. We begin with a glyph group from the codices whose semantic interpretation is well known and beyond dispute, namely the one for "turkey" (it regularly accompanies depictions of turkeys in both the Dresden and Madrid codices; see Fig. 15.5, top section, where the glyph group accompanies a turkey shown hanging from a noose). The glyph group involves two main signs compounded, read here in left-to-right order:

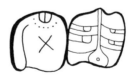

We have several hypotheses to begin with: (1) that the codices are twelfth- to fourteenth-century Yucatec; (2) that the sixteenth-century Yucatec words for turkey might well be the same as the earlier ones; and (3) that the compound is a phonetic construction written according to the principle of synharmony. We also have a fact: one of the sixteenth-century Yucatec words for turkey was *cutz*, according to contemporary colonial dictionaries.

We now bring Landa's "alphabet" (Fig. 15.9) into play. Notice that Landa frequently matches more than one glyph with each letter of the alphabet, and in some cases, the letters of the alphabet are accompanied by vowels; let us assume that these are syllables. Noting the similarity of our first glyph in the compound for turkey to the glyph over Landa's *cu* (they both have the X-shape inside, for example), we hypothesize that this glyph is indeed the syllabic sign for *cu*, and

Fig. 15.9. The Landa "alphabet."

the word being spelled in the codices is *cutz*. This generates a second hypothesis, which is that the second glyph in our compound is the synharmonic syllabic sign *tzu*, for a spelling in which the second vowel is only conventional, not real phonetically. This can be tested by finding *independent* uses of the two glyphs for which our values provide successful analyses.

For example, our *cu* glyph is also found in the following glyph group (the first glyph is eroded):

This group is on p. 19 of the Dresden Codex (see Fig. 14.3), immediately over the column of day signs in the top section (see Fig. 16.4 for the day signs), where it is third in reading order, the eroded glyph is first, and the other glyph is second. We know the meaning of the glyph group; it is one of the two numbers mentioned above that are actually spelled out rather than entered in bar-and-dot notation in the Dresden Codex. Because of the mathematical structure of the almanac it is in, we can calculate which number it ought to be, namely eleven. The colonial Yucatec word for eleven was *buluc*. By Knorozov's principle, then, our three glyphs should read *bu*[eroded]-*lu-c(u)*; in other words, the placement of *cu* in the third position is predicted by our hypotheses. And we have generated yet another hypothesis: that the second glyph is *lu*. In fact, the glyphic compound *tzu-l(u)* occurs frequently in the codices:

Its meaning too has long been known: it is the domestic dog. If all our hypotheses so far are correct, there should have been a word *tzul* meaning domestic dog in Yucatec, and there was indeed just such a word.

In this way one can proceed from hypothesis to hypothesis, each one generating the next in a logical chain that would very unlikely be due to chance. It is this type of argument that persuaded many modern researchers of the essential correctness of the principles. So why did this not convince Thompson? Why was Knorozov unable to proceed directly to a correct and complete syllabary? And why did not Landa's "alphabet" prove as effective in Maya decipherment as the Rosetta stone had for Egyptian?

Essentially, the answer is that Maya writing was a mixed system, usually much more complex than the purely phonetic and neatly synharmonic spellings that the words above suggest. Even in the codices, which are generally more phonetic than the Classic inscriptions, many words are only partially phonetic, and many are purely logographic. Phonetic spellings are often not synharmonic (e.g., *ku-ch(i)* for *kuch* "vulture"). Moreover, because the script was in use for at least 1,500 years, it is no surprise that we find (as in English) "fossilized" spellings, that is, spellings that were once phonetically or pictographically representative, but which lost this characteristic through language change, borrowing of written forms from one language to another, etc. Small wonder that Thomas, Whorf, and Knorozov were unable to leap from their initial insights to the overall phonetic breakthrough they sought. To experts who firmly believed the system was logographic, it was only too easy to demolish the overblown claims, misidentifications, and other errors, rejecting the good with the bad. Yet Knorozov's insights were of a higher order than those of Thomas and Whorf, and he won a following that they had not. Today almost all specialists in Maya writing agree that the system was logosyllabic, and that it displayed increasing phoneticism over time.

## The Current Status of Decipherment

Proceeding along the lines of the chained hypotheses above, several scholars have added convincing readings of specific glyphs as well as new insights into the nature of the script. In 1973, when Floyd Lounsbury deciphered the compound prefix T168, long suspected of being a personal title, as *ahau*, "lord" (Fig. 15.10; see also Fig. 15.7, which shows T168 as a constant prefix on emblem glyphs), he was able to demonstrate his reading by an ingenious argument that set a standard for later work. Lounsbury showed that the individual elements of the prefix were to be read *AH* (logograms are transcribed in capitals) and *po*, respectively, for an original title of *ahpo* that is attested only in colonial Quichean, where it meant "lord"; whether this title was simply a variant of colonial Quichean *ahpop* (see Chapter 8) or a completely separate title has not been determined. Lounsbury then showed that this title was often accompanied by a suffixed T130, which he read as the syllable *wa*. The Classic Maya, he argued, had adopted an original written title *ahpo*, probably from a highland language, but substituted their own term *ahau* for it, and indicated this with the suffixed *wa*. Since Lounsbury's publication, the validity of these syllabic readings has been repeatedly confirmed. But their real significance does not lie in the specific values; Lounsbury showed how phonetic signs, such as *wa*, could be used to partially indicate the reading of a logogram when the word was not fully spelled phonetically (i.e., as a phonetic *complement*), and he showed not only that a historical explanation for a fossilized spelling was necessary, but that it could also implicate other languages in the history of the script.

James Fox and John Justeson, in several recent coauthored papers, have added a large number of glyphs to the known Maya syllabary, but their work too has had implications beyond the specific decipherments. They show that glyphs that are phonetically equivalent can be used in alternative spellings of the same word, and that this was done in the codices for aesthetic effect. Perhaps most important, they were able to resolve a major stumbling block for many in accepting syllabic values for Maya signs: they demonstrated that a large number of Maya glyphs were *polyvalent* (had two or more values), and explained the development of polyvalence for each sign historically in terms of specific changes in the language or in the script, or of borrowings from one written language to another, doing for individual glyphs what Lounsbury had done for glyph groups. In separate work, Justeson made significant advances in our understanding of the aesthetic conventions of Maya writing and of Maya literacy and scribal practice generally.

We now have at least the rough outlines of a Maya syllabary (Fig. 15.10), along with a considerable understanding of its associated orthographic rules and the origins of individual values. And we can now answer the riddle of the Landa "alphabet." A number of signs in the Landa manuscript resemble some in the syllabary. In each case, a simple hypothesis concerning Landa's actual procedure explains how the letter value he assigned is actually in accord with the accepted syllabic value: Landa was asking his informant, not to write the glyphs for the sounds of Yucatec, but to write the glyphs for the sounds of the *names of the letters* in the Spanish alphabet! These are, of course, mostly one-syllable words,

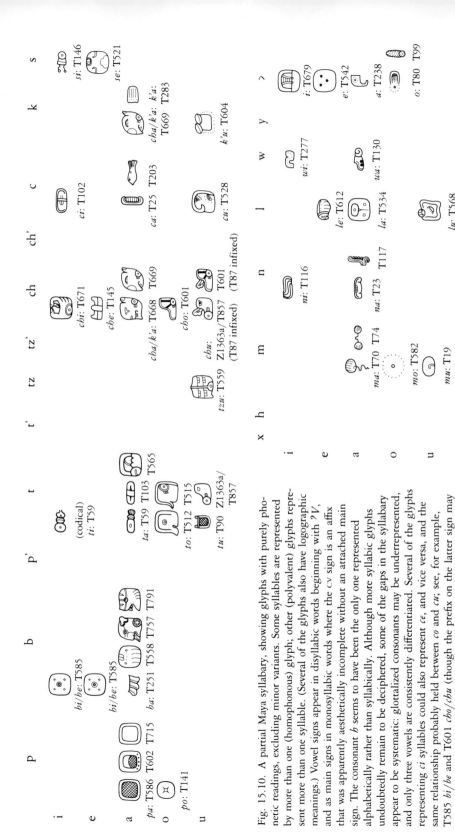

Fig. 15.10. A partial Maya syllabary, showing glyphs with purely phonetic readings, excluding minor variants. Some syllables are represented by more than one (homophonous) glyph; other (polyvalent) glyphs represent more than one syllable. (Several of the glyphs also have logographic meanings.) Vowel signs appear in disyllabic words beginning with ʔV, and as main signs in monosyllabic words where the CV sign is an affix that was apparently aesthetically incomplete without an attached main sign. The consonant *b* seems to have been the only one represented alphabetically rather than syllabically. Although more syllabic glyphs undoubtedly remain to be deciphered, some of the gaps in the syllabary appear to be systematic: glottalized consonants may be underrepresented, and only three vowels are consistently differentiated. Several of the glyphs representing *ci* syllables could also represent *ce*, and vice versa, and the same relationship probably held between *co* and *cu*; see, for example, T585 *bi/be* and T601 *cho/cbu* (though the prefix on the latter sign may consistently mark the *cbu* usage). (T857 was reassigned by Thompson from T515; 1363a in Zimmermann's catalogue.)

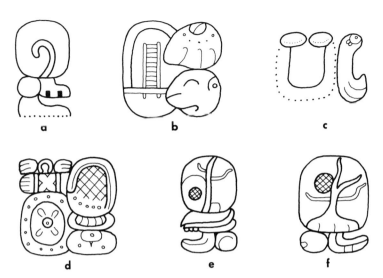

Fig. 15.11. Some syllabic spellings and complementations: (*a*) the month Muan, spelled *mu-wa-n(e)*; (*b*) the glyph group for armadillo, Yucatec *ibach*, spelled *i-ba-ch(a)*; (*c*) the glyph group for vulture, Yucatec *kuch*, spelled *ku-ch(i)*; (*d*) Pacal, a ruler of Palenque, spelled with a glyph depicting a shield (*pacal*) complemented by the syllables *pa-ca-l(a)*; (*e*) the Cholan month *uniw*, or *onew*, spelled with the main sign possibly depicting an avocado tree and fruit (see also Fig. 15.7*e*) plus the syllabic complements *ne-w(a)*; (*f*) the month *uniw* with only one phonetic complement, *w(a)*.

as in English, but the words are not the same as the phonetic values of the letters; and some are of more than one syllable, such as *f* (*efe*) and *h* (*hache*). Landa's informant responded with the glyphs corresponding to the most prominent syllables he heard. For example, Landa's *cu* (hard *c*) comes where the letter *q* (pronounced *cu*) occurs in alphabetical order, and the associated glyph is now known to have had the syllabic value *cu* along with several logographic values. For Landa's *h* the informant responded with the syllabic sign *che*, the second syllable of the Spanish word *hache*. Could Landa have been that naive? Confusion of sounds with letters was even more common in his day than in ours, but we are still not sure what Landa's intentions were; in the text he implies that he was teaching the Maya to write with their own characters according to Spanish (alphabetic) rules. Was he describing the pre-Columbian system, or a now-lost Maya-Spanish hybrid?

We are not sure how many more syllabic signs we can expect to decipher, and the number of available texts is limited. We cannot foresee how many equivalent and polyvalent signs there were. And syllabaries do not always, or even usually, have separate signs for every possible syllable. For example, the Maya syllabary appears to be lacking in signs for several of the glottalized consonants, though the set for *k* leads us to expect sets for others; but it is possible that some signs could serve for both a plain consonant and its glottal-ized counterpart. For most consonants it has been possible to decipher signs for a consonant + *a* (*ca*), but signs for *ci* are often used for *ce* and vice versa, just as signs for *cu* are used for *co* and vice versa, occasionally with minor infixes apparently signaling the difference. Thus the syllabary seems to represent a three-vowel system, with precision at the five-vowel level perhaps only in an early stage of development.

Some glyph values and fossilized glyph groups clearly had their immediate origins among Cholan writers even though they were used by Yucatecans. The syllabic sign *chi*, for example, was also used as a logogram for "deer" (Yucatec *ceh*) and the Yucatec day Manik. The sign was therefore polyvalent in Yucatec, but the values were nearly equivalent in Cholan, where the word for "deer" and the day sign were both *chih*. Many of the glyph groups signifying the month names (see Figs. 15.11 and 16.5) are easy to explain on the basis of Cholan origins. For example, the glyph group for the Yucatec month Kankin has a logogram followed usually by the phonetic complement *wa*, occasionally by *ni* and *wa*, leading us to expect a month name ending in *-niw* or *-new*. This does not fit the Yucatec name, but it does fit the Cholan *uniw*. Similarly, the Yucatec month Tzec, spelled with prefixed *se* and suffixed *ca* in the codices, is spelled *ca-se-w(a)* in the Classic texts, and the Cholan name for the month was *caseu*. In the Landa versions of the Yucatec month spellings, syllabic signs are added to the fossilized traditional spellings to give the current Yucatec pronun-ciations of the names. For example, the Landa spelling for the Yucatec month Zip, traditionally spelled with the logograms *ik* and *kat* (the Cholan name was *ik kat*, "black cross"), has a prefixed syllabic sign *si* in Landa's spelling.

The ultimate origins of Maya writing, however, are still obscure. The earliest known lowland Maya text is Tikal Stela 29, dated at 292 B.C. (though there are earlier Maya monuments without writing). Scholars are sure that its ancestors can be found at Preclassic sites in highland Guatemala, along the Pacific piedmont of Guatemala, in the Isthmus of Tehuantepec, and in Oaxaca, but its development is hard to trace in detail because of the paucity of glyphic texts from this period. Of these, perhaps the mostly clearly Maya in nature is the famous Late Preclassic inscription on Kaminaljuyu Stela 10 (Fig. 15.12), which seems to begin with a time count of 15 uinals, and to contain the "capture" compound. Inscriptions at sites such as El Baúl, Abaj Takalik, Chiapa de Corzo, and Tres Zapotes have Maya-like dates and the predecessors of some Maya (and Central Mexican) glyphs, but these areas were not Mayan-speaking in colonial times and we cannot yet ascertain their pre-Columbian linguistic affiliations. Internal evidence from the script itself may eventually implicate some non–Greater Lowland Mayan languages in the origins of glyph values (for example, Lounsbury's reference to Quichean), but that evidence is still insufficient at this time.

What, then, can be read of Maya writing now? We have the syllabary, still

Fig. 15.12. Preliminary drawing of Kaminaljuyu Stela 10, by James Porter. Note the fragments remaining from a lightly incised hieroglyphic text to the right of the sacred round date in the upper left corner, and the more complete inscription to the right of the sacred round date in the lower center. The lower inscription, if read left-to-right, top-to-bottom in columns of two, apparently begins with a count of 15 uinals (300 days).

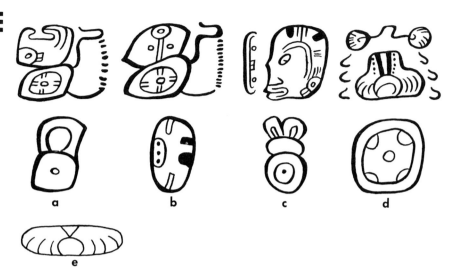

a      b      c      d

e

Fig. 15.13. The direction and color glyphs: (*a*) west (Yucatec *chikin*) and its associated color, black (Yucatec *é:k*); (*b*) east (Yucatec *likin*, earlier *lakin*) and its associated color, red (Yucatec *chac*); (*c*) north (Yucatec *xaman*) and its associated color, white (*sac*); (*d*) south (Yucatec *nohol*) and its associated color, yellow (Yucatec *kan*); and (*e*) the colors blue and green (Yucatec *ya?x*), associated with the center.

incomplete, and we have a large number of glyphs and glyph groups that we can interpret and, to some extent, actually read, usually because they are accompanied by one or more phonetic complements. Apart from the calendrical and astronomical glyphs (see Chapter 16), we have the glyphs for the colors and directions (Fig. 15.13), which are associated in the Maya texts and in Mesoamerican cultures generally in the following manner: east/red, north/white, west/black, south/yellow, center/blue-and-green (Mayan languages did not distinguish blue from green as abstract colors). Glyphs for many deities (see Chapter 14 and Fig. 14.5), animals, plants, and other objects have been identified through phonetics and context; some of these (Fig. 15.14) clearly represent their meanings pictographically, e.g., turkey, vulture, leaf-nosed bat, dog, armadillo, and gopher, though they may be found phonetically spelled as well.

Glyphs corresponding to various parts of speech—verbs, nouns, adjectives, and particles—have been identified, as well as glyphs for various grammatical prefixes and suffixes. Generally, the main signs in Maya writing represent logograms, and the affixes represent either phonetic complements or (logographic or phonetic) grammatical affixes, but this generalization has many exceptions, too. The ordering of glyphs in Maya texts reflects the grammatical structure of the languages (e.g., the Yucatec codices are ordered verb-object-subject, which corresponds to Yucatec usage), but the glyphic texts can be highly abbreviated, sometimes almost telegraphic or mnemonic.

Many glyphic identifications are being made as a direct result of advances in understanding the scenes accompanying the inscriptions. The iconography of such scenes gives crucial clues to the content of the texts, and in many cases, individual elements (such as implements, items of clothing, etc.) first identified through extensive comparison of such scenes have eventually turned out to be depicted by individual glyphs.

More glyphs of social and historical importance have been identified. To the emblem glyphs and glyphs for birth, accession, death, titles, capture, and captor deciphered by Berlin and Proskouriakoff have been added more emblem glyphs and titles, a glyph for captive, glyphs for marriage, and a glyph for numerical position in the dynastic line. Personal names and titles have also been identified, and many of these can be read phonetically. Pacal, a ruler of Palenque, for example, has in his name glyphs a shield (*pacal*) that is often accompanied by the phonetic spelling *pa-ca-l(a)*. Texts naming rulers also name their predecessors, and the associated genealogical relations are explicitly stated with kinship glyphs. Linda Schele, Peter Mathews, and Floyd Lounsbury have together been instrumental in establishing the genealogical nature of these expressions, and have proposed that the actual meanings include "child of man," "child of woman," and "child of parent (sex unspecified)," distinctions which are common in Mayan languages. They have also proposed that the line of succession in the Maya states was from father to son, as is reflected in interpretations elsewhere in this book. Recently, however, Fox and Justeson have proposed new decipherments of several of the kinship expressions that seem to indicate that

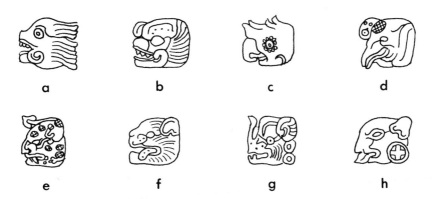

Fig. 15.14. Examples of glyphs depicting recognizable animal heads: (*a, b*) variants of a glyph for fish (T738a, T738c); (*c*) macaw (T744b); (*d*) vulture (T747a); (*e*) jaguar (T751b); (*f*) dog (T752); (*g*) leaf-nosed bat (T756a); (*h*) gopher (T757).

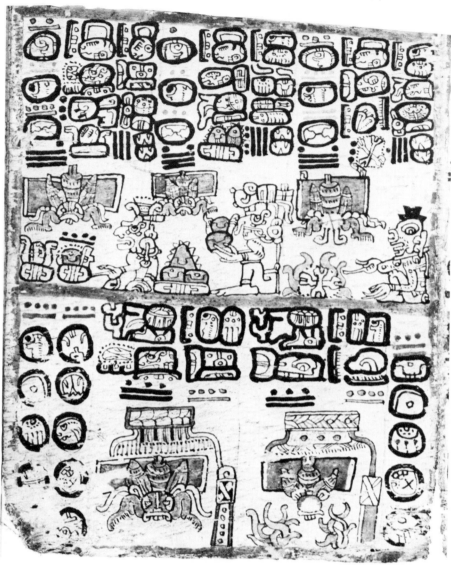

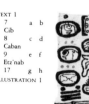

Fig. 15.15 (*facing page*). From the Madrid Codex, p. 103, part of a section on beekeeping. The illustrations and glyphic texts of the top half are separated and analyzed below the figure as an aid to understanding the explanation below; both the schematization and the translations are by James A. Fox. Successive stations in the calendrical framework give auguries and ritual information, but the complex interpretations necessary to understand them are not given here. Syllabic signs are transliterated in lowercase italics, logographic signs in italic small capitals; when the English meaning for a sign is known, but the exact Yucatec word is not, the meaning is given in small capitals.

*Illustration 1.* Bee descending from hive over seated god Itzamna and offerings of an unidentified animal and some sort of maize (toasted?). The number 9 above the maize probably counts the number of items to be offered.

| Text 1 | a | b | c | d |
|---|---|---|---|---|
| Glyphs | *u-pa-cha* | *u-pa-cha* | ITZAMNA-*na* | AHAU-IL-IL |
| Yucatec | *u-pach* | *u-pach* | *itzam na* | *ahau-l-il* |
| Meaning | he takes | he takes | Itzamna | lord |

| | e | f | g | h |
|---|---|---|---|---|
| Glyphs | 3-OC-*wa* | *h*-HA?-IL | [offering] | 15-[offering] |
| Yucatec | *noh-oc-wah* | *ha?-il* | ? | 15 ? |
| Meaning | big feast | rain | [offering] | 15 [offering] |

Translation: "Lord Itzamna takes his honey; big feast [and] rain [are the auguries]; [?] and 15 [?] [are the offerings]."

In glyph group *b*, *u-pa-cha* is almost certainly a scribal error for *u-*CÀ:B-*ba* ("his honey"), as in Texts 2 and 3. In Yucatec, 3 and 9 are used metaphorically for "big, many"; see group *e* for an example.

*Illustration 2.* Bee descending, seated god Chac, offerings of maize in hand and maize with superimposed iguana symbol in dish.

| Text 2 | a | b | c | d |
|---|---|---|---|---|
| Glyphs | *u-pa-cha* | *u-*CÀ:B-*ba* | *cha-ci* | ?-WATER-MAIZE |
| Yucatec | *u-pach* | *u-cà:b* | *chac* | ? *ha?-kan* |
| Meaning | he takes | his honey | Chac [the rain god] | ? water, maize |

| | e | f | g | h |
|---|---|---|---|---|
| Glyphs | *tu-?-na* | *ah-po*/AHAU-*le* | MAIZE, IGUANA | 19-[offering] |
| Yucatec | *t-u-?* | *ahau-le?* | *kan, hù:h* | 19 ? |
| Meaning | in his ? | noose? | maize, iguana | 19 [offering] |

Translation: "Chac takes his honey; ? water [and] maize, in his ? [the] noose [are the auguries]; maize, iguana, and 19 [?] [are the offerings]."

The glyph for the day Kan is used for maize throughout the codices, as it is here in groups *d* and *g*; it is often (but not here) suffixed with T130 (*wa*), perhaps for *kan wah* "yellow food," presumably a metaphor for maize (*ixim*).

*Illustration 3.* Bee (headless) descending, etc., seated death god before burning crossed bones.

| Text 3 | a | b | c | d |
|---|---|---|---|---|
| Glyphs | *u-pa-cha* | *u-*CÀ:B-*ba* | DEATH GOD | *tu*-DEATH |
| Yucatec | *u-pach* | *u-cà:b* | *cisin* | *t-u-*[*cim-il?*] |
| Meaning | he takes | his honey | Cisin | in his death |

| | e | f | g | h |
|---|---|---|---|---|
| Glyphs | *u-*MUC | *h*-HA? /CHANGE-*IL* | 3-BURNING BONES | 16-[offering] |
| Yucatec | *u-muc* | *ha?-il*/CHANGE | 3 ?? | 16 ? |
| Meaning | its omen | change [from?] rain | 3 (or many) burning bones | 16 [offering] |

Translation: "Cisin takes his honey; death [is] its omen; rain [stops?]; many burning bones [and] 16 [?] [are the offerings]."

The rain glyph has an infixed swastika-like sign meaning change.

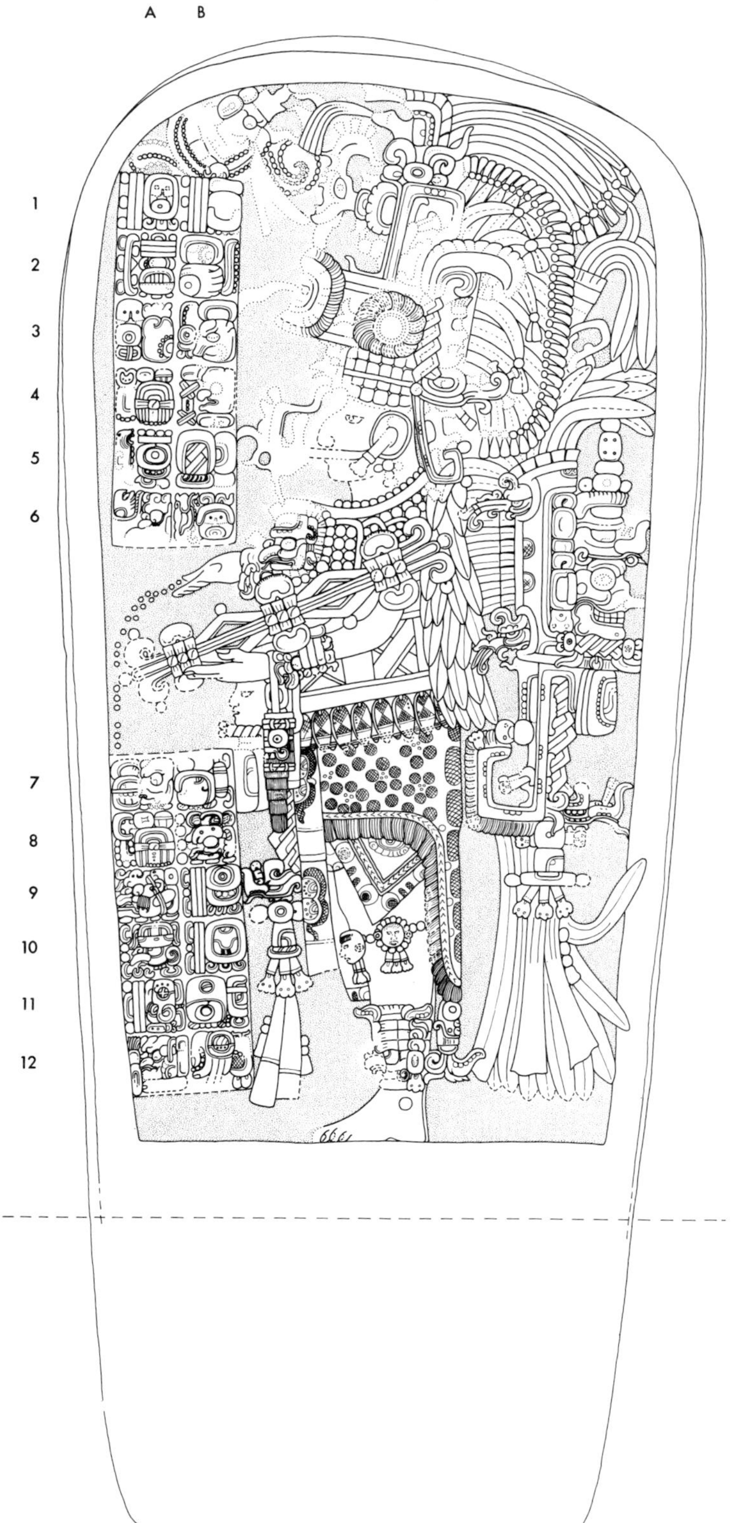

A
B
1
2
3
4
5
6
7
8
9
10
11
12

Fig. 15.16. Translation of Tikal Stela 22 (*facing page;* see also Fig. 11.18), by Christopher Jones. Some English words have been interpolated to make the cryptic Maya text more understandable.

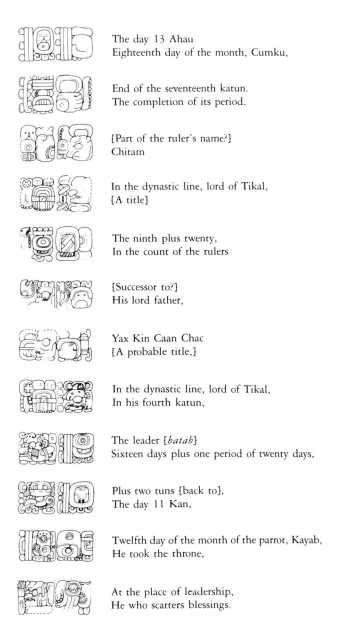

The day 13 Ahau
Eighteenth day of the month, Cumku,

End of the seventeenth katun.
The completion of its period.

[Part of the ruler's name?]
Chitam

In the dynastic line, lord of Tikal,
[A title]

The ninth plus twenty,
In the count of the rulers

[Successor to?]
His lord father,

Yax Kin Caan Chac
[A probable title,]

In the dynastic line, lord of Tikal,
In his fourth katun,

The leader [*batab*]
Sixteen days plus one period of twenty days,

Plus two tuns [back to],
The day 11 Kan,

Twelfth day of the month of the parrot, Kayab,
He took the throne,

At the place of leadership,
He who scatters blessings.

Maya succession was from a ruler to his nephew, who married the ruler's daughter in a system of cousin marriage. The nephew moved in from another city, and the ruler's son(s) moved away to rule elsewhere. In their theory, the female line remained constant at a given place, and the required alliances gave political solidarity to entire regions; such systems were used elsewhere in pre-Columbian Mesoamerica, notably among the Mexica. Though this theory explains the prominence of women in Classic inscriptions, and seems to be more in accord with the apparent phonetic readings of the kin terms involved, neither theory is well established at the moment, and debate continues.

Glyphic texts on Maya ceramic vessels and murals have in the main resisted decipherment, partly because their aesthetically pleasing but highly cursive style makes them difficult to identify, and partly because they have long been virtually ignored by writing specialists owing to the relative inaccessibility of published texts. Recently, however, Michael Coe has made an exciting break-through in the ceramic texts associated with Maya burials. Coe noticed that the "primary" texts (those appearing in a horizontal ring around the vessel or, failing that, in vertical columns), although they may bear different glyphs, nearly always show any particular glyph in the same order with respect to any other glyph, as if each vessel had on it a selection from some long text that itself is in a rigid order. The master text, which appears fully on no single vessel, Coe called the "Primary Standard Sequence," and suspected it might be a set of standard ritual incantations and other burial texts something like the Egyptian *Book of the Dead*. Since the scenes on the vessels often depict characters and events from the *Popol Vuh* underworld mythology, Coe's proposal seems reasonable, but specific portions of the text remain to be interpreted.

Recent progress in decipherment has thus negated earlier claims that Maya writing would never be read in any detail. And in response to those who might complain that even these advances leave us with nothing but the most boring sort of history—lists of rulers and the formal events of their lives, all with associated dates—one might reflect how colorful this information must be to scholars who have long had to be content with hundreds of dates, exact to the very day, but with none of the corresponding events ascertained at all. Even this limited sort of information can lead to discoveries important to historians and archaeologists. The codices, too, offer us a fascinating insight into the spiritual life of the Postclassic Maya.

It is often asked what percentage of the glyphs or inscriptions can be read, and to this question only the vaguest of answers can be given. Some texts are almost completely understood; others lie in relative obscurity in spite of progress. As examples of the amount and kind of information available to scholars from the best-understood records, Fig. 15.15 presents a decipherment of a page from the Madrid Codex, and Fig. 15.16 a translation of Tikal Stela 22.

**16**

# ARITHMETIC, CALENDRICS, AND ASTRONOMY

The sciences they taught were the computation of the years, months and days, the festivals and ceremonies, the administration of the sacraments, the fateful days and seasons, their methods of divination and their prophecies.
—Landa's *Relación de las cosas de Yucatán* (Tozzer 1941: 27)

Knowledge of arithmetical, calendrical, and astronomical matters was seemingly more highly developed by the ancient Maya than by any other New World peoples. The inscriptions and writings dealing with these matters have been largely understood since the nineteenth century; nonetheless, further progress has been made in this century. Like the medieval alchemists of our own Western tradition, the ancient Maya pursued these realms for both mystical and practical purposes. Numbers, time, and the cosmos were ruled by supernatural forces (see Chapter 14). By discovering and recording regularities in these forces, therefore, the Maya believed they were in a position to better understand and even predict events. These regularities were expressed in the various cycles of the calendar; thus, to the ancient Maya each passing cycle brought with it the possibility of repeated destiny—the idea of cyclic history. Of course, the calendrical system was also used to record the events of history, the reigns of rulers, their conquests and achievements, and other earthly matters.

## Arithmetic

It now appears that by the Late Preclassic period the Maya had begun to use a system of numeration by position, involving the use of the mathematical concept of zero, a notable intellectual accomplishment and, perhaps, the earliest known instance of this concept. The ancient Maya also settled on the vigesimal system of counting, which is based on a position shift at twenty (rather than at ten, as in our decimal system).

In writing their numbers, the Maya commonly used a bar-and-dot notation. In this system, the dot (●) has a numerical value of one, and the bar (━━━) a numerical value of five. A shell ( ⬭ ) had the value of zero or

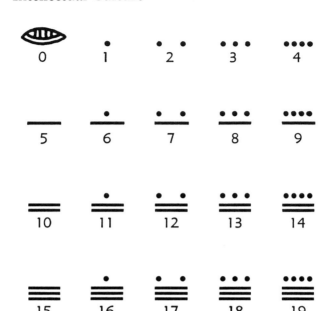

Fig. 16.1. Glyphs for zero and the numbers one to nineteen inclusive.

"completion." Combinations of the bar and dot symbols represented the numbers one to nineteen (Fig. 16.1). The numbers above nineteen were indicated on the basis of position. This system is just as useful as our own decimal place system. Besides being base twenty instead of base ten, it differs in that, whereas we use unique symbols for the values zero to nine, the Maya use three symbols, the shell, bar, and dot.

Maya bar-and-dot notation was simpler and much more efficient for mathematical calculations than the contemporary Roman system used in the Old World. Instead of three symbols, the Roman system required seven (I, V, X, L, C, D, and M), and in combining these, a symbol following one of equal or greater value adds to its value (LXXVI = 76), and a symbol preceding one of greater value subtracts from its value (XC = 90). In order to write the same numbers in Maya bar-and-dot notation, one employs fewer symbols and only one arithmetical process, addition. And the concept of regular position shifts—the foundation of the vigesimal and decimal systems—is wholly lacking in Roman notation.

In our decimal system, the positions to the left of the decimal point increase by powers of ten. In Maya mathematical calculations the values of the positions increase by powers of twenty from bottom to top. Note, however, that the place notational system was not often used in calendrical inscriptions, so that the usual order is from top to bottom (see below). Another exception was made in counting calendrical time, for, as will be explained later, the third time unit (the tun) was obtained by multiplying the value of the second position by eighteen rather than by twenty.

To illustrate the Maya vigesimal mathematical system at work (Fig. 16.2), the number twenty is represented by a single dot in the second order ("20's") and a shell in the first order, symbolizing zero units in this position. Examples of other numbers recorded in this system are also shown. The ease of adding Maya numbers is also demonstrated: 10,951, the sum of the numbers in the two preceding columns, is obtained simply by combining the bars and dots of 806 and 10,145 to arrive at this total.

According to Bishop Diego de Landa, the Maya vigesimal system was used by merchants to keep track of their commercial dealings. Maya merchants used counters, often cacao beans, to make their computations on the ground or any available flat surface.

An alternative notational system was employed by the ancient Maya to record numbers on some calendrical inscriptions. This less commonly used method is known as the head-variant system, relying on a series of distinctive anthropomorphic-deity head glyphs to represent zero and the numbers one to thirteen (Fig. 14.9). The head-variant system is thus comparable to our Arabic notation, where ten unique symbols represent zero and the nine digits. In the Maya system the head-variant glyph for ten is a death's head, and in forming the head variants for the numbers fourteen to nineteen the fleshless lower jaw is used to represent the value of ten. For example, if the fleshless jaw is attached to the head glyph that designates six, characterized by crossed elements in each

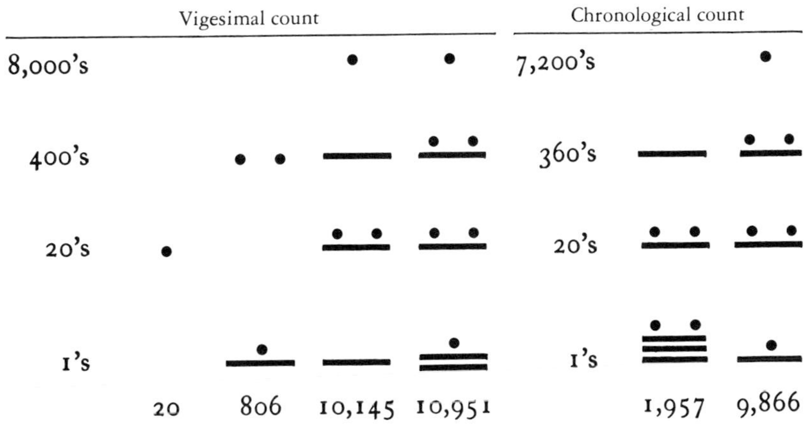

| Vigesimal count | | | | | Chronological count | | |
|---|---|---|---|---|---|---|---|
| 8,000's | | • | • | | 7,200's | | • |
| 400's | | • • | — | •• | 360's | — | •• |
| 20's | • | •• | •• | | 20's | •• | •• |
| 1's | | • | — | • | 1's | •• | • |
| | 20 | 806 | 10,145 | 10,951 | | 1,957 | 9,866 |

Fig. 16.2. Examples of Maya positional mathematics.

eye, the resulting head symbolizes sixteen. It has been suggested that the heads representing numbers one to thirteen are those of the Oxlahuntiku, the Thirteen Deities of the Upper World (see Chapter 14).

## The Calendar

The Maya calendar was far more complex than the system we use, for it served a variety of purposes, both practical and esoteric (such as astrological divination). The full knowledge of the Maya calendar must have been guarded by the ruling elite, since it was undoubtedly a source of great power. The calendar demonstrated to the populace that the rulers held close communion with the supernatural forces that governed the cosmos. One might assume, however, that even the poorest farmer had some knowledge of the basic system, by which to guide his family's daily life.

In the Maya calendrical system, records were kept of a series of recurring cycles of time based on the movements of celestial deities (sun, moon, and the planet Venus being the most prominent). In this system any given date would recur at cyclic intervals, just as a date in our calendar recurs every 365 days. These cycles were compounded into much greater cycles, and by counting from a single beginning date, the system could be used for establishing absolute chronology. In an absolute chronological system, any given date is unique, as July 4, 1776, is in our own system.

### BASIC UNITS AND CYCLES

The unit of the Maya calendar was the day, or kin. The second order of units, composed of twenty kins, was the uinal, roughly the equivalent of our month. In a perfect vigesimal system, the third order would be 400 (20 × 20 × 1), but at this point the Maya introduced a variation for calendrical reckoning. The third order, the tun, was composed of eighteen uinals, or 360 (instead of 400) kins. This was done, apparently, to create a closer approximation to the length of the solar year (365 days).

Above the third order the unit or progression was uniformly twenty, as is seen in the numerical values of all nine orders of time periods:

| | |
|---|---|
| 20 kins | = 1 uinal, or 20 days |
| 18 uinals | = 1 tun, or 360 days |
| 20 tuns | = 1 katun, or 7,200 days |
| 20 katuns | = 1 baktun, or 144,000 days |
| 20 baktuns | = 1 pictun, or 2,880,000 days |
| 20 pictuns | = 1 calabtun, or 57,600,000 days |
| 20 calabtuns | = 1 kinchiltun, or 1,152,000,000 days |
| 20 kinchiltuns | = 1 alautun, or 23,040,000,000 days |

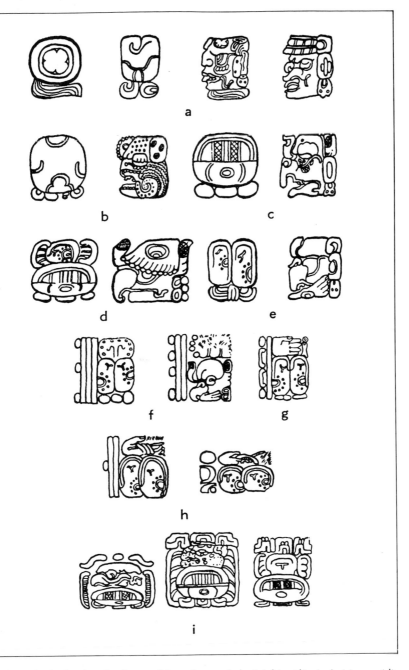

Fig. 16.3. Glyphs for the nine known Maya time periods: (*a*) kin; (*b*) uinal; (*c*) tun; (*d*) katun; (*e*) baktun; (*f*) pictun; (*g*) calabtun; (*h*) kinchiltun; (*i*) alautun, or long-count introductory glyph.

(The period of the fifth order was originally called the "cycle" by investigators. "Baktun" may have been the ancient name, and is the term now in use among Maya scholars.) The normal and head-variant glyphs for these time periods, about which more below, are given in Fig. 16.3.

The three most common cyclic counts used by the ancient Maya—the 260-day almanac, the 365-day vague year, and the 52-year calendar round—are very old concepts, shared by all Mesoamerican peoples. The treatment of these three cycles will be followed by a description of a chronological system unique to the Maya: the long count (or Initial Series) and its derivatives, period-ending and short-count dating. The long count operated independently of the 260- and 365-day cycles; it functioned as an absolute chronology by tracking the number of days elapsed from a zero date, to reach a given day recorded by these lesser cycles.

### THE ALMANAC OF 260 DAYS

The sacred almanac of 260 days, or "count of days," determined the Maya pattern of ceremonial life and provided a basis of prophecy. Birth dates were recorded by this almanac and the patron deity of the particular day became closely associated with the person's destiny. Among the Cakchiquel Maya of the Guatemalan highlands, where the 260-day almanac is still used, parents assigned their children given names from their birth dates.

The almanac was not divided into months, but was a single succession of 260 days, each designated by prefixing a number from one to thirteen before one of twenty Maya day names. The Yucatec names are given below, and their corresponding hieroglyphs are shown in Fig. 16.4.

| Imix | Cimi | Chuen | Cib |
|------|------|-------|-----|
| Ik | Manik | Eb | Caban |
| Akbal | Lamat | Ben | Etz'nab |
| Kan | Muluc | Ix | Cauac |
| Chicchan | Oc | Men | Ahau |

The almanac had no day name without an accompanying number. Since each of the day names had a number prefixed to it, the calendar ran: 1 Ik, 2 Akbal, 3 Kan, 4 Chicchan, 5 Cimi, and so on. The fourteenth name, Men, had the number 1 again; next came 2 Cib; and so on. The first name, Ik, on the second time around, had the number 8. Not until every one of the thirteen numbers had been attached in turn to every one of the twenty day names was an almanac cycle complete. Since 13 and 20 have no common factor, 260 days had to elapse before 1 Ik recurred and a new 260-day cycle began.

### THE VAGUE YEAR OF 365 DAYS

The vague year, or *haab*, was composed of nineteen months—eighteen months (uinals) of 20 days each and a closing month of 5 days, making a total

Fig. 16.4. Glyphs for the twenty Maya days: (*a*) Imix; (*b*) Ik; (*c*) Akbal; (*d*) Kan; (*e*) Chicchan; (*f*) Cimi; (*g*) Manik; (*h*) Lamat; (*i*) Muluc; (*j*) Oc; (*k*) Chuen; (*l*) Eb; (*m*) Ben; (*n*) Ix; (*o*) Men; (*p*) Cib; (*q*) Caban; (*r*) Etz'nab (*s*) Cauac; (*t*) Ahau.

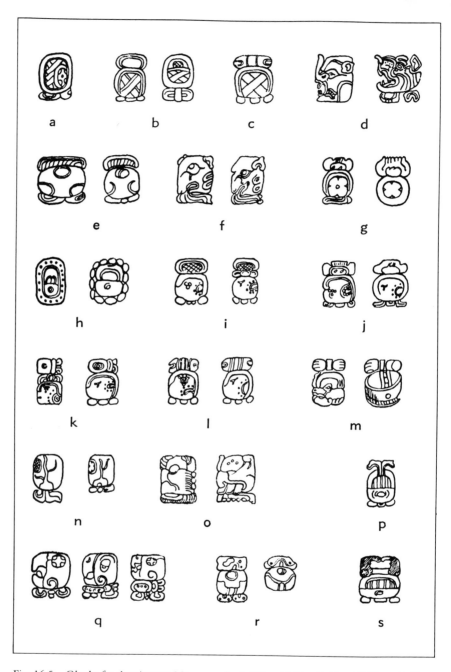

Fig. 16.5. Glyphs for the nineteen Maya months: (*a*) Pop; (*b*) Uo; (*c*) Zip; (*d*) Zotz; (*e*) Tzec; (*f*) Xul; (*g*) Yaxkin; (*h*) Mol; (*i*) Chen; (*j*) Yax; (*k*) Zac; (*l*) Ceh; (*m*) Mac; (*n*) Kankin; (*o*) Muan; (*p*) Pax; (*q*) Kayab; (*r*) Cumku; (*s*) Uayeb.

of 365 positions in the calendar year. The vague year approximated the solar year, which is actually slightly longer than 365 days. The nineteen monthly divisions in Yucatec are given below and their corresponding hieroglyphs are shown in Fig. 16.5.

| Pop | Xul | Zac | Pax |
|-----|-----|-----|-----|
| Uo | Yaxkin | Ceh | Kayab |
| Zip | Mol | Mac | Cumku |
| Zotz | Chen | Kankin | Uayeb |
| Tzec | Yax | Muan | |

In order to show how the 260 days of the almanac were combined with the 365 positions of the *haab*, they may be graphically represented on two cog-wheels (Fig. 16.6). The smaller wheel, A, has 260 cogs, one for each day of the almanac, and the larger wheel, B, has 365 cogs, one intercog space for each day of the *haab*.

Before the two wheels are joined, we must know two additional facts about the ancient Maya calendar. First, the Maya New Year's Day was written 1 Pop, although the previous day was often referred to as "the seating of Pop" (expressed as 0 Pop), when the Pop influence began to be felt. Second, because of the permutations of the 52-year cycle, only four days of the almanac could ever occupy the first position of the *haab*, or of any of its months. In Classic times these were the days Akbal, Lamat, Ben, and Etz'nab, known as year-bearers. Since each of these four day names had the numbers 1 to 13 prefixed to them in turn, only 52 (4 × 13) days of the almanac could begin the *haab* or any of its months. These 52 possibilities fell on the following days:

| | | | | | | | | | |
|---|---|---|---|---|---|---|---|---|---|
| 1 | Akbal | 1 | Lamat | 1 | Ben | 1 | Etz'nab | 1 | Akbal |
| 2 | Lamat | 2 | Ben | 2 | Etz'nab | 2 | Akbal | 2 | Lamat |
| 3 | Ben | 3 | Etz'nab | 3 | Akbal | 3 | Lamat | | etc. |
| 4 | Etz'nab | 4 | Akbal | 4 | Lamat | 4 | Ben | | |
| 5 | Akbal | 5 | Lamat | 5 | Ben | 5 | Etz'nab | | |
| 6 | Lamat | 6 | Ben | 6 | Etz'nab | 6 | Akbal | | |
| 7 | Ben | 7 | Etz'nab | 7 | Akbal | 7 | Lamat | | |
| 8 | Etz'nab | 8 | Akbal | 8 | Lamat | 8 | Ben | | |
| 9 | Akbal | 9 | Lamat | 9 | Ben | 9 | Etz'nab | | |
| 10 | Lamat | 10 | Ben | 10 | Etz'nab | 10 | Akbal | | |
| 11 | Ben | 11 | Etz'nab | 11 | Akbal | 11 | Lamat | | |
| 12 | Etz'nab | 12 | Akbal | 12 | Lamat | 12 | Ben | | |
| 13 | Akbal | 13 | Lamat | 13 | Ben | 13 | Etz'nab | | |

By the time of the Spanish Conquest, the Maya year-bearers had shifted forward to the days named Kan, Muluc, Ix, and Cauac.

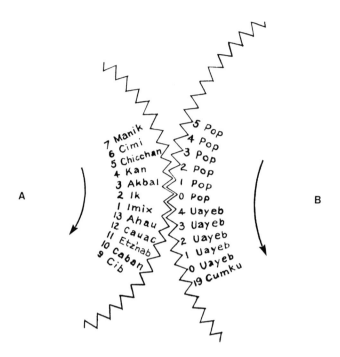

Fig. 16.6. Diagram illustrating the meshing of the 260-day almanac (left) with the 365-day year (right).

THE CALENDAR ROUND

In order to complete the designation of any day in the Maya calendar round, it was also necessary to add to the 260-day almanac designations the corresponding position that it occupied in the *haab*, the 365-day vague year.

When the two wheels are meshed, the cog of Wheel A, 2 Ik, fits into the space on Wheel B corresponding to 0 Pop, giving the almanac designation of this day as 2 Ik 0 Pop. Now our problem is to find the number of complete revolutions each wheel will have to make before 2 Ik will again mesh with 0 Pop.

We must first ascertain the least common denominator of 260 and 365. Both numbers are divisible by 5; 260 gives a quotient of 52, and 365 gives a quotient of 73, so the least common multiple of 260 and 365 is 5 × 52 × 73, or 18,980. Therefore, Wheel A will make 73 revolutions and Wheel B will

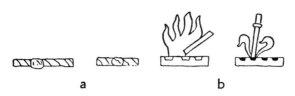

a                              b

Fig. 16.7. Mexica glyphs for the *xiuhmolpilli*, or 52-year period: (*a*) two examples of the knot; (*b*) two examples of the stick and drill for kindling the Sacred Fire.

make 52 revolutions before the two wheels have returned to their original positions, making a total of 18,980 elapsed days, or 52 vague years.

Once every 52 years, then, any given year-bearer coincided with the first day of the year. Thus any Maya who lived more than 52 years began to see New Year's Days of the same name repeat themselves. We do not know the ancient Maya name or hieroglyph for this 52-year period, but modern students of the Maya calendar designate it the *calendar round*.

None of the other peoples of Mesoamerica made use of time periods longer than this 18,980-day period. The Mexica (Aztecs), for example, conceived time as an endless succession of these 52-year periods and gave to them the name *xiuhmolpilli*, meaning "year bundle."

The Mexica had two special glyphs for this period, arising from their beliefs concerning it. The first was a knot indicating that the bundle of 52 years had been tied up, and the second was the fire drill and stick for kindling the Sacred Fire (Fig. 16.7). The Mexica believed that the world would come to an end at the close of one of these 52-year periods, and on the last night of the *xiuhmolpilli*, the population of Tenochtitlan (Mexico City) withdrew to the hills surrounding the city to await the dawn. When the sun rose on that morning, there was general rejoicing, the Sacred Fire was rekindled, the houses were cleaned and set in order, and the business of life resumed. The gods had given mankind another 52-year lease on life.

## THE LONG COUNT, OR INITIAL SERIES

Most peoples have realized the advantage of having a fixed point from which their chronological records could be counted, but the ancient Maya seem to have been among the first to use this basic concept. The events selected by different societies as starting points for their chronologies may be either specific or hypothetical.

The most familiar chronology of the first type is the Gregorian calendar, starting at the birth of Christ. The Greeks reckoned time by four-year periods called Olympiads, beginning with the earliest Olympic festival for which the winner's name was known, in 776 B.C.

Other chronologies begin with hypothetical starting points, for example, the supposed date of the creation of the world. The era of Constantinople, the chronological system used by the Greek Church, begins with a creation date corresponding to 5509 B.C. The Jewish calendar begins with an equivalent date of 3761 B.C.

The ancient Maya reckoned their chronology from a fixed point corresponding to the end of the preceding great cycle of thirteen baktuns (a period of approximately 5,128 solar years). The beginning date of the current great cycle, 13.0.0.0.0 4 Ahau 8 Cumku (corresponding to a day in 3114 B.C.), probably refers to an important event in the past, such as the creation of the current world in the Maya cosmology, and precedes the earliest contemporary Maya date (Stela 2 at Chiapa de Corzo; see Chapter 3) by over 3,000 years. According to the generally accepted calendrical correlation (see below), the current great cycle will end on December 21, 2012 (see Appendix B).

Great-cycle dates open most Classic Maya inscriptions, and so were named the Initial Series by Alfred Maudslay in the nineteenth century. Because Initial Series dates were reckoned from a fixed point in the distant past, this form of chronology also came to be known as the *long count*. Long-count texts first appear on Late Preclassic monuments in the southern Maya area, and are later found throughout the Maya lowlands during the Classic period, providing dedicatory dates for monuments and other inscriptions.

The long-count date fixes a given calendar-round day within the great cycle of thirteen baktuns (1,872,000 days). It is preceded by a standardized and oversized glyph, usually four times as large as the following hieroglyphs, known as the introductory glyph (Fig. 16.8). The only part of this introductory glyph that varies is the central element. A series of forms for this variable element corresponds to each of the nineteen months of the *haab*, or vague year. These variable elements are probably forms of the name glyphs for the patron deities of the *haab* months.

The following five glyph blocks record the number of baktuns, katuns, tuns, uinals, and kins that have elapsed from the beginning of the current great cycle. Remember that in its application to the long count, the Maya modified their vigesimal system to record twenty units of each order except for uinals, where only eighteen units were counted (360 kins). The first part of the calendar-round date, the almanac designation, follows, and after a series of intervening glyphs the second part of the calendar round date, the *haab* designation, closes the long count. The system can be better understood by closer examination.

The unit of the long count is the day (kin), and that of our chronology is the year, but the two systems are similar in their methods of recording. When we write the date Friday, January 1, 1982, we mean that 1 period of one thousand years, 9 periods of one hundred years, 8 periods of ten years, and 2 periods of one year have elapsed since the beginning point in our chronology to reach the

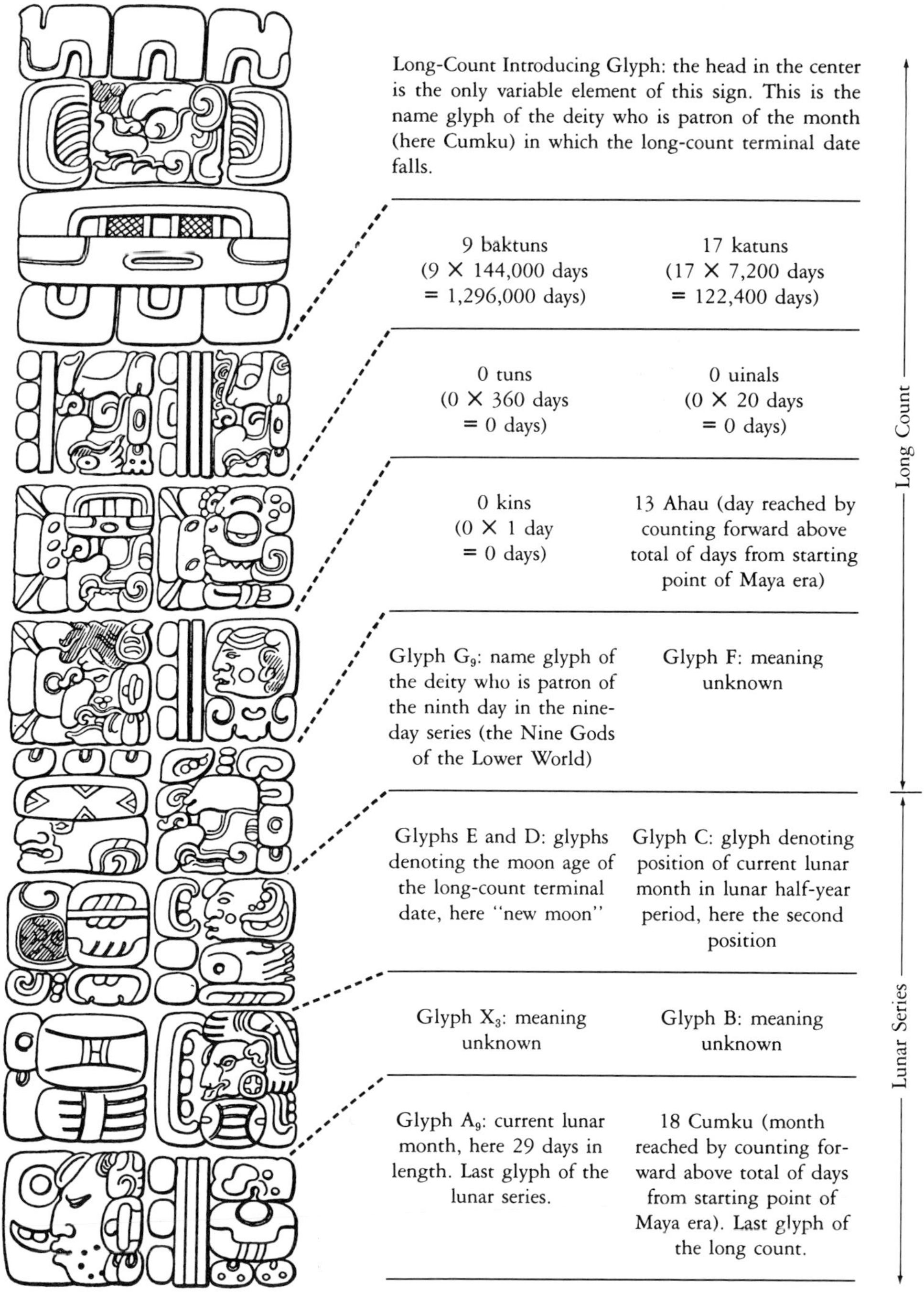

Long-Count Introducing Glyph: the head in the center is the only variable element of this sign. This is the name glyph of the deity who is patron of the month (here Cumku) in which the long-count terminal date falls.

| | |
|---|---|
| 9 baktuns (9 × 144,000 days = 1,296,000 days) | 17 katuns (17 × 7,200 days = 122,400 days) |
| 0 tuns (0 × 360 days = 0 days) | 0 uinals (0 × 20 days = 0 days) |
| 0 kins (0 × 1 day = 0 days) | 13 Ahau (day reached by counting forward above total of days from starting point of Maya era) |
| Glyph G₉: name glyph of the deity who is patron of the ninth day in the nine-day series (the Nine Gods of the Lower World) | Glyph F: meaning unknown |
| Glyphs E and D: glyphs denoting the moon age of the long-count terminal date, here "new moon" | Glyph C: glyph denoting position of current lunar month in lunar half-year period, here the second position |
| Glyph X₃: meaning unknown | Glyph B: meaning unknown |
| Glyph A₉: current lunar month, here 29 days in length. Last glyph of the lunar series. | 18 Cumku (month reached by counting forward above total of days from starting point of Maya era). Last glyph of the long count. |

Long Count

Lunar Series

Fig. 16.8. Example of a long-count date, from the inscription on the east side of Monument 6 (Stela E), Quirigua, Guatemala.

day Friday, January 1. When the ancient Maya recorded a long-count date given in arabic notation as 9.17.0.0.0 13 Ahau 18 Cumku, the first five places corresponded to 9 periods of 144,000 days (9 baktuns), 17 periods of 7,200 days (17 katuns), 0 periods of 360 days (0 tuns), 0 periods of 20 days (0 uinals), and 0 periods of 1 day (0 kins) that had elapsed since the beginning point in their chronology to reach the day 13 Ahau 18 Cumku.

In the long count, the calendar-round day in the sacred 260-day almanac, in this case 13 Ahau, is usually found in the sixth position after the introductory glyph, immediately following the kin notation.

Glyph G follows the almanac day in the seventh position after the introductory glyph. Each of the nine possible forms for Glyph G corresponds to one of the Bolontiku, or Nine Gods of the Lower World, and represents the particular deity who was the patron of the day recorded by the long count (see Chapter 14). In this particular example, this was the sun deity, patron of the ninth day. Following Glyph G is Glyph F, probably naming a particular Bolontiku as "lord of the night."

Between Glyph F and the *haab* date there is usually a group of six glyphs designated the lunar (formerly supplementary) series. They appear to give information about the age of the moon on the date recorded, the length of the lunar month in which the long-count date fell, the number of the particular lunation in the lunar half-year period, and some other undetermined information. The *haab* day and month glyphs, here 18 Cumku, follow and close the long-count calendrical inscription.

### THE SECONDARY SERIES

In addition to the dedicatory date of the monument, other dates are often included in the inscriptions. To express a single day by means of the long count, ten different glyphs were necessary. This method of dating was accurate but cumbersome, and its repetition for every additional date in an inscription was superfluous. If one date in an inscription was fixed, other dates could be calculated from it. Such derived dates have been called *secondary series.*

This was done by simply recording the time interval elapsed before or after the base date. Secondary series dates consist of the number of days (distance numbers) to be counted forward or backward from the base date to arrive at the new calendar-round position. The distance numbers are usually in ascending order (kins, uinals, tuns, and so forth), rather than the descending order of the long count.

For example, a long-count date of 9.16.0.0.0 2 Ahau 13 Tzec might be followed by distance numbers of 11 kins and 8 uinals (171 days) and the calendar-round date of 4 Chuen 4 Kan. This indicates that a count of 171 days (forward in this case) will reach the date 9.16.0.8.11 4 Chuen 4 Kan.

Initially, secondary-series dates were thought to be a calendar-correction formula, somewhat like our leap-year correction. However, the known instances of secondary-series dates span intervals as short as one day and perhaps as long as millions of years. Thus the secondary series probably served a variety of purposes, but in most cases they seem to refer to cyclical antecedents used by lords to legitimize their royal ancestry and their right to rule. In some cases these inscriptions refer to dates deep in the mythical past. For example, several extremely long calculations into the past have been proposed from secondary-series dates on two monuments at Quirigua, presumably to probe the mythological past. Monument 6 (Stela F) records a date of 1 Ahau 13 Yaxkin, calculated to be some 91,683,930 tuns (over 90 million years) earlier than the long-count date of 9.16.10.0.0 1 Ahau 3 Zip (A.D. 761). But this is nothing compared to a secondary-series date on Monument 4 (Stela D), calculated to be 411,863,930 tuns (over 400 million years) before the long-count date of 9.16.15.0.0 7 Ahau 18 Pop.

## PERIOD-ENDING DATES AND THE SHORT COUNT

By the middle of the Late Classic period, long-count dating began to pass out of use, to be replaced by an abbreviated system termed period-ending dating. By this method only a specific time period and the date upon which it ended are stated. In it the ten glyphs needed to express the long-count date 9.16.0.0.0 2 Ahau 13 Tzec are reduced to three, namely, Katun 16 2 Ahau 13 Tzec (Fig. 16.9; see also the opening of Tikal Stela 22 text, Fig. 15.12). Not computed over such a long period as a long-count cycle, a period-ending date was exact to a day within a cyclic period of nearly 19,000 years.

By Late Postclassic times the Maya chronological system had gone under further abbreviation, so that accuracy within a period of only about 256 years (260 tuns) could be achieved. This new system, recorded in the *u kahlay katunob,* or "count of the katuns," is called by Maya students the *short count.*

In our previous example, the long-count date 9.16.0.0.0 2 Ahau 13 Tzec, a katun ending of the long count (the day upon which this katun ended), was 2

a            b            c

Fig. 16.9. Period-ending date of Katun 16, on 2 Ahau 13 Tzec, given in the long count as 9.16.0.0.0 2 Ahau 13 Tzec: (*a*) end of Katun 16; (*b*) 2 Ahau; (*c*) 13 Tzec.

Ahau. In the *u kahlay katunob* everything was eliminated except this ending day; all other time periods were suppressed. This particular katun was known simply as Katun 2 Ahau.

This method of dating had the merit of requiring only one glyph to express it—any given day Ahau—plus the understanding that this day ended some katun of the long count. There were only thirteen differently designated katuns in this method of dating (1 Ahau, 2 Ahau, 3 Ahau, etc.), and since each katun equals 19.71 of our years, a katun of any given designation would return after a lapse of thirteen katuns, 13 × 19.71 years, or 256¼ years. If a Katun 2 Ahau ended in 751, another Katun 2 Ahau ended in 1007, and another in 1263.

Each katun in the *u kahlay katunob* was named after its last day, but the numbers did not follow each other in ascending numerical sequence. It follows from the arithmetic (7200 ÷ 13 = 553 with a remainder of 11) that the number of the day Ahau with which each successive katun ended was two less than that of the last day of the preceding katun: Katun 13 Ahau, Katun 11 Ahau, etc. (see Appendix B). This round of the katuns was represented graphically by the ancient Maya as a wheel, the periphery of which was divided into sections, one for each of the thirteen differently numbered katuns.

Landa describes and illustrates one of these katun wheels (Fig. 16.10):

Not only did the Indians have a count for the year and months, as has been said and previously set out, but they also had a certain method of counting time and their affairs by their ages, which they counted by twenty-year periods, counting thirteen twenties, with one of the twenty signs of their months, which they call Ahau, not in order, but going backward as appears in the following circular design. In their language they call these [periods] katuns, with these they make a calculation of their ages that is marvelous, thus it was easy for the old man of whom I spoke in the first chapter [of Landa's original manuscript] to recall events that had taken place three hundred years before. Had I not known of these calculations, I should not have believed it possible to recall thus after such a period.

The direction of movement is counterclockwise, in order that the katuns shall pass the cross at the top in the proper sequence, the days Ahau decreasing by two. The words in the center of Landa's wheel read, "They call this count in their language *wazlazon katam* [more properly *wazaklom katun*] which means the round [or return] of the epochs [katuns]."

The katun from which this round was counted seems to have been a Katun 8 Ahau. The repetition of the sequence began after each Katun 8 Ahau was completed, and these katuns were called *uudz katunob*, "the katuns that are doubled back."

Each of the thirteen katuns had its patron deity, its prophecies, and its special ceremonies. A series of eleven katuns, part of the *u kahlay katunob*, is presented in the Paris Codex, beginning with a Katun 4 Ahau (perhaps A.D. 1224–44) and closing with a Katun 10 Ahau (perhaps 1421–41). One of the intermediate

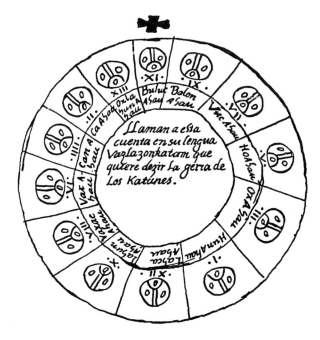

Fig. 16.10.  Katun wheel, after Landa's *Relación de las cosas de Yucatán.*

katuns, a Katun 7 Ahau (perhaps 1323–42) has been reproduced in part in Fig. 14.7.

The *u kahlay katunob*, or short count, was a kind of historical synopsis presented in a succession of approximately twenty-year periods, and so long as the sequences remained unbroken it was accurate enough for ordinary purposes. At the time of the Spanish Conquest, this record, if we can trust its ordering, stretched back through 62 katuns, to 9.0.0.0.0 (A.D. 435), a period of eleven centuries.

## THE CORRELATION OF THE MAYA CALENDAR

As we have seen, the Maya calendar was based on the basic Mesoamerican 52-year cycle, or calendar round, determined by the permutation of a 260-day almanac and the 365-day vague year. The combination of numbers one to thirteen and twenty named days produced the 260-day almanac (13 × 20 = 260); the vague year was composed of eighteen named months composed of twenty days (numbered zero to nineteen), along with the final five-day period.

The long-count system, or Initial Series, used by the ancient Maya was probably developed during the Late Preclassic in the southern Maya area, and is found throughout the lowlands during the Classic era. It recorded calendar-round dates within a great cycle of thirteen baktuns (1,872,000 days, or some 5,128 years), thus fixing any given day within the current great cycle, which began in 3114 B.C. To do this, a modified vigesimal numerical system was used to record (in reverse order) the number of kins (days), uinals (20 kins), tuns (18 uinals, or 360 days), katuns (20 tuns, or 7,200 days), and baktuns (20 katuns, or 144,000 days) elapsed from the beginning of the current great cycle or zero date. Long-count dates may be expressed in our arabic numerals, as in 9.15.10.0.0, referring to 9 baktuns (1,296,000 days), 15 katuns (108,000 days), 10 tuns (3,600 days), zero uinals, and zero kins to reach the calendar-round date 3 Ahau 3 Mol (June 30, A.D. 741).

Once a given calendrical inscription established a long-count date, any other date could be recorded by giving the number of days (distance numbers) to count forward or backward from the long-count position. Some Classic texts recorded an abbreviated or period-ending date, composed of the katun number and the calendar-round date. Thus, the previously given long-count date could also be recorded as simply Katun 15 3 Ahau 3 Mol. By the Late Postclassic the even briefer short count was used, which recorded only the day on which the katun ended, in this case, Katun 3 Ahau.

Because the long-count system was no longer in use by the time of the Spanish Conquest, the Maya long count cannot be directly correlated with the European calendar. We do have correlations with the short-count system then in use, however, since sixteenth-century documents record *u kahlay katunob* dates corresponding to days in the Julian calendar. These include the founding of Mérida on January 6, 1542. By comparing dates such as these, scholars have been able to conclude that a Katun 13 Ahau of the short count ended sometime during the Julian year 1539. Assuming continuity with the old long count, the problem becomes one of determining which Katun 13 Ahau long-count position might correspond to the recorded short-count Katun 13 Ahau. In other words, the correlation problem becomes a question of integrating the Postclassic short count with the earlier long-count system.

The generally accepted correlation, and the one followed throughout this book, is Goodman-Martínez-Thompson (the GMT correlation), which places the long-count katun ending of 11.16.0.0.0 13 Ahau 8 Xul on November 14, 1539 (Gregorian). This correlation is in best accord with chronological evidence from both archaeological and historical sources. Numerous other correlations have been proposed, however. One of these, the Spinden correlation, also generally satisfies the documentary evidence, and in some ways is in better accord with the archaeological data from the northern lowlands (although it is in less agreement with the evidence from archaeology in the rest of the Maya area). The Spinden correlation would require all Maya dates to be placed 260 years earlier than the GMT correlation, since it establishes the Katun 13 Ahau short-count date at 12.9.0.0.0 in the long count. Another correlation, advanced by

George Vaillant, places Katun 13 Ahau at 11.3.0.0.0; this would add 260 years to the dates given by the GMT correlation, placing the end of the Classic period at about 1150 and greatly compressing the Postclassic era. Though J. Eric Thompson and several other scholars advocate the 11.16 (GMT) correlation, they do not rule out the 11.3 correlation. Additional correlations, based on astronomical criteria such as the lunar tables in the Dresden Codex, tend to lack support from archaeological or historical sources.

An opportunity to test these various correlations came with the advent of radiocarbon dating. Although not infallible, radiocarbon dating can increase the certainty of archaeological chronologies if used with care, and if multiple tests produce consistent results. The tests were run with sapodilla wood samples from the dated lintels preserved at Tikal. The earliest tests, before the radiocarbon method was perfected, seemed to favor the Spinden correlation. However, a much larger sample was later tested, using an improved radiocarbon procedure. In one of these later tests, twelve samples were dated from Temple IV. Of these, ten were consistent with the age span predicted by the GMT correlation (A.D. 741–51), and only one fell within the span based on the Spinden correlation (A.D. 481–91). This, and the one remaining sample that fell halfway between these two spans, were probably from older beams reused in Temple IV. This test, along with those based on samples from other Tikal temples, offers strong support for the GMT correlation.

On the basis of the GMT correlation, the long-count katun and half-katun endings from 8.0.0.0.0 to 13.0.0.0.0 are given in Appendix B of this book. The same appendix includes instructions on how to convert Maya long-count dates to our calendar and vice versa.

## Astronomy

Most of our knowledge of ancient Maya astronomical calculations, which provided the basis for their complex calendar, comes from the texts carved on monuments or written in the surviving codices. In addition, archaeological remains indicate that some of the structures built by the Maya served astronomical functions. Examples include preserved monumental and architectural alignments, such as Stelae 10 and 12 at Copan (Fig. 16.11) and the more complex Group E assemblage at Uaxactun (Fig. 11.21). Although the simple sighting devices that the Maya apparently used have not survived, there can be little doubt that architectural alignments preserve some of the means by which ancient astronomical observations were made.

THE SUN AND MOON

The Maya had a fixed calendar year of only 365 days with which to measure an astronomical phenomenon which, according to modern measurements, re-

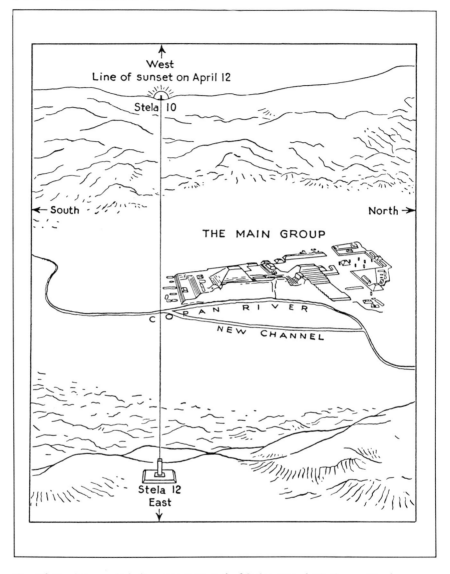

Fig. 16.11. Astronomical alignment composed of Stelae 10 and 12, Copan, Honduras.

quires 365.2422 days to complete. The Maya probably realized the discrepancy between their vague year and the true solar year; but although earlier theories credited the Maya with fixing the length of the year more accurately than does the Gregorian calendar, there is no evidence to support this idea at present.

The Maya had also made advances in measuring the exact length of a lunation. According to the perfected observation of astronomers, this period is a little over 29.53059 days. Since Maya arithmetic had no fractions (or decimal points), how did the priests measure such a complex fraction as 53,059/-100,000 of a day? The result was accomplished much as we keep our own calendar year in harmony with the true year by the leap-year correction. We have three years of 365 days each, followed by a fourth that is 366 days long. Centuries divisible by 400 are leap years (i.e., A.D. 400, 800, 1200, etc.); the others are not (see Appendix B). Our process gives a slight overcorrection every four years, compensated for by a slight undercorrection once every century. This system of successive adjustments keeps the calendar closely in harmony with the natural year.

At first, the Maya may have worked from a revolution of the moon composed of 30 days, but they soon saw that the actual new moons were falling short of this. Next, they may have allowed 29 days for a lunation, only to discover that the moons were exceeding 29 days in length. When this happened, they may next have tried alternating lunations of 29 and 30 days.

But even this correction failed them, although more slowly. Every two lunations reckoned this way gave an average lunation of 29.5 days, but the exact figure is a little longer. This kind of lunar calendar gained on the actual phenomenon at the rate of 3,059+/100,000 a day every lunation, an error that reached an entire day every 2⅔ years. At the beginning of the Late Classic period, at Copan, a new method for determining the average lunation appears to have been discovered, and was soon accepted by most lowland Maya centers. If 4,400 days equaled 149 moons, the resulting lunation value (29.53020) was certainly close enough to the actual period to minimize further discrepancies.

On pages 51–58 of the Dresden Codex, 405 consecutive lunations (about 32¾ years) are presented, arranged in 69 groups. Sixty of these groups are composed of six lunations each, the other nine of five each. In the 60 six-lunation groups, each totals either 178 days or 177 days, depending on whether three or four 30-day months have been used, giving 30 + 29 + 30 + 29 + 30 + 30 = 178 days, or 30 + 29 + 30 + 29 + 30 + 29 = 177 days. Each of the 9 five-lunation groups totals 148 days, or 30 + 29 + 30 + 29 + 30 = 148. These pages of the Dresden Codex are a solar eclipse table, since the closing days of each of these groups are days upon which, under certain conditions, a solar eclipse would be visible somewhere on the earth. The extra 30-day lunar months are so skillfully interpolated that nowhere throughout these 405 successive lunations does the discrepancy between the calendar placement and the actual appearance of new moons amount to one day.

## VENUS

Venus was one of the most important stars observed by the ancient Maya astronomers. There seem to have been at least two names for it: Noh ek, "the great star," and Xux ek, "the wasp star." Landa mentions Venus as the morning star, but gives no specific name for it: "They used the Pleiades and Gemini as guides by night, so as to know the hour of the Morning Star."

The planet Venus makes one synodical revolution in almost exactly 583.92 days. (The individual revolutions run in series of five—approximately 580, 587, 583, 583, and 587 days each, but any five consecutive revolutions average about the same length.) The Maya called this period 584 days, but they knew that this value was a bit too high.

Venus in its synodical revolution divides into four periods; (1) after inferior conjunction it is the morning star for about 240 days; (2) it then disappears for about 90 days during superior conjunction; (3) it reappears as the evening star for another 240 days; then (4) it disappears again for 14 days during inferior conjunction. The Maya assigned slightly different values to these four phases of Venus, although the total number of days in one revolution always remained 584. According to Maya astronomy, Venus was the morning star for 236 days; invisible during superior conjunction for 90 days; the evening star for 250 days; and invisible during inferior conjunction for 8 days. It has been suggested that the lengths of these four Venus phases were arbitrarily fixed to agree with lunations.

Ascribing 584 days to one synodical revolution of Venus made it too long by 8/100 of a day. The Maya were aware of this error and knew how to correct it. One of their important ceremonial periods was the time unit composed of five synodical revolutions of Venus (5 × 584 = 2,920 days), for they had also discovered that this period was equal to eight of their calendar years (8 × 365 = 2,920 days), a coincidence that was useful to them. It combined eight Earth years with five Venus years and supplied a convenient period for correcting the Venus calendar, which was falling behind the apparent Venus year at the rate of two-fifths of a day every eight calendar years.

As presented in the Dresden Codex, the Venus calendar is really three distinct calendars, each composed of 65 synodical revolutions of the planet. Each of the three Venus calendars is equal to 104 Earth years, but there is an overlap between the first and second, and another overlap between the second and third. The corrections were inserted at these points, at which the calendar Venus-year of 584 days overran the synodical Venus-year. By the end of the fifty-seventh Venus-solar period of this first calendar, the accumulated error had reached eight days. By dropping back eight days from this date, the zero date of the second calendar is reached. At the end of the sixty-first Venus-solar period of the second calendar, an error of four days had accumulated, and by dropping back four days from this point in the second calendar, the zero date of the third calendar is reached. By the use of this table the Venus-solar period was kept in harmony with the movements of the planet for 384 years before the accumulated error began to render the table useless.

There is some evidence that the ancient Maya observed and recorded the movements of other planets. Mars has a synodical period of about 780 days, and some scholars have pointed to the tables in the Dresden Codex dealing with multiples of 78 as being reckonings for the movements of Mars. However, J. Eric Thompson has argued persuasively against this. The other planets readily visible to the naked eye, Mercury and Jupiter, were also of probable interest to the ancient Maya astronomers, and recently Fox and Justeson have demonstrated a reference to Saturn on a Classic Maya inscription (Dumbarton Oaks Relief Panel 1).

The Pleiades were called *tzab* in Yucatec Mayan, the word for the rattles of a rattlesnake, perhaps because of their fancied resemblance. Gemini was *aac*, "the tortoise."

The ancient Maya may have had their own zodiac, composed of thirteen houses, and it may be that this zodiac is represented on pages 23 and 24 of the Paris Codex. If so, the first three signs, or houses, seem to have been Scorpion, Tortoise, and Rattlesnake. These are the first three figures shown hanging from a constellation band in the middle section of page 24 (Fig. 15.4).

The North Star was also of great importance to the Maya. Its apparent immobility and the orderly procession of the other constellations around it made it a dependable beacon. Because of the regularities in the alignments of many Maya structures, there can be little doubt that the North Star and other celestial bodies were used to guide the orientation of buildings.

### ASTRONOMICAL OBSERVATORIES

It may be asked how the ancient Maya achieved such a high degree of astronomical accuracy without the instruments upon which modern astronomers depend. However, if the lines of sight are sufficiently long, accuracy to within less than a day's error may be achieved in fixing the synodical or apparent revolution of many heavenly bodies. Maya temples are sufficiently high to obtain clear lines of sight from their summits to distant points on the horizon. A pair of crossed sticks or similar sighting devices were probably set up on top of pyramids. From this as a fixed observation point, the place where the sun, moon, or planets rose or set was noted with reference to some natural feature on the horizon. When the heavenly body under observation rose or set behind this same point a second time, it had made one complete synodical revolution.

Although the three known Maya codices contain no representations of observatories, pictures of them are found in the Mexican codices (Fig. 16.12). In the Nuttall Codex, in the doorway of a temple is a pair of crossed sticks, and looking out through them is the head of a man. In the Selden Codex, an eye

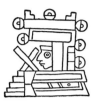

Fig. 16.12. Representations of astronomical observatories in the Mexican codices: (*left*) from the Nuttall Codex; (*center*) from the Selden Codex; (*right*) from the Bodleian Codex.

appears in the notch made by a pair of crossed sticks in the temple doorway. Another Mexican codex, the Bodleian, shows an eye between two crossed sticks, a star descending into a notch, and two observers. With such simple instruments the ancient Maya probably also predicted eclipses and the heliacal risings and settings of the morning and evening stars.

The ancient Maya accumulated and recorded a considerable body of astronomical knowledge, including the cycles of the moon and Venus. Their solar eclipse tables appear to have allowed them to make accurate predictions. And they seem to have observed and recorded other planetary cycles and astronomical phenomena, although the evidence for this knowledge is a matter of dispute among scholars. But it must be remembered that to the ancient Maya, these celestial objects represented deities. Observations and accurate calculations were undertaken to better predict the events on earth they believed these deities controlled. There is no evidence that the ancient Maya understood these movements as Kepler and Copernicus did.

# EPILOGUE

# THE SPANISH CONQUEST

11 Ahau was when the mighty men arrived from the east. They were the ones who first brought disease here to our land, the land of us who are Maya, in the year 1513. —*Book of Chilam Balam* of Chumayel (Roys 1967: 138)

Forty-nine years have passed since the Castilians came to Xepit and Xetulul. On the day 1 Ganel the Quiches were destroyed by the Castilians. Tunatiuh Avilantaro, as he was called, conquered all the towns. Their countenances were previously unknown, and the people rendered homage to sticks and stones.
—*Annals of the Cakchiquels* (Brinton 1885: 177)

Tragically, contacts between alien societies often begin in peace and end in war. Such was the case in the sixteenth century when the expanding nations of Europe encountered the unexpected, a whole New World populated by an array of cultures isolated from the rest of the human race. The destructive consequences of this contact, now well known, represent one of the most catastrophic episodes in human history. In Mesoamerica and in the Andes, traditions of civilization thousands of years old were terminated by the Spanish Conquest. For the Maya, this military conquest was especially long and brutal, stretching over a period of nearly two hundred years before the last stronghold of Maya independence was destroyed. (Most of the Maya region was subdued by the mid-sixteenth century, but it took the Spaniards another 150 years to crush the powerful Itza of the Peten. See Table 16.) In many ways, the Maya were ill prepared for this assault, for on the eve of the Spanish Conquest the independent states of both the Yucatan and the highlands were preoccupied with local conflicts that were to aid the cause of the invaders.

## First Contacts, 1502-25

The first recorded contacts between the Maya and Europeans occurred several decades before dreams of wealth and glory brought the armies of the conquistadores to the shores of Mesoamerica. During the final voyage of Columbus, a Maya oceangoing trading canoe was sighted in the Gulf of Honduras (see Chapter 10). Subsequent voyages of exploration resulted in a series of contacts between the Spanish and Maya settlements along the coast of the Yucatan.

By 1511 the Spanish had established several colonies in the Caribbean, with

TABLE 16
*Summary of Events of the Spanish Conquest Period*

| Date | Event |
|---|---|
| 1502 | Maya trading canoe contacted during Columbus's fourth voyage in the Gulf of Honduras. |
| 1511 | Shipwrecked Spaniards captured on the east coast of the Yucatan. |
| 1515 or 1516 | *Mayacimil,* "the easy death" epidemic of smallpox (?), spreads among the Maya of the Yucatan. |
| 1517 | Córdoba expedition defeated in battle with the Maya after landing in Campeche. |
| 1518 | Grijalva expedition circumnavigates the Yucatan Peninsula. |
| 1519 | Cortés expedition sails along the coast of the Yucatan before landing on the Gulf coast to begin the conquest of Mexico. |
| 1519–21 | Cortés, aided by native forces, leads the conquest of the Mexica (Aztecs) and the destruction of their capital, Tenochtitlan. |
| 1523–24 | Alvarado, aided by Mexican and Cakchiquel Maya forces, leads the conquest of the Quiche Maya; the Quiche capital destroyed, and most Quiche leaders killed. |
| 1524 | Alvarado founds the first Spanish capital of Guatemala at Iximche, the former capital of the Cakchiquel Maya (July 25). |
| 1524–25 | Cortés expedition to Honduras passes through the Maya lowlands and discovers the independent city of Tayasal, capital of the Itza Maya. |
| 1527 | Second capital of Guatemala founded at Ciudad Vieja after a Cakchiquel-led revolt is subdued by Spanish forces. |
| 1527–28 | First unsuccessful attempt to conquer the Yucatan led by Montejo the Elder. |
| 1531–35 | Second unsuccessful attempt to conquer the Yucatan led by Montejo the Elder. |
| 1540–46 | Successful conquest of the Yucatan led by Montejo the Younger; Spanish capital at Mérida founded January 6, 1542. |
| 1618 | Fathers Fuensalida and Orbita visit Tayasal (October). |
| 1697 | Tayasal, last capital of the Itza Maya, captured and destroyed by forces led by Martin de Ursua. |

their capital at Havana, Cuba. In that year a Spanish official named Valdivia set out from Darien (part of present-day Panama) in a caravel for the island of Santo Domingo to report to its governor about the quarrels between Diego de Nicuesa and Vasco Nuñez de Balboa. Near Jamaica the caravel foundered and sank, but Valdivia and eighteen sailors escaped in a small boat, without sails and without food. The Yucatan Current carried the survivors westward for fourteen days, during which time seven men died. The survivors were cast upon the east coast of the Yucatan Peninsula, where further misfortunes were in store. They were seized by an unfriendly Maya lord, who sacrificed Valdivia and four companions and gave their bodies to his people for a feast. Gerónimo de Aguilar, Gonzalo de Guerrero, and five others were spared for the moment as being too thin for this cannibalistic ceremony. Says Aguilar, in describing their situation, "I together with six others remained in a coop, in order that for another festival that was approaching, being fatter, we might solemnize their banquet with our flesh."

Aguilar and his companions escaped and fled to the country of another lord, an enemy of the first chieftain. This second lord enslaved the Spaniards, and soon all of them died except Aguilar and Guerrero. Aguilar was serving still another Maya chieftain when Cortés reached the Yucatan in 1519. Guerrero in the meantime had drifted farther south and entered the service of Nachan Can, lord of Chetumal, whose daughter he married. He rose to a powerful position in that province. When Cortés's messengers offered to take Guerrero back to the Spaniards he declined, choosing to spend his life with his Maya family. Aguilar suggests that Guerrero was ashamed to rejoin his countrymen "because he has his nostrils, lips, and ears pierced and his face painted, and his hands tattooed . . . and on account of the vice he had committed with the woman and his love for his children."

The pestilence of 1515 or 1516, the *mayacimil* or "easy death," which was characterized by great pustules that "rotted their bodies with a great stench so that the limbs fell to pieces in four or five days," may have been smallpox, perhaps introduced among the Maya by survivors of the Valdivia expedition or transmitted overland from Darien by Indian traders.

## THE FRANCISCO HERNÁNDEZ DE CÓRDOBA EXPEDITION, 1517

Early in 1517, Francisco Hernández de Córdoba sailed westward from Santiago de Cuba in search of slaves. It is not clear exactly where he first sighted the Yucatan mainland, but it is believed that he first landed at Isla Mujeres, on the northeastern coast. After leaving this island, Córdoba turned northwest to Cabo Catoche and then, skirting along the north coast of the Peninsula, sailed southward as far as Bahía de Campeche, where he landed on February 23, 1517. At Campeche the Spaniards heard of a large town called Champoton, farther south along the coast, where they next landed. The lord of Champoton received the Spaniards with open hostility, and a fight ensued. In spite of the gunfire, which the Maya encountered for the first time in this battle, they fought bravely, inflicting heavy losses on the better-armed Spaniards. Córdoba himself received 33 wounds and "sadly returned to Cuba" to report the new land as very rich, because of the gold trinkets he had found. He died of his wounds shortly after his return.

## THE JUAN DE GRIJALVA EXPEDITION, 1518

Diego de Velásquez, governor of Cuba, was greatly excited by the reports of gold, and fitted out another expedition of four ships and two hundred men under command of his nephew, Juan de Grijalva. Francisco de Montejo, the future conqueror of Yucatan, was also a member of this second expedition, which left Cuba in April 1518.

Grijalva's pilot was Anton de Alaminos, who had piloted the Córdoba expedition. The first landing was made at Isla de Cozumel, off the east coast, where the Maya fled at sight of the Spaniards. Grijalva continued southward along the coast, passing three large sites, one of which is described as follows:

We followed the shore day and night, and the next day toward sunset we perceived a city or town so large, that Seville would not have seemed more considerable nor better; one saw there a very large tower; on the shore was a great throng of Indians, who bore two standards which they raised and lowered to signal us to approach them; the commander [Grijalva] did not wish it. The same day we came to a beach near which was the highest tower we had seen. . . . We discovered a wide entrance lined with wooden piles set up by fishermen.

The largest of the sites seen by Grijalva was probably the ancient town of Zama (perhaps the archaeological site Tulum), and the "highest tower" was almost certainly the Castillo of Tulum. The large bay was Bahía de la Ascensión, so named because it was discovered on Ascension Thursday, 1518.

This was the southernmost point reached. From here Grijalva sailed north again and around the Peninsula to Campeche on the west coast. Continuing southward from Campeche, he discovered Laguna de Términos, named Río San Pablo and Río San Pedro, and entered Río Tabasco. In this region considerable treasure was obtained, including the first Mexica (Aztec) turquoise mosaic work the Spaniards had seen. Following the Gulf coast northward, Grijalva first heard of the Mexica nation, presumably at some place on the Veracruz coast, and finally reached as far north as Río Pánuco. On the return voyage to Cuba, the armada put in at Champoton to avenge the defeat of Córdoba, the year before. Here the Maya again attacked the Spaniards fiercely, killing one and wounding 50 others, including Grijalva. From Champoton, Grijalva returned to Havana, after having been away for five months.

## THE HERNÁN CORTÉS EXPEDITION, 1519

The voyage of Grijalva caused tremendous excitement in Cuba. The Yucatan was thought to be a land of gold and plenty, awaiting only the adventurous to seize its riches. A third expedition was fitted out, consisting of eleven ships, five hundred men, and some horses. Hernán Cortés was put in command of the armada, and with him went a number of other captains: Francisco de Montejo, Pedro de Alvarado, Diego de Ordaz, Gonzalo de Sandoval, Cristóbal de Olid, and Bernal Díaz del Castillo, most of them destined to win fame in the conquest of Mexico.

The armada first anchored off Isla de Cozumel, where Cortés spent some days. Idols in the temples were destroyed, and a cross was erected in one of them. While there, Cortés learned of the presence of "bearded men" on the mainland. These seemed to be Europeans, and Cortés sent messengers to summon them. In this manner Gerónimo de Aguilar was rescued, and later served Cortés well as interpreter.

Leaving Cozumel, the armada sailed around the north coast of the Peninsula and continued on to Rio Tabasco, which was renamed Grijalva in honor of its discoverer. In Tabasco, Cortés was given a beautiful young Indian girl named Marina. Her father, who was a chief, seems to have died when she was young. She was given by her mother to people in Xicalango, who later gave her to others in Tabasco, and these gave her to Cortés. Marina spoke both Mayan and Nahuatl, and Aguilar spoke Mayan and Spanish, so the two of them supplied Cortés with a means of communicating in Nahuatl with the Mexica. They played vital roles in the conquest of Mexico.

## THE CORTÉS EXPEDITION THROUGH THE MAYA LOWLANDS, 1524-25

Hernán Cortés and his party were the first Europeans to pass through the central and southern Maya lowlands, when in 1524–25 they crossed this region on a march from Mexico to Honduras, only a few years after the conquest of the Mexica.

In 1524, Cortés sent one of his captains, Cristóbal de Olid, to subdue Honduras. Olid seized the opportunity to rebel against his leader and to set himself up independently. When news of this defection reached Mexico, Cortés set out from Tenochtitlan (present-day Mexico City) on October 12, 1525, to march to Honduras, a six-month trip.

This formidable undertaking constitutes one of the most sustained efforts in military history. Because of the difficult character of the terrain, the attendant hardships and privations were almost beyond endurance and the army was always just one step ahead of actual starvation.

Cortés was accompanied by about 140 Spanish soldiers, 93 of them mounted, and by more than 3,000 Indians from Mexico, with 150 horses, a herd of pigs, artillery, munitions, and supplies. Because he dared not leave them behind, he also took Cuauhtemoc, Cohuanacox, and Tetlepanquetzal, the deposed rulers of Tenochtitlan, Texcoco, and Tlacopan. To transport such a large body of men across this wilderness would tax the strength and endurance of a well-organized modern army. When it is remembered that this expedition was undertaken in the early years of the sixteenth century, Cortés's outstanding qualities of leadership are magnified to almost unbelievable proportions.

Cortés entered the Maya area in what is now central Tabasco and crossed the Río Usumacinta just below the modern town of Tenosique. Pushing eastward, he reached Acalan, ruled by a Chontal Maya lord named Paxbolon Acha, toward the close of February 1525. Somewhere near the western frontier of this province occurred the blackest deed of Cortés's career—the summary execution of the last Mexica emperor, Cuauhtemoc, and his fellow ruler, Tetlepanquetzal, lord of Tlacopan.

When these princes had surrendered at Tenochtitlan, Cortés had promised them their lives, but here in the wilds of Acalan his promise was broken. The two eyewitnesses to this tragedy who have left accounts of it are Cortés himself and one of his captains, Díaz del Castillo; both agree that there was a conspiracy among the Mexica lords to fall upon the Spaniards and slay them. That this was no idle fear is confirmed by a recently discovered document in the files of the Archives of the Indies at Seville. This document, dated 1612, is a petition from the Chontal ruler of that day, a grandson of Paxbolon Acha. It appeals to the Crown of Spain for a pension for himself, because of his grandfather's services nearly a century earlier. The petitioner relates that Cuauhtemoc approached his grandfather and urged him to join the conspiracy against the Spaniards, pointing out how Cortés was abusing and robbing the Chontal. According to the testimony of his grandson, Paxbolon Acha was wary of these counsels and betrayed the conspiracy to the Spanish leader.

The danger was obviously great. The Spaniards were tremendously outnumbered by their own Indian troops, and immediate action was imperative. Cortés arrested the two leaders and hanged them without delay. Pablo Paxbolon, however, says in his account of the affair that the lords were beheaded. A Mexica hieroglyphic manuscript dating from the middle sixteenth century seems to indicate that both accounts may be correct. This manuscript portrays Cuauhtemoc's headless body hanging by its feet from a tree. The body of the dead ruler is swathed in bandages—the Mexica symbol denoting death—and his name glyph, an eagle, is attached to his head.

Cortés, with six hundred Chontal Maya as carriers, left Acalan on March 5, 1525, and reached the shores of a large lake eight days later. Here Canek, the Itza ruler, met Cortés on the northern shore of the lake. Cortés had the Catholic priests with the expedition celebrate Mass, which so impressed Canek that he promised to destroy his idols and replace them with the worship of the Cross. He invited Cortés to visit Tayasal, the Itza capital, and the invitation was accepted. Cortés took with him twenty Spanish soldiers, while the rest of the army proceeded around the lake and met him on the southern shore.

The army next entered a terrible terrain, the rugged country on the western flanks of the Maya Mountains. Here they encountered a pass so tortuous it took the tired army twelve days to travel twenty miles. During this time more than two-thirds of the horses were lost.

Emerging from this pass, they reached a large river swollen by the torrential rains that had never ceased falling. Turning upstream, they encountered a series of "terrifying and impetuous rapids." Today these same rapids are ironically known as "Gracias a Dios." It took the army two days to find its way over the rapids, and more horses were lost in the crossing. Beyond lay the village of Tenciz, which the crippled force reached on April 15, the Saturday before Easter, in 1525.

After leaving Tenciz, the army became lost in a wilderness of hills north of Lago de Izabal. The Indian guides deserted here, and had it not been for the capture of an Indian boy, who finally led them out, they would all have died of starvation.

Just beyond this point, Cortés heard definite news of the Spaniards he was seeking. To the delight of the exhausted army, it was learned that Nito, the object of their wanderings, lay only two days' journey ahead.

The final lap of this odyssey took the Spaniards three days before they finally emerged on the northwestern bank of Río Dulce opposite Nito; here Cortés was met by Diego Nieto representing the authorities of the settlement. Cortés and ten or twelve companions crossed immediately to the other side of the river and the rest of the army straggled in during the next five or six days.

On his march across the Maya area, Cortés visited the site of only one important Maya center, Tayasal, though he must have passed within a few miles of several others, notably Palenque, Laguna Perdida, Itsimte, Polol, Motul de San José, Ixkun, and Pusilha, ending his journey at Nito, not far from Quirigua.

## The Period of Conquest, 1524-1697

The conquest of both the Mexican and Maya peoples was facilitated by the superior arms of the Spanish, since they alone possessed firearms and cavalry. But other factors were just as important. In the first place, the Spanish could not have succeeded without the assistance of Mexican and Maya warriors who joined their cause. For the native armies, the principal motive for these alliances was the vengeance of past grievances. In Mexico, the Tlaxcalans joined Cortés to defeat their traditional enemy, the Mexica. In the Maya highlands, the Cakchiquel joined Alvarado for a time and helped vanquish their old enemies, the Quiche. Thus, in the conquest of the Maya the Spanish frequently took advantage of preexisting rivalries among the independent states of both the Yucatan and the highlands.

A second factor contributing to the Spanish success cannot be overestimated. The Europeans brought with them a series of Old World diseases for which the Maya and other New World peoples had no immunities. As a result, epidemics often decimated armies and entire populations before the battle lines were ever drawn.

## The Conquest of the Southern Maya by Pedro de Alvarado, 1524-27

After the fall of Tenochtitlan, the Mexica capital, in 1521, Cortés received representatives from various powers seeking to express their allegiance to the new masters of Mexico. Several accounts mention that one delegation came to Tenochtitlan from the Cakchiquel capital of Iximche, and possibly another from the Quiche capital of Utatlan.

In the following year, Cortés sent a small party of Mexican allies to reconnoiter the borders of the southern Maya area. They went to the province of Soconusco, on the Pacific coast of what is now Chiapas, where they met delegations from both Iximche and Utatlan. Cortés reported that both highland Maya states declared their vassalage to the King of Spain on that occasion. But, according to his account, he learned later that the Cakchiquel and Quiche

have not kept faith, but are molesting the towns of Soconusco because they are our friends. On the other hand, the Christians [native allies in Soconusco] have written me that they [the highland Maya] constantly send messages to excuse themselves, saying that these things had been done by others, and that they had no part in it. So, to learn the truth of this, I dispatched Pedro de Alvarado with 80 horsemen and 200 foot soldiers, amongst whom were many crossbowmen and musketeers; he took four field pieces and artillery, and a great supply of ammunition and powder.

The departure of Alvarado's expedition was delayed. But by the time it was ready to leave, on December 6, 1523, Cortés had seen fit to strengthen his "fact-finding mission" to 120 cavalry (with 50 spare horses), 300 infantry, and an unspecified number of Mexican warriors, along with the four artillery pieces.

The leader of this force, Pedro de Alvarado, had served as Cortés's principal captain throughout the trials of the conquest of Mexico. Díaz del Castillo had served with Alvarado, and described him in his *True History of the Conquest of New Spain*: "He was about thirty-four years old when he came here, of good size, and well proportioned, with a very cheerful countenance and a winning smile, and because he was so handsome the Mexicans gave him the name of *Tonatio*, which means the Sun."

But Alvarado was also infamous for his cruelty and his inhuman treatment of his foes. While in temporary command of the Spanish army in Tenochtitlan he led a brutal massacre of the Mexica. And his conquest of Guatemala was punctuated by numerous reports of similar events. According to Bartolomé de Las Casas, Alvarado's Maya conquests were heinous: "He advanced killing, ravaging, burning, robbing, and destroying all the country wherever he came, under the pretext, namely, that the Indians should subject themselves to such inhuman, unjust and cruel men, in the name of the unknown King of Spain, of whom they had never heard and whom they considered to be much more unjust and cruel than his representatives."

Las Casas goes on to itemize the atrocities committed by Alvarado during the conquest of the southern Maya area. There is no reason to reject Las Casas's account, for Alvarado's own letters, which provide the best history of the conquest of Guatemala, allude to the terror tactics he employed against the defenseless populace: "And, after entering in the houses we struck down the people, and continued the pursuit as far as the market place and a half a league beyond. . . ."

In late 1523 Alvarado's force marched from Mexico to Soconusco, following the ancient trade route from Tehuantepec along the Pacific coast. No opposition appeared until the Spanish reached Río Samala, in what is now western Guatemala. There, in the coastal province held by the Quiche, a native force tried and failed to block Alvarado's progress. Once across the river, the invaders rampaged through the nearby settlements to strike terror into the Quiche who still resisted.

From this point, Alvarado turned north to attack the heartland of the Quiche state, crossing over the mountain pass and into the rich valley of Quetzaltenango. Another battle was fought in the pass, but after the contingent of Mexican warriors was driven back by the Quiche, a charge by the Spanish cavalry brought victory, for "as they had never seen horses they showed much fear, and we made a very good advance and scattered them and many of them died."

Alvarado's force was soon able to enter the deserted city of Xelahu, the major center in the valley. Xelahu was called Quetzaltenango by Alvarado's Mexican allies. Most place names in the southern Maya area today bear Nahuatl names, because the Mexicans served as interpreters for the new masters of the land.

Six days later a climactic battle was fought in the valley of Quetzaltenango, as the Quiche made yet another attempt to stop the invaders.

We commenced to crush them and scattered them in all directions and followed them in pursuit for two leagues and a half until all of them were routed and nobody was left in front of us. Later we returned against them, and our friends [the Mexican allies] and the infantry made the greatest destruction in the world at a river. They surrounded a bare mountain where they had taken refuge, and pursued them to the top, and took all that had gone up there. That day we killed and imprisoned many people, many of whom were captains and chiefs and people of importance.

One of the Quiche commanders that led the fight against the Spanish was Tecun Uman, a hero of his people. But Tecun Uman and many other leaders were killed in battle, and the Quiche resistance was nearly exhausted. The Quiche then sued for peace, offering tribute, and invited Alvarado to enter their capital, Gumarcaaj, known as Tecpan Utatlan in Nahuatl. The ever-suspicious Alvarado sensed a trap, believing that the Quiche "would lodge me there, and that when thus encamped, they would set fire to the town some night and burn us all in it, without the possibility of resistance." Nevertheless, Alvarado accepted the Quiche offer and ordered his force to proceed to Utatlan.

When the Spanish came to Utatlan (Fig. 6.18), Alvarado believed that his fears were well founded.

And in truth their evil plan would have come to pass but that God our Lord did not see good that these infidels should be victorious over us, for this city is very, very strong, and there are only two ways of entering it; one of over thirty steep stone steps and the other by a causeway. . . . And as we rode up and I could see how large the stronghold was, and that within it we could not avail ourselves of the horses because the streets were so narrow and walled in, I determined at once to clear out of it on to the plain . . . and outside the city were many warriors, and as they saw me pass out on to the plain, they retreated, but not so much that I did not receive much harm from them. But I concealed it all so that I might capture the chiefs who were taking flight, and by the cunning with which I approached them, and through presents which I gave them, the better to carry out my plan, I took them captive and held them prisoners in my camp.

The chiefs Alvarado captured by his cunning were the highest officials of Utatlan, Oxib-Queh, the *ahpop* of the Quiche, and the *ahpop c'amha*, Beleheb-Tzy. "And as I knew them to have such a bad disposition towards the service of His Majesty, and to insure the good and peace of this land, I burnt them, and sent to burn the town and destroy it. . . ."

With Utatlan destroyed, and its rulers dead, Alvarado sent a delegation to Tecpan Quauhtemalan ("City of Guatemala," or Iximche), the Cakchiquel capital, asking them to join him in the final defeat of the Quiche. The Cakchiquel were, until the arrival of the Spanish, the paramount power in the highlands, and the traditional enemy of the Quiche. According to Alvarado, they sent a force of four thousand warriors, although the *Annals of the Cakchiquels* mentions only four hundred, and joined the Spanish against the Quiche.

From Utatlan, Alvarado was received by his new Cakchiquel allies into their capital of Iximche. The Cakchiquel appear to have thought that they could use their new alliance to vanquish another of their enemies, the Tzutuhil. At the request of the Cakchiquel, Alvarado sent two messengers to the Tzutuhil capital, Tecpan Atitlan. And when the news arrived that they had been killed, the Spanish and their Cakchiquel allies attacked the Tzutuhil. After being defeated in a battle on the shores of Lago de Atitlan, the Tzutuhil offered tribute and became vassals of the King of Spain.

From the highlands, Alvarado launched a further expedition to the Pacific coast and eastward to conquer the Pipil province of Cuscatlan, in what is now El Salvador. He then returned to the Maya highlands, and on July 25, 1524, founded the first Spanish capital of the province of Guatemala, at Iximche. But the first capital was short lived, for as related in the *Annals of the Cakchiquels*, the oppressive policies of the Spanish brought revolt from their former allies.

There was no fighting and Tunatiuh (Tonatio, "the Sun," as Alvarado was known) rejoiced when he entered Iximche. Thus did the Castilians enter of yore, O my children; but it was a fearful thing when they entered; their faces were strange, and the chiefs took them for gods. . . . Then Tunatiuh began to ask the chiefs for money. He wished that they should give him jars full of precious metals, and even their drinking cups and crowns. Not receiving anything, Tunatiuh became angry and said to the chiefs: "Why have you not given me the metal? If you do not bring me the precious metal in all your towns, choose then, for I shall burn you alive and hang you." Thus did he speak to the chiefs.

War soon broke out again, and the Spanish were driven from their new capital at Iximche. For the next several years the highland Maya, led by the Cakchiquel, fought a desperate campaign in an attempt to drive the Spanish from the highlands. But in the end the Maya were defeated. On November 22, 1527, a new Spanish capital was founded at the foot of Agua volcano, now known as Ciudad Vieja. Fourteen years later it was destroyed by a mudslide from the volcano, and the colonial capital was reestablished nearby in the city now known as Antigua Guatemala. With the highlands more or less subdued, the Spanish could turn their attention to the Maya of the north.

## The Conquest of Yucatan by the Montejos, 1527-46

The conquest of the Yucatan lasted for twenty years, and may be divided into three active phases, separated by two quiescent periods:

First phase (1527-28): Conquest of Yucatan attempted from the east
First interval (1528-31)
Second phase (1531-35): Conquest of Yucatan attempted from the west
Second interval (1535-40)
Third phase (1540-46): Conquest of Yucatan completed from the west

Francisco de Montejo was a member of both the Grijalva and the Cortés expeditions. He did not take part in the conquest of Mexico, however, having been sent to Spain in 1519 by Cortés in charge of the King's share of the treasure that had been collected. At the same time Montejo was to plead Cortés's cause at the Spanish court, because irregularities in connection with Cortés's departure from Cuba had brought him into open rupture with Diego de Velásquez, the governor of Cuba.

During the seven years Montejo was at court, he applied to the King of Spain on his own behalf for permission to conquer the Yucatan. In a royal decree, dated December 8, 1526, Montejo was granted the hereditary title of Adelantado, and was authorized to raise an army for the conquest and colonization of the Peninsula.

### FIRST PHASE: CONQUEST ATTEMPTED FROM THE EAST, 1527-28

The Montejo armada, consisting of three ships and four hundred men, set sail from Spain in 1527, with Alonso d'Avila as second in command. A stop was made at Santo Domingo to pick up supplies and horses, and one ship was left behind to bring additional supplies later. The two other ships made Isla de Cozumel toward the end of September, where Ah Naum Pat, the lord of Cozumel, received them peaceably. After a brief stop, the ships sailed for the mainland, where Montejo took possession of the land in the name of God and the King of Castile, somewhere near the town of Xelha in Ekab.

To quell a mutiny among his troops, Montejo set fire to his two ships. Leaving 40 men at Xelha under command of d'Avila, and another 20 at the nearby town of Pole, he set out with 125 men on a tour of the towns and villages in the northeastern corner of the Peninsula. None of the towns visited survives today, and even the location of most of them is unknown: Xamanha, Mochis, and Belma; the last may perhaps be identified with the modern settlement of El Meco. Here the chiefs of the surrounding towns were called together to swear allegiance to the Spanish crown.

From Belma the little army proceeded to Conil in Ekab, a settlement that is said to have been composed of five thousand houses; here the Spaniards rested for two months. They left Conil in the spring of 1528 for the capital of Chauaca, where the first serious encounter with the Indians took place. The Maya, abandoning the town in the night, attacked vigorously the next morning, but were defeated.

From Chauaca the army moved to Ake, 16 km north (10 mi.) of the modern town of Tizimin. There a great battle took place, in which more than 1,200 Maya were killed. In this action

the Indians appeared with all the arms which they use in the wars: quivers of arrows, poles with their tips hardened by fire, lances with points of sharp flints, two-handed swords of very strong woods inset with obsidian blades, whistles, and beating the shells of great turtles with deer horns, trumpets of large conch-shells of the sea; naked except for the shameful parts which were covered with a cloth, [their bodies] daubed with earth of divers colors, so they appeared as most ferocious devils; their noses and ears pierced with nose- and ear-plugs of bone and stones of varied colors.

As a result of this battle all the neighboring Maya chiefs surrendered.

From Ake, the Spaniards went to Sisia and Loche, and then returned to Xelha by an inland route. At Xelha, Montejo found his first settlement in desperate straits. Of the 40 Spaniards he had left there, only 12 remained, and all 20 of those stationed at Pole had been massacred. Of the 125 Spaniards who had accompanied him on his journey, only 60 returned. The entire force must now have numbered fewer than a hundred men.

The third vessel of the flotilla having arrived from Santo Domingo, Montejo decided to continue exploration of the coast to the south. D'Avila was sent overland, and Montejo sailed southward. He discovered a settlement called Chetumal on a good bay and learned that Gonzalo de Guerrero, a Valdivia survivor, was in the vicinity. Although Montejo sent messengers to persuade him to rejoin his countrymen, Guerrero again refused. The Adelantado and d'Avila failed to meet in Chetumal, as the Maya purposely kept them apart by false reports. D'Avila, after waiting some time, made his way back to Xelha and moved the Spanish settlement from this location to the nearby town of Xamanha.

After waiting in vain for d'Avila to appear at Chetumal, Montejo continued southward to Río Ulúa in Honduras and then turned back, rejoining his lieutenant at Xamanha. Late in 1528, leaving d'Avila at Xamanha as lieutenant governor, Montejo sailed around the northern coast of the Peninsula and returned to New Spain (Mexico), ending the first attempt to conquer the Yucatan.

Montejo, having secured an appointment as *alcalde mayor* of Tabasco, left Mexico City for that province in 1529, taking with him his son, also named Francisco de Montejo. They succeeded in pacifying the province and founded the town of Salamanca at Xicalanco near the north coast of Tabasco.

D'Avila was brought back from the east coast of the Yucatan and sent to reduce Acalan south and east of Laguna de Términos. Montejo did not long enjoy his new position in Tabasco, however; the former governor, regaining power there, threw Montejo into prison. Later the Adelantado was allowed to rejoin his son at Xicalanco, and both father and son moved over to Champoton in southwestern Yucatan, where d'Avila had already preceded them.

## SECOND PHASE: CONQUEST ATTEMPTED FROM THE WEST, 1531-35

From Champoton the Adelantado moved to Campeche. With this as a base of operations, the second attempt to reduce the Yucatan was launched. D'Avila was sent to Chauaca in the east. On his way there he passed through Mani, where the Xiu gave him a friendly reception; finally he reached Chetumal in the far southeast, where he founded Villa Real, or "royal town." The natives here resisted so stubbornly that d'Avila found himself obliged to abandon the newly founded town and to embark in canoes for Honduras. He got as far as Trujillo before turning back, after an absence of two years.

After the departure of d'Avila for the east in 1531, the Montejos withstood a strong attack at Campeche in which the elder Montejo nearly lost his life. The Spaniards, however, won the battle, which resulted in the surrender of Ah Canul, north of Campeche.

Montejo next sent his son to conquer the northern provinces, instructing him to divide among his followers the services of the Indians encountered. The younger Montejo first went to the province of the Cupules, to the site of the former Itza capital at Chichen Itza, where he was received somewhat reluctantly by the Cupul ruler, Naabon Cupul. Montejo, finding the population submissive, founded the first Ciudad Real, or "royal city," at Chichen Itza, and divided the towns and villages of the region among his soldiers, each Spaniard being allotted the services of two or three thousand Indians.

The Cupules soon became dissatisfied under Spanish rule. After six months of the foreign yoke, Naabon Cupul tried to kill Montejo but lost his own life in the attempt. The death of their ruler increased the hatred of the Cupules for the Spaniards, and about the middle of 1533 they blockaded the small Spanish garrison at Chichen Itza. Fortunately for the invaders, however, the Xiu, Chel, and Pech groups of the western peninsula remained faithful.

The younger Montejo, seeing the countryside roused against him, decided to abandon the royal city, which was probably no more than a small military camp, and to rejoin his father in the west. To accomplish this maneuver, according to an early chronicler, he resorted to the following ruse:

... finally one night they abandoned the town, leaving a dog attached to the clapper of a bell, and a little bread placed at one side so that he could not reach it; and the same day they wearied the Indians with skirmishes, so that they should not follow them. The dog rang the bell in his efforts to reach the bread, which greatly astonished the Indians, who thought the Spaniards wished to attack them; later when they learned how they had been tricked they resolved to look for the Spaniards in all directions, as they did not know which road they had taken. And those who had taken the same road overtook the Spaniards, shouting loudly as at people who were running away, because of which six horsemen awaited them in an open place and speared many. One of the Indians seized a horse by the leg and felled it as though it were a sheep.

Young Montejo finally reached Dzilam in the province of the Chels, where the young lord, Namux Chel, received him with friendship. Later in the spring of 1534 Montejo rejoined his father at Dzibikal in Chakan near T'ho (the present Mérida).

Meanwhile, the Adelantado had advanced inland as far as Mani and visited the Xiu ruler there. Throughout the Conquest, the Xiu repeatedly showed their friendship for the Spaniards, and it was largely owing to their aid that Spanish authority was established permanently. The Montejos met at Dzibikal, and shortly afterward the Adelantado founded the second royal city at Dzilam, where the Spaniards are said to have "suffered many privations and dangers."

When the Adelantado determined to return to Campeche, the friendly Namux Chel offered to conduct him there, accompanied by two of his cousins. The cousins were taken in chains, perhaps as hostages, though Namux Chel was provided with a horse for the long overland journey. Montejo left his son at Dzilam to carry on the work of conquest and pacification as best he might. The Adelantado was well received by the Indians around Campeche, where he was presently joined by d'Avila and shortly afterward by his son, who found his position at Dzilam no longer tenable.

At this point the conquest of the Yucatan received a setback. News of the conquest of Peru and of the riches to be had there reached the disheartened followers of Montejo at Campeche. The Spaniards had been fighting through northern Yucatan for seven years, and had found no more gold than would fill a few helmets. They had begun to realize that there would be no rich rewards such as the soldiers of Cortés had reaped in Mexico, and such as the companions of Pizarro were now gaining in Peru. The Adelantado could no longer hold together his already depleted forces. The little army dwindled until it became necessary to abandon the conquest of the Peninsula a second time. Late in 1534 or early in 1535, the Adelantado withdrew from Campeche to Veracruz with the remnant of his army.

Since he had first visited Honduras in 1528, the Adelantado had been petitioning the Spanish king for the governorship of that province. Combined with the *adelantazgo* of Yucatan and certain administrative rights in Tabasco and Chiapas, this would have given him jurisdiction over all of what is now southern Mexico and northern Central America. In answer to his petitions, Montejo was named governor and captain general of Honduras-Hibüeras in 1535, although notice of the appointment did not reach him until after he had left Yucatan for Tenochtitlan. He did not actually return to Honduras until 1537.

The Honduras episode was unsuccessful from the outset. Montejo found himself seriously involved with another Adelantado, Pedro de Alvarado, who had been named governor and captain general of Guatemala by royal appointment. But Alvarado also claimed jurisdictional rights over Honduras as well as Guatemala, and in August 1539 Montejo was obliged to give up his interests in Honduras-Hibüeras to Alvarado. Montejo returned to Tabasco, where his son was acting as lieutenant governor and captain general during his father's absence.

In 1535 the Franciscan Brother Jacobo de Testera had gone to Champoton to subdue the Yucatan by peaceful means. The Crown had promised him that all Spanish soldiers would be excluded from the country until he had first made an attempt to subjugate it by preaching. He was having some success at this when Captain Lorenzo de Godoy appeared at Champoton with Spanish soldiers sent by Montejo the Younger to subdue the region. Trouble between Testera and Godoy broke out, and the priest returned to Mexico.

Under Godoy, affairs at Champoton went from bad to worse. The Couohs of the surrounding region became more and more warlike until, in 1537, Montejo the Younger was obliged to send his cousin from Tabasco to take charge of the situation. The new Spanish leader was more politic than Godoy and persuaded the Indians to be less hostile, but want and misery continued and this last Spanish toehold in the Yucatan became more and more precarious.

## THIRD PHASE: CONQUEST COMPLETED FROM THE WEST BY FRANCISCO DE MONTEJO THE YOUNGER, 1540-46

The Adelantado was now about 67 years old and had been trying unsuccessfully for 13 years to conquer the Yucatan. He was weary, disillusioned, impoverished, and resolved to entrust the active prosecution of the conquest to his son.

In 1540 the Adelantado drew up a formal document turning over the conquest of the Yucatan to his son and giving him elaborate instructions. Early in 1541 Montejo the Younger left Tabasco for Champoton, where his cousin had already been stationed for more than two years. Shortly after his arrival,

Montejo moved his headquarters to Campeche, which was the first permanent Spanish *cabildo*, or town government, to be set up in the northern Maya area. The army again numbered between three and four hundred soldier-colonists under the command of Montejo, the son, with his cousin as second in charge.

Early in 1541 Montejo summoned the Maya lords to Campeche to render submission to the Spanish crown. The Xiu ruler and a number of neighboring caciques obeyed the summons, but the province of Ah Canul refused. Montejo dispatched his cousin to subdue the Ah Canules, while he remained behind to await the arrival of new recruits. His cousin met the Ah Canules in Chakan, near T'ho, and defeated them. In the late summer of 1541 Montejo the Younger, on his way from Campeche to T'ho, met more of the Xiu chieftains at Tuchicaan and received their submission. In the early fall of 1541 he reached the site of T'ho, and on the following January 6, 1542, he founded "The Very Noble and Very Loyal City of Mérida," setting up the second Spanish *cabildo* in the northern Maya area.

Seventeen days after the founding of Mérida, Spanish sentries stationed at the base of the pyramid where Montejo's army was encamped sighted a throng of Indians escorting a young Maya lord, seated in a palanquin. From the deference shown him it was obvious that he was a person of high degree. The Spaniards were terrified, fearing an immediate attack in force, but the Indian lord made signs that he came in peace, bringing with him food, which the Spaniards direly needed.

Through an interpreter, this Indian indicated that he was the lord Tutul Xiu, supreme ruler of Mani, that he admired the bravery of the white men, and that he wanted to know them and see some of their religious ceremonies. Montejo ordered the chaplain of the army to celebrate "a solemn Adoration of the Holy Cross," in which all the Spanish soldiers took part. The Xiu ruler was deeply impressed, and said that he wished to become a Christian. He stayed at the Spanish camp for two months, during which time he was instructed in the Catholic faith and baptized Melchor.

The results of this visit were far-reaching. Since the fall of Mayapan a century earlier, the Xiu province of Mani had been the most powerful political unit in northern Yucatan, and its peaceful submission to the Spaniards was followed by that of other western provinces. Before leaving Mérida, Melchor promised to send ambassadors to the other Maya lords, urging them to give obedience to Montejo, and the pacification of the west was accomplished without further fighting. However, the east still remained unconquered.

After the submission of the western provinces, Montejo the Younger sent his cousin to Chauaca. All the eastern lords received him peacefully except the Cochua chieftains. After a brief though bitterly contested campaign against the Cochua lords, Montejo defeated them.

Next the Cupules, incited by their priests, revolted and were subdued. Montejo finally reached the east coast at Pole, in Ekab, and tried to cross to Isla de Cozumel, but was prevented from doing so by stormy weather. In the attempt, however, nine Spaniards were drowned and a tenth was killed by the Maya. Exaggerated reports of these losses encouraged both the Cupules and the Cochuas to revolt again.

Landa describes the unrest among the eastern Maya: "The Indians received with sorrow the yoke of slavery, but the Spaniards had the towns of the country well divided into *repartimientos* [individual holdings]." The eastern provinces, Cupul, Cochua, Sotuta, and Chetumal, and to a lesser degree that of the Tazes, managed to retain their independence, and it was obvious that further military action against them would be necessary.

The conquest of the Yucatan was drawing to a close, but one more revolt was to occur before final Spanish victory. This revolt involved a conspiracy of almost all of the eastern provinces, and the night of November 8, 1546, was chosen for the uprising. Through information from friendly natives, Mérida and Campeche had word of the impending revolt, but in the east the surprise was complete. Says a contemporary Spanish writer:

Late in the year of '46 the natives of all these provinces, of the Cupules, Tazes, and Chikin Cheles rose and rebelled against His Majesty, making a great massacre of the Spanish *encomenderos* [those among whom the Indians had been divided] of whom they killed eighteen Spaniards who were in their towns, where they sacrificed them . . . and besides more than four hundred Indian free-men who served the Spaniards as servants, without leaving anything alive, if it was a thing that savoured of the Spanish, including the herds and other things, until help came from the city of Mérida in the same year and the natives became peaceful again, the culprits being punished.

When the revolt began, both the younger Montejos were in Campeche, awaiting the arrival of the Adelantado from Chiapas. The Adelantado reached Mérida in December, raised additional troops from his plantations at Champoton and Campeche, and placed them under the command of the nephew. After losing twenty Spaniards and several hundred of the contingent of friendly Indians, they defeated the coalition of the eastern Maya chieftains in a single engagement. With these victories the conquest of the Yucatan was brought to a successful conclusion.

## The Independent Itza, 1525-1696

With the conquest of the Yucatan completed (1546), there remained only one independent Maya group—the powerful Itza nation, centered in the lake region of the Peten. The Itzas were able to resist the Spaniards and to maintain their political independence for another century and three-quarters.

Tayasal, the Itza capital, was a long distance both from Mérida in northern Yucatan and from Antigua, the Spanish capital in the southern highlands. For nearly a century after Cortés had visited Tayasal in 1525, neither Yucatan nor Guatemala attempted to reduce the remote and hostile province of the Itza. Between 1550 and 1556 Franciscan missionaries had made evangelizing expeditions from Campeche into Acalan and had persuaded the Chontal Maya of that region to move nearer to Campeche, where they could be instructed in the Catholic faith, but the warlike Itza, farther to the southeast, were left alone.

In 1618 two Franciscans, Fathers Bartolomé de Fuensalida and Juan de Orbita, having secured permission to attempt to Christianize the Itza peaceably, set out from Mérida for Tayasal. They left Mérida in the spring of 1618, traveling by way of Laguna de Bacalar, and were accompanied by the *alcalde* of Bacalar and a number of Indian converts. With the delays incident to travel, the fathers did not reach Tayasal until nearly six months later. Canek, the Itza ruler, received them with friendliness.

They remained at Tayasal for some days, attempting to Christianize the Itza, but Canek, though interested in the services held by the missionaries, refused to renounce his own religion. He believed that the time had not yet arrived when, according to their ancient prophecies, the Itza were to accept a new faith.

The fathers were shown a large idol in the form of a horse, called Tzimin Chac, the "thunder horse." When Cortés had visited Tayasal, he left a lame horse with the Canek of that day, promising to return for it himself or to send for it. After Cortés's departure, the Itza treated the horse as a god, offering it fowl, other meats, and flowers, on which diet the horse died. The Itza, terrified at the death of a god on their hands, made a stone idol of the horse, which they worshiped in order to prove they were not responsible for its death. When Father Orbita saw this image, he became so infuriated at the idolatry that he smashed the image into bits. The Itza, outraged at such a sacrilege, tried to kill the missionaries, but Father Fuensalida seized the occasion to preach a sermon of such eloquence that the tumult subsided and the missionaries' lives were spared. When the fathers saw that they were making no progress in Christianizing the Itza, they took friendly farewell of Canek, who seems to have borne them no ill will for destroying the idol. Father Fuensalida reached Mérida on December 8, 1618, but Father Orbita remained at Tipu, a small settlement near Laguna de Bacalar.

The fathers set out from Tipu for Tayasal a second time in September of the following year, accompanied by some Tipu Indians as guides and servants. They reached the Itza capital at the beginning of October and remained there for eighteen days. Although Canek was at first friendly, the Tipu Indians were suspicious of the Itza and deserted in a body; later, however, three of them came back to serve the fathers. The Itza priests were becoming jealous of the influence of the Catholic missionaries and persuaded Canek's wife to urge her husband to expel them. The fathers' house was surrounded by armed Indians; the fathers themselves were hustled into a canoe with their Tipu servants and told never to return, as the Itza wanted no more of their religion. Father Orbita made some resistance, but a young Itza warrior seized the collar of his habit and twisted it so violently that Orbita fell to the ground senseless. The party was shoved off in a canoe without food or drink, the Itza hoping they would die of hunger on the long trip back to Tipu.

The Tipu Indians, however, had managed to secrete a little food, and the five subsisted on this until they reached Tipu. The fathers rested there for a few days, but, seeing that the time was not opportune for further attempts to convert the Itza, they left Tipu and returned to Mérida.

Three years later, in 1622, the governor of the Yucatan authorized Captain Francisco de Mirones to conduct a military expedition against the Itza. On March 30 of that year, Mirones with 20 Spaniards and 140 Indians left Hopelchen in Campeche for the Itza country. A Franciscan missionary, Father Diego Delgado, joined the army later. The force marched to Sacalum, where Mirones's treatment of the Indians was such that Father Delgado decided to leave the soldiers and go on without them. He left camp secretly and proceeded to Tayasal by way of Tipu, taking with him 80 converted Tipu Indians. Father Delgado and his Indians were escorted to Tayasal by the Itza with a great show of friendship. On reaching the town, however, all were seized and sacrificed to the Itza idols.

News of the death of Father Delgado reached Mérida slowly, but as soon as the authorities at the capital heard of it they sent word to Captain Mirones at Sacalum to be on his guard. However, the news came too late. On February 2, 1624, the Spaniards at Sacalum were all in the village church, without arms, when the Indians fell upon them and slaughtered them.

These two massacres put a stop to all attempts either to Christianize or to conquer the Itza. When, about twelve years later, the Tipu Indians began to apostatize, returning to their former idolatry, the last link of friendly Indian contact between northern Yucatan and the province of the Itza was severed. And thus affairs remained for nearly three-quarters of a century. The Spanish continued to consolidate their positions in the Yucatan and in Guatemala, but the territory lying between remained unconquered and un-Christianized, a continual irritation to both the military and ecclesiastical authorities of the two provinces.

In June 1695, Martin de Ursua, governor of the Yucatan, sent a contingent of Spanish soldiers and Indians to the village of Cauich in northern Campeche, to start building a road to the Peten. Toward the end of the month, the road builders reached a village called Nohthub in southern Campeche, where three Franciscans headed by Father Andres de Avendaño joined them. The priests were soon disgusted by the Spanish captain's treatment of the Indians, and they returned to Mérida.

On December 15, 1695, Father Avendaño again left Mérida for the province of the Itza, accompanied by two other Franciscans, four Indian singers from the Yucatan, and three Indian guides. Instead of going around by way of Tipu,

Father Avendaño followed the new road as far south as it had been built and then pushed on through the forests with his Indian guides.

They reached the lake on January 13, 1696, and were given a boisterous reception by the Chakan Itza living at the western end. The next day Canek met them at the village of the Chakan Itza, having crossed from Tayasal with an escort of 80 canoes. The fathers remained at Tayasal for three and a half days, and baptized more than three hundred Indian children. Father Avendaño urged Canek and his councilors to surrender to the Crown of Spain and accept Christianity. The Itza council took this proposal under consideration, but their final decision was that the time had not yet arrived when their prophecies had foretold that they should give up the worship of their old gods. They promised that if Governor Ursua would send the fathers back in another four months, the Itza would become vassals of the Spanish king and embrace Christianity.

Canek, learning of a plot among the Chakan Itza to waylay and kill the fathers on their return trip, persuaded Avendaño to return to Mérida by the longer though safer route through Tipu. On the night of January 17, 1696, the three fathers with their Indians from Yucatan, after taking an affectionate farewell of Canek and his family, embarked in a canoe.

From this point on, bad luck and increasing hardships beset the fathers. The promised guides to Tipu were not forthcoming, and after waiting two days the fathers set out on January 20 on the long, dangerous return journey to northern Yucatan. At the end of five days the party came to a large stream, probably the Rio Holmul, which they followed for another five days, becoming hopelessly lost. At this point they determined to strike west, hoping to reach the road that Ursua was having built from Cauich to the shores of the lake. They pushed on in this direction for fifteen days more, living on a meager diet of wild honey, green mammee, and palm nuts. On the fourth day of this exhausting trek Avendaño became so weak that the two other Franciscans, taking one of the four Indians as a guide, pushed on in the hope of locating some frontier settlement and bringing back help and supplies.

After six more days of slow, painstaking progress, Father Avendaño came upon the ruins of an ancient city, which he describes as follows:

With so few comforts and so many hardships my strength was failing rapidly, which brought home to me the truth of the adage that the Biscayans, my countrymen, have, namely, that "the belly supports, or carries the legs, and not the legs, the belly."

Among these high mountains which we passed there are a number of ancient buildings; among them I recognized some as living places, and although they were very high and my strength very little, I climbed them, but with difficulty. They are in the form of a convent with small cloisters and many rooms for living, all roofed, surrounded by a terrace and whitened with lime inside, which latter abounds in these parts, because all the hills are of limestone; and these said buildings are of such form that they did not appear like those of this province [Yucatan] which latter are entirely of dressed stone put together without mortar, especially as to their arches, but these [in Peten] are of stone masonry plastered over with lime.

The archaeological site best answering this description is Tikal. He was, perhaps, the first European to see this greatest of all ancient Maya centers.

Father Avendaño traveled westward and northward for another three days until his strength gave out altogether. He ordered the Indians to leave him propped against a tree with a lighted fire and a gourd of water, and to push on for help. The next morning his Indians returned with ten carriers. After leaving Avendaño the day before, they had come out on a trail that led them to Chuntuqui on the new road from Cauich. Here they found some Indian carriers and took them back to rescue the father. The Indians carried him in a hammock to Chuntuqui, where they arrived on February 19, 1696, after being lost for 31 days. At Chuntuqui he found the two other Franciscans who had left him 18 days before in search of help. After resting at Chuntuqui for a few days, Avendaño and his companions continued to Mérida, where they reported on their mission.

## The Conquest of the Itza, 1696-97

Although the road from Cauich to the Peten had been opened for 80 km (50 mi.) beyond Chuntuqui by September 1695, heavy rains prevented supplies from being transported along this route. Road gangs were obliged to return to Zucthok, north of the present boundary between Mexico and Guatemala, until the rainy season was over.

As the result of an embassy from Canek, which reached Mérida in December 1695, Ursua became convinced that the Itza were at last ready to submit to Spanish rule. He ordered Captain Paredes, who was still at work on the road, to proceed to Tayasal. Paredes, unable to comply with the order in person, sent Captain Pedro de Zubiaur with 60 Spanish soldiers, some Indian warriors, and Father San Buenaventura, to take possession of the province.

By this time the road had advanced to within 32 km of the lake, and Zubiaur's command reached the shore on January 18, 1696. Zubiaur had expected a peaceful reception by the Itza, but as the Spaniards approached the lake, they saw a flotilla of canoes filled with armed Indians advancing toward them. Leaping ashore, the Itza attacked vigorously, seizing some of the Indians from the Yucatan as prisoners. Father San Buenaventura, a lay Franciscan brother, and a Spanish soldier were also made prisoners, and a fourth Spaniard was killed in the fight. The Itza numbered about two thousand.

Battle having been forced upon them, the Spaniards defended themselves bravely, but finding his force outnumbered, Zubiaur withdrew to the main camp of Captain Paredes. A second and larger Spanish force was dispatched to the lake a day or so later. When it met with a similar hostile reception, further attempts to press the attack were discontinued.

The news of the Chakan Itza's hostility to Father Avendaño and of Zubiaur's defeat reached Ursua at the same time, and made it evident that the Itza were to be reduced only by military force. One hundred extra soldiers, shipwrights, and carpenters were needed to build a dugout and a galley to navigate the lake, in order to dominate Tayasal and the other villages. The men were recruited in Mérida and sent to Paredes with instructions to press forward the work of opening the road the remaining 32 km. However, Ursua at this time became engaged in a lawsuit with a political rival; he ordered Captain Paredes to retire to Campeche to await his coming with larger forces the next year.

The close of 1696 and the beginning of 1697 were spent in reassembling the army at Campeche. This army consisted of 235 Spanish soldiers, 120 Indian muleteers and road workers, and a number of Indian carriers. The infantry, artillery, and supply trains were sent ahead under Paredes, with orders to Zubiaur to proceed to within 8 km of the lake with the ship carpenters and caulkers. There they were to cut and trim sufficient timber for a galley and a dugout, and to await the arrival of the rest of the army. Ursua followed shortly with the cavalry, his personal suite, and the rest of the supplies. He left Campeche on January 24, 1697. On March 1, the needed timber ready, the whole army moved forward to the shore of the lake, where a fortified camp was built.

For the next twelve days the Itza made hostile demonstrations against the Spanish camp. Flotillas of canoes maneuvered in front of the camp daily. Companies of painted warriors surrounded it on the land side, beating their war drums and threatening the Spaniards with death and sacrifice. On March 10, a number of canoes were seen approaching the camp from the direction of Tayasal, the first canoe carrying a white flag. It was an embassy from Canek, consisting of the Itza high priest and other chiefs, who came to offer peace. Ursua received them in a friendly manner, and through them invited Canek to visit the Spanish camp the third day hence. The embassy was dismissed after being given a number of gifts, and the camp settled down to await the arrival of the Itza ruler.

On the appointed day, the Itza ruler did not appear. Instead, a great flotilla of canoes was seen moving across the lake toward the camp, while on shore companies of warriors threatened to attack. However, as night fell, both canoes and land forces withdrew. Ursua called a council of war of all his officers and requested each to give his opinion as to what should be done. They agreed that further efforts to reduce the Itza by peaceable means were useless and that the only course was to conquer them by force of arms. A decree was read to the army ordering the attack on Tayasal the following morning.

On March 13, before dawn, Mass was celebrated, breakfast was eaten, and the soldiers selected for the attack embarked on the galley. Ursua took with him 108 Spanish soldiers, the vicar-general of the army, and a nephew of Canek, who had shown himself friendly to the Spanish cause. He left behind, as a garrison, 127 Spaniards and all the Indian bowmen, road workers, and servants.

The galley swept toward Tayasal at dawn. The order of the preceding day was read again aboard ship; the vicar-general urged all who had sinned to ask forgiveness and granted a general absolution.

Soon those on the galley saw canoes putting out from the shore in two flanking squadrons, the occupants shouting and threatening with their weapons. Ursua ordered the oarsmen to row with all speed toward the town itself, which was now clear in the morning light. The number of canoes grew so rapidly that, as the galley neared shore, they formed a crescent around it, cutting it off from the lake. The Spaniards were now close enough to see the fortifications that had been built against them and the multitude already under arms waiting to defend the town.

Having come within bowshot of the galley, the Itza began to discharge a hail of arrows. In spite of this attack, Ursua still held back, shouting above the tumult, "No one fire, for God is on our side and there is no cause for fear." The Itza pressed closer, the arrows fell more thickly, and still Ursua held fire, shouting that no one was to discharge a shot, under pain of death. The Itza, mistaking this restraint for cowardice, mocked the Spaniards as not only already vanquished but killed and eaten.

Finally the Spanish general made one last appeal. The galley was slowed down and through an interpreter he told the Itza that the Spaniards came in peace and friendship. Unless the Itza laid down their arms, he said, they alone would be responsible for the slaughter that would follow. Although the Itza heard Ursua's plea, they again mistook his forbearance for weakness. Jeering at the Spaniards, they let fly more arrows. In spite of the congestion on the galley, only two Spaniards were wounded—Sergeant Juan González and a soldier named Bartolomé Durán.

Durán, infuriated, ignored Ursua's orders not to begin fighting, and discharged his harquebus at the Itza. The others followed his example until firing from the galley became general. The Spaniards, not waiting for the galley to ground, leaped into the water, firing their guns. Even here Ursua showed mercy, for he prevented his men from discharging the artillery. Had this been brought into action, the slaughter would have been frightful, for the enemy were numerous and closely packed.

Having gained the shore, the Spaniards continued firing with such effect that the Itza were soon in full flight. Everyone who could took to the lake, swimming frantically for the opposite shore. The stretch of water that separated Tayasal from the mainland was so thick with people that swimming was almost impossible and many perished.

Ursua and the victorious Spaniards pressed up the hill, while the galley was rowed back and forth, the men shooting from its deck. The Itza in the canoes sought to escape by hurling themselves into the lake and swimming for the mainland, so that soon the entire population of Tayasal was in the water.

Upon reaching the highest temple, Ursua planted the royal standard. From this temple, Ursua with his principal captains and the two Catholic priests gave thanks to God for their victory and for having preserved them from any loss of life. On every side there were congratulations; Ursua thanked his officers and men for their bravery and constancy, which had made possible the whole undertaking. The amenities being concluded, and finding themselves masters of the town, Ursua formally renamed Tayasal "Nuestra Señora de los Remedios y San Pablo de los Itzaes."

Ursua and the vicar-general made a tour of the temples, breaking the idols found in them as well as in the dwellings of the Itza. So vast was the number of idols that their destruction took the entire Spanish force from nine in the morning to half past five in the afternoon. As the final act of the day, Ursua selected the principal temple, where human sacrifice had recently been offered to the Itza deities, to be the sanctuary of the Christian God. Thus, in the morning of a single day the power of the Itza was crushed, and the last independent Maya political entity was brought under the domination of the Spanish crown.

The conquest of the Maya by the Spanish was obviously a long and brutal process, a campaign that ultimately succeeded in destroying the last remnants of ancient Maya civilization. In succeeding so well, of course, the conquest also marked the beginning of the modern Maya. But as is often said, that is another story indeed.

# APPENDIXES

# APPENDIX A

# EARLIEST AND LATEST LONG-COUNT DATES
# AT SELECTED MAYA SITES

| Site | Earliest long-count date | Latest long-count date |
|---|---|---|
| Chiapa de Corzo | 7.16.3.2.13 (?) (Stela 2) | |
| Tres Zapotes | 7.16.6.16.18 (Stela C) | |
| Abaj Takalik | 7.16?.?.?.? (Stela 2) | 8.4.5.17.11 (Stela 5) |
| El Baúl | 7.19.15.7.12 (Stela 1) | |
| Tikal | 8.12.14.8.15 (Stela 29) | 10.2.0.0.0 (Stela 11) |
| Uaxactun | 8.14.10.13.15 (Stela 9) | 10.3.0.0.0 (Stela 12) |
| Xultun | 8.15.0.0.0 (?) (Stela 12) | 10.3.0.0.0 (Stela 10) |
| Yaxha | 8.16.0.0.0 (Stela 5) | 9.18.3.0.0 (Stela 13) |
| El Zapote | 8.17.1.5.3 (Stela 4) | 9.0.0.0.0 (Stela 5) |
| Balakbal | 8.18.9.17.18 (Stela 5) | |
| Uolantun | 8.18.13.5.11 (Stela 1) | |
| Piedras Negras | 9.0.0.0.0 (Altar 1) | 9.19.0.0.0 (Altar 3) |
| Altar de Sacrificios | 9.1.0.0.0 (Stela 10) | 10.1.0.0.0 (Stela 22) |
| Copan | 9.1.10.0.0 (Stela 20) | 9.18.10.0.0 (Altar 61) |
| Naranjo | 9.2.0.0.0 (Stela 41) | 9.19.10.0.0 (Stela 32) |
| Oxkintok | 9.2.0.0.0 (Doorjamb) | |
| Quirigua | 9.2.3.8.0 (Monument 21) | 9.19.0.0.0 (Structure 1B-1) |
| Chichen Itza | 9.2.10.0.0 (Temple of Initial Series) | |
| Caracol | 9.2.10.0.0 (Stela 9) | 10.1.0.0.0 (Stela 17) |
| Yaxchilan | 9.4.0.0.0 (Stela 7) | 9.18.17.12.6 (Lintel 10) |
| Calakmul | 9.4.0.0.0 (Stela 43) | 9.19.0.0.0 (Stela 64) |
| Naachtun | 9.4.10.0.0 (Stela 23) | 9.16.10.0.0 (Stela 10) |
| Kuna-Lacanha | 9.6.0.11.0 (Stela 2) | 9.15.15.0.0 (Lintel 1) |
| Tulum (Xelha?) | 9.6.10.0.0 (Stela 1) | |
| Ojo de Agua | 9.7.15.0.0 (Stela 1) | |
| Ichpaatun | 9.8.0.0.0 (Stela 7) | |

| Site | Earliest long-count date | Latest long-count date |
|---|---|---|
| Pusilha | 9.8.0.0.0 (Stela D) | 9.15.0.0.0 (Stela E) |
| Tonina | 9.8.0.0.0 (Monument 106) | 10.4.0.0.0 (Monument 101) |
| El Encanto | 9.8.4.9.1 (Stela 1) | |
| Bonampak | 9.8.9.0.0 (Lintel 6) | 9.18.0.0.0 (Lintel 3) |
| Palenque | 9.8.9.13.0 (Hieroglyphic Staircase) | 9.17.13.0.7 (Tablet 96 Glyphs) |
| El Tortuguero | 9.8.10.0.0 (Stela 6) | 9.14.0.0.0 (Stela 2) |
| Coba | 9.9.0.0.0 (Stela 6) | 9.12.12.0.5 (Stela 20) |
| Uxul | 9.9.0.0.0 (Stela 3) | 9.16.0.0.0 (?) |
| Chinikiha | 9.9.2.8.4 (Throne) | |
| Chinkultic | 9.9.5.0.0 (?) | 10.0.15.0.0 (Stela 1) |
| Tzibanche | 9.9.5.0.0 (?) | 10.4.0.0.0 (Jade gorget) |
| El Pabellón | 9.10.0.0.0 (Stela 1) | |
| Isla de Jaina | 9.11.0.0.0 (Stela 1) | |
| Dos Pilas | 9.11.10.0.0 (Hieroglyphic Staircase 2) | 9.15.4.6.4 (Stela 16) |
| Pestac | 9.11.12.9.6 (Stela 1) | |
| El Amparo | 9.11.13.0.0 (Altar 1) | |
| Edzna | 9.12.0.0.0 (Stela 18) | 9.18.10.0.0 (Stela 5) |
| Tila | 9.12.13.0.0 (Stela B) | 10.0.0.0.0 (Stela A) |
| Oxpemul | 9.12.15.0.0 (Stela 15) | 10.0.0.0.0 (Stela 7) |
| Tzendales | 9.12.19.6.9 (Temple of Initial Series) | |
| Aguateca | 9.13.0.0.0 (Stela 5) | 9.18.0.0.0 (Stela 7) |
| Pixoy | 9.13.1.3.2 (Stela 5) | |
| Ucanal | 9.13.10.0.0 (Stela 10) | 10.1.0.0.0 (Stela 4) |
| Machaquila | 9.14.0.0.0 (Stela 13) | 10.0.10.0.0 (Stela 5) |
| El Palmar | 9.14.0.0.0 (Stela 10) | 10.2.15.0.0 (Stela 41) |
| La Florida | 9.15.0.0.0 (Stela 9) | 9.16.15.0.0 (Stela 7) |
| Itsimte | 9.15.0.0.0 (Stela 5) | 9.17.5.0.0 (Altar 1) |
| Itzan | 9.15.4.15.3 (Stela 17) | 9.19.12.8.18 (Stela 6) |
| Laguna Perdida | 9.15.11.2.17 (Altar) | |
| Xcalumkin | 9.15.12.6.9 (Temple of Initial Series) | |
| Seibal | 9.15.15.0.0 (Hieroglyphic Staircase A-1) | 10.3.0.0.0 (Stela 20) |
| La Amelia | 9.16.9.4.19 (Hieroglyphic Staircase) | 9.18.13.17.1 (Stela 2) |
| Holactun | 9.16.13.0.0 (Temple of Initial Series) | |
| La Honradez | 9.17.0.0.0 (Stela 7) | 9.18.0.0.0 (Stela 4) |
| Nakum | 9.17.0.0.0 (Stela U) | 10.1.0.0.0 (Stela D) |
| El Cayo | 9.17.1.5.8 (Lintel 1) | |
| Polol | 9.17.7.0.4 (Stela 4) | 9.18.0.0.0 (Stela 1) |
| Ixkun | 9.17.9.0.13 (Stela 2) | 9.18.10.0.0 (Stela 5) |

| Site | Earliest long-count date | Latest long-count date |
|---|---|---|
| El Caribe | 9.17.10.0.0 (Stela 2) | |
| Ixtutz | 9.17.10.0.0 (Stela 4) | |
| La Milpa | 9.17.10.0.0 (Stela 7) | |
| La Muñeca | 9.17.10.0.0 (Stela 5) | 10.3.0.0.0 (Stela 1) |
| Los Higos | 9.17.10.7.0 (Stela 1) | |
| La Mar | 9.17.15.0.0 (Stela 1) | 9.18.15.0.0 (Stela 2) |
| Aguas Calientes | 9.17.16.6.1 (Stela 1) | |
| Cancuen | 9.18.0.0.0 (Stela 2) | 9.18.10.0.0 (Stela 1) |
| Poco Uinic | 9.18.0.0.0 (Stela 3) | |
| Tayasal | 9.18.0.0.0 (Lintel 1) | 10.2.0.0.0 (Flores Stela 1) |
| Hatzcab Ceel | 9.19.0.0.0 (Altar 2) | |
| Xunantunich | 10.0.0.0.0 (Stela 9) | 10.1.0.0.0 (Stela 1) |
| Ixlu | 10.1.10.0.0 (Stela 1) | 10.2.10.0.0 (Stela 2) |
| Comitan | 10.2.5.0.0 (Stela 1) | |
| Sacchana | 10.2.5.0.0 (Stela 1) | 10.2.10.0.0 (Stela 2) |
| Jimbal | 10.2.10.0.0 (Stela 1) | 10.3.0.0.0 (Stela 2) |
| Uxmal | 10.3.17.14.1 (Capstone) | |

# APPENDIX B

# THE CONVERSION OF MAYA AND GREGORIAN CHRONOLOGIES

The conversion of the Maya and Gregorian calendars, one to the other, is accomplished by the use of Julian Day Numbers (JDN's) and a correlation constant. There are computer programs for this operation, but it can also be done rather easily on a pocket calculator, along with pencil and paper.

JDN's are a standard chronological reference used by astronomers and other scholars to count the days from a base date of January 1, 4712 B.C. JDN's for the centuries of our era are given in Table B.1. Subtracting the correlation constant from a given JDN yields the corresponding day number in Maya chronology, the count of days from the Maya "zero" date of 4 Ahau 8 Cumku, 3114 B.C. (Conversely, when the correlation constant is added to a Maya day number, it yields the corresponding JDN.) A variety of correlation constants has been proposed, corresponding to each of the Maya calendrical correlations (see Chapter 16). The generally accepted correlation used here (by which the short-count date of Katun 13 Ahau corresponds to the long-count date 11.16.0.0.0) is calculated from the original correlation constant of 584,280 (Goodman 1905); the constant was later corrected by Thompson (1935) to 584,285 and finally to the figure generally used today, 584,283 (Thompson 1950).

To convert a Maya long-count date to the Gregorian system, begin by calculating its equivalent JDN. This is done by the use of the correlation constant, 584,283, for the 11.16.0.0.0 date (other correlations use 489,383, for the 12.9.0.0.0 date, and 679,183, for the 11.3.0.0.0 date). A given long-count date, 9.15.6.14.6, for instance, is first converted into its Maya day number by multiplying and adding the days of its component units. In this case, $9 \times 144,000$ (baktuns) + $15 \times 7,200$ (katuns) + $6 \times 360$ (tuns) + $14 \times 20$ (uinals) + $6 \times 1$ (kins) = 1,406,446. This Maya day number is then added to the correlation constant (1,406,446 + 584,283 = 1,990,729) to give its corresponding JDN. From this JDN, the nearest *smaller* JDN for which an equivalent Gregorian date is known is then subtracted, using values like those given in Table B.1. Using our example and selecting the closest smaller JDN to 1,990,729 (in this case, that for A.D. 700), it can be seen that the remainder of 13,999 days corresponds to 38 years, 129 days (13,999 ÷ 365 + a remainder of 129). However, it must be remembered that in the Gregorian calendar (but not the Maya calendar) every fourth year adds one leap day. Leap centuries are those that end in 00 and are divisible by 400 (A.D. 400, 800, 1200, 1600, etc.). If we then subtract the number of leap days between A.D. 700 and 738 (9) from the 129-day remainder, we find that the Maya long-count date 9.15.6.14.6 corresponds to day 120 of A.D. 738, or May 1.

To convert a Gregorian date to the Maya long count, the procedure is reversed, and a little more complex. As before, first convert a given Gregorian date, March 16, 1940, for example, to its equivalent JDN (2,415,021 + 40 × 365 + 75 + 10 leap days = 2,429,706). The correlation constant is then subtracted to yield the Maya day number (2,429,706 − 584,283 = 1,845,423). This Maya day number is next divided by the baktun, katun, tun, uinal, and kin values as follows:

$$1,845,423 \div 144,000 = 12 \text{ baktuns} + 117,423$$
$$117,423 \div 7,200 = 16 \text{ katuns} + 2,223$$
$$2,223 \div 360 = 6 \text{ tuns} + 63$$
$$63 \div 20 = 3 \text{ uinals} + 3$$
$$3 \div 1 = 2 \text{ kins}$$

This produces the long-count date 12.16.6.3.3.

To determine the calendar-round positions for this date, divide the Maya day number by 13, 20, and 365 to yield the remainders for each:

$$1,845,423 \div 13: \text{ remainder of } 8$$
$$1,845,423 \div 20: \text{ remainder of } 3$$
$$1,845,423 \div 365: \text{ remainder of } 348$$

The day number in the 260-day almanac, the first component of the calendar-round date, is determined by adding the first remainder to 4 (8 + 4 = 12). If the result exceeds 13, subtract 13 from this sum. The corresponding day in the 260-day almanac is found by using the value of the second remainder above (3) to determine the number of days after Ahau (see Fig. 16.4). These steps are done because the beginning of the current Maya calendrical era was on the calendar-round date 4 Ahau 8 Cumku. By counting 3 positions from Ahau the day Akbal is arrived at, so that the complete 260-day almanac date is 12 Akbal.

The vague-year day and month position (Fig. 16.5) is determined by counting the

TABLE B.1

*Julian Day Numbers (JDN's) for January 1 of the Years A.D. 0–2000*

| Year | JDN | Year | JDN | Year | JDN |
|---|---|---|---|---|---|
| 0 | 1,721,060 | 700 | 1,976,730 | 1400 | 2,232,400 |
| 100 | 1,757,585 | 800 | 2,013,254 | 1500 | 2,268,924 |
| 200 | 1,794,104 | 900 | 2,049,779 | 1600 | 2,305,448 |
| 300 | 1,830,633 | 1000 | 2,086,303 | 1700 | 2,341,973 |
| 400 | 1,867,157 | 1100 | 2,122,827 | 1800 | 2,378,497 |
| 500 | 1,903,682 | 1200 | 2,159,351 | 1900 | 2,415,021 |
| 600 | 1,940,206 | 1300 | 2,195,876 | 2000 | 2,451,545 |

number of days after 8 Cumku equal to the third remainder calculated above (348). There are 17 days from 8 Cumku to 0 Pop, the beginning of a new vague year (12 days remaining in Cumku and 5 days in Uayeb), so that by subtracting 17 from 348, and counting forward the resulting number of days (331), the day 11 Kayab is reached. Thus the complete long-count date for March 16, 1940, is 12.16.6.3.3 12 Akbal 11 Kayab.

Table B.2 provides the conversions of Maya long-count dates to their Gregorian equivalents for the katun and half-katun endings from 8.0.0.0.0 to 13.0.0.0.0 on the basis of the GMT (or 11.16) correlation. This is an increase over the time span included in the earlier editions of this work. Note that in these previous editions the Gregorian date equivalents were based on the 584,285 correlation constant (Thompson 1935; Morley 1937–38). Since the correlation constant of 584,283 (Thompson 1950) is now generally preferred, it has been used to calculate the Gregorian dates in the following table, and the Gregorian dates that appeared in the earlier editions have been corrected by two days.

TABLE B.2

*Correlation of Maya and Gregorian Chronologies*
*According to the Goodman-Martínez-Thompson (GMT) Correlation*

| Katun or half-katun ending in the Maya long count (Initial Series) | | | Katun ending in the Maya short count (the *u kahlay katunob*) | Gregorian equivalent A.D. (584,283 correlation constant) |
|---|---|---|---|---|
| 8.0.0.0.0 | 9 Ahau | 3 Zip | Katun 9 Ahau | 41, September 6 |
| 8.0.10.0.0 | 8 Ahau | 18 Cumku | | 51, July 15 |
| 8.1.0.0.0 | 7 Ahau | 8 Pax | Katun 7 Ahau | 61, May 24 |
| 8.1.10.0.0 | 6 Ahau | 18 Mac | | 71, April 2 |
| 8.2.0.0.0 | 5 Ahau | 8 Zac | Katun 5 Ahau | 81, February 9 |
| 8.2.10.0.0 | 4 Ahau | 18 Mol | | 90, December 18 |
| 8.3.0.0.0 | 3 Ahau | 8 Xul | Katun 3 Ahau | 100, October 26 |
| 8.3.10.0.0 | 2 Ahau | 18 Zip | | 110, September 4 |
| 8.4.0.0.0 | 1 Ahau | 8 Pop | Katun 1 Ahau | 120, July 13 |
| 8.4.10.0.0 | 13 Ahau | 3 Kayab | | 130, May 22 |
| 8.5.0.0.0 | 12 Ahau | 13 Kankin | Katun 12 Ahau | 140, March 30 |
| 8.5.10.0.0 | 11 Ahau | 3 Ceh | | 150, February 6 |
| 8.6.0.0.0 | 10 Ahau | 13 Chen | Katun 10 Ahau | 159, December 15 |
| 8.6.10.0.0 | 9 Ahau | 3 Yaxkin | | 169, October 24 |
| 8.7.0.0.0 | 8 Ahau | 13 Zotz | Katun 8 Ahau | 179, September 2 |
| 8.7.10.0.0 | 7 Ahau | 3 Uo | | 189, July 11 |
| 8.8.0.0.0 | 6 Ahau | 18 Kayab | Katun 6 Ahau | 199, May 20 |
| 8.8.10.0.0 | 5 Ahau | 8 Muan | | 209, March 29 |
| 8.9.0.0.0 | 4 Ahau | 18 Ceh | Katun 4 Ahau | 219, February 5 |
| 8.9.10.0.0 | 3 Ahau | 8 Yax | | 228, December 14 |
| 8.10.0.0.0 | 2 Ahau | 18 Yaxkin | Katun 2 Ahau | 238, October 23 |
| 8.10.10.0.0 | 1 Ahau | 8 Tzec | | 248, August 31 |
| 8.11.0.0.0 | 13 Ahau | 18 Uo | Katun 13 Ahau | 258, July 10 |
| 8.11.10.0.0 | 12 Ahau | 13 Cumku | | 268, May 18 |
| 8.12.0.0.0 | 11 Ahau | 3 Pax | Katun 11 Ahau | 278, March 27 |
| 8.12.10.0.0 | 10 Ahau | 13 Mac | | 288, February 3 |
| 8.13.0.0.0 | 9 Ahau | 3 Zac | Katun 9 Ahau | 297, December 12 |
| 8.13.10.0.0 | 8 Ahau | 13 Mol | | 307, October 22 |
| 8.14.0.0.0 | 7 Ahau | 3 Xul | Katun 7 Ahau | 317, August 30 |
| 8.14.10.0.0 | 6 Ahau | 13 Zip | | 327, July 9 |
| 8.15.0.0.0 | 5 Ahau | 3 Pop | Katun 5 Ahau | 337, May 17 |
| 8.15.10.0.0 | 4 Ahau | 18 Pax | | 347, March 26 |

TABLE B.2 (*continued*)

| Katun or half-katun ending in the Maya long count (Initial Series) | | Katun ending in the Maya short count (the *u kahlay katunob*) | Gregorian equivalent A.D. (584,283 correlation constant) |
|---|---|---|---|
| 8.16.0.0.0 | 3 Ahau 8 Kankin | Katun 3 Ahau | 357, February 1 |
| 8.16.10.0.0 | 2 Ahau 18 Zac | | 366, December 11 |
| 8.17.0.0.0 | 1 Ahau 8 Chen | Katun 1 Ahau | 376, October 19 |
| 8.17.10.0.0 | 13 Ahau 18 Xul | | 386, August 28 |
| 8.18.0.0.0 | 12 Ahau 8 Zotz | Katun 12 Ahau | 396, July 6 |
| 8.18.10.0.0 | 11 Ahau 18 Pop | | 406, May 15 |
| 8.19.0.0.0 | 10 Ahau 13 Kayab | Katun 10 Ahau | 416, March 23 |
| 8.19.10.0.0 | 9 Ahau 3 Muan | | 426, January 30 |
| 9.0.0.0.0 | 8 Ahau 13 Ceh | Katun 8 Ahau | 435, December 9 |
| 9.0.10.0.0 | 7 Ahau 3 Yax | | 445, October 17 |
| 9.1.0.0.0 | 6 Ahau 13 Yaxkin | Katun 6 Ahau | 455, August 26 |
| 9.1.10.0.0 | 5 Ahau 3 Tzec | | 465, July 4 |
| 9.2.0.0.0 | 4 Ahau 13 Uo | Katun 4 Ahau | 475, May 13 |
| 9.2.10.0.0 | 3 Ahau 8 Cumku | | 485, March 21 |
| 9.3.0.0.0 | 2 Ahau 18 Muan | Katun 2 Ahau | 495, January 28 |
| 9.3.10.0.0 | 1 Ahau 8 Mac | | 504, December 7 |
| 9.4.0.0.0 | 13 Ahau 18 Yax | Katun 13 Ahau | 514, October 16 |
| 9.4.10.0.0 | 12 Ahau 8 Mol | | 524, August 24 |
| 9.5.0.0.0 | 11 Ahau 18 Tzec | Katun 11 Ahau | 534, July 3 |
| 9.5.10.0.0 | 10 Ahau 8 Zip | | 544, May 11 |
| 9.6.0.0.0 | 9 Ahau 3 Uayeb | Katun 9 Ahau | 554, March 20 |
| 9.6.10.0.0 | 8 Ahau 13 Pax | | 564, January 27 |
| 9.7.0.0.0 | 7 Ahau 3 Kankin | Katun 7 Ahau | 573, December 5 |
| 9.7.10.0.0 | 6 Ahau 13 Zac | | 583, October 14 |
| 9.8.0.0.0 | 5 Ahau 3 Chen | Katun 5 Ahau | 593, August 22 |
| 9.8.10.0.0 | 4 Ahau 13 Xul | | 603, July 2 |
| 9.9.0.0.0 | 3 Ahau 3 Zotz | Katun 3 Ahau | 613, May 10 |
| 9.9.10.0.0 | 2 Ahau 13 Pop | | 623, March 19 |
| 9.10.0.0.0 | 1 Ahau 8 Kayab | Katun 1 Ahau | 633, January 25 |
| 9.10.10.0.0 | 13 Ahau 18 Kankin | | 642, December 4 |
| 9.11.0.0.0 | 12 Ahau 8 Ceh | Katun 12 Ahau | 652, October 12 |
| 9.11.10.0.0 | 11 Ahau 18 Chen | | 662, August 21 |
| 9.12.0.0.0 | 10 Ahau 8 Yaxkin | Katun 10 Ahau | 672, June 29 |
| 9.12.10.0.0 | 9 Ahau 18 Zip | | 682, May 8 |
| 9.13.0.0.0 | 8 Ahau 8 Uo | Katun 8 Ahau | 692, March 16 |
| 9.13.10.0.0 | 7 Ahau 3 Cumku | | 702, January 24 |
| 9.14.0.0.0 | 6 Ahau 13 Muan | Katun 6 Ahau | 711, December 3 |
| 9.14.10.0.0 | 5 Ahau 3 Mac | | 721, October 11 |
| 9.15.0.0.0 | 4 Ahau 13 Yax | Katun 4 Ahau | 731, August 20 |
| 9.15.10.0.0 | 3 Ahau 3 Mol | | 741, June 28 |
| 9.16.0.0.0 | 2 Ahau 13 Tzec | Katun 2 Ahau | 751, May 7 |
| 9.16.10.0.0 | 1 Ahau 3 Zip | | 761, March 15 |
| 9.17.0.0.0 | 13 Ahau 18 Cumku | Katun 13 Ahau | 771, January 22 |
| 9.17.10.0.0 | 12 Ahau 8 Pax | | 780, November 30 |
| 9.18.0.0.0 | 11 Ahau 18 Mac | Katun 11 Ahau | 790, October 9 |
| 9.18.10.0.0 | 10 Ahau 8 Zac | | 800, August 17 |
| 9.19.0.0.0 | 9 Ahau 18 Mol | Katun 9 Ahau | 810, June 26 |
| 9.19.10.0.0 | 8 Ahau 8 Xul | | 820, May 4 |
| 10.0.0.0.0 | 7 Ahau 18 Zip | Katun 7 Ahau | 830, March 13 |
| 10.0.10.0.0 | 6 Ahau 8 Pop | | 840, January 20 |
| 10.1.0.0.0 | 5 Ahau 3 Kayab | Katun 5 Ahau | 849, November 28 |
| 10.1.10.0.0 | 4 Ahau 13 Kankin | | 859, October 7 |
| 10.2.0.0.0 | 3 Ahau 3 Ceh | Katun 3 Ahau | 869, August 15 |
| 10.2.10.0.0 | 2 Ahau 13 Chen | | 879, June 24 |
| 10.3.0.0.0 | 1 Ahau 3 Yaxkin | Katun 1 Ahau | 889, May 2 |
| 10.3.10.0.0 | 13 Ahau 13 Zotz | | 899, March 11 |
| 10.4.0.0.0 | 12 Ahau 3 Uo | Katun 12 Ahau | 909, January 18 |

TABLE B.2 (*continued*)

| Katun or half-katun ending in the Maya long count (Initial Series) | | Katun ending in the Maya short count (the *u kahlay katunob*) | Gregorian equivalent A.D. (584,283 correlation constant) |
|---|---|---|---|
| 10.4.10.0.0 | 11 Ahau 18 Kayab | | 918, November 27 |
| 10.5.0.0.0 | 10 Ahau 8 Muan | Katun 10 Ahau | 928, October 5 |
| 10.5.10.0.0 | 9 Ahau 18 Ceh | | 938, August 14 |
| 10.6.0.0.0 | 8 Ahau 8 Yax | Katun 8 Ahau | 948, June 22 |
| 10.6.10.0.0 | 7 Ahau 18 Yaxkin | | 958, May 1 |
| 10.7.0.0.0 | 6 Ahau 8 Tzec | Katun 6 Ahau | 968, March 9 |
| 10.7.10.0.0 | 5 Ahau 18 Uo | | 978, January 16 |
| 10.8.0.0.0 | 4 Ahau 13 Cumku | Katun 4 Ahau | 987, November 25 |
| 10.8.10.0.0 | 3 Ahau 3 Pax | | 997, October 3 |
| 10.9.0.0.0 | 2 Ahau 13 Mac | Katun 2 Ahau | 1007, August 13 |
| 10.9.10.0.0 | 1 Ahau 3 Zac | | 1017, June 21 |
| 10.10.0.0.0 | 13 Ahau 13 Mol | Katun 13 Ahau | 1027, April 30 |
| 10.10.10.0.0 | 12 Ahau 3 Xul | | 1037, March 8 |
| 10.11.0.0.0 | 11 Ahau 13 Zip | Katun 11 Ahau | 1047, January 15 |
| 10.11.10.0.0 | 10 Ahau 3 Pop | | 1056, November 23 |
| 10.12.0.0.0 | 9 Ahau 18 Pax | Katun 9 Ahau | 1066, October 2 |
| 10.12.10.0.0 | 8 Ahau 8 Kankin | | 1076, August 10 |
| 10.13.0.0.0 | 7 Ahau 18 Zac | Katun 7 Ahau | 1086, June 19 |
| 10.13.10.0.0 | 6 Ahau 8 Chen | | 1096, April 27 |
| 10.14.0.0.0 | 5 Ahau 18 Xul | Katun 5 Ahau | 1106, March 7 |
| 10.14.10.0.0 | 4 Ahau 8 Zotz | | 1116, January 14 |
| 10.15.0.0.0 | 3 Ahau 18 Pop | Katun 3 Ahau | 1125, November 22 |
| 10.15.10.0.0 | 2 Ahau 13 Kayab | | 1135, October 1 |
| 10.16.0.0.0 | 1 Ahau 3 Muan | Katun 1 Ahau | 1145, August 9 |
| 10.16.10.0.0 | 13 Ahau 13 Ceh | | 1155, June 18 |
| 10.17.0.0.0 | 12 Ahau 3 Yax | Katun 12 Ahau | 1165, April 26 |
| 10.17.10.0.0 | 11 Ahau 13 Yaxkin | | 1175, March 5 |
| 10.18.0.0.0 | 10 Ahau 3 Tzec | Katun 10 Ahau | 1185, January 11 |
| 10.18.10.0.0 | 9 Ahau 13 Uo | | 1194, November 20 |
| 10.19.0.0.0 | 8 Ahau 8 Cumku | Katun 8 Ahau | 1204, September 28 |
| 10.19.10.0.0 | 7 Ahau 18 Muan | | 1214, August 7 |
| 11.0.0.0.0 | 6 Ahau 8 Mac | Katun 6 Ahau | 1224, June 15 |
| 11.0.10.0.0 | 5 Ahau 18 Yax | | 1234, April 24 |
| 11.1.0.0.0 | 4 Ahau 8 Mol | Katun 4 Ahau | 1244, March 2 |
| 11.1.10.0.0 | 3 Ahau 18 Tzec | | 1254, January 9 |
| 11.2.0.0.0 | 2 Ahau 8 Zip | Katun 2 Ahau | 1263, November 18 |
| 11.2.10.0.0 | 1 Ahau 3 Uayeb | | 1273, September 26 |
| 11.3.0.0.0 | 13 Ahau 13 Pax | Katun 13 Ahau | 1283, August 5 |
| 11.3.10.0.0 | 12 Ahau 3 Kankin | | 1293, June 13 |
| 11.4.0.0.0 | 11 Ahau 13 Zac | Katun 11 Ahau | 1303, April 23 |
| 11.4.10.0.0 | 10 Ahau 3 Chen | | 1313, March 1 |
| 11.5.0.0.0 | 9 Ahau 13 Xul | Katun 9 Ahau | 1323, January 8 |
| 11.5.10.0.0 | 8 Ahau 3 Zotz | | 1332, November 16 |
| 11.6.0.0.0 | 7 Ahau 13 Pop | Katun 7 Ahau | 1342, September 25 |
| 11.6.10.0.0 | 6 Ahau 8 Kayab | | 1352, August 3 |
| 11.7.0.0.0 | 5 Ahau 18 Kankin | Katun 5 Ahau | 1362, June 12 |
| 11.7.10.0.0 | 4 Ahau 8 Ceh | | 1372, April 20 |
| 11.8.0.0.0 | 3 Ahau 18 Chen | Katun 3 Ahau | 1382, February 27 |
| 11.8.10.0.0 | 2 Ahau 8 Yaxkin | | 1392, January 6 |
| 11.9.0.0.0 | 1 Ahau 18 Zotz | Katun 1 Ahau | 1401, November 15 |
| 11.9.10.0.0 | 13 Ahau 8 Uo | | 1411, September 24 |
| 11.10.0.0.0 | 12 Ahau 3 Cumku | Katun 12 Ahau | 1421, August 2 |
| 11.10.10.0.0 | 11 Ahau 13 Muan | | 1431, June 11 |
| 11.11.0.0.0 | 10 Ahau 3 Mac | Katun 10 Ahau | 1441, April 19 |
| 11.11.10.0.0 | 9 Ahau 13 Yax | | 1451, February 26 |
| 11.12.0.0.0 | 8 Ahau 3 Mol | Katun 8 Ahau | 1461, January 4 |
| 11.12.10.0.0 | 7 Ahau 13 Tzec | | 1470, November 13 |
| 11.13.0.0.0 | 6 Ahau 3 Zip | Katun 6 Ahau | 1480, September 21 |

TABLE B.2 (*continued*)

| Katun or half-katun ending in the Maya long count (Initial Series) | | Katun ending in the Maya short count (the *u kahlay katunob*) | Gregorian equivalent A.D. (584,283 correlation constant) |
|---|---|---|---|
| 11.13.10.0.0 | 5 Ahau 18 Cumku | | 1490, July 31 |
| 11.14.0.0.0 | 4 Ahau 8 Pax | Katun  4 Ahau | 1500, June 9 |
| 11.14.10.0.0 | 3 Ahau 18 Mac | | 1510, April 18 |
| 11.15.0.0.0 | 2 Ahau 8 Zac | Katun  2 Ahau | 1520, February 25 |
| 11.15.10.0.0 | 1 Ahau 18 Mol | | 1530, January 3 |
| 11.16.0.0.0 | 13 Ahau 8 Xul | Katun 13 Ahau | 1539, November 12 |
| 11.16.10.0.0 | 12 Ahau 18 Zip | | 1549, September 20 |
| 11.17.0.0.0 | 11 Ahau 8 Pop | Katun 11 Ahau | 1559, July 30 |
| 11.17.10.0.0 | 10 Ahau 3 Kayab | | 1569, June 7 |
| 11.18.0.0.0 | 9 Ahau 13 Kankin | Katun  9 Ahau | 1579, April 16 |
| 11.18.10.0.0 | 8 Ahau 3 Ceh | | 1589, February 22 |
| 11.19.0.0.0 | 7 Ahau 13 Chen | Katun  7 Ahau | 1599, January 1 |
| 11.19.10.0.0 | 6 Ahau 3 Yaxkin | | 1608, November 9 |
| 12.0.0.0.0 | 5 Ahau 13 Zotz | Katun  5 Ahau | 1618, September 18 |
| 12.0.10.0.0 | 4 Ahau 3 Uo | | 1628, July 27 |
| 12.1.0.0.0 | 3 Ahau 18 Kayab | Katun  3 Ahau | 1638, June 5 |
| 12.1.10.0.0 | 2 Ahau 8 Muan | | 1648, April 13 |
| 12.2.0.0.0 | 1 Ahau 18 Ceh | Katun  1 Ahau | 1658, February 20 |
| 12.2.10.0.0 | 13 Ahau 8 Yax | | 1667, December 30 |
| 12.3.0.0.0 | 12 Ahau 18 Yaxkin | Katun 12 Ahau | 1677, November 7 |
| 12.3.10.0.0 | 11 Ahau 8 Tzec | | 1687, September 16 |
| 12.4.0.0.0 | 10 Ahau 18 Uo | Katun 10 Ahau | 1697, July 25 |
| 12.4.10.0.0 | 9 Ahau 13 Cumku | | 1707, June 4 |
| 12.5.0.0.0 | 8 Ahau 3 Pax | Katun  8 Ahau | 1717, April 12 |
| 12.5.10.0.0 | 7 Ahau 13 Mac | | 1727, February 19 |
| 12.6.0.0.0 | 6 Ahau 3 Zac | Katun  6 Ahau | 1736, December 28 |
| 12.6.10.0.0 | 5 Ahau 13 Mol | | 1746, November 6 |
| 12.7.0.0.0 | 4 Ahau 3 Xul | Katun  4 Ahau | 1756, September 14 |
| 12.7.10.0.0 | 3 Ahau 13 Zotz | | 1766, July 24 |
| 12.8.0.0.0 | 2 Ahau 3 Pop | Katun  2 Ahau | 1776, June 1 |
| 12.8.10.0.0 | 1 Ahau 18 Pax | | 1786, April 10 |
| 12.9.0.0.0 | 13 Ahau 8 Kankin | Katun 13 Ahau | 1796, February 17 |
| 12.9.10.0.0 | 12 Ahau 18 Zac | | 1805, December 26 |
| 12.10.0.0.0 | 11 Ahau 8 Chen | Katun 11 Ahau | 1815, November 5 |
| 12.10.10.0.0 | 10 Ahau 18 Xul | | 1825, September 13 |
| 12.11.0.0.0 | 9 Ahau 8 Zotz | Katun  9 Ahau | 1835, July 23 |
| 12.11.10.0.0 | 8 Ahau 18 Pop | | 1845, May 31 |
| 12.12.0.0.0 | 7 Ahau 13 Kayab | Katun  7 Ahau | 1855, April 9 |
| 12.12.10.0.0 | 6 Ahau 3 Muan | | 1865, February 15 |
| 12.13.0.0.0 | 5 Ahau 13 Ceh | Katun  5 Ahau | 1874, December 24 |
| 12.13.10.0.0 | 4 Ahau 3 Yax | | 1884, November 2 |
| 12.14.0.0.0 | 3 Ahau 13 Kankin | Katun  3 Ahau | 1894, September 11 |
| 12.14.10.0.0 | 2 Ahau 3 Tzec | | 1904, July 21 |
| 12.15.0.0.0 | 1 Ahau 13 Uo | Katun  1 Ahau | 1914, May 30 |
| 12.15.10.0.0 | 13 Ahau 8 Cumku | | 1924, April 7 |
| 12.16.0.0.0 | 12 Ahau 18 Kankin | Katun 12 Ahau | 1934, February 14 |
| 12.16.10.0.0 | 11 Ahau 8 Mac | | 1943, December 24 |
| 12.17.0.0.0 | 10 Ahau 18 Yax | Katun 10 Ahau | 1953, November 1 |
| 12.17.10.0.0 | 9 Ahau 8 Mol | | 1963, September 10 |
| 12.18.0.0.0 | 8 Ahau 18 Tzec | Katun  8 Ahau | 1973, July 19 |
| 12.18.10.0.0 | 7 Ahau 8 Zip | | 1983, May 28 |
| 12.19.0.0.0 | 6 Ahau 3 Uayeb | Katun  6 Ahau | 1993, April 5 |
| 12.19.10.0.0 | 5 Ahau 13 Pax | | 2003, February 12 |
| 13.0.0.0.0 | 4 Ahau 3 Kankin | Katun  4 Ahau | 2012, December 21 |

# REFERENCE MATTER

# BIBLIOGRAPHIC SUMMARIES

Our fascination with the rich culture of the Maya has led to a broad and varied literature about the people and their culture. Topics here follow those in text, and full citations are given in the Bibliography.

## Introduction

Summaries of the history of early explorers and theories dealing with the ancient Maya and other New World peoples may be found in Wauchope (1962, 1965). There are a number of general books dealing with Maya civilization. Works such as those by Spinden (1917, 1928), Gann and Thompson (1931), Brainerd (1954), Thompson (1954a, 1966), and the earlier editions of this volume by Morley (1946) and Morley and Brainerd (1956), although out of date, remain landmarks in the history of Maya studies. More current but generally briefer accounts of Maya civilization include studies by Culbert (1974), Benson (1977a), Stuart and Stuart (1977), M. Coe (1980), Hammond (1982), and Henderson (1981).

General treatments of the historical development of the Maya and other Mesoamerican peoples, including the post-Conquest period, are provided in Helms (1975), Wolf (1959), and Farriss (n.d.). Accounts of specific changes wrought by the Spanish include LaFarge & Byers (1931), Scholes (1933), Scholes & Roys (1938), and Roys (1952). Regional ethnohistorical and ethnographical studies of Maya peoples include Redfield (1941) and Steggerda (1941) for Yucatan; Villa Rojas (1934) for Quintana Roo; Tozzer (1907) and Scholes & Roys (1948) for Campeche; Thompson (1930) for Belize; Vogt (1969) for highland Chiapas; and McBryde (1947), Miles (1957), and King (1974) for highland Guatemala. Specific examples of surviving ancient Maya practices and beliefs may be found in LaFarge (1947), Oakes (1951), Reina (1962), and D. Thompson (1960), among others. For the codices (manuscripts) prepared by the ancient Maya, see Chapter 15 and its bibliographic summary.

One of the earliest accounts of the looting of ancient Maya archaeological remains is Saville (1893). More recent descriptions of this destruction may be found in Coggins (1972), Robertson (1972b), and Sheets (1973). Meyer (1977) provides a general work concerned with the plundering of the past and its consequences.

## Chapter 1: The Setting

The traditional definition of the Mesoamerican culture area is provided by Kirchhoff (1952). Cultural and historical syntheses of this area may be found in Wolf (1959) and Helms (1975). The *Handbook of Middle American Indians* (*HMAI*) contains comprehensive summaries of what is known about the past and present native peoples in Mesoamerica, including environmental and linguistic data. The boundaries of the Maya area may be traced from the distribution of present and past Maya languages (McQuown 1956; Kaufman 1964). The difficulty of defining the southeastern boundary of the Maya area in prehistoric times has been dealt with by Lothrop (1939), Longyear (1947), Thompson (1970), Sharer (1974), and Andrews V (1977), among others.

### NATURAL AND CULTURAL SUBDIVISIONS OF THE MAYA AREA

Versions of the overly simplified highland-lowland environmental dichotomy may be found in most works dealing with the Maya (see, for instance, M. Coe 1966: 19–27; Sanders 1973). More recent studies have begun to examine and define the diversity of environmental conditions, even within what was once described as the "homogeneous" or "redundant" lowlands (several of these redefined views may be found in Harrison & Turner 1978; see also Sanders 1977).

Geographical descriptions of the Maya area include works by Huntington (1912), Sapper (1896), Tamayo (1964), and West (1964). Shattuck (1933) and Escoto (1964) may be consulted for climatological information. Botanical studies include those by Carnegie Institution of Washington (1935, 1940), Lundell (1937), Standley (1930), and Wagner (1964). Treatments of faunal distributions may be found in Griscom (1932), Murie (1935), Schmidt & Andrews (1936), and L. Stuart (1964).

Specific studies dealing with the environment of the Maya area may be found in several selections. McBryde (1947) furnishes a landmark report on the cultural geography of southwestern Guatemala. There is a series of works concerning the mineralogical resources important to the ancient Maya, including obsidian (Sheets 1976a; Sidrys, Andresen & Kimberlin 1976). The most important obsidian deposits are those at El Chayal (Coe & Flannery 1964; Sheets 1975) and Ixtepeque (Graham & Hester 1968). Jadeite sources are documented in the middle Motagua valley (Foshag & Leslie 1955; Hammond et al. 1977).

The karst topography typical of the northern highlands and southern lowlands is well described by Siemens (1978). The tectonic activity of the southern Maya region has been the subject of numerous studies, including a report of the most recent severe earthquake (Plafker 1976) and the uncovering of the remains from ancient volcanism at Cerén, El Salvador (Sheets 1979a). Pearse, Creaser, and Hall (1936) provide a classic study of Yucatecan cenotes.

## Chapter 2: The Origins of Maya Civilization

The developmental and chronological subdivisions most commonly used in Mesoamerican prehistory were proposed and defined by Willey and Phillips (1958). Sanders and Price (1968) provide a more explicitly evolutionary summary of the development of Mesoamerican civilization.

### THE ORIGINS OF HIGHLAND AND COASTAL CULTURAL TRADITIONS

MacNeish (1964a,b) outlines the sequence of cultural development in the Tehuacan valley (see also the final reports of the Tehuacan Project, especially Byers 1967; MacNeish, Peterson & Flannery 1970; Johnston 1972). The excavations at Santa Marta cave are described by MacNeish and Peterson (1962). Brown (1979, 1980) and Brown and Majewski (1979) report the preagricultural sites from the Guatemalan highlands. The problem of recovery of early sites in the Maya highlands is outlined by Sedat and Sharer (1972). MacNeish, Wilkerson, and Nelken-Terner (1980) provide a preliminary report of the ongoing Belize coast archaeological survey. The dating of early occupation at Cuello, Belize, is based on radiocarbon determinations (Hammond et al. 1976). The early ceramics from Cuello are described by Pring (1979). Evidence of Early Preclassic occupation from the cave of Loltun, Yucatan, is based on pottery reported by Mercer (1975) and E. Thompson (1897a) and on the recent excavations by Velázquez (1980). The Mani pottery was described by Brainerd (1958). The early settlers of the Pacific coast are known from sites such as La Victoria (M. Coe 1961), Salinas la Blanca (Coe & Flannery 1967), and Alta Mira (Green & Lowe 1967). A summary of this early occupation is provided by Lowe (1977); but see also Shook & Hatch (1979).

The earlier ceramic traditions from lowland South America are reported by Reichel-Dolmatoff (1965) for Puerto Hormiga, Colombia, and by Meggers, Evans, and Estrada (1965) for Valdivia, Ecuador. The precocious development of settled village life on the coast of Ecuador has been revealed by excavations at Real Alto (Lathrap, Marcos & Zeidler 1977).

### THE OLMEC, MESOAMERICA'S FIRST CIVILIZATION

General treatments of Olmec civilization are furnished by Bernal (1969) and M. Coe (1965, 1968). The occupational sequence at the Olmec site of San Lorenzo is summarized by M. Coe (1970); Coe and Diehl (1980) provide the final reports of the research at this site. The excavations at La Venta are reported in Drucker (1952), Drucker, Heizer & Squier (1955), Heizer (1968), and Heizer, Graham & Napton (1968). Clewlow (1974) presents a study of Olmec sculpture and its distribution (see also Stirling 1965). Evidence for Olmec interaction in other regions of Mesoamerica is furnished by Grove et al. (1976) for Chalcatzingo, J. Graham (1979) for Abaj Takalik, Sharer (1974) for Chalchuapa, and Flannery (1968) for the valley of Oaxaca. The relationships between the Olmec and the ancient Maya are also discussed by M. Coe (1965, 1977) and Lowe (1977).

THE PRELUDE TO MAYA CIVILIZATION

The most recent compendium of views regarding the origins of the ancient Maya is a volume edited by Adams (1977), although portions of this work are rendered somewhat out-of-date by more recent archaeological discoveries. For references to the specific factors discussed in this section, see the bibliographic summaries for Chapters 7 (Subsistence), 8 (Organization), 10 (Trade), and 14 (Ideology).

## Chapter 3: The Preclassic Maya

The archaeological investigations in the Maya highland area include those at Kaminaljuyu (see Maudslay 1889–1902) reported in Kidder (1961), Kidder, Jennings & Shook (1946), Shook & Kidder (1952), Sanders & Michels (1977), Michels (1979a,b), and Wetherington (1978) and the excavations at Chalchuapa (Sharer 1978a). Descriptions of the Verapaz Project's research are in Sedat & Sharer (1972) and Sharer & Sedat (1973). Demarest (in press) summarizes the excavations at Santa Leticia. For a general treatment of highland archaeology up to the early 1960's, see Borhegyi (1965a,b).

Investigations on the Pacific coast mentioned are those by Burkitt (1930a) at Chocola and the excavations at Izapa (Ekholm 1969), Bilbao (L. Parsons 1967–69), El Balsamo (Shook & Hatch 1978), and Abaj Takalik (J. Graham 1977, 1979; Graham, Heizer & Shook 1978); see also Shook (1965, 1971).

THE MIDDLE PRECLASSIC

Evidence for Olmec trade in obsidian from the Guatemalan highlands may be found in Cobean et al. (1971). Olmec interaction and trade in the southern Maya area and beyond into South America is discussed by Sharer (1974, in press); see also M. Coe (1965, 1977). The Olmec ties seen at Padre Piedra are reported by Sorenson (1956) and Navarrete (1960). Thompson (1943a) described the Olmec boulder sculpture at Abaj Takalik, and the recent discoveries of additional Olmec sculptures at the site are reported by J. Graham (1977, 1979) and Graham, Heizer, and Shook (1978). The Olmec-style fragment at La Lagunita is published by Ichon (1977a). The Las Victorias boulder sculptures at Chalchuapa are described by Boggs (1950; see also D. Anderson 1978), and additional evidence of Olmec interaction at the site is discussed by Sharer (1974). The Olmec-style "blood-letter" from Seibal is reported by Willey (1978a). The Xoc sculpture is described by Ekholm (1973).

THE LATE PRECLASSIC

Miles (1965) discusses many examples of southern Maya sculpture that reached their peak of development in the Late Preclassic (see also Proskouriakoff 1971). The sculptural style continuities between the Middle Preclassic Olmec, the Late Preclassic southern Maya, and the Classic Maya are discussed by M. Coe (1965), J. Graham (1979), and Quirarte (1973, 1977). The development of Maya hieroglyphic writing in this area is considered in Campbell, Justeson & Norman (1980), Prem (1971), J. Graham (1971), and Sharer & Sedat (1973); see also Thompson (1941, 1943a) and Proskouriakoff (1965). The question of early Oaxacan writing and its origins is reviewed by Caso (1965) and Marcus (1980). Stela C at Tres Zapotes is reported by Stirling (1940). Prem (1971) discusses the dates assigned for Chiapa de Corzo Stela 2 and El Baúl Stela 1 (see also Thompson 1943a; J. Graham 1971). The Abaj Takalik Stela 5 dates are from Graham, Heizer & Shook (1978). The monuments from Izapa are fully documented by Norman (1973), and Chalchuapa Monument 1 is illustrated and discussed by Sharer (1974; see also D. Anderson 1978). The origins and distribution of Usulutan ceramics are treated by Demarest and Sharer (in press: a).

The evidence for the interaction among southern Maya sites during the Late Preclassic, and its role in the development of civilization in this region, is summarized by Lowe (1977) and Demarest and Sharer (in press: b). The proposed linguistic correlates for this development are advanced by Josserand (1975), Campbell (1976), and Kaufman (1976).

THE MAYA LOWLANDS IN THE LATER PRECLASSIC

The correlation of the Mamom- and Chicanel-period transition with earlier riverine settlements and later expansion into open forest environments was hypothesized by Sharer and Gifford (1970) and further documented by Puleston and Puleston (1971). Examples of Middle Preclassic lowland architecture include those at Cuello (Hammond 1977a) and Altar de Sacrificios (A. Smith 1972). Late Preclassic architecture at Tikal is discussed by W. Coe (1965a, 1967). Structure E-VIII-sub at Uaxactun is reported by Ricketson and Ricketson (1937). The Late Preclassic architecture at Cerros, Belize, is described by Freidel (1977), who also discusses regional interaction and the symbolic distinctions between highland and lowland architectural traditions (1979a,b). Pendergast (1981) summarizes the Late Preclassic development at Lamanai, including the construction of the mammoth structure N10-43. The recent research at El Mirador, the largest Late Preclassic site yet discovered in the lowlands, is reviewed by Matheny (1980).

THE PROTOCLASSIC AND THE DECLINE OF THE SOUTHERN MAYA

The decline of the southern Maya has been noted by several scholars (see, for instance, Shook & Proskouriakoff 1956; Borhegyi 1965a). The link of this decline with evidence for a volcanic eruption was first seen at Chalchuapa (Sharer 1969). The identification of this eruption with the Ilopango volcano was proposed by Sheets (1971), who also documented the widespread environmental and cultural disruptions caused by this eruption (1979a). The cultural consequences of the Ilopango disaster have been seen as causing migrations northward into the Maya lowlands (Sheets 1971) and disrupting the southern Maya trade network (Sharer 1975, in press). Dahlin (1979) suggests that Ilopango refugees introduced cacao plantation agriculture into the rich river valleys of the eastern lowlands, stimulating the economic growth of the region in the Classic era. Sharer (1974) also proposes that the decline of the southern Maya encouraged the subsequent intrusion by Teotihuacan into this area.

## Chapter 4: The Classic and the Rise of the Lowland Maya

Accounts of several of the pioneering lowland Maya explorations may be found in Stephens (1841, 1843), Maudslay (1889–1902), Maler (1901, 1903, 1908a,b, 1911), and Tozzer (1907, 1911, 1913). Thompson (1965a) provides a fairly recent synthesis of the archaeology of the lowland area. The basic reports of excavations at the lowland sites mentioned include Merwin & Vaillant (1932) for Holmul; Wauchope (1934), Ricketson & Ricketson (1937), and A. Smith (1937, 1950) for Uaxactun; Morris, Charlot & Morris (1931), Ruppert (1931, 1935, 1943), and Pollock (1937) for Chichen Itza; Thompson (1939a) for San José; Satterthwaite (1943, 1944a,b, 1944 & 1954, 1952) for Piedras Negras; Willey et al. (1965) for Barton Ramie; Shook et al. (1958), Adams et al. (1961), and Carr & Hazzard (1961) for Tikal; Pendergast (1969, 1979) and Mathews & Pendergast (1979) for Altun Ha; Willey & Smith (1969), A. Smith (1972), and Willey (1973) for Altar de Sacrificios; Willey (1975, 1978b) for Seibal; Hammond (1975) for Lubaantun; Andrews & Andrews (1980) for Dzibilchaltun; Adams (1975) and Andrews V & Andrews (1979) for Becan; and Ruz (1952a,b, 1955, 1958a,b,c, 1962) for Palenque.

Few publications are yet available dealing with the most recent lowland excavations. However, some reports have appeared, including T. Hester (1979) for Colha; Baudez (1978a,b, 1979a,b) for Copan; Hammond (1978a) for Cuello; Sharer (1978b), Ashmore (1979), and Schortman & Urban (in press) for Quirigua; Becquelin & Baudez (1979) for Tonina; Matheny (1980) for El Mirador; and Pendergast (1981) for Lamanai. The art historical works mentioned are Spinden (1913) and Proskouriakoff (1950).

### THE SOUTHERN MAYA AREA IN THE CLASSIC

For reports of excavations at Kaminaljuyu, Bilbao, and Abaj Takalik, see the Chapter 3 Bibliographic Summary. Additional sites mentioned are Zaculeu (Woodbury & Trik 1953), Chitinamit-Atitlan (Lothrop 1933), Zacualpa (Wauchope 1948, 1975), and other highland-area sites (see, for instance, Ichon 1977a, 1979; Brown 1979; Becquelin 1969; Shook, Hatch & Donaldson 1979; A. Smith 1955; A. Smith & Kidder 1943; and Walters 1980).

### PRIMARY CENTERS: THE EMERGENCE OF STATES IN THE MAYA LOWLANDS

Studies dealing with the origins and definition of preindustrial states include Childe (1954), R. M. Adams (1966), and Service (1975). Webb (1973) and Webster (1977) discuss this issue with particular regard to the lowland Maya. The identification of emblem glyphs with specific centers was proposed by Berlin (1958), and the decipherment of the emblem-glyph prefix was advanced by Lounsbury (1973). The first dynastic histories were worked out by Proskouriakoff (1960, 1961, 1963, 1964), and Thompson (1973a) discusses Maya rulers and their supernatural connections. The four-tiered hierarchy of Classic-period sites is described by Marcus (1976). Haviland (1967, 1968, 1977) discusses the origins and nature of ruling lineages at Tikal and other Classic sites. Freidel (1979a) provides a stimulating contribution to the issue of the origins of lowland civilization.

## THE PROTOCLASSIC

The diagnostic Protoclassic pottery assemblage is based on the tomb wares from Holmul (Merwin & Vaillant 1932), and further refined as the Floral Park Complex at Barton Ramie (Gifford 1976). Evidence for an indigenous Protoclassic cultural development is presented by W. Coe (1965a), Culbert (1977a), and Pring (1976, 1977), among others. The thesis of outside interaction has been advanced in Willey & Gifford (1961), Sharer & Gifford (1970), Sheets (1976b, 1979b), and Dahlin (1979), among others. Willey (1977) provides a recent synthesis of these views.

## THE EARLY CLASSIC

The excavations in Tikal's North Acropolis are summarized by W. Coe (1962, 1965a, 1967). Tikal's Early Classic dynastic history was initially proposed by Coggins (1975; see also Coggins 1976, 1979; Shook 1960; C. Jones & Satterthwaite in press). The first study of the Leyden Plate was published by Morley and Morley (1939). Proskouriakoff (1963, 1964) has outlined the Yaxchilan dynastic sequence, but see also Marcus (1976). Tikal's connections to the southeastern lowlands have been proposed in Sharer (1978b, in press) and C. Jones & Sharer (1980). Baudez (1978a, 1980) reports the newly found Stela 35 at Copan. The discovery of Monument 26 at Quirigua is described by Ashmore, Schortman, and Sharer (in press), and C. Jones (in press) provides a full description of the stela.

The Early Classic burial interpretations are from Rathje (1970). C. Jones (1977) outlines several of Tikal's strategic advantages that seem to have contributed to its Early Classic dominance. He has also postulated Tikal's role as a trading power (Jones 1979); see also Rathje (1977). Puleston and Callender (1967) report the defensive earthworks at Tikal; Ruppert and Denison (1943) describe the discovery of the moat and rampart at Becan. Evidence for initial lowland contact with Teotihuacan is presented by Pendergast (1971). The various interpretations for the Tikal-Kaminaljuyu-Teotihuacan connections are considered by Ball (1980), Cheek (1977b), Coggins (1975), Miller (1978), and Santley (1980), among others.

## THE MIDDLE CLASSIC HIATUS

Proskouriakoff (1950) notes the occurrence of a hiatus in monument activity at most lowland sites. The hiatus has been defined at Tikal by Coggins (1975). Willey (1974) advances the thesis that the causes of the hiatus were linked with the decline of Teotihuacan. A recent compilation of papers dealing with this era has been published (Pasztory 1978).

## THE LATE CLASSIC

The epigraphic evidence bearing on the structure of Late Classic lowland society is summarized by Marcus (1976b). The characterizations founded on ceramic data are given by Willey, Culbert, and Adams (1967). Tikal's Late Classic dynastic history has been reconstructed by C. Jones (1977); see also Coggins (1975). The Twin Pyramid complex at Tikal is analyzed by C. Jones (1969), and interpreted in light of

Teotihuacan influence by Coggins (1976). Ah Cacau's tomb under Temple I is described by Trik (1963).

Palenque's dynastic sequence has been proposed by Mathews and Schele (1974), Lounsbury (1974), and Schele (1978), following contributions by Berlin (1965, 1970). The tomb of Pacal under the Temple of the Inscriptions is described by Ruz (1952a,b, 1955), who has disputed its occupant's age at death (1977).

As mentioned, Proskouriakoff (1963, 1964) proposed the initial reconstruction of Yaxchilan's ruling dynasty; see also Kelley (1976). Earlier, she proposed the first Maya dynastic reconstruction based on the monuments from Piedras Negras (Proskouriakoff 1960, 1961). Historical details in the relationships between these centers and other Usumacinta sites are postulated by Marcus (1976b).

Copan's dynastic history has been the subject of several studies (Kelley 1962b, Pahl 1976, Riese 1980, and Marcus 1976b). Kelley (1962b) outlined the Late Classic rulers at Quirigua (see also Marcus 1976b). An expanded dynastic and archaeological reconstruction for Quirigua is given in Sharer (1978b) and C. Jones & Sharer (1980).

THE TERMINAL CLASSIC

Specific evidence for cultural changes during this era are provided by Culbert (1974) for Tikal; Sabloff and Willey (1967) for Seibal; and Sharer (1978b, n.d.) for Quirigua. For other references, see the bibliographic summaries for Chapters 6 and 7.

## Chapter 5: The Decline of the Classic Maya

Much of the material in this chapter is based on a treatment of the subject published elsewhere (Sharer 1982). The issue of the collapse of Classic lowland Maya society is most thoroughly treated in the published symposium referred to in this chapter (Culbert 1973).

W. Coe (1968: 175) discusses the continuity of occupation at Tikal after the Late Classic florescence (see also Adams & Trik 1961). Continued occupation in Belize is best exemplified at Lamanai (Loten n.d.).

The early discovery of Maya sites (see Stephens 1841, 1843) and theories about their origins are summarized by Willey and Sabloff (1974), and treated more specifically by Wauchope (1962, 1965).

Culbert (1974: 113) discusses the issue of cultural processes within ancient Maya society as a key to unraveling the causes of the collapse. Willey undertook the pioneering application of settlement archaeology in the Maya area at Barton Ramie (Willey et al. 1965). The distinction between internal and external collapse theories follows Sabloff (1973a).

THEORIES EMPHASIZING INTERNAL FACTORS

The possibility that earthquakes caused disruptions in the central lowlands was raised by Mackie (1961). Tectonic activity along the Motagua fault and its possible implications for Classic-period Quirigua are summarized by Sharer and Bevan (n.d.); see also the Bibliographic Summary for Chapter 3. Adams (1973a) reviews the possible consequences of hurricanes in the Maya area.

The evidence for the presence of various epidemic and endemic diseases among the ancient Maya, and the possible consequences, is summarized by Shimkin (1973). Spinden (1928: 148) advances the proposal that yellow fever may have contributed to the collapse. The analogy to medieval Europe, using depopulation caused by the bubonic plague, was proposed by Adams and Smith (1977). The definitive study of ancient Maya disease and nutritional status was undertaken by Saul (1973) on the basis of skeletal material from Altar de Sacrificios. Haviland (1967) provides a similar study for Tikal.

The possible destructive consequences of swidden agriculture, as proposed by Cook (1921), was followed by Morley (1946: 71-72) to explain the abandonment of the central lowlands. Cooke (1931) postulates that the lowland *bajos* were silted-up lakes, but the study of Bajo de Santa Fe by Cowgill and Hutchinson (1963) tends to contradict this thesis. However, recent analyses of cores from several central Peten lakes (Deevey et al. 1979) indicates that heavy Late Classic occupation greatly accelerated the rate of silt deposition and phosphorus accumulation in these lakes.

The ecological theories based on a posited subsistence failure were introduced by Meggers (1954) and expanded by several authors, including Sanders (1962, 1963). Sanders (1973) also advances the theory of grassland swiddening. Ancient agricultural use of lowland grasslands (savannas) is indirectly supported by new settlement data published in D. Rice & P. Rice (1979), P. Rice & D. Rice (1979). Ricketson and Ricketson (1937: 12) were among the first to hold that the ancient Maya did not rely on swidden agriculture. The *bajo* theory has been reintroduced by Harrison (1977) and further discussed by Turner and Harrison (1978). Current ecological theories now assume a diverse subsistence base for the lowland Maya (Harrison & Turner 1978) that nonetheless could have been overwhelmed by overpopulation (Culbert 1974: 115-17; Sharer 1977: 544-48).

Archaeological evidence for ancient violence provided by monument mutilation has been advanced for Piedras Negras (Satterthwaite 1937a: 20) and Tikal (Satterthwaite 1958). However, W. Coe (1962: 484-97) sees this as reflecting customary ritual behavior, not revolt, a view in accord with present evidence. The popular-revolt theory is most often associated with Thompson (1954a, 1966), but was also accepted by Morley and Brainerd (1956), Altschuler (1958), and Culbert (1974), among others, although Becker (1979) points to the absence of this idea in Thompson's scholarly works. A recent article by Hamblin and Pitcher (1980) attempts to resurrect the class revolt theory, but this argument is weakened by acceptance of outmoded ideas about the ancient Maya.

Rathje (1971, 1973) sees the collapse as owing to economic failure, whereas Webb (1964, 1973) advances the thesis of economic and political competition from rival Mexican states. The conclusion quoted from the collapse symposium is by Willey and Shimkin (1973: 491). The view that the Classic Maya elite actively attempted to counter growing stresses within their society is provided by Culbert (1977b: 526-28) and Sharer (1977: 544-48).

The Maya concept of cyclic history was used by both Coggins (1975) and C. Jones (1977) to interpret archaeological evidence from Classic-period Tikal. The application of a revitalization model (A. Wallace 1956) was proposed by Ashmore and Sharer (1975) and Dahlin (1976) for Classic Tikal, and more recently for the Postclassic Maya by Fry (1979). Puleston (1979) details the possible role of beliefs in cyclic history in the demise of the Classic Maya.

Internal warfare as a factor in the Classic collapse has been advanced by G. Cowgill (1979). Evidence for conflict is provided by walled centers (see, for instance, Webster 1979; D. Rice & P. Rice 1981). The striking portrayal of warfare in the Bonampak murals may be found in Ruppert, Thompson & Proskouriakoff (1955). Epigraphic evidence for a Late Classic conflict between Copan and Quirigua, first pointed out by Proskouriakoff (1973), is summarized and presented with supportive archaeological evidence by Sharer (1978b).

THEORIES EMPHASIZING EXTERNAL FACTORS

Sabloff (1973a: 37) discusses the recent rise in popularity of external theories for the Classic Maya collapse (see also Erasmus 1968). Foreign invasion has been proposed by G. Cowgill (1964), and in the specific case of Altar de Sacrificios, by Adams (1973b). Sabloff and Willey (1967) provide the definitive discussion of the postulated role of invasion in the collapse, using Seibal as a case study. The link of these apparent conquests with the expansion of the Putun Maya is advanced by Thompson (1970: 3–47). However, Culbert (1974: 111) sees foreign invasion as more of a response to an already failing system, rather than as a cause for that failure.

Webb (1973) proposes that the Maya collapse was due to a failure to cope with changing economic and political conditions in neighboring Mesoamerican states. Specifically, Sabloff and Rathje (1975b) see changes in long-distance trade routes as a crucial factor. C. Jones (1979) accepts this thesis in the case of Tikal. The proposed mid-Classic hiatus as a preenactment of the collapse was proposed by Willey (1974).

## Chapter 6: The Postclassic Maya

The traditional definition of the Postclassic period is based on the developmental criteria outlined by Willey and Phillips (1958). The *Book of Chilam Balam* of Chumayel, quoted at several points in this chapter, has been translated by Roys (1933) and Brotherston (1979). Bishop Diego de Landa's account of Postclassic Yucatecan society, also quoted here, was translated with extensive footnotes by Tozzer (1941). An overall synthesis of Yucatecan prehistory may be found in Andrews IV (1965). A thematic summary of the lowland Postclassic period is provided by Freidel (n.d.).

THE EARLIER PERIODS IN YUCATAN IN RETROSPECT

The importance of the salt trade in Yucatan is documented by A. Andrews (1980a,b). The development of Komchen and Dzibilchaltun and their external relationships are summarized by Andrews V (1982). Vlcek, Gonzalez, and Kurjack (1978) report the similar career and status of Chunchucmil. Freidel (1978, 1979a) reviews the evidence for early coastal trade in Yucatan, with special reference to the site of Cerros. Coastal sites in northern Yucatan are reported by Eaton (1978). The changing pattern of ceramic affiliations seen at Edzna are summarized by Forsyth (1979). General summaries of the architectural styles and regional characteristics of this period can be found in Ball (1974a, 1977a, 1979), Andrews V (1979a,b), Potter (1977), and Pollock (1980).

## THE TRANSITION FROM CLASSIC TO POSTCLASSIC IN YUCATAN

This era is also summarized by Ball (1974a, 1977a) and Andrews V (1979a,b). The definitive study of the Putun (Chontal) Maya is by Scholes and Roys (1948), with more recent interpretations provided by Thompson (1966, 1970), A. Andrews and Robles (n.d.), and Sabloff (1977). Litvak-King (1972) discusses Xochicalco, and the murals at Cacaxtla are described in Abascal et al. (1976) and Lopez & Molina (1976); the pottery affiliations are reported by Wheaton (1976). Moreno (1959) considers ethnohistorical evidence of possible Putun incursions into central Mexico during the Terminal Classic. The evidence of foreign occupation at Seibal is treated by Sabloff and Willey (1967) and Sabloff (1973b), and interpreted as a Putun conquest by Ball (1974a), who also identified Seibal as Chakanputun. Miller (1977a) discusses the murals from the ball court at Chichen Itza (Temple of the Jaguars) and their intriguing links to the history of the Itza, or Putun Maya.

## THE DOMINANCE OF CHICHEN ITZA

An appealing popular account of the archaeological investigations at Chichen Itza is by Morris (1931). Details of this research are given by Morris, Charlot, and Morris (1931) for the Temple of the Warriors; Pollock (1937) for the Casa Redonda; Ruppert (1931, 1935, 1943) for the Temple of the Wall Panels, Caracol, and Mercado, respectively (see also Ruppert 1952); and Lothrop (1952) and Proskouriakoff (1974) for materials recovered from the Cenote of Sacrifice. Acosta (1956, 1960), Covarrubias (1954), Joyce (1927), Keleman (1943), and Toscano (1944) provide material for the comparison of Tula-Toltec and Early Postclassic Yucatec art and architecture. The suggestion of Tula's possible derivation from Chichen Itza is raised by Kubler (1961).

The site of Tulum is described by Lothrop (1924), Sanders (1960), and Miller (1977b, in press). Miller (in press) also reports on investigations at the nearby site of Tancah. The murals at Santa Rita were discovered by Gann (1900, 1918), and the recent work at Nohmul and Santa Rita is reported by D. Chase (1981). Recent investigations on Isla de Cozumel are described by Sabloff and Rathje (1975a). The report of the Quirigua Chacmool is by Saville (1893) and, later, by Richardson (1940), but see also Sharer (n.d.).

## THE LATE POSTCLASSIC AND THE DOMINANCE OF MAYAPAN

The Mayapan investigations are published by Bullard (1952), Pollock (1954), Proskouriakoff (1954, 1955), and R. Smith (1954, 1971). Descriptions of specific Mayapan buildings are furnished by Shook (1954), Shook and Irving (1955), P. Smith (1955), and Thompson (1954b). The site map that illustrates the settlement pattern of Mayapan was done by M. Jones (1952). Roys (1943, 1965) provides summaries of Late Postclassic lowland society.

The question about the location of Tayasal is summarized by A. Chase (1976), who favors its identification with the site of Topoxte (see Bullard 1970). Its traditional placement at Lago Peten Itza is defended by Jones, Rice, and Rice (1981).

## THE SOUTHERN MAYA AREA IN THE POSTCLASSIC

The principal ethnohistorical sources that are readily available in English translation remain the *Popol Vuh* (Recinos 1950; Edmonson 1971) and the *Annals of the Cakchiquels* (Recinos & Goetz 1953). The major highland Maya sources are described by Carmack (1973).

For studies of the Cotzumalhuapan style and the debate regarding its chronological setting, see Thompson (1943b, 1948), Shook (1965), L. Parsons (1967–69), and Pasztory (1978). A reconnaissance of highland sites of the Terminal Classic and Early Postclassic periods is reported by A. Smith (1955); see also A. Smith & Kidder (1951), Burkitt (1930b), Gruhn & Bryan (1976), Dillon (1978), Borhegyi (1965a), and A. Smith (1965). Fox (1980) summarizes the evidence and interpretations leading to the postulation of two distinct waves of Mexicanized Maya intrusions into the highlands. The Toltec connections with Postclassic highland society are treated by Carmack (1968); see also Navarrete (1976).

The shifts in Early Postclassic highland settlement have been identified by Shook and Proskouriakoff (1956), A. Smith (1955), Borhegyi (1965b), and Brown (1980), among others. The Early Postclassic highland ruling lineages are identified by Fox (1980). The excavations at Chitinamit-Atitlan are reported by Lothrop (1933), and the possible *tzompantli* at Chalchitan is mentioned by A. Smith (1955: 14). The excavations at Chitinamit are summarized by Brown (n.d.)

Excavations at Late Postclassic highland sites include those by Woodbury and Trik (1953) at Zaculeu; Wauchope (1948, 1975) at Zacualpa; Lehmann (1968) at Mixcu Viejo; Guillemin (1965, 1967) at Iximche; and Ichon (1975, 1977b) at Pueblo Viejo Chicaj and Los Cimientos-Chustum, respectively. The ethnohistorical and archaeological evidence dealing with the Utatlan Quiche is presented by Carmack (1973), Fox (1978), Wallace and Carmack (1977), especially the papers by Wallace and Stewart, and Carmack and Weeks (1981); for an alternative view, see Brown (n.d.).

## Chapter 7: Subsistence Systems

Until quite recently the idea that ancient Maya subsistence was based on swidden agriculture (Cook 1921) could be found in most general works dealing with the Maya (see, for instance, Brainerd 1954; Morley & Brainerd 1956; Thompson 1954a, 1966; M. Coe 1966), as well as in technical studies (such as Lundell 1933; Meggers 1954; Hester 1954; Altschuler 1958; Dumond 1961; U. Cowgill 1962; Sanders 1973). The swidden thesis was based on studies of contemporary Maya milpa agriculture (Stadelman 1940; Reina 1967; Carter 1969) and on the colonial accounts of Landa (1938; Tozzer 1941) and other chroniclers.

Problems with the swidden thesis were noted by the results of the first comprehensive survey of domestic remains in the central lowlands, carried out at Uaxactun; the survey revealed evidence of Classic-period populations too large to have been supported by shifting agriculture (Ricketson & Ricketson 1937). During this same time several investigators reported evidence of agricultural terraces (Joyce 1926; Thompson 1931; Lundell 1933) that indicated ancient intensive cultivation. But for the most part these findings were ignored and the swidden idea prevailed.

The demise of the swidden thesis resulted from a combination of archaeological evidence gathered over the past decade that demonstrates high population densities and a variety and intensity of ancient Maya subsistence technology (Harris 1972, 1978; Siemens & Puleston 1972; Turner 1974, 1978a; Hammond 1978b; Vlcek, Gonzalez & Kurjack 1978).

SUBSISTENCE SYSTEMS AVAILABLE TO THE ANCIENT MAYA

Overall summaries of subsistence alternatives used by, or available to, the ancient Maya may be found in Wilken (1971), Turner & Harrison (1978), and Willey (1978c).

The wild-food resources available to the Maya are referenced in Chapter 1 (see also Lundell 1938; Roys 1931). Gann (1918) discusses Maya hunting-and-gathering practices. Urban (1978) has determined the increasing frequency over time of deer skeletal remains at Tikal. Aquatic resources are well summarized in Lange (1971), but see also Puleston & Puleston (1971). D. Rice (1978) provides the evidence for decreasing utilization of freshwater mollusks in the Classic-period Peten.

Animal husbandry is reported by Landa (1938; Tozzer 1941) in the colonial era. Thompson (1974) proposed that the Maya once raised fish in artificial channels, such as those reported along the Río Candelaria in Campeche (Siemens & Puleston 1972). The raising of food animals by the Maya is also discussed by Turner and Harrison (1978).

The central importance of agricultural growth for the development of civilization has been considered by numerous scholars (see, for instance, Childe 1954; Carneiro 1967; Boserup 1965). In the case of the ancient Maya, this question has been discussed in Sanders (1977), Netting (1977), D. Rice (1978), Turner & Harrison (1978), and others. Specific agricultural systems and methods used by the Maya are outlined by Turner (1974, 1978b), Puleston (1978), Netting (1977), and Wiseman (1978). Several staple crops have been proposed as supplements to maize and other traditional cultigens, including root crops (Bronson 1966) and ramon, or breadnut (Puleston 1968).

Continuous field cultivation, with minimal or no fallowing, is discussed by Turner (1978b) and Wiseman (1978), and evidence of field boundaries is reported by Eaton (1975). The use of agricultural terraces is reported in Turner (1974, 1978b) and Healey, van Waarden & Anderson (n.d.). Kirke (1980) describes agricultural methods and capabilities in the Belize valley.

Household gardening is proposed by Puleston (1968, 1978) and Netting (1977), among others (see also Puleston 1971; Reina & Hill 1980). Arboriculture is also discussed by Puleston (1968, 1971, 1978), and Wiseman (1978) distinguishes between monocropping and intercropping plantation techniques.

Hydraulic-cultivation technology (Denevan 1970; Armillas 1971) among the Maya has been reviewed by Matheny (1976), with special regard to Edzna. Evidence of raised-field systems has been reported by Siemens and Puleston (1972), Olsen et al. (1975), and Harrison (1977, 1978); see also Puleston (1977).

The development of Maya subsistence systems through time has been reviewed by Puleston and Puleston (1971), Puleston (1978), Turner and Harrison (1978), and Willey (1978c). D. Rice (1978) provides a detailed and well-documented study of the growth of population and the changes in subsistence methods around Lago Yaxha, in the central lowlands (see also Deevey et al. 1979).

## Chapter 8: The Organization of Society

The basic premises and results of archaeological research devoted to ancient settlement may be found in such works as Willey (1953, 1956), Chang (1972), Ucko, Tringham & Dimbleby (1972), and Flannery (1976).

Summary studies of ancient Maya settlement archaeology may be found in Haviland (1966) and the collection of papers from a recent advanced seminar on lowland settlement (Ashmore 1981b), especially those by Willey, Ashmore, Ashmore and Willey, and Hammond and Ashmore. Shook and Proskouriakoff (1956), Borhegyi (1965b), and Fox (1978) provide settlement information from the southern Maya area. Central and southern lowland settlement is dealt with by Bullard (1960), Willey and Bullard (1965), D. Rice (1976), Rice and Puleston (1981), Hammond (1981), and Leventhal (1981). Sanders (1960), Andrews IV (1965), Harrison (1981), Kurjack and Garza (1981), and Freidel (1981a) present summaries of northern lowland settlement.

### SETTLEMENT UNITS IN THE MAYA LOWLANDS

The basic units of settlement remains in the lowlands discussed in this section are defined by Ashmore (1981a). For variations in the approach to the definition of Maya centers, see Bullard (1960), W. Haviland (1970), D. Wallace (1977), and Turner, Turner, & Adams (1981). The view of Classic lowland Maya sites as non-urban ceremonial centers (Morley & Brainerd 1956; Thompson 1954a, 1966; Sanders & Price 1968) is in contrast to their being seen as having once possessed many urban characteristics and functions (W. Haviland 1970; Becker 1979). The specific examples of site definition mentioned in this chapter are Tikal (W. Haviland 1970; Puleston 1974), Lubaantun (Hammond 1975), and Quirigua (Sharer 1978b; Ashmore 1979); see also Kurjack & Andrews (1976).

The definition of sociopolitical realms beyond the site level has been approached by Hammond (1974), who used Thiesson polygons, by Marcus (1973, 1976), who used central-place models and the distribution of emblem glyphs (also see Chapter 15), and by Adams and Jones (1981), who used the number of courtyard groups.

### EVIDENCE FROM ETHNOHISTORICAL STUDIES

Cline (1972-75) provides a thorough background and guidance for the use of ethnohistorical sources in Mesoamerican studies. Specific ethnohistorical research dealing with ancient Maya organization includes the landmark study by Scholes and Roys (1948) of the Putun Maya, and more recent works such as that by Carmack (1973) concerning the Quiche Maya. An example of the combination of archaeological and ethnohistorical approaches is provided by Wallace and Carmack (1977). Sanders (1981) uses ethnographic analogy to help reconstruct ancient lowland sociopolitical organization.

The organization of northern lowland Maya society at the time of the Spanish Conquest, based primarily on Landa (1938; Tozzer 1941), was reconstructed by Roys (1943, 1965). The description of Postclassic Quiche organization is after Carmack (1977), based on accounts given in the *Popol Vuh* (Recinos 1950, Edmonson 1971) and other ethnohistorical sources.

RECONSTRUCTING THE ORGANIZATION OF SOCIETY

The basically egalitarian model of sociopolitical organization is described by Vogt (1961, 1964). The two-class, or reciprocal "priest-peasant," model is presented in varying forms by Brainerd (1954), Thompson (1954a, 1966), Morley and Brainerd (1956), Bullard (1964), and Sanders and Price (1968). The "multiple-class" model is implied or described in works by W. Haviland (1968, 1977), Adams (1970), and Becker (1973), and forms a basis for the contributions in the recent lowland settlement volume (Ashmore 1981b).

Specific social organizational principles, such as those derived from patrilineal descent, are discussed by W. Haviland (1968, 1977) for the Classic lowland Maya, and by Carmack (1977) and D. Wallace (1977) for the Postclassic Quiche; see also Tozzer (1907) for a description of Lacandon social organization. Classic-period elite marriage alliances are discussed by Molloy and Rathje (1974). The operation of a feudal principle within Classic lowland society is postulated by Adams and Smith (1981), and seems to underlie the analysis of Postclassic Quiche society presented by Carmack (1977).

The specific example of the social and political fortunes of the occupants of Tikal's group 7F-1 results from research by W. Haviland (1981). The strengths and weaknesses in Maya political authority are discussed by Marcus (1974), Coggins (1975), Haviland (1977), Carmack (1977), and Freidel (1981b), among others (see also the bibliographic summary for Chapter 4). An overall summary of these various issues is provided by Willey (1980). The suggestions of an ancient Maya quadripartite cosmological or political order are discussed by Barthel (1968) and Marcus (1976).

## Chapter 9: Everyday Life

The bulk of the material presented in this chapter is from Landa (1938; Tozzer 1941), and pertains to the Yucatec Maya of the early colonial period. Although it can be reasonably assumed that many of the customs described by Landa were little changed from earlier eras, it is also certain that some had changed. Some aspects of ancient Maya daily life can be inferred from archaeological evidence, such as dress and appearance (from murals and pottery figurines), family organization (from the size and patterning of settlement remains; see Chapter 8), and burial customs. But most aspects of everyday life leave little archaeological trace, so that reliance on colonial-period documents is important and necessary.

Most native Maya sources offer scant information about the non-elite population, as Carmack (1977) notes in his reconstruction of Postclassic Quiche society. Apart from Landa and a few other Spanish writers, therefore, we can offer only hypothetical reconstructions, such as those presented by Thompson (1954a, 1966), to gain a glimpse of daily life in Classic times.

As might be expected, most of the available archaeological evidence from the Classic era concerns the ruling elite, whose costumes and activities were depicted in sculpture (Proskouriakoff 1950) and in paintings, at Bonampak (Ruppert, Thompson, & Proskouriakoff 1955) and elsewhere. For more information about ancient Maya burial practices, see the summary by Ruz (1965).

## Chapter 10: Trade and External Contact

### PREHISTORIC TRADE IN MESOAMERICA

The treatment of the role of trade in prehistoric societies, such as Mesoamerica, is based primarily on papers found in two recent works, edited by Sabloff and Lamberg-Karlovsky (1975) and by Earle and Ericson (1977). Summaries of trade in prehistoric Mesoamerica are provided in Chapman (1957), Dillon (1975), and Lee & Navarrete (1978). Regional trade in the Valley of Mexico was defined by Sanders (1956); more recently research in this same area has been reported in a volume edited by Wolf (1976) and in the archaeological-ecological work by Sanders, Parsons, and Santley (1979). One of the best studies of regional trade in the contemporary Maya area is McBryde's study (1947) of southwestern Guatemala. Tourtellot and Sabloff (1972) discuss the distinction between utilitarian ("useful") and exotic ("functional") exchange for the ancient Maya. The best-known model, proposing that utilitarian trade fostered the complex sociopolitical organization of the prehistoric Olmec and Maya, is that of Rathje (1971; see also Rathje, Gregory & Wiseman 1978). Several critiques of this model have been published, including those by Dillon (1975), Culbert (1977b), and Sharer (1977).

### GOODS AND MECHANISMS IN LONG-DISTANCE TRADE

The examples of long-distance trade goods cited in this chapter were compiled from several authoritative ethnohistorical sources, especially Cortés (1928) and Landa (1938; Tozzer 1941). Recent studies of the subject are provided by papers in Thompson (1970) and Lee & Navarrete (1978). Blom (1932) provides a definitive work dealing with Maya trade. Maya merchants and markets at the time of the Spanish Conquest were described by Landa (1938), Fuentes y Guzmán (1932-34), Las Casas (1909), and Benzoni (1970). The possible market at Tikal, recognized from archaeological indications, is identified by W. Coe (1967) and C. Jones (1979). The Mexica market at Tlatelolco is known from ethnohistorical descriptions, especially Sahagún (1946) and Díaz del Castillo (1963). The Iximche market was described by Las Casas (1909: 623-24). The use of trade fairs by the ancient Maya in Classic and Postclassic times has been proposed by Freidel (1981b) and Feldman (1978). The *pochteca* is described by Sahagún (1946) and Duran (1965), and there is a recent examination of this institution by Bittman and Sullivan (1978).

LATE PRECLASSIC TRADE

The model for the fall of the Olmec is based on Rathje (1971). The archaeological and ecological data bearing on the rise of Teotihuacan is reported by Sanders, Parsons, and Santley (1979). Recent archaeological research in the southern Maya area is reported by Lowe, Lee, and Martinez (1973) at Izapa, L. Parsons (1967–69) at El Baúl, J. Graham (1979) at Abaj Takalik, and Sharer (1974, 1978a) at Chalchuapa. The problem of the fate of the southern Maya was defined by Shook and Proskouriakoff (1956) and further dealt with by Lowe (1977). The evidence and theories dealing with Ilopango volcanism and the possible migration of refugees is based on Sharer (1969, 1974), Sharer & Gifford (1970), and Sheets (1971, 1976b, 1979a). The consequences of this volcanic disaster in severing the coastal trade routes was proposed by Sharer (1975). Dahlin (1979) advances the theory that refugees from the Ilopango region introduced cacao plantations into the eastern lowlands. The Late Preclassic coastal trading network in Yucatan has been postulated by Freidel (1978, 1979a), based on research at Cerros, the salt trade has been examined by A. Andrews (1980a,b), and the trade relationships with Komchen are described by Andrews V (1982).

CLASSIC TRADE: TEOTIHUACAN AND THE LOWLAND MAYA

For a summary of the recent archaeological mapping project at Teotihuacan, see Millon (1973); other Teotihuacan sources include Sanders, Parsons & Santley (1979). Santley (1980) provides an appraisal of the role of Teotihuacan in Mesoamerican long-distance trade, especially in regard to obsidian. The Teotihuacan colonization of Kaminaljuyu was first documented by Kidder, Jennings, and Shook (1946), and later reinforced by more recent archaeological research at the same site (Sanders & Michels 1977). L. Parsons (1967–69) defined this Teotihuacan interaction in the Maya area as a "Middle Classic" phenomenon, which was further explored in a recent symposium (Pasztory 1978). Willey (1974) has proposed the thesis that the lowland mid-Classic hiatus was caused by the decline of Teotihuacan.

Obsidian trade in the Maya area is described by Hammond (1972), Sidrys (1976), and Santley (1980). The discussion of Tikal as a Classic-period trading center is based on the thesis of C. Jones (1977, 1979). Specific works providing evidence for obsidian trade at Tikal are discussed by Moholy-Nagy (1975, 1976).

See Chapter 4 for additional references regarding the origins and development of lowland Maya trading centers, the epigraphic evidence for a Teotihuacan-Tikal alliance, and the interrelationships of Classic-period centers. Other papers relevant to trade and the Classic lowland Maya include A. Andrews (1980a), Andrews V (1977), Ball (1977a), Freidel (1978), Rathje (1977), and Webb (1973).

TRADE IN THE POSTCLASSIC

The arguments presented by Thompson (1970) provide the basis for the Putun Maya reconstruction. Much of Thompson's evidence was based on the work of Scholes and Roys (1948), who also reported the Mexican-Maya trading center at

Xicalango, and is reinforced by recent archaeological investigations, including those documenting a "foreign" takeover at Seibal (Sabloff & Willey 1967). Other treatments of Postclassic Maya exchange networks are provided in A. Andrews (1978, 1980a,b), and in Sabloff & Rathje (1975a), which also reports the archaeological investigation of the port of trade on Isla de Cozumel (see also Sabloff & Freidel 1975). The consequences for the Classic lowland Maya precipitated by the expansion of sea trade is best treated by Sabloff and Rathje (1975b). The encounter by Columbus with a Maya sea-trading canoe is recounted by Las Casas (1957). Chapman (1957) is the standard work dealing with Postclassic ports of trade. The continuance of traditional Maya overland exchange networks into the colonial era is discussed in G. Jones (1977).

## Chapter 11: Architecture and Archaeological Sites

### ARCHITECTURE

For studies of pre-Columbian architecture, including that of the ancient Maya, see Marquina (1951) and Kubler (1962). Totten (1926), Proskouriakoff (1946), Pollock (1965), A. Smith (1965), and G. Andrews (1975) provide works dealing specifically with Maya architecture and site planning (see also Wauchope 1938). For the northern lowlands, see Potter (1977); Pollock (1980) is a recently published definitive study of Puuc architecture.

### ARCHAEOLOGICAL SITES

The best-known nineteenth-century descriptions of Maya sites are those of Stephens (1841, 1843) and Maudslay (1889-1902). The studies by Morley (1920, 1937-38) remain essential sources for their catalogues of monuments and brief descriptions of lowland sites. The corpus of known Maya inscriptions is being updated by I. Graham (1975, 1978, 1979, 1980), Graham and Von Euw (1975, 1977), and Von Euw (1977, 1978), and Kudlek (1977) gives a listing of dated monuments by site.

Detailed reports of surveys and investigations at the individual sites discussed in this chapter are many. For early reports of Tikal, see Maler (1911) and Tozzer (1911). Of the multitude of works resulting from the Tikal Project, some of the more useful and accessible reports include Shook et al. (1958), Adams et al. (1961), the site map (Carr & Hazard 1961), Jones & Satterthwaite (in press), and a series of articles by W. Coe (1962, 1965a, 1967) and W. Haviland (1967, 1970, 1977). The specific ties between Tikal's dynastic history and its architectural remains are provided by Coggins (1975, 1976, 1979) and Jones (1977), and the Temple I tomb is described by its discoverer, Aubrey Trik (1963).

For Uaxactun, see Ricketson (1933), Ricketson & Ricketson (1937), Wauchope (1934), Kidder (1947), A. Smith (1937, 1950), and R. Smith (1937, 1955). For El Mirador, see Madeira (1931), I. Graham (1967), and Matheny (1979). For Calakmul, see Ruppert & Denison (1943). For Nakum, see Tozzer (1913) and Hellmuth (n.d.). For Naranjo and Yaxha, see Maler (1908a) and Hellmuth (1971a,b, 1972); Naranjo is also described by I. Graham (1975).

For Becan, see Ruppert & Denison (1943). Recent research is summarized in J. Andrews (1976), Adams (1975), and Andrews V & Andrews (1979), and more detailed reports include Ball (1974b, 1977b), P. Thomas (1980), and Webster (1976).

The research at Altun Ha is reported by Pendergast (1965, 1969, 1971, 1979). For Xunantunich, see Maler (1908a), Satterthwaite (1950b), and Mackie (1961). For Caracol, see Satterthwaite (1950a, 1954), Willcox (1954), A. Anderson (1958), and Beetz (1980). The Lubaantun investigations are reported in Gann (1904–5), Joyce (1926), Joyce, Clark & Thompson (1927), and Hammond (1975).

The ruins of Altar de Sacrificios and Seibal are described by Maler (1908b). The recent research at Seibal is reported by Tourtellot (1970), J. Graham (1973), A. Smith (1977), and Willey (1975, 1978a,b). For the excavations at Altar de Sacrificios, see Willey & Smith (1963, 1969), A. Smith (1972), Adams (1971), Saul (1972), J. Graham (1972), and Willey (1972, 1973).

Maler (1903) describes Yaxchilan; see also Graham and Von Euw (1977) and I. Graham (1979). The site of Piedras Negras is also described by Maler (1901), and its later investigation is reported by Mason (1931, 1932), Satterthwaite (1937a,b, 1943, 1944a,b, 1944 & 1954, 1952), and W. Coe (1959). For Bonampak, see Ruppert, Thompson & Proskouriakoff (1955).

Research at Palenque is described in Blom & La Farge (1926–27), Ruz (1952a,b, 1955, 1958a,b,c, 1962), R. Rands & B. Rands (1959), B. Rands & R. Rands (1961), Acosta (1977), Robertson (1974, 1976), and Robertson & Jeffers (1978). For Tonina, see Becquelin & Baudez (1975, 1979), Becquelin & Taladoire (1979), and Becquelin (1979).

Gordon (1896), Morley (1920), Trik (1939), Stromsvik (1942, 1952), and Longyear (1944) treat past investigations at Copan. Copan is also conveniently described by Nuñez Chinchilla (1963). The recent Copan valley settlement research is reported by Willey, Leventhal and Fash (1978), Leventhal (1981), and Willey and Leventhal (1979). The Proyecto Copan investigations are summarized by Baudez (1978a,b, 1979a,b); see also Pahl (1977). For Quirigua, see Hewett (1911, 1912, 1916), Morley (1935), Ricketson (1935), Stromsvik (1941), and Becker (1972). Work of the recent project is summarized in Sharer (1978b, 1980), Ashmore & Sharer (1978), Jones & Sharer (1980), Ashmore (1979, 1980a,b), Schortman (1980), and Schortman & Urban (in press).

For Coba, see Thompson, Pollock, & Charlot (1932), Villa Rojas (1934), and Benavides (1979). The Dzibilchaltun research is reported in Andrews IV (1975), Andrews V (1982), Ball & Andrews (1975), Kurjack (1974), Stuart et al. (1979), and the final report by Andrews IV & Andrews (1980).

For Uxmal, see Blom (1930) and Morley (1910, 1970), and for Labna, E. Thompson (1897b); architectural summaries of these and other Puuc sites are provided by Pollock (1980). Research at Chichen Itza is reported by Morris, Charlot, and Morris (1931), Pollock (1937), Ruppert (1931, 1935, 1943, 1952), Lothrop (1952), and Proskouriakoff (1974). For Tulum, see Lothrop (1924), Sanders (1960), Barrera R. (n.d.), and Miller (1977b, in press). Kowalski (1980) presents evidence for the dynastic sequence at Uxmal.

## Chapter 12: Ceramics

For the archaeologist the two classic works concerned with ceramic studies are those edited by Matson (1956) and by Shepard (1971). The question of deriving ceramic chronologies has been treated by numerous scholars, including Ford (1962), and the definition of ceramic complexes for Maya pottery is best described by Gifford (1976, especially Chapter 1).

The specific-site pottery sequences used in Table 12 are based on research at Uaxactun (R. Smith 1955), Barton Ramie (Gifford 1976), Cuello (Pring 1979), Altar de Sacrificios (Adams 1971), Becan (Ball 1977b), Mayapan (R. Smith 1971), Dzibilchaltun (Ball & Andrews 1975), Bilbao (Parsons 1967–69), Kaminaljuyu (Kidder 1961; Wetherington 1978), Chalchuapa (Sharer 1978a), and Salinas la Blanca (Coe & Flannery 1967).

### A CHRONOLOGICAL REVIEW OF MAYA POTTERY

The materials in this section are based largely on the individual ceramic studies cited above (see also Culbert 1963; Fry & Cox 1974; Sabloff 1975; Forsyth 1979; Warren 1961; Ekholm 1969; and Willey et al. 1980), together with the available regional synthesis for the Maya lowlands in Willey, Culbert & Adams (1967) and Smith & Gifford (1965); similar studies for the highlands are provided by Rands & Smith (1965), and for Yucatan by Brainerd (1958). Specific studies of the earliest known New World pottery include those from the Tehuacan valley, Mexico (MacNeish, Peterson & Flannery 1970), and from Valdivia, Ecuador (Meggars, Evans & Estrada 1965). The Early Preclassic coastal pottery traditions from the Maya area are known from Chiapas (Green & Lowe 1967; Lowe 1977) and Belize (Pring 1979).

The various interpretations regarding the ancient functions of Maya ceramic figurines are discussed by Borhegyi (1950) and Kidder (1965); for general summaries of pottery figurines, see R. Rands (1965b) and R. Rands & B. Rands (1965). The Teotihuacan-style figurine cache from Becan is described by Ball (1974b). The interpretation of the Altar Vase follows Adams (1971). The northern highland polychromes mentioned here are illustrated in Gordon & Mason (1925–43), and the mercantile interpretation is suggested by Thompson (1970: 137).

R. Thompson (1958) describes the k'abal slow-wheel technique for making pottery in the Yucatan. The technical analysis of plumbate ceramics was first presented by Shepard (1948). The Late Postclassic pottery traditions of the central Peten lake region were first formulated by Bullard (1970), and later modified by P. Rice (1979). The ceramics of the Postclassic Maya highlands are summarized by Wauchope (1970).

### PATTERNS OF HOUSEHOLD AND INDUSTRIAL CERAMIC PRODUCTION

Much of the material in this section is based on the author's observations of contemporary Maya pottery making. The most thorough published studies of pottery making in the Maya area are those by R. Thompson (1958) for the Yucatan and by Reina and Hill (1978) for the Guatemalan highlands.

## Chapter 13: Arts and Crafts

Excellent treatments of Maya art may be found in Spinden (1913), Kubler (1962), and Proskouriakoff (1965); more general surveys of Mesoamerican art include those by Covarrubias (1954), Joyce (1927), and Keleman (1943).

### STONE AND WOOD SCULPTURE

The definitive treatise on Maya sculpture is Proskouriakoff (1950). Some of the best illustrations of Maya stone and wood sculpture may be found in Catherwood (1844; see also Stephens 1841, 1843), Maudslay (1889–1902; see also Maudslay & Maudslay 1899), Greene (1967), and Greene, Rands & Graham (1972). Excavations in the flint-tool manufacturing center of Colha are described by T. Hester (1979). The quarry stumps on the Quirigua monuments are reported by Stromsvik (1942).

The early sculptures of the southern Maya area are discussed by Miles (1965), Proskouriakoff (1971), and Kubler (1971); see also the Chapter 3 bibliographic summary. Tikal Stela 29 (Shook 1960) and the other Tikal monuments are reported in C. Jones & Satterthwaite (in press). Morley (1937–38) provides the standard reference for most Classic-period lowland monuments, along with the more recent corpus prepared by I. Graham (1975).

### STUCCO MODELING

The stucco reliefs of Palenque are illustrated by Maudslay (1889–1902); for references to other stucco work, including the Temple of the Inscriptions tomb, see the Chapter 4 bibliographic summary. Robertson (1977) presents a thorough analysis of the ancient stucco and painting techniques used at Palenque. The Comalcalco stucco reliefs are reported by Blom and LaFarge (1926–27) and G. Andrews et al. (1967).

### PAINTING

The Preclassic wall paintings at Tikal are discussed by Coggins (1975). See A. Smith (1950) in regard to the Uaxactun Structure B-XIII paintings, and L. Smith (1934) and R. Smith (1955) for the Uaxactun pottery vessels. The Bonampak murals are illustrated and discussed by Ruppert, Thompson, and Proskouriakoff (1955). See the Chapter 11 bibliographic summary for references to Chichen Itza, Santa Rita, and Tulum. Thompson (1973b) and C. Jones (1975) report several painted capstones from the northern lowlands. Studies of Maya paint colors (Shepard 1971) have focused on the identity of the distinctive blue pigment (Arnold & Bohor 1975; Littmann 1980). Illustrations of Maya vase paintings may be found in Gordon & Mason (1925–43) and M. Coe (1973, 1975a). M. Coe and Quirarte (1976, 1979) provide iconographic studies of vase painting; see also the bibliographic summary for Chapter 12.

LAPIDARY ART AND MOSAICS

Digby (1972), Easby (1961), and Kidder (1951) discuss Maya jadeite carvings; in addition, see R. Rands (1965a) and Woodbury (1965). The Leyden plaque is described by Morley and Morley (1939). The jades from the Cenote of Sacrifice at Chichen Itza are fully reported by Proskouriakoff (1974). Pendergast (1969) reports the Altun Ha jadeite sculpture of Kinich Ahau. The jadeite mosaic mask and vases from Tikal are illustrated by W. Coe (1975). Maya jadeite sources are identified by Foshag and Leslie (1955) and Hammond et al. (1977).

METALWORK

Bray (1977) and Pendergast (1962) provide descriptions of Maya metalwork. The metal artifacts from Copan are reported by Stromsvik (1942), and the copper from Quirigua by Lothrop (1952) and Sharer et al. (1979). The metal objects recovered from the Cenote of Sacrifice at Chichen Itza are described by Lothrop (1952).

CHIPPED STONE

Maya chipped-stone artifacts are the subject of a volume edited by Hester and Hammond (1976). Examples of eccentric chipped-stone work may be found in Stromsvik (1942) and Morley (1935). Technical studies of chipped-stone artifacts include those by W. Coe (1959), Lee (1969), Sheets (1972, 1975; see also Sheets 1976a), and Willey (1978a).

TEXTILES

Ancient Maya textiles are discussed by Mahler (1965). The weaving of the Lacandon is described by Tozzer (1907), and contemporary highland Maya textiles are discussed by Osborne (1935, 1965).

BASKETRY AND MATTING

Robicsek (1975) provides a study of ancient Maya mat symbolism; see also Lounsbury (1973). Osborne (1965) treats contemporary highland Maya basketry, matting, and other handicrafts.

FEATHERWORK

Sources quoted referring to ancient Maya featherwork include Fuentes y Guzmán (1932–34) and Las Casas (1909). Barrera Vásquez (1939) provides a study of Maya featherworking, and Sahagún (1946) describes Aztec featherwork.

## Chapter 14: Ideology

The primary sources for our understanding of ancient Maya ideology are discussed by Thompson (1970: 159–65). The concept of *cuxolalob*, and the Maya view of the world, are described by Brotherston (1979), on the basis of an analysis of passages in the *Book of Chilam Balam* of Chumayel (Roys 1933). The general aspects of formal Maya religion (the ancient priesthood and rituals) are treated by Thompson (1970: 165–96).

Landa (1938; see also Tozzer 1941) remains the best source of information on Postclassic Maya religious practices and beliefs, including the series of rituals described in this chapter (see also Herrera 1726–30). The worship of idols and the practice of human sacrifice in the Postclassic and during earlier eras is discussed by Thompson (1970: 175–91). A volume dealing with human sacrifice in Mesoamerica has been edited by Benson (in press). The Bonampak murals are reproduced by Ruppert, Thompson, and Proskouriakoff (1955). The example of apparent Late Preclassic mass human sacrifice is reported by Fowler (1979).

Divination and the use of consciousness-altering substances by the ancient Maya have been discussed by several scholars, including Thompson (1970: 185). Divination and other uses of psychotropic substances, common among pre-Columbian Mesoamerican societies, are still practiced in some areas today (see Furst 1976). Landa (1938) verifies the use of alcohol. Thompson (1946) and, more comprehensively, Robicsek (1978) have studied the use of tobacco. The consumption of hallucinogenic mushrooms has been proposed by Borhegyi (1961), and continued use by the Lacandon is reported by Robertson (1972a). The possible uses of peyote, morning glory, *Bufo marinus* poison, and other substances in Mesoamerica is reviewed by Furst (1976). Dobkin de Rios (1974) also proposes the utilization of some of these substances by the ancient Maya, suggesting the water lily as an undocumented possibility. Gage describes the mixture of substances in seventeenth-century highland brews (Thompson 1958: 225). The evidence for ancient Maya use of narcotics and hallucinogens, especially as administered in enemas, is described by Furst and Coe (1977).

TRANSFORMATIONS BY OUTSIDERS

The ideological changes wrought by the Spanish Conquest have been studied by numerous scholars, including Chamberlain (1948), Roys (1943), Scholes (1933), and Scholes and Roys (1938) in Yucatan. Among the most useful treatments of the interaction between western European and Maya ideology are those by Edmonson (1960), Madsen (1960), and D. Thompson (1960). The consequences of Spanish attempts at conversion and the continuities of native Maya beliefs in twentieth-century Maya communities in Yucatan and Quintana Roo are described by Redfield (1941), Redfield and Villa Rojas (1934), Villa Rojas (1955), and Saville (1921). The War of the Castes has been well studied by Reed (1964).

Similar information about the contemporary beliefs of Maya peoples in Belize is provided by Thompson (1930) and Muntsch (1943). The beliefs and rituals of the Lacandon have been reported by Tozzer (1907), Amram (1942), and Thompson (1952), among others.

Las Casas (1909) is the primary source regarding the Verapaz and other highland areas. Descriptions of the syncretism of Maya and Christian ideologies in a series of highland Maya communities may be found in Bunzel (1952), LaFarge (1927, 1947), Oakes (1951), Siegel (1941), and Wagley (1949), and others. Specific examples of continuities in the ancient Maya calendrical system may be found in these studies and in LaFarge & Byers (1931).

COSMOLOGY

Ancient Maya cosmology and characteristics of Maya "deities" are described by Landa (1938) and further discussed by Thompson (1934, 1939b, 1970: 179–96). The tombs of Late Classic rulers are described by Ruz (1954) at Palenque and by Trik (1963) at Tikal. Coggins (1975) provides a stimulating interpretation of the ideological meaning of materials recovered from the tombs excavated at Tikal. The case for a monotheistic quality in Maya ideology is best presented by Freidel (1979b). Some of the interpretations of myth and ritual, based on scenes on painted pottery, are provided by M. Coe (1973, 1975a). The parallels between Maya and Mexican deities as depicted in the Maya codices are reviewed by Kelley (1976). Descriptions of Mexica (Aztec) ideology at the time of the Spanish Conquest are provided by Díaz del Castillo (1963), Caso (1936), and Vaillant (1941).

MAYA DEITIES

Most of the common Maya deities have been identified from the Dresden, Paris, and Madrid codices (1880; 1887; 1869–70 and 1892, respectively). The most accepted classification, and the one followed here, was proposed by Schellhas (1904). Other classifications are provided by Seler (1902–23), and Zimmermann (1956). Kelley (1976: 61–105) provides a good recent summary of the deity classification and problems in identification. Thompson (1970: 197–329) presents a thorough description of both the well-known and lesser-known Maya deities, arguing strongly for the primacy of Itzamna. The case for the Tlaloc origins for the manikin-scepter deity (God K) at Tikal is detailed by Coggins (1979).

## Chapter 15: Language and Writing

The estimate of the number of speakers of Mayan languages is from Kaufman (1974). The map of Mayan languages is based on that of Fox (1978). Basic references on Mayan languages include a comprehensive bibliography by Campbell et al. (1978) and several articles in the linguistics volume of the *Handbook of Middle American Indians*, edited by McQuown (1967). See also the survey of Mesoamerican Indian languages by Kaufman (1974), and the many articles on Mayan languages in the *International Journal of American Linguistics*, the *Journal of Mayan Linguistics*, and the *Mayan Linguistics Newsletter*.

HISTORY OF THE MAYAN LANGUAGES

Surveys of Mayan historical linguistics are found in Campbell (1977) and Fox (1978). For the classification of Mayan, see the above and articles by Kaufman (1974) and McQuown (1956). For a discussion of linguistics in colonial New Spain, see McQuown (1976). The glottochronological findings are based on Swadesh (1967). Principles of historical inference from language differentiation and distribution were pioneered by Sapir (1916), and have been applied to Maya by Diebold (1960), McQuown (1964), and Kaufman (1969). Cultural inferences from the reconstructed Proto-Mayan vocabulary have been made by Sapper (1897), Kaufman (1964), and

McQuown (1964). The characterization of a reconstructed language as a "glorious artifact" is in Haas (1969).

The subgrouping and relationships of Mixe-Zoquean are discussed by N. Thomas (1974), Witkowski & Brown (1978), and Brown & Witkowski (1979). Campbell and Kaufman (1980) have been reluctant to accept the proposed close relationship of Mayan and Mixe-Zoquean. For an analysis of borrowings within and outside Mayan, see Kaufman (1973, 1976), Josserand (1975), Campbell (1977), Fox (1979), and Campbell, Justeson & Norman (1980).

The close relationship of Chorti, Chol, and Cholti was independently established by Charencey (1872), Sapper (1897), and Gates (1920). Kaufman and Norman (1982) give a preliminary reconstruction of Proto-Cholan. For the former existence of a Cholan belt in the Maya heartland, see Sapper (1897), Thompson (1938), and Gates (1920). For inscriptional evidence bearing on the linguistic identity of the Classic Lowland Maya, see Fox & Justeson (in press: a).

## THE STRUCTURE OF MAYAN LANGUAGES

The phonology of the Yucatecan languages has been treated by Fisher (1973). For a description of colonial Yucatec, with special attention to early sources and orthographic conventions, see McQuown (1967). For Mayan morpheme structure, see Fox (1978). For Yucatec grammar, see Tozzer (1921), Andrade (1955), Blair (1964), and McClaran (1973). Sources for the phonology and grammar of Cholan languages include studies of Chorti (Fought 1967), Cholti (Moran 1935), Chol (Attinasi 1973), colonial Chontal (Smailus 1975a), and modern Chontal (Keller 1959).

Mayan numeral systems are discussed in Thompson (1950). For Mayan numeral classifiers, see B. Berlin (1968). For positional verbs, see MacLeod (1982).

Important dictionaries of Greater Lowland Mayan languages include works on Yucatec (Martínez-Hernandez 1930), Chol (Aulie & Aulie 1978), Cholti (Moran 1935), Chorti (Wisdom 1950), and Tzotzil (Laughlin 1975). For botanical terminology, see the monographs by Berlin, Breedlove, and Raven (1974) and Roys (1931). For zoological terminology, see Hunn (1977) and Roys (1931). Mayan languages have figured prominently in the work on universals of color terminology by Berlin and Kay (1969). See Eggan (1934), Miles (1957), and Fox & Justeson (1982) for Mayan kinship terminology. Early dictionaries have been studied for social content (Miles 1957), agricultural content (Marcus 1982), and physico-geographical content (Álvarez 1980).

Studies of discourse include collections of diverse Mayan texts (Furbee 1976; Furbee-Losee 1979, 1980), Chorti texts (Fought 1972, in press), Yucatec texts (Andrade 1971; Smailus 1975b), and Tzotzil tales and dreams (Laughlin 1976, 1977); a monograph on Lacandon dreams (Bruce 1975); and works on Tzotzil ritual humor (Bricker 1973) and gossip (J. Haviland 1977). Highland Guatemalan gestural systems have been studied by Du Bois (1978).

## MAYA DOCUMENTS OF THE COLONIAL PERIOD

For an introduction to colonial documents in indigenous languages, see Volume 15 of the *Handbook of Middle American Indians*, edited by Cline (1975). For translations and analyses of the *Books of Chilam Balam*, see Roys (1933), Makemson (1951),

Craine & Reindorp (1979), and Edmonson (1982). For translations and discussions of the *Popol Vuh*, see Recinos (1950) and Edmonson (1971); the latter includes the Quiche text and is the only attempt to preserve the original poetic structure in translation. For *Popol Vuh* themes in Mesoamerican art and on Maya ceramic vessels, see Norman (1973) and M. Coe (1973).

## ANCIENT MAYA WRITING

Many scholars have used writing as a criterion for the definition of civilization, among them Morgan (1877) and Childe (1954). For general works on Maya writing, see Thompson (1950, 1972a), Kelley (1976), H. Berlin (1977), Justeson (1978), and Campbell & Justeson (in press). For other Mesoamerican writing systems, see Benson (1973), M. Smith (1973), and Marcus (1980). For a discussion of the Andean *quipu*, see Ascher & Ascher (1981). For the traditional view that Maya writing was not used for recording history, see Goodman (1897), Teeple (1926), Morley (1946), and Thompson (1950). See Stephens (1841), Morley (1915), and Spinden (1917: 113) for earlier opinions to the contrary.

## PRE-COLUMBIAN MAYA TEXTS

The description of the destruction of ancient Maya books by Landa is from Tozzer (1941: 169). For a survey, census, and bibliography of pre-Columbian codices, see the articles by Glass (1975) and Glass and Robertson (1975) in Volume 14 of the *Handbook of Middle American Indians*, edited by Cline (1975). A complete facsimile of the Dresden Codex, painted by A. Aglio, was published in Volume 3 of Kingsborough (1831–48). The first photographic facsimile (1880) was that of Förstemann, in color. The second edition, made in 1892, was reprinted in 1962. Other important editions are those of Thompson (1972b) and Anders (1975); Anders's edition shows the present condition of the codex, which sustained water damage during World War II. Black-and-white plates of the Paris Codex were first published in 1864; these are reproduced with the modern color edition by Anders (1968). The two fragments of the Madrid Codex were first published in 1869–70 (the Tro portion) and 1883 (the Cortés portion); the former was in color, the latter in black and white. The second edition of the Cortés portion (1892) was in color. A modern color facsimile of both portions has been published by Anders (1967). The Anders editions (1967, 1968, 1975) are all screenfold (i.e., they reproduce the original folded-screen format of the codices). Black-and-white freehand facsimiles of all three codices were published by Villacorta and Villacorta (1933). For commentaries on the codices and discussions of their manufacture, see Von Hagen (1944), Zimmermann (1956), Anders (1967, 1968), and Thompson (1972b); Knorozov (1982) also provides a commentary. The Maya provenance of the codices is discussed in Thompson (1972b), and the stylistic comparisons with Tancah and Tulum are discussed by Miller (1982). A facsimile, with discussion, of the Grolier Codex appears in M. Coe (1973); Thompson (1972b) gives a negative assessment of its authenticity.

Pre-Columbian Maya texts on stone, wood, and bone are illustrated in many sources; some of the most important are Maudslay (1889–1902), Maler (1901, 1903, 1908a,b, 1911), Morley (1920, 1937–38), Greene, Rands & Graham (1972), J.

Graham (1972), I. Graham (1967, 1975, 1978, 1979, 1980, 1982), Graham & Von Euw (1975, 1977), and Von Euw (1977, 1978). For a review of the *Corpus,* see Fox (1980). Illustrations are also found throughout the Palenque Round Table publications (Robertson 1974, 1976, 1980; Robertson & Jeffers 1978). Mayer (1978) furnishes a useful catalogue of unprovenanced (primarily looted) Classic monuments now in Europe. For illustrations of Maya ceramic vessels bearing hieroglyphic texts, most also unprovenanced, see especially M. Coe (1973, 1975a).

DECIPHERING MAYA WRITING

For the place of Maya writing in a general typology of writing systems, see Justeson (1978). See Thompson (1950, 1972a) and Kelley (1976) for basic introductions to the structure of glyphic texts, and Riese (1971), Kubler (1973), and Kelley (1976) for more advanced treatment.

See Tozzer (1941) for a detailed commentary on the life and work of Landa. Many important early German works have been translated; see Förstemann (1904, 1906), Schellhas (1904), and Seler (1904). For Goodman's contributions, see Goodman (1897) and the discussion in Thompson (1950). For other important early works on calendrics and astronomy, see Morley (1915) and Teeple (1926, 1931). Tozzer and Allen (1910) made an important study of animal figures and associated glyphs in the codices.

For a survey of H. Berlin's and Proskouriakoff's early discoveries, see Kelley (1976) and the original articles by Berlin (1958) and Proskouriakoff (1960, 1963, 1964). Proskouriakoff (1961) also wrote a popularized account of her findings. Bowditch's and Morley's prescient insights are found in Bowditch (1901) and Morley (1915). Thompson lived to see the decipherment of historical inscriptions from several Classic-period centers, and graciously acknowledged that his earlier view had been incorrect (Thompson 1971: v).

For early attempts at phonetic decipherment, see C. Thomas (1882, 1893), Whorf (1933, 1942), and Knorozov (1958, 1967). The most devastating critique of Knorozov was by Thompson (1953). The chain of phonetic decipherment is based partly on Kelley (1976).

THE CURRENT STATUS OF DECIPHERMENT

For significant recent work on phoneticism in Maya writing, see Lounsbury (1973), Fox & Justeson (1980), Knorozov (1982), and Campbell & Justeson (in press); in the latter work, see Fox & Justeson (in press: b) for a discussion of polyvalence, and Fox & Justeson (in press: a) for glyphic evidence bearing on the identification of the languages of the inscriptions and codices.

For discussions of early Maya and pre-Maya inscriptions, see M. Coe (1976), J. Graham (1977), Graham, Heizer & Shook (1978), Kelley (1976), and Marcus (1976a). For efforts to identify and read the glyph elements and combinations representing (logographically or phonetically) Mayan grammatical morphemes, see Thompson (1950), Kelley (1976), Schele (1980), Fox & Justeson (in press: b), and MacLeod (1982).

For kinship decipherments and associated cultural and political inferences, see

Mathews & Schele (1974), W. Haviland (1977), G. Jones (1977), Schele (1978), Sharer (1978b), Mathews (1980), Schele, Mathews & Lounsbury (n.d.), and Fox & Justeson (1982). Marcus (1976b) discusses the political implications of the distribution of emblem glyphs. For a discussion of texts on ceramic vessels, see M. Coe (1973).

## Chapter 16: Arithmetic, Calendrics, and Astronomy

### ARITHMETIC

The arithmetic of the ancient Maya is discussed by Morley (1915), Thompson (1942, 1950, 1971), Satterthwaite (1947), and Lounsbury (1976), among others. A recent treatment of computations using Maya numerals is provided in Lambert, Ownbey-McLaughlin & McLaughlin (1980).

### THE CALENDAR

Landa (1938; Tozzer 1941) describes the basic Maya calendrical system as it existed in the Yucatan during the early colonial era. This account includes versions of the standard Mesoamerican 260-day almanac and the 365-day vague year, so that the Yucatec names for these calendrical units have been used by Maya scholars ever since. For general summaries of the entire system, see Morley (1915), Thompson (1950, 1971), and Kelley (1976).

The long-count dates, or Initial Series (Maudslay 1889–1902), recorded in Classic-period inscriptions is discussed by Morley (1915, 1925), Spinden (1924, 1930), Thompson (1950, 1971), and Satterthwaite (1965), among others. The assumed calendrical zero date was proposed by Beyer (1936). The standard letter-designation scheme used in referring to the supplementary series was proposed by Morley (1916; see also Andrews IV 1951); Thompson (1929) demonstrated that Glyph G of this series referred to any one of the nine Bolontiku. Teeple (1931), Thompson (1950, 1971), and several other scholars have discussed the lunar series glyphs. Thompson (1950, 1971) provides the standard reckoning for the distance-number inscriptions, arguing for the reading of calculations into the distant past on Quirigua Stelae D and F.

Period-ending dating is discussed by Thompson (1950, 1971) and Satterthwaite (1965), as well as the Maya short-count system recorded by Landa (1938; Tozzer 1941).

The correlation of the Maya and European calendars is discussed by Andrews IV (1940), Beyer (1935), Kidder and Thompson (1938), Palacios (1932), and Thompson (1935, 1950), among others. The GMT correlation was built on the one first proposed by Goodman (1905), later modified by Martínez and finally by Thompson (1927; see also 1935). Other correlations mentioned are discussed by Spinden (1924) and Vaillant (1935). Satterthwaite and Ralph (1960) report the radiocarbon dates from Tikal and their implications for the correlation question. Sidrys, Krowne, and Nicholson (1975) provide a computer program for the conversion of long-count dates to the Gregorian calendar.

ASTRONOMY

Maya astronomy is summarized by Teeple (1931) and Kelley and Kerr (1973), and M. Coe (1975b) discusses astronomical knowledge in ancient Mesoamerica. Knowledge of Venus and other planets is considered by Teeple (1926), Kelley (1975), Fox and Justeson (1978), and Aveni (1979). Thompson (1972b) explores the postulated recording of Mars and other planetary cycles. The Maya "zodiac" is summarized by Kelley (1976). Astronomical observatories and astronomical alignments of Maya architecture are discussed by Ricketson and Ricketson (1937), Aveni (1975), Hartung (1975), and Aveni, Gibbs, and Hartung (1975); see also the bibliographic summary for Chapter 11.

## Epilogue: The Spanish Conquest

Firsthand accounts of the Spanish Conquest and colonization of Mexico may be found in Díaz del Castillo (1963) and Sahagún (1946). The march by Cortés and his party across the Peten is described by Díaz del Castillo (1963).

The conquest of Guatemala is related in the sparse words of Alvarado (1924) himself. The highland Maya version of the conquest forms part of the *Popol Vuh* (Recinos 1950; Edmonson 1971) and the *Annals of the Cakchiquels* (Recinos & Goetz 1953). Fuller accounts may be found in Ximenez (1929–31) and Fuentes y Guzmán (1932–34). Las Casas (1909) provides a harsh denunciation of Alvarado and his military campaign.

The early Spanish voyages and the conquest of the Yucatan are related in a variety of works. Those in the Spanish language include Ancona (1889), Carrillo y Ancona (1937), Lizana (1893), and Scholes et al. (1936). Accounts in English include Blom (1936), Chamberlain (1948), Farriss (in press), Means (1917), and Roys (1952). The account of the final conquest of the Tayasal Itza is related by Villagutierre (1933).

# BIBLIOGRAPHY

Abbreviations used for frequently cited publications and institutions:

A       *Archaeology*
AA      *American Anthropologist*
AAnt    *American Antiquity*
APA     *Archaeoastronomy in Precolumbian America* (A. F. Aveni, ed.). Austin: University of Texas Press, 1975
BAE     Bureau of American Ethnology, Smithsonian Institution
CCM    *Ceramica de Cultura Maya*
CIW     Carnegie Institution of Washington
           CAA    *Contributions to American Archaeology* (or *Anthropology and History*)
           NMA    *Notes on Middle American Archaeology and Ethnology*
DO       Dumbarton Oaks, Trustees for Harvard University, Washington, D.C.
ECAUY   Escuela de Ciencias Antropologicas de la Universidad de Yucatán
ECM     *Estudios de Cultura Maya*
FMAS    Field Museum of Natural History, Anthropological Series. Chicago
HMAI    *Handbook of Middle American Indians* (R. Wauchope, general ed.). 15 vols. Austin: University of Texas Press, 1964–75
ICA      International Congress of Americanists
IJAL     *International Journal of American Linguistics*
IMS      Institute for Mesoamerican Studies, State University of New York, Albany
INAH    Instituto Nacional de Antropología e Historia, Mexico
JFA      *Journal of Field Archaeology*
MARI    Middle American Research Institute, Tulane University
MCM    Microfilm Collection of Manuscripts on Middle American Cultural Anthropology, Regenstein Library, University of Chicago
NWAF   New World Archaeological Foundation, Brigham Young University
PMAE   Peabody Museum of Archaeology and Ethnology, Harvard University
SA       *Scientific American*
SAR     School of American Research, Advanced Seminar Series, Santa Fe, New Mexico
SWJA    *Southwestern Journal of Anthropology*

UCARF   University of California Archaeological Research Facility, University of
           California, Berkeley
UM       University Museum, University of Pennsylvania, Philadelphia
WA       *World Archaeology*


Abascal, R., P. Davila, P. J. Schmidt, and D. Z. Davila. 1976. *La arqueología del sur-oeste de Tlaxcala*. Primera Parte. Suplemento, Comunicaciónes Proyecto Puebla-Tlaxcala. Puebla, Mexico: Fundacion Alemána para la investigación científica.

Acosta, J. R. 1956. Exploraciones arqueológicas en Tula, Hidalgo, Temporadas VI, VII, y VIII. *INAH Anales* 8: 37-115.

————. 1960. Las exploraciones arqueológicas en Tula, Hidalgo, durante la XI temporada, 1955. *INAH Anales* 11: 39-72.

————. 1977. Excavations at Palenque, 1967-1973. In Hammond 1977b: 265-85.

Adams, R. E. W. 1970. Suggested Classic-Period Occupational Specialization in the Southern Maya Lowlands. In PMAE Papers, Vol. 61: 489-502.

————. 1971. *The Ceramics of Altar de Sacrificios*. PMAE Papers, Vol. 63(1).

————. 1973a. The Collapse of Maya Civilization: A Review of Previous Theories. In Culbert 1973: 21-34.

————. 1973b. Maya Collapse: Transformation and Termination in the Ceramic Sequence at Altar de Sacrificios. In Culbert 1973: 133-63.

————, comp. 1975. Preliminary Reports on Archaeological Investigations in the Río Bec Area, Campeche, Mexico. In MARI Publication 31: 103-46.

————, ed. 1977. *The Origins of Maya Civilization*. SAR. Albuquerque: University of New Mexico Press.

————. 1980. Swamps, Canals, and the Locations of Ancient Maya Cities. *Antiquity* 54: 206-14.

————. 1981. Settlement Patterns of the Central Yucatan and Southern Campeche Regions. In Ashmore 1981b: 211-57.

Adams, R. E. W., and R. C. Aldrich. 1980. A Reevaluation of the Bonampak Murals: A Preliminary Statement on the Paintings and Texts. In Robertson 1980: 45-59.

Adams, R. E. W., V. L. Broman, W. R. Coe, W. A. Haviland, R. E. Reina, L. Satterthwaite, E. M. Shook, and A. S. Trik. 1961. *Tikal Report* Nos. 5-10. UM Monographs, 20.

Adams, R. E. W., and R. C. Jones. 1981. Spatial Patterns and Regional Growth among Maya Cities. *AAnt* 46: 301-22.

Adams, R. E. W., and W. D. Smith. 1977. Apocalyptic Visions: The Maya Collapse and Mediaeval Europe. *A* 30: 292-301.

————. 1981. Feudal Models for Classic Maya Civilization. In Ashmore 1981b: 335-49.

Adams, R. E. W., and A. S. Trik. 1961. Temple I (Str. 5D-1): Post-constructional Activities. *Tikal Report* No. 7. In UM Monograph 20: 113-47.

Adams, R. M. 1966. *The Evolution of Urban Society*. Chicago: Aldine.

Altschuler, M. 1958. On the Environmental Limitations of Maya Cultural Development. *SWJA* 14: 189-98.

Alvarado, P. de. 1924. *An Account of the Conquest of Guatemala in 1524*. Translated by S. J. Mackie. New York: The Cortes Society.

Alvarez, C. 1980. *Diccionario etnolingüístico del idioma Maya Yucateco colonial*. Vol. I. *Mundo Físico*. Mexico City: Universidad Nacional Autónoma de México.

Amram, D. W. 1942. The Lacandon, Last of the Maya. *El Mexico Antiguo* 6: 15-26.

Ancona, E. 1889. *Historia de Yucatán*. 2nd ed. 4 vols. Barcelona: Raviratta.

Anders, F., ed. 1967. *Codex Tro-Cortesianus (Codex Madrid), Museo de América, Madrid*. Graz: Akademische Druck- und Verlagsanstalt.

# 638    Bibliography

————, ed. 1968. *Codex Peresianus (Codex Paris), Bibliothèque Nationale, Paris.* Graz: Akademische Druck- und Verlagsanstalt.

————, ed. 1975. *Codex Dresdensis, Sächsische Landesbibliothek Dresden.* Graz: Akademische Druck- und Verlagsanstalt.

Anderson, A. H. 1958. More Discoveries at Caracol, British Honduras. *33rd ICA Actas* 2: 211-18.

Anderson, D. 1978. Monuments. In *The Prehistory of Chalchuapa, El Salvador* (R. J. Sharer, general editor), UM Monograph 36(1): 155-80.

Andrade, M. J. 1955. A Grammar of Modern Yucatec. *MCM*, No. 41.

————. 1971. Yucatec Maya Texts. *MCM*, No. 108.

Andrews, A. P. 1978. Puertos costeros del Postclasico Temprano en el norte de Yucatán. *ECM* 11: 75-93.

————. 1980a. The Salt Trade of the Ancient Maya. *A* 33(4): 24-33.

————. 1980b. Salt-Making, Merchants and Markets: The Role of a Critical Resource in the Development of Maya Civilization. Unpublished doctoral dissertation, University of Arizona.

Andrews, A. P., and F. Robles C. N.d. Chichen Itzá and Cobá: An Itza-Maya Standoff in Early Postclassic Yucatan. In Chase & Rice (n.d.).

Andrews, E. W., IV. 1940. Chronology and Astronomy in the Maya Area. In *The Maya and Their Neighbors* (C. L. Hay and others, editors): New York: Appleton Century. 150-61.

————. 1951. The Maya Supplementary Series. 39th *ICA Selected Papers* 1: 123-41.

————. 1965. Archaeology and Prehistory in the Northern Maya Lowlands: An Introduction. In *HMAI* 2: 288-330.

————. 1975. Progress Report on the 1960-1964 Field Seasons NGS-Tulane University Dzibilchaltun Program. In MARI Publication 31: 23-67.

Andrews, E. W., IV, and E. W. Andrews V. 1980. *Excavations at Dzibilchaltun, Yucatan, Mexico.* MARI Publication 48.

Andrews, E. W., V. 1977. The Southeastern Periphery of Mesoamerica: A View from Eastern El Salvador. In Hammond 1977b: 113-34.

————. 1979a. Some Comments on Puuc Architecture of the Northern Yucatan Peninsula. In *The Puuc: New Perspectives* (L. Mills, editor): 1-17. Pella, Iowa: Central College Press.

————. 1979b. Early Central Mexican Architectural Traits at Dzibilchaltun, Yucatan. 42nd ICA *Actas* 8: 237-49.

————. 1981. Dzibilchaltun. In *HMAI Supplement 1* (J. A. Sabloff, ed.): 313-41. Austin: University of Texas Press.

Andrews, E. W., V, and A. P. Andrews. 1979. NGS-Tulane University Program of Archaeological Research in the Yucatan Peninsula, Mexico. *National Geographic Society Research Reports, 1970 Projects*: 7-22.

Andrews, G. F. 1969. *Edzna, Campeche, Mexico—Settlement Patterns and Monumental Architecture.* Eugene: University of Oregon.

————. 1975. *Maya Cities: Placemaking and Urbanization.* Norman: University of Oklahoma Press.

Andrews, G. F., D. Hardesty, C. Kerr, F. E. Miller, and R. Mogul. 1967. *Comalcalco, Tabasco, Mexico—An Architectonic Survey.* Eugene: University of Oregon.

Andrews, J. M. 1976. Reconnaissance and Archaeological Excavations in the Río Bec Area of the Maya Lowlands. *NGS Research Reports, 1968 Projects*: 19-27.

Armillas, P. 1971. Gardens on Swamps. *Science* 174: 653-61.

Arnold, D. E., and B. F. Bohor. 1975. Attapulgite and Maya Blue. *A* 28: 23-29.

Arqueta, J. G. 1979. Introducción al patron de asentamiento del sitio de Cobá, Quintana Roo. Thesis, Escuela Nacional de Antropología e Historia, Mexico.

Ascher, M., and R. Ascher. 1969. Code of Ancient Peruvian Knotted Cords (Quipus). *Nature* 222: 529-33.

————. 1981. *Code of the Quipu*. Ann Arbor: The University of Michigan Press.

Ashmore, W. A., ed. 1979. *Quirigua Reports I* (R. J. Sharer, general ed.), Papers 1–5, Site Map. UM Monograph 37.

————. 1980a. The Classic Maya Settlement at Quirigua. *Expedition* 23(1): 20–27.

————. 1980b. Discovering Early Classic Quirigua. *Expedition* 23(1): 35–44.

————. 1981a. Some Issues of Method and Theory in Lowland Maya Settlement Archaeology. In Ashmore 1981b: 37–70.

————, ed. 1981b. *Lowland Maya Settlement Patterns*. SAR. Albuquerque: University of New Mexico Press.

Ashmore, W. A., E. M. Schortman, and R. J. Sharer. In press. The Quirigua Project: 1979 Season. In *Quirigua Reports II* (E. M. Schortman and P. A. Urban, eds.), UM Monograph.

Ashmore, W. A., and R. J. Sharer. 1975. A Revitalization Movement at Late Classic Tikal. Paper presented at the Area Seminar in Ongoing Research, West Chester State College.

————. 1978. Excavations at Quirigua, Guatemala: The Ascent of an Elite Maya Center. *A* 31(6): 10–19.

Ashmore, W. A., and G. R. Willey. 1981. An Historical Introduction to the Study of Lowland Maya Settlement Patterns. In Ashmore 1981b: 3–18.

Attinasi, J. J. 1973. Lak T'an: A Grammar of the Chol (Mayan) Word. Doctoral dissertation, University of Chicago.

Aulie, H. W., and E. W. Aulie. 1978. *Diccionario Ch'ol-Español, Español-Ch'ol*. Serie de Vocabularios y Diccionarios Indígenas Mariano Silva y Aceves, No. 21. Mexico City: Insituto Lingüístico de Verano.

Aveni, A. F. 1975a. Possible Astronomical Orientations in Ancient Mesoamerica. In Aveni 1975b: 163–90.

————, ed. 1975b. *Archaeoastronomy in Precolumbian America*. Austin: University of Texas Press.

————. 1979. Venus and the Maya. *American Scientist* 67: 274–85.

Aveni, A. F., S. L. Gibbs, and H. Hartung. 1975. The Caracol Tower at Chichen Itza: An Ancient Astronomical Observatory? *Science* 188: 977–85.

Ball, J. W. 1974a. A Coordinate Approach to Northern Maya Prehistory: A.D. 700–1200. *AAnt* 39: 85–93.

————. 1974b. A Teotihuacan-Style Cache from the Maya Lowlands. *A* 27(1): 2–9.

————. 1977a. An Hypothetical Outline of Coastal Maya Prehistory: 300 B.C.–A.D. 1200. In Hammond 1977b: 167–96.

————. 1977b. *The Archaeological Ceramics of Becan, Campeche, Mexico*. MARI Publication 43.

————. 1978. Archaeological Pottery of the Yucatan—Campeche Coast. In MARI Publication 46: 76–146.

————. 1979. Southern Campeche and the Mexican Plateau: Early Classic Contact Situation. 42nd *ICA Actas* 8: 271–80.

————. 1980. Ceramics and Central Mexican Highland–Maya Lowland Classic-Period Social Interactions: A Theoretical Perspective. Paper presented at the DO Symposium on Mesoamerican Highland-Lowland Interaction, Washington, D.C.

Ball, J. W., and E. W. Andrews V. 1975. The Polychrome Pottery of Dzibilchaltun, Yucatan, Mexico: Typology and Archaeological Context. In MARI Publication 31: 227–47.

Barrera Rubio, A. 1978. Settlement Patterns in the Uxmal Area, Yucatan, Mexico. Paper presented at the 43rd Annual Meeting of the Society for American Archaeology, Tucson.

————. 1980. Mural Paintings of the Puuc Region in Yucatan. In Robertson 1980: 173–82.

————. N.d. Littoral-Marine Economy at Tulum, Quintana Roo, Mexico. In Chase & Rice (n.d.).

Barrera Vásquez, A. 1939. Algunos datos acerca del arte plumaria entre los mayas. *Cuadernos Mayas* No. 1. Mérida.

Barthel, T. 1968. El complejo "emblema." *ECM* 7: 159-93.

Baudez, C. F. 1978a. Segundo informe sobre las actividades del proyecto. Copan: Proyecto Arqueológico Copán.

————. 1978b. Tercer informe sobre las actividades del proyecto. Copan: Proyecto Arqueológico Copán.

————. 1979a. Cuarto informe sobre las actividades del proyecto. Copan: Proyecto Arqueológico Copán.

————. 1979b. Quinto informe sobre las actividades del proyecto. Copan: Proyecto Arqueológico Copán.

————. 1980. Iconography and History of Copan. Paper presented at the 45th Annual Meeting of the Society for American Archaeology, Philadelphia.

Becker, M. J. 1972. Plaza Plans at Quirigua, Guatemala. *Katunob* 8(2): 47-62.

————. 1973. Archaeological Evidence for Occupational Specialization Among the Classic-Period Maya at Tikal, Guatemala. *AAnt* 38: 396-406.

————. 1979. Priests, Peasants and Ceremonial Centers: The Intellectual History of a Model. In Hammond & Willey 1979: 3-20.

Becquelin, P. 1969. Archeologie de la Region de Nebaj (Guatemala). *Memoires de l'Institut d'Ethnologie* No. 2. Paris.

————. 1979. Tonina: A City State of the Western Maya Periphery. Paper presented at the 43rd ICA, Vancouver.

Becquelin, P., and C. F. Baudez. 1975. Architecture et Sculpture a Tonina, Chiapas, Mexique. 41st *ICA Actas* 1: 433-35.

————. 1979. *Tonina, une Cité Maya du Chiapas*. Études Mesoamericaines 6(1). Mexico: Mission Archéologique et Ethnologie Française au Mexique.

Becquelin, P., and E. Taladoire. 1979. Excavations at Tonina, Chiapas, Mexico, the Fourth Field Season (1979). Paper presented at the 43rd ICA, Vancouver.

Beetz, C. P. 1980. Caracol Thirty Years Later: A Preliminary Account of Two Rulers. *Expedition* 22(3): 4-11.

Benavides Castillo, A. 1976. El sistema prehispanico de comunicaciones terrestres en la region de Cobá, Quintana Roo, y sus implicaciones sociales. Thesis, Universidad Nacional Autónoma de México.

————. 1979. Cobá y Tulum: Adaptación al medio ambiente y control del medio social. Paper presented at the 43rd ICA, Vancouver.

Benson, E. P., ed. 1968. *Dumbarton Oaks Conference on the Olmec*. Washington, D.C.: DO.

————, ed. 1973. *Mesoamerican Writing Systems*. Washington, D.C.: DO.

————. 1977a. *The Maya World*. Revised ed. New York: Crowell.

————, ed. 1977b. *The Sea in the Pre-Columbian World*. Washington, D.C.: DO.

————, ed. In press. *Pre-Columbian Human Sacrifice*. Washington, D.C.: DO.

Benzoni, G. 1970. *History of the New World*. Translated by W. H. Smith. New York: Lenoz Hill.

Berdan, F. F. 1978. Ports of Trade in Mesoamerica: A Reappraisal. In Lee & Navarrete 1978: 187-98.

Berlin, B. 1968. *Tzeltal Numeral Classifiers: A Study in Ethnographic Semantics*. The Hague: Mouton.

Berlin, B., D. E. Breedlove, and P. H. Raven. 1974. *Principles of Tzeltal Plant Classification*. New York: Academic Press.

Berlin, B., and P. Kay. 1969. *Basic Color Terms: Their Universality and Evolution*. Berkeley: University of California Press.

Berlin, H. 1958. El glifo "emblema" en las inscripciones mayas. *Journal de la Société des Américanistes* 47: 111-19.

————. 1959. Glifos nominales en el sarcófago de Palenque. *Humanidades* 2(10): 1-8.

————. 1965. The Inscription of the Temple of the Cross at Palenque. *AAnt* 30: 330-42.

————. 1970. The Tablet of the 96 Glyphs at Palenque, Chiapas, Mexico. In MARI Publication 26: 137–49.

————. 1977. *Signos y Significados en las Inscripciones Mayas.* Guatemala: Instituto Nacional del Patrimonio Cultural de Guatemala.

Bernal, I. 1969. *The Olmec World.* Translated from the Spanish by D. Heyden and F. Horcasitas. Berkeley: University of California Press.

Beyer, H. 1931. The Analysis of the Maya Hieroglyphs. *Internationales Archiv für Ethnographie* 31: 1–20.

————. 1935. On the Correlation between Maya and Christian Chronology. *Maya Research* 2(1): 64–72.

————. 1936. The True Zero Date of the Maya. *Maya Research* 3: 202–4.

————. 1937. *Studies on the Inscriptions at Chichen Itza.* CIW Publication 483, CAA No. 21.

Bittman, B., and T. D. Sullivan. 1978. The Pochteca. In NWAF Paper 40: 211–18.

Blair, R. W. 1964. Yucatec Maya Noun and Verb Morphology. Doctoral dissertation, Indiana University. Also in *MCM*, No. 109.

Blom, F. 1930. Uxmal: The Great Capital of the Xiu Dynasty of the Maya. *Art and Archaeology* 30: 198–209.

————. 1932. *Commerce, Trade and Monetary Units of the Maya.* MARI Publication 4.

————. 1936. *The Conquest of Yucatan.* Boston: Houghton Mifflin.

Blom, F., and O. La Farge. 1926–27. *Tribes and Temples.* MARI Publications 1 and 2.

Boggs, S. H. 1950. Olmec Pictographs in the Las Victorias Group, Chalchuapa Archaeological Zone, El Salvador. *CIW NMA* No. 99.

Borhegyi, S. F. 1950. A Group of Jointed Figurines in the Guatemala National Museum. *CIW NMA* No. 100.

————. 1961. Miniature Mushroom Stones from Guatemala. *AAnt* 26: 498–504.

————. 1965a. Archaeological Synthesis of the Guatemalan Highlands. In *HMAI* 2: 3–58.

————. 1965b. Settlement Patterns of the Guatemalan Highlands. In *HMAI* 2: 59–75.

Boserup, E. 1965. *The Conditions of Agricultural Growth: The Economics of Agrarian Change under Population Pressure.* Chicago: Aldine.

Bowditch, C. P. 1901. *Notes on the Report of Teobert Maler in Memoirs of the Peabody Museum, Vol. II, No. I.* PMAE.

————. 1910. *The Numeration, Calendar Systems and Astronomical Knowledge of the Mayas.* Cambridge, Mass.: The University Press.

Brainerd, G. W. 1954. *The Maya Civilization.* Los Angeles: Southwest Museum.

————. 1958. *The Archaeological Ceramics of Yucatan.* Anthropological Records, No. 19. University of California.

Brasseur de Bourbourg, C. E. 1866. *Palenque et autres ruines de l'ancienne civilisation du Mexique.* Paris: Bertrand.

Bray, W. 1977. Maya Metalwork and Its External Connections. In Hammond 1977b: 365–403.

Bricker, V. R. 1973. *Ritual Humor in Highland Chiapas.* Austin: University of Texas Press.

Brinton, D. G. 1882. *The Maya Chronicles.* Brinton's Library of Aboriginal American Literature, No. 1. Philadelphia.

————. 1885. *The Annals of the Cakchiquels. The Original Text with a Translation, Notes and Introduction.* Brinton's Library of Aboriginal American Literature, No. 6. Philadelphia.

————. 1895. *A Primer of Mayan Hieroglyphs.* University of Pennsylvania Series in Philology, Literature and Archaeology, Vol. 3(2). Philadelphia.

Bronson, B. 1966. Roots and the Subsistence of the Ancient Maya. *SWJA* 22: 251–59.

Brotherston, G. 1979. Continuity in Maya Writing: New Readings of Two Passages in the Book of Chilam Balam of Chumayel. In Hammond & Willey 1979: 241–58.

Brown, C., and S. Witkowski. 1979. Aspects of the Phonological History of Mayan-Zoquean. *IJAL* 45: 34–47.

Brown, K. L. 1977. The Valley of Guatemala: A Highland Port of Trade. In Sanders & Michels 1977: 205-395.

—————. 1979. Ecology and Settlement Systems in the Guatemalan Highlands. Paper presented at the 44th Annual Meeting of the Society for American Archaeology, Vancouver.

—————. 1980. A Brief Report on Paleo-Indian-Archaic Occupation in the Quiche Basin, Guatemala. *AAnt* 45: 313-24.

—————. N.d. Postclassic Relationships between the Highland and Lowland Maya. In Chase & Rice (n.d.).

Brown, K. L., and T. Majewski. 1979. Culture History of the Central Quiche Area. Paper presented at the Popol Vuh Conference, Santa Cruz del Quiche, Guatemala.

Bruce, R. D. 1975. *Lacandon Dream Symbolism: Dream Symbolism and Interpretation among the Lacandon Maya of Chiapas, Mexico.* Mexico City: Ediciones Euro-Americanas Klaus Thiele.

Bullard, M. R., and R. J. Sharer. N.d. The Pottery of Quirigua, Guatemala. *Quirigua Reports.* UM Monograph.

Bullard, W. R., Jr. 1952. Residential Property Walls at Mayapan. *CIW Current Reports,* Department of Archaeology, No. 3.

—————. 1960. Maya Settlement Pattern in Northeastern Peten, Guatemala. *AAnt* 25: 355-72.

—————. 1964. Settlement Pattern and Social Structure in the Southern Maya Lowlands During the Classic Period. Paper presented at the 35th ICA, Mexico City.

—————. 1970. Topoxte, A Postclassic Site in Peten, Guatemala. In PMAE Papers, Vol. 61: 245-307.

Bunzel, R. 1952. *Chichicastenango, A Guatemalan Village.* American Ethnological Society Publication 22. Locust Valley, N.Y.

Burkitt, R. 1930a. Excavations at Chocola. *UM Journal* 15: 115-44.

—————. 1930b. Explorations in the Highlands of Western Guatemala. *UM Journal* 21: 41-72.

Byers, D. S., ed. 1967. *The Prehistory of the Tehuacan Valley.* Vol. 1: *Environment and Subsistence.* Austin: University of Texas Press.

Campbell, L. R. 1976. The Linguistic Prehistory of the Southern Mesoamerican Periphery. *XIV Mesa Redonda, Sociedad Mexicana de Antropología* 1: 157-83.

—————. 1977. *Quichean Linguistic Prehistory.* University of California Publications in Linguistics, No. 81. Berkeley, Los Angeles, London: University of California Press.

————— (with P. Ventur, R. Stewart, and B. Gardner). 1978. *Bibliography of Mayan Languages and Linguistics.* IMS Publication No. 3.

Campbell, L. R., and J. S. Justeson, eds. In press. *Phonetic Studies in Mayan Hieroglyphic Writing.* IMS.

Campbell, L. R., J. S. Justeson, and W. C. Norman. 1980. Foreign Influence on Lowland Mayan Language and Script. Paper presented at the DO Symposium on Mesoamerican Highland-Lowland Interaction, Washington, D.C.

Campbell, L. R., and T. S. Kaufman. 1980. On Mesoamerican Linguistics. *AA* 82: 850-57.

Carlson, J. B. 1980. On Classic Maya Monumental Recorded History. In Robertson 1980: 199-203.

Carmack, R. M. 1968. Toltec Influences on the Postclassic Culture History of Highland Guatemala. In MARI Publication 26: 49-92.

—————. 1973. *Quichean Civilization.* Berkeley: University of California Press.

—————. 1977. Ethnohistory of the Central Quiche: The Community of Utatlan. In Wallace & Carmack 1977: 1-19.

—————. 1981. *The Quiche Mayas of Utatlan.* Norman: University of Oklahoma Press.

Carmack, R. M., and J. M. Weeks. 1981. The Archaeology and Ethnohistory of Utatlan: A Conjunctive Approach. *AAnt* 46: 323-41.

Carnegie Institution of Washington. 1935. *Botany of the Maya Area.* CIW Publication 461.
————. 1940. *Botany of the Maya Area.* CIW Publication 522.
Carneiro, R. L. 1967. On the Relationship Between Size of Population and Complexity of Social Organization. *SWJA* 23: 234-43.
————. 1970. A Theory of the Origin of the State. *Science* 169: 733-38.
Carr, R. F., and J. E. Hazard. 1961. *Map of the Ruins of Tikal, El Peten, Guatemala.* Tikal Report No. 11, UM Monograph 21.
Carrillo y Ancona, C. 1937. *Historia Antigua de Yucatán.* Mérida: Tipográfica Yucateca.
Carter, W. E. 1969. *New Lands and Old Traditions: Kekchi Cultivators in the Guatemalan Lowlands.* Latin American Monograph No. 6. Gainesville: University of Florida Press.
Caso, A. 1936. *La religión de los Aztecas.* Mexico: Imprenta mundial.
————. 1965. Sculpture and Mural Painting of Oaxaca. In *HMAI* 3: 849-70.
Catherwood, F. 1844. *Views of Ancient Monuments in Central America, Chiapas, and Yucatan.* New York: Barlett and Welford.
Chamberlain, R. S. 1948. *The Conquest and Colonization of Yucatan, 1517–1550.* CIW Publication 582.
Chang, K. C. 1972. *Settlement Patterns in Archaeology.* Reading, Mass.: Addison-Wesley Modules in Anthropology, No. 24.
Chapman, A. M. 1957. Port of Trade Enclaves in Aztec and Maya Civilizations. In *Trade and Market in the Early Empires* (K. Polanyi, C. Arensberg, and H. Pearson, editors). Glencoe: Free Press.
Charencey, H. de. 1872. Recherches sur les lois phonétiques dans les idiomes de la famille Mame-Huastèque. *Revue de Linguistique et de Philologie Comparée* 5: 129-67.
Chase, A. F. 1976. Topoxte and Tayasal: Ethnohistory in Archaeology. *AAnt* 41: 154-67.
————. 1979. Regional Development in the Tayasal-Paxcaman Zone, El Peten, Guatemala: A Preliminary Statement. *CCM* 11: 87-119.
Chase, A. F., and P. M. Rice, eds. N.d. The Lowland Maya Postclassic: Questions and Answers.
Chase, D. Z. 1981. The Maya Postclassic at Santa Rita Corozal. *A* 34(1): 25-33.
Cheek, C. D. 1977a. Excavations at the Palangana and the Acropolis, Kaminaljuyu. In Sanders & Michels 1977: 1-204.
————. 1977b. Teotihuacan Influence at Kaminaljuyu. In Sanders & Michels 1977: 441-52.
————. 1980. The Developmental Sequence in the Plaza, The Main Group, Copan, Honduras. Paper presented at the 44th Annual Meeting of the Society for American Archaeology, Philadelphia.
Childe, V. G. 1954. *What Happened in History.* Harmondsworth: Penguin.
Clewlow, C. W. 1974. *A Stylistic and Chronological Study of Olmec Monumental Sculpture.* UCARF Contribution 18.
Cline, H. F. 1944. Lore and Deities of the Lacandon Indians, Chiapas, Mexico. *Journal of American Folklore* 57: 107-15.
————, ed. 1972-75. Guide to Ethnohistorical Sources. In *HMAI* 12-15.
Cobean, R., M. Coe, E. Perry, K. Turekian, and D. Kharkar. 1971. Obsidian Trade at San Lorenzo Tenochtitlan, Mexico. *Science* 174: 666-71.
Coe, M. D. 1961. *La Victoria: An Early Site on the Pacific Coast of Guatemala.* PMAE Papers, Vol. 53.
————. 1965. The Olmec Style and Its Distribution. In *HMAI* 3: 739-75.
————. 1966. *The Maya.* New York: Praeger.
————. 1968. *America's First Civilization.* New York: American Heritage.
————. 1970. The Archaeological Sequence at San Lorenzo Tenochtitlan, Veracruz, Mexico. In UCARF Contribution 8: 21-34.
————. 1973. *The Maya Scribe and His World.* New York: Grolier Club.

————. 1975a. *Classic Maya Pottery at Dumbarton Oaks*. Washington, D.C.: DO.

————. 1975b. Native Astronomy in Mesoamerica. In Aveni 1975b: 3–31.

————. 1976. Early Steps in the Evolution of Maya Writing. In *Origins of Religious Art & Iconography in Preclassic Mesoamerica* (H. B. Nicholson, ed.): 107–22. Los Angeles: UCLA Latin American Center Publications/Ethnic Arts Council of Los Angeles.

————. 1977. Olmec and Maya: A Study in Relationships. In Adams 1977: 183–95.

————. 1980. *The Maya*. Rev. and enlarged ed. London and New York: Thames and Hudson.

Coe, M. D., and R. A. Diehl. 1980. *In the Land of the Olmec*. 2 vols. Austin: University of Texas Press.

Coe, M. D., and K. V. Flannery. 1964. The Pre-Columbian Obsidian Industry of El Chayal, Guatemala. *AAnt* 30: 43–49.

————. 1967. *Early Cultures and Human Ecology in South Coastal Guatemala*. Smithsonian Contributions to Anthropology, 3. Washington, D.C.

Coe, W. R. 1959. *Piedras Negras Archaeology: Artifacts, Caches and Burials*. UM Monograph 18.

————. 1962. A Summary of Excavation and Research at Tikal, Guatemala: 1956–61. *AAnt* 27: 479–507.

————. 1965a. Tikal, Guatemala, and Emergent Maya Civilization. *Science* 147: 1401–19.

————. 1965b. Tikal: Ten Years of Study of a Maya Ruin in the Lowlands of Guatemala. *Expedition* 8(1): 5–56.

————. 1967. *Tikal, A Handbook of the Ancient Maya Ruins*. Philadelphia: University Museum, University of Pennsylvania.

————. 1968. Tikal: In Search of the Mayan Past. In *The World Book Yearbook*: 160–90. Field Educational Enterprises.

————. 1975. Resurrecting the Grandeur of Tikal. *National Geographic* 148(6): 792–95.

Coggins, C. C. 1972. Archaeology and the Art Market. *Science* 175: 263–66.

————. 1975. Painting and Drawing Styles at Tikal: An Historical and Iconographic Reconstruction. Unpublished doctoral dissertation, Harvard University.

————. 1976. Teotihuacan at Tikal in the Early Classic Period. 42nd *ICA Actes* 8: 251–69.

————. 1979. A New Order and the Role of the Calendar: Some Characteristics of the Middle Classic Period at Tikal. In Hammond & Willey 1979: 38–50.

Cook, O. F. 1921. Milpa Agriculture: A Primitive Tropical System. *Annual Report of the Smithsonian Institution, 1919*: 307–26. Washington, D.C.

Cooke, C. W. 1931. Why the Mayan Cities of the Peten District, Guatemala, Were Abandoned. *Journal of the Washington Academy of Sciences* 21(13): 283–87.

Cortés, Hernán. 1928. *Five Letters of Cortes to the Emperor* (1519–1526). Translated by J. B. Morris. New York: Norton.

Covarrubias, M. A. 1954. *The Eagle, the Jaguar, and the Serpent: Indian Art of the Americas*. New York: Knopf.

Cowgill, G. L. 1964. The End of the Classic Maya Culture: A Review of Recent Evidence. *SWJA* 20: 145–59.

————. 1979. Teotihuacan, Internal Militaristic Competition, and the Fall of the Classic Maya. In Hammond & Willey 1979: 51–62.

Cowgill, U. M. 1962. An Agricultural Study of the Southern Maya Lowlands. *AA* 64: 273–86.

Cowgill, U. M., and G. E. Hutchinson. 1963. *El Bajo de Santa Fe*. American Philosophical Society Transactions 53 (7).

Craine, E. R., and R. C. Reindorp, ed. and trans. 1979. *The Codex Pérez and the Book of Chilam Balam of Maní*. Norman: University of Oklahoma Press.

Culbert, T. P. 1963. Ceramic Research at Tikal, Guatemala. *CCM* 1: 34–42.

————, ed. 1973. *The Classic Maya Collapse.* SAR. Albuquerque: University of New Mexico Press.

————. 1974. *The Lost Civilization: The Story of the Classic Maya.* New York: Harper and Row.

————. 1977a. Early Maya Development at Tikal, Guatemala. In Adams 1977: 27–43.

————. 1977b. Maya Development and Collapse: An Economic Perspective. In Hammond 1974b: 509–30.

Dahlin, B. H. 1976. An Anthropologist Looks at the Pyramids: A Late Classic Revitalization Movement at Tikal, Guatemala. Unpublished doctoral dissertation, Temple University.

————. 1978. Figurines. In *The Prehistory of Chalchuapa, El Salvador* (R. J. Sharer, general ed.), UM Monograph 36(2): 134–211.

————. 1979. Cropping Cash in the Protoclassic: A Cultural Impact Statement. In Hammond & Willey 1979: 21–37.

Deevey, E. S., D. S. Rice, P. M. Rice, H. H. Vaughan, M. Brenner, and M. S. Flannery. 1979. Maya Urbanism: Impact on a Tropical Karst Environment. *Science* 206: 298–306.

del Rio, A. 1822. *Description of the Ruins of an Ancient City Discovered near Palenque, in the Kingdom of Guatemala, in Spanish America* [translated from the Spanish]. London: Berthoud and Suttaby, Evance and Fox.

Demarest, A. A. 1981. Santa Leticia and the Development of Complex Society in Southeastern Mesoamerica. Unpublished doctoral dissertation, Harvard University.

————. In press. Informe preliminar sobre las excavaciones efectuadas en 1977 en la finca "Santa Leticia," Departamento de Ahuachapan, El Salvador. *Museo Nacional de El Salvador Anales.*

Demarest, A. A., and R. J. Sharer. In press: a. The Origins and Evolution of the Usulutan Ceramic Style. *AAnt.*

————. In press: b. Interregional Patterns in the Late Preclassic of Southeastern Mesoamerica: A Definition of Highland Ceramic Spheres. In *The Southeast Maya Periphery* (P. Urban and E. Schortman, eds.). Austin: University of Texas Press.

Denevan, W. M. 1970. Aboriginal Drained-Field Cultivation in the Americas. *Science* 169: 647–54.

Díaz del Castillo, B. 1963. *The Conquest of New Spain.* Translation and Introduction by J. M. Cohen. Baltimore: Penguin.

Diebold, A. R., Jr. 1960. Determining the Centers of Dispersal of Language Groups. *IJAL* 26: 1–10.

Digby, A. 1972. *Maya Jades.* London: Trustees of the British Museum.

Dillon, B. D. 1975. Notes on Trade in Ancient Mesoamerica. In UCARF Contribution 24: 80–135.

————. 1977. *Salinas de los Nueve Cerros, Guatemala.* Socorro, N.M.: Ballena Press.

————. 1978. A Tenth-Cycle Sculpture from Alta Verapaz, Guatemala. In UCARF Contribution 36: 39–46.

Dobkin de Rios, M. 1974. The Influence of Psychotropic Flora and Fauna on Maya Religion. *Current Anthropology* 15: 147–64.

Dresden Codex. 1880. *Die Maya-Handschrift der Königlichen Bibliothek zu Dresden.* Edited by E. Förstemann. Leipzig: Röder. Second ed., 1892, reprinted as *Codex Dresdensis: Die Maya-Handschrift in der Sächsischen Landesbibliothek Dresden.* Foreword by E. Lips. Berlin: Akademie-Verlag, 1962. (See also Anders 1975; Kingsborough 1831–48; Thompson 1972b; Villacorta & Villacorta 1933.)

Drucker, P. 1952. *La Venta, Tabasco: A Study of Olmec Ceramics and Art.* BAE Bulletin 153.

Drucker, P., R. F. Heizer, and R. J. Squier. 1955. *Excavations at La Venta, Tabasco, 1955.* BAE Bulletin 170.

Du Bois, J. W. 1978. Mayan Sign Language: An Ethnography of Non-Verbal Communication. Paper presented at the 77th Annual Meeting of the American Anthropological Association, Los Angeles.

Dumond, D. E. 1961. Swidden Agriculture and the Rise of Maya Civilization. *SWJA* 17: 301–16.

Duran, D. 1965. *Historia de las Indias de Nueva España y islas de tierra firme*. Mexico: Editoria Nacional.

Earle, T. K., and J. E. Ericson, ed. 1977. *Exchange Systems in Prehistory*. New York: Academic Press.

Easby, E. 1961. The Squier Jades from Tonina, Chiapas. In *Essays in Pre-Columbian Art and Archaeology* (S. K. Lothrop and others, eds.): 60–80. Cambridge: Harvard University Press.

Eaton, J. D. 1975. Ancient Agricultural Farmsteads in the Río Bec Region of Yucatan. In UCARF Contribution 27: 56–82.

————. 1978. Archaeological Survey of the Yucatan—Campeche Coast. MARI Publication 46: 1–67.

Edmonson, M. S. 1960. Nativism, Syncretism and Anthropological Science. In MARI Publication 19: 181–203.

————. 1967. Classical Quiche. In *HMAI* 5: 249–67.

————. 1971. *The Book of Counsel: The Popol Vuh of the Quiche Maya of Guatemala*. MARI Publication 35.

————, ed. & trans. 1982. *The Ancient Future of the Itza: The Book of Chilam Balam of Tizimin*. Austin: University of Texas Press.

Edwards, C. R. 1978. Precolumbian Maritime Trade in Mesoamerica. In Lee & Navarrete 1978: 199–209.

Eggan, F. 1934. The Maya Kinship System and Cross-Cousin Marriage. *AA* 36: 188–202.

Ekholm, S. M. 1969. *Mound 30a and the Early Preclassic Ceramic Sequence of Izapa, Chiapas, Mexico*. NWAF Paper 25.

————. 1973. *The Olmec Rock Carving at Xoc, Chiapas, Mexico*. NWAF Paper 32.

Erasmus, C. J. 1968. Thoughts on Upward Collapse: An Essay on Explanation in Anthropology. *SWJA* 24: 170–94.

Escoto, J. A., 1964. Weather and Climate of Mexico and Central America. In *HMAI* 1: 187–215.

Farriss, N. In press. *Maya Society Under Colonial Rule: The Collective Enterprise of Survival*. Princeton, N.J.: Princeton University Press.

Feldman, L. H. 1978. Moving Merchandise in Protohistoric Central Quauhtemallan. In NWAF Paper 40: 7–17.

Fernández, M. A., and H. Berlin. 1954. Drawing of Glyphs and Structure XVIII, Palenque. *CIW NMA* No. 119.

Fettweis-Vienot, M. 1980. Las pinturas murales de Coba. *ECAUY Boletín* 7(40): 2–50.

Fisher, W. M. 1973. Towards the Reconstruction of Proto-Yucatec. Doctoral dissertation, University of Chicago.

Flannery, K. V. 1968. The Olmec and the Valley of Oaxaca: A Model for Interregional Interaction in Formative Times. In Benson 1968: 79–117.

————, ed. 1976. *The Early Mesoamerican Village*. New York: Academic Press.

Folan, W. J., G. E. Stuart, L. A. Fletcher, and E. R. Kintz. 1977. El proyecto cartográfico arqueológico de Cobá, Quintana Roo. *ECAUY Boletín* 4(22, 23): 14–81.

Follett, P. H. F. 1932. *War and Weapons of the Maya*. MARI Publication 4.

Foncerrada de Molina, M. 1980. Mural Painting in Cacaxtla and Teotihuacan Cosmopolitism. In Robertson 1980: 183–98.

Ford, J. A. 1962. *A Quantitative Method for Deriving Cultural Chronology*. Technical Manual 1, Department of Social Affairs, Pan American Union. Washington, D.C.

Förstemann, E. W. 1904. Translations of Various Papers. In BAE Bulletin, 28: 393–590.

———. 1906. *Commentary on the Maya Manuscript in the Royal Public Library of Dresden.* PMAE Papers, Vol. 4(2).

Forsyth, D. 1979. An Analysis of the Prehispanic Ceramics of Edzna, Campeche, Mexico. Unpublished doctoral dissertation, University of Pennsylvania.

Foshag, W. F., and R. Leslie. 1955. Jade from Manzanal, Guatemala. *AAnt* 21: 81–82.

Fought, J. G. 1967. Chorti (Mayan): Phonology, Morphophonemics, and Morphology. Doctoral dissertation, Yale University.

———. 1972. *Chorti (Mayan) Texts.* Philadelphia: University of Pennsylvania Press.

———. In press. Cyclical Patterns in Chorti (Mayan) Literature. In *HMAI Supplement 2* (M. S. Edmonson, ed.). Austin: University of Texas Press.

Fowler, W. R., Jr. 1979. Evidence of Preclassic-Period Human Sacrifice at Chalchuapa, El Salvador. Paper presented at the 44th Annual Meeting of the Society for American Archaeology, Vancouver.

Fox, J. A. 1978. Proto-Mayan Accent, Morpheme Structure Conditions, and Velar Innovations. Doctoral dissertation, University of Chicago.

———. 1979. The Etymology of Quichean *kumats* 'snake' and the Linguistic Affiliation of the Olmecs. In *Proceedings of the Annual Symposium of the Deseret Language and Linguistic Society* (J. S. Robertson, ed.). Provo, Utah: Brigham Young University Press.

———. 1980. [Review of] *Corpus of Maya Hieroglyphic Inscriptions.* (Ian Graham and Eric Von Euw, eds.). *AAnt* 45: 210–11.

Fox, J. A., and J. S. Justeson. 1978. A Mayan Planetary Observation. In UCARF Contribution 36: 55–59.

———. 1980. Maya Hieroglyphs as Linguistic Evidence. In Robertson 1980: 204–16.

———. In press: a. Classic Maya Dynastic Alliance and Succession. In *HMAI*, Supplement 2: *Ethnohistory* (V. R. Bricker and R. M. Spores, eds.). Austin: University of Texas Press.

———. In press: b. Hieroglyphic Evidence for the Languages of the Classic Maya. In Campbell & Justeson in press.

———. In press: c. Polyvalence in Mayan Hieroglyphic Writing: New Readings. In Campbell & Justeson in press.

Fox, J. W. 1978. *Quiche Conquest: Centralism and Regionalism in Highland Guatemalan State Development.* Albuquerque: University of New Mexico Press.

———. 1980. Lowland to Highland Mexicanization Processes in Southern Mesoamerica. *AAnt* 45: 43–54.

Freidel, D. A. 1977. A Late Preclassic Monumental Mayan Mask at Cerros, Northern Belize. *JFA* 4: 488–91.

———. 1978. Maritime Adaptation and the Rise of Maya Civilization: A View from Cerros, Belize. In Stark & Voorhies 1978: 239–65.

———. 1979a. Culture Areas and Interaction Spheres: Contrasting Approaches to the Emergence of Civilization in the Maya Lowlands. *AAnt* 44: 36–54.

———. 1979b. World Image and World View: The Structural Foundations of Lowland Maya Civilization. Paper presented at the 43rd ICA, Vancouver.

———. 1981a. Continuity and Disjunction: Late Postclassic Settlement Patterns in Northern Yucatan. In Ashmore 1981b: 311–32.

———. 1981b. The Political Economics of Residential Dispersion among the Lowland Maya. In Ashmore 1981b: 371–82.

———. N.d. The Lowland Maya Postclassic: Summation of the Major Themes. In Chase & Rice (n.d.).

Freidel, D. A., and R. M. Leventhal. 1975. The Settlement Survey. In *A Study of Changing Precolumbian Commercial Systems* (J. A. Sabloff and W. L. Rathje, eds.). PMAE Monograph 3: 60–76.

Fry, R. E. 1979. Nativistic Movements among the Postclassic Lowland Maya. Paper presented at the 78th Annual Meeting of the American Anthropological Association, Cincinnati.

Fry, R. E., and S. C. Cox. 1974. The Structure of Ceramic Exchange at Tikal, Guatemala. *JFA* 1: 209–25.

Fuentes y Guzmán, F. A. 1932–34. *Historia de Guatemala o Recordación Florida.* Guatemala: Biblioteca Goathemala.

Furbee, L., ed. 1976. *Mayan Texts I.* IJAL, Native American Texts Series, Vol. 1(1). Chicago: University of Chicago Press.

Furbee-Losee, L., ed. 1979. *Mayan Texts I².* IJAL, Native American Texts Series, Monograph No. 3. Chicago: University of Chicago Press.

————, ed. 1980. *Mayan Texts III.* IJAL, Native American Texts Series, Monograph No. 5. Chicago: University of Chicago Press.

Furst, P. T. 1976. *Hallucinogens and Culture.* San Francisco: Chandler and Sharp.

Furst, P. T., and M. D. Coe. 1977. Ritual Enemas. *Natural History* 86(3): 88–91.

Gann, T. W. F. 1900. Mounds in Northern Honduras. BAE Annual Report 19(2): 655–92.

————. 1904–5. Report of a Visit to the Ruins on the Columbia Branch of the Río Grande in British Honduras. *Proceedings of the Society of Antiquaries of London* 20: 27–32.

————. 1918. *The Maya Indians of Southern Yucatan and Northern British Honduras.* BAE Bulletin 64.

————. 1927. *Maya Cities, a Record of Exploration and Adventure in Middle America.* London: Duckworth.

Gann, T. W. F., and J. E. S. Thompson. 1931. *The History of the Maya from the Earliest Time to the Present Day.* New York: Scribner's.

Gates, W. 1920. The Distribution of the Several Branches of the Mayance Linguistic Stock. In Morley 1920: Appendix XII.

————. 1937. *Yucatan Before and After the Conquest, by Friar Diego de Landa, with Other Related Documents.* Translation and Notes. Baltimore: Maya Society Publication No. 20.

————. 1938. *A Grammar of Maya.* Baltimore: Maya Society Publication No. 13.

Gifford, J. C. 1976. *Prehistoric Pottery Analysis and the Ceramics of Barton Ramie in the Belize Valley.* Compiled by C. A. Gifford. PMAE Memoirs, Vol. 18.

Glass, J. B. 1975. A Survey of Native Middle American Pictorial Manuscripts. In *HMAI* 14: 3–80.

Glass, J. B., and D. Robertson, 1975. A Census of Native Middle American Pictorial Manuscripts. In *HMAI* 14: 81–280.

Goodman, J. T. 1897. The Archaic Maya Inscriptions. Appendix to Maudslay 1889–1902.

————. 1905. Maya Dates. *AA* 7: 642–47.

Gordon, G. B. 1896. *Prehistoric Ruins of Copan, Honduras.* PMAE Memoirs, Vol. 1(1).

Gordon, G. B., and J. A. Mason. 1925–43. *Examples of Maya Pottery in the Museum and in Other Collections.* 3 vols. Philadelphia: University Museum, University of Pennsylvania.

Graham, I. 1967. *Archaeological Explorations in El Peten, Guatemala.* MARI Publication 33.

————. 1975. *Corpus of Maya Hieroglyphic Inscriptions.* Vol. 1: *Introduction.* PMAE.

————. 1978. *Corpus of Maya Hieroglyphic Inscriptions.* Vol. 2, Part 2: *Naranjo, Chunhuitz, Xunantunich.* PMAE.

————. 1979. *Corpus of Maya Hieroglyphic Inscriptions.* Vol. 3, Part 2: *Yaxchilan.* PMAE.

————. 1980. *Corpus of Maya Hieroglyphic Inscriptions.* Vol. 2, Part 3: *Ixkun, Ucanal, Ixtutz, Naranjo.* PMAE.

————. 1982. *Corpus of Maya Hieroglyphic Inscriptions.* Vol. 3, Part 3: *Yaxchilan.* PMAE.

Graham, I., and E. Von Euw. 1975. *Corpus of Maya Hieroglyphic Inscriptions.* Vol. 2, Part 1: *Naranjo.* PMAE.

————. 1977. *Corpus of Maya Hieroglyphic Inscriptions.* Vol. 3, Part 1: *Yaxchilan.* PMAE.

Graham, J. A. 1971. Commentary on Calendrics and Writing. In UCARF Contribution 11: 133–40.

————. 1972. *The Hieroglyphic Inscriptions and Monumental Art of Altar de Sacrificios.* PMAE Papers, Vol. 64(2).

————. 1973. Aspects of Non-Classic Presences in the Inscriptions and Sculptural Art of Seibal. In Culbert 1973: 207–17.

————. 1977. Discoveries at Abaj Takalik, Guatemala. *A* 30: 196–97.

————. 1979. Maya, Olmecs and Izapans at Abaj Takalik. *42nd ICA Actes* 8: 179–88.

Graham, J. A., R. F. Heizer, and E. M. Shook. 1978. Abaj Takalik 1976: Exploratory Investigations. In UCARF Contribution 36: 85–110.

Graham, J. A., and R. Hester. 1968. Notes on the Papalhuapa Site, Guatemala. In UCARF Contribution 5: 101–25.

Green, D. F., and G. W. Lowe. 1967. *Altamira and Padre Piedra, Early Preclassic Sites in Chiapas, Mexico.* NWAF Paper 20.

Greene, M. 1967. *Ancient Maya Relief Sculpture.* New York: Museum of Primitive Art.

Greene, M., R. L. Rands, and J. A. Graham. 1972. *Maya Sculpture from the Southern Lowlands, the Highlands, and Pacific Piedmont Guatemala, Mexico, Honduras.* Berkeley, Calif.: Lederer, Street and Zeus.

Griscom, L. 1932. *The Distribution of Birdlife in Guatemala.* American Museum of Natural History Bulletin, Vol. 64. New York.

Grove, D. C., K. G. Hirth, D. E. Bugé, and A. M. Cyphers. 1976. Settlement and Cultural Development at Chalcatzingo. *Science* 192: 1203–10.

Gruhn, R., and A. L. Bryan. 1976. An Archaeological Survey of the Chichicastenango Area of Highland Guatemala. *CCM* 9: 75–119.

Guillemin, J. F. 1965. *Iximche: Capital del Antiguo Reino Cakchiquel.* Guatemala: Instituto de Antropología e Historia.

————. 1967. The Ancient Cakchiquel Capital of Iximche. *Expedition* 9(2): 22–35.

Guthe, C. E. 1932. The Maya Lunar Count. *Science* 75: 271–77.

Haas, M. L. 1969. *The Prehistory of Languages.* The Hague: Mouton.

Hamblin, R. L., and B. L. Pitcher. 1980. The Classic Maya Collapse: Testing Class Conflict Hypotheses. *AAnt* 45: 246–67.

Hammond, N. 1972. Obsidian Trade Routes in the Mayan Area. *Science* 178: 1092–93.

————. 1974a. The Distribution of Late Classic Maya Major Ceremonial Centres in the Central Area. In Hammond 1974b: 313–34.

————, ed. 1974b. *Mesoamerican Archaeology: New Approaches.* Austin: University of Texas Press.

————. 1975. *Lubaantun, A Classic Maya Realm.* PMAE Monograph 2.

————. 1977a. The Earliest Maya. *SA* 236(3): 116–33.

————, ed. 1977b. *Social Process in Maya Prehistory, Essays in Honour of Sir J. Eric S. Thompson.* New York: Academic Press.

————. 1978a. *Cuello Project 1978 Interim Report.* Archaeological Research Program, Douglas College, Rutgers University, Publication 1. New Brunswick, N.J.

————. 1978b. The Myth of the Milpa: Agricultural Expansion in the Maya Lowlands. In Harrison & Turner 1978: 23–34.

————. 1980. Early Maya Ceremonial at Cuello, Belize. *Antiquity* 54: 176–90.

————. 1981. Settlement Patterns in Belize. In Ashmore 1981b: 157–86.

————. 1982. *Ancient Maya Civilization.* New Brunswick, N. J.: Rutgers University Press.

Hammond, N., and W. A. Ashmore. 1981. Lowland Maya Settlement: Geographical and Chronological Frameworks. In Ashmore 1981b: 19–36.

Hammond, N., A. Aspinall, S. Feather, J. Hazelden, T. Gazard, and S. Agrell. 1977. Maya Jade: Source Location and Analysis. In *Exchange Systems in Prehistory* (T. K. Earle and J. E. Ericson, eds.): 35–67. New York: Academic Press.

Hammond, N., D. Pring, R. Berger, V. Switsur, and A. Ward. 1976. Radiocarbon Chronology for Early Maya Occupation at Cuello, Belize. *Nature* 260: 579–81.

Hammond, N., and G. R. Willey, eds. 1979. *Maya Archaeology and Ethnohistory*. Austin: University of Texas Press.

Harris, D. R. 1972. Swidden Systems and Settlement. In Ucko, Tringham & Dimbleby 1972: 245-62.

————. 1978. The Agricultural Foundations of Lowland Maya Civilization. In Harrison & Turner 1978: 301-23.

Harrison, P. D. 1977. The Rise of the Bajos and the Fall of the Maya. In Hammond 1977b: 469-508.

————. 1978. Bajos Revisited: Visual Evidence for One System of Agriculture. In Harrison & Turner 1978: 247-53.

————. 1981. Some Aspects of Preconquest Settlement in Southern Quintana Roo, Mexico. In Ashmore 1981b: 259-86.

Harrison, P. D., and B. L. Turner, eds. 1978. *Pre-Hispanic Maya Agriculture*. Austin: University of Texas Press.

Hartung, H. 1975. A Scheme of Probable Astronomical Projections in Mesoamerican Architecture. In Aveni 1975: 191-204.

Haviland, J. B. 1977. *Gossip, Reputation and Knowledge in Zinacantan*. Chicago: University of Chicago Press.

Haviland, W. A. 1966. Maya Settlement Patterns: A Critical Review. In MARI Publication 26: 21-47.

————. 1967. Stature at Tikal, Guatemala: Implications for Ancient Maya Demography and Social Organization. *AAnt* 32: 316-25.

————. 1968. Ancient Lowland Maya Social Organization. In MARI Publication 26: 93-117.

————. 1970. Tikal, Guatemala, and Mesoamerican Urbanism. *WA* 2: 186-98.

————. 1977. Dynastic Genealogies from Tikal, Guatemala: Implications for Descent and Political Organization. *AAnt* 42: 61-67.

————. 1981. Dower Houses and Minor Centers at Tikal, Guatemala: An Investigation into the Identification of Valid Units in Settlement Hierarchies. In Ashmore 1981b: 89-117.

Healey, P. F., M. van Waarden, and T. Anderson. N.d. Ancient Maya Agricultural Terraces of the Cayo District, Belize: A Preliminary Report. In *Agricultura Intensiva Precolumbino* (W. M. Denevan, ed.). Mexico City: Instituto Indigenista Interamericano.

Heizer, R. F. 1968. New Observations on La Venta. In Benson 1968: 9-40.

Heizer, R. F., J. A. Graham, and L. K. Napton. 1968. The 1968 Investigations at La Venta. In UCARF Contribution 5: 127-54.

Hellmuth, N. M. 1971a. Possible Streets at a Maya Site in Guatemala. New Haven, Conn.: mimeographed.

————. 1971b. Preliminary Report on Second-Season Excavations at Yaxha, Guatemala. New Haven, Conn.: mimeographed.

————. 1972. Excavations Begin at Maya Site in Guatemala. *A* 25: 148-49.

————. N.d. Nakum, Guatemala: A New Sketch Map of the Classic Maya Ruins.

Helms, M. W. 1975. *Middle America: A Cultural History of Heartland and Frontiers*. Englewood Cliffs, N.J.: Prentice-Hall.

Henderson, J. S. 1979. *Atopula, Guerrero and Olmec Horizons in Mesoamerica*. Yale University Publications in Anthropology, No. 77. New Haven.

————. 1981. *The World of the Ancient Maya*. Ithaca, N.Y.: Cornell University Press.

Henderson, J. S., I. Sterns, A. Wonderly, and P. A. Urban. 1979. Archaeological Investigations in the Valle de Naco, Northwestern Honduras: A Preliminary Report. *JFA* 6: 169-92.

Herrera, A. 1726-30. *Historia General de los hechos de los Castillanos en las Islas i Tierra Firme del Mar Oceano*. 5 vols. Madrid: Imprenta real de Nicolas Rodriguez Franco.

Hester, J. A., Jr. 1954. Natural and Cultural Bases of Ancient Maya Subsistence Economy. Unpublished doctoral dissertation, University of California, Los Angeles.

Hester, T. R., ed. 1979. *The Colha Project: A Collection of Interim Papers.* Center for Archaeological Research, University of Texas. San Antonio.

Hester, T. R., and N. Hammond, eds. 1976. *Maya Lithic Studies: Papers from the 1976 Belize Field Symposium.* San Antonio: University of Texas.

Hewett, E. L. 1911. Two Seasons' Work in Guatemala. *Bulletin of the Archaeological Institute of America* 2: 117-34.

————. 1912. The Excavations at Quirigua in 1912. *Bulletin of the Archaeological Institute of America* 3: 163-71.

————. 1916. Latest Work of the School of American Archaeology at Quirigua. In *Holmes Anniversary Volume Anthropological Essays* (F. W. Hodge, ed.): 157-62. Washington, D.C.

Holmes, W. H. 1895-97. *Archaeological Studies among the Ancient Cities of Mexico. Part I: Monuments of Yucatan. Part II: Monuments of Chiapas, Oaxaca and the Valley of Mexico.* Field Columbian Museum, Anthropological Series, I. Chicago.

Hunn, E. 1977. *Tzeltal Folk Zoology: The Classification of Discontinuities in Nature.* New York: Academic Press.

Huntington, E. 1912. The Peninsula of Yucatan. *Bulletin of the American Geographical Society* 44: 801-22.

Ichon, A. 1975. *Organización de un centro Quiché protohistórico: Pueblo Viejo Chichaj.* Instituto de Antropológia e Historia Publicación Especial No. 9, Guatemala.

————. 1977a. *Les sculptures de la Lagunita, El Quiche, Guatemala.* Paris: Centre National de la Recherche Scientifique.

————. 1977b. A Late Postclassic Sweathouse in the Highlands of Guatemala. *AAnt* 42: 203-9.

————. 1979. *Rescate arqueológico en la cuenca del Río Chixoy.* Guatemala City: Informe Preliminar, Mision Científica Franco-Guatemalteca.

Johnston, F. 1972. *Chronology and Irrigation* (R. S. MacNeish, general ed.). Vol. 4: *The Prehistory of the Tehuacan Valley.* Austin: University of Texas Press.

Jones, C. 1969. The Twin Pyramid Group Pattern: A Classic Maya Architectural Assemblage at Tikal, Guatemala. Unpublished doctoral dissertation, University of Pennsylvania.

————. 1975. A Painted Capstone from the Maya Area. In UCARF Contribution 27: 83-110.

————. 1977. Inauguration Dates of Three Late Classic Rulers of Tikal, Guatemala. *AAnt* 42: 28-60.

————. 1979. Tikal as a Trading Center. Paper presented at the 43rd ICA, Vancouver.

————. In press. Monument 26, Quirigua, Guatemala. In *Quirigua Reports II* (E. M. Schortman and P. A. Urban, eds.). UM Monograph.

Jones, C., and L. Satterthwaite. In press. The Monuments and Inscriptions. *Tikal Report* No. 38A. UM Monograph 44.

Jones, C., and R. J. Sharer. 1980. Archaeological Investigations in the Site-Core of Quirigua. *Expedition* 23(1): 11-19.

Jones, G. D., ed. 1977. *Anthropology and History in Yucatan.* Austin: University of Texas Press.

Jones, G. D., D. S. Rice, and P. M. Rice. 1981. The Location of Tayasal: A Reconsideration in Light of Peten Maya Ethnohistory and Archaeology. *AAnt* 46: 530-47.

Jones, M. R. 1952. *Map of the Ruins of Mayapan, Yucatan, Mexico. CIW Current Reports,* Department of Archaeology, No. 1.

Josserand, J. K. 1975. Archaeological and Linguistic Correlations for Mayan Prehistory. *41st ICA Proceedings* 1: 501-10.

Joyce, T. A. 1926. Report on the Investigations at Lubaantun, British Honduras, in 1926. *Journal of the Royal Anthropological Institute* 56: 207-30.

————. 1927. *Maya and Mexican Art.* London: The Studio.

Joyce, T. A., J. C. Clark, and J. E. S. Thompson. 1927. Report on the British Museum Expedition to British Honduras. *Journal of the Royal Anthropological Institute* 57: 295-323.

Justeson, J. S. 1978. Mayan Scribal Practice in the Classic Period: A Test-case of an Explanatory Approach to the Study of Writing Systems. Doctoral dissertation, Stanford University.

Kaufman, T. S. 1964. Materiales lingüísticos para el estudio del las relaciones internas y externas de la familia de idiomas Mayanos. In *Desarrollo cultural de los mayas* (E. Z. Vogt and A. Ruz L., eds.): 86–136. Mexico City: Universidad Nacional Autonoma de Mexico.

———. 1969. *Some Recent Hypotheses on Mayan Diversification.* Language Behavior Research Laboratory, Working Paper No. 26. University of California, Berkeley.

———. 1973. Areal Linguistics in Middle America. In *Current Trends in Linguistics,* Vol. 11 (T. A. Sebeok, ed.): 459–83. The Hague: Mouton.

———. 1974. Mesoamerican Indian Languages. *Encyclopaedia Britannica* (15th ed.) 11: 959–63.

———. 1976. Archaeological and Linguistic Correlations in Mayaland and Associated Areas of Mesoamerica. *WA* 8: 101–18.

Kaufman, T. S., and W. N. Norman. 1982. An Outline of Proto-Cholan Phonology and Morphology. In Campbell & Justeson in press.

Keleman, P. 1943. *Medieval American Art.* 2 vols. New York: Macmillan.

Keller, K. C. 1959. The Phonemes of Chontal. *IJAL* 25: 44–53.

Kelley, D. H. 1962a. A History of the Decipherment of Maya Script. *Anthropological Linguistics* 4(8): 1–48.

———. 1962b. Glyphic Evidence for a Dynastic Sequence at Quirigua, Guatemala. *AAnt* 27: 323–35.

———. 1975. Planetary Data on Caracol Stela 3. In Aveni 1975: 257–62.

———. 1976. *Deciphering the Maya Script.* Austin: University of Texas Press.

Kelley, D. H., and K. A. Kerr. 1973. Mayan Astronomy and Astronomical Glyphs. In Benson 1973: 179–215.

Kidder, A. V. 1937. *Notes on the Ruins of San Agustin Acasaguastlan, Guatemala.* CIW Publication 456, CAA No. 15.

———. 1947. *The Artifacts of Uaxactun, Guatemala.* CIW Publication 576.

———. 1951. Artifacts. In *Excavations at Nebaj, Guatemala,* CIW Publication 594: 32–76.

———. 1961. Archaeological Investigations at Kaminaljuyu, Guatemala. In American Philosophical Society Proceedings, 105: 559–70.

———. 1965. Preclassic Pottery Figurines of the Guatemala Highlands. In *HMAI* 2: 146–55.

Kidder, A. V., J. D. Jennings, and E. M. Shook. 1946. *Excavations at Kaminaljuyu, Guatemala.* CIW Publication 561.

Kidder, A. V., and J. E. S. Thompson. 1938. The Correlation of Maya and Christian Chronology. In CIW Publication 501: 493–510.

King, A. 1974. *Copan and the Verapaz: History and Culture Process in Northern Guatemala.* MARI Publication 37.

Kingsborough, E. K. 1831–48. *Antiquities of Mexico.* 9 vols. London: Aglio.

Kirchhoff, P. 1952. Mesoamerica. In *Heritage of Conquest* (S. Tax, ed.): 17–30. Glencoe: Free Press.

Kirke, C. M. 1980. Prehistoric Agriculture in the Belize River Valley. *WA* 11: 281–87.

Knorozov, Y. V. 1958. The Problem of the Study of the Maya Hieroglyphic Writing. *AAnt* 23: 284–91.

———. 1967. *The Writing of the Maya Indians.* English translation by S. Coe of Chapters 1, 6, 7, and 9 of *Pis'menost Indeitsev Maiia.* Moscow-Leningrad: Academy of Sciences. PMAE Russian Translation Series, No. 4.

———. 1982. *Maya Hieroglyphic Codices.* S. Coe, trans. IMS.

Kowalski, J. K. 1980. A Historical Interpretation of the Inscriptions of Uxmal. Paper presented at the 4th Mesa Redonda, Palenque, Mexico.

Kubler, G. 1961. Chichen Itza y Tula. *ECM* 1: 47–80.

————. 1962. *The Art and Architecture of Ancient America: The Mexican, Maya, and Andean Peoples.* Baltimore, Md.: Pelican History of Art.

————. 1971. Commentary on Early Architecture and Sculpture in Mesoamerica. In UCARF Contribution 11: 157–68.

————. 1973. The Clauses of Classic Maya Inscriptions. In Benson 1973: 145–64.

Kudlek, M. 1977. Computer Printout of Dated Maya Monuments by Ceremonial Center. Hamburg: University of Hamburg.

Kurjack, E. B. 1974. *Prehistoric Lowland Maya Community and Social Organization: A Case Study at Dzibilchaltun.* MARI Publication 38.

Kurjack, E. B., and E. W. Andrews V. 1976. Early Boundary Maintenance in Northwest Yucatan, Mexico. *AAnt* 41: 318–25.

Kurjack, E. B., and S. Garza T. 1981. Precolumbian Community Form and Distribution in the Northern Maya Area. In Ashmore 1981b: 287–310.

LaFarge, O. 1927. Adaptations of Christianity among the Jacalteca Indians of Guatemala. *Thought* (December): 1–20.

————. 1947. *Santa Eulalia.* Chicago: University of Chicago Press.

LaFarge, O., and D. Byers. 1931. *The Year Bearer's People.* MARI Publication 3.

Lambert, J. B., B. Ownbey-McLaughlin, and C. D. McLaughlin. 1980. Maya Arithmetic. *American Scientist* 68: 249–55.

Landa, D. de. 1938. *Relación de las cosas de Yucatán.* Mérida: Edición Yucateca.

Lange, F. W. 1971. Marine Resources: A Viable Subsistence Alternative for the Prehistoric Lowland Maya. *AA* 73: 619–39.

Las Casas, B. de. 1909. *Apologética historia de las Indias.* 2 vols. Madrid: Serrano y Ganz.

————. 1957. *Historia de las Indias.* Madrid: Ediciones Atlas.

Lathrap, D. W., J. G. Marcos, and J. Zeidler. 1977. Real Alto: An Ancient Ceremonial Center. *A* 30(1): 2–13.

Laughlin, R. M. 1975. *The Great Tzotzil Dictionary of San Lorenzo Zinacantan.* Smithsonian Contributions to Anthropology, No. 19. Washington, D.C.: Smithsonian Institution Press.

————. 1976. *Of Wonders Wild and New: Dreams from Zinacantan.* Smithsonian Contributions to Anthropolgy, No. 22. Washington, D.C.: Smithsonian Institution Press.

————. 1977. *Of Cabbages and Kings: Tales from Zinacantan.* Smithsonian Contributions to Anthropology, No. 23. Washington, D.C.: Smithsonian Institution Press.

Lee, T. A. 1969. *The Artifacts of Chiapa de Corzo, Chiapas, Mexico.* NWAF Paper 26.

Lee, T. A., and C. Navarrete, eds. 1978. *Mesoamerican Communication Routes and Cultural Contacts.* NWAF Paper 40.

Lehmann, H. 1968. *Mixco Viejo: Guia de las ruinas de la plaza fuerte Pokoman.* Guatemala: Tipografía Nacional.

Leventhal, R. M. 1979. Settlement Patterns at Copan, Honduras. Unpublished doctoral dissertation, Harvard University.

————. 1981. Settlement Patterns in the Southeast Maya Area. In Ashmore 1981b: 187–210.

Lincoln, C. E. 1980. A Preliminary Assessment of Izamal, Yucatan, Mexico. Unpublished senior honors thesis, Tulane University.

Littmann, E. R. 1980. Maya Blue: A New Perspective. *AAnt* 45: 87–100.

Litvak-King, J. 1972. Las relaciones externas de Xochicalco: Una evaluación de su significado. *Anales de Antropología* 9: 53–76.

Lizana, B. de. 1893. *Historia de Yucatan. Devocionario de Nuestra Señora de Izmal y conquista espiritual impresa en 1633.* 2nd edition. Mexico City: Museo Nacional de Mexico.

Longacre, R. 1967. Systematic Reconstruction and Comparison. In *HMAI* 5: 117–59.

Longyear, J. M. 1944. *Archaeological Investigations in El Salvador.* PMAE Memoirs, Vol. 9(2).

————. 1947. *Cultures and Peoples of the Southeastern Maya Frontier.* CIW Theoretical Approaches to Problems, No. 3.

————. 1952. *Copan Ceramics: A Study of Southeastern Maya Pottery.* CIW Publication 597.

Lopez, D., and D. Molina. 1976. Los Murales de Cacaxtla. *INAH Boletín* 16(2): 3-8.

Loten, S. H. N.d. Lamanai Postclassic. In Chase & Rice (n.d.).

Lothrop, S. K. 1924. *Tulum. An Archaeological Study of the East Coast of Yucatan.* CIW Publication 335.

————. 1933. *Atitlan: An Archaeological Study of the Ancient Remains on the Borders of Lake Atitlan, Guatemala.* CIW Publication 444.

————. 1939. The Southeastern Frontier of the Maya. *AA* 41: 42-54.

————. 1952. *Metals from the Cenote of Sacrifice, Chichen Itza, Yucatan.* PMAE Memoirs, Vol. 10(2).

Lounsbury, F. G. 1973. On the Derivation and Reading of the "Ben-Ich" Prefix. In Benson 1973: 99-143.

————. 1974. The Inscription of the Sarcophagus Lid at Palenque. In Robertson 1974 (Part II): 5-19.

————. 1976. Maya Numeration, Computation, and Calendrical Astronomy. In *Dictionary of Scientific Biography* (C. C. Gillispie, ed.): 759-818.

Lowe, G. W. 1962. *Mound 5 and Minor Excavations, Chiapa de Corzo, Chiapas, Mexico.* NWAF Paper 12.

————. 1977. The Mixe-Zoque as Competing Neighbors of the Early Lowland Maya. In Adams 1977: 197-248.

Lowe, G. W., P. Agrinier, J. A. Mason, F. Hicks, and C. E. Rozaire. 1960. *Excavations at Chiapa de Corzo, Chiapas, Mexico.* NWAF Papers 8-11 (issued as Publication No. 7).

Lowe, G. W., T. A. Lee, and E. Martínez E. 1973. *Izapa: An Introduction to the Ruins and Monuments.* NWAF Paper 31.

Lundell, C. L. 1933. The Agriculture of the Maya. *Southwest Review* 19: 65-77.

————. 1937. *The Vegetation of Peten.* CIW Publication 478.

————. 1938. Plants Probably Utilized by the Old Empire Maya of Peten and Adjacent Lowlands. *Papers of the Michigan Academy of Science, Arts, and Letters* 24: 37-56.

Mackie, E. W. 1961. New Light on the End of Classic Maya Culture at Benque Viejo, British Honduras. *AAnt* 27(2): 216-224.

MacLeod, B. 1982. Cholan and Yucatecan Verb Morphology and Glyphic Verbal Affixes in the Inscriptions. In Campbell & Justeson in press.

MacNeish, R. S. 1964a. Ancient Mesoamerican Civilization. *Science* 143: 531-37.

————. 1964b. The Origins of New World Civilization. *SA* 211(5): 29-37.

MacNeish, R. S., and F. A. Peterson. 1962. *The Santa Marta Rock Shelter, Ocozocoantla, Chiapas, Mexico.* NWAF Paper 14.

MacNeish, R. S., F. A. Peterson, and K. V. Flannery. 1970. *The Prehistory of the Tehuacan Valley.* Vol. 3: *Ceramics.* Austin: University of Texas Press.

MacNeish, R. S., S. J. K. Wilkerson, and A. Nelken-Terner. 1980. *First Annual Report of the Belize Archaic Archaeological Reconnaissance.* Andover, Mass.: Robert F. Peabody Foundation for Archaeology, Phillips Academy.

Madeira, P. C. 1931. An Aerial Expedition to Central America. *UM Journal* 22(2).

Madrid Codex. 1869-70. *Manuscrit Troano: Études sur le système graphique et la langue des mayas* [Tro Fragment]. C. E. Brasseur de Bourbourg, comp. Paris: Imprimerie Impériale.

————. 1892. *Códice Maya denominado cortesiano que se conserva en el Museo Arqueológico Nacional* [Cortés Fragment]. Madrid: Hecha y publicada bajo la dirección de Dios y Delgado y López de Ayala y del Hierro.

————. 1930. Facsimile of combined fragments issued by Artes e Industrias Gráficas. Madrid: Matev. (See also Anders 1967; Villacorta & Villacorta 1933.)

Madsen, W. 1960. Christo-Paganism. In MARI Publication 19: 105-79.

Mahadevan, I. 1977. *The Indus Script.* Memoirs of the Archaeological Survey of India, No. 77. New Delhi: Tata Press.

Mahler, J. 1965. Garments and Textiles of the Maya Lowlands. In *HMAI* 3: 581–93.

Makemson, M. W. 1951. *The Book of the Jaguar Priest: A Translation of the Book of Chilam Balam of Tizimin*. New York: Schuman.

Maler, T. 1901. *Researches in the Central Portion of the Usumatsintla Valley. Report of Explorations for the Museum, 1898-1900*. PMAE Memoirs, Vol. 2(1).

———. 1903. *Researches in the Central Portions of the Usumatsintla Valley. Reports of Explorations for the Museum*. PMAE Memoirs, Vol. 2(2).

———. 1908a. *Explorations in the Department of Peten, Guatemala, and Adjacent Region. Topoxte; Yaxha; Benque Viejo; Naranjo*. PMAE Memoirs, Vol. 4(2).

———. 1908b. *Explorations of the Upper Usumatsintla and Adjacent Region. Altar de Sacrificios; Seibal; Itsimté-Sácluk; Cankuen*. PMAE Memoirs, Vol. 4(1).

———. 1911. *Explorations in the Department of Peten, Guatemala. Tikal*. PMAE Memoirs, Vol. 5(1).

Marcus, J. 1973. Territorial Organization of the Lowland Classic Maya. *Science* 180: 911–16.

———. 1974. The Iconography of Power Among the Classic Maya. *WA* 6: 83–94.

———. 1976a. The Origin of Mesoamerican Writing. In *Annual Review of Anthropology* (B. Siegel, A. Beals, and S. Tyler, eds.) 5: 35–67.

———. 1976b. *Emblem and State in the Classic Maya Lowlands*. Washington D.C.: DO.

———. 1980. Zapotec Writing. *SA* 242(2): 50–64.

———. 1982. The Plant World of the Sixteenth- and Seventeenth-Century Lowland Maya. In *Maya Subsistence: Studies in Memory of Dennis E. Puleston* (K. V. Flannery, ed.): 239–73. New York: Academic Press.

Marquina, I. 1951. *Arquitectura prehispánica*. Mexico City: Instituto Nacional de Antropología e Historia.

Martínez-Hernandez, J. H., ed. 1930. *Diccionario de Motul, Maya Español, atribuido a Fray Antonio de Ciudad Real, y Arte de Lengua Maya por Fray Juan Coronel*. Mérida: Talleres de la Compania Tipográfica Yucateca.

Mason, J. A. 1931. A Maya Carved Stone Lintel from Guatemala. *UM Bulletin* 3(1): 5–7.

———. 1932. Excavations at Piedras Negras. *UM Bulletin* 3(6): 178–79.

Matheny, R. T. 1976. Maya Lowland Hydraulic Systems. *Science* 193: 639–46.

———. 1979. El Mirador, Peten, Guatemala: Report of the 1979 Season. Paper presented at the 43rd ICA, Vancouver.

———, ed. 1980. *El Mirador, Peten, Guatemala, an Interim Report*. NWAF Paper 45.

Mathews, P. 1980. Notes on the Dynastic Sequence of Bonampak, Part 1. In Robertson 1980: 60–73.

Mathews, P., and D. M. Pendergast. 1979. The Altun Ha Jade Plaque: Deciphering the Inscription. In UCARF Contribution 41: 197–214.

Mathews, P., and L. Schele. 1974. Lords of Palenque—the Glyphic Evidence. In Robertson 1974 (Part I): 63–75.

Matson, F. R. 1956. *Ceramics and Man*. Chicago: Aldine.

Maudslay, A. P. 1889-1902. *Biología Centrali Americana: Archaeology*. 5 vols. London: R. H. Porter and Dulau and Co.

Maudslay, A. P. and A. C. Maudslay. 1889. *A Glimpse at Guatemala, and Some Notes on the Ancient Monuments of Central America*. London: Murray.

Mayer, K. H. 1978. *Maya Monuments: Sculptures of Unknown Provenience in Europe*. Translated by S. L. Brizee. Ramona, Calif.: Acoma.

McBryde, F. W. 1947. *Cultural and Historical Geography of Southwest Guatemala*. Institute of Social Anthropology Publication 4, Smithsonian Institution, Washington, D.C.

McClaran, M. 1973. Lexical and Syntactic Structures in Yucatec Maya. Doctoral dissertation, Harvard University.

McQuown, N. 1955. The Indigenous Languages of Latin America. *AA* 47: 501–70.

————. 1956. The Classification of Maya Languages. *IJAL* 22: 191–95.

————. 1964. Los orígenes y la diferenciación de los mayas según se infiere del estudio comparativo de las lenguas mayanas. In *Desarrollo cultural de los mayas* (E. Z. Vogt and A. Ruz L., eds.): 49–80. Mexico City: Universidad Nacional Autonoma de Mexico.

————. 1967. Classical Yucatec (Maya). In *HMAI* 5: 201–47.

————. 1976. American Indian Linguistics in New Spain. In *American Indian Languages and American Linguistics: Papers of the Second Golden Anniversary Symposium of the Linguistic Society of America, held at the University of California, Berkeley, on November 8 and 9, 1974* (W. Chafe, ed.). Lisse, Belgium: Peter de Ridder Press.

Means, P. A. 1917. *History of the Spanish Conquest of Yucatan and of the Itzas*. PMAE Papers, Vol. 7.

Meggers, B. J. 1954. Environmental Limitation on the Development of Culture. *AA* 56: 801–24.

Meggers, B. J., C. Evans, and E. Estrada. 1965. *Early Formative Period of Coastal Ecuador: The Valdevia and Machalilla Phases*. Smithsonian Contributions to Anthropology, 1. Washington, D.C.

Mercer, H. C. 1975. *The Hill-Caves of Yucatan*. Reprint of 1896 ed., with an introduction by J. E. S. Thompson. Norman: University of Oklahoma Press.

Merwin, R. E., and G. C. Vaillant. 1932. *The Ruins of Holmul, Guatemala*. PMAE Memoirs, Vol. 3(2).

Meyer, K. E. 1977. *The Plundered Past*. New York: Atheneum.

Michels, J. W., ed. 1979a. *Settlement Pattern Excavations at Kaminaljuyu, Guatemala*. Pennsylvania State University Press Monograph Series on Kaminaljuyu. University Park.

————. 1979b. *The Kaminaljuyu Chiefdom*. Pennsylvania State University Press Monograph Series on Kaminaljuyu. University Park.

Miles, S. W. 1957. The Sixteenth-Century Pokom Maya: A Documentary Analysis of Social Structure and Archaeological Setting. *Transactions of the American Philosophical Society* 47: 731–81.

————. 1965. Sculpture of the Guatemala-Chiapas Highlands and Pacific Slopes and Associated Hieroglyphs. In *HMAI* 2: 237–75.

Miller, A. G. 1977a. "Captains of the Itza": Unpublished Mural Evidence from Chichen Itza. In Hammond 1977b: 197–225.

————. 1977b. The Maya and the Sea: Trade and Cult at Tancah and Tulum. In Benson 1977b: 97–138.

————. 1978. A Brief Outline of the Artistic Evidence for Classic-Period Culture Contact between Maya Lowlands and Central Mexican Highlands. In Pasztory 1978: 63–70.

————. 1980. Art Historical Implications of Quirigua Sculpture. Paper presented at the 45th Annual Meeting of The Society for American Archaeology, Philadelphia.

————. 1982. *On the Edge of the Sea: Mural Painting at Tancah-Tulum, Quintana Roo, Mexico*. Washington, D.C.: DO.

Millon, R., ed. 1973. *Urbanization at Teotihuacan, Mexico*. Vol. 1: *The Teotihuacan Map*. Austin: University of Texas Press.

Moholy-Nagy, H. 1975. Obsidian at Tikal, Guatemala. *41st ICA Actas* 1: 511–18.

————. 1976. Spatial Distribution of Flint and Obsidian Artifacts at Tikal, Guatemala. In Hester & Hammond 1976: 91–108.

Molloy, J. P., and W. L. Rathje. 1974. Sexploitation among the Late Classic Maya. In Hammond 1974b: 431–44.

Moran, F. 1935. *Arte y Diccionario en Lengua Cholti: A Manuscript Copied from the Libro Grande of Fray Pedro Moran of about 1625*. Baltimore: Maya Society Publication No. 9.

Moreno, W. J. 1959. Sintesis de la historia pretolteca de mesoamerica. In *Esplendor del Mexico Antiguo* (C. Cook de Leonard, ed.): 1019–1108. Mexico City: Centro Investigaciones Antropológicos.

Morgan, L. H. 1877. *Ancient Society*. New York: Holt.

Morley, S. G. 1910. Uxmal—A Group of Related Structures. *American Journal of Archaeology*, ser. 2, 14: 1-18.

—————. 1911. The Historical Value of the Books of Chilam Balam. *American Journal of Archaeology*, ser. 2, 15: 195-214.

—————. 1915. *An Introduction to the Study of the Maya Hieroglyphs*. BAE Bulletin 57.

—————. 1916. The Supplementary Series in the Maya Inscriptions. In *Holmes Anniversary Volume Anthropological Essays* (F. W. Hodge, ed.). 366-96. Washington, D.C.

—————. 1920. *The Inscriptions at Copan*. CIW Publication 219.

—————. 1925. The Earliest Mayan Dates. *Compte-Rendu of the 21st ICA* 2: 655-67.

—————. 1935. *Guide Book to the Ruins of Quirigua*. CIW Supplemental Publication 16.

—————. 1937-38. *The Inscriptions of the Peten*. 5 vols. CIW Publication 437.

—————. 1946. *The Ancient Maya*. Stanford, Calif.: Stanford University Press.

—————. 1953. *La civilización maya*. Translation by A. Recinos. 2nd ed. Mexico City: Fondo de Cultura Económica.

—————. 1970. The Stela Platform at Uxmal, Yucatan, Mexico. Edited and annotated by H. E. D. Pollock. In MARI Publication 26: 151-80.

Morley, S. G., and G. W. Brainerd. 1956. *The Ancient Maya*. 3rd ed. Stanford, Calif.: Stanford University Press.

Morley, S. G., and F. R. Morley. 1939. *The Age and Provenance of the Leyden Plate*. CIW Publication 509, CAA No. 24.

Morris, A. A. 1931. *Digging in Yucatan*. New York: Doubleday, Doran.

Morris, E. H., J. Charlot, and A. A. Morris. 1931. *The Temple of the Warriors at Chichen Itza, Yucatan*. CIW Publication 406.

Muntsch, A. 1943. Some Magico-Religious Observations of the Present-Day Maya Indians of British Honduras and Yucatan. *Primitive Man* 16(1): 31-44.

Murie, A. 1935. Mammals from Guatemala and British Honduras. In University of Michigan Museum of Zoology, Miscellaneous Publications, 26: 7-30. Ann Arbor.

Navarrete, C. 1960. *Archaeological Explorations in the Region of the Frailesca, Chiapas, Mexico*. NWAF Paper 7.

—————. 1976. Algunas influencias Mexicanas en el area maya meridional durante el postclasico tardio. *Estudios de Cultura Nahuatl* 14: 345-82.

Netting, R. M. 1977. Maya Subsistence: Mythologies, Analogies, Possibilities. In Adams 1977: 299-333.

Norman, V. G. 1973. *Izapa Sculpture*. NWAF Paper 30.

Nuñez Chinchilla, J. 1963. *Copan Ruins*. Publications of the Banco Central de Honduras. Tegucigalpa.

Oakes, M. 1951. *The Two Crosses of Todos Santos*. New York: Pantheon.

Olsen, G. W., A. H. Siemens, D. E. Puleston, G. Cal, and D. Jenkins. 1975. Ridged Fields in British Honduras. *Soil Survey Horizons* 16: 9-12.

Osborne, L. de Jongh. 1935. *Guatemala Textiles*. MARI Publication 6.

—————. 1965. *Indian Crafts of Guatemala and El Salvador*. Norman: University of Oklahoma Press.

Pahl, G. W. 1976. The Maya Hieroglyphic Inscriptions of Copan: A Catalog and Historical Commentary. Unpublished doctoral dissertation, University of California, Los Angeles.

—————. 1977. The Inscriptions of Río Amarillo and Los Higos: Secondary Centers of the Southeastern Maya Frontier. *Journal of Latin American Lore* 3: 133-54.

Paillés, H. M. 1978. The Process of Transformation at Pajón: A Preclassic Society Located in an Estuary in Chiapas, Mexico. In Stark & Voorhies 1978: 81-95.

Palacios, E. J. 1932. Maya-Christian Synchronology or Calendrical Correlation. In MARI Publication 4: 147-80.

————. 1933. *El calendario y los jeroglíficos cronográficos mayas*. Mexico City: Editorial cultura.

Paris Codex. 1887. *Manuscrit hiératique des anciens Indiens de l'Amérique centrale conservé à la Bibliothèque Nationale de Paris; avec une introduction par Leon de Rosny*. 2nd ed. Paris: Maisonneuve et cie., Libraires de la Sociedad Ethnographie. Reissued "under the care of" William E. Gates, 1909. (See also Anders 1968; Villacorta & Villacorta 1933.)

Parsons, J. R. 1972. Archaeological Settlement Patterns. *Annual Review of Anthropology* 1: 127–50.

Parsons, L. A. 1967–69. *Bilbao, Guatemala*. 2 vols. Milwaukee Public Museum Publications in Anthropology, Nos. 11 and 12.

Pasztory, E., ed. 1978. *Middle Classic Mesoamerica*. New York: Columbia University Press.

Pearse, A. S., E. P. Creaser, and F. G. Hall. 1936. *The Cenotes of Yucatan, a Zoological and Hydrographic Survey*. CIW Publication 457.

Pendergast, D. M. 1962. Metal Artifacts in Prehispanic Mesoamerica. *AAnt* 27: 520–45.

————. 1965. Maya Tombs at Altun Ha. *A* 18(3): 210–17.

————. 1969. *Altun Ha, British Honduras (Belize): The Sun God's Tomb*. Royal Ontario Museum Art and Archaeology Occasional Paper 19. Toronto.

————. 1971. Evidence of Early Teotihuacan-Lowland Maya Contact at Altun Ha. *AAnt* 36: 455–60.

————. 1979. *Excavations at Altun Ha, Belize, 1964–1970*. Vol I. Toronto: Royal Ontario Museum.

————. 1981. Lamanai, Belize: Summary of Excavation Results 1974–1980. *JFA* 8: 29–53.

Plafker, G. 1976. Tectonic Aspects of the Guatemala Earthquake of 4 February 1976. *Science* 193: 1201–8.

Pollock, H. E. D. 1937. *The Casa Redonda at Chichen Itza, Yucatan*. CIW Publication 456, CAA No. 17.

————. 1954. Department of Archaeology. *CIW Yearbook* 53: 263–67.

————. 1965. Architecture of the Maya Lowlands. In *HMAI* 2: 378–440.

————. 1980. *The Puuc, an Archaeological Survey of the Hill Country of Yucatan and Northern Campeche, Mexico*. PMAE Memoirs, Vol. 19.

Pollock, H. E. D., R. L. Roys, T. Proskouriakoff, and A. L. Smith. 1962. *Mayapan, Yucatan, Mexico*. CIW Publication 619.

Potter, D. F. 1977. *Maya Architecture of the Central Yucatan Peninsula, Mexico*. MARI Publication 44.

Prem, H. J. 1971. Calendrics and Writing in Mesoamerica. In UCARF Contribution 11: 112–32.

Pring, D. C. 1976. Outline of the Northern Belize Ceramic Sequence. *CCM* 9: 11–51.

————. 1977. Influence or Intrusion? The "Protoclassic" in the Maya Lowlands. In Hammond 1977b: 135–65.

————. 1979. The Swasey Ceramic Complex of Northern Belize. In UCARF Contribution 41: 215–29.

Proskouriakoff, T. 1946. *An Album of Maya Architecture*. CIW Publication 558. Reprinted by the University of Oklahoma Press, 1963.

————. 1950. *A Study of Classic Maya Sculpture*. CIW Publication 593.

————. 1954. Mayapan, Last Stronghold of a Civilization. *A* 7(2): 96–103.

————. 1955. The Death of a Civilization. *SA* 192(5): 82–88.

————. 1960. Historical Implications of a Pattern of Dates at Piedras Negras. *AAnt* 25: 454–75.

————. 1961. The Lords of the Maya Realm. *Expedition* 4(1): 14–21.

————. 1963. Historical Data in the Inscriptions of Yaxchilan (Part I). *ECM* 3: 149–67.

————. 1964. Historical Data in the Inscriptions of Yaxchilan (Part II). *ECM* 4: 177–202.

————. 1965. Sculpture and Major Arts of the Maya Lowlands. In *HMAI* 2: 469–97.

————. 1971. Early Architecture and Sculpture in Mesoamerica. In UCARF Contribution 11: 141-56.

————. 1973. The Hand-Grasping-Fish and Associated Glyphs on Classic Maya Monuments. In Benson 1973: 165-73.

————. 1974. *Jades from the Cenote of Sacrifice, Chichen Itza, Yucatan, Mexico.* PMAE Memoirs, Vol. 10(1).

Puleston, D. E. 1968. *Brosimum alicastrum* as a Subsistence Alternative for the Classic Maya of the Central Southern Lowlands. Unpublished master's thesis, University of Pennsylvania.

————. 1971. An Experimental Approach to the Function of Classic Maya Chultuns. *AAnt* 36: 322-35.

————. 1974. Intersite Areas in the Vicinity of Tikal and Uaxactun. In Hammond 1974b: 303-11.

————. 1977. The Art and Archaeology of Hydraulic Agriculture in the Maya Lowlands. In Hammond 1977b: 449-67.

————. 1978. Terracing, Raised Fields, and Tree Cropping in the Maya Lowlands: A New Perspective on the Geography of Power. In Harrison & Turner 1978: 225-45.

————. 1979. An Epistemological Pathology and the Collapse, or Why the Maya Kept the Short Count. In Hammond & Willey 1979: 63-74.

Puleston, D. E., and D. W. Callender, Jr. 1967. Defensive Earthworks at Tikal. *Expedition* 9(3): 40-48.

Puleston, D. E., and O. S. Puleston. 1971. An Ecological Approach to the Origins of Maya Civilization. *A* 24(4): 330-37.

Quirarte, J. 1973. *Izapa-Style Art: A Study of Its Form and Meaning.* Studies in Pre-Columbian Art and Archaeology, No. 10. Washington, D.C.: DO.

————. 1976. The Underworld Jaguar in Maya Vase Painting: An Iconographic Study. *New Mexico Studies in the Fine Arts* 1: 20-25.

————. 1977. Early Art Styles of Mesoamerica and Early Classic Maya Art. In Adams 1977: 249-83.

————. 1979. The Representation of Underworld Processions in Maya Vase Painting: An Iconographic Study. In Hammond & Willey 1979: 117-48.

Rands, B. C., and R. L. Rands. 1961. Excavations in a Cemetery at Palenque. *ECM* 1: 87-106.

Rands, R. L. 1965a. Jades of the Maya Lowlands. In *HMAI* 3: 561-80.

————. 1965b. Classic and Postclassic Pottery Figurines of the Guatemalan Highlands. In *HMAI* 2: 156-62.

Rands, R. L., and B. C. Rands. 1959. The Incensario Complex of Palenque, Chiapas, Mexico. *AAnt* 25: 225-36.

————. 1965. Pottery Figurines of the Maya Lowlands. In *HMAI* 2: 535-60.

Rands, R. L., and R. E. Smith. 1965. Pottery of the Guatemalan Highlands. In *HMAI* 2: 95-145.

Rathje, W. L. 1970. Socio-Political Implications of Lowland Maya Burials: Methodology and Tentative Hypotheses. *WA* 1: 359-74.

————. 1971. The Origin and Development of Classic Maya Civilization *AAnt* 36: 275-85.

————. 1973. Classic Maya Development and Denouement: A Research Design. In Culbert 1973: 405-56.

————. 1977. The Tikal Connection. In Adams 1977: 373-82.

Rathje, W. L., D. A. Gregory, and F. A. Wiseman. 1978. Trade Models and Archaeological Problems: Classic Maya Examples. In NWAF Paper 40: 147-75.

Rau, C. 1879. *The Palenque Tablet in the United States National Museum, Washington, D.C.* Smithsonian Contributions to Knowledge, Vol. 22(5). Washington, D.C.

Recinos, A. 1950. *Popol Vuh: The Sacred Book of the Ancient Quiche Maya.* English translation by S. G. Morley and D. Goetz. Norman: University of Oklahoma Press.

Recinos, A., and D. Goetz. 1953. *The Annals of the Cakchiquels.* Norman: University of Oklahoma Press.

Redfield, R. 1941. *The Folk Culture of Yucatan.* Chicago: University of Chicago Press.

—————. 1956. *The Little Community.* Chicago: University of Chicago Press.

Redfield, R., and A. Villa Rojas. 1934. *Chan Kom: A Maya Village.* CIW Publication 448.

Reed, N. 1964. *The Caste War of Yucatan.* Stanford, Calif.: Stanford University Press.

Reichel-Dolmatoff, G. 1965. *Excavaciones arqueológicas en Puerto Hormiga, Departamento de Bolívar.* Publicaciones de la Universidad de los Andes, Antropología 2. Bogotá.

Reina, R. E. 1962. The Ritual of the Skull of Peten, Guatemala. *Expedition* 4(4): 26–36.

—————. 1966. *The Law of the Saints: A Pokomam Pueblo and Its Community Culture*: Indianapolis: Bobbs-Merrill.

—————. 1967. Milpas and Milperos: Implications for Prehistoric Times. *AA* 69: 1–20.

Reina, R. E., and R. M. Hill II. 1978. *The Traditional Pottery of Guatemala.* Austin: University of Texas Press.

—————. 1980. Lowland Maya Subsistence: Notes from Ethnohistory and Ethnography. *AAnt* 45: 74–79.

Rice, D. S. 1976. Middle Preclassic Maya Settlement in the Central Maya Lowlands. *JFA* 3: 425–45.

—————. 1978. Population Growth and Subsistence Alternatives in a Tropical Lacustrine Environment. In Harrison & Turner 1978: 35–61.

Rice, D. S., and D. E. Puleston. 1981. Ancient Maya Settlement Patterns in the Peten, Guatemala. In Ashmore 1981b: 121–56.

Rice, D. S., and P. M. Rice. 1979. Introductory Archaeological Survey of the Central Peten, Savanna, Guatemala. In UCARF Contribution 41: 231–77.

—————. 1981. Muralla de Leon: A Lowland Maya Fortification. *JFA* 8: 271–88.

Rice, P. M. 1979. Ceramic and Nonceramic Artifacts of Lakes Yaxha-Sacnab, El Peten, Guatemala. *CCM* 11: 1–85.

Rice, P. M., and D. S. Rice. 1979. Home on the Range: Aboriginal Maya Settlement in the Central Peten Savannas. *A* 32(6): 16–25.

Richardson, F. B. 1940. Non-Maya Monumental Sculpture of Central America. In *The Maya and Their Neighbors* (C. L. Hay and others, eds.): 395–416. New York: Appleton Century.

Ricketson, O. G. 1931. *Excavations at Baking Pot, British Honduras.* CIW Publication 403, CAA No. 1.

—————. 1933. The Culture of the Maya. Excavations at Uaxactun. In CIW Supplemental Publication 6: 1–15.

—————. 1935. Maya Pottery Well from Quirigua Farm, Guatemala. *Maya Research* 2: 103–5.

Ricketson, O. G., and A. V. Kidder. 1930. An Archaeological Reconnaissance by Air in Central America. *Geographical Review* 20: 177–206.

Ricketson, O. G., and E. B. Ricketson. 1937. *Uaxactun, Guatemala, Group E, 1926–1937.* Publication 477.

Riese, B. 1971. *Grundlagen zur Entzifferung der Mayahieroglyphen, Dargestellt an den Inschriften von Copan.* Beiträge zur mittelamerikanischen Völkerkunde, 11. Hamburgisches Museum für Völkerkunde und Vorgeschichte. Munich: Kommissionsverlag Klaus Renner.

—————. 1980. Late Classic Relationships between Copan and Quirigua: Some Epigraphic Evidence. Paper presented at the 45th Annual Meeting of the Society for American Archaeology, Philadelphia.

Rivet, P. 1954. *Cités maya.* 4th ed. Paris: Guillot.

Robertson, M. G. 1972a. The Ritual Bundles of Yaxchilan. Paper presented at the Tulane University Symposium on the Art of Latin America, New Orleans.

—————. 1972b. Monument Thievery in Mesoamerica. *AAnt* 37: 147–55.

————, ed. 1974. Parts I and II, *Primera Mesa Redonda de Palenque*. Pebble Beach, Calif.: The Robert Louis Stevenson School.

————, ed. 1976. The Art, Iconography and Dynastic History of Palenque. Part III, *Segunda Mesa Redonda de Palenque*. Pebble Beach, Calif.: The Robert Louis Stevenson School.

————. 1977. Painting Practices and Their Change Through Time of the Palenque Stucco Sculptors. In Hammond 1977b: 297–326.

————, ed. 1980. Vol. V, *Third Palenque Round Table, Part 2*. Austin: University of Texas Press.

Robertson, M. G., and D. C. Jeffers, eds. 1978. Vol. IV, *Tercera Mesa Redonda de Palenque*. Palenque: Pre-Columbian Art Research Center.

Robicsek, F. 1972. *Copan: Home of the Mayan Gods*. New York: Museum of the American Indian, Heye Foundation.

————. 1975. *A Study in Maya Art and History: The Mat Symbol*. New York: Museum of the American Indian, Heye Foundation.

————. 1978. *The Smoking Gods*. Norman: University of Oklahoma Press.

Robles Castella, J. F. 1980. La secuencia cerámica de la región de Cobá, Quintana Roo. Thesis, Escuela Nacional de Antropología e Historia, Mexico.

Rosny, L. de. 1875. *L'interpretation des anciens textes mayas*. Paris: Société Américaine de France.

Roys, R. L. 1931. *The Ethno-Botany of the Maya*. MARI Publication 2.

————. 1933. *The Book of Chilam Balam of Chumayel*. CIW Publication 438.

————. 1943. *The Indian Background of Colonial Yucatan*. CIW Publication 548. Reprinted by the University of Oklahoma Press, 1972.

————. 1952. *Conquest Sites and the Subsequent Destruction of Maya Architecture in the Interior of Northern Yucatan*. CIW Publication 596, CAA No. 54.

————. 1965. Lowland Maya Society at Spanish Contact. In *HMAI* 3: 659–78.

————. 1967. *The Book of Chilam Balam of Chumayel*. Introduction by J. E. S. Thompson. Republication of the original CIW edition (1933). Norman: University of Oklahoma Press.

Ruppert, K. J. 1931. *Temple of the Wall Panels*. CIW Publication 403, CAA No. 3.

————. 1935. *The Caracol at Chichen Itza, Yucatan, Mexico*. CIW Publication 454.

————. 1943. *The Mercado, Chichen Itza, Yucatan, Mexico*. CIW Publication 546, CAA No. 43.

————. 1952. *Chichen Itza: Architectural Notes and Plans*. CIW Publication 595.

Ruppert, K. J., and J. H. Denison. 1943. *Archaeological Reconnaissance in Campeche, Quintana Roo, and Peten*. CIW Publication 543.

Ruppert, K. J., E. M. Shook, A. L. Smith, and R. E. Smith. 1954. Chichen Itza, Dzibiac, and Balam Canche, Yucatan. *CIW Yearbook* 53: 286–89.

Ruppert, K. J., J. E. S. Thompson, and T. Proskouriakoff. 1955. *Bonampak, Chiapas, Mexico*. CIW Publication 602.

Ruz Lhuillier, A. 1952a. Exploraciones en Palenque: 1950. *INAH Anales* 5: 25–45.

————. 1952b. Exploraciones en Palenque: 1951. *INAH Anales* 5: 47–66.

————. 1954. La Pirámide-tumba de Palenque. *Cuadernos Americanos* 74: 141–59.

————. 1955. Exploraciones en Palenque: 1952. *INAH Anales* 6: 79–110.

————. 1958a. Exploraciones arqueológicas en Palenque: 1953. *INAH Anales* 10: 69–116.

————. 1958b. Exploraciones arqueológicas en Palenque: 1954. *INAH Anales* 10: 117–84.

————. 1958c. Exploraciones arqueológicas en Palenque: 1955. *INAH Anales* 10: 185–240.

————. 1958d. Exploraciones arqueológicas en Palenque: 1956. *INAH Anales* 10: 241–99.

————. 1962. Exploraciones arqueológicas en Palenque: 1957. *INAH Anales* 14: 35–90.

————. 1965. Tombs and Funerary Practices in the Maya Lowlands. In *HMAI* 2: 441–61.

————. 1977. Gerontocracy at Palenque? In Hammond 1977b: 287-95.

Sabloff, J. A. 1973a. Major Themes in the Past Hypotheses of the Maya Collapse. In Culbert 1973: 35-40.

————. 1973b. Continuity and Disruption During Terminal Late Classic Times at Seibal: Ceramic and Other Evidence. In Culbert 1973: 107-33.

————. 1975. *Excavations at Seibal, Department of the Peten, Guatemala: The Ceramics.* PMAE Memoirs, Vol. 13(2).

————. 1977. Old Myths, New Myths: The Role of Sea Traders in the Development of Ancient Maya Civilization. In Benson 1977b: 67-88.

Sabloff, J. A., and D. A. Freidel. 1975. A Model of a PreColumbian Trading Center. In Sabloff & Lamberg-Karlovsky 1975: 369-408.

Sabloff, J. A., and C. C. Lamberg-Karlovsky, eds. 1975. *Ancient Civilization and Trade.* SAR.

Sabloff, J. A., and W. R. Rathje, eds. 1975a. *A Study of Changing PreColumbian Commercial Systems.* PMAE Monograph 3.

————. 1975b. The Rise of a Maya Merchant Class. *SA* 233(4): 72-82.

Sabloff, J. A., and G. R. Willey. 1967. The Collapse of Maya Civilization in the Southern Lowlands: A Consideration of History and Process. *SWJA* 23: 311-36.

Sahagún, B. de. 1946. *Historia general de las cosas de la Nueva España.* Mexico City: Editoria Nueva España. 2nd ed., with numeration, notes, and appendixes by A. M. Garibay K., 1969. Mexico City: Biblioteca Porrúa.

Sanders, W. T. 1956. The Central Mexican Symbiotic Region. In Willey 1956: 115-27.

————. 1960. *Prehistoric Ceramics and Settlement Patterns in Quintana Roo, Mexico.* CIW Publication 606, CAA No. 60.

————. 1962. Cultural Ecology of the Maya Lowlands, I. *ECM* 2: 79-121.

————. 1963. Cultural Ecology of the Maya Lowlands, II. *ECM* 3: 203-41.

————. 1973. The Cultural Ecology of the Lowland Maya: A Re-Evaluation. In Culbert 1973: 325-65.

————. 1977. Environmental Heterogeneity and the Evolution of Lowland Maya Civilization. In Adams 1977: 287-97.

————. 1981. Classic Maya Settlement Patterns and Ethnographic Analogy. In Ashmore 1981b: 351-69.

Sanders, W. T., and J. W. Michels, eds. 1977. *Teotihuacan and Kaminaljuyu: A Study in Prehistoric Cultural Contact.* Pennsylvania State University Press Monograph Series on Kaminaljuyu. University Park.

Sanders, W. T., J. R. Parsons, and R. S. Santley. 1979. *The Basin of Mexico.* New York: Academic Press.

Sanders, W. T., and B. J. Price. 1968. *Mesoamerica: The Evolution of a Civilization.* New York: Random House.

Santley, R. S. 1980. Obsidian Trade and Teotihuacan Influence in Mesoamerica. Paper presented at the DO Symposium on Mesoamerican Highland-Lowland Interaction, Washington, D.C.

Sapir, E. 1916. *Time Perspective in Aboriginal American Indian Culture: A Study in Method.* Canada, Department of Mines, Geological Survey, Memoir 90, Anthropological Series No. 13. Ottawa: Government Printing Bureau. 87 pp. Reprinted in *Selected Writings of Edward Sapir in Language, Culture, Personality* (D. Mandelbaum, ed.): 389-462. Berkeley and Los Angeles: University of California Press, 1968.

Sapper, K. 1896. *Sobre la geografía física y la geología de la península de Yucatán.* Instituto Geología No. 3, Mexico.

————. 1897. *Das Nördliche Mittel-Amerika Nebst einem Ausflug nach dem Hochland von Anahuac: Reisen und Studien aus den Jahren 1888–1895.* Braunschweig: F. Vieweg und Sohn.

Satterthwaite, L. 1937a. Thrones at Piedras Negras. *UM Bulletin* 7(1): 18–23.

————. 1937b. Identification of Maya Temple Buildings at Piedras Negras. *Publications of the Philadelphia Anthropological Society* 1: 161–77.

————. 1943. *Piedras Negras: Architecture Part I, Introduction.* UM.

————. 1944a. *Piedras Negras Archaeology: Architecture Part II, Temples.* UM.

————. 1944b. *Piedras Negras Archaeology: Architecture Part IV, Ball Courts.* UM.

————. 1944, 1954. *Piedras Negras Archaeology: Architecture Part VI, Unclassified Buildings and Substructures.* UM.

————. 1947. *Concepts and Structures of Maya Calendrical Arithmetic.* Joint Publications, Museum of the University of Pennsylvania and the Philadelphia Anthropological Society, No. 3.

————. 1950a. Reconnaissance in British Honduras. *UM Bulletin* 16(1): 21–37.

————. 1950b. Plastic Art of a Maya Palace. *A* 3: 215–22.

————. 1952. *Piedras Negras Archaeology: Architecture Part V, Sweathouses.* UM.

————. 1954. Sculptured Monuments from Caracol, British Honduras. *UM Bulletin* 18(1–2): 1–45.

————. 1958. The Problem of Abnormal Stela Placements at Tikal and Elsewhere. *Tikal Report* No. 3. In UM Monograph 15: 61–83.

————. 1965. Calendrics of the Maya Lowlands. In *HMAI* 3: 603–31.

Satterthwaite, L., and E. K. Ralph. 1960. New Radiocarbon Dates and the Maya Correlation Problem. *AAnt* 26: 165–84.

Saul, F. P. 1972. *The Human Skeletal Remains of Altar de Sacrificios, An Osteobiographic Analysis.* PMAE Papers, Vol. 63(2).

————. 1973. Disease in the Maya Area: The Precolumbian Evidence. In Culbert 1973: 301–24.

Saville, M. 1893. Vandalism Among the Antiquities of Yucatan and Central America. *Archaeologist* 1: 91–93.

————. 1921. *Reports on the Maya Indians of Yucatan.* Heye Foundation, Indian Notes and Monographs, Vol. 9(3). New York.

Schele, L. 1978. Genealogical Documentation on the Tri-Figure Panels at Palenque. In Robertson & Jeffers 1978: 41–70.

————. 1980. Verb Morphology and Syntax of the Maya Hieroglyphic Writing System. Doctoral dissertation, University of Texas.

Schele, L., P. Matthews, and F. Lounsbury. N.d. Parentage and Spouse Expressions from Classic Maya Inscriptions.

Schellhas, P. 1904. *Representations of Deities of the Maya Manuscripts.* PMAE Papers, Vol. 4 (1): 1–47.

Schmidt, K. P., and E. W. Andrews IV. 1936. Notes on Snakes from Yucatan. In Field Museum of Natural History Zoological Series, 20(18): 167–87. Chicago.

Scholes, F. V. 1933. The Beginnings of Hispano-Indian Society in Yucatan. *Scientific Monthly* 44: 530–38.

Scholes, F. V., C. R. Menéndez, J. I. Rubio M., and E. Adams, eds. 1936. *Documentos para la historia de Yucatán. Tomo I. 1550–1561.* Mérida: Tipográfia Yucateca.

Scholes, F. V., and R. L. Roys. 1938. *Fray Diego de Landa and the Problem of Idolatry in Yucatan.* Cooperation in Research CIW Publication 501.

————. 1948. *The Maya Chontal Indians of Acalan-Tixchel.* CIW Publication 560.

Schortman, E. M. 1980. Archaeological Investigations in the Lower Motagua Valley. *Expedition* 23(1): 28–34.

Schortman, E. M., and P. A. Urban, eds. In press. *Quirigua Reports II* (R. J. Sharer, general ed.), Papers 6–14. UM Monograph.

Sedat, D. W., and R. J. Sharer. 1972. Archaeological Investigations in the Northern Maya Highlands: New Data on the Maya Preclassic. In UCARF Contribution 16: 23–35.

Seler, E. 1902-23. *Gesammelte abhandlungen zur Amerikanischen Sprach und Alterthumskunde.* 5 vols. Berlin: Ascher, Behrend.

————. 1904. English translations of nine of Seler's articles. In BAE Bulletin 28: 353-91.

Service, E. R. 1975. *Origins of the State and Civilization.* New York: Norton.

Sharer, R. J. 1969. Chalchuapa: Investigations at a Highland Maya Ceremonial Center. *Expedition* 11(2): 36-38.

————. 1974. The Prehistory of the Southeastern Maya Periphery. *Current Anthropology* 15(2): 165-87.

————. 1975. The Southeastern Periphery of the Maya Area: A Prehistoric Perspective. Paper presented at the 74th Annual Meeting of the American Anthropological Association, San Francisco.

————. 1977. The Maya Collapse Revisited: Internal and External Perspectives. In Hammond 1977b: 532-52.

————, general ed. 1978a. *The Prehistory of Chalchuapa, El Salvador.* 3 vols. UM Monograph 36. Philadelphia: University of Pennsylvania Press.

————. 1978b. Archaeology and History at Quirigua, Guatemala. *JFA* 5(1): 51-70.

————. 1980. The Quirigua Project, 1974-1979. *Expedition* 23(1): 5-10.

————. 1982. Did the Maya Collapse? A New World Perspective on the Demise of Harappan Civilization. In *Harappan Civilization: A Contemporary Perspective* (G. A. Possehl, ed.). American Institute of Indian Studies, New Delhi: Oxford and IBH.

————. In press. Lower Central America as Seen from Mesoamerica. In *Central American Archaeology* (D. Stone and F. Lange, eds.). SAR.

————. N.d. Terminal Events in the Southeastern Lowlands: A View from Quirigua. In Chase & Rice (n.d.).

Sharer, R. J., and B. Bevan. In press. Quirigua and the Earthquake of February 4, 1976. In Schortman & Urban in press.

Sharer, R. J., and J. C. Gifford. 1970. Preclassic Ceramics from Chalchuapa, El Salvador, and Their Relationships with the Maya Lowlands. *AAnt* 35: 441-62.

Sharer, R. J., C. Jones, W. A. Ashmore, and E. M. Schortman. 1979. The Quirigua Project: 1976 Season. In *Quirigua Report I* (W. A. Ashmore, ed.), UM Monograph 37: 45-73.

Sharer, R. J., and D. W. Sedat. 1973. Monument 1, El Porton, Guatemala, and the Development of Maya Calendrical and Writing Systems. In UCARF Contribution 18: 177-94.

Shattuck, G. C. 1933. *The Peninsula of Yucatan, Medical, Biological, Meteorological and Sociological Studies.* CIW Publication 431.

Sheets, P. D. 1971. An Ancient Natural Disaster. *Expedition* 13(1): 24-31.

————. 1972. A Model of Mesoamerican Obsidian Technology Based on Preclassic Workshop Debris in El Salvador. *CCM* 8: 17-33.

————. 1973. The Pillage of Prehistory. *AAnt* 38: 317-20.

————. 1975. A Reassessment of the Precolumbian Obsidian Industry of El Chayal, Guatemala. *AAnt* 40: 98-103.

————. 1976a. Islands of Lithic Knowledge and Seas of Ignorance in the Maya Area. In Hester & Hammond 1976: 1-9.

————. 1976b. The Terminal Preclassic Lithic Industry of the Southeast Maya Highlands: A Component of the Protoclassic Site-Unit Intrusions in the Lowlands. In Hester & Hammond 1976: 55-69.

————. 1979a. Maya Recovery from Volcanic Disasters, Ilopango and Ceren. *A* 32(3): 32-42.

————. 1979b. Environmental and Cultural Effects of the Ilopango Eruption in Central America. In *Volcanic Activity and Human Ecology* (P. D. Sheets and D. K. Grayson, eds.): 525-64. New York: Academic Press.

Shepard, A. O. 1948. *Plumbate: A Mesoamerican Trade Ware.* CIW Publication 573.

————. 1971. *Ceramics for the Archaeologist.* 7th printing. CIW Publication 609.

Shimkin, D. B. 1973. Models for the Downfall: Some Ecological and Cultural-Historical Considerations. In Culbert 1973: 269–99.

Shook, E. M. 1954. The Temple of Kukulcan at Mayapan. *CIW Current Reports*, No. 20.

——. 1960. Tikal Stela 29. *Expedition* 2(2): 29–35.

——. 1965. Archaeological Survey of the Pacific Coast of Guatemala. In *HMAI* 2: 180–94.

——. 1971. Inventory of Some Preclassic Traits in the Highlands and Pacific Guatemala and Adjacent Areas. In UCARF Contribution 11: 70–77.

Shook, E. M., W. R. Coe, V. L. Broman, and L. Satterthwaite. 1958 *Tikal Reports* Nos. 1–4. UM Monograph 15.

Shook, E. M., and M. P. Hatch. 1978. The Ruins of El Balsamo, Department of Escuintla, Guatemala. *Journal of New World Archaeology* 3(1): 1–38.

——. 1979. The Early Preclassic Sequence in the Ocos-Salinas La Blanca Area, South Coast of Guatemala. In UCARF Contribution 41: 143–95.

Shook, E. M., M. P. Hatch, and J. K. Donaldson. 1979. Ruins of Semetabaj, Dept. Solola, Guatemala. In UCARF Contribution 41: 7–142.

Shook, E. M., and W. Irving. 1955. Colonnaded Buildings at Mayapan. *CIW Current Reports*, No. 20.

Shook, E. M., and A. V. Kidder. 1952. *Mound E-III-3, Kaminaljuyu, Guatemala.* CIW Publication 596, CAA No. 53.

Shook, E. M., and T. Proskouriakoff. 1956. Settlement Patterns in Mesoamerica and the Sequence in the Guatemalan Highlands. In Willey 1956: 93–100.

Sidrys, R. V. 1976. Classic Maya Obsidian Trade. *AAnt* 41: 449–64.

Sidrys, R. V., J. Andresen, and J. Kimberlin. 1976. Obsidian Sources in the Maya Area. *Journal of New World Archaeology* 1: 1–14.

Sidrys, R. V., C. M. Krowne, and H. B. Nicholson. 1975. A Lowland Maya Long Count/ Gregorian Conversion Computer Program. *AAnt* 40: 337–44.

Siegel, M. 1941. Religion in Western Guatemala: A Product of Acculturation. *AA* 43: 62–76.

Siemens, A. H. 1978. Karst and the Pre-Hispanic Maya in the Southern Lowlands. In Harrison & Turner 1978: 117–43.

Siemens, A. H., and D. E. Puleston. 1972. Ridged Fields and Associated Features in Southern Campeche: New Perspectives on the Lowland Maya. *AAnt* 37: 228–39.

Smailus, O. 1975a. *El Maya-Chontal de Acalan: Análisis Lingüístico de un Documento de los Años 1610–12.* Centro de Estudios Mayas, Cuaderno 9. Mexico City: Universidad Nacional Autónoma de México.

——. 1975b. *Textos Mayas de Belice y Quintana Roo: Fuentes para una Dialectología del Maya Yucateco.* Indiana 3. Beiträge zur Völker und Sprachenkunde, Archäologie und Anthropologie des Indianischen Amerika. Berlin: Gebr. Mann Verlag.

Smith, A. L. 1934. *Two Recent Ceramic Finds at Uaxactun.* CIW Publication 436, CAA No. 5.

——. 1937. *Structure A-XVIII, Uaxactun.* CIW Publication 483, CAA No. 20.

——. 1950. *Uaxactun, Guatemala: Excavations of 1931–37.* CIW Publication 588.

——. 1955. *Archaeological Reconnaissance in Central Guatemala.* CIW Publication 608.

——. 1965. Architecture of the Maya Highlands. In *HMAI* 2: 76–94.

——. 1972. *Excavations at Altar de Sacrificios, Architecture, Settlement, Burials and Caches.* PMAE Papers, Vol. 62(2).

——. 1977. Patolli at the Ruins of Seibal, Peten, Guatemala. In Hammond 1977b: 349–63.

Smith, A. L., and A. V. Kidder. 1943. *Explorations in the Motagua Valley, Guatemala.* CIW Publication 546, CAA No. 41.

——. 1951. *Excavations at Nebaj, Guatemala.* CIW Publication 594.

Smith, M. E. 1973. *Picture Writing from Ancient Southern Mexico: Mixtec Place Signs and Maps.* Norman: University of Oklahoma Press.

Smith, P. E. 1955. Excavations in Three Ceremonial Structures at Mayapan. *CIW Current Reports*, No. 21.

Smith, R. E. 1937. *A Study of Structure A-I Complex at Uaxactun*. CIW Publication 456, CAA No. 19.

————. 1954. Explorations on the Outskirts of Mayapán. *CIW Current Reports*, No. 18.

————. 1955. *Ceramic Sequence at Uaxactun, Guatemala*. 2 vols. MARI Publication 20.

————. 1971. *The Pottery of Mayapan*. 2 vols. PMAE Papers, Vol. 66.

Smith, R. E., and J. C. Gifford. 1965. Pottery of the Maya Lowlands. In *HMAI* 2: 498–534.

Smithsonian Institution. 1904. *Mexican and Central American Antiquities, Calendar Systems, and History*. Twenty-four papers by E. Seler, E. Förstemann, P. Schellhas, C. Sapper, and E. P. Dieseldorff, translated from the German under the supervision of C. P. Bowditch, BAE Bulletin 28.

Sorenson, J. L. 1956. An Archaeological Reconnaissance of West-Central Chiapas, Mexico. In NWAF Paper 1: 7–19.

Spinden, H. J. 1913. *A Study of Maya Art*. PMAE Memoirs, Vol. 6.

————. 1917. *The Ancient Civilizations of Mexico and Central America*. American Museum of Natural History Handbook Series, No. 3. New York.

————. 1924. *The Reduction of Maya Dates*. PMAE Papers, Vol. 6(4).

————. 1928. *The Ancient Civilizations of Mexico and Central America*. 3rd ed., rev.

————. 1930. *Maya Dates and What They Reveal*. Brooklyn Institute of Arts and Sciences, Vol. 4(1). New York.

Stadelman, R. 1940. *Maize Cultivation in Northwestern Guatemala*. CIW Publication 523, CAA No. 33.

Standley, P. C. 1930. *Flora of Yucatan*. Field Museum of Natural History Publication 279, Botanical Series Vol. 3(3). Chicago.

Stark, B. L., and B. Voorhies, eds. 1978. *Prehistoric Coastal Adaptations: The Economy and Ecology of Maritime Middle America*. New York: Academic Press.

Steggerda, M. 1941. *Maya Indians of Yucatan*. CIW Publication 531.

Stephens, J. L. 1841. *Incidents of Travel in Central America, Chiapas and Yucatan*. 2 vols. New York: Harper. Reprinted by Dover, 1962.

————. 1843. *Incidents of Travel in Yucatan*. 2 vols. New York: Harper. Reprinted by Dover, 1963.

Stewart, R. 1977. Classic to Postclassic Period Settlement Trends in the Region of Santa Cruz del Quiche. In Wallace & Carmack 1977: 68–81.

Stirling, M. W. 1940. An Initial Series from Tres Zapotes, Vera Cruz, Mexico. *National Geographic Society Mexican Archaeology Series*, Vol. 1(1).

————. 1965. Monumental Sculpture of Southern Veracruz and Tabasco. In *HMAI* 3: 716–38.

Stone, D. Z. In press. Cacao and the Maya Traders. In *Central American Archaeology* (D. Stone and F. Lange, eds.). SAR.

Stromsvik, G. 1942. *Substela Caches and Stela Foundations at Copan and Quirigua*. CIW Publication 528, CAA No. 37.

————. 1952. *The Ball Courts of Copan, with Notes on Courts at La Union, Quirigua, San Pedro Pinula and Asunción Mita*. CIW Publication 596, CAA No. 55.

Stuart, G. E., J. C. Scheffler, E. B. Kurjack, and J. W. Cottier. 1979. *Map of the Ruins of Dzibilchaltun, Yucatan, Mexico*. MARI Publication 47.

Stuart, G. E., and G. S. Stuart. 1977. *The Mysterious Maya*. Washington, D.C.: National Geographic Society.

Stuart, L. C. 1964. Fauna of Middle America. In *HMAI* 1: 316–62.

Swadesh, M. 1961. Interrelaciones de las lenguas Mayenses. *INAH Anales* 13: 231–67.

————. 1967. Lexicostatistic Classification. In *HMAI* 5: 79–115.

Tamayo, J. L. 1964. The Hydrography of Middle America. In *HMAI* 1: 84-121.

Teeple, J. E. 1926. Maya Inscriptions: The Venus Calendar and Another Correlation. *AA* 28: 402-8.

————. 1931. *Maya Astronomy.* CIW Publication 403, CAA No. 2.

Thomas, C. 1882. A Study of the Manuscript Troano. In *U.S. Department of the Interior, Contributions to North American Ethnology*, 5: 1-237.

————. 1893. Are the Maya Hieroglyphs Phonetic? *AA* (o. s.) 6: 241-70.

Thomas, N. D. 1974. *The Linguistic, Geographic, and Demographic Position of the Zoque of Southern Mexico.* NWAF Paper 36.

Thomas, P. M., Jr. 1974. Prehistoric Settlement at Becan: A Preliminary Report. In MARI Publication 31: 139-46.

————. 1980. *Prehistoric Maya Settlement Patterns at Becan, Campeche, Mexico.* MARI Publication 45.

Thompson, D. E. 1960. Maya Paganism and Christianity. In MARI Publication 19: 1-35.

Thompson, E. H. 1897a. Cave of Loltun, Yucatan. In PMAE Memoirs, Vol. 1(2): 49-72.

————. 1897b. *The Chultunes of Labna.* PMAE Memoirs, Vol. 1(3).

Thompson, J. E. S. 1927. A Correlation of the Mayan and European Calendars. In FMAS, 17(1): 1-22.

————. 1929. Maya Chronology: Glyph G of the Lunar Series. *AA* 31: 223-31.

————. 1930. *Ethnology of the Maya of Southern and Central British Honduras.* FMAS, 17(2).

————. 1931. *Archaeological Investigations in the Southern Cayo District, British Honduras.* FMAS, 17(2).

————. 1932. The Solar Year of the Mayas at Quirigua, Guatemala. In FMAS, 17(4): 365-421.

————. 1934. *Sky-Bearers, Colors and Directions in Maya and Mexican Religion.* CIW Publication 436, CAA No. 10.

————. 1935. *Maya Chronology: The Correlation Question.* CIW Publication 456, CAA No. 14.

————. 1938. Sixteenth- and Seventeenth-Century Reports on the Chol Mayas. *AA* 40: 584-604.

————. 1939a. *Excavations at San Jose, British Honduras.* CIW Publication 506.

————. 1939b. *The Moon Goddess in Middle America.* CIW Publication 509, CAA No. 29.

————. 1941. *Dating of Certain Inscriptions of Non-Maya Origin.* CIW Theoretical Approaches to Problems, No. 1.

————. 1942. *Maya Arithmetic.* CIW Publication 528, CAA No. 36.

————. 1943a. Some Sculptures from Southeastern Quetzaltenango, Guatemala. *CIW NMA* No. 17.

————. 1943b. A Trial Survey of the Southern Maya Area. *AAnt* 9: 106-34.

————. 1944. *The Fish as a Maya Symbol for Counting and Further Discussion of Directional Glyphs.* CIW Theoretical Approaches to Problems, No. 2.

————. 1945. A Survey of the Northern Maya Area. *AAnt* 11: 2-24.

————. 1946. Some Uses of Tobacco Among the Maya. *CIW NMA* No. 61.

————. 1948. *An Archaeological Reconnaissance in the Cotzumalhuapa Region, Escuintla, Guatemala.* CIW Publication 574, CAA No. 44.

————. 1950. *Maya Hieroglyphic Writing: An Introduction.* CIW Publication 589. Reprinted by the University of Oklahoma Press, 1960 and 1971.

————. 1952. Waxen Idols and a Sacrificial Rite of the Lacandon. *CIW NMA* No. 109.

————. 1953. [Review of] La antigua escritura de los pueblos de América Central (Y. V. Knorozov). *Yan: Ciencias Antropológicas* 2: 174-78. Mexico City: Centro de Investigaciones Antropológicas de México.

———. 1954a. *The Rise and Fall of Maya Civilization.* Norman: University of Oklahoma Press.

———. 1954b. A Presumed Residence of Nobility at Mayapán. *CIW Current Reports,* No. 19.

———. 1958. *Thomas Gage's Travels in the New World.* Edited with an Introduction by J. E. S. Thompson. Norman: University of Oklahoma Press.

———. 1959. Systems of Hieroglyphic Writing in Middle America and Methods of Deciphering Them. *AAnt* 24: 349-64.

———. 1962. *A Catalog of Maya Hieroglyphs.* Norman: University of Oklahoma Press.

———. 1965a. Archaeological Synthesis of the Southern Maya Lowlands. In *HMAI* 2: 331-59.

———. 1965b. Maya Hieroglyphic Writing. In *HMAI* 3: 632-58.

———. 1966. *The Rise and Fall of Maya Civilization.* 2nd ed., rev. Norman: University of Oklahoma Press.

———. 1970. *Maya History and Religion.* Norman: University of Oklahoma Press.

———. 1971. *Maya Hieroglyphic Writing: Introduction.* 3rd ed. Norman: University of Oklahoma Press.

———. 1972a. *Maya Hieroglyphs Without Tears.* London: Trustees of the British Museum.

———. 1972b. *A Commentary on the Dresden Codex.* American Philosophical Society Memoir, Vol. 93.

———. 1973a. Maya Rulers of the Classic Period and the Divine Right of Kings. In *The Iconography of Middle American Sculpture.* New York: The Metropolitan Museum of Art.

———. 1973b. The Painted Capstone at Sacnicte, Yucatan, and Two Others at Uxmal. *Indiana* 1: 59-63.

———. 1974. "Canals" of the Río Candelaria Basin, Campeche, Mexico. In Hammond 1974b: 297-302.

———. 1975. The Grolier Codex. In UCARF Contribution 27: 1-9.

Thompson, J. E. S., H. E. D. Pollock, and J. Charlot. 1932. *A Preliminary Study of the Ruins of Coba, Quintana Roo, Mexico.* CIW Publication 424.

Thompson, R. H. 1958. *Modern Yucatecan Maya Pottery Making.* Memoirs of the Society for American Archaeology, No. 15. Salt Lake City.

Toscano, S. 1944. *Arte precolumbino de México y de la América Central.* Mexico City: Universidad Nacional Autónoma de México.

Totten, G. O. 1926. *Maya Architecture.* Washington, D.C.: Maya Press.

Tourtellot, G. 1970. The Peripheries of Seibal: An Interim Report. In PMAE Papers, Vol. 61: 405-21.

Tourtellot, G., and J. A. Sabloff. 1972. Exchange Systems among the Ancient Maya. *AA* 37: 126-35.

Tozzer, A. M. 1907. *A Comparative Study of the Mayas and the Lacandones.* Archaeological Institute of America. New York: Macmillan.

———. 1911. *A Preliminary Study of the Prehistoric Ruins of Tikal, Guatemala; a Report of the Peabody Museum Expedition, 1909–1910.* PMAE Memoirs, Vol. 5(2).

———. 1912. The Value of Ancient Mexican Manuscripts in the Study of the General Development of Writing. *Smithsonian Institution Annual Report, 1911:* 493–506. Washington, D.C.

———. 1913. *A Preliminary Study of the Prehistoric Ruins of Nakum, Guatemala.* PMAE Memoirs, Vol. 5(3).

———. 1921. *A Maya Grammar with Bibliography and Appraisement of the Works Noted.* PMAE Papers, Vol. 9.

———. 1941. *Landa's Relación de las cosas de Yucatán.* PMAE Papers, Vol. 28.

———. 1957. *Chichen Itza and Its Cenote of Sacrifice.* PMAE Memoirs, Vols. 11 and 12.

Tozzer, A. M., and G. M. Allen. 1910. *Animal Figures in the Maya Codices.* PMAE Papers, Vol. 4(3).

Trik, A. S. 1939. *Temple XXXII at Copan.* CIW Publication 509, CAA No. 27.

————. 1963. The Splendid Tomb of Temple I, Tikal, Guatemala. *Expedition* 6(1): 2-18.

Turner, B. L. 1974. Prehistoric Intensive Agriculture in the Maya Lowlands. *Science* 185: 118-24.

————. 1978a. The Development and Demise of the Swidden Thesis. In Harrison & Turner 1978: 13-22.

————. 1978b. Ancient Agricultural Land Use in the Central Maya Lowlands. In Harrison & Turner 1978: 163-83.

Turner, B. L., and P. D. Harrison. 1978. Implications from Agriculture for Maya Prehistory. In Harrison & Turner 1978: 337-73.

Turner, E. S., N. I. Turner, and R. E. W. Adams. 1981. Volumetric Assessment, Rank Ordering and Maya Civic Centers. In Ashmore 1981b: 71-88.

Ucko, P. J., R. Tringham, and G. W. Dimbleby, eds. 1972. *Man, Settlement and Urbanism.* London: Duckworth.

Urban, P. A. 1978. An Analysis of Mammalian Fauna from Tikal, El Peten, Guatemala. Unpublished master's thesis, University of Pennsylvania.

Vaillant, G. C. 1935. Chronology and Stratigraphy in the Maya Area. *Maya Research* 2: 119-43.

————. 1944. *The Aztecs of Mexico. Origin, Rise and Fall of the Aztec Nation.* New York: Doubleday. Reprinted by Pelican, 1950.

Velázquez Valadez, R. 1980. Recent Discoveries in the Caves of Loltun, Yucatan, Mexico. *Mexicon* 2: 53-55.

Villacorta, J. A., and C. A. Villacorta. 1927. *Arqueología Guatemalteca.* Guatemala: Tipografía Nacional.

————. 1933. *Códices mayas reproducidos y desarrollados.* Guatemala: Tipografía Nacional.

Villagra, A. 1949. Bonampak, la ciudad de los muros pintados. *INAH Anales* 3 (Supplement).

Villagutierre Soto-Mayor, J. de. 1933. *Historia de la conquista de la Provincia de el Itzá.* Guatemala: Biblioteca Goathemala.

Villa Rojas, A. 1934. *The Yaxuna–Coba Causeway.* CIW Publication 436, CAA No. 9.

————. 1955. *The Maya of East-Central Quintana Roo.* CIW Publication 559.

Vlcek, D. T. 1978. Muros de delimitación residencial en Chunchucmil. *ECAUY Boletín* 5(28): 55-64.

Vlcek, D. T., S. García de Gonzalez, and E. B. Kurjack. 1978. Contemporary Farming and Ancient Maya Settlements: Some Disconcerting Evidence. In Harrison & Turner 1978: 211-23.

Vogt, E. Z. 1961. Some Aspects of Zinacantan Settlement Patterns and Ceremonial Organization. *ECM* 1: 131-45.

————. 1964. Some Implications of Zinacantan Social Structure for the Study of the Ancient Maya. *35th ICA Actas* 1: 307-19.

————. 1969. *Zinacantan: A Maya Community in the Highlands of Chiapas.* Cambridge, Mass.: Harvard University Press.

Von Euw, E. 1977. *Corpus of Maya Hieroglyphic Inscriptions.* Vol. 4, part 1: *Itzimte, Pixoy, Tzum.* PMAE.

————. 1978. *Corpus of Maya Hieroglyphic Inscriptions.* Vol. 5, part 1: *Xultun.* PMAE.

Von Hagen, V. 1944. *The Aztec and Maya Papermakers.* New York: Augustin.

Voorhies, B. 1978. Previous Research on Nearshore Coastal Adaptations in Middle America. In Stark & Voorhies 1978: 5-21.

Wagley, C. 1949. *The Social and Religious Life of a Guatemala Village.* AA Memoir No. 71.

Wagner, P. L. 1964. Natural Vegetation of Middle America. In *HMAI* 1: 216-64.

Wallace, A. F. C. 1956. Revitalization Movements. *AA* 58: 264-81.

Wallace, D. T. 1977. An Intra-Site Locational Analysis of Utatlan: The Structure of an Urban Site. In Wallace & Carmack 1977: 20-54.

Wallace, D. T., and R. M. Carmack, eds. 1977. *Archaeology and Ethnohistory of the Central Quiche*. IMS Publication No. 1.

Walters, G. R. 1980. A Summary of the Preliminary Results of the 1979 San Augustin Acasaguastlan Archaeological Project. *Mexicon* 2: 55-56.

Warren, B. W. 1961. The Archaeological Sequence at Chiapa de Corzo. In *Los mayas del sur y sus relaciones con los nahuas meridionales*. Mexico City: Sociedad Mexicana de Antropología.

Wauchope, R. 1934. *House Mounds of Uaxactun, Guatemala*. CIW Publication 436, CAA No. 7.

————. 1938. *Modern Maya Houses*. CIW Publication 502.

————. 1948. *Excavations at Zacualpa, Guatemala*. MARI Publication 14.

————. 1949. Las edades de Utatlán e Iximché. *Antropología e Historia de Guatemala* 1: 10-22.

————. 1962. *Lost Tribes and Sunken Continents*. Chicago: University of Chicago Press.

————, general ed. 1964-76. *Handbook of Middle American Indians*. Vols. 1-16. Austin: University of Texas Press.

————. 1965. *They Found the Buried Cities*. Chicago: University of Chicago Press.

————. 1970. Protohistoric Pottery of the Guatemalan Highlands. In PMAE Papers, Vol. 61: 89-244.

————. 1975. *Zacualpa, El Quiche, Guatemala. An Ancient Provincial Center of the Highland Maya*. MARI Publication 39.

Webb, M. 1964. The Postclassic Decline of the Peten Maya: An Interpretation in the Light of a General Theory of State Society. Unpublished doctoral dissertation, University of Michigan.

————. 1973. The Peten Maya Decline Viewed in the Perspective of State Formation. In Culbert 1973: 367-404.

Webster, D. L. 1976. *Defensive Earthworks at Becan, Campeche, Mexico*. MARI Publication 41.

————. 1977. Warfare and the Evolution of Maya Civilization. In Adams 1977: 335-72.

————. 1979. Three Walled Sites of the Northern Maya Lowlands. *JFA* 5: 375-90.

West, R. C. 1964. Surface Configuration and Associated Geology of Middle America. In *HMAI* 1: 33-83.

Wetherington, R. K., ed. 1978. *The Ceramics of Kaminaljuyu, Guatemala*. Pennsylvania State University Press Monograph Series on Kaminaljuyu. University Park.

Wheaton, T. R. 1976. La cerámica clásica del area de Huejotzingo, Puebla. *Proyecto Puebla-Tlaxcala Comunicaciones* 13: 25-31.

Whorf, B. J. 1933. *The Phonetic Value of Certain Characters in Maya Writing*. PMAE Papers, Vol. 13(2).

————. 1942. Decipherment of the Linguistic Portion of the Maya Hieroglyphs. *Smithsonian Institution Annual Report, 1941*: 479-502.

Wilkin, G. C. 1971. Food Producing Systems Available to the Ancient Maya. *AAnt* 36: 432-48.

Willcox, H. 1954. Removal and Restoration of the Monuments of Caracol. *UM Bulletin* 18(1-2): 46-72.

Willey, G. R. 1953. *Prehistoric Settlement Patterns in the Virú Valley, Peru*. BAE Bulletin 155.

————, ed. 1956. *Prehistoric Settlement Patterns in the New World*. Viking Fund Publications in Anthropology, No. 23. New York.

————. 1956. The Structure of Ancient Maya Society: Evidence from the Southern Lowlands. *AA* 58: 777-82.

————. 1972. *The Artifacts of Altar de Sacrificios*. PMAE Papers, Vol. 64(1).

————. 1973. *The Altar de Sacrificios Excavations, General Summary and Conclusions.* PMAE Papers, Vol. 64(3).

————. 1974. The Classic Maya Hiatus: A Rehearsal for the Collapse? In Hammond 1974b: 417-44.

————, general ed. 1975. *Excavations at Seibal, Department of Peten, Guatemala.* PMAE Memoirs, Vol. 13(1, 2).

————. 1977. The Rise of Maya Civilization: A Summary View. In Adams 1977: 383-423.

————. 1978a. Artifacts. In *Excavations at Seibal*, PMAE Memoirs, Vol. 14(1): 1-189.

————, general ed. 1978b. *Excavations at Seibal, Department of Peten, Guatemala.* PMAE Memoirs, Vol. 14(1-3).

————. 1978c. Pre-Hispanic Maya Agriculture: A Contemporary Summation. In Harrison & Turner 1978: 325-35.

————. 1980. Towards an Holistic View of Ancient Maya Civilization. *Man* 15: 249-66.

————. 1981. Maya Lowland Settlement Patterns: A Summary Review. In Ashmore 1981b: 385-415.

Willey, G. R., and W. M. Bullard, Jr. 1965. Prehistoric Settlement Patterns in the Maya Lowlands. In *HMAI* 2: 360-77.

Willey, G. R., W. R. Bullard, Jr., and J. B. Glass. 1955. The Maya Community of Prehistoric Times. *A* 8(1): 18-25.

Willey, G. R., W. R. Bullard, Jr., J. B. Glass, and J. C. Gifford. 1965. *Prehistoric Maya Settlements in the Belize Valley.* PMAE Papers, Vol. 54.

Willey, G. R., T. P. Culbert, and R. E. W. Adams. 1967. Maya Lowland Ceramics: A Report from the 1965 Guatemala City Conference. *AAnt* 32: 289-315.

Willey, G. R., and J. C. Gifford. 1961. Pottery of the Holmul I Style from Barton Ramie, British Honduras. In *Essays in Pre-Columbian Art and Archaeology* (S. K. Lothrop and others, eds.): 152-70. Cambridge, Mass.: Harvard University Press.

Willey, G. R., and R. M. Leventhal. 1979. Prehistoric Settlement at Copan. In Hammond & Willey 1979: 75-102.

Willey, G. R., R. M. Leventhal, and W. L. Fash, Jr. 1978. Maya Settlement in the Copan Valley. *A* 31: 32-43.

Willey, G. R., and P. Phillips. 1958. *Method and Theory in American Archaeology.* Chicago: University of Chicago Press.

Willey, G. R., and J. A. Sabloff. 1974. *A History of American Archaeology.* San Francisco: Freeman.

Willey, G. R., R. J. Sharer, R. Viel, A. A. Demarest, R. M. Leventhal, and E. M. Schortman. 1980. A Study of Ceramic Interaction in the Southeastern Maya Periphery. Paper presented at the 45th Annual Meeting of the Society for American Archaeology, Philadelphia.

Willey, G. R., and D. B. Shimkin. 1973. The Maya Collapse: A Summary View. In Culbert 1973: 457-502.

Willey, G. R., and A. L. Smith. 1963. New Discoveries at Altar de Sacrificios. *A* 16(2): 83-89.

————. 1969. *The Ruins of Altar de Sacrificios, Department of Peten, Guatemala, An Introduction.* PMAE Papers, Vol. 62(1).

Willson, R. W. 1924. *Astronomical Notes on the Maya Codices.* PMAE Papers, Vol. 6(3).

Wisdom, C. 1940. *The Chorti Indians of Guatemala.* Chicago: University of Chicago Press.

————. 1950. Materials on the Chorti Language. *MCM*, No. 28.

Wiseman, F. M. 1978. Agricultural and Historical Ecology of the Maya Lowlands. In Harrison & Turner 1978: 63-115.

Witkowski, S. R., and C. H. Brown. 1978. Mesoamerican: A Proposed Language Phylum. *AA* 80: 942-44.

Woodbury, R. B. 1965. Artifacts of the Guatemalan Highlands. In *HMAI* 2: 163–79.
Woodbury, R. B., and A. S. Trik. 1953. *The Ruins of Zaculeu, Guatemala.* 2 vols. Richmond, Va.: William Byrd Press.
Wolf, E. R., ed. 1959. *Sons of the Shaking Earth.* Chicago: University of Chicago Press.
———, ed. 1976. *The Valley of Mexico.* SAR.
Ximenez, F. 1929–31. *Historia de la provincia de San Vicente de Chiapa y Guatemala.* 3 vols. Guatemala: Sociedad de Geografía e Historia de Guatemala.
Zeitlin, R. N. 1978. Long-Distance Exchange and the Growth of a Regional Center on the Southern Isthmus of Tehuantepec, Mexico. In Stark & Voorhies 1978: 183–210.
Zimmermann, G. 1956. *Die Hieroglyphen der Maya Handschriften.* Hamburg: Cram, de Gruter.

# ILLUSTRATION CREDITS

Figs. 2.1 and 2.2. N. Hammond, Corozal Project.

Fig. 2.3. R. J. Sharer, Chalchuapa Project.

Fig. 2.4. J. A. Graham, Abaj Takalik Project.

Fig. 3.1. From R. J. Sharer and W. A. Ashmore, *Fundamentals of Archaeology* (Menlo Park, Calif.: Benjamin/Cummings, 1979), Fig. 5.4, p. 152; by permission.

Fig. 3.2. From Shook & Kidder 1952, Fig. 15; by permission of CIW.

Fig. 3.3. From R. J. Sharer and W. A. Ashmore, *Fundamentals of Archaeology* (Menlo Park, Calif.: Benjamin/Cummings, 1979), Fig. 7.6, p. 222; by permission.

Fig. 3.4. Chalchuapa Project.　　　Fig. 3.5. NGS.

Fig. 3.6. U.S. National Museum.　　Fig. 3.7. PM.

Figs. 3.8 and 3.9. J. A. Graham, Abaj Takalik Project.

Fig. 3.10. From Greene, Rands & Graham 1972, Plate 202; by permission.

Fig. 3.11. UM.

Fig. 3.12. Chalchuapa Project (drawing by W. R. Coe).

Fig. 3.13. R. J. Sharer, Verapaz Archaeological Project.

Fig. 3.14. *Above*, UM; *right*, J. A. Graham, Abaj Takalik Project; *lower left*, W. R. Coe, TP.

Fig. 3.15. D. M. Pendergast, Lamanai Project.

Fig. 3.16. D. A. Freidel, Cerros Project.

Fig. 3.17. W. R. Coe, TP.　　　　　Fig. 3.18. R. Velazquez V., Proyecto Loltun.

Figs. 3.19 and 3.20. CIW.　　　　　Figs. 3.21 and 3.22. R. J. Sharer.

Figs. 4.1 and 4.2. After Marcus 1976b, Figs. 1.7 and 1.8; by permission of Dumbarton Oaks, Washington, D.C.

Fig. 4.3. R. T. Matheny, © copyright 1980 El Mirador Project.

Figs. 4.4–4.6. W. R. Coe, TP.　　　Figs. 4.7 and 4.8. CIW.

Fig. 4.9. PM.　　　　　　　　　　　Fig. 4.10. TAM.

Figs. 4.11 and 4.12. W. R. Coe, TP.

Fig. 4.13. CIW.

Fig. 4.14. *Upper left*, J. Hairs; *two right*, rubbings by J. M. Keshishian, QP.

Fig. 4.15. CIW.

Fig. 4.16. After Marcus 1976b, Fig. 3; by permission of Dumbarton Oaks, Washington, D.C.

Fig. 4.17. G. Holton, TP.　　　　　Fig. 4.18. W. R. Coe, TP.

Fig. 4.19. TP.　　　　　　　　　　　Fig. 4.20. S. Greco.

Figs. 4.21 and 4.22. A. Ruz L.

Fig. 4.23. Rubbing by M. Greene Robertson.

Fig. 4.24. Maudslay 1889–1902, Vol. II, Plates 86 and 87.

Fig. 4.25. *Left two and right*, UM; *center*, MN.

Fig. 4.26. UM.　　　　　　　　　　Fig. 4.27. CIW.

Fig. 4.28. R. J. Sharer, QP.　　　　Fig. 4.29. PM.

Figs. 6.1 and 6.2. E. W. Andrews V, Komchen Project.

Fig. 6.3. CIW.

Figs. 6.4. *Above*, from Proskouriakoff 1946, plate on p. 53; by permission of CIW. *Below*, J. W. Ball, Becan Project.

Fig. 6.5. CIW.　　　　　　　　　　Fig. 6.6. *Above*, CIW; *below*, FG.

Fig. 6.7. EC.　　　　　　　　　　　Fig. 6.8. CIW.

Fig. 6.9. INAH.　　　　　　　　　　Fig. 6.10. D. Z. Chase.

Figs. 6.11–6.13. A. G. Miller, Tancah Project.

Fig. 6.14. A. F. Chase, Tayasal Project.

Fig. 6.15. From Greene, Rands & Graham 1972, Plate 189; by permission.

Figs. 6.16 and 6.17. R. J. Sharer.

Fig. 6.18. D. T. Wallace, from Wallace & Carmack 1977; by permission.

Figs. 6.19 and 6.20. R. J. Sharer.　　Fig. 7.1. TAM.

Fig. 7.2. G. G. Healey.　　　　　　Fig. 7.3. P. D. Sheets, Proyecto Protoclasico.

Fig. 7.4. R. T. Matheny, Edzna Project.

Figs. 7.5–7.7. B. L. Turner, Pulltrouser Swamp Project (Fig. 7.7 courtesy of the Royal Air Force).

Fig. 7.8. A. H. Siemens, from Siemens & Puleston 1972, Fig. 4; by permission of the Society for American Archaeology.

Fig. 8.1. After Eaton 1975, Fig. 5; by permission.

Fig. 8.2. W. A. Ashmore.

Fig. 8.3. From Hammond 1975 (copyright 1975 by the President and Fellows of Harvard College), after Fig. 43; by permission

Fig. 8.4. MARI.

Fig. 8.5. PM.

Figs. 9.1 and 9.2. TAM.

Fig. 9.3. *Upper two*, A. Galindo; *lower two*, CIW.

Fig. 9.4. TAM.

Fig. 10.1. A. P. Andrews.

Figs. 11.1 and 11.2. TAM.

Fig. 11.3. *Top two*, D. F. Wagner; *below*, F. R. Morley.

Fig. 11.4. CIW.

Fig. 11.5. EC.

Fig. 11.6. TP.

Fig. 11.7. O. Imboden, courtesy of G. E. Stuart, NGS.

Figs. 11.8–11.20. W. R. Coe, TP.

Figs. 11.21 and 11.22. TAM.

Figs. 11.23–11.25. R. T. Matheny, El Mirador Project.

Fig. 11.26. CIW.

Fig. 11.27. J. W. Ball, Becan Project.

Figs. 11.28–11.31. D. M. Pendergast, Altun Ha Project.

Fig. 11.32. G. R. Willey, Seibal Project.

Fig. 11.33. G. R. Willey, Altar de Sacrificios Project.

Fig. 11.34. CIW.                     Fig. 11.35. PM.

Fig. 11.36. T. Proskouriakoff.          Fig. 11.37. UM.

Fig. 11.38. O. Imboden, courtesy of G. E. Stuart, NGS.

Fig. 11.39 and 11.40. Museo Nacional de Antropología, Mexico.

Fig. 11.41. B. Edgerton.                Fig. 11.42. PM.

Fig. 11.43. TAM.                        Fig. 11.44. CIW.

Fig. 11.45. M. J. Becker, Proyecto Copan.

Fig. 11.46. *Left*, CIW; *right*, Maudslay 1889–1902, Vol. I, Plate 86.

Figs. 11.47–11.50. QP.

Fig. 11.51. UM.

Fig. 11.52. CIW.

Figs. 11.53–11.55. E. W. Andrews V, MARI.

Fig. 11.56. UM and Fairchild Aerial Surveys.

Figs. 11.57 and 11.58. TAM.

Fig. 11.59. *Above*, F. R. Morley; *below*, FG.

Figs. 11.60 and 11.61. CIW.

Fig. 11.62. EC.

Fig. 11.63. CIW.

Fig. 11.64. UM and Fairchild Aerial Surveys.

Figs. 11.65 and 11.66. TAM.          Fig. 11.67. FG.

Fig. 11.68. EC.                        Fig. 11.69. *Above*, FG; *below*, EC.

Fig. 11.70. INAH.                      Fig. 11.71. CIW.

Fig. 11.72. EC.                        Fig. 11.73. Museum Library, UM.

# 676    Illustration Credits

Figs. 11.74–11.77. A. G. Miller, Tancah-Tulum Project.

Fig. 12.1. *a–d*, from Sharer 1978a; by permission. *e–g*, from Pring 1976, Fig. 1; by permission.

Fig. 12.2. From Dahlin 1978; by permission.

Fig. 12.3. *a–e*, from Sharer 1978a; by permission. *f*, from Gifford 1976 (copyright 1976 by the President and Fellows of Harvard College), Fig. 27p; by permission.

Fig. 12.4. From Dahlin 1978; by permission.

Fig. 12.5. From Sharer 1978a; by permission.

Figs. 12.6 and 12.7. W. R. Coe, TP.

Figs. 12.8. *a*, *b*, from Sharer 1978a; by permission. *c*, from Gifford 1976 (copyright 1976 by the President and Fellows of Harvard College), Fig. 72a; by permission.

Fig. 12.9. From Sharer 1978a; by permission.

Fig. 12.10. *a–c*, from Gifford 1976 (copyright 1976 by the President and Fellows of Harvard College), Figs. 96i, 88o, 88a; by permission. *Below*, W. R. Coe, TP.

Fig. 12.11. *Top two*, W. R. Coe, TP; *below*, J. W. Ball, Becan Project.

Fig. 12.12. From Sharer 1978a; by permission.

Fig. 12.13. W. R. Coe, TP.

Fig. 12.14. G. E. Stuart, NGS.

Fig. 12.15. TAM.

Fig. 12.16. Museo Arqueológico, Etnográfico e Histórico, Campeche.

Fig. 12.17. PM.

Figs. 12.18 and 12.19. CIW.

Fig. 12.20. From Gifford 1976 (copyright 1976 by the President and Fellows of Harvard College), Figs. 171g, 192v, 196a,b; by permission.

Fig. 12.21. From Sharer 1978a; by permission.

Fig. 12.22. *Above*, PM; *below*, CIW.

Figs. 13.1 and 13.2. TAM.　　　　　Figs. 13.3 and 13.4. CIW.

Fig. 13.5. TAM.　　　　　Fig. 13.6. PM.

Figs. 13.7 and 13.8. CIW.　　　　　Fig. 13.9. UM.

Figs. 13.10 and 13.11. School of American Research, Santa Fe, New Mexico.

Fig. 13.12. TAM.　　　　　Figs. 13.13 and 13.14. INAH.

Fig. 13.15. *Left*, INAH; *right*, EC.　　　　　Fig. 13.16. FG.

Fig. 13.17. Museum für Völkerkunde, Basel.

Fig. 13.18. TAM.

Fig. 13.19. Maudslay 1889–1902, Vol. IV, Plate 33.

Fig. 13.20. A. Ruz L.　　　　　Fig. 13.21. MARI.

Fig. 13.22. PM.　　　　　Fig. 13.23. W. R. Coe, TP.

Figs. 13.24–13.27. G. G. Healey.　　　　　Figs. 13.28–13.32. TAM.

Fig. 13.33. A. G. Miller, Tancah-Tulum Project.

Figs. 13.34–13.41. TAM.

Fig. 13.42. *Upper left*, S. Stubbs; *lower left*, CIW; *upper pair*, MARI; *lower pair*, PM.

Fig. 13.43. Secretaría de Agricultura y Fomento, Mexico.

Fig. 13.44. CIW.

Fig. 13.45. R. J. Sharer, Verapaz Archaeological Project.

Fig. 13.46. A. Ruz L.

Fig. 13.47. EC.

Fig. 13.48. Museo de Arqueología e Historia, Mérida.

Fig. 13.49. W. R. Coe, TP.

Fig. 13.50. R. J. Sharer, Verapaz Archaeological Project.

Fig. 13.51. W. R. Coe, TP.

Figs. 13.52 and 13.53. TAM.

Fig. 13.54. *Upper two*, Museo Nacional de Antropología, Mexico; *below*, PM.

Fig. 13.55. TAM.                          Fig. 13.56. CIW.

Fig. 13.57. TAM.                          Fig. 13.58. PM.

Figs. 13.59 and 13.60. TAM.               Fig. 13.61. C. Jones, QP.

Fig. 13.62. Museo Arqueológico, Etnográfico e Histórico, Campeche

Fig. 14.1. TAM.                           Fig. 14.2. G. G. Healey.

Figs. 14.3–14.8. TAM.                     Fig. 14.9. CIW.

Figs. 14.10–14.13. TAM.

Fig. 15.1. C. Beetz, after Fox 1978.

Fig. 15.2. Classification follows Fox 1978.   Fig. 15.3. After Willey 1978a, Fig. 77.

Fig. 15.4. TAM.                           Fig. 15.5. Museum Library, UM.

Figs. 15.6–15.8. C. Beetz, from drawings by J. A. Fox.

Fig. 15.9. Tozzer 1941; by permission of PM.

Fig. 15.10. J. A. Fox, inked by C. Beetz.

Fig. 15.11. C. Beetz, from drawings by J. A. Fox.

Fig. 15.12. J. Porter, courtesy of J. Graham.

Fig. 15.13. *Four directions*, TAM (hardbound); "*center*," C. Beetz, from a drawing by J. A. Fox.

Fig. 15.14. After Thompson 1962, glyphs on pp. 316, 326, 330, 336, 340, 343, 350; by permission of University of Oklahoma Press.

Fig. 15.15. Museum Library, UM; decipherment by J. A. Fox.

Fig. 15.16. C. Jones, TP.                 Figs. 16.1–16.12. TAM.

# INDEX